Drumbeats

That Changed the World

To Eileen,

whose forty years of
cheerful encouragement have
brightened the journey,

and to

that great company of
missionaries, then and now,
whose lives
are the substance of this account.

Drumbeats

That Changed the World

A History of

The Regions Beyond Missionary Union

and

The West Indies Mission

1873–1999

By Joseph F. Conley

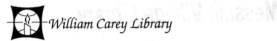

William Carey Library

P.O. Box 40129
Pasadena, CA 91114

For information please contact World Team International

USA
1431 Stuckert Rd.
Warrington, PA 18976
Phone: (215) 491-4900
1-800-967-7109
E-mail: wt-usa@worldteam.org

Australia
P.O. Box 217, Ringwood East
Victoria 3135, Australia
Phone: 61-3-9879-6377
Fax: 61-3-9879-6388
E-mail: wt-australia@worldteam.org

Canada
2476 Argentia Rd #203
Mississauga, ON L5N 6M1
Phone: (905) 821-6300
1-800-610-9788
Fax: (905) 821-6325
E-mail: infocanada@Worlteam.org

Extracts fron the work of Michele Guinness in *The Guiness Legend* are reproduced by permission of Hodder and Stoughton, Limited. Citations from *Cannibal Valley* by permission of Christian Publications, Camp Hill, PA. Scripture references are from the King James Version of the Bible unless otherwise noted.

Library of Congress Cataloging-in-Publication Data

Conley, Joseph F., 1928-
   Drumbeats that changed the world : a history of the Regions Beyond Missionary Union and the West Indies Mission, 1873-1999 / Joseph F. Conley.
      p.cm.
   Includes bibliographical references and index.
   ISBN 0-87808-603-X (alk. paper)
      1. Regions Beyond Missionary Union--History. 2. West Indies Mission--History. I. Title.

BV2361.R44 C66 2000
266'.023'0601'--dc21

00-057189

 6 5 4 3 2 1
04 03 02 01 00

Printed in the United States of America

Contents

Part 1
The First 70 Years
The Regions Beyond Missionary Union
1873–1945

Part 2
Headwaters
The West Indies Mission
1900–1945

Part 3
When The Lights Came on Again
The Regions Beyond Missionary Union
The Postwar Years
1945–1995

Part 4
A Mission Grows
The West Indies Mission
The Postwar Years
1945–1995

Chapter   Page

Part 5
Treading a New Path
The Merger of RBMU and Worldteam
1995–2000

Introduction

Joe Conley renders admirable service to the World Team family in this fascinating account of the history of the Regions Beyond Missionary Union (RBMU) and the West Indies Mission (WIM). Singularly qualified for the assignment, Joe had spent several years with RBMU as a missionary to Peru, when one of God's surprising course corrections brought him and his family home in 1962. He gave the next twenty-five years to mission administration, twenty-three of them as the US director of RBMU.

His grasp of the ethos of the two agencies bears witness to a lifelong interaction with the global missionary community. It likewise evidences singular diligence in a two-year research project, in which he traces more than a century of adventure in world evangelization. In the process, he has brought to light many intriguing details of the origins of both missions, valuable missiological insights, and calls us to praise God for the astonishing harvest gathered through the obedience of many.

Walk through this book as I have done and you will marvel at the sovereign work of the Holy Spirit in the great mission of the Church. You will rejoice in the exploits of ordinary people whose extraordinary service has become part of the eternal record, forever written in heaven. Their drumbeats have resonated throughout the earth, and they have truly changed our world.

Albert Ehmann,
International Director, World Team International
31 March 2000

About This Story . . .

When asked to write a history of our two mission agencies I knew that I faced a formidable assignment. Some likened it to coiling barbed wire with bare hands. An equally valid metaphor might be that of making bricks without straw. Original documentation on the early development of the *Regions Beyond Missionary Union* is mostly archived in Edinburgh, Scotland,[1] so that I have had to lean heavily on secondary sources. These appear in the endnotes and in the bibliographies. *The West Indies Mission* story presented an even greater challenge. Since my working years were spent with RBMU, the WIM learning curve was daunting, and significant critical material came to hand only late in the writing process.

This attempt to recast the 122-year history of the RBMU and the 67-year pilgrimage of the West Indies Mission[2] is rooted in three facts. First, most accounts are now either out of print or otherwise remain inaccessible to the average reader. Second, in 1995, two agencies united to form a new mission called *World Team*. For new workers joining the Mission, a comprehensive survey of its dual roots offers continuity with a rich and fruitful past. Institutional memories are instructive guideposts. World Team is new, but it is not a tyro on the missions scene. Third, this account will introduce missionaries and World Team partners to the other half of the family. When the two agencies entered corporate wedlock on 3 June 1995, most members did not know the people in the other mission! This record offers linkage.

Throughout this work, the evolution of agency names is contemporized in context. At times, initials are used to designate these titles (see list of acronyms). The older of the two began (1873) as *the East London Institute for Home and Foreign Missions* (ELI), a missionary training school. With expansion into new facilities in 1878, the name was prefixed as "*Harley College, the East London Institute for Home and Foreign Missions.*" With its venture into Africa, the missionary arm of the ELI became the *Livingstone Inland Mission* (LIM). In turn, it became the *Congo Balolo Mission* (CBM), *the Regions Beyond Missionary Union* (RBMU), and (in North America only) *RBMU International*. Likewise, the younger of the two agencies began as *Los Pinos Nuevos Bible Institute* (The New Pines Bible Institute, known in North America as the Cuba Bible Institute). From that effort flowed the West Indies Mission (WIM), later changed to *Worldteam*. When the two agencies merged in 1995, a new name—World Team (two words)—was adopted.

Since World War II is indisputably the watershed of twentieth century missions, I have used the end of the conflict (1945) as the major dividing point of this material. Parts One and Two deal with pre-war RBMU and WIM, respectively. Likewise, Parts Three and Four deal with postwar RBMU and WIM. Part Five addresses the merger and post-merger events. Some liberties are taken with these time frames in the interests of chapter continuity.

I have purposely given more attention to the earlier history and principal figures of both agencies, since this material is furthest from the reach of the present mission family and is rapidly fading from living memory. The Livingstone Inland Mission, precursor of RBMU, existed from 1878 to 1884 before being turned over to the American Baptists. This segment of the story is largely absent from available RBMU publications. It is both fascinating and seminal. For the same reasons more detailed attention has been given to the historical antecedents and early history of the Cuba Bible Institute, which became the West Indies Mission. No attempt has been made to provide exhaustive coverage of the more recent work of either mission, neither of the fields themselves nor of the hundreds of missionaries who have mustered to Christ's service under their banner during 125 years. Since mission is always affected by, and conducted within the flow of secular history, I have tried wherever possible to set the unfolding drama of these agencies in the wider historical context of world events.

I owe much to many. The Reverend Elmer Lavastida, son of the co-founder of the West Indies Mission kindly gave me interview time and shared his 1998 (then unpublished) thesis in Spanish, *Trayectoria Pastoral*—the story of his father, B. G. Lavastida. June Vetter's earlier unpublished work on the Worldteam story gave valuable introduction to that mission, and early in the project was my primary source. Mrs. Vetter had drawn from live interviews with Elmer and Evelyn Thompson, from their personal papers, and from the family letters of Roger Kirk and Hattie Monge—the latter lent by Muriel Hansen, Evelyn Thompson's sister. Late in the writing process, some of Hattie Kirk Monge's autobiography and some of Roger Kirk's letters came to hand, allowing me to document these early events.

Mark Sirag provided a treasure-trove in the form of his mother's newsletters from 1935 forward—an arsenal of information on RBMU's beginnings in North America and Borneo. Canadian RBMU archives yielded early correspondence between Annie G. Soper and members of the Simmonds family. Also shared was correspondence of Ebenezer G. Vine and relevant Canada Council minutes.

Special thanks to Ed Walker, who shared his personal papers and provided critical leads to Worldteam sources. Allen Thompson's clear recall and transparent sharing of personal documents spared me from leaps of imagination in reconstructing the later Worldteam story. Extensive interviews with David Hartt, Patrick Arnold, and other Worldteam veterans greatly helped to flesh out my understanding of the West Indies Mission. Thanks to Don and Eunice Richter, Max Inglis, the editors at William Carey Library, and to the World Team secretaries. Their investment of time and expertise in review of the manuscript is priceless.

In pursuit of historical accuracy, I have—wherever possible—submitted field-specific chapter drafts to senior missionaries of both agencies. Their insights, suggestions, and affirmations have helped to assure a reliable history. Countless e-mails, postal mail, and telephone conversations have combined to produce this record.

Beginning in 1964 and over a period of twenty-three years as director of American RBMU, I edited the North American quarterly, *Regions Beyond.* This material has been a fertile source of information. Personal visits to all former RBMU fields and years of interaction with their development have earned the writer some degree of authority in treating the subject. A fascination with mission history—specifically with that of RBMU—has developed familiarity with vintage volumes no longer in print. The nineteenth and early twentieth centuries, free of computers and video, produced graphic and gifted writers whose copious legacy rivals that of celluloid and videotape. I am indebted to Michele Guinness, whose definitive work on the Guinness family in *The Guinness Legend,* yielded intimacies drawn from family records not otherwise available to this writer.

I have likewise drawn from previous issues of the *Whitened Harvest,* later, *Harvest,* and later still, *Worldteam* magazine, the organs of the old West Indies Mission. The historical threads of the two missions are remarkably interwoven in a way that defies explanation apart from the design of a sovereign Providence. Wherever practical, direct quotations are indicated by indentation. Some anecdotal material has been adapted for the sake of clarity, brevity, and style, but always with sensitivity to the intent of the author. If the covers of this book seem too far apart, the index may help you find what you are looking for.

Lastly, this account is not a study in comparative missiological methods. These have varied from country to country, and have evolved empirically over time, as the tensions inevitable to the growth of both church and mission have required. Missiological insights appear incidentally throughout the narrative, but not with studied intent. The only exception is the later Worldteam history, where the metamorphosis of that mission from a general mission agency to a single-vision church planting task force *is* both the story and a lesson in creative missiology.

The primary purpose of this narrative is to portray in broad stroke the unfolding drama of redemption through the narrow window of two mission societies. Reflection on these events and their principal figures will lead to the ascription of glory and honor to our Lord Jesus Christ, Lord of the Harvest. May it also help us to esteem the vision and sacrifice of those who made it happen and bring inspiration to those who follow in their steps.

Joseph F. Conley
Deerfield Beach, Florida,
March 31, 2000

Preface

History is a neglected means of grace. *"As I was with Moses, so will I be with you,"* was God's reassurance to Joshua. The promise should inspire and buttress our own faith and obedience as it did for Moses' understudy.

Because the God of creation is the primal Missionary, the Bible that reveals him is a missionary book. Scripture and history are the progressive revelation of God's redemptive purpose for Earth's peoples. For that reason, the history of missions is the progressive assimilation and execution of that purpose by his people, consummating in the ultimate, universal exaltation of Jesus Christ. Grasping this fact not only helps us to understand history, it sets before us a new, triumphant agenda for life. Solomon affirmed that *"The path of the just is as the shining light that shines brighter and brighter to the dawning of the perfect day."*[3] This metaphor of Christian experience forecasts the certain triumph of the missionary enterprise as global evangelization accelerates with a breadth and intensity never before experienced.

The legacies of Regions Beyond Missionary Union and Worldteam present us with a great cloud of witnesses. Having written history, they trace the path to victory and call us to follow. Not only have they lifted thousands into the joyous knowledge of our God and Savior, they have in the process effected social change, liberated men and women from the bondage of ignorance, educated the masses, paved the way to religious freedom, healed the sick, and fed the hungry.

RBMU and Worldteam were two agencies with differing personas and emphases. Two groups of people who pledged allegiance to their Lord within a family of their peers to obey Christ's last command. Without knowing much about each other, they were bound by a commonality of purpose: to bring the lost peoples of Earth to the lodestar of history—the universal worship of the Lord, Jesus Christ. They were—and are—ordinary people, familiar with failure, fears, tears, and triumph. They weathered disease, early death, upheavals of war, unexplained reversals, personal tragedies of sacrifice and martyrdom, hard soil, unrequited labor, and family separations borne courageously for the sake of the Name. In the power of the Holy Spirit, they defied the darkness, sundered chains, revolutionized societies, shared in joyous harvest, and changed their world. *"Their voice has gone out into all the earth, their words to the ends of the world."*[4]

It is axiomatic that any work of God will be assailed by difficulties, not only from without, but also from within the company of the committed. Our Lord had a Judas, a revolutionary, and a tax collector in his band. It is a tribute to his wise and conciliatory leadership that he held them together in productive harmony. The superlative apostle Paul had tensions with John Mark. The Biblical record reports these departures from our shining ideal with a sometimes-shocking transparency, but also with didactic purpose. It is this: God achieves his ends through flawed and imperfect people—he has no other variety with which to work.

No honest history of missions will gloss the tensions, rivalries, jealousies, divisions, moral failures, discouragements, and dropouts that have marred the work of global evangelization. These are present wherever God's people join hands and heart to do his work. Maturity will anticipate the fact. Honesty will accept it. Wisdom will learn from the experience of failure and move forward redemptively in each situation, ever learning, but undismayed and undeterred in the pursuit of our goal—the supreme exaltation of Jesus Christ. This is the grand motivation of history. It is the confident and certain outcome of missions. The bottom line is simple and compelling: *We Win!* The God of Peace *shall* bruise Satan under our feet. Jesus Christ shall be satisfied. That is what he said: *"All that the Father gives me will come to me."* (John 6:37 NIV)

Lastly, to stand on the threshold of a new millennium is a unique moment for our generation. Reflection on what God has done is an exercise from which we may draw inspiration and confident expectation for what lies ahead.

On 3 June 1995, RBMU International, earlier known as The Regions Beyond Missionary Union, and Worldteam—formerly the West Indies Mission— united their forces and their resources to become a new International mission agency called World Team. But we're ahead of the story. . . .

Acronyms Used in This Work

ABCCOP	Alliance of Bible Christian Communities of the Philippines
ABMU	American Baptist Missionary Union
ABWE	Association of Baptists for World Evangelism
ADIBEL	Association of Bible Churches of Lima
AETAL	Bible Inst. & Seminary Accrediting Assoc. for Latin America
AI	Advance International
AIBC	Association of Ifugao Bible Churches
AIENOP	Association of Evangelical Churches of Northeastern Peru
ANBC	All Nations Bible College
APCM	Asia Pacific Christian Mission
C MA	Christian and Missionary Alliance
CADELU	Community of the Assoc. of Evangelical Churches of Lulonga
CBI	Cuba Bible Institute
CBM	Congo Balolo Mission
CFS	Congo Free State
CIM	China Inland Mission
CIS	Commonwealth of Independent States
CIU	Columbia International University
DNG	Dutch New Guinea
DR	Dominican Republic
DTL	Door to Life Ministries
ECWI	Evangelical Churches of the West Indies
EID	Evangelism-In-Depth
ELI	East London Institute for Home and Foreign Missions
ESI	Evangelical Seminary of Indonesia
ETANI	Evangelical Trust Association of North India
EUSA	Evangelical Union of South America
FCS	Free Church of Scotland
GMU	Gospel Missionary Union
GPPIK	Fellowship of Gospel Proclaiming Churches (Kalimantan)
GR	Gospel Recordings

HECA	Highland Evangelical Church Association (Philippines)
IBL	Institut Biblique Lumière (Haiti)
ICM	Maringa Christian Institute
IHBR	Iglesia Hispana de Boca Raton
LAM	Latin America Mission
LEP	Least-evangelized People *See also* UPG
LIM	The Livingstone Inland Mission
MAF	Mission Aviation Fellowship
MBI	Moody Bible Institute
MEBSH	Mision Evangelique Baptiste d'Sud Haiti
MTO	Mission to Orphans
OMF	Overseas Missionary Fellowship
PBI	Prairie Bible Institute
PIM	Peru Inland Mission
PT	Project Timothy
RBMU	Regions Beyond Missionary Union
SAKIJ	Irian Jaya Bible and Vocational Institute
SAM	Sekolah Alkitab Maranata (Maranatha Bible Institute)
SBI	Simpson Bible Institute
SEND	Formerly known as the Far Eastern Gospel Crusade
SGM	Scripture Gift Mission
SMU	Swedish Missionary Union
SVM	Student Volunteer Movement
TEAM	The Evangelical Alliance Mission
TEE	Theological Education by Extension
UFM	Unevangelized Fields Mission
UMN	United Mission to Nepal
UPG	Unreached People Groups
WAC	Women's Army Corps
WBT	Wycliffe Bible Translators
WIM	West Indies Mission
WIN	Institute for Church Planting
WT	World Team
WTA	World Team Associates
WTE	World Team Essentials

Part 1

The First Seventy Years

The Regions Beyond Missionary Union

1873–1945

Congo Drums

One of our carriers was a very clever drumbeater. He could send any message by his talking drum. Although we did not understand what he was saying, it was a pleasure to listen to its rhythm.

Messages are normally sent in the cool of the evening, since sound carries better than at midday. However, in the early mornings—four or five a.m.—we heard the drums beating in village after village. We asked our drummer what was going on. "Oh," he replied, "just sending the news." We objected that most people were asleep at that time and not likely to hear the drum. Our informant agreed but said that did not matter—they had heard the news already. Early morning news was sent daily to the spirits of dead ancestors and friends! They believe that those who pass on are interested in what happens in their old homes.

Likae was the drummer in our caravan. My husband asked him: If he could send messages to the dead, would he send a message for us to the living? "Yes," he replied, "but what would be the subject?" My husband explained that it would be a gospel message—to be sent in the quiet of the evening when people could think about it. He gave the drummer an outline and Likae went off to see how he might work it out in his code words. Later, he came by and offered to try to send it that evening. Here is what he drummed out on the night air:

> The Creator who made men, the Owner of the forest, sent his only Son to die on a tree with a crosspiece, and he received a spear wound. He died for us all because he loved us. He died for those who grip the spear and shield (men) and he died for those who bear child (women), and for those who recline on chairs (old folk) and for those who run about with pattering feet (little children). He is not dead. He is alive and with us now. When you go into the forest, he accompanies you. Believe and love him in your heart; speak to him in the forest, or by the stream, or in your village. He hears you. Do not forget: he never leaves you. On a journey, he is always with you.

The message went on the air that evening. It drew attention, stimulated interest, and brought a lot of people to the gospel service the next morning—especially older folk. Others who would not normally attend a service came, seeking information about that remarkable Person of whom they had heard the night before. It became our custom when on the road to send a gospel message to all who had ears to hear our wireless news. We shall never know how many listened to it and told it to others, but we believe that God blessed the effort.

—Lily Ruskin, in *Ruskin of Congo*

1

The Man Who Beats the Drum

The man who beats the drum does not know how far the sound will go.

—Congolese proverb

Western Blizzard

Jeremiah Lanphier paced the floor, fear wrestling with faith. Three weeks before, he had distributed a handbill announcing a prayer meeting to be held every Wednesday at 12:00 noon, beginning September 23. It would last just an hour. It was for businessmen. But this was New York City. Would they come?

Lanphier had just accepted appointment as a city missionary with the Old North Dutch Church in downtown Manhattan. Membership was down. With his engaging manner and gifts of exhortation, Lanphier seemed the ideal candidate to infuse new life into the Old North Church. In 1857, like a lot of others, Old North needed something new.

America was in turmoil. The third great economic panic in American history—dubbed The Western Blizzard—had collapsed the blazing prosperity of the previous seven years (1850–56). Gold fever in California had catalyzed explosive growth of the railroads, fueling a frenzied stock market. Prosperity had "caught the public fancy, and turned men's hearts from God."[5] Bank fraud and inflated stocks fed the collapse of Wall Street. Hundreds of businesses failed. The railroads followed. Factories closed, leaving thousands unemployed. On September 12, the sidepaddle steamer, *Central America*, went down in a hurricane off Cape Hatteras, taking four hundred lives and $1.6 million in California gold. News of the disaster triggered fresh panic. By 19 October 1857—the worst point of the freefall—"the hearts of the American people were weaned from speculation and uncertain gain, while hunger and despair stared them in the face."[6]

A Nation Turns to Prayer

The panic drove thousands into churches and tent meetings, where they prayed for "an end to bloodshed in Kansas, civil strife in the cities, and a return to prosperity." Even the secular press bowed its head when "the usually staid *Journal of Commerce* asked its readers to

> Steal awhile away from Wall Street
> And every worldly care,
> And spend an hour about mid-day
> In humble, hopeful prayer." [7]

At 12:00 noon on 23 September 1857, Lanphier opened the door of the consistory building of the North Dutch Church on Fulton Street and took his seat. Ten minutes passed. No one came. At 12:25, Lanphier was still alone. Then, at 12:30, a step was heard on the stairs and the first person appeared. Soon six were present and the prayer meeting began.

The following Wednesday, twenty supplicants arrived. On October 7, forty intercessors were present. Encouraged, Lanphier conferred with others and decided to hold the meeting daily instead of weekly. The now-famous Fulton Street gathering quickly spilled over into daily prayer meetings at one hundred fifty locations throughout Manhattan and Brooklyn.[8] Within six months, ten thousand businessmen were gathering daily for prayer in New York City, and within two years, a million converts had poured into American churches.

> A divine influence seemed to pervade the land, and men's hearts were strangely warmed by a Power that was outpoured in unusual ways. There was no fanaticism . . . It seemed to many that the fruits of Pentecost had been repeated a thousandfold. At any rate, the number of conversions reported soon reached the total of fifty thousand weekly, a figure borne out by church statistics showing an average of ten thousand additions to church membership a week for a period of two years.[9]

In the same week, apparently unconnected to the American panic, revival swept the city of Hamilton in faraway Canada. The Great Awakening of 1858–59 had begun. It would set in motion the greatest wave of world evangelization the world had yet seen.

The man who beats the drum does not know how far the sound will go. So runs the Congolese proverb. The apothegm has practical meaning for the Congolese. Village drums in thatch roofed gazebos perch atop conical anthills twenty feet high. They waft their melodic cadences across the forest canopy. These are the *talking drums* by which villages discourse with one another. The signal may travel for miles. Just how far is limited by humidity, temperature, air currents, and other such factors. Once the drummer sends his message these forces take over. He really does not know how far the sound will go. While there were many factors and hidden antecedents to the *Great Awakening*, the now-famous Fulton Street Prayer Meeting was a primary trigger. Lay missionary Lanphier had beat the drum. He could never have guessed how far the sound would go.

The Spreading Flame

The awakening in North America could not be contained. Overleaping national boundaries, the spreading flame burned its way across the Atlantic. First to feel its glow was Ireland, in 1858. The revival then moved—in order—to Scotland, and England. Sweden and Norway followed. There was one notable exception: revival failed to touch those Roman Catholic countries where the Bible was not in the hands of the people.[10]

Alexander Whyte, renowned scholar and pulpiteer of Free St. George's in Edinburgh, then a student/teacher at King's College, Aberdeen, wrote to John Dickson:

> Are not these great days of the Son of Man? Are you getting any news of such work in Ireland and the West of Scotland? If you have read any account of the awakening, you will know that it had its origin in answer to a prayer meeting held in Kells schoolroom by four young men, and you will find John Wallace the first of them.

Then, advising his academic friend of what to expect from Wallace, he says:

> He is a poor, uneducated, working Irishman—a few years ago a wild, drunken, cock-fighting Irishman. Now he is an eminently spiritual man of God. He has, I think, the strongest hold on God's promises and faithfulness of any man I ever met. He mispronounces fearfully . . . is far from the clerical type, but he is a jewel of the first water in rough setting. His kindness, humility, sympathy, Christ-like walk, cheerfulness, and quiet humor make him a most pleasant companion . . . Think of it, the origin of the Irish Revival which has brought tens of thousands to Christ . . . is spreading through England, Scotland, and Wales . . . We are honored in having him under the same roof.[11]

The spiritual firestorm that swept North American and British churches brought immeasurable blessing to the nations of the Earth. It was a matter of cause and effect. J. Edwin Orr, noted historian of revival movements, affirmed that wherever God moves in a revival way, the effects will be felt on the mission fields of Earth within ten years. It is a fact of history. William Temple's axiom was operational: "No one can possess or be indwelt by the Holy Spirit and keep that Spirit to himself. He flows. If he is not flowing, he is not there."[12] He was there. And he was flowing.

Divine Symbiosis

The Great Awakening of 1858 is the preamble to the story of our two mission agencies, for the history of missions is essentially the history of revival. Beginning with Pentecost, mission and revival have been inseparable, concurrent, and functionally synonymous. Mission is the spontaneous expression of God's nature. Awakened men and women, ardent with the love of Christ, will love God's world, for mission flows from God-likeness. It is impossible to explain the birth, growth, and accomplishments of the Regions Beyond Missionary Union and the West Indies Mission apart from the outpouring of the Holy Spirit in the revival of 1858 and 1859. That Awakening was the spring. It began as a trickle. It became a river, flowing from the throne of God and of the Lamb, bringing healing to many nations.

2

A Shining Light

The spirit of Revival that broke out in Britain and America had taken hold of me. I was prepared for it though I knew it not, but only yearned to be a burning and a shining light for God among men.

—H. Grattan Guinness

Brewers, Bankers—and Henry

Henry Grattan Guinness is not as well known today than the beverage that sports the family name in British pubs. His name, however, shines with a luster brighter than that on the gilded label of a bottle of stout. As his chronicler explains, "When the first Arthur Guinness founded a small brewery on the banks of the River Liffey in Dublin, he could not have foreseen the dynasty of brewers and bankers that would emerge. But there was another side to the family: several generations of brilliant clergymen and missionaries, perhaps the greatest of whom was Henry Grattan Guinness, the Billy Graham of his day."[13]

Multi-gifted and born to privilege, the Irish orator with the silver voice became one of the outstanding preachers of the nineteenth century—on a par with Spurgeon and Moody, affirmed J. Edwin Orr. More remarkable, Guinness and his illustrious family became primary catalysts of the astonishing worldwide missionary effort flowing from the Great Awakening. So much so, that when John Mott read the telegram announcing Guinness' death to the delegates of the 1910 World Missionary Conference in Edinburgh, Scotland, "A wave of sorrow passed over the assembly." So noted Joseph Adams, a former Guinness student. "We all felt that the Church of Christ Militant had lost one of its great missionary leaders. To those who had known him intimately and loved him dearly there came a feeling of personal loss."[14]

Birth and Background

Henry Grattan Guinness was born in 1835 in Dublin to Irish Protestant parents, both Nonconformists,[15] and both widowers. His mother, Jane Lucretia, beautiful and gifted as a pianist, had lost her first husband in a duel. His father, Captain John Grattan Guinness, at fifty-two was retired from army service with the East India Company. It was the second marriage for both. They named their first son, Henry Grattan, after John Grattan's cousin, "Ireland's most celebrated politician."[16] Life had smiled on Henry. He was gifted with an instinct for leadership, an eloquence of speech, a magnetic personality, and the ability to move men. Much of this asset he drew from his mother, who could point to a long pedigree of distinguished musicians and composers. He remembered her as "a gifted woman, constantly occupied with Christian activities." Lucretia's spiritual activism reached into the community, providing schools for children, engaging in Biblical dialog with Jewish people, working for the rehabilitation of prostitutes, visiting the sick, and witnessing of Christ to all she met. Henry would later say of her, "Whatever love I have had for nature, for history, and for literature, has been derived from her, and also whatever gift I may possess as a public speaker."[17]

On the other side of the ledger "Guinness men were either intensely shrewd and practical or spiritual and other-worldly, and when they were the latter they were hopelessly impractical." So notes Michele Guinness, the family chronicler. In the case of Henry and his father, both "lived half in this world and half in the next, and left the lesser, mundane necessities of life, such as food and finance, to the practical good sense of their spouses."[18] Fortunately, God had someone in mind that would provide Henry with that practical good sense.

Conversion and Patagonia

Henry Grattan Guinness was converted in 1853 through his brother, Wyndham, a sailor. Returning home to Cheltenham after a long sea voyage, he spoke to Henry of the need of Christ in his life. That night Henry became a changed man. He at once decided to serve Christ and purposed to give his life to the people of Patagonia in Argentina's frigid Southern Cone. He had been greatly moved by the life of Captain Allen Gardiner, a former British naval officer turned missionary. Together with six companions, Gardiner had died of starvation on the bleak and wintered shores of Tierra del Fuego. Irresistibly drawn to the shining hero, young Guinness began to prepare himself for the venture, but it was not to be. Ill health firmly closed the door.

While recuperating in southern Ireland, Guinness came under deep conviction of sin. Restless and dissatisfied with his spiritual life, he longed for holiness and a life of usefulness in the Lord's service. He emerged from this crisis "consumed with evangelistic zeal" and threw himself into fearless witness among the Roman Catholics of southern Ireland. The effort nearly ended his life when he was beaten by angry mobs of country people, encouraged by the Roman priests.[19] At the urging of his ever-practical mother, Henry entered New College, London, but not for long. Distributing thousands of tracts to passersby on the streets of London offered a more attractive exercise than books. Moreover, finding places to preach in the open air seemed to satisfy an irrepressible sense of call. Henry would become a great lover of books and a renowned writer. But not just yet. He left London College and plunged into ministry.

Ordination and Ministry

Henry was ordained on Wednesday, 29 July 1857 in Moorfields Tabernacle, London. Just twenty-one, he immediately launched an evangelistic tour throughout the whole of Wales. During this itinerary, he addressed congregations in churches and in the open air 142 times in eighty places, reaching 100,000 people.[20] Revival was in the air, and it was a time "when theatres, music-halls, concert halls, or any buildings capable of seating an audience were filled with people, some of them waiting from early morning to get places at an evening service."

Peregrinations in Scotland followed the Welsh tour; then he went on to the Continent. Returning to England, he addressed yet more meetings. Then it was back to Ireland and a succession of engagements that reached every town in the Emerald Isle. A second tour in Ireland was conducted the following year, just before he left in the fall for the United States. A very young Grattan Guinness had been invited to help sustain the awakening that was sweeping North America. It would be the first of many visits. He arrived in Philadelphia in November 1858 "to a punishing schedule, preaching as often as thirteen times a week" to the crowds that pressed to hear him—sailors, riggers, stevedores, firefighters, students, children, and criminals. Then it was on to New York and other American and Canadian towns, "preaching a minimum of nine sermons a week for six or seven months."[21] Drained by the exercise, he returned to Ireland for a time of rest. He found recovery during the summer of 1860 at Ilfracombe, a resort town on the North Devon coast. He also found a wife.

Fanny Fitzgerald

Fanny Fitzgerald was twenty-nine and not particularly attractive. Nevertheless, the Irish lass had a mind, a gifted pen, and a pedigree. Her father had been a member of one of Ireland's most illustrious aristocratic families—"a long line of adventurers who had played a leading role in the conquest of Ireland."[22] He was also a distinguished journalist and editor of a newspaper—gifting that Fanny would inherit and effectively employ. Nevertheless, for all his favored heritage, Major Edward Fitzgerald was overcome by the storms of life—a divorce, the loss of his son, and the death of his second wife.

Despondent, he threw himself overboard from a Channel steamer, leaving four girls without a parent. Fanny was second of the four, and eight years old. She was taken in and brought up by a Quaker couple, who nurtured her in Quaker ways.[23]

Marriage and Ministry

Henry was completely smitten by Fanny Fitzgerald. Bypassing her more attractive sister, he concluded that Fanny "was no ordinary woman" and followed her to her home in Bath to pursue the relationship. The romance blossomed, and in October 1860, Henry Grattan and Fanny Fitzgerald blended their lives and embarked on an incredible career. They would have thirty-eight years together.

Some months after their wedding, the couple sailed for America, "that I might there resume my evangelistic work," said Henry. The trip was prognostic. Incessant travel—transatlantic crossings, trips to Ireland, England, Scotland, Wales, and the Continent—marked their first twelve years together. In the process, they raised a cosmopolitan family.

Of their eight children, only two were born in the same city, and only four would survive. H. Grattan Jr., affectionately known as "Harry," arrived in Toronto on 2 October 1861. Geraldine, who married Dr. Howard Taylor and became Hudson Taylor's biographer, was a Christmas package, presented in Liverpool on Christmas Day 1862. Lucy, who with her husband Karl Kumm, founded the Sudan United Mission, joined the family in July 1865. Whitfield, who became a medical missionary to China, made his debut in Paris in 1869.

God births and gifts great men for special tasks in history, then discards the mold. There are no duplicates. Indisputably, Henry Grattan Guinness was custom-created for the Great Awakening. On reaching his twenty-first birthday—the year before the Revival—he confided to his diary that his only ambition was "to live preaching and to die preaching: to live and die in the pulpit; to preach to perishing sinners till I drop down dead."[24] And preach he did. As his gifts became visible, invitations multiplied—on both sides of the Atlantic.

Learning to Walk

For all the intellectual endowment by which he might have commanded a fortune, H. Grattan Guinness lived frugally and walked in daily dependence upon God's promised provision. Both Hudson Taylor's life and his maxim, "God's work done in God's way will never lack God's supply," strongly influenced Guinness. The euphoria of revival had moved men to believe God and to test the divine promise, *"See if I will not throw open the floodgates of heaven and pour out so much blessing that you will not have room enough for it."*[25] George Mueller had found it so. Tom Barnardo likewise. Both founded great orphanages. These men—and Hudson Taylor—were Guinness' contemporaries. The tide of blessing lifted all their boats. Guinness would later write:

> Looking back over the ministry of those days I recall the fact that it was boldly undertaken in faith, and largely unrecompensed in character. It was wholly unsalaried. Never, as far as I remember, in the course of a long ministry, have I made any bargain for fee or reward. My Uncle, Arthur Guinness of Beaumont, had left me £400 as a legacy, and when my mother needed pecuniary help I gave her this sum, and went down to Birmingham to preach the gospel, knowing no one and with half a crown in my pocket. When speaking there in the open air in what was called the Bull Run, a brother in the Lord came forward and asked me to his house, and from that day I have never lacked a home to shelter in, or provision for daily needs.[26]

Walking by faith seemed to come with relative ease to Guinness. He was more a visionary than an administrator. Managing the day-to-day affairs of meeting budgets and feeding a growing student body, as they would later do, fell largely to Fanny. Her more commonsensical bent knew that trusting God must necessarily be accompanied by practical measures. When it came to making needs known, her pragmatism was unabashed. Speaking of the East London Institute—the missionary training college they established—she affirmed:

> We commenced the Institute with nothing in hand—no premises, no furniture, no linen, china, cutlery, no educational apparatus, no mission hall, and without funds in hand, but with the conviction that if it were of God and for his glory, he would send the means of supply.[27]

Affairs of the Purse

As in every work of God, the exercise of finding God's supply was often difficult. The Guinnesses, however, were not in the dark as to Heaven's purpose in the often-mysterious tension that seems to exist between God's supply and our demand. She wrote:

> Money matters are certainly not for the present joyous, but grievous. We do greatly dislike them. Sometimes regretting the amount of thought, energy, attention and prayer which it has been needful to devote to the question of ways and means, we have wondered why the blessed Master, who could so easily have done it, did not send us adequate and regular supplies. Deuteronomy 8 solves the problem: "He humbled thee and suffered thee to hunger and fed thee with manna that He might make thee to know that man does not live by bread alone." Money matters may be, must be, a means of grace to those whose only banker is their heavenly Father.[28]

Notwithstanding, Guinness piety was no head-in-the-clouds idealism. They held faith in refreshing balance with a down-to-earth pragmatism:

> As to our mode of raising funds—said Fanny—we rely mainly on prayer to God; but believing that prayer and effort are not antagonistic, we take means to make our little undertaking and its requirements known to fellow-Christians whom we think likely to sympathize in it. We do not expect God to do for us by a miracle that which we can do for ourselves, that is, give information of the nature and needs of our work. [But] we do entirely trust him to do that which we cannot do— open the hearts of his people to sustain it.[29]

This approach to financing would mark the Mission for a hundred years.

Although his formal theological training was never completed, Guinness never decried education. He was a student of history, of the Scriptures, and of the sciences. Half a century of such discipline produced a plethora of books on prophetic subjects and on Romanism, science, and philosophy. At one time, more than 50,000 copies of his books were in circulation. Brown University (Providence, Rhode Island) recognized this in 1899, conferring on him the Doctor of Divinity degree.[30] His ventures into astronomy as a key to Biblical prophecy would win him a fellowship in the Royal Astronomical Society.

The Church Awakens

The Awakening of 1858–59 had stirred the churches of North America and Britain to a fresh sense of the authority of Scripture and the primacy of prayer—two elements that distinctly marked the revival movement. As our Lord had opened the long-dimmed eyes of his disciples to the missionary message of the Old Testament and its focus on the ethnic groups of earth,[31] so the Holy Spirit opened the eyes of the late nineteenth century Church to the call of an unevangelized world. The spirit of joyous sacrifice was moving through the churches, and missionary volunteers seemed to abound. This work of the Spirit would not go uncontested.

An Old Foe in Fresh Garb

In 1866, Guinness became incensed with the deepening insinuation of Darwinism into the working class society of London. Popularized by the release of *Origin of Species* (1859), Darwin's plausible theory of natural selection had begun to grip public imagination. By substituting a purposeless materialistic process for the Creator, it was now possible to be "an intellectually fulfilled atheist." No longer confined to the intelligentsia, the evolutionary notion had launched its sinister assault on the common people. To combat this fresh strategy from the nether regions, a new weapon was needed and H. Grattan Guinness knew what it was. He determined to launch a counterculture of his own.

The Dublin Apologetics Class

Ill equipped in the skills of Christian apologetics, he began to develop an arsenal of Christian evidences, conducting lively debates in homes with proponents of the new secularism. The debates drew public attention. In the same year—1866—Guinness started a theology class for young men in his Dublin home. He purposed to arm them with appropriate evidential weapons.[32] He and Fanny were hopeful of beginning "a training home for evangelists and missionaries." They could not have known it then, but the reverberations of their drumbeat would echo far beyond the Emerald Isle.

China Comes to Dublin

To this apologetics class in Dublin in 1866 the thirty-one-year-old Guinness invited James Hudson Taylor, who the previous year had founded the China Inland Mission (CIM). Taylor likewise was a product of the revival. He and Guinness had chanced to meet in Liverpool and the youthful revivalist instinctively saw what an infusion of encouragement the now-famous missionary might bring to his students. Seizing the moment, he invited Taylor to address the class. Taylor agreed. Guinness took an earlier channel steamer, and went ahead to make preparations. What happened next was recalled years later by Mrs. Howard Taylor:[33]

> [Mr. Guinness] had much to tell about the new Mission, and especially its leader, who in faith was attempting no less a task than the evangelization of inland China. The young men assembled at the hour of Mr. Taylor's arrival were on the tiptoe of expectation. John McCarthy was there, and Charles Fishe and his brother, little thinking they were that night to hear the call of God to their life work . . . Mr. and Mrs. Guinness, too, were unconsciously waiting the touch that was to lead first themselves, then all their children, into the work of foreign missions.[34]

The Door Closes—Again

Ten candidates for China resulted from that visit, but not the personal commission that Henry and Fanny had hoped for. Hudson Taylor gently advised them that perhaps they were not meant to go themselves, but would they not devote their experience and talents to the important task of training others to go?[35] Again, God was closing a door—as he had done in the case of Patagonia—that he might open another. It would be the great work of their lives. However, Henry and Fanny were not yet ready to revise their agenda.

Taylor's Radical Strategy

By 1873 Hudson Taylor's China Inland Mission was eight years old and about to become the largest mission in China. Taylor's strategy was shrewd, unprecedented, and successful: Recruit missionary candidates across denominational lines and turn them loose. Under the umbrella of the China Inland Mission, he gave freedom to the new pioneers to develop Christian communities within defined geographical areas where they might retain their denominational distinctives—Presbyterians, Baptists, Methodists, *et al.* It was the gospel in thirty-three flavors. But it was the gospel! In inland China there had been no gospel. The plan worked. Within eight years, the CIM had fielded more than 1,000 missionaries.

Until Hudson Taylor's time most denominational missions had confined their ministry to the major coastal centers of the countries they served. The new vision focused on the vast and unreached populations of the interior of these countries. The day of the *inland* missions had dawned—the China Inland Mission, the Africa Inland Mission, the Sudan Interior Mission. This passion for the unreached interior populations of the great continents shaped Guinness' thinking and would, in 1878, birth the Livingstone Inland Mission to Central Africa, precursor of the Regions Beyond Missionary Union.

H. Grattan Guinness
Founder of the Regions Beyond Missionary Union.

3

Ashes That Lit a Fire

Never, as far as I remember, in the course of a long ministry, have I made any bargain for fee or reward. My Uncle, Arthur Guinness of Beaumont, had left me £400 as a legacy, and when my mother needed pecuniary help I gave her this sum, and went down to Birmingham to preach the gospel, knowing no one and with half a crown in my pocket.

—H. Grattan Guinness

France and Spain

Henry and Fanny pondered Hudson Taylor's suggestion, but ideas, like seeds, need time to germinate. Not until 1873—seven years after Taylor's visit to Dublin—would the East London Institute for Home and Foreign Missions bud and flower. While the Guinnesses mused the idea of a training school, they plunged themselves into their first love: evangelistic ministry.

In 1868 they crossed the Channel to France to lend a hand with an evangelistic campaign, *Evangèlization Populaire*. They spent eighteen months pioneering in Paris and the provinces, with the exception of a three-month excursion to Switzerland. While in France, the Guinness children became fluent in French, an asset that would later serve young Harry well in Congo. At the outbreak of the Franco-Prussian war in 1870, they returned to England.[36]

Guinness could barely speak French, but he was not one to be troubled by petty handicaps. In a few months, he addressed more than seven hundred meetings. Exhausted, and with eyes inflamed, he went to Switzerland for a rest. On his return, he traveled through Spain. What happened here changed the course of his life. Michele Guinness, in her definitive biography of the Guinness family, relates the event:

Some workmen in Madrid were constructing a new road near the city. As they cut through the top of a hill, they noticed that between the usual layers of red gravel there was a large stratum of soft black dust. When they examined the layer more closely, they found bits of bone and hair and realized they had discovered human remains. This was the site of the *Quemadero*,[37] the burning place of the Spanish inquisition. Thousands of Protestant "heretics" had been tortured and killed on this spot.[38]

The Spanish Inquisition

The Inquisition's bloody engine brought its reign of terror to Spain in 1483 under the blessing of Queen Isabella and with the support of Pope Alexander VI, purportedly to promote "the purity of faith, nation, and people." Balancing this altruism—at least in equal measure—was the insatiable materialistic appetite of the aristocracy. The sought-for purity was achieved under the inquisitor Torquemada, who began the process by driving the Jews out of Spain. They were the lucky ones. In its 330 years of existence in Spain alone, the Inquisition had 323,362 persons put to death by fire, and 17,659 burned in effigy.[39]

Guinness' biographer continues:

> News of the finding spread quickly round the town and Henry, who happened to be in Madrid, went to have a look. The workmen went on digging, exposing yet more gruesome evidence of the most barbaric cruelty, rusty chains and nails, instruments of torture, the remains of two hands clasped in prayer and transfixed by a huge iron nail, the ribs of a victim with a spear protruding from them. Any attempt to separate the relics from the surrounding substances failed. They simply crumbled into dust. As Guinness stood among the ashes of so many martyrs, tears welled up in his eyes. None of his study of church history had caused him the sense of grief and revulsion which he felt now as he touched and examined the ghastly evidence of religious cruelty. He collected a heap of ashes, folded them tenderly in a Spanish newspaper, and took them home to his hotel.[40]

The Madrid visit took place in the Spring of 1870 on the eve of the great ecumenical council in Rome, in which the Vatican Council proclaimed the infallibility of the Pope (then Pius IX). Both incidents profoundly influenced Guinness, giving fresh vigor and direction to his ministry from that point forward. Newly minted Roman pretensions to infallibility now combined with the horror of the Madrid experience to drive him more deeply into the study of prophecy. He became an increasingly ardent and eloquent champion of Reformation truth. The ashes from the Quemadero remained on his desk, and at times were brought to the lectern when he preached, a carbonized symbol of all that was wrong with Rome.[41]

Guinness' diatribes against the Roman Catholic system flowed from an informed scholarship with respect to the papacy and its dark history of suppressing the truth and those who proclaimed it. He spoke with incandescent eloquence of the ruthless persecution of the Albigenses, of the Waldenses, and of the massacre of 22,000 French Protestants known as the Huguenots. He decried the expulsion of 50,000 Protestants from France—the deadly work of the Inquisition—and the unretracted audacity of the Council of Trent (1547), that placed tradition on an equal level of authority with the biblical record.[42] Typical of his oratorical eloquence is this extract from one of his lectures:

> Ride forth, fair flower of France! Strive, ye brave Huguenots, for your country's freedom and the faith of the gospel! But Paris shall run with your blood; ye shall fall like leaves from a tree shaken by tempest; ye shall lie in heaps, like rubbish in the streets; your bodies shall choke the streams, they shall rot in rivers, they shall hang in chains, they shall be shoveled into cemeteries, or buried in dung heaps. Rome shall ring her joy-bells and sing her *Te Deums,* and fill her cathedrals and palaces with acclamations because the massacre of St. Bartholomew has overthrown for a time, the work of the Reformation in France.[43]

Historicist Views

Guinness became a committed historicist in his interpretation of the book of Revelation, specifically identifying the "beast" of Revelation 13 and the "Little Horn" of Daniel 7 as the same entity, both metaphors depicting the papal system.[44] For Guinness, the *Man of Sin*, of whom the Apostle Paul speaks (2 Thess. 2.4) was neither Jewish nor a single individual but represented the long succession of Roman Popes—in a word, the papal dynasty. It was the Jesuit Ribera, Guinness affirmed, who at the close of the sixteenth century first introduced futurist interpretations of Antichrist—relegating his appearance to "some final spasm" at the close of the age. This was done to deflect public attention from the true nature of the papacy as the foe of truth.[45]

Nor was it the temple in Jerusalem into which this usurper had come, but into that greater temple, the Church of the Lord Jesus Christ, his rightful throne pre-empted by a succession of great pretenders—the long line of Roman Catholic popes. In this conviction, Guinness was in good company. The reformers agreed, as did the divines who put together the Westminster Confession of Faith.

Marshaling convincing arguments from both Scripture and the Church Fathers, Guinness identified the much debated *he who hinders,* who would be *taken out of the way* (1 Thess. 2:6,7) as Imperial Rome before its collapse in 476 A. D. Until that time, he maintained, the strong arm of Roman secular authority had restrained the lethal ascendancy of the papacy. Once Rome *pagan* had been taken out of the way, the path was clear for Rome *papal* to rise unchallenged in the sixth century. With the fall of imperial Rome, the "beast" laid aside its secular garb and donned the ornate robes of an absolute politico-religious papacy.

The Guinness outrage flowed from a genuine anguish for the millions whose blind allegiance had deprived them of the liberating freedom of the gospel. If his charges seem inflammatory to the late twentieth century ear, it must be remembered that he spoke in a day when Romanist pretensions to absolute ecclesiastical and civil authority were far less subject to the restraints of social and political correctness prevailing one hundred years later.

The Purpose of Prophecy

Notwithstanding, Henry Grattan Guinness rode no eschatological hobbyhorse. If with unrelenting fervor he challenged the arrogance and barbarisms of popery, he also tirelessly pursued the salvation of a lost humanity. For Guinness the study of prophecy was no doctrinaire exercise to titillate the overfed and the curious. It was a wake-up call to world evangelization. Christ would soon return, and there was a world to be won. Prophecy was fuel for faith, calling the Church to bold venture in winning the lost. It moved Guinness to tireless effort in spreading the gospel. He founded the East London Institute in the "eschatological consciousness" of the swift approach of the end of the age, and for the same reasons he promoted the formation of missionary training schools in the United States with like philosophy and objective.

This was clear from his prodigious evangelistic ministry through which thousands came to Christ around the world. His absorption with Bible prophecy led to the writing of scholarly books, such as *Light for the Last Days*, *The Approaching End Of The Age*, and *Romanism and the Reformation*.[46] More important, his transparent love for the lost bore the irrefutable hallmark of authenticity, for it won the allegiance of his children, all of whom became ardent missionaries. The astonishing array of missionary effort and mission agencies that flowed from the influence of his pen and pulpit bear ample witness.

Times of the Gentiles

One other achievement of Guinness' biblical research is fascinating. It arose from his study of the works of the Swiss astronomer, Jean Philippe Loys de Cheseaux, who in 1754 had been able to reconcile the difference between the lunar and the solar calendars.[47] Michele Guinness explains:

> De Cheseaux, who had been trying to establish the date of the cruci-
> fixion, fell upon the fact that 315 years constituted such a soli-lunar cy-
> cle, the sun and moon coming to within three hours, twenty-four sec-
> onds of absolute agreement. No sooner had he discovered that cycle
> than, to his excitement, he realized that 315 was a quarter of 1260, the

number of "days" mentioned in the book of Revelation as having significance for the end of the age. Therefore 1260 years, as a multiple of 315, was itself a soli-lunar cycle.

But even more extraordinary, when he examined it closely he discovered that 1260 years was the time it took for the sun and moon to move into conjunction within an hour of each other. Guinness had found the key: 1260 years was a complete cycle of time, bringing the lunar and solar calendars into almost total harmony."[48]

This discovery explained for Guinness the enigmatic use of "day" in prophecy as representing a soli-lunar "year." Before Cheseaux, the solar and lunar cycles had been perceived as irreconcilable. It was now clear that Scripture's use of the word "day" in place of "year" was intentional—until the astronomical precision of the luni-solar year should be discovered. The stellar heavens were, in fact, a giant prophetic clock in perfect harmony with Biblical revelation. When Guinness saw the remarkable connection between the stellar vault and the prophetic Scriptures, he became an avid astronomer, and acquired a telescope on which he had the text engraved, *Holiness to the Lord*. He was honored with a fellowship in The Royal Astronomical Society and his astronomical tables became a standard in observatories throughout the world.[49]

These computations are set out fully in *Light for the Last Days*.[50] In that book, he pointed to 1917 as a crucial year for Jewish restoration. At the end of the last paragraph of the book of Ezekiel, Guinness had penciled the date 1948 (He died in 1910). It was the logical projection of the 1,260th year marking the times of the Gentiles. On 15 May 1948, Israel became a nation.[51]

4

The East London Institute

The vision of faith has ideas about the future, which are God's ideas. God himself is the one who 'summons things that are not yet in existence as if they already were.' Vision is not a matter of seeing what is and asking why. It is far more a matter of seeing what has never yet been and asking why not."

—Os Guinness

No Place to Take a Family

By 1872, Hudson Taylor's suggestion had germinated in Guinness' thinking. The conviction that God was calling them to a wider service was ready to flower. In November, while in Armagh, the decision was made. Henry noted simply in his diary, "The Cloud Moves—may I have grace to follow." They would attempt to start a missionary training college in London. Putting shoes to their purpose, they took the channel steamer to England and began to tramp the wintry streets of London in search of a location.[52]

London's East End had an unsavory reputation. In 1873 it was a slum, graphically depicted by Charles Dickens, Lucy Guinness, and other writers.[53] Squalor and wretchedness had been the human price of the Industrial Revolution. A place of disease, poverty, the stench of street refuse, and run-down tenements, the East End was home to the marginalized and the serfdom of the lords of industry. It was no place to take a family, and certainly, no place to start a school. But Mile End Waste thronged with hucksters and human traffic. For Guinness, it was a magnet.

Though born to wealth and privilege, he had always been attracted to the disadvantaged. As a young man, he had preached in the worst of London's slums. Now facing the challenge of locating a training school, he was drawn to this unpromising setting, so full of dangers for a tender family. Guinness was bent on training missionaries. He was certain that anyone who could not make it in London's East End would be unlikely to survive the rigors of the Congo. He explained, "we . . . established our Missionary College in a neighborhood whose only attraction was the sphere it afforded for evangelistic and philanthropic work."[54]

Another—perhaps subliminal—factor that played in this unlikely choice was the fact that years before in this very neighborhood, in a small crowded home on Coburn Street, Hudson had welcomed his first volunteers for China. Taylor was Guinness' hero, and his walk of faith and missionary methods posed an ideal. He later recalled:

> Strangely enough, Harley House—for more than thirty years our Missionary Training Institute—is but a few steps from Coburn, where Mr. Taylor received his first volunteers for the China Inland Mission.
>
> When I visited the small, crowded home of the outgoing Lammermuir party, [little] did I imagine that close to that spot we were to build a college that should train more than a thousand evangelists for the foreign field . . . About a hundred of our students have become missionaries in China, some of them being numbered among the martyrs of the Boxer Outbreak.[55]

The East End offered a bonanza of practical ministry opportunities, and Henry tried to find a house near to the Mile End Waste, a kind of open market thronged with hucksters who plied their wares among the crowds. He discovered what he was looking for at 29 Stepney Green. It was just the spot for training missionary candidates in open air preaching. The Institute opened for business in March 1873[56] with six resident students. In the first year, there were one hundred applications. They had room for thirty-two.[57]

Harley College

By the end of the first year they had outgrown the Stepney Green property, and acquired *Harley House*, two miles east, in Bow.[58] In keeping with the English custom of giving names to private residences, Harley House would become the cognomen for mission headquarters for generations to come. To accommodate the unremitting expansion of the student body, adjoining properties were secured and extensions added. The rule was never to refuse a suitable volunteer. They were accepted in faith that God would provide.

With the growth of the Institute, mission halls were opened throughout East London. Students deployed to preach the gospel until they were reaching 12,000 people weekly. A mission yacht, The *Evangelist,* ferried students and their message to seamen and their ships. Foreign mission rallies spun off throughout the country. The expansion led to construction of a new, two-story facility. It opened in 1878 as Harley College. Then came a women's branch, a women's medical department, and a publishing division.[59]

If euphoric enthusiasm for evangelism marked the East London Institute, it was but part of the wider tide of blessing flowing from an awakened church, as Betty Pritchard relates:

> Dr. Barnardo, the young Tom [of Guinness' Dublin Bible Class], now living opposite Harley House, the home of the Institute, had bought a public house and converted it into a mission hall holding 1,500. [It became the largest orphanage in England]. Bryant and May's match factory was close by, giving opportunity for working men's clubs and night schools, Bible classes for converts, [and] meetings for women and girls. Not far from Harley House stood the East London Tabernacle with its Sunday school of hundreds of children. This building held 2,000 and was always packed to the doors. Moody pitched his great iron hall behind it for his mission of the early 80s and the Guinness children as well as the students threw themselves into the work of this Mission.[60]

The East London Institute

The ELI was a novel departure in British education. Essentially a missionary training institution, the Institute was specifically vocational in purpose, since all applicants came with the declared intention of finding their life work on the foreign field. It was *international*, with twenty nationalities represented in the student body. It was also *interdenominational*, matriculating students from a variety of denominational backgrounds. Nor was ELI a proprietary school. Trainees were freely returned to their own sending agencies, and as many as forty denominations counted Harley men within their ranks.

Most of the new wave of volunteers had little formal education. Existing denominational agencies had their own standards and were equipped to send out their own. However, most applicants lacked the primary education on which to build effective cross-cultural ministry skills. The challenge was formidable. In addition to a comprehensive Bible program, a general education department addressed English language and literature, rhetoric, logic, psychology, ethics, and Greek. Apologetics, theology, and homiletics were not omitted.

The missions department covered world religions and the history of missions. The practical training department reviewed health management, dispensary work, and offered medical training in local hospitals. Weekend preaching found a ready outlet in many districts of the great city. Not least, the daily walk with God was honed through treatment of such practical themes as the prayer life, believing God, and that ever-elusive quality—"mutual forbearance!" Happily free of legalism, the entire curriculum stressed that conduct must be "inspired by principles rather than by rules."[61]

Remarkably, the college was a resident school, operated by faith, charged no tuition fees, and offered no salaries. In the wake of revival, reliance entirely upon God had become the hallmark of an increasing number of missionary societies, of which Harley College was but one. Hudson Taylor's walk of faith in the birth of the China Inland Mission had impressed Guinness. So had George Mueller, who was feeding thousands of orphans in London with no subsidy but God's supply.

Cliff College

In time, the college diversified to accommodate the variety of academic strata reflected in the volunteers. In 1875 friends of H. Grattan Guinness gifted Cliff House—a large country mansion and estate in Derbyshire—for his personal country retreat. It became a training center for workers going to Congo. Under the direction of principal Rattray, "Cliff" combined an academic base with training in survival skills for missionary candidates. Many of the applicants were armed with little more than the conviction that they had a message to deliver to the dark places of earth.

Doric Lodge, the distaff counterpart of Harley College, provided an equally diversified curriculum, plus the addition of midwifery training. In 1889, the Lodge expanded to *Bromley Hall*, an old mansion, and was later directed by Mrs. Fanny Newell, a graduate who had been widowed in Peru in 1902. It was here that Annie Soper, pioneer of RBMU's later work in inland Peru, would take her training. Through Fanny Newell, she would hear the call to the land of the Incas.

Harley College, the first missionary training school in Britain, 1873.

5

How Far the Sound Would Go

Every revival of religion in the homelands is felt within a decade on the foreign mission fields. The records of missionary enterprise and pages of missionary biography following 1860 are full of the clearest evidence of the stimulating effect of the revival throughout the world.

—J. Edwin Orr

The Global Influence of H. Grattan Guinness

Hudson Taylor's quiet suggestion that Guinness start a missionary training college soon re-echoed in other lives and in the formation of other mission agencies. The effects were staggering in their magnitude and enduring in their global consequence. The ELI grew into a popular, multi-school complex, which by 1915 had equipped 1500 men and women for missionary service. Not a few graduates launched new mission societies. Others were absorbed by forty different denominational agencies.

With the glow of the 1858/59 revival still diffusing throughout North America and Britain, the cadences of Jeremiah Lanphier's drumbeat were already resonating around the world. Grattan Guinness' oratorical gifts had brought him to North America in 1858, a mere youth of twenty-three. The Awakening had come to Hamilton, Ontario the previous October—almost simultaneously with the Fulton Street prayer meeting in New York City. It was only the beginning.

A. B. Simpson and the C&MA

While Guinness was preaching in Chatham, western Ontario, his pungent discourses produced deep conviction in a timid fifteen-year-old. Albert B. Simpson, born on Prince Edward Island, grew up in Chatham. Depressed and fearful for his life following a near-drowning experience, the sensitive teenager gave his heart to Christ.[62] Simpson quickly distinguished himself as a gifted preacher of the gospel and at twenty-one took the pulpit of prestigious Knox

Presbyterian Church in Hamilton, Ontario, a post he held with distinction for nine years.[63] In 1883, Simpson founded the *Missionary Training Institute,* the first Bible college in North America and forerunner of *Nyack College.*

Simpson was strongly influenced by Grattan Guinness, and the Nyack institute was "conceived in eschatological consciousness," drawing its philosophy, objectives and structure from the ELI founded nine years earlier by Guinness.[64] Five years later (1887), Simpson founded the Christian and Missionary Alliance (C&MA). When he died in 1919, the C&MA was worldwide, and at the end of the century was ministering in fifty-seven countries with 2.4 million members in 10,000 churches.

William Coit "Daddy" Stevens

One of Simpson's admirers was William Coit Stevens, who left the Presbyterian pastorate to collaborate with the new Alliance movement. A "classic linguist, he acquired skills in Latin, Greek and Hebrew, in addition to German and French." Stevens was a graduate of Union Seminary and had done two years of graduate work in Germany. He brought high credentials to his post as principal of Simpson's Missionary Training Institute, having already organized the C&MA Gospel Tabernacle in Los Angeles, and having worked the West Coast from Canada to Mexico as an Alliance Superintendent. Utterly without pretensions, he held his earned degrees with disarming modesty while refusing several honorary degrees, preferring to be called, simply, "Pastor Stevens."[65] This self-effacing attitude and disdain for academic acclaim would later play a formative role in the lives of two principal figures in the World Team story.

Both Simpson and Stevens wanted to move the Nyack Schools toward junior and liberal arts college status, and ultimately to university level. But the time was not ripe. By 1914, a bias was slowly building within the C&MA against higher education because "the liberal movement had its support mainly in denominational universities and seminaries." Wartime financial shortfall was another factor. The dreams of Stevens for higher education at the Nyack schools "were rejected by the General Council in 1914." Having left the Presbyterian Church to follow Simpson, Stevens had become staunchly nonsectarian. He now judged that the Alliance was moving away from its traditional interdenominational stance and was no longer a purely fraternal movement.[66]

Midland Bible Institute

In 1914, after thirteen years at Nyack, Stevens resigned, later moving to Kansas City, where in 1918 he founded the Midland Bible Institute. The school survived for just five years, but it was long enough to shape two students who would add their own drumbeat to those of Jeremiah Lanphier, Hudson Taylor, and Grattan Guinness.

Leslie E. Maxwell

Leslie E. Maxwell was the eldest of five children. Upon the death of his father, he was left with the care of his mother, his siblings, and the family farm in Salina, Kansas. His desire to attend Moody Bible Institute (MBI) was thus thwarted by family responsibilities. Chicago was too far away. His pastor—a Moody graduate—was on the board of the small school that W.C. Stevens had started the year before in Kansas City. Midland Bible Institute was struggling with just four teachers and a handful of students, but it was closer than Chicago, and "Daddy" Stevens enjoyed the reputation of being "deep in the Word." Maxwell enrolled. With classes held only in the mornings, he was free to work half time for the support of his family.

Shaping an Ethos

Leslie E. Maxwell enjoyed instant rapport with Stevens, and for four years, the godly academician infused young Maxwell with the tools, spirit, values, and graces that had endeared Stevens to lovers of God, his work, and his world. This included the Search Question Method, an inductive approach to Bible Study, which Stevens seems to have developed. On 22 September 1922, L. E. Maxwell finished his studies at Midland. Seventeen days later, he held his first session with eight students in Three Hills, Alberta in what would become Prairie Bible Institute (PBI). Two of the eight would play a large role in the West Indies Mission—Evelyn and Muriel McElheran. A year later, Midland Bible Institute closed.

While Maxwell was busy launching Prairie Bible Institute, Colorado-born Elmer V. Thompson was still immersed in studies—first at Midland (his time there had overlapped with that of Maxwell), then at the Simpson Bible Institute (SBI) in Seattle, Washington, where he followed Principal Stevens when Midland closed in 1923. Thompson graduated from SBI on 13 May 1925.[67] As fellow students at Midland, Maxwell and Thompson connected in a linkage that would lead to the formation of the West Indies Mission. Both men had been deeply influenced by Stevens. He disdained the mad rush to academic credentials as a substitute for the dynamic of the Holy Spirit, a perception that became part of his legacy to Leslie Maxwell and Elmer Thompson. They would transmit this influence to hundreds of students in Canada and in Cuba.

Thompson Goes to Prairie

In 1925, Leslie Maxwell, now principal of Prairie Bible Institute, was looking for help. The school was growing and he needed additional teachers. Logically, he turned for advice to his former professor, now teaching at Simpson Bible College in Seattle. Did Stevens have a student who might join the staff at PBI? Stevens had just the man. He tapped Elmer V. Thompson, who was about to graduate in May. Maxwell had just married Pearl Plummer and a trip to the big city seemed a great way to spend their honeymoon. The newlyweds took the train and—never one to miss an opportunity—Maxwell began married life with a rigorous week of ministry to the students at Simpson College. While in Seattle, he conferred with Elmer Thompson and the two reached an accord: Thompson would join the Prairie Bible Institute staff. The stage had been set for what God was about to do.

Elmer Thompson graduated from SBI in May 1925, joining the PBI faculty in the fall. He taught for two years.[68] The two men forged a lifelong friendship, collaborating in education and world missions—Leslie E. Maxwell, as founder and principal of Prairie Bible Institute, and Elmer V. Thompson, as cofounder and director of the West Indies Mission. Just how that happened is another story to which we will return.

The Qua Iboe Mission

Back at Harley College, a letter reached H. Grattan Guinness. In 1887, a merchant in Nigeria regularly gathered African villagers on Sundays for Christian instruction. Out of this came a request from some West African chiefs for a resident missionary. On a day in June, when the request reached Guinness in London, he shared the letter at mealtime with his students. One responded. Samuel A. Bill, from Belfast, established the Qua Iboe Missionary Association, so named for a small stream that empties into the Gulf of Guinea. His boyhood friend, Archie Bailie, joined him the following year. One of the first *Ibunos* to come to faith was David Ekong, son of a principal chief. He became a primary figure in the growth of a truly indigenous movement among the Ibunos. In 1984 the name of the mission was changed to the Qua Iboe Fellowship to express its missionary partnership with the church. In 1995 the Qua Iboe church had 1,100 congregations and nearly 150,000 members.[69]

The Sudan United Mission

Lucy Guinness, gifted writer, pianist, missions activist, and daughter of H. Grattan Guinness, married Karl Kumm, a young German who had trained at Harley College. They began the *Sudan United Mission* (SUM) in 1904, another story to which we shall return. In 1961, SUM had 60 stations in Nigeria. The Mission was later reorganized as Action Partners, and in 1991 took over the RBMU–UK work in Zaire (Congo).

The Latin America Mission

In 1894, Lucy Guinness, reckoned to be "the finest Christian editor in the British Isles,"[70] published the book, *South America: The Neglected Continent.*[71] Until then, South America had been neglected by evangelical missions As late as 1910 the great Edinburgh World Missionary Conference—in deference to Roman Catholic presence—refused to recognize Latin America as a legitimate field for Protestant missions. Guinness' book greatly influenced the cause of Protestant missions in Latin America.

Harry Strachan and Susan Beamish were among the students of Grattan Guinness at Harley College. Harry applied to RBMU for service in Congo, but his offer was declined on medical grounds. Instead, he and Susan went to Argentina. An inveterate traveler, he did the work of an itinerant evangelist throughout South and Central America, and together in 1921 the Strachans founded the Latin America Mission [LAM] in Costa Rica. Later, they founded the Costa Rica Bible Institute. [72] Strachan groomed the first convert of Annie G. Soper from inland Peru, graduating Vicente Coral from the Costa Rica Bible Institute in 1937. Coral became the first president of *the Association of Evangelical Churches* [AIENOP] in inland Peru. Hattie Kirk, the first missionary to go to Cuba with what would become the West Indies Mission, had also sat under Strachan's ministry in Costa Rica. We shall later meet both Vicente Coral and Hattie Kirk.

Help For Brazil Mission

Another Guinness student, James Fanstone, served seven years in Brazil in Pernambuci. He married Bessie Baird, a Scottish lass from Doric Lodge, the midwifery training division of Harley College. Together they founded the Help for Brazil Mission, which in 1911 merged with the RBMU work in Peru and Argentina to become the Evangelical Union of South America. [73]

North Africa Mission

In the 1880s Grattan Guinness, George Pearse, and other leaders in the 1859 revival in Great Britain joined in founding the North Africa Mission. It later became Arab World Ministries. The mission sought a foothold in Morocco, Tunis, and Algeria. [74]

Gospel Missionary Union

A series of meetings held in Kansas City by H. Grattan Guinness with a dozen men resulted in six volunteering for service and six others offering to provide their support. The result was the formation of the Gospel Missionary Union [GMU]. [75]

Evangelical Union of South America

In 1893 three Englishmen arrived independently in Peru from Harley College in London—Adam Robert Stark, John L. Jarrett, and Frederick J. Peters. Their interest had been awakened by reports of colporteur Francisco G. Penzotti's imprisonment for selling Bibles in Arequipa, a city in the southern Peruvian Andes. [76] They laid the foundations of the first RBMU work in Peru, which in 1911 joined with the Help For Brazil Mission to become the Evangelical Union of South America. [EUSA] [77]

Gordon College and the American Baptists

Driven by ill health, Guinness spent 1899 in the United States, travelling as far as California and Mexico. The following year he returned again to the States, preaching wherever he went. These visits prompted the formation of two Bible schools—one in Minneapolis, presided over by Dr. Henry Mabie, who later became secretary of the American Baptist Missionary Union (ABMU). The other school, founded in Boston under the guidance of Dr. A. J. Gordon, became Gordon College.[78] Mabie recalled the Minneapolis visit:

> About this time, Dr. H. Grattan Guinness made repeated visits to America, once with Mrs. Guinness. He was full of enthusiasm for the Congo [and] gave thrilling accounts of the China Inland and other missions, [including] his own training-school in East London, which had then sent out about twelve hundred missionaries to different parts of the world . . . His public addresses, his conversation and prayers, took a deep hold upon me.

> This was reinforced by the accounts of what Dr. A. J. Gordon, in Boston, was doing in the way of recruiting and training candidates. I also felt drawn out to do something in the way of establishing a similar agency. The Student Volunteer Movement . . . had been largely stimulated by the influence of Drs. Ashmore, Pierson, and Guinness, with all of which I also had close personal relations. I, with others, finally started a small recruiting and training institute in Minneapolis.[79]

While some launched new mission agencies, scores of Guinness' students distinguished themselves in the cause of world evangelization. James Chalmers and Oliver Tompkins, two graduates of Harley College, laid down their lives in Papua New Guinea. About a hundred became members of the China Inland Mission, many losing their lives in the Boxer uprising of 1902. William Newell paved the way for constitutional religious liberty in Peru, while John Ritchie's tireless efforts led to the formation of the IEP (The Evangelical Church of Peru)—at one time the largest evangelical group in the country.[80]

Grattan and Fanny Guinness' literary gifts were passed on primarily to two of their children—Lucy and Geraldine. Geraldine married Howard Taylor, Hudson Taylor's son. She gave literary visibility to the China Inland Mission (CIM)[81] in her classic works, *The Growth of a Soul*, and *The Growth of a Work*, the story of Taylor and the CIM. Henry Grattan Guinness epitomized the wisdom of the Congo proverb—"The man who beats the drum does not know how far the sound goes." The reverberations of his obedience still echo throughout the earth. Nevertheless, in 1873 he had only begun the subject of this story.

6

Heal This Open Sore

Future missionaries will see conversions following every sermon. We prepare the way for them. May they not forget the pioneers who worked in the thick gloom with few rays to cheer except such as flow from faith in God's promise. We work for a glorious future which we are not destined to see.

—David Livingstone

The Bloody Traffic

Starting a foreign mission agency had never occupied the thinking of Henry and Fanny Guinness. For five years (1873–1877) the flow of missionary volunteers through the East London Institute absorbed the academic energies of the legendary couple. Finding resources for the not-for-profit Institute had already stretched faith to the limit. The premises now housed 170 students. Launching a mission agency in addition to carrying the already heavy overhead of the college would put presumption at odds with Providence. This conservatism was about to change.

David Livingstone's life and work was the turning point. Unwittingly, the Scottish explorer inspired the founding of RBMU. By sheer determination and dauntless tenacity, the famed missionary rose from an impoverished boyhood in the mills of Blantyre, Scotland, to secure a medical degree and go to Africa. He was there for thirty years. His first tour with the Church Missionary Society was not particularly successful. His second, an expedition to the Zambesi, ended in failure. His third assignment was sponsored by the Royal Geographical Society and occupied the last eight years of his life. It secured his place in history. This third and final mission accomplished two things: suppression of the Arab slave traffic—what Wilberforce had called "the bloody traffic"—and the long-sought identification of the headwaters of the River Nile.

Just before he died Livingstone had written, "All I can add in my solitude is may heaven's richest blessings come down on everyone, American, English, or Turk, who will help heal this open sore of the world." Etched on his memorial in Westminster Abbey, the famous words laid down the gauntlet. H. Grattan Guinness and the fervent young men and women at the East London Institute were listening. It was a challenge they could not ignore.

Livingstone's Strange Partnership

Earlier explorers had disputed the source of the Nile and they looked for an answer. Slavery had been outlawed throughout the British Empire in 1834, but while naval blockades curtailed the horrific traffic from West Africa, they offered little deterrent to the inhuman merchandising conducted by Arab slavers on the other side of the continent. Just off Africa's East Coast lay the island of Zanzibar, hub of the Arab slave trade and embarkation point for "80,000 to 100,000 captives brutally kidnapped and dragged from the African interior each year."[82] Since Zanzibar was also the gateway to any hope of access to the source of the Nile, Livingstone's course was clear.

Livingstone hated Zanzibar and all it stood for, yet he had little choice but to close his eyes to the Arab traffic. He made friends with the perpetrators and used the aid of their caravans to penetrate the continent. No one else knew the way. Curiously, the Arabs befriended the explorer and provided essential protection and supply—in spite of their knowledge that English law forbade slavery and prosecuted slavers.

Henry Morton Stanley

Livingstone left England for the last time on 13 August 1865. When he sailed from Zanzibar for the mainland on 19 March 1866, only one white man would see him alive again. By 1871, no one had heard from him for five years. Charles Gordon Bennett, pioneer of tabloid journalism and owner of the New York Herald, had an instinct for a story. By this time, Livingstone was rumored to be dead and was no longer newsworthy. Bennett knew that finding Livingstone would be the journalistic scoop of the century. It was a gamble, but worth the risk. Calling Welsh-born journalist Henry Morton Stanley to his Paris office, he gave him a purse and a commission: "Find Livingstone!" Amazingly, Stanley caught up with Livingstone at Ujiji on the northeastern shore of Lake Tanganyika. He bonded immediately with the old doctor, stayed five months, and wept when they parted.[83]

Stanley's journalistic accounts appeared regularly in American and British newspapers. Livingstone, whose search for the beginnings of the Nile had ended in disappointment, profoundly influenced Stanley. The river that Livingstone had thought to be the source of the Nile was in reality the *Chambesi* in northwestern Zambia. Since it conjoined with the Lualaba—which deceptively flowed north (in the same direction as the Nile)—he assumed it was the Nile. Worn out and probably obsessed with his quest, Livingstone confidently reported the Chambesi to be the source of the Nile. It was not. What he had discovered in the Chambesi was of far greater importance to his lifelong mission. The Chambesi was in fact the headwater of the River Congo. It would remain for Stanley, after Livingstone's death, to follow the Lualaba across the continent to its estuary in the Atlantic.[84]

Livingstone died in May 1873—the same year the East London Institute was founded. After the death of his hero, Stanley resolved to return to Africa to trace the Lualaba north and finally finish Livingstone's work. Backed by the London Daily Telegraph and the New York Herald, he did exactly that in a feat of exploration that ranks with Livingstone's transcontinental journey. The result was to prove to a waiting world that the Lualaba was the Congo.

On 9 August 1877, Henry Morton Stanley, gaunt and exhausted, reached the port of Boma, sixty miles upriver from the mouth of the Congo. In exactly 999 days since leaving Zanzibar, he had crossed the African continent from east to west. At a cost of 170 of his men, he had followed the tortuous course of the Congo River for nearly three thousand miles from its rise in Zambia to the Atlantic Ocean. In a heroic display of endurance, he had achieved what Livingstone had failed to do. He had raised the curtain on the mystery of Central Africa, and had fulfilled Livingstone's dream—to open Central Africa for "Commerce, Christianity, and Civilization."

By the fall of 1877, Stanley's reports had been published in the British and American newspapers. Stanley received a hero's welcome. Thanks largely to his greatest admirer, David Livingstone would be forever lionized in the hearts of the British people. The Zanzibar slave market had closed, never to reopen. Charles Gordon Bennett had achieved the journalistic scoop of the century. Within six months, the first Protestant mission society was pioneering the lower Congo.

7

Frail Craft on a Troubled Sea

Although I cannot report any conversions, yet both Mr. Harvey and I are of the opinion that at three of our stations a crisis is at hand, when some will come out boldly for Christ.

—Henry Craven, first LIM missionary to Congo

A Step Ahead of Stanley

The Guinnesses' keen leadership instincts and their heartbeat for world missions sensed the import of Stanley's achievement and seized the moment.

"Even before the astonishing news of a grand waterway into the heart of Africa had reached our shores," Fanny wrote, "many hearts had been yearning to get beyond the narrow belt of maritime country in which alone missions *on the west coast* (of Africa) then existed . . . Some of us were yearning . . . even before Stanley's letters appeared—to attempt privately a new departure with a view to *interior* gospel work."[85]

"Some of us" had included Robert Arthington, "the miser of Leeds," a man of means, abstemious in lifestyle, but a generous benefactor of missions. As "the first Protestant to realize the importance of the Congo as a route for missionary advance into central Africa," Arthington wrote to Harley House suggesting that a mission be sent to the "King of Kongo," and offered £50 toward expenses. Guinness declined the gesture, knowing well that ten times that sum would not begin to finance such a venture.[86]

Alfred Tilly

Baptist pastor Alfred Tilly was more practical. Tilly was from Cardiff, and was one of the directors of the English Baptist Missionary Society. Eager to do something on behalf of Central Africa, he lamented the disproportionate expenditure of men and money on Africa's coastal regions while the interior remained unevangelized. Moreover, Tilly had friends. Better still, they were friends with means. He enlisted the sympathy of the well-known Messieurs Cory, of Cardiff. Both men were able and willing to help underwrite the venture. Thus armed with the means, all they needed now were the men to launch the endeavor. For that the Cardiff preacher turned to Mr. and Mrs. Guinness and the East London Institute. His goal was disarmingly simplistic, perhaps naive: "to attempt to send a few evangelists" into the interior of Congo.

New Mission with an Old Name

In the spring of 1877, while Stanley was still struggling through his heroic descent of the Congo, the principals met with Mr. James Irvine, of Liverpool, "a gentleman well acquainted with West Africa." This handful of visionaries resolved, "in prayerful dependence on Divine assistance," to lose no time in sending volunteers on a mission to Central Africa. Mrs. Guinness would recall:

> On the publication of Mr. Stanley's letters in the autumn of 1877, we at once resolved to attempt an entrance into Africa by the new route [that is, via the West Coast rather than the East]; and formed ourselves into a committee for the conduct of a mission for which we adopted the name, THE LIVINGSTONE INLAND MISSION," later adding, "the first word recalled *an example*; the second defined *an aim*."[87]

Other friends joined the committee,[88] and the East London Institute furnished the volunteers for what would prove to be a dangerous and deadly pioneer service:

> A few friends, mostly members of the committee, contributed the means required to start with, and the Rev. Alfred Tilly, though engaged in active pastoral duties, acted as secretary for the first three years.

Even as Stanley was finishing his epic journey, the people at Harley House were gathering funds and making plans for the Congo venture. In January 1878 the frail craft of the new Mission was launched on what proved to be "a very troubled sea." The Livingstone Inland Mission (LIM) would be the first evangelical mission to enter the Congo.

River of Legend

Congo's fabled river was the key to the evangelization of Central Africa. Nearly 3000 miles of waterway drained the Central African plateau, home to a (then) estimated 30 million Bantu tribal people. Four hundred years earlier (1484–85), the Portuguese had entered the mouth of the Congo in the west, only to turn back. Arab slavers funneled their human booty through Zanzibar on the East Coast. Between the two extremes lay an area the size of Europe, virtually unknown.

Two barriers defied the opening of Central Africa. Until the Livingstone expeditions, no one knew where the Congo River began. The Congo basin was a blank on the 1876 map of The Royal Geographical Society.[89] Henry Morton Stanley, building on the work of his Scottish hero, would not determine the river's source with certainty until 1877. The second obstacle was equally forbidding. Approaching the Congo eastward from the Atlantic, no one knew what lay upstream beyond the notorious cataracts, 232 miles in length. They stood sentinel-like, one hundred miles from the estuary, guarding the green labyrinth of rain forest and roaring defiance to all challengers.

The River Congo also confused any would-be explorer—it is the only major river in the world to cross the equator twice. It begins by flowing north for hundreds of miles as the Lualaba, then traces a northwesterly arc for hundreds of miles more before beginning its southwesterly race for the Atlantic. This northerly flow of the Lualaba deceived Livingstone and led to his fatal miscalculation.

The Name That Failed

Stanley had tried to change the name of the river in honor of his hero, but there were no takers. The idea of a "Livingstone River" failed to capture public imagination. For starters, the historic Kingdom of Kong near the river's mouth had given the river its name, and so held a natural association. There was a second problem. Throughout its course of nearly 3,000 miles, the river changes its local name nearly every time it receives a fresh tributary. At its rise in the mountains west of Lake Nyassa, where Livingstone first saw it in January 1867, it is the Chambesi. It then becomes the Luapula, then the Luvua, then the Lualaba, and finally, the Congo. "Congo" had become a basket designation for these collective affluents. The name stuck. Exuding mystery, "*Congo*" even sounded like a drumbeat. It resonated with African authenticity.

The Cataracts

For centuries, the cataract zone held hostage the untapped wealth of Central Africa. The same was true of the (then) estimated 30 million Bantu people who still awaited the Good News. Pedestrian portage of goods and supplies around the cataracts meant an arduous trek of at least six days. This called for body-bruising negotiation of rocky trails, exhausting climbs, and frequent palavers with local chiefs over rights of passage. Moreover, the trail was punctuated with the bones of hapless porters, left to die where they fell. Eventually a railroad on the south bank would circumvent the cataract zone, connecting the lower river port of Matadi with Malebo (Stanley) Pool. However, in 1878 this was a dream, still twenty years away.[90]

Missionaries and commercial interests knew that if a way could be found to circumvent the cataract region, steamers could be launched on the upper river, and a new world would open, fulfilling Livingstone's vision. In its flow toward the Atlantic, the river widens to a lake-like width of four to ten miles in the area known as Stanley (Malebo) Pool, still high in the central plain. Here it begins a drop of 900 feet over a course of two hundred miles, dramatically contracting to an impetuous torrent a few hundred yards wide. It then gushes through tremendous mountain gorges in a series of cataracts, tumbling downward to Yellala, where it resumes its tranquil flow for a hundred miles to the Atlantic as the Lower Congo.

Journalist Stanley described the river's fury:

> [It was] no longer a stately stream whose mystic beauty, noble grandeur, and gentle uninterrupted flow fascinated us, despite the savagery of its peopled shores; but a furious river rushing down a steep bed, obstructed by heaps of lava, projecting barriers of rock and lines of immense boulders, winding in crooked course through deep chasms, and dropping down over terraces in a long series of falls, cataracts and rapids. Our frequent contest with the savages culminated in tragic struggles with the mighty river as it pushed and roared through the deep, yawning pass that leads from the broad tableland of Central Africa down to the Atlantic Ocean.[91]

Congo's cataracts defied all challengers.

A Thousand Miles of Waterway

Approaching from the Atlantic, and once beyond the cataracts at Stanley (Malebo) Pool, the river again becomes navigable for a thousand miles as far as Kisangani and the Wyoma (Stanley) Falls, its navigational head. Half a dozen major affluents flowing north and west pour their contents into the main river creating a network of several thousand miles of navigable waterway. This water network offered access to unreached tribal populations. This was *Balolo* country—the Upper Congo. It was the ultimate objective of the fledgling Mission. However, ten years would pass before it could be realized.

The First LIM Party: 1878

Henry Craven, of Liverpool, was the first of the LIM pioneers. In February 1878 he and Strom, a Danish sailor, landed at Matadi, "the place of stones."[92] Strom would eventually break off the venture. Craven would have just seven years. His short run did not lack triumphs. He had been able to develop a Congo–English, English–Congo dictionary with a list of useful sentences for missionaries and travelers in the Cataract Region. Add to that the firstfruits of Central Africa.

N'dambi and *Pukamoni*, Congo youths, had served as language informants to Craven at Palabala, one of four stations constructed on the lower river. They became the first converts of the LIM and accompanied Mr. and Mrs. Craven to England in the summer of 1881. They were baptized on 31 July 1882 in the East London Tabernacle—the same day the final revision of the Congo grammar was sent to press.[93] Francis and Robert Walker, as the boys were later named, returned to Africa at the close of the year and remained useful to the Mission. However, the cost had been steep.

By the time of this first baptism—five years into the effort—four men and women had laid down their lives in the assault on Congo's forests, James Telford being the first. Hugh McKergow, Adam McCall, and Mary Richards followed.[94] A fifth, Mr. Charles Harvey, was invalided home. Craven, while not the first casualty, would join their ranks two years later. In his last report to Harley House, he wrote: "Although I cannot report any conversions, yet both Mr. Harvey and myself are of the opinion that at three of our stations a crisis is at hand, when some will come out boldly for Christ."[95] He was right.

The Steamer Livingstone: 1881

With four LIM stations already in place on the lower river, it was clear that a steamboat was necessary to service the one hundred miles of navigable waterway between Banana and Matadi. LIM's first steam launch, *The Livingstone*, was secured—a forty-foot mahogany copper-clad hull with a seven-foot beam, equipped with awnings and with both sail and oars, thus hedging all bets on the availability of wood and coal on the river. A two-decker with twin stacks, she was launched from Forrest's Yard, Limehouse, on the Thames on the 9 March 1881. She could carry ten or twelve passengers and four or five tons of cargo. The vessel was laded onto the steamship *Corisco*, and with four LIM missionaries aboard, piggybacked to Banana.[96] May 6 marked her maiden voyage on the lower Congo.[97]

The Livingstone now played a critical role in the titanic struggle to construct and supply stations along the lower river, all of them on the south bank, the north bank being French territory. Bases sprang up at Palabala, Banana (later moved to Mukimvika) Matadi Minkanda, Banza Manteka, Bemba, and Manyanga. It was a rare location that was not marked by a missionary grave. At Banana, disembarkation port for Atlantic steamers, the headstones told the story—nearly all were under forty years of age.

ELI Takes the Reins

About this time, Baptist pastor Alfred Tilly was having second thoughts about the Congo venture. The administrative care of the Mission that he had carried for three years as secretary had come into tension with his pastoral duties. However, something deeper seemed to trouble Tilly. His desire to see the

LIM fully self-supporting in Congo had not materialized. Heavy demand for funding continued. Guinness understood what Tilly seems to have been slower to grasp—Congo was not a place for colonists, where missionaries might homestead, raise foodstuffs, and quickly become self-sufficient. That might come later, but for the present, the Congo venture was a raw-boned pioneer thrust into a hostile environment. Continued heavy capital investment was essential to maintain the costly logistical supply line, already three hundred miles in length. In October of 1880, in good spirit and without injury to relationships, Baptist pastor Alfred Tilly resigned as secretary of the LIM.

Fanny Guinness' administrative acumen made her the logical choice to replace Tilley, so it was no surprise when they asked her to fill the vacancy and become secretary to the committee on which she had already been serving from the start of the work. The Guinnesses had no desire to assume so large a responsibility without condition, so they countered with a proposal: Let the LIM become a subset of the East London Institute, which would assume sole responsibility for its support and management. The original committee would be free to remain as a council of reference. Agreement was unanimous, and in October of 1880, the fledgling Mission was integrated with the East London Institute for Home and Foreign Missions. Administration of the LIM was now firmly in the hands of Henry and Fanny Guinness.[98]

Expendable

For a brief moment, Adam McCall flashed like a meteor against the darkness of Congo's night. An architect and surveyor by profession, he had already spent seven years in Africa (1872–1879) before sensing God's call upon his life. Traveling 15,000 miles throughout Cape Colony, the Orange Free State, Griqualand, West Natal, Transvaal, Bechuanaland, the Matabele country, he had trekked the Zambesi Valley and had viewed Victoria Falls. Two years in the civil service of the South African government had further seasoned him in the lore of the continent.

Still unconverted, he returned to England in 1878, intending to return to the Zambesi to photograph the region. However, special services in his home town of Leicester led to his conversion. Suddenly, "all his desires and feelings about life were changed . . . Old things passed away; all things became new to him! He could no longer live for mere self-pleasing. His earnest inquiry was, 'Lord, what wilt thou have me to do?'"[99]

McCall wasted no time. Offering his services to the LIM, he crammed a twelve-month course in theology and medicine, shuttling between the ELI and London Hospital. He quickly won the affectionate regard of all who knew him, inspiring four students at the Institute to form a Congo team under his leadership—McKergow, Harvey, Lanceley, and Clarke.

By February, 1880, LIM had been two years in Africa—long enough to realize that the goal of reaching the Upper Congo would prove a more daunting task than expected. Construction of well-stocked supply bases would be imperative along the three hundred-mile route. Barter goods, shelter, and provisions were essential to supply newly arriving missionaries on their trek to the Upper River. Logistics posed a formidable priority. It was here that Adam McCall would shine.

The Expedition

In March, McCall launched LIM's most highly organized expedition. The plan was to reach Banana (at the mouth of the Congo) by the end of April, traverse the one hundred navigable miles to Yellala Falls, then negotiate the 232-miles of cataracts, reaching Stanley Pool by early June—all in one dry season. No one had ever been able to do this.

Well primed through his earlier Africa experience, McCall prepared meticulously. McKergow, a Scottish carpenter, had already gone ahead to construct a station on the river to receive the initial party. Among them was Charles Harvey, well equipped as teacher, translator, and earnest preacher. Clarke, of Aberdeen, had been a custom house officer, gifted with a good head and skilled hands.

Passage to Congo by the mail steamers from Liverpool was prohibitively expensive. Delays were common as the ships called frequently at West African ports. However, the West Africa Steamship Company ran cargo vessels to the Congo. Less costly, and with accommodations for only a handful of passengers, a cargo ship passage was ideal. Agreement was reached to have the steamer *Vanguard* do a direct run, calling first at Tenerife, in the Canary Islands, where they would take on twenty donkeys for caravan use. They would then proceed to Sierra Leone to contract the services of twenty-five porters for a year, and from there, direct to Banana, Congo's Atlantic port.[100] This unexpected opportunity called for an earlier departure than originally planned, and the passages were booked by faith without the necessary funds at hand.

McCall and his party sailed from Plymouth in March 1880. By the end of April, the *Vanguard* reached Banana. Then, at Boma, sixty miles upriver, they were greeted by the news of Charles Petersen's death from fever at Banza Manteka, in the cataract zone. Petersen was the second casualty of the new mission, James Telford having been the first.

Race for the Pool

Reaching Matadi (Yellala Falls—the farthest navigable point on the lower river), the party raced to complete a supply base, but progress was thwarted by delays in arrival of goods and timber. By September, hopes had dimmed of reaching Stanley Pool before the rainy season. The use of donkeys for transport proved futile, aborting repeated efforts. The animals were unable to negotiate the rocky terrain, and some drowned in the river crossings. The hired porters refused to carry, too timid to venture into the unknown. The struggle with heavy loads over rocky paths, punctuated by treacherous river crossings, drained the energies of man and beast. On reaching Banza Manteka, McCall weathered a severe liver flare-up, a recurrence of his experience in Zambesi years before. It was an ominous sign. By the end of October, they had reached Bemba, still short of their goal to reach the pool. Then the rains came.

Final Voyage

The men were now assailed by storms, and with the river swollen, further advance was impossible. The party settled down to language-learning, establishing friendly linkage with the locals, and construction of housing. With the dawn of 1881, reversals continued. On February 4, underlined in black in his diary, McCall received news of the death of his father, the demise of Hugh McKergow, and the destruction of the new Matadi station by tornado. More cheering was the arrival of nine new missionaries in three parties—April, May, and July. Meanwhile, field leader McCall gave himself to the oversight of station construction and meeting new arrivals at Banana, now facilitated by the use of the SS *Livingstone*, which could do the Banana—Matadi run in one-and-one half days.

Months passed and McCall's health worsened. He knew he must seek medical help. He left Banana on 8 October 1881, anticipating a brief convalescence in England. As the outbound mail steamer moved into the estuary, McCall watched the long snow-white outbuildings of Banana slip past, gleaming in the sunlight against the bright green foliage. He confided to his diary, "May God preserve and protect our beloved Mission and all our dear brethren till I come back!"[101]

The three-week voyage stretched into six, as the steamer sluggishly skirted the Gulf of Guinea, stopping frequently at ports to discharge and take on cargo. McCall's condition worsened. By the time the vessel reached Madeira in the Canaries, the young pioneer was gravely ill.

News of McCall's condition reached England by telegraph. His mother and brother traveled through the night from Leicester to Southampton in a grim race to see him. They were already on the deck of the Madeira-bound *Garth Castle* when a telegram broke the news that Adam McCall could not have many hours to live. A storm was blowing. Should they go on? With no time to deliberate, they wired Madeira to advise they were starting. The normal run to Madeira was four days, but the gale rose to hurricane strength, boiling the Atlantic. For 36 hours the *Garth Castle* lay to, her fires extinguished. Passengers were now in fear for their own safety, and it seemed that "the family tie just severed by death, was by death to be speedily reunited."[102]

The *Garth Castle* weathered the storm, reaching Madeira two days behind schedule. The weather had turned and the sun was brightly shining, but too late. Early in the morning of November 25, Adam McCall, director of LIM's Congo field, had been released into the presence of his Lord, mute witness to the aphorism another Harley missionary would later write to his mother, "Africa kills all her lovers."[103] McCall's missionary career had lasted twenty-one months. His own prayer had been prophetic "If it please Thee to take myself instead of the work that I would do for Thee, what is that to me? Thy will be done."[104]

Promising prospects had once more been shattered by the unexplained, and faith was left to lean on the providence of God. Scarcely two years into his mission, in the vigor of young manhood, "his heart overflowing with earnest purpose to carry the gospel of Christ into the great Congo Valley,"[105] Adam McCall had already finished his course.

Assault of Doubt

McCall's death stunned the staff at Harley House. As the LIM wrestled with the grim statistics of attrition, misgivings haunted the leadership, Ought we to go on with such a mission? Was there a message in this seeming waste of life? Could God himself be closing this door upon a presumptuous venture? The exquisite torture of this spiritual dilemma was hardly new. John the Baptist's plaintive question pulsed with the same pathos in the stony silence of the unexplained, *"Are you he who should come, or look we for another?"[106]* Nonetheless, for the Harley staff, the counterpoint was equally insistent: "How could we drop a work for which lives had been sacrificed?"[107]

Sierra Leone Model

History ministers grace to those who study it. Not lost on the Guinnesses as they worked through another tragedy was the fact that in the first twenty years of the Church Missionary Society's work in Sierra Leone, also on Africa's West Coast, fifty-three missionaries had died at their posts. Four of five new workers going out in 1823 had died within six months. Of six going out in 1825, two had fallen within four months, while the following year two of three new arrivals had succumbed within six months.

Nevertheless, Guinness noted, "there was never wanting a constant supply of laborers." As for the issue from this deadly sowing, 32,000 of Sierra Leone's population of 37,000 had become professing Christians. Within thirty-three years, the British colony for freed slaves had supplied fifty educated native pastors for the work in West Africa.[108] The beleaguered leadership at the LIM steadied themselves. The assault of doubt must be met from the ultimate Mission Manual: *"Except a corn of wheat fall into the ground and die, it abides alone. But if it die, it brings forth much fruit."[109]*

The Church Missionary Society (CMS) work in Sierra Leone had suggested an unwelcome—perhaps inevitable—paradigm for what lay before the young LIM in Congo. One certainty had become inescapable: Mission is cruciform. But beyond death, there must also be resurrection. Beyond sowing, there must be a harvest. The LIM was just four years into her mission and the harvest was yet to come.

Prince of Missionaries

David Livingstone had been rashly accused of abandoning the tasks of missionary for those of the geographer and explorer or at best that of philanthropist. Livingstone had not been successful as a church planter, but he paved the way for those who would. Fanny Guinness understood the distinction and did not attempt to conceal her admiration for the great explorer:

> It was [his] high and holy purpose of opening up a new world to the gospel that impelled and sustained this prince of missionaries throughout thirty years of weary pilgrimage and terrible sufferings . . . [He] betook himself to the task of introducing to the knowledge and sympathies of the Christian church an entire continent, cursed under the withering blight of heathenism, and crushed under the cruel yoke of slavery.[110]

Role of the Pioneer

Livingstone had forged his philosophy of mission on the anvil of his own gifting and his experience in South Africa. Successful mission, he maintained, could only be carried out in the wake of colonization, and colonization presupposed exploration. He had a clear grasp of the role of the pioneer in a primitive context:

> My views of what is missionary duty are not so contracted as those of persons whose ideal of a missionary is a dumpy sort of man with a Bible under his arm. I have labored in bricks and mortar, at a forge and carpenter's bench, as well as in preaching and in medical practice. I feel that I am not my own, and that I am equally serving Christ when shooting a buffalo for my men or taking an astronomical observation.[111]

Adam McCall's short and deadly tour in Congo must be weighed in these terms. His contemporary and colleague, Henry Craven, the first LIM worker, wrote home, " I can report no conversion."[112] Could McCall report any conversion? We do not know. We do know that he engineered construction of the bases on the Lower Congo that made possible the outreach of the LIM to the thousands of miles of waterway on the Upper River. He paved the way for others, and in this, he served his generation by the will of God. Those who knew him best paid him the tribute that says it all: "[He was] a bright, brave, dauntless, spirited man, full of energy and resource, strong in purpose, amiable in disposition, and devoted in heart."

The fourth year of the LIM (1881), was its first under the sole management of the East London Institute. Although marred by McCall's untimely death, it had been a year of advance, with nine new workers going out in three detachments, all "eager to close up the ranks and fill the posts of those who had fallen."[113] Four years of planning, expenditure, and sacrifice were about to pay off.

SS Henry Reed

While the SS *Livingstone* served as LIM's workhorse on the lower river, the mission's goal lay beyond the cataracts, on the upper river. Achieving that would require a second vessel, but also posed the larger question: How to get a steamboat past 232 miles of cataracts and onto the upper river above Stanley Pool? Akin to the question, "How do you eat an elephant?" there was but one logical answer: "One bite at a time." The steamer would have to be built in Britain, taken to bits, shipped to Congo, portaged over the cataracts, and reassembled.

Henry and Margaret Reed had been close friends of the Guinnesses and had entertained both H. Grattan and Dr. Harry on their evangelistic visits to Tasmania, and it was in their home that Harry had found Annie Reed, his bride-to-be. "After the death of her husband in 1880, Margaret Reed continued to make generous gifts to the causes of her choice, her first being the presentation to the LIM of a second steamer for use in the upper Congo. It was to be called the *Henry Reed* in memory of her late husband."[114]

While the *Henry Reed* was under construction on banks of the Thames, plans were laid to transport the vessel from London to Stanley Pool. Henry Craven had taken out stores and provisions for the 1,000 carriers who would be needed. He also took barter goods for contracting with the fresh carrier crews that would be required along the way. With preparations underway, construction was begun on a shed at Stanley Pool where the dismembered steamer would be reassembled.

The vessel was a wood-burner, seventy-one feet in length with a ten-foot beam, and three feet deep. Her shallow draft of twelve to fourteen inches was necessary to negotiate the sandbars and uncertain river channels. For the same reasons, the designers opted for a stern paddle wheel as opposed to twin screws. She weighed fourteen tons and could carry sixteen tons of cargo. Fourteen tons of gross weight translated to five hundred man-loads to be portaged around the cataract region. Sixteen thousand rivets were required to bolt her plates together, a serious task for missionary amateurs in Africa.

The *Henry Reed* was shipped in sections to Rotterdam, and there loaded on the Dutch steamer *Afrikaan,* bound for Banana, the Congo's Atlantic port. It took 1000 porters to carry the sections of the dismembered steamer the 232 miles from Tundwa to the pool. Arriving in April, assembly began and the *Henry Reed* was launched safely on 24 November 1881 in the cove at Leopoldville. The Upper Congo was finally accessible.[115]

8

Pentecost on the Congo

A great yearning for souls took possession of me. I could not sleep for it sometimes, and had to pray God to take it away, for it was consuming me. But there was no sign of blessing.

—Henry Richards

Prize and Process: 1879–1884

When Henry Richards left England he was neither prepared for the prize that awaited him nor the process it would exact. Arriving at Banza Manteka on the Lower River (1879), he little guessed that six years would pass before he felt any degree of usefulness:

> Of course, I had at first to build and plant and get acclimatized—he explained—Then I had to learn the language. No easy task when you have no teacher and no books. It was years before I could understand and enjoy hearing it, and before I could use it with any power.[116]

The indifference of the people was deadly and discouraging. Illness compounded the mystery of what seemed to be a lack of blessing on his efforts. Forced to return to England, the sense of failure continued to gnaw at his inner peace.

> I felt I must be blessed if I was to be made a blessing. When I got back, my one desire was for converts. A great yearning for souls took possession of me. I could not sleep for it sometimes, and had to pray God to take it away, for it was consuming me. But there was no sign of blessing. I resolved to go elsewhere if the Word bore no fruit at Banza Manteka. First, I had to ask myself—what was the fault? I was preaching the truth, and the people listened; but they did not seem to feel in the least interested.

As Richards pursued the longed-for harvest, the Holy Spirit began to awaken him to a missing element in his ministry:

> As I read, I began to see I had been trying the wrong way to do good to the heathen. I had been much occupied with many things, and the one great thing to which a missionary should devote himself mainly, if not exclusively, *preaching*, had not been made prominent enough. It is so easy in Congo to get distracted. There is so much to do. Building, planting, ordinary business of various sorts, learning the language, teaching, writing, traveling—all these things are apt to squeeze preaching into a corner.[117]

When reminded that even missionaries in the homelands are affected by the same distractions, he replied, "Yes, but the consequences are more serious there. Preaching—'the foolishness of preaching'—is God's one great ordinance for the salvation of men." [118]

The Ngangas

As Richards began to experience a greater power in his preaching, the son of a local chief professed conversion. The impact was explosive. A movement began, but met with opposition. Like the silversmiths of Ephesus, the medicine men of Banza Manteka—the *ngangas*—feared the loss of their craft and their living. An American observer, Mr. T. T. France, wrote: "We fail to get a hearing when it is known that the chief or the *nganga* does not wish the gospel to be preached in the village . . ."[119]

When Lukongo carriers traveling up and down the river saw the people throwing away their idols and turning to God, they were amazed that no ill befell the converts and that the heavens did not fall or the earth swallow them up. The fact that no harm befell those who quit following the *ngangas* and threw away their *nkissis*, or charms, held strong appeal. When dire predictions of death and disaster went unfulfilled, many were led to see through the deceptions that had been practiced upon them. The blessing brought Richards little rest:

> When the revival came, I was no longer satisfied with occasional services and regular Sunday work. I gave myself to preaching daily—twice a day. One year I preached seven hundred times. In addition, the people do not care for short sermons. They like a full hour or hour and a half. They have so much to learn.[120]

Hunger for God melted the former indifference, and the people demonstrated a ready appetite for preaching and teaching. Work schedules were rearranged to accommodate two daily services. "I asked them to choose their own time. They fixed one o'clock, when all their fieldwork is done and they have had their mid-day meal. Again, later in the evening, they come freely and eagerly."

Richards had broken with traditional approaches to mission. He viewed the establishing of schools as "a waste of time"—but only in the initial stages. "When the people are converted, then have schools for the Christians, that they may learn how to read the word of God." [121]

When Harvest Came

Revival touched the lower Congo in 1884 and by 1887 more than a thousand converts had been added to the churches. In 1889 alone, 950 were baptized and the Banza Manteka church boasted fifteen hundred members. Converts went out as evangelists to the surrounding villages, pleading with the people to turn from wooden and rag idols to God. The ingathering became a folk movement. One visitor assessed the phenomenon:

> The *nkimba,* the *nkissis,* the poison-giving, the throat-cutting, the demoniacal yells, the diabolical dance, and witchcraft, are things of the past here. '*Old things have passed away, and behold, all things are become new.* '[122]

Henry Richards had witnessed the first Pentecost on the Congo—and the first church. Banza Manteka, the third of the LIM stations, had become the first Christian parish on David Livingstone's river. Two thousand were baptized during the stirring. In other stations similar awakenings occurred. By the end of the century Banza Manteka missionaries had nearly three thousand pupils in sixty schools. Hundreds were being baptized each year and added to the fellowship.[123] After Grattan Guinness transferred the promising field to the American Baptists, the awakenings continued. Those who were there affirmed: "We are in the midst of a revival that equals the Banza Manteka Pentecost in intensity and surpasses it in extent."[124]

Retrenchment: 1884

While the LIM was thriving on the Lower Congo, increasing administrative demands had begun to strain the resources of the slender staff at Harley House. The elder Guinnesses were carrying the daily administration of Harley College, Doric Lodge, and Berger Hall.

They were training and supporting more than a hundred students, who were going overseas at the rate of one a week. At the same time they were corresponding with hundreds more who were already in the fields. In addition, the conduct of home missions required constant oversight, as this was the means by which LIM students received their practical training in evangelism. Mrs. Guinness also edited *Regions Beyond,* the mission magazine.[125] It would enjoy a continuity of one hundred years.

The LIM also had an adolescent's appetite for money. It was not easy to find. Fanny Guinness wrote:

> As to finances . . . the Mission was our second, and not our first, responsibility. We were bound first to pray and labor for the large and constantly increasing needs of the Institute, which never was intended to be a Missionary Society, though a number of missions in various parts of the world owe to it, directly or indirectly, their existence. Its great object was and is to help to multiply missionaries, to induce, prepare, and help young Christian workers to evangelize among the heathen in the regions beyond, according to the command of Christ.[126]

As unremitting demand exacted its toll, the Guinnesses were no longer able to do justice to the LIM, believing that "it could be no longer managed as a subsidiary of our East London Training Institute," wrote Fanny. It had become "important enough to rank as one of the principal enterprises of a great missionary society [and was] fast outgrowing the parent institution, and becoming the larger enterprise of the two. We had but a fraction of time and attention to devote to it, and yet it demanded a great share of both."

Then Mrs. Guinness suffered a stroke—a warning that after twenty-five years of intense ministry it was time to take some slack. Henry Grattan likewise sensed that it was time for a change of pace. His prophetic books had been well received and he was eager to give more time to writing. Cliff House, in the gentle hills of Derbyshire, was far from London's din. It was the ideal place.

What God Had Wrought

In seven years of existence, the Livingstone Inland Mission had fulfilled its original agenda, and had planted stations at intervals through seven hundred miles of country, right to the interior. Although LIM was the youngest in the family of Central Africa Missions, Fanny noted that "No other had then either so large a staff or so many mission stations in working order. It had also accomplished much literary work, nor had spiritual blessings been lacking."

Baptists Take the Challenge

The steamer *Henry Reed* had been carried up to Stanley Pool, reconstructed at Leopoldville, and was afloat on the Upper Congo, ready to deploy evangelists throughout the interior. Twenty-five devoted men and women were in the country. The Holy Spirit was regenerating human hearts and confirming the word with signs following. Notwithstanding, the Harley staff was looking for a way out:

> We were prayerfully considering the best course to take under the circumstances when we heard from the American Baptist Missionary Union [ABMU] that they were looking for a good opening in Central Africa. [They felt] that it was their special duty—as having a large con-

stituency of colored churches—to do something for the evangelization of the Negro's fatherland."[127]

The news seemed to ring with the promise of relief, and the Guinnesses took it as guidance, immediately corresponding with ABMU Secretary, Dr. J. N. Murdock, of Boston. Murdock was already known to the Guinnesses through their visits to United States, and they arranged for Murdock and Dr. Crane, also of the ABMU executive committee, to come to Britain to assess the work and policies of the LIM and the possibility of transfer.

The ABMU agreed to adopt the LIM work and promised "vigorously to prosecute it." They would also take over the existing staff—its members having consented to the transfer—together with "all the stations, steamers, and property of the Mission."[128]

While the LIM was non-denominational, the ABMU was constitutionally Baptist, but in full accord with the principle of conducting its work "in the spirit of large-hearted charity which recognizes that the essential points on which Christians are agreed are much more important than the secondary points on which they differ." In fact, many of the staff of the LIM were Baptists, and the only other mission in the country was the English Baptist Missionary Society.

LIM was confident that the union was a wise move. They had no desire to introduce a second denomination into the field. Their reasoning may draw a smile, but they felt there was "something appropriate in an arrangement which placed in American hands the first mission to be established in the Congo, as the great river had been opened to the world through American capital and enterprise."(ibid.)

Like the Amputation of a Limb: 1884

With anguished reluctance, the work of the LIM was transferred to the ABMU in 1884. To Dr. Harry Guinness, "it seemed like the amputation of a limb." With the LIM out of the picture, some Swedish missionaries who had been part of that effort withdrew to form their own society. It became the Swedish Missionary Union (SMU).[129]

At the time of the handover, LIM had seven operational bases, extended along seven hundred miles.[130] Twenty-four missionaries were in place—"all that remained of twice that number who had gone out during the seven years since the arrival of the first party at Banana in 1878. A few had proved unsuitable and had been recalled, two or three had been invalided home, and a few had retired, while eleven plus one Congolese worker had laid down their lives."(ibid., 401) The seven LIM stations were all on the south side of the river, and all but one in the Congo Free State. In six years, the fragile dream of 1878 had become an accomplished fact.

A Remnant Remains

Many LIMers chose to remain in Congo to carry on their work under the Baptists.[131] One of them had other notions. For John McKittrick, the "immensely likeable"[132] Irishman from Belfast, the American Baptist policy of consolidation was disappointing. The Baptists had no plans to extend their lines to the upper river, where McKittrick wanted to go. After four years with the Baptists, he had been working at Equator station, the most advanced outpost of the mission. Just before furlough, he obtained permission to do an exploratory canoe journey into Balolo territory. His adventure would mark the beginning of a century of ministry in Congo's heartland. What he brought back with him would raise eyebrows and ignite fresh fire in British churches.

Steam launch SS *Pioneer*, donated by the Belfast YMCA and shipped to Congo in April 1889. See page 74.

9

The Congo Balolo Mission

Gentlemen, find out the will of God for your generation, and then, as quickly as possible, get into line.

—Harry Guinness

Harry the Splendor

By 1887, H. Grattan Guinness and his gifted spouse had exhausted their considerable energies. Launching Britain's first college for the training of missionaries and birthing the first Protestant mission to the Congo had demanded all they had to give. They gave it heroically. It would fall to their son to carry their vision into the new century.

Henry Grattan Guinness II was born in Toronto, Canada, on 2 October 1861. Bearing the same name as his renowned father, he was affectionately known as "Harry" to avoid confusion. We so refer to him in this account. On both sides, he claimed descent from a long line of Irish ancestors: landowners, soldiers, sailors, clergymen, barristers, and musicians. Like his father, Harry Guinness was multi-gifted, a natural born leader, orator, musician, and a motivator of people. What his father may have lacked in practical skills, Harry made up for. He was a perfect blend of the visionary qualities of his father and the practical attributes of his mother.

He entered the London Hospital in 1880 and on completion of his medical studies five years later, spent two years in evangelistic ministry in Australia and Tasmania, finding time while there to meet and—upon his return to London—marry Annie Reed.[133]

His biographer paints a stunning portrait:

> [Harry was] a keen athlete, tall, handsome, with bright blue eyes and a ringing laugh, an atmosphere of vigorous health, moral and physical,

radiated from him. He also possessed that higher histrionic power which enables a man to focus and express in his own person the character in which he stands forth—in his case a champion of "the Faith once for all delivered to the saints." It was not that he eclipsed others. On the contrary, he illuminated them. When he appeared on the scene almost everybody felt and knew they were at their best—ten times themselves! Everybody wanted to do their utmost for him as leader, and to let him enjoy all the credit.[134]

His devoted sister summed it in a word—"Harry is a splendor." (ibid.)

Harry Guinness began his preaching career at the age of eighteen, and continued it until the day he was stricken with his fatal illness on 10 April 1915. According to his mother's journal, before May of 1884 he had preached 235 times, seldom, if ever, without witnessing conversions that stood the test of time. While Harry's natural gifts are not to be minimized, it must be noted that they were aflame in an atmosphere of pure oxygen. C. W. Mackintosh described the environment that had catalyzed Harry's gifts:

> He had grown up in the afterglow of the great mid-century revival; it inspired all his convictions, and now a new one seemed to be dawning. It was the era of Moody and Sankey's second campaign in England—of the Salvation Army's chief triumphs. The Consecration teaching at Mildmay [a Bible conference], and the Keswick Convention for the Promotion of Practical Holiness were rousing Christians to a higher ideal of life and service . . . New Missions were being organized in every direction, and old Missions were taking on a new lease of life. Not only were the meetings of leading evangelists thronged, but also the humblest gatherings where the simple Gospel was proclaimed, and from the first, the young preacher had the happiness of knowing that he did not labor in vain. "The Lord their God was with them, and the shout of a King was among them."[135]

Harry would soon be called upon to provide shape and structure to the enterprise his parents had launched. The work of the ELI now included oversight of Harley College in London, Doric Lodge for deaconesses, also in London, and Cliff College in Derbyshire. The three divisions accommodated one hundred students. Screening missionary candidates was in itself time-consuming, since the number of volunteers always exceeded the ability to accommodate them.

All this administrative responsibility would fall upon a very young man. In 1884, when the LIM withdrew from Congo, Harry was just twenty-three. Fund raising had become a daily challenge to faith, since the operation was without endowment or subscribers. Moreover, the paper shuffle was not Harry's first love. His best gifts lay elsewhere. Contemporaries at the London Hospital had predicted a brilliant medical career, while his successes in Australia marked him as a gifted evangelist. Nevertheless, he felt he owed it to his parents to relieve them in the work to which their powers were no longer equal. While he wrestled with the decision, a letter from his wise and insightful mother afforded a rare gem of Biblical advice.

Mother's Advice

I have learned by experience that the call of God varies as we pass through life. What is a duty at one time becomes a folly, if not a sin, at another. For Elijah to have lingered in the wilderness by the brook Kidron, *though* God had sent him there—when he ought to appear before Ahab and Israel, would have been a terrible mistake. For Luther to have tried to continue his public ministry when the Lord wanted him to prepare in the Wartburg a German translation of his Word would have been a fatal folly . . .

Our times are in his hands, and it is useless for us to say, Such and such shall be my career through life. Not without many a painful and disappointing exercise of heart did I learn this lesson! The blessed Master has every right to say to his servant, Go here, or Go there—do this or do that, and He says it in many ways. The servant alone can hear the voice at times, though there are generally providential indications to confirm his impression,

The *Mother of Congo* buttressed her case with an appeal to the urgency of the times and to her clear sense of Harry's appointment with destiny:

A widespread and deep awakening is taking place all over England on the subject of missions. The Institute *ought* to be enlarged, extended, and improved . . . The world's need is tremendous, the time is short, and the volunteers are many. There are two hundred and fifty millions [pounds sterling] of money *hoarded* every year in England—surplus accumulations of rich and poor—in Banks—yet little more than one million is given to Missions!

But, above all, the time is short. We must not think only of what we can do ourselves, but of what we can do *through others*. Motive power is a great thing, and organizing power. You have fallen, my son, on very solemnly momentous days! God give you wisdom and grace to use your precious ten talents to the full. How best to do this, we will pray over and talk over when you come.[136]

For Harry, his mother's letter was "the parting of the ways," and he affirmed, "I knew and felt it was the guidance of God. Not for five minutes was I in doubt of this."[137] He took the job.

Harry Takes the Helm

In June of 1887, a youthful Harry Guinness—now twenty-six—assumed the leadership of his parents' work. They bedecked him with the ponderous title, *Honorary Secretary of the East London Training Institute for Home and Foreign Missions*. Reluctantly, he had jumped into a growing and demanding operation. Simultaneously, he became London director for the Livingstone Inland Mission, allowing his parents to retire to the relative comfort and seclusion of Cliff House in Derbyshire. H. Grattan Guinness at fifty-two would now devote himself to the writing that would further distinguish him.

The Helpers' Union

Harry had written his wife in 1888 to unveil an idea that would effectively mobilize the British public. He and his sister Lucy conceived a plan to enlist participation of churches and nonprofessionals in a *Helper's Union* to encourage people to pray, study, and act on behalf of foreign missions. The effort was patterned after "Carey's Weekly Penny," a similar plan set up in 1792. In the Helpers' Union plan, every member received a missionary box designed to graphically portray the proportion of Christians to the yet-unreached populations of the world. Cards were distributed designating an unevangelized region for each day of the month. In 1892, the Helpers' Union was formally launched with 8000 helpers in place. Within fifteen years, the "Carey" boxes had generated an income of £50,000.

Beyond the Cataracts

John McKittrick, "the immensely likeable Irishman," was working under the Baptists in 1888 when he ventured his canoe survey of the upper river. His eye was on Balololand, a vast, unevangelized area with an estimated ten million inhabitants, lying south of the great horseshoe bend of the river. The Balolo, (iron people) were of the Bantu family of languages. The prefix, *ba,* translates, *people*, and combines with *lolo*, meaning, *iron*. Expert bronze artisans, the Balolo were well-equipped with agricultural implements and weapons, and employed the former effectively in the cultivation of maize and manioc.[138] Since Balolo country was eight hundred miles up river from the Atlantic, "Balolo" became a loose designation for the Upper Congo.

McKittrick knew that his vision for the Balolo could not be fulfilled with the American Baptists, who had no desire to extend their work that far north, and he determined to return to England to make his case for LIM's re-entry of Congo.[139] He was warmly received on the survey and enlisted Bompele, a Balolo lad, to accompany him to England. Bompele was from the region near the Lulonga River's confluence with the Congo. McKittrick knew that a live African in British churches could be his best argument for LIM's reopening of its Congo work. He was not disappointed.

Once back at Harley House, McKittrick's visit kindled high enthusiasm. Bompele's fifteen-month stay in Britain was a hit with English audiences. Harry Guinness backed the venture. His youthful vigor blended with the complementary gifts of his Australian wife, Annie, to take up the gauntlet. Everyone agreed: The LIM would return to the Congo.

The summer of 1888 saw the great world missionary convention assemble at London's Exeter Hall. Dr. Murdock of the ABMU was present. For four years, his board had efficiently conducted the work of the old LIM, and Harry Guinness took advantage of Murdock's visit to discuss plans.

Guinness had once superimposed a same-scale map of Europe on the Congo basin. The area LIM now contemplated was as large as Germany. Beyond the cataracts, however, the region could easily be worked by river launch along the six navigable tributaries flowing northwesterly into the Congo. On the map, the six affluents looked like tendrils hanging from a branch. Collectively, they represented 2,000 miles of navigable waterway, both banks studded with towns and villages.

Discussions with Murdock were amiable. The Baptists readily agreed to release McKittrick to the new venture. Ever generous, they further agreed to lend the old LIM steamer *Henry Reed* for one year. The new enterprise took the name, Congo Balolo Mission (CBM), and adopted for its sphere the six southern tributaries of the Congo beyond Equatorville—the Lulonga, Maringa, Lopori, Ikelemba, Juapa, and Bosira.

First CBM Party: 1889

McKittrick's enthusiasm was contagious, and a party of seven volunteers readily assembled under his leadership. Not least of these was Dora Fooks, Harry Guinness' cousin, whom John had just married. She was already seasoned by five years of mission work among the Syrians of Lebanon and Damascus. A second volunteer was Miss de Haile. Her vision for the Congo had been tried by fire. Her fiancé, Alexander Cowe, a Baptist missionary to Congo, had died after just three weeks in Africa. He had preached but once.

Peter Whytock, a Scot, was a veteran of some years in Port Said. Gustav Haupt, "a beloved and esteemed German brother,"[140] was an earnest preacher and soul winner. James Todd was from Glasgow, while Mr. Blake of Ipswich completed the advance team. All but de Hailes were products of the East London Institute for Home and Foreign Missions. Bompele, the Congolese lad who had accompanied McKittrick to England, would return with the team. The send-off for the pioneer party was at Exeter Hall, 26 March 1889. Bompele addressed the English audience:

> Isn't it a shame? Shame to keep gospel to yourself—Not meant for English only! My people wanting gospel—Isn't it a shame? Isn't it?[141]

Tumbling in broken English from the lips of the Balolo lad, the terse appeal carried emotional impact, riveting the hundreds of Christians gathered in the great hall. On the platform were the first eight missionaries to leave for Africa with the new Congo Balolo Mission. John McKittrick, the athletic Irishman from Belfast, was the team captain. In three years, he would be dead.[142]

SS *Pioneer*

Since the steamer *Henry Reed* would be theirs for a year only, they immediately began to look for funds to construct a new vessel. They did not have to wait long. Enthusiasm was running high, and the young men of the Belfast YMCA gifted £500, while an anonymous Irish friend provided the balance with a single gift of £900! Aptly named *Pioneer,* the sixty-foot, twenty-three-ton sidepaddle steamer was launched at Wivenhoe, Essex, on 28 October 1889. Like her predecessor, *Henry Reed,* she was shipped to Congo (December 1889) in plates and sections, then rebuilt, and fitted at Stanley Pool.[143]

Meanwhile, the CBM vanguard had sailed from England on 18 April 1889, reaching Matadi four months later, ninety-three miles upriver from the mouth of the great river.[144] The six-day trek around the cataracts brought them to Stanley Pool and the old LIM base.[145] Within a year, using the borrowed *Henry Reed,* they would establish two stations, one on the Lulonga and other on the Maringa at its confluence with the Lopori. CBM would soon have three stations—Bonginda, Lulonga, and Ikau. In March 1891, a fourth post was opened at Bongandanga on the Lopori.

The Reception

Dora McKenzie was on deck as the stern-wheeler *Henry Reed* gently nosed into the Lulonga River at its confluence with the Congo. It was 24 August 1889, and the first party of CBM missionaries was about to keep their destiny with the Balolo people. News of their approach had preceded them, "telegraphed" by rhythmic drumbeat as village after village passed the news up the line. A phalanx of armed men awaited them, lining the left bank—"as far as the eye could reach." Their "threatening looks and wild gesticulations" needed no interpretation. All had turned out to witness the arrival of the mysterious *smoke-canoe*—except the women and children, who were safely out of sight.

Since any attempt to land could be dangerous, the *Reed* proceeded upstream until, with the villages behind them, they cast anchor and spent the night. In the morning they continued up river, passing more populous districts until they came to the village of Bonginda. Here they determined to establish friendly contact. The blast from the *Reed's* whistle and the smoke from her stack sent wary spectators scurrying into the bush, but after several hours of patient entreaty and a few beads tossed on the bank, the landing zone was soon swarming with friendly faces, now innocent of fear and distrust. McKenzie described the event:

> The old chief, MATA IBENGE, came in state to visit us, bringing a long train of wives and slaves and invited us to land . . . The bodies of all alike were covered with a mixture of palm oil and camwood, and decorated with a variety of tattoo marks . . . The chiefs were distinguished by their headdresses, which were made of monkey skin. A great palaver was arranged and attended by hundreds of these wild-looking people. A heated discussion took place as to whether we would be allowed to settle among them . . . The expressive gestures of the orators told us plainly whether they were speaking for or against us. Amid furious excitement, the king's chief speaker, old Mata Lokota . . . declared in our favor. Presents were exchanged and we took possession of our new home. Now for the first time, we had opportunity of declaring our message to the Balolo people. As our interpreter finished, a murmur of assent went round and our hearts were thrilled as Mata Lokota rose and replied, "These words are good, white man; you shall be our father and we will be your children."

The Congo Balolo Mission party had received a hearty welcome and their beachhead seemed secure, but the battle had just begun. Chief Mata Ibenge became the inveterate enemy of the missionaries, vowing to kill anyone who taught them the language, and preventing those who would bring them food. Collaborating with three other unfriendly chiefs, he orchestrated a plot to kill them all, burn the station, and seize their goods. Likewise, the witch doctors, whose power was now threatened, had used all their arts to drive out the missionaries. On the set day, all the men and boys in the employ of the Mission fled.

> "We surmised that something was wrong," McKenzie recalled. "As we waited and watched, one of our boys—Nyanga—crept up to the back of the house and told us the terrible scheme to destroy us all, which was to be carried out that night. We could do nothing but cast ourselves on GOD. Within an hour we heard the whistle of a steamer, and realized with deep thankfulness that our lives were spared."

In the morning, the missionaries went straight to Mata Ibenge demanding that he call a palaver so that they might inquire directly of the people the reason for the antagonism. Hundreds gathered in the palaver house, but when the discussion was raised, it was clear that most of the people had known nothing of Ibenge's designs. Both the chief's authority and that of the witch doctors eroded and the tide began to turn. Within three years of their arrival, the missionaries had won the respect of the old king, and McKenzie reported:

A great change had come over the people of the district. Fighting had practically ceased among [them], and young folk who, before the advent of the white men would not have dared to go alone beyond their village for fear of being kidnapped and sold as slaves, moved about freely and unmolested. Spears and other weapons were buried . . . We invited all . . . to come and talk their palavers on the mission station. In many cases this was done. This occupied a great deal of the missionary's time . . . but by this means bloodshed was avoided, and frequently palavers which had lasted for more than a generation were amicably settled."[146]

Buried Stones

Harry Guinness took his medical degree in Brussels in January 1891 and sailed for Congo in March, the hold of the SS *Afrikaan* full of gunpowder and gin.[147] McKittrick had planned two exploratory trips with Guinness, one to the north to contact the fierce and cannibalistic *Ngombe*, while a second trip south would try to define the limits of the Balolo tribe. Heading north on foot from the Bongandanga station, they narrowly escaped being massacred on the third day, and their party beat a terrified retreat through the forest, armed Ngombe in hot pursuit. Regrouping in the safety of Bongandanga, they set out a few days later to do the second trip, only to find the entire district at war. Both Guinness and McKittrick fell ill with fever, but McKittrick's condition worsened. They returned to McKittrick's home at Bonginda, where he succumbed on November 22. His young wife, Dora, was at his side.

Harry took the funeral service. "We buried him next day close by his house," Guinness reported, "and close to the chapel in which he had so often told out the old, old story." Grief notwithstanding, he went on to write, "We could not but rejoice the next day . . . as we baptized the first five converts of the Balolo Mission." Twenty-five others were awaiting immersion. Immediately after the baptisms, Harry Guinness started home with his young widowed cousin.[148]

If McKittrick's death was the first taste of Calvary for the new Mission, it would not be the last. The first six years of the CBM were marked by six graves. Of the first thirty-five CBM missionaries to go to Congo, only six would survive into the new century. Twelve gave their lives in their first year of service, and twelve in their second and third. More remarkable is the fact that in the face of these grim statistics, volunteers continued to pour into Africa in a suicidal stream. Gustav Haupt, whose own grave lies next to that of John McKittrick, understood. He wrote of his fallen comrades, "They are buried stones for the future building of God."[149]

10

The Enemy

Now, in the twentieth year of the Mission, thirty-six members of our Congo band have joined the company of those who are in the immediate presence of their Lord. In 1896, our black year, seven of our fellow workers were called to higher service. It is the price that must be paid for the salvation of Congoland.

—Harry Guinness

Blackwater Fever

Central Africa remained unexplored until the late nineteenth century, but not for want of men who tried. In 1569, the Portuguese *Diego Cam* had probed the lower and middle Zambesi in search of gold. The party succumbed to disease, hostile tribal attacks, and all their horses died. In 1805, a Scottish surgeon, Mungo Park, set out to discover the source of the Niger River. Within six months, all in his party were dead. Their fate remained unknown for five years. In 1816, Captain James Tuckey, R.N. sailed up the lower Congo as far as the cataracts. Despite a reported favorable climate, within three months eighteen men had died from "an intense remittent fever with black vomit." Similar results attended many other expeditions.[150]

The tsetse fly killed horses. Malaria killed people. In its worst form they called it *blackwater fever*, sometimes, *hematuria*. Both terms described symptoms of the virulent form of the disease in which the presence of blood darkens the urine. The malarial parasite, introduced to the human bloodstream through the bite of the female anopheles mosquito, penetrates the blood cells, multiplies within the cell envelope, breaks down, digests the hemoglobin, and bursts the hemoglobin cell, releasing toxins into the bloodstream. The predominant African type, *plasmodium falciparum,* was the most malignant variety, often resulting in quick death.[151]

In the early days of the CBM, no one yet suspected the anopheles mosquito as the carrier of the deadly plasmodium. It was assumed that the sickness derived from exposure to the damp air near the ground. This was the "bad air"—the *"mal air."* The misdiagnosis stuck. It gave us a new word, *malaria.* The bite of the infected female anopheles was not identified as the vector until 1897. Since the *mal air* was believed never to rise higher than six feet above the ground, young missionaries built their sleeping platforms on poles—six feet above ground. It did no good.[152] Back at Harley College, the students had given Congo a macabre nickname. They called it "the shortcut to heaven."

Explorer Henry Morton Stanley in his long African experience had survived "over great and slight" without knowing why. He alludes to 260 other Europeans in Africa being "as ignorant as myself of the causes of these fevers."

> I may have suffered over one hundred before suspecting that many of these were preventable in other ways than by taking quinine and its preliminary remedies, or that there were other causes of fever besides malaria and miasma." [153]

In time, Stanley became certain of the cause of his fevers. Who could contest the authority bestowed by his years in Congo? The fevers—he maintained—were due to "Drafts, Malaria, and Alcohol." Chills were to be avoided at all costs, as the currents of cool air blowing through the Congo gorge were thought certain to be a culprit. Malaria, on the other hand, was due simply to bad air. Stanley affirmed that "if men inhale poison, they will suffer from it just as surely as they imbibe it."

The source of this "bad air" was decomposing vegetation on the jungle floor, "a steamy atmosphere, rising up with the clouds of moisture . . . from old, decaying grass at the base of the green shoots, or from the decaying leaves at the base of the beautiful bananas." Years of experience confirmed that this miasma was "more pernicious to health than life on a dunghill in an unfloored house in Europe . . . On open ground the air diffuses this pestilential vapor, heavy with putrefaction and decay . . ."[154] But conventional wisdom failed to stay death's grim hand.

Quinine

Both Stanley and Livingstone had used quinine to combat the deadly fevers, as had some of the LIM pioneers. So did Adam McCall on his final and fatal voyage to England. Quinine is the alkaloid extracted from the bark of the *cinchona* tree. This tree appears on the Peruvian coat of arms, since its remedial bark was first discovered in that country. The alkaloid is lethal to the malarial parasite. In use since 1820, when Italian chemists isolated it, quinine was a classic example of empirical treatment. It worked, but no one knew why. So, why were the early pioneers of the LIM unable to make effective use of the prophylactic? Although serious side effects could result from large doses of the substance, the alternative was hardly a choice.[155] For this writer, the question remains unanswered. What is clear is that the greatest obstacle to missions and to the exploration of Central Africa was neither slavery nor savagery nor the impassable cataracts of the River Congo. Only the conquest of lethal fly and waterborne diseases would make possible the opening of the Dark Continent.

Sleeping Sickness

Another enemy of gospel advance was sleeping sickness. Of the first 115 members of the church in Bongandanga, the CBM's fourth station, and where the Ruskins made their home, eighty-five died within a few years. Many succumbed to smallpox, accidents, or other ailments, but sleeping sickness was the most dreaded reaper. Livingstone wrote that the tsetse fly "was fatal to horses and cattle and a barrier to progress." [156] For this reason, horses could not be used in Equatorial Africa. In 1900, no cure was known. Nationals viewed it with such superstition that they refused even to name it.

Rumor circulated that it was contracted through closing ones eyes in prayer. The Ruskins advised the congregation to refrain from closing their eyes—just bowing the head at prayer would suffice. Members feared even to pray about the disease lest the mere mention of the name might increase the number of cases. The hysteria was warranted. No one ever recovered from sleeping sickness. Gradually, faith won the day, and believers began to pray earnestly for deliverance. The Lord heard. At that time, the Lopori river was infested with the Tsetse fly, carrier of the disease. So God sent another fly, new to the missionaries. This chased the Tsetse. Both expats and nationals noticed the phenomenon. They thanked God and took courage.[157] Not long after Bongandanga was opened in March 1891, the Anglo-Belgian Rubber Company settled not far from the Mission. This would bring a yet more lethal enemy to the hapless Congolese.[158]

Mr. and Mrs. E. A. Ruskin, Congo Pioneers

11

This Magnificent African Cake

You have come to tell us of salvation from sin, but have you no word of salvation from rubber?

—Congolese victim of the rubber
atrocities

Congo's Hinge of Fate

David Livingstone's exploits had failed to rouse British imperial interests in the Congo. Henry Morton Stanley knew that Central Africa was a commercial bonanza, free for the taking. As a loyal Brit, he wanted Queen Victoria to be first in line. Hoping to awaken the nation, he embarked on the lecture circuit and wrote a plethora of newspaper articles, painting Congo as a goldmine of economic opportunity. He consulted with powerful political figures, including the Prince of Wales and Baron Rothschild, but Britain was not interested in the high-risk venture of an African colony, and his pleas went unheeded.[159]

Fanny Guinness was not pleased. She understood the hinge-points of history and the far-reaching consequences of political whim. She lamented, "We [Great Britain] declined it and left the post of honor to Catholic Belgium."[160] Britain's default now forced Stanley into one of the less noble chapters of his life and embroiled him in one of the darkest sagas of African history. It also guaranteed a difficult path for Protestant missions.[161]

Leopold II

King Leopold II of Belgium (d.1909) was a cunning and avaricious entrepreneur who had been looking for a colony to enhance Belgium's stature within the European community of nations. Reports of Congo's wealth caught Leopold's imagination, but the Belgian's ambition to establish a colony in Congo was not shared by his government. Like Britain, they wanted no part of it.

Forced to find other means to fulfill his personal ambitions, Leopold contrived a philanthropic and scientific venture that he called the *International Africa Association,* with headquarters in Brussels. The IAA would dedicate its efforts to the suppression of the slave traffic and the development of commerce, while protecting the Congolese from exploitation. Inviting an impressive array of explorers and geographers, Leopold convened the conference on 11 September 1876. Guests were lavishly entertained, and in his welcome he assured the delegates:

> In bringing you to Brussels I was in no way motivated by selfish designs . . . if Belgium is small, she is happy and satisfied with her lot. My only ambition is to serve her.[162]

His sincerity may be judged by what he wrote to the Belgian ambassador in London a few months later: "I do not want to miss a good chance of getting us a slice of this magnificent African cake."[163] The ruse was successful. Europe took the bait. Leopold emerged a hero, a champion of the oppressed African. By a carefully orchestrated deception, he had successfully masked his real purpose. With Europe duped, Leopold was free to pursue a predatory policy of ruthless exploitation and personal aggrandizement. It would decimate the population of Central Africa.

Stanley's failure to interest the British government in the country he had opened was gleefully welcomed by Leopold, who had already unsuccessfully courted Stanley's cooperation. With Britain out of the way, the Belgian king had no fear. Leopold would never personally visit Congo, but he needed an experienced agent to execute his scheme for the opening of Central Africa. Stanley fit the bill perfectly. His skills and long experience in Congo only awaited a commission. Leopold now found in Stanley a sympathetic ear.[164]

Congo Free State

Stanley's triumphant descent of the Congo River in 1877 proved that Central Africa's wealth was at last accessible. Now in the employ of Leopold, he returned to Congo to negotiate trading agreements with tribal chiefs, signing a hundred contracts with as many groups. A rush of European nations followed—Portugal, France, and Germany—all jostling for a slice of the African cake. Within seven years, bickering was rife. To resolve the disputes, an international arbitration conference convened in Berlin in 1884, establishing the *Congo Free State* (CFS). Even the United States was party to the agreement, though not a signatory.

The CFS charter championed the protection of missionaries, scientists, and explorers, suppression of the slave trade, civilization of the natives, and taxes or duties equivalent to the value of services rendered to navigation itself.

While the agreement made concessions to Portugal and France, it effectively deeded most of the Congo basin to the aspirations of its founder," Leopold II. He had pulled off the largest personal land grab in history. But the Belgian king—who had invested a considerable personal fortune in the initial development of his trading empire—was just getting started.[165]

Red Rubber

When Scottish veterinarian John Boyd Dunlop fashioned the first pneumatic bicycle tire for his ailing son in 1888, rubber became one of the hottest commodities on the world market. Wild, latex-bearing plants abounded in tropical Congo, and Leopold discovered that his private estate in the heart of Africa could be a lucrative producer of what the world wanted. He turned Congo into a vast rubber farm.[166] The wild latex required no cultivation and could be harvested immediately and at will. The only requirement to reap this bonanza was labor, and with an indigenous slave population already in place there was no shortage. Nor was there any lack of agents to expedite Leopold's predatory designs.

He established a system of extraction that paid the natives for their work, not in money, but in worthless goods.[167] Enforcement of rubber quotas became ruthless and barbaric. It was achieved by beatings, shootings, amputation of hands, feet, or ears, burning of villages, and chaining the uncooperative to trees where they were left to die. Entire populations were decimated in the process. Roger Casement, the British Consul, estimated three million deaths under Leopold's regime.[168] The system worked well until an astute advocate exposed the fraud.

Leopold Exposed

Twenty-eight-year-old Edmond Morel was a clerk with the *Elder Dempster* shipping line, and a correspondent for *The West African Mail*. What caught his eye was the disparate balance of trade between Liverpool, Amsterdam, and the Congo port of Matadi. Millions of pounds sterling in rubber was coming out of Congo. What was going in was not the equivalent in trade goods, but arms and ammunition—the means to continue extortion of the rubber quotas. Morel's weekly articles in *The West African Mail* documented the outrage and fired the British parliament to investigate.[169]

Darwinian Logic

In 1888, the life of African blacks was held in small regard. In the academic halls and drawing rooms of England, Darwin's concept of natural selection was bearing its bitter fruit. If survival of the fittest was a natural process, the fit were free to accelerate that process with impunity. Inferior races might be used, then discarded. Serious discussions focused on whether the Negroid people were truly human. One group concluded that pygmies in particular were an early stage in the evolutionary process.[170] In 1906, at New York's Bronx Zoo, Ota Benga—a Congolese pygmy—had been exhibited in a monkey cage.[171] With God safely removed from the equation, the business of rubber extraction could proceed with little to disturb the conscience.

Silence of the Missionaries

The early silence of RBMU missionaries in the face of these atrocities eludes explanation until we remember that by the time the Congo Free State (1885–1908) was established, the Congo basin had effectively become Belgian soil. By virtue of the rights accorded at the 1884 Berlin conference, Leopold was both proprietor and host to the missionaries. To expose the atrocities of their unscrupulous benefactor was to risk expulsion from the country. The viability of all that the missionaries had worked for was at stake. This explains why missionaries—as RBMU's Lily Ruskin tells us—were constantly at pains to distance themselves from Belgian traders.

Cruel treatment by agents of the trading companies spawned bitter Congolese antagonism against Europeans, including missionaries. To African eyes white skin was a common denominator shared alike by both missionaries and the sadistic enforcers of Leopold's policies. To avoid guilt by association, missionaries shunned the use of commercial steamers, which regularly plied the Upper River.[172] Beyond this mute gesture, their lips were sealed. However, even this failed to exonerate the Message-bearers in Congo eyes:

> "Sit down, white man," said the native chief to Mr. Padfield, who was preaching in a Congo village he had not previously visited. "Sit down and listen to me. You have come to tell us of salvation from sin, but have you no word of salvation from rubber?"[173]

Such rebukes cut deeply.

While the rubber business exacted its toll from the Congolese, missionaries were not exempt from a different cost. What they either witnessed or knew is reflected in Mrs. Ruskin's remarks years later:

> We were in the midst of what were rightly called Congo atrocities. It is not my wish to recount any of the terrible and horrible things that took place in the early years of this century right up to 1910; but it was a hard time. The mental strain told upon us and left its mark for years. One tries not to remember some of the happenings of those dark days when we suffered with our dear people; looking back it is like the remembrance of a horrible nightmare.[174]

Even the courageous Ed Ruskin, who lived and worked on the river throughout the entire process, refused to report the genocidal tactics of the Belgian agents. He kept diaries and notes but never aired them. When Leopold was finally deposed, Ruskin refused to discuss the matter and burned his records, explaining:

> The government of *Congo Belge* has done its best to put things right and has very largely succeeded. I shall never bring up what I know.[175]

Was Ruskin's silence bought in some degree by the services he personally rendered to Leopold? English Baptist missionary George Grenfell had charted thousands of miles of the Congo River basin, an achievement of great value to Leopold. Ruskin likewise had been courted by Leopold to negotiate treaties with tribal chiefs. His translation work had rendered similar service to the king's enterprises. The Belgian king was a shrewd manipulator and carefully cultivated the favor of those who served his ends. In his Brussels palace, he had entertained both Ruskin and Grenfell.[176] However, in a less diplomatic approach, the missionaries had been warned to keep hands off. The May 1891 issue of *Regions Beyond* reported the burning of African towns by state officials, while the BMS noted that the Congo regime "was bearing heavily upon both Africans and Europeans." Such negative publicity hardly pleased Leopold, and some missionaries "had been told very emphatically that 'preaching the gospel and teaching' is their vocation, and that the administration of the country is not for them to meddle with."[177] For some, silence became the price of ministry.

Guinness Incredulous

What Ruskin and other CBM missionaries knew about the Congo atrocities was at first largely unknown to Dr. Harry Guinness and his mother. They refused to believe the stories of European savagery, preferring to regard the allegations as isolated incidents—the excesses of irresponsible agents.[178] That Leopold could be complicit in such atrocities defied credibility. In defense of the Belgians, there was no denying that their presence was gradually establishing law and order along the river and its tributaries. Tribal warfare was diminishing, the flow of liquor had been stopped, and Arab slave raiders were no longer trafficking in human life. Leopold had worked to suppress the slave traffic in keeping with the well-publicized humanitarian aims of the International Africa Association. This provided the necessary cover for his other interests. Moreover, Belgian officials were courteous to missionaries and Mrs. Guinness was completely taken in. Confidently, she wrote (1890) in lavish praise of Leopold's altruism, referring to him as "the philanthropic and generous monarch" who had instigated measures for Congo's good, bearing the expenses out of his private purse.[179]

Harry Goes to Brussels

Guinness awoke to reality in 1895 when the first documented reports of the rubber atrocities reached Harley House. The following year undeniable confirmation came from E. V. Sjöblom, a Swedish missionary and former Harley student. He shared a grisly account:

> On December 14, 1895 my friend, Mrs. Banks, had been crossing the station compound at Bolengi, when she saw a poor woman being beaten by a native sentry. On inquiring what was the matter, the sentry replied,
>
> "She has lost one!"
>
> "One what?" inquired Mrs. Banks.
>
> "Why, one of the hands," said the sentry.
>
> Then Mrs. Banks noticed that the basket on the back of the woman was filled with human hands. She immediately called her husband and Rev. Sjöblom, and the hands were counted in her presence. There were eighteen in all, and the angry sentry still asserted that there ought to have been nineteen. Some of these smoked hands were those of children, some of women and some of men.
>
> "Where are you taking these?" asked one of the missionaries.
>
> "To the white man [The Congo Free State official] to whom I must prove that I have been diligent in pushing the rubber business, and who would punish me if I did not compel the people to bring in a sufficient quantity."[180]

Armed with incontrovertible data, Harry Guinness immediately went to Brussels for an audience with Leopold. The king received him courteously and gave him extended opportunity to speak, and then responded, "You are an excellent young man, but you must not believe what the natives say!" Guinness countered with the evidence, including Mrs. Banks' testimony about the severed hands. Leopold promised an inquiry, requesting the names of officials whom the missionaries thought should be removed. Several were removed, only to appear later in other regions where they pursued the same actions with even less compunction.[181] As Harry later realized, Leopold's action was merely placatory and intended "to throw dust in the eyes of Europe."[182]

Congo Reform Association

By 1904, widespread public outcry called for stronger measures, and in March, the *Congo Reform Association* was established. For three years, Dr. Harry Guinness conducted a vigorous public campaign, bringing to bear his power over audiences and his intimate first hand knowledge of the Congo scene, and the indignation of God through the witness of Scripture. He had marshaled his facts, complete with import and export records revealing the disproportion between the value of the rubber exports and the barter trinkets given in exchange. The atrocities were reported objectively, and documented without histrionics. Guinness presented his report to the British Foreign Secretary, and in 1907 while en route to Peru, met personally with President Theodore Roosevelt, since America had been party to the international agreement, though not a signatory. In 1908, a fifty-page paper, *The Congo Crisis*, called Protestant Europe to prayer.[183]

Leopold's Death

Under the pressure of public outrage, King Leopold abdicated in 1904, but continued his proxy administration of the Congo Free State. International intervention finally forced Belgium to negotiate annexation of the king's African preserve. By the time Christian Churches raised formal protest at Albert Hall—presided over by the Archbishop of Canterbury—the Congo Free State had already been annexed by Belgium. A month later, on December 17, Leopold died.[184] Reforms began immediately under Albert, his successor, but with Leopold's infrastructure still in place, it would take years for the changes to trickle down for the benefit of all affected Congolese. Clearly a part of the process, Christian voices had demonstrated the dynamic power of the gospel for social and humanitarian reform. Another drumbeat had made the world a better place. Notwithstanding, Europe's legacy of barbarism had sunk deep into the soul of the Congolese people. Like invisible ink, it would disappear for a few decades, only to reappear under the right conditions—but with a terrible vengeance. In 1960, conditions would be right.

Congo's Unfinished Task

In 1908, Dr. Harry Guinness summarized the challenge that still beckoned the CBM:

> Missionary effort has only touched the fringe of Upper Congo need. In the vast territory . . . in which the [CBM] is at work, we have only been permitted to occupy a comparatively restricted area. The Lomami River, navigable for seven hundred miles beyond its junction with the Congo, remains entirely unreached. [As far as we know], its large population speaks the Lomongo language with which our missionaries are familiar. [Nonetheless], they have only known the iron oppression of the rubber tyranny . . . As to the Juapa, Bosira, Momboyo, and other vast affluents of the Ruki system of rivers, what of their peoples? These are all included in the horseshoe bend of the Congo, which the CBM ought to reach.

> We began to establish a station at Moniaca [Bonyeka]. The vast amount of rubber that has been derived from this part of Congo tells its own story of what must have taken place where missionaries have been forbidden to enter.[185]

Britain's default to "Catholic Belgium" had begun to exact its toll upon Protestant missions. Harry Guinness continued his retrospect:

Now in the twentieth year of the Mission, thirty-six members of our
Congo band have joined the company of those who are in the immediate presence of their Lord. In 1896, our black year, no fewer than seven
were called to higher service, and this high rate of mortality has not
been confined to the CBM. It is the price that must be paid for the salvation of Congoland.[186]

12

If I Will That He Tarry

Picture the lives of these missionaries. Isolated by hundreds of miles of forest and waterways from the nearest of their kind. Set down in the midst of cannibal communities, their nearest neighbors—representatives of the State—frankly inimical to their labors. So, cut off that the warning whistle of the "Pioneer" as it threads its tortuous way through the shallows of the little creek, is the sweetest music.

—Edgar Wallace, British journalist

Edward Algernon Ruskin

Africa's high mortality rate assured a short and deadly race for many of the early pioneers. But not for all. God's ways with his own must often remain veiled in mystery until that Daybreak when all is made clear. Jesus said as much. Just after Peter learned of the death he would face, he nodded in John's direction and asked Jesus, *"And what shall this man do?"* The Lord's reply forever speaks to those perplexed by life's disparities. *"If I will that he tarry till I come, what is that to thee? Follow me."*[187]

Few of the early Congo pioneers were as measurably productive or enjoyed so long a tenure in the service of the Congolese as Edward Algernon Ruskin and his wife, Lily. Entering Harley College on 6 January 1892, he moved on to Cliff College the following October, where he reveled in Greek, and where he remained, "just long enough to learn his own ignorance, and a few other things medical."

Lily Wall had always wanted to be a missionary, and on hearing of the work in Congo through Dr. and Mrs. Grattan Guinness, the call came. She entered Doric lodge for training and took a diploma in midwifery. During Edward Ruskin's ten-month furlough, he and Lily met. They already knew that "the inclining of the heart of each to the other even before they had seen each other" had been of God's design, as Lily Ruskin noted; and that the furlough meeting was simply a "ratification of the mystic union"*[188]* already established. They were married on 1 August 1898, and sailed together from Liverpool three days later aboard the SS *Niger*. Mr. James Irvine, one of the directors of the Mission, was at the docks to see them off. Lily recalls, "I remember the dear old gentleman placing his hand on my shoulder and saying, 'Goodbye, dear, the Lord bless you. I hope you will get on all right.'"[189] Twenty-six ports and six weeks later they arrived at Matadi.

Forty-Four Years in Congo

Edward Ruskin brought his bride to Bongandanga, where he had arrived as a single missionary four years earlier (29 July 1894). This would be their only home during the forty-four years of Ruskin's Congo life.

Ruskin's achievements were formidable and abiding. A gifted linguist, he soon became fluent in Lomongo and then defined the grammar. His tenacity in developing a vocabulary and pursuing the right turn of phrase earned him the nicknames, "The one who pesters us with questions," and "He who carries the little book to write words." He collected words like a philatelist collects stamps. He would pay cash for them when necessary, and linguistic *bon mots* like ice being "sleeping water" and love translating "to feel pain for," were worth their weight in gold when turning a sermon illustration. Ruskin soon discovered that while Lomongo contained many words for vices there were few to express virtues, so that some words had to be lifted and infused with new meanings, while other concepts had to be embodied in brief phrases.

Linguistic Achievements

During his first three years in Congo, Ruskin traveled an estimated 4000 miles by canoe along the tributaries through regions "teeming with hippos, elephants, a few crocodiles, and coveys of birds by day, mosquitoes and other insects buzzing all night in their myriads."[190] His name is forever linked with the Lomongo Bible. By 1908, he had printed the Lomongo New Testament on the mission presses at Bongandanga. Costs were underwritten by the British and Foreign Bible Society. The Ruskins published *Outlines of the Grammar of the Lomongo Language*.

By 1930 they had "the supreme joy of seeing the whole Bible printed in the Lomongo language." [191] During this translation process, they were hard at work on the Lomongo dictionary, a work in two sections, half of the 650 pages devoted to both English and French equivalents of Lomongo, the other half providing the Lomongo equivalents of English. The dictionary was published in 1928, followed by the *Grammar* in 1934 and the *Notes on the Lingombe Grammar* in 1937.

In addition, they had many schoolbooks to their credit, and were honored by Leopold, the Belgian king. In one of his last official acts in Congo, Ruskin presided over the opening of the Mompono Bible Institute in 1938. His lustrous niche in the early history of the Congo mission is secure.

Angel of the Lord and an Umbrella

In March 1895, Ruskin led an expedition to the upper Lopori River district, notorious for its cannibalistic residents. Having decided not to take a gun, it proved difficult to hire a crew of carriers to accompany him to the forbidden region. The first crew summarily resigned upon hearing that they would be unprotected by a firearm. The second crew abandoned the contract for fear of cannibals. A third crew stayed the course.

On arriving at Bongila, a war whoop suddenly rang through the forest and a party of savages confronted Ruskin, yelling, "Spear him! Spear him now!" As they rushed at him, they suddenly became terrified, covering their eyes as if dazzled. Uttering a weird cry, "A-a-ah!" they disappeared into the forest. The strange phenomenon was repeated further on. In the village, plans for killing him were discussed in his presence. Deciding it was unwise to remain, he sent the carriers on ahead, while he himself brought up the rear, walking backward to keep his eyes on his pursuers. However, the heat was intense and the road bad, so commending himself to God, he turned his back on his assailants and marched forward, at the same time putting up his umbrella. In an instant, the alarming sound of many moving feet convinced him that he was about to be speared in the back, but turning around, he found that the whole lot had stampeded into the bush. Ruskin had no doubt that the Angel of the Lord had intervened to save him, using an umbrella!

Years later Lily Ruskin reflected:

> That is how the Ekoutshi district was entered. There are now schools and churches there, and a goodly number of Christians, some of them being sons and daughters of the men who took part in the incidents above mentioned. At one baptismal service, the son of one of the attackers—now an elder of the church—entered the water with my husband and assisted him in baptizing several of his own people.
>
> On our last journey through the district, a very old man in one village called out as we passed, "White man, I know the use of an umbrella now! I was there in the crowd when we thought it was a gun. When you explained it was to cover your head from the sun, we said you must be as soft as a white ant to need such a thing! We were foolish, but we did not know any better![192]

Where to Write Your Prayers

The witty and irreverent British journalist Edgar Wallace visited the CBM work about 1907. He toured the Upper River on the CBM Steamer, *Livingstone*, Belgian traders having refused to take him for obvious reasons. He described his days on the *Livingstone*—his respectful sufferance of on-board morning prayers, and his interview with a Congolese victim of the rubber atrocities. Then, assuring his readers that he would not be a missionary on the Congo for £5,000 a year, Wallace lavished his admiration for the CBM missionaries:

> Already to me the Congo is as a dreadful nightmare, a bad dream of death and suffering. Such a dream as one sees o' nights when nothing is right, when every law of man and nature is revolted, and the very laws of life are outraged.
>
> A bad dream, save only in this, that mingled with the mad delirium of lawlessness, runs a brighter theme . . . of men and women . . . living their lives and dying their deaths at humanity's need; who are creating a manhood from a degraded race; who are making Christians and citizens. Hard, bitterly hard is the work; full of disappointment and rebuff, but steadfastly and unflinchingly, these brave soldiers of the Nazarene are fighting his fight.
>
> I am grateful to them for this: that they made me feel ashamed; ashamed of my futile life by the side of their great achievements. In England I met a smug Christian, and told him of these missionaries. "We owe them our prayers," he said sententiously. I laughed.
>
> "Write your prayers on the back of a five-pound note and send the note to the Congo Balolo Mission."[193]

13

The Congo Church

Then what does the heart of the Savior suffer when he looks down from his heaven upon such a scene as this? Does he see some sitting in comfortable ease at home who should be helping us on the field? I implore you to commune with God on the matter, and if he says, "Go!" then come over and help us! If not, then willingly give to him of your substance, to enable us to do more for the sufferers who remain.

—Kate Butler of Congo

CBM at Twenty-Five Years

By 1916 the Congo Balolo Mission was firmly established throughout an area the size of England. Forty-one missionaries were deployed in nine stations strung out over five hundred miles of rain forest—Lulonga, Ikau, Bongandanga, Baringa, Mompono, Yuli, Yoseki, Bosodjafo, Munda, and Etoka. The number of communicants, while "not large" had been won at the cost of thirty-eight lives.[194] Forty years later, in 1955, there were 32,000 members on the church rolls, 9,000 children in schools, nineteen pastors, and eighty-eight evangelists.[195]

The Hospitals—Baringa, Yoseki, Yuli

Founded in 1932, the Baringa Hospital quickly grew to a staff of three doctors attending 50,000 patients annually. A second hospital was opened in 1945 at Yoseki, the Mission's easternmost base. Three years later, RBMU launched a third hospital at Yuli, the indirect result of a 1948 plane crash that took the lives of a pastor and two missionaries. The trio was flying to England to seek funds for a new medical work when tragedy struck. The Yuli Hospital became their memorial.[196]

Mompono Bible School

On 16 April 1938, the Bible School was opened at Mompono, the aging Ruskins presiding at the ceremony. It had earlier been an Evangelists' Training School under the direction of Mr. and Mrs. Carpenter. With the new construction, including an assembly hall and four classrooms, the Mompono Bible School received its first class of thirteen students representing four mission stations and three different tribal groups.

Baringa Leprosy Colony

In the same year, the Baringa Leprosy Colony was opened with the admission of eighty patients to the first forty huts. Organized on the pattern of a village, each patient had a garden plot to cultivate his own food. A brick church was opened on Christmas Day 1941 and a dispensary in 1943. This was followed in 1945 with construction of a brick school. At the colony, Congo drums were still the means of communication as Dr. Edgar Wide noted:

> Between the church and the dispensary stands a huge anthill. Perched on top of this is a hut sheltering three drums. Quite often, just after dawn, the sound of these drums can be heard four miles away at Baringa, calling the [patients] to morning worship. Every Sunday morning as the drums throb, the church is filled with a motley crowd—adults and children, crippled and active, some semi-naked and some brightly clad, some converted and some still in darkness. The drums call the people not only to worship and witness, but to wrestle with their disease.[197]

In later years the incidence of leprosy would decrease in Congo with the advent of modern treatment, but in the pre and post-World War II years the Mission ministered at times to as many as 2,000 patients in several leprosaria.[198] The Belgian government honored Dr. Edgar Wide for his work with leprosy patients. In the quiescent decade of the 1930s all seemed well in Congoland, and the association of RBMU churches (CADELU) was robust. In 1939 no one could have guessed the trial by fire that lay ahead.

14

Lucy Guinness Kumm

*Up the white stairway of these scintillating summits thought
climbs to their Creator. Inscrutable, divine, they stand there,
eloquent of him and of humanity's nothingness . . . There is
eternal Holiness. There is a changeless power and stainless
purity, far above the sorrow and sinning of the world. These
are the real things, these alone are the real things . . . God! He
has room. He has time. He has means. He has purposes. And
He has need of thee.*

—Lucy Guinness

Light for the Darkness

She opened India with her pen. The third of Grattan Guinness' surviving children arrived in July 1865—the same month that marked the end of the American Civil War. Her parents called her Lucy—from lumière, meaning, *light*—"hoping that God would make her a light to those in darkness."[199] They named her well.

Lucy's cosmopolitan upbringing prepared her to touch her world for God. Studies in Paris were followed—at seventeen—by two and a half years of schooling in Australia and Tasmania. Once back in England, Harley House for Lucy was an international Grand Central Station, and living there in the atmosphere of missions brought the world to her doorstep.

In London, she identified with the disadvantaged. Her father wrote, "we had established our Missionary College in a neighborhood [in London] whose only attraction was the sphere it afforded for evangelistic and philanthropic work." In order to become thoroughly acquainted with their ways and needs, she worked for a time in one of the East End factories, living in lodgings among the disadvantaged. She subsequently embodied her impressions in a book entitled, *Only a Factory Girl.* This led to the establishment of a home for these girls.[200]

By Pen and Pulpit

When her mother was no longer able, she edited the _Regions Beyond_ magazine for eight or nine years. In 1890, at twenty-five, she accompanied her father to America, where she "traveled far and wide through the United States, visiting and speaking on behalf of missions at women's colleges, and founding many new branches of the Student Volunteer Movement."[201] She edited her sister Geraldine's widely distributed, _Letters from the Far East,_ which focused evangelical attention on China and the China Inland Mission.

In 1898, Lucy traveled across India with her father, visiting Bombay, Madras, Calcutta, Benares, and other centers. She authored the illustrated volume, _Across India at the Dawn of the Twentieth Century._ Empire-conscious Brits bought hundreds of copies. Packed with mission statistics, _Across India_ showcased her descriptive literary skills and revealed her eloquent and facile pen as deserving of the encomium, "the most gifted editor in the British Isles." Its pathos revealed something deeper—the almost genetic compassion of the Guinness family for a lost humanity.

It might be Henry's white-hot anger on seeing the ashes of the martyrs at the infamous Quemadero in Madrid. It might be Lucy's refusal of medical treatment in her terminal illness so that she might finish writing her plea for Congo's violated humanity. Whatever the occasion, the Guinness heart seemed unaffectedly broken with the things that break the heart of God.

Britain's Opium Revenue

Nor was spiritual bondage the only servitude attacked by the Guinness pen. Eloquent polemics were hurled at Britain's Indo-Chinese opium revenue, which even in 1906 exceeded three million pounds annually, and though morally indefensible, was justified at the highest levels by the threadbare argument that "if we don't ruin China someone else will, or she will ruin herself."[202]

Romance on the Nile

Lucy was unmarried and thirty-three when her mother died in 1898. Her older and only sister, Geraldine, was married to Howard Taylor and serving with the China Inland Mission on the other side of the world. H. Grattan felt that Lucy needed a change of scenery and took her to Egypt, where they visited various missions and ascended the Nile as far as the first cataract. Here she met Dr. Karl Kumm, a young German missionary, who acted as guide and interpreter for Guinness and his daughter. A mutual affection soon developed. The chemistry led to a second visit to the land of the Pharaohs and to a new chapter in Lucy's life. It would also initiate a fresh drumbeat in world evangelization.

Karl Kumm

Grattan, Lucy, and Karl met at Aswan, seven hundred miles up the Nile; where seventy-one years later the Soviet Union would complete construction of one of the world's largest dams. Kumm was returning from an evangelistic tour among the Arabs of the Sahara. Lucy's attention—and her father's—was quickly captured by the handsome German's account of his contact with the *Bishareen*. True to character, Grattan Guinness seized the initiative. Here is the gist of his account:

> During our stay at Aswan the condition of the Bishareen of the neighboring desert, and the Nubians, whose country begins at the first cataract and stretches five hundred miles up the Nile, attracted our attention. Dr. Kumm collected from the Bishareen a vocabulary of the principal words in their language, and I secured the services of a Christian Copt to teach in a school. I also contracted with Ali Hissein, a Nubian who had been trained in our College, to evangelize the Nubians. We gathered several of the wild Bishareen into a building we hired for a school, and began a work that subsequently grew into the Sudan Mission.
>
> Ten years before, I had been deeply interested in the needs of the Sudanese, and had lectured on the subject in the United States, publishing a little mission paper called *'The Sudan.'* Because of this effort more than twenty secretaries of the Young Men's Christian Association in Kansas and Nebraska volunteered to go as missionaries to the Sudan. Several of these went to Sierra Leone, and established a chain of stations extending from that spot to the upper waters of the Niger. The missionaries suffered at first severely from fever; several died, but with a diminished staff of workers, the mission that had become associated with the work of Dr. Simpson, of New York City, continues to the present day.[203]

The Sudan United Mission

On this historic spot the Sudan United Mission was conceived. On 11 January 1900, Lucy Guinness and Karl Kumm joined hands above the clasped hands of two Bishareen in token of Grattan Guinness' consent to the union. They were married on February 3 at Cairo in the American Mission Church.

To Lucy and her husband, the evangelization of the Sudan was "the most pressing mission question of the hour."[204] Fifty million Sudanese populated an area between the Niger and the Nile, equal in size to Europe, but with only "half a dozen mission stations on its borders."[205] Guinness foresaw what was coming:

The Mohammedans are rapidly absorbing the pagan populations of the Sudan into Islam and threaten soon to engulf the whole region in the anti-Christianism of their creed.[206]

Driven by their vision, Lucy and Karl went on to barnstorm England, Scotland, and Ireland, visiting "the most influential Christian ministers in the land" and forming councils in London, Edinburgh, and Dublin. They recruited workers for the venture, and raised the funds to send them out.

The Kumms took the gospel message to Africa's largest country, but they would not be together for long.[207] In July 1906, Karl had sailed for Britain to speak at Keswick. During his absence, Lucy had been living and writing in a cottage in Northfield, Massachusetts on the grounds of D. L. Moody's famed Bible conference, where both she and her father had ministered. Her health, never strong, had suffered severely from the strain of multiplied responsibilities. On August 12, following two unsuccessful surgeries for an ectopic pregnancy, Lucy Guinness Kuhm's light flickered and went out. Writing furiously to the end, she had completed *Our Slave State,* an impassioned brief on behalf of the Congolese. It was never used. Dr. G. Campbell Morgan, Dr. Henry Mabie, and Dr. R. A. Torrey paid their tributes at the memorial service, and her remains were laid to rest in a portion of the D. L. Moody family lot.

15

Graveyard of Missions

Visit this place as I have done and it will wring your heart. Here is a little fragment of North India containing nearly the whole population of Australia, yet if you were to take out all the Christians and put them in Albert Hall it would be only half full.

— A visitor to North Bihar

The Turbid Flood

Lucy's Guinness' work, *Across India at the Dawn of the Twentieth Century,* not only captured empire-conscious Brits; it lifted the horizons of the twelve-year-old Congo Balolo Mission. "Again we stand at Benares," Guinness wrote, "that ancient center of gross idolatry with its eight hundred temples on the banks of the Ganges, or row up the river for miles witnessing the superstitious worship of congregated thousands seeking to wash away their sins in its turbid flood."[208] The province of Bihar in North India had a population of twenty million. Lucy described it as "the most neglected Indian mission field."[209] One hundred years later it had earned an even sadder epithet—"the graveyard of missions."

Lucy did more than write. Her untiring energy in missionary recruitment effectively catapulted the CBM into its second field. Embodying the fervor of an evangelist, she stormed British churches with their gospel responsibility to "the empire." So effective were her pleas to the students at Harley College that pith-helmeted ambassadors were on their way to the subcontinent within a year of her India visit.

Banks and Hicks

Towards the end of 1899, Harley College men, George Hicks and Alex Banks, arrived at Dinapore. In this city a hundred years earlier, Henry Martyn had lifted his famous prayer, "What a wretched life shall I lead if I do not exert myself from morning till night in a place where through whole territories, I seem to be the only light." Where Banks and Hicks were going, they *would* be the only lights. Henry Martyn could have told them what to expect. Dying at thirty-one, he had seen no convert. If Africa had "killed all her lovers," India would smother hers with indifference.

Bihar

The province of Bihar nestles at the foot of the Himalayas in northeast India. Cradled in the alluvial plain of the mighty Ganges River, they called it, "the Garden of India," for Mother Ganges (*Gunga Mataji*) nourished its verdant expanses and the productive soil drew people like a magnet. Even in 1897 twenty million people crowded into a space little larger than the state of Florida. It would later become the most densely populated acreage on earth. Bihar then had but fifteen missionaries, but in the district of Champaran, with two million inhabitants, there was no missionary witness at all.

George Banks and Alex Hicks camped in a mango grove in the town of Motihari, Champaran's administrative center. The town became the first base of the Mission in India. Soon joined by John Z. Hodge and Peter Wynd, the team established stations at Siwan, Champatia (1905), and Gopalganj, opening a girls' school at Raxaul, a town on the Nepal border, and orphanages at Motihari and Siwan. Hodge was a gifted public advocate for missions, and his book, *Christ or Caste,* opened the eyes of his generation to the formidable obstacles facing those who dared to assault Hinduism.[210]

Hinduism

Hinduism shocked Peter Wynd. "Their religion is disgusting," he wrote. "It effectively shuts out God for it confounds him with His works and exalts His immanence until His personality is lost sight of . . . We are entrusted with the gospel and it is required in a steward that he be found faithful."[211]

Among the staff at Harley House, North Bihar quickly won a reputation for impermeability to the gospel message. The grim statistics of Hinduism and caste bound eighty percent of the population. Abject poverty afflicted most Biharis, who from earliest memory were besieged by an endless cycle of drought, earthquakes, floods, and famine. Suffering and disease dulled the collective mind, producing a jaded, almost colorless profile—a daunting prospect for all but the rarest breed of missionary. It was why Gordon Guinness would later call Bihar, "The forgotten frontier."

Twenty Years Without a Convert

Herbert and Elizabeth Pritchard spent a lifetime in Bihar province with little to show for it in terms of evangelistic head counts. The emotional stamina and spiritual maturity implicit in such a record of endurance is humbling. The writer felt the pathos in 1969 outside the leprosy clinic in Muzaffarpur, when

Herbert Pritchard confided, "I have preached here for twenty years without seeing a single convert." The Author of missions, our Lord Jesus Christ, had laid down the law of sowing and reaping, often mysterious to our eyes, when he declared: *I sent you to reap that upon which you bestowed no labor. Other men labored and you are entered into their labors.*[212] The principle should invoke humility in those privileged to reap ready harvests. It should likewise infuse great encouragement in those who have borne the burden and the heat of the day with few results. The Bihar pioneers and many of their successors are among the "other men" who sowed that others might reap.

The Mission Takes a New Name

With work established in north India, the twelve-year-old Congo Balolo Mission had outgrown its name. New horizons demanded a more comprehensive title. Just as David Livingstone had provided the inspiration for entering Africa, his philosophy of ministry had also struck a lively chord with Guinness. The Scottish explorer affirmed that he "would never build upon another man's foundation" and that he would "always work beyond another man's line of things." [213]

Long before Livingstone, Paul the Apostle had expressed the same pioneering philosophy to the church at Corinth when he declared his purpose *To preach the gospel in the regions beyond you, and not to boast in another man's line of things made ready to our hand.*[214] Paul's burden had been to take the message to earth's frontiers, where Christ was not yet named. The text seemed to define the young mission perfectly. The people at Harley House agreed: *Regions Beyond Missionary Union* would be the new name.[215]

While the word *union* rings with different connotations in the modern ear, at the turn of the twentieth century, "union" was conventional nomenclature for designating mission and church agencies. Moreover, in the heyday of colonialism, few objected to the word, *missionary*, and that was what RBMU was all about—fulfilling Christ's mandate. The term would later become offensive to some third-world governments and the name would have to change again to accommodate international mood swings, but in 1900 the designation was apt and would remain so for the next eighty years.

Early Work

The first four pioneers in Bihar Province were joined by their chosen partners early in the century, "two of them the prettiest girls in Doric Lodge," reported Betty Pritchard.

> Twelve others had been added to their number over the years and they had pushed out from Motihari and Siwan, establishing stations at Gopalganj and Champatia. They opened the work in the forestlands of the Tharuhat (a twenty-five mile strip co-extensive with the Nepal-India border

and home to two million Tharus, an aboriginal tribe of uncertain origins). Hundreds of Hindu and Muslim lads passed through the RBMU school at Siwan, having been taught daily of Jesus Christ and his salvation, and both boys and girls were being cared for in the Mission's orphanages.[216]

However, gospel results in Bihar failed to match the joyful harvest the Mission was experiencing in Congo. Diligent and faithful preaching seemed like firing pebbles against an impregnable fortress of Bihari apathy and indifference. While not totally without encouragement—the RBMU task force did see God at work in a few lives—Christian groups remained "pitifully small, producing no leaders who could take over the care of the churches." Betty Pritchard tells us that the tiny, struggling clusters of believers lacked the inspirational factors that normally attend a growing church—the crowded meetings, the joyful uplift of exuberant congregational singing, and the challenge of frequent conversions. So disheartening was the work in North Bihar that the Mission decided to suspend the sending of further recruits to India. Then something happened to rescind that decision.[217]

Hope Dawns in the Thirties

About 1935, a friend of the Mission sent funds to Harley House specifically designated to send two new workers to India. Gordon Guinness, son of Dr. Harry Guinness, had returned as chairman of the RBMU board and again urged advance into the eastern part of North Bihar. His visit to Raxaul in 1927 had kindled hope that Nepal would soon open to the gospel and that RBMU missionaries in Bihar might be the first to enter. From 1935 to 1937, nine new workers went out, seven of them fired with the hope of an early entry into Nepal. As it turned out, only three of the seven would get to Nepal.

The coming of reinforcements infused hope and expectation into the beleaguered Bihari team. The fresh troops had come armed with the provocative teaching of Roland Allen's book, *Paul's Method or Ours?* Their coming threatened to turn the Bihar field upside down. Betty Pritchard recalled:

> They realized quickly, however, that Bihar was not going to yield all that easily to such methods. Not one of the small Christian groups appeared fit to be left. No one had emerged showing any particular concern for the welfare of the churches. Most of the Christians had been drawn from Hinduism, which does not attempt to proselytize and they had no concern for the plight of the millions around them, living in darkness. To evangelize was the missionary's work along with those whom he paid to do it.[218]

Even so, plans were laid for fresh advance in North Bihar. Surveys were conducted. Then, in 1939, Britain was plunged into a global conflict that touched all corners of the empire, including India. A year later, five RBMU men were conscripted into the Indian army. They were away for six years. Those left behind struggled with a depleted staff. Even Dr. Cecil Duncan was swallowed up in the war effort and the Duncan Hospital at Raxaul was closed. Once again it seemed that God had drawn a curtain over North Bihar, as if to say, "Not yet."

Just before the war, a visitor from the more spiritually fertile South Bihar had come north to serve as best man for one of the new crop of RBMU missionaries. He wrote, "Visit this place as I have done and it will wring your heart. Here is a little fragment of North India containing nearly the whole population of Australia, yet if you were to take out all the Christians and put them in Albert Hall it would be only half full."[219]

RBMU's Australia Council

Notwithstanding, one bright note emerged from North Bihar's wartime struggles. In 1942, the "Quit India" uprising threatened a complete breakup of mission work. Seeds of deep mistrust between foreigners and national Christians were sown that would later bring a harvest of sorrow. The uprising against foreign missionaries forced closure of the Australian Nepalese Mission (ANM), whose missionaries had been working to the northeast of RBMU's Bihar field. ANM personnel, endangered by local unrest, were obliged to take refuge in Motihari. Here they were unexpectedly thrust into a close-quarters fellowship with RBMU personnel. The effect was a joyous camaraderie of mutual encouragement between the two groups, and led to the ANM's merger with RBMU. By the end of 1943, the RBMU had a new council in Melbourne, Australia.[220]

The Duncan Hospital, Raxaul, North India—Gateway to Nepal

16

A Very Able Major

Wearing Indian dress will not make you an Indian. Instead, learn their language thoroughly and learn to love them sincerely. Then you can wear a top hat and a frock coat and they will receive you!

—Missionary from Landour

Ernest W. Oliver

When eighteen-year-old Ernest W. Oliver announced his plans to become a missionary, his mother countered, "Who do you think you are? David Livingstone?" Coming from the godly matriarch who had led him to Christ, Ernest knew the question was no put-down. It was more an expression of incredulous surprise. In the Oliver home, aspiring to the missionary life was to reach for the highest rung on the ladder of Christian duty. Sure of his call, he remained undaunted. From his baptism at fifteen, Oliver's gifts in communication found ample exercise in preaching in churches, mission halls, and in the open air. Three years at the Hammersmith School of Art further honed his skills in speech and drama. A six-year apprenticeship to an architectural artist developed an expertise in calligraphy and led to his crafting all the lettering for the Shakespeare Memorial Theatre in Stratford-on-Avon, the stonemasonry drawings for the Guildford Cathedral, and other public works of eminence.

All Nations Bible College (ANBC) had been founded in 1923 to replace RBMU's Harley Missionary Training College, which had closed during World War I. Here Ernest Oliver took his formal missionary training. In the early thirties ANBC, like many of its counterparts, was strong on the devotional life and commitment to missions, but had little to offer in terms of the sophisticated missiological curricula which mark today's missionary training. Nonetheless, on-the-job discovery soon made up for these deficits, and in twenty-two years of subsequent teaching at mission colleges in Britain, Ernest

Oliver made sure that his students would not confront the challenges of cross-cultural ministry with the same handicaps he had taken to India in 1935.

He had entered All Nations Bible College aspiring to service in Congo, but in 1934, a devastating earthquake shook Nepal and the contiguous Ganges Valley of India's Bihar province. In a college prayer meeting that followed, the event became a Divine semaphore. Ernest Oliver's focus had been redirected to Nepal, a country still closed to the gospel. That focus would never waver.

No Short Terms!

Oliver landed in Bombay on Armistice Day, 1935, but in the battle for the soul of India and Nepal, there would be no armistice. To begin with, Margaret was not with him. Most mission society rules were unbending, and RBMU was no exception. A man was required to pass two language exams before being permitted to marry. So Ernest worked and waited for his fiancée at Motihari. Margaret Honeywood came out three years later. They were married on 26 October 1938. There were no short terms. Mission commitment was for life. Scheduled for seven years, Oliver's first term stretched to eleven, thanks to the war. He jumped into his tour of duty with few clues about what to expect. For starters, he did not know what living stipend he might expect from RBMU. It turned out to be $50 per month.

Oliver quickly distinguished himself as a brilliant linguist. He would later serve as first class interpreter in the Hindi language for the Indian army and was one of the group of nine young people "who took the Bihar field by storm" in 1935–37.

Dress Will Not Make You an Indian

A two-month camping trip among the villages of the Nepal border in 1937–38 revealed Oliver's cultural sensitivity and care for the masses. With one or two exceptions, none of the RBMU missionaries to that point had troubled to learn the Bhojpuri dialect, spoken throughout North Bihar. Conventional wisdom affirmed that speaking the dialect of the disadvantaged diminished the respect of a foreigner before the people. Oliver was not convinced. The camping trip allowed him to break from the sheltered isolation of the missionary community and savor the life of the peasants who made up the bulk of India's population. An old Methodist missionary at Landour, versed in Islamics, had given him sage advice: "Wearing Indian dress will not make you an Indian. Instead, learn their language thoroughly and learn to love them sincerely. Then you can wear a top hat and a frock coat ant they will receive you!" Oliver's sojourn among the peasants of the Nepal border proved the point. Throughout his years in Nepal and India, he built his service on its wisdom.

World War II pre-empted personal agendas throughout the empire. India was no exception. In 1941, Ernest Oliver was one of five RBMU men conscripted for the duration. He served in Iraq and Iran as leader of the Cipher Team for the Sixth Indian Division of the Tenth army, a special assignment being the decoding and delivery of a "scathing personal message" from Winston Churchill to British general Auchinleck. Excellent Hindi opened the door to ministry to Indian Christian troops on Sundays. In addition, the Hammersmith School of Art came in handy. Countering the standard ribald fare of the local military gazette, he drew—on request—a series of political cartoons for the paper. Promoted to the rank of major, he served the remaining war years as recruiting officer in Lucknow.

Betty Pritchard, missionary to Bihar, remembers Ernest Oliver as a clear thinker, well received by both missionaries and nationals, controlled in speech, able to analyze complex situations and broker solutions with economy of language. These qualities led to his return to India in 1947 to take the reins of the RBMU field. From that vantage, he became God's instrument in the opening of the work in Nepal in 1954, to which we shall return in a later chapter.

Abilities Equal to My Tasks

Oliver's leadership skills were to elevate him to still greater responsibilities in missions. As a shy and timid youngster he had been weaned from the prayer, "Give me tasks equal to my ability," and had begun to pray, "Give me abilities equal to my tasks." The prayer was answered, as prayer often is, in incremental ascents. In 1961, he was called from India to the post of executive secretary to the London Board of RBMU. From 1966–1983 the Mission seconded him part time to Britain's Evangelical Missionary Alliance, a role which facilitated cooperation among the evangelical mission agencies of Great Britain and their partnership with national churches overseas. In 1970, he brought together three independent missionary training institutions in a merger, forming the All Nations Christian College, which he served as chairman until 1980.[221]

17

Neglected Continent

While efforts to spread Christianity in other parts of the world are carried on with vigor, all animation dies when South America is but hinted at. Collective voices seem to say with a soft murmur, 'It is the natural inheritance of Pope and pagan— let it alone.'

—Allen Gardiner

Lucy's Book

Twenty-six-year-old Harry Guinness had no sooner taken the reins of the CBM than he headed for South America. Some Harley College men had gone out independently to Peru and Argentina. Guinness planned to unite their efforts under the administrative umbrella of the Mission.

In 1894 his sister, Lucy, had edited and largely written a 180-page work entitled, *South America, The Neglected Continent,* in which she summarized the activity of Protestant missions among its (then) thirty-seven million people. As usual, Lucy's work was "crowded with facts" and "bright with diagrams and illustrations."[222] The neglect of South America as a legitimate concern for evangelical missions was due to the dominance of Roman Catholicism throughout the continent. The great 1910 world missionary conference in Edinburgh added fuel to this notion when in deference to the Roman Catholic presence it refused to acknowledge South America as a field for Protestant missionary work. However, not everyone had neglected the great continent.

Children of the Sun

RBMU's first appearance in Peru did not result from a corporate decision by the Mission. Several efforts in South America were undertaken by the personal initiative of former Harley students, while the East London Institute acted as a clearing agency for collecting and sending out funds and reinforcements.[223] Robert Stark, Frederick J. Peters, and John L. Jarrett were three graduates of Harley College whose interest in Peru had been awakened by reports of colporteur Penzotti's imprisonment. An agent of the American Bible Society, Penzotti had been jailed in Callao for eight months, his books confiscated. He was released from prison in 1891, free to circulate the Bible. Penzotti had won the first battle for religious liberty in Peru.[224] Peru had long been famed as the showcase of Spanish conquest and plunder since the crushing of the Inca empire in 1532. In all South America, Peru, with its three millions of people and its one Protestant pastor, was the most neglected of all. Since Peru's constitution made all public worship illegal save for that of the Roman Catholic Church, any evangelical venture into the land of the Incas was an invitation to trouble.[225]

Navel of the Empire

Following some deputation in the States and Canada, the trio arrived in Peru in March 1894. After some months of language study in Callao, Lima's port city, they moved to the capital, where they began meetings on 2 September 1894 on a street called Polvos Azules, and soon established a church. However, their objective lay beyond Lima. Cuzco, the ancient capital of the Inca empire and home of the Quechua people, was their goal. Peters and Jarrett arrived in Cuzco—among the Children of the Sun—on 4 July 1895.[226]

They met with fury. Cuzco was a hotbed of Romanism, and led by the local bishop, a crowd threatened the prefect with revolution and bloodshed if the heretics were allowed to remain. At the height of the tension, Jarrett came down with smallpox and Peters had to nurse him while keeping the authorities at bay. The prefect placed armed militia around their residence to protect the pair from threatened violence. Immediately upon Jarrett's recovery, the men were summoned before the prefect and ordered to leave within 24 hours. They declined to do so without written orders. Further threats from the priests intimidated the prefect and the written order "of the Supreme Government" was issued.

Escape from Cuzco

As cathedral bells tolled, a "great multitude" assembled in Cuzco's main square to accelerate and celebrate the departure of the heretics. Handbills were distributed "To thank God and the prefect for the expulsion of the heretics." The authorities had planned for an escort to Lima via Arequipa and the coast, but by this time, the crowd had become an "expectant mob," and the missionaries quickly saw that the handful of soldiers would afford little defense against the frenzied populace. Worse, the procession was led by the sacred Roman images, and to remain on their mounts in the presence of these would court death. They decided to risk all and go overland alone. While the escort waited in the square, Jarrett and Peters mounted their horses and stole out of the city by the back streets.

With Jarrett still weakened by smallpox, five hundred miles on horseback now lay between the fugitives and the relative safety of Lima. The descent from Cuzco's 11,300-foot elevation took three tortured weeks, at times skirting the snowline, where they endured cold, rain, and hunger.

Arriving in Lima, Jarrett and Peters discovered that the government had not, in fact, ordered their expulsion. On the contrary, the authorities had requested the prefect of Cuzco to give the missionaries all possible protection. The matter was taken up in Congress, creating a stir throughout the country, and resulted in the payment of a small indemnity to the missionaries. It was just enough to cover the entire expense of their venture. The Protestant cause was advanced, the offending prefect was removed, and "many another authority [was] guided in his conduct toward Bible sellers and preachers by what happened in Cuzco in 1895."

Second Venture

The Jarretts returned to Cuzco in 1896, but again met with violent opposition incited by the local priests. They were boycotted, spat upon, stoned, mobbed, slandered, and insulted. Martial law was frequently invoked; regular troops from Lima were often called in, as the local police were unreliable. After eight months' of struggle, Jarrett's school was shut down in spite of good enrollment. Jarrett and his wife were now without a residence, as no one would rent them property.

In a Monastery Garden

The Jarretts left Cuzco, but not before a bizarre incident left them with a ray of hope. A letter from a monk was mysteriously delivered to Jarrett, stating that he had been watching the missionary couple and had read their literature and found he drawn to their message. Admitting that the persecution inflicted on the couple exhibited very little of the Spirit of Jesus Christ, the monk requested more literature. Would Jarrett write?

Following instructions, the missionary went by night to the monastery and from a window high up on the wall at a given signal, a letter came down on a string. A parcel was put in its place and went up out of sight. Many such letters passed between the two, but they were unable to talk. One night, after the usual signal under the window, Jarrett went around the building to a little back door, where, after the creaking of bolts, the door opened and he found himself in the presence of his friend. Several of these clandestine meetings took place as Jarrett helped the young monk with his struggle into the light.

One such tryst produced a warning. His monastic friend had been to a meeting of the priests presided over by the bishop, where it was agreed that expulsion of the missionaries could no longer be delayed. Jarrett's life was now in danger. It was time to go. The following day the town roughs assembled to incite a demonstration. That night, Jarrett and the monk prolonged what was to be their final garden visit. Suddenly, another priest appeared with two men. While the two blocked the exit, the priest ran to sound the alarm.

The Great Escape

Jarrett's friend led him pell-mell through the rambling halls of the monastery, and commending him to God, summarily thrust him through a door. Finding himself in another large garden, Jarrett saw that a fourteen-foot wall blocked his escape. Now frantic, having incited the barking of dogs, he found a sapling which had been cut for building purposes. With this aid, he made it to the top of the wall, only to face a twenty-foot drop to the riverbed. At three o'clock in the morning and with dogs barking, options were few. Jarrett dropped the twenty feet, some bushes breaking his fall, "not very pleasantly." It was the end of the first attempt at Protestant work anywhere in the interior of Peru.[227]

Reinforcements and Harry's Visit

Other workers arrived—Harry Backhouse, Robert Lodge, Robert Stark and his wife, William and Fanny Newell, Fred Peters and his wife. Lodge died of typhoid fever while on a trip to La Paz with Jarrett. He occupied the first missionary grave in the Andes. In September 1897, Dr. Harry Guinness went to Peru, visiting Cuzco during his stay. It was the first of three visits he would make.[228]

Guinness had made the trip to organize the work of Harley College missionaries who had gone to Peru independently, and to bring them under the umbrella of RBMU. The time was ripe. To this point, their work had been supported and coordinated by friends in Toronto.[229] Persecution had won sympathy for the missionaries, and others were ready to join them. But the move to establish a formal RBMU presence in the country was marred by another dark event. Harry Backhouse, who had arrived in October 1895, succumbed to typhoid in January 1898, shortly after Guinness returned to England.

Third Assault on Cuzco

On 9 December 1898, three couples—Jarrett, Peters, and Newell—reached Cuzco to begin anew, only to encounter bitter opposition from a handful of radical Romanists, who sent a formal protest to the Central Government in Lima. This time, however, the tide was turning, and a petition from the mayor of Cuzco and several leading citizens assured the authorities in Lima that no state of alarm existed. The protest was dropped, and the missionaries, securing residence, opened a photographic studio. This enabled them to identify with the business community in Cuzco while avoiding the stigma of overt evangelism, still prohibited by law.

A large farm for the education and training of Quechua Indians was purchased at Urco, twenty miles away. In Cuzco, the number of converts grew and a thriving church was established. Then, in 1902, another blow fell. William Newell died of typhoid fever. His wife, Fanny, returned to England where she took a post as matron instructor at RBMU's Bromley Hall, school of missionary nursing.[230] Though widowed, Fanny had not lost her love for Peru and shared her burden for that land with the aspiring missionary midwives under her care. One of them was a frail young woman named Annie G. Soper.

The Peru Task Force

By October of 1908, RBMU had two couples in Cuzco—the A. Stuart McNairns and the Searses—and a Miss Pinn. Mr. and Mrs. Job and Mr. and Mrs. Payne staffed the farm at Urco. The Roman stronghold of Arequipa hosted a team comprising Mr. and Mrs. Hercus, Mr. Millham, and Miss Newton, while in Lima, the Jarretts, the Watsons, the Austins, and Mr. John Ritchie carried on their ministries. Ritchie would prove to be an able administrator, organizing the *Iglesia Evangélica Peruana* (IEP—The Evangelical Church of Peru) which later became the largest evangelical church association in the country.[231]

As related elsewhere, after the death of Henry Grattan Guinness in 1910, RBMU's work in Peru and Argentina was merged (1911) with that of the Help for Brazil Mission and other work, forming the Evangelical Union of South America. Harry Guinness' death in 1915 further weakened the mission. The rebirth of RBMU work in Peru would now depend on a couple of English nurses.

Annie G. Soper and the first five students to go to the
Costa Rica Bible Institute. *Left:* Vicente Coral.

18

Beyond the Ranges

When the darkness is dense, one candle is like the sun. Four years in Cuzco may be more valuable than forty in England. Life is not measured by years, but by consecration. [232]

—Principal Forbes Jackson, Harley College

The Lame Take the Prey

When RBMU work in Peru and Argentina reorganized in 1911 as the Evangelical Union of South America (EUSA), Annie Georgina Soper was twenty-eight years of age. She took a post as Sister-Tutor at Bromley Hall, the London maternity hospital where aspiring RBMU missionary candidates came for midwifery training. Here she came under the spell of Matron Fanny Newell, widowed in 1902, when her missionary husband succumbed to typhoid in Cuzco. Soper was captured by Newell's tales of Peru's *Children of the Sun,* and later wrote, "I was very fond of Mrs. Newell, and . . . with deep affection . . . look back on those days at Bromley Hall . . . They influenced my early life."[233]

Of eleven siblings—nine brothers and two sisters—Annie was the youngest. She lost her father when she was three, her mother when she was ten. It was a large brood, but the senior Sopers seem to have parented well, for at seven years of age Annie returned from Sunday school one day to tell her mother, "there was nothing spiritual in the lesson." When her mother died, William, her oldest brother, provided a home for the family and became Annie's confidant and protector. He talked her into going to a Brethren assembly, where at fifteen she was converted. At twenty-two, she entered nurses' training in London's St. Giles Hospital.

Shattering disappointment followed the three-year internship. Through a complete physical breakdown, Annie Soper came to grips with God, realizing that she had never truly surrendered her life to Christ. Her nephew, Leonard

Soper, described her as "dangerously ill," and between "periods of great pain and unconsciousness," the promise was made to the Lord that if he gave her health and strength, her life would be devoted to his service. Then he added, "It was in St. Giles Hospital, Camberwell, that the Peru Inland Mission was born."[234]

What Soper lacked in physical robustness, she compensated with iron determination! On health grounds, she was turned down by several mission agencies. Undaunted, she crossed the Atlantic to attend Toronto Bible Institute, because "Canada was a step closer" to her goal. Here she met Arthur and Ada Simmonds, who became her lifelong friends and benefactors.

Dos de Mayo Hospital

A cable reached her in 1915 at Simmonds' church—Emmanuel Baptist in Toronto—offering the post of director of nursing at the Dos de Mayo (May 2) hospital in Lima. The appeal was from John Ritchie, one of RBMU's early pioneers in Peru, and a graduate of Harley College. Soper needed no urging. The students of Toronto Bible Institute[235] came to see her off. Assembled on the station platform, they lifted the chorus, *The Lord bless thee and keep thee.* She never forgot that moment.

With neither mission board nor patron other than friends at Emmanuel Baptist, and with the world at war, Annie G. Soper steamed 'round Cape Horn and took up her duties training Peruvian nurses in Lima's Dos de Mayo Hospital. In 1916, hygienic conditions were virtually unknown, and Soper's innovations were not always welcome, but the Lima hospital was the bridgehead Annie had looked for. In July, 1919 she was joined by Rhoda Gould, also a nurse.[236] Rhoda would be Annie's companion and coworker for the next thirty-eight years. However, the real work of their lives was not in Lima. It lay beyond the ranges.

The Other Side of the Mountain

In 1919, Dr. A.M. Renwick[237] of the Free Church of Scotland traveled through Peru's department of San Martin and visited the provincial capital of Moyobamba.[238] The exotic-sounding name derived from an Indian word, *mayupampa,* meaning "a circular plain." Moyobamba was the second oldest Spanish town east of the Andes—after Chachapoyas—and had been founded by the conquistadors on the site of an Inca settlement. Laced with four hundred years of history, Moyobamba had the ring of romance and mystery. But neither of these qualities had fired Renwick to share his discovery. He had surveyed Peru's unreached interior provinces with a missionary eye.

"Moyobamba would be an ideal center," he enthused. "The Bible is an unknown book [and] the place is abandoned because of the difficulty of access." Shooting to kill, Renwick looked straight at Annie and said, "Cannot you go, Miss Soper?" There was no escape. "From that moment," she confessed, "I do not think Moyobamba was long out of my thoughts."[239] Returning to England, she looked for a mission agency to join, but no society was yet prepared to undertake work so deep in the interior of Peru.[240] Their misgivings were warranted. Annie Soper was seriously ill with a hemorrhaging stomach ulcer. She submitted to a gastrectomy. On one occasion her brother and his wife talked with her far into the night "to dissuade her from what seemed to be a most dangerous venture." While they failed in their attempt, Annie "had triumphed by the early hours of the morning."[241] She looked up her colleague, Rhoda, who had earlier returned to England. The disfranchised pair borrowed passage money from the EUSA and returned to Peru. EUSA's John Ritchie had called Soper to Lima in the first place.[242] In June 1922, they set out for Moyobamba.

The Trek

Peru's topography divides the California-size country neatly into three well-defined zones. The entire coast of Peru is desert, its desperately needed rainfall denied by the cold Pacific Humboldt Current. The Andes rise abruptly from the coastal plain. Thrusting their bleak, denuded peaks into the sky, they form a spine that runs the entire length of the country. Beyond this majestic barrier are the forested eastern slopes of the mountains. This piedmont is known as the *montaña*, and gradually descends in rugged beauty until it melts into the steaming flats of the Amazon basin, a region known as the *selva*.

Moyobamba is in the eastern Andean foothills, five hundred miles north of Lima in San Martin, one of Peru's twenty-four states, called *departamentos*. Getting there was a challenge. The shortest route was to travel north by ship the four hundred miles from Lima's port of Callao to the coastal city of Pacasmayo. From there the trans-Andean trip was a mere 185 miles, but with a difference. There were no roads and no planes. Just mules.

The English nurses, both thirty-nine, contracted with muleteers to make the assault on the mountain chain. The journey took them through Cajamarca, Calendin, and Chachapoyas. Cajamarca—at 9,000 feet—was the site of Inca emperor Atahualpa's overthrow by Pizarro's forces in 1532. Atahualpa had been strangled and his troops massacred. Calvin Mackay of the Free Church of Scotland had moved here with his family the year before Soper's trip. For Annie and Rhoda, the stopover would have been a welcome break among friends. The journey took five weeks[243] and climaxed with their triumphant arrival in Moyobamba on 27 July 1922.[244]

The Moyobamba plan had called for the nurses to join the staff of the Free Church of Scotland—Renwick, remember, was a FCS man—and for a time, they did so. Later, however, the FCS felt unable to accept responsibility for the six orphans the women had by then adopted. In any case, by 1929 the FCS had decided to establish their own base in Moyobamba.

The Town

If getting there had been a triumph, Moyobamba was anything but jubilant at Soper's arrival. "We certainly had no welcome," she wrote. "We found a strong Roman Catholic town, much sickness and poverty, gross immorality, and no knowledge of the gospel whatsoever." The priest tried to prevent their staying and the people were at first suspicious, but the medicine dispensed by kindly hands soon defused the opposition. With a government hospital lying empty, there had been no medical caregiver in Moyobamba. The nurses opened a dispensary. In Lima, Soper had directed the first school of nursing in Peru. With her reputation thus established, the authorities turned over the hospital building to the British missionaries.

The antagonism they had met from the nuns in Lima's Dos de Mayo Hospital resurfaced in Moyobamba. Determined resistance from Roman priests contested every step. Receiving Protestant literature was forbidden. The women countered by wrapping medicine in gospel tracts. Attempts were made upon their lives; political pressures were employed to oust them. Love won. Eduardo Cifuentes and Manuel Morias became their first converts. Within two years they dedicated the first evangelical church in Moyobamba. When an unwanted infant was left in a bundle of rags on the waiting room floor, the mandate came with compelling clarity: *Take this child and nurse it for me.* Frankie became the first of a stream of children who found refuge in the country orphanages of Moyobamba and Lamas. As the work grew, Annie Soper was no stranger to the discouragements and obstacles that every work for God must face. To her diary she lamented:

> What with constant headache, neuralgia, backache, and general weariness, I seem to have no power to fight at all. It seems as though everyone has forsaken us.

In 1927 Soper returned to England for furlough, bringing with her Frankie and eleven-year-old Martina. Great blessing attended her stay.[245] In 1928, she returned to Lima not only with the children but also with her twenty-six-year-old niece, Ellen Kathleen Soper, William Soper's only daughter. Kathleen was a surprise. At eleven years of age she had purposed to be a missionary to Peru, but had never shared her secret, not even with her parents. Kathleen and her aunt Annie landed in Peru in December 1928, and proceeded to Moyobamba.[246]

Lamas

Within eight years of their arrival under the FCS, Soper and Gould had planted the first evangelical church in the city, established an orphanage and a hospital, and had sent Eduardo Cifuentes and Manual Morias off to Bible school in Costa Rica. But Moyobamba was not to be their resting-place. With the arrival of Free Church of Scotland doctor, Kenneth Mackay, their services to Moyobamba had become redundant—the town proving "too small for two such strong personalities [Soper and Mackay]."[247]

Forty miles to the southeast (five days on foot) was the town of Lamas, where one hundred people had signed a petition inviting them to come. The women made the move to Lamas in October 1929, and immediately secured a site for the construction of the orphanage—they had left the eleven children in Moyobamba with Kathleen. Here in Lamas the guiding Cloud would settle, and here it would remain.

Eight months later, with housing secured in Lamas, Soper made the five-day trek back to Moyobamba to retrieve Kathleen and her brood of eleven. She described the ordeal to A.C. Simmonds:

> "We are now definitely established here [in Lamas] . . . the children were all ill and [we] had a formidable journey back. The rains were heavy—the mud so deep that the animal could not get through with me on his back. So I was forced to walk for five days, wading through mud knee deep with huge stones, tree roots, and trunks of fallen trees scattered everywhere. Such dense forest that often we had to force our way through. On the second day I took off shoes and stockings, thinking that I could walk better like the natives—barefooted—but at the end of the day the skin of my feet was torn off in many places and made walking a misery.

> Twice night came on while we were still struggling through mud and forest. Once I was alone in dense darkness in the forest for more than an hour, having lost the boy who came with us. Eventually we had to sleep by the wayside in a tiny hut made with palm leaves, too exhausted to go farther. Wet through with drenching rain [and] having to wade through many rivers, we arrived safely in Lamas and have not even had a cold.[248]

So wrote the wisp of a woman who had been rejected by ten mission agencies!

By this time, Annie's brother, William, had retired from government service and assumed responsibility in representing the fledgling Mission, keeping books, tracking donors, and publishing the newsletter, *The Lamas Evangel*, which he began in January 1933. He became their fervent advocate. With the new work in Lamas, it was time to give the mission a new name. The Peruvian Inland Mission seemed to fit. Later they would make a semantic adjustment and change it to The Peru Inland Mission (PIM).

Eyebrow of the Jungle

The town of Lamas sits atop a hill of red clay in Peru's eastern piedmont, sometimes referred to as the "eyebrow of the jungle" (*ceja de la selva*). At

2,500 feet of elevation, the town commands a panorama of the valley, which melds into the larger and more important center of Tarapoto, 14 miles away. The valley between is a patchwork of *chacras*—the small family farms from which the people wrest a living. This *montaña*—in its way, the most beautiful of Peru's smorgasbord of landscapes—is a showcase of rolling hills, verdant and forested, rifted by swift currents racing toward the Amazon basin and their destiny with the Atlantic, 2,000 miles away.

In 1930 Lamas was postcard picturesque—adobe houses with whitewashed facades, roofed mostly with palm thatch, sometimes with crudely formed tiles. Freestanding tamped-earth walls offered little protection against earthquakes, assuring that homes rarely exceeded two stories. Uninviting streets were paved with the same red clay, always rutted with fissures eroded by frequent tropical rains. The people were *mestizos*—as are the majority of Peruvians—the word meaning "mixed," for their faces reveal the blend of Spanish and Indian blood going back to the invasion of the conquistadors, four hundred years earlier. For the new Mission, the modest elevation offered a more refreshing climate for the missionaries and their new work. Tamped earth walls surrounding the PIM complex—orphanage, hospital, Bible school, and missionary apartments—offered a further degree of insulation from Lamas town life and from the distant bustle of commercial Tarapoto. In the 1930s, the mission 'compound' was still in vogue as a prudent means of assuring privacy and viability for the missionary community.

Sprinkled among the predominant Spanish-speaking mestizo communities were the Quechua *barrios*—smaller settlements of Lowland Indians who had resettled in the *montaña* when they fled their mountain homes before the Spanish invaders. More colorful and distinctive in dress than their mestizo neighbors, the Quechua were disdained as social inferiors, exploited by the *patron* system, and largely neglected by early mission efforts. Nevertheless, they were there, intermingling on a daily basis in the street markets of Lamas. Annie Soper could not ignore them. Nor would God.

God Gives the Harvest

Soper and Gould attacked their work with tireless industry, evangelizing through their daily medical clinic, wrapping medicines in gospel tracts, and conducting Sunday schools and gospel services. Eduardo Cifuentes, first convert of their work in Moyobamba and graduate of the Costa Rica Bible Institute, joined them in Lamas and became an important figure in preaching and teaching. Kathleen Soper, Annie's niece and a certified teacher, opened a British school—La Escuela Britanica. It became very popular.[249] Their ranks were further reinforced when music teacher Lucy Kisky joined them the same year. In every community of believers—however primitive—the Holy Spirit has gifted some to lead the Church. Almost immediately upon their arrival in Lamas God brought them such a man.

Vicente Coral kneeled one night at the feet of Annie Soper, pretending to pray. Inebriated as usual, Coral had earned his reputation as the village drunk. It was not hard to get drunk in Lamas. There was no shortage of cantinas and every house had its *cantaro*—a clay pot filled with *chicha,* home-brewed beer made from corn or sugar cane. Life was hard in Lamas, and chicha provided some escape. Vicente Coral, however, seemed to escape with chronic frequency. On the night he feigned repentance, Coral was too drunk to get converted and Soper brushed him off with an imperious, "Go home!" But he returned, bought a Bible, and together with his wife, Manuela, was gloriously converted. They were among the firstfruits of many.

By 1933, the Lamas congregation had grown to one hundred members, and Coral was to play a singular role in the life of evangelical churches yet unborn. The first evangelical church in Lamas was erected the following year, seating four hundred. Five hundred were present for the dedication. Then—just when the Peru Inland Mission was ready to stretch its wings—a curious thing happened.

Harry Strachan, founder of the Costa Rica Bible Institute, was flying to Iquitos when engine trouble forced his amphibian to an emergency landing on the Mayo River. While waiting for the aircraft to be repaired and knowing that Annie Soper and Eduardo Cifuentes were nearby, he trekked up to Lamas—about two hours on foot. Strachan's powerful ministry lifted the Lamas church to even greater visibility. That was when he met Vicente Coral and saw his potential for gospel work. Strachan seized the moment: Would Vicente be interested in taking studies in Costa Rica?

A Mere Handful of Women

In January 1934 Annie Soper and Lucy Kisky set out from Lamas on an evangelistic tour, which introduced them to scores of villages along the vast network of tributaries flowing eastward into the Huallaga River. Accompanied by three young men they headed for the large town of Yurimaguas, first by canoe, then by the relative comfort of balsa raft on the Huallaga River—downstream, of course! Stopping at villages along the way, they administered medicine and shared the gospel. In Yurimaguas, they engaged three Indians to ferry them on their return journey—upstream—by canoe along the Cainarachi River to the point where it became no longer navigable. The rest of the return journey to Lamas was overland. Hands-on contact with "the hidden and appalling needs of [this vast] forest" left an abiding impression on the women:

> We are conscious of our calling. We are tent-dwellers and feel the same urge upon us as was felt by our Lord. There are still many "other

sheep" which we must tell. The injustice of the position struck me anew—1900 years after Christ's last word to his followers, and yet there are numbers hidden away in corners such as we have visited whom no one has felt responsible to tell. Practically all this region is virgin soil . . .[250]

The region *was* virgin soil. And it was *vast*. An endless network of swift streams flowed into the Huallaga River—the Mayo, Sisa, Sapo, Biabo, Cainarachi, and the Shanusi, to name a few. All were dotted with towns and villages along their banks. All were without the gospel. This grapevine of tributaries extended eighty miles from east to west and the same from north to south—6,000 square miles of montaña, selva, and "a mere handful of women."

Training Nationals

The trip awakened Annie Soper to the urgency of starting a Bible institute for the training of evangelists and pastors. The job was too big for "a handful of women," and Soper knew what to do:

We have both come back convinced that we must get some of the young men into training. We have called together a missionary council to see who could and would be willing to go to Costa Rica Bible College. I figure that six could go with what [we have in hand]. I have written by airmail to the wife of the principal of the College, Mr. Strachan.[251]

Soper knew that the move would put heavy pressures on the budget, and that sending off their most promising young men would leave the church work short handed:

Just what we will do without them, I do not know. Don Vicente [Coral] wants to go. It means providing for his wife and children—but he has the making of a splendid worker.[252]

Within the year, five young people were ready for Costa Rica. Each was a seminal investment in the evangelization of the Huallaga basin. Strachan's visit had lit Vicente Coral's fires. The first to go, he trekked alone across the Andes and caught a ship for Costa Rica.[253] He was followed later by four others.

The writer will not forget his visit years later to Coral's humble Lamas home. At 88, the old warrior had long been a pillar in the churches of the eastern Andes. He pointed to his diploma from the Costa Rica Bible Institute. It still hung proudly on the whitewashed wall. It was dated December 1937 and was signed by Harry Strachan.[254]

The Conversion of Vicente Coral

The conversion of Vicente Coral was radical, dramatic, and abiding. Candidly, he had shared his transformation:

To live in the darkness of this world is an incomparable torment. I was born in Lamas, a remote town in the interior of Peru. While still a child, I was taken to live with my father in the town of Iquitos. After his death, I went to live with my grandmother and grew to manhood while with her. I was a child of corruption . . . [and] found myself in the darkness of vice and intemperate drinking. I followed the ways of Satan, hoping always that their end would be happiness and progress . . . In the whirlpool of this miserable life I formed my home . . . I became a habitual drunkard and smoker, absolutely lost. My life as a husband, father, citizen, was a failure. But with all this, I was a good Christian according to the Roman Catholic Church.

This was my state when the Lord sent his servants to my town in 1930. In the height of my transgression, I bought a Bible on Good Friday. Then that happy day arrived when the Lord took compassion on me and I came to know him when nearly thirty-one years of age. From that time a new life opened before me . . . in place of misery, happiness and peace now reigned in my home.

Seeing my town and the surrounding villages in the same plight, I decided to leave my home and go to prepare for service in the Bible Institute of Costa Rica. During the three years of preparation, the Lord has protected me and the family I had to leave behind. Now I am almost ready to return to my home to preach the good news. For thirty-one years, I was dead, but for seven years I have been alive unto Christ.[255]

Coral wrote these words from the Costa Rica Bible Institute at the close of 1937. Fifty years of ministry lay before him.

Reinforcements

Rye Lane Baptist Chapel in Peckham, England, was Annie Soper's home church and became a fertile source of new recruits. Pastor Theodore M. Bamber was a warm-hearted advocate for the Peru Inland Mission. Nurse Eleanor Wohlfarth arrived in Lamas in 1933. Mary Taverner, Jessie Norton, and Myrtle Cooper went out in 1935, followed by Gladys Tyley and Edyth Vinall. By 1936, The Peru Inland Mission had a complement of eleven—all women, and nearly all nurses. A friend wrote from Winnipeg, marveling that "a mere handful of women could so attack this stronghold of Satan and drive such a wedge into the enemy's ranks."[256] But the wedge would be contested.

Opposition to the evangelical message consistently marked Rome's response to Protestant advance throughout Latin America. When authorities refused burial to evangelicals in the Lamas cemetery, the believers secured their own plot and—in keeping with local custom—built a wall around it. They then erected wooden gates, over which they sculpted the text, *Jesus said, I am the resurrection and the life, he that believeth in me though he were dead yet shall he live.* That was 1934.[257] Later the opposition set fire to the gates. Children faced priest-instigated discrimination in the classroom. Village churches were padlocked. These practices continued for years, and in subtler forms, well beyond the Second Vatican Council (1962–1965).

The Lowland Quechua

Few cared for Peru's Lowland Quechua. They were a community apart, distinctive in dress, isolated by language, and disdained as social inferiors. Annie Soper shared her first impressions of the San Martin Quechua:

> I wish you could see the Indians here today. It is a religious holiday. [They dress] ridiculously, with faces painted, and many [of them] intoxicated, go dancing round the streets, beating drums and tin cans, making hideous noise. This ends up in the [RC] church. The poor things have no opportunity to learn anything of real Christianity. We have not made much progress with the language. It is very difficult.[258]

The Quechua populating San Martin had fled before Spanish troops four hundred years earlier. As the PIM work grew, the tyranny of the urgent and the difficulty of the Quechua language combined to focus most of the Mission's energies on the mestizo population, but from the outset the Lowland Quechua people presented a mute appeal that Soper could not escape:

> Our hearts ache for them, not yet released from slavery . . . their lot is hard in the extreme. The burden bearers of everyone [they have] few rights [and are] absolutely chained by the intricate system of Rome. Their masters [*patrones*] do everything possible to prevent their education . . . How we long to get the glorious news of the gospel to them.[259]

Notwithstanding, in 1939—seventeen years after Soper's arrival in Moyobamba—she would admit:

> Though many among [the rest of] the population have found Christ as their Savior, and fill us with joy . . . yet we hardly know of one pure [blooded] Indian who has grasped the message of salvation . . ."[260]

Edyth Vinall

Soper wrote that note from the village of Sisa, on the banks of the river by the same name. The town was separated from Lamas by twenty miles—parts of them nearly vertical—and fifteen hours of tortuous trek across a ridge of hills, stunning in their beauty, but devastating in their toll upon all but the most robust traveler. Sisa was a major center of lowland Quechua population and the post of Edyth Mary Vinall, a single nurse who had joined the PIM stalwarts in 1937. Edyth shared Annie's love for the Quechua and worked diligently to win them, learning their language, doing translation, and developing Sunday

schools and Bible studies. In 1946 she took the ultimate step of cultural identification—against the protests of her family—and married Misael Tuanama.
Conventional missiological wisdom of the day called for Edyth's resignation
from the PIM (cross-cultural marriages were frowned upon). She did so, but
remained in the Sisa Valley for many years—supported independently—but
in a happy continuity of fellowship with her PIM colleagues. The marriage
was short. Within two years, Misael Tuanama succumbed to tuberculosis.

A Forgotten People

Meanwhile, the 30,000 Lowland Quechua in San Martin province remained
largely without the gospel. Even the Spanish-speaking evangelical churches
of the Huallaga Valley seemed to hold no special sense of burden for their
Indian neighbors—geographically so near, but culturally, so distant. All that
was to change. The Quechua knew there was a penalty attached to sin, but
demonstrated little confidence in their Roman mentors, as Peggy Myhill explained:

> Edyth Vinall had gone to visit a sick Indian, but found the priest al-
> ready in the house performing the *Last Rites*. When the cleric had left,
> two old Indian men knelt down in turn to be flogged three times. They
> took the punishment without flinching, then rose up to kiss the dying
> man, while many gathered round to sing a chorus—*Perdonado* [par-
> doned].

Edyth had come to tell them of another who had taken the punishment for
their sins—sins that no amount of self-imposed punishment could absolve.[261]
The PIM decision to launch the Quechua work had been made in January
1939. The mandate had been clear—*God hath set the land before thee. Go up
and possess it.* Edyth Vinall drew inspiration from the knowledge that "so
many prayer partners at home are taking such a lively interest in these Indians, [and that this] would contribute to the reaping of a glorious harvest in the
near future." However, evangelizing the Quechua posed problems, as Soper
noted:

> Their language is difficult, and we do not have time to learn it prop-
> erly." Nor was medical help—the normal bridge into a wary culture—
> much help. "If we attend them, their masters make them pay big fees . .
> . the poor things haven't money to pay, so they have to work for ever so
> long or they are put in prison . . . consequently many are afraid to come
> to us." We are hoping to begin a school for Indians very shortly . . .
> This is going to bring a storm of protest upon our heads . . . as the
> commercial people do not want the Indians educated. At present they
> are slaves, and most unjustly treated.[262]

Then, when they least expected it, another billow of sorrow broke upon the cadre of the valiant. Kathleen Soper—just ten years in Peru—fell ill with typhoid fever and died nine days later. Back in England, 19 January 1938 was a dark day for William Soper. Kathleen was his only daughter.

The PIM was still "a mere handful of women" when Kathleen Soper was taken—ten, to be exact. Peruvian Vicente Coral was busy with evangelistic work, and Demetrio Cordoba was conducting an Indian school at Santa Ana, a village on the west bank of the Mayo; but no expatriate men had yet joined the Lamas Mission. So, when twenty-four-year-old Denis Tompson signed up, it was a groundbreaking event. Tompson reached Peru in May 1938, but expectations dimmed when, within a few weeks, he contracted tuberculosis. Invalided home under the care of Jessie Norton, he succumbed to the disease on 16 February 1940. First, Kathleen. Now Denis. The PIM was left to ponder the inscrutable.

Adding to these solar plexus blows was Rome's continuing harassment. In 1939, the Lamas Hospital was shut down—one of several priest-instigated actions based on spurious legal pretext. Open-air meetings were forbidden upon pain of imprisonment, as was distribution of gospel literature. The women of the Lamas Mission needed an ombudsman, and God sent one. The PIM gender hurdle was at last overcome with the arrival of Edward "Ted" James Ball in 1940. Ted had been brought up in Argentina, and blessed with flawless Spanish and a clear mind, he was immediately welcomed both by his fellow Brits and by Peruvians. From a potential matrimonial field of ten single ladies, he chose Eileen Davis. They were married 25 September 1942. Vicente Coral performed the ceremony.

The Lamas Bible School

Two years after Kathleen's death, the Lamas Bible School opened on 22 April 1940, with seven male students. Ernest and Effie Olsen, independent missionaries in Iquitos, came through to lead the three-month effort. Vicente Coral and Lucy Kisky filled out the teaching staff. Classes ran mornings, Tuesday through Saturday, with work projects in the afternoons and village evangelism Saturday evenings. During these tours hundreds heard the gospel and many professed Christ.[263]

The outbreak of World War II brought no noise of battle to Peru. Manuel Prado, who was elected to the presidency in 1939, aligned Peru with America's interests during the war and remained an ally. For the PIM, the cost of the conflict came in other ways—delayed furloughs, diminished remittances, and the "gnawing anxiety" over the safety of parents and relatives as German air raids unleashed death and destruction upon the homeland. For the PIMers, the lines were more than poetry—*They also serve who only stand and wait.*

19

Ebb Tide

Go on and preach His gospel, for he has it in his seven-sealed book that there will be a time of refreshing till all the ends of the earth shall see the salvation of God. See that you are doing your utmost to hasten that kingdom. For whatever else is shipwrecked on the face of God's earth, the kingdom of the Lord Jesus Christ is sure to come into harbor.

—Alexander Whyte

Fanny Guinness

By 1908, RBMU had established a vigorous and viable profile. Ninety-one missionaries made up the force—twenty-two in Argentina, sixteen in Peru, forty-two in Congo, and eleven in India. Canadian and American boards of the Mission had been established as a result of Dr. Harry Guinness' visit to North America. Nevertheless, factors were already at work that would siphon off the energies of the Mission. Mrs. Fanny Guinness, affectionately known as the "Mother of Congo" was called Home in 1898, following a seven-year illness. Her death was the first break in the original team. Other more serious assaults were to come.

Boer War

British eyes were on the gold fields of Transvaal in South Africa and long-standing tensions erupted when the Dutch Afrikaners declared war on 11 October 1899. The Boer conflict lasted nearly three years, cost £200 million, and exacted 22,000 British lives. Matriculations at Harley began to fall off. Loss of income forced the surrender of Cliff College, the beautiful country manor house in Derbyshire. It passed into the hands of Thomas Cook of the Joyful News Mission. He and Samuel Chadwick turned it into an establishment for the training of village missioners.

Queen Victoria

When Queen Victoria died in 1901 on the Isle of Wight, it was the end of an era. Her pleasure-loving son, Edward VII, abandoned the abstemious quality of his mother's rule and gave us the Edwardian Era, marked by opulence and a *bon vivant* lifestyle. Cultural change invaded the British Church. Foreign missions, borne on the vigor of the revival movement and fueled by national heroes like David Livingstone had been respectable pursuits of high society. Under Edward, public interest dried up almost instantly. However, the worst blow was yet to come.

Death of Grattan Guinness

The silver tongue that for thirty-seven years had been the voice of the RBMU was stilled on 21 June 1910. Coincidentally, but appropriately, his passing occurred during the Edinburgh Conference on World Missions. At seventy-five, and after fifty years of service, Henry Grattan Guinness was with his Lord. The light at Harley College had gone out.

The EUSA

Bereft of its driving force, facing economic shortfalls and the burgeoning administrative responsibilities of its South American fields, the RBMU fell upon hard times. In 1911 the decision was made to release the work in South America. The ministries in Peru and Argentina were joined with the Help For Brazil Mission and reorganized as the Evangelical Union of South America (EUSA).

Harley College Closes

The ominous cloud of World War I had long loomed on the horizon. When it struck on 28 July 1914, it unleashed the most horrific bloodbath in recorded history. The global conflict cost eight million lives. Harley College closed. There were no men and there was no money. The land where the new college had been built had been acquired through the London City Council on condition that a new building be in place by 1908. The cost of the new construction imposed an impossible burden on an already-strained operating budget. The City Council requisitioned the land and the buildings became a center for the housing and care of Belgian refugees. Harley House was finally sold for £3,000 to a spice company for warehouse space. It had been the Guinness home for forty years.[264]

Death of Harry Guinness

Indirectly, the war would deal yet another blow to RBMU. In April 1910 Harry Guinness had returned to Congo to "mark the [rubber] reforms already in progress."[265] He fell seriously ill in Leopoldville, where Belgian doctors insisted on his return to England. Symptoms persisted, but remained undiagnosed.

He never fully recovered. Notwithstanding, he conducted an intensive five-month preaching tour in India.[266] Then, with the war raging, he had been conducting mission work among the soldiers in the YMCA huts in England when prostrated by his final illness on 10 April 1915. After three unsuccessful operations, he died on 25 May 1915. He was fifty-three.

Curtailment

For RBMU the third decade of the new century hardly qualified as "the Roaring Twenties." They were more like a whimper. The work in Peru and Argentina had been ceded to the EUSA, and the only remaining fields of operation were Congo and the Province of Bihar in North India. The Mission moved into a holding pattern. No new missionaries were sent out. Furloughs were postponed, except for medical emergency. Mission finances were exhausted. Even the *Regions Beyond* monthly paper was curtailed. The work remained in the hands of a board of directors. However, the difficulties were not confined to missions. The whole of British society had been wounded, as Betty Pritchard explained:

> Disillusioned with postwar Britain, harassed and impoverished by unemployment, strikes, and lockouts on a tremendous scale, so many tied to the despair and indignity of the dole, people were seeking to drown their depression in a frantic search for pleasure. God and his word were disregarded and interest in missions was almost dead.[267]

Frederick B. Meyer

The hiatus would last for two decades, but during this nadir of the Mission's history, one luminous name shines like a star glimpsed through clouds scudding across the night sky. Frederick B. Meyer had become associated with Grattan Guinness and the East London Institute in 1887 while carrying out his own pastoral ministry at Melbourne Hall, Leicester.

Fourteen years earlier, a twenty-six-year-old Meyer had endorsed Moody and Sankey at the outset of their 1873 campaign in the city of York. The endorsement transformed the reception of the American evangelists from one of cool British reluctance to warm and enthusiastic welcome. Churches and chapels opened their arms to the American evangelists. The encounter also changed F.B. Meyer, who saw in Moody a power he himself longed for and which was wonderfully granted. Meyer attributed his newfound anointing in pointing men to God to his brush with Moody, and the two became fast friends. Moody's promotion of Meyer's work contributed largely to the sale of more than five million copies of his books and pamphlets in his lifetime.[268]

Moody and Meyer

At the time of his meeting with Grattan Guinness in 1887, Meyer was a rising luminary in Bible conference ministry and a prolific author of expository and devotional literature. He was a frequent speaker at the Northfield Conference in Massachusetts that had been started by Moody, and at the Keswick convention in England's Lake District, where he became one of the best loved figures. "With his shining white hair, his chiseled features and benevolent smile, it was said of him that he was a saint and looked it."[269]

F.B. Meyer had published a monthly paper called, *Word and Work*, and he now combined his own magazine with *Regions Beyond*, and from that time his articles and sermons appeared regularly in the East London Institute magazine. He also lectured regularly to Harley students, becoming, in 1898, a co-director of the Mission. During a protracted illness of Dr. Harry Guinness, Meyer resided at Harley House for eighteen months, overseeing the day-to-day operation of the Mission. He remained a director of the RBMU with only one break until his death in 1929.[270]

Gordon Guinness

In April 1927, the Reverend Gordon Guinness—son of Dr. Harry Guinness—joined the Board of Directors, eventually becoming acting director and general secretary. Unfortunately, illness cut short his work although he was able to visit India and write the book, *The Quest of the Nepal Border*. This book would later influence RBMU personnel in India, and propelled the Mission into the world's only Hindu kingdom. Later, he played an important part in bringing the Mission through a particularly difficult period, and became president of RBMU.

Little expansion was possible during the twenties. The war had exhausted everyone, physically and economically. There was a shortage of money for missionary work, and times were hard. The work on the fields was consolidated. In Congo, however, the British and Foreign Bible Society agreed to print the first Lomongo Bible. The New Testament in Lingombe and the Gospels and Acts in the Longando languages were also printed. This magnum achievement was the work of Mr. and Mrs. Ruskin and their helpers. Later, plans were laid to move the church in Congo toward greater autonomy and self-dependence by reducing the amount of foreign funding, while principles of self-government, self-support and self-propagation were taught.[271]

Cecil Duncan

In India, the appointment of Dr. Cecil Duncan in March 1928 would have far reaching consequences for RBMU. Duncan had gone to India independently, and had built a hospital at Raxaul on the border of India and Nepal.[272] It would become one of the largest training hospitals in India and a primary factor in the opening of Nepal to the gospel. In 1938, a forward move was launched in India with a survey of the needs in Bihar Province. As the challenge rang out, new recruits began to come forward, and income began to improve.

Meanwhile someone already within the ranks of RBMU was about to breathe fresh life into an old mission and lift it to new and exciting horizons on the other side of the world. In 1939, Ebenezer G. Vine was named General Secretary of the RBMU in London. Dark clouds again loomed on the global horizon. Adolph Hitler's invasion of Poland on 1 September 1939 plunged Europe into darkness. It would be six years before the lights came on again "all over the world."[273] When they did, it would be a very different world.

Annie G. Soper
Founder of the Peru Inland Mission

Sirag Wedding Party at the Home of E.G. Vine, 1935
Seated: Bill and Sylvia Sirag. *Standing, left to right*:
Eunice Vine, David Belamy, Mrs. E. G. (Elizabeth) Vine,
Bertel G. Vine

Sylvia Sirag brought Ebenzer G. Vine to
North America.

Part 2
Headwaters
The West Indies Mission
1900–1945

20

Where It All Began

The most glorious triumphs of Christ are spiritual. His noblest work is that wrought in the secret of the soul. Not the conquest of Kingdoms, but self-conquest; not the renunciation of anything external, merely, but self-renunciation; not the consecration of substance, but self-consecration in the service of God and man—these are the hardest deeds to accomplish, and the most divine attainments. They shine with the peculiar light of Calvary.

—H. Grattan Guinness

Remember the Maine

The explosion shattered the darkness of Havana's waterfront. Chaos reigned as panic-stricken Cubans left the revelry of Carnivale and rushed to the site of the blast. Twenty thousand pounds of brown powder[274] in the forward ammunition magazines of the USS *Maine* had erupted with a roar, shredding the tied-up American battleship into twisted scrap. Of the complement of 350 officers and crew, most of them asleep, 267 died. At 9:40 p.m. on 15 February 1898, Cuban history turned a corner. The incident sparked war between the United States and Spain. By the end of the year, Teddy Roosevelt had led his famous charge on San Juan Hill (16 July 1898) and Spain had withdrawn from Cuba, ceding Cuba, Puerto Rico, Guam, and the Philippines to the United States.[275] For the next thirty years, Cuba would be a ward of her giant neighbor to the north. America had overnight become a world power. For Cuba, the long chafing Iberian yoke had been broken, and the door to Protestant missions—barely ajar—had been opened wide.[276]

Cuban Fears

Christopher Columbus claimed Cuba for Spain in 1492 during his first visit to the Americas, bequeathing the Spanish language and Roman Catholicism to the island. In 1511, Spanish colonists began importing African slave labor.

The native Carib population was soon decimated. As the years passed, exploitative Spanish rule became onerous, then obnoxious to the Cuban people. At the time of the Maine incident, Cuban patriots, long fighting for independence from Spain, were at the same time fearful of annexation by the United States. They had reason. American expansionists had long eyed the Spanish colony, just ninety miles from the US mainland.

On March 22, five weeks after the sinking, a Spanish board of inquiry attributed the destruction of the American battleship to an internal explosion, thereby denying external sabotage. However, a US naval court of inquiry found to the contrary, and disputed the Spanish report. When the American version of the disaster was made public on March 28, a note from the ambassadors of six great powers was sent to President McKinley, calling for a peaceful solution to the Cuban problem. The Spanish queen regent, María Cristina, acting on papal advice, ordered a suspension of hostilities against Cuban insurgents to "facilitate peace negotiations," but the die was cast. President McKinley sent a war message to Congress on April 11.

The Spanish-American War

On April 19, a joint resolution of the US Congress recognized Cuban independence and authorized McKinley to demand Spanish withdrawal from the island. Disclaiming any intention to annex Cuba, US Army forces under Major General William Rufus Shaffer arrived off Santiago on June 20, disembarking two days later with the famed Rough Riders of Colonel Wood and Lieutenant Colonel Theodore Roosevelt. In a swift and decisive victory, Cuba was freed from the control of an absolute religious–political monarchy.[277]

The Galling Iberian Yoke

Alone among the Latin American republics, Cuba had continued to chafe under Spanish rule long after her South American neighbors had won their struggle for independence from Spain. Liberator San Martín had championed freedom for Argentina, Chile, and Peru, while Simon Bolívar had overthrown the hated rule of Iberia in Venezuela, Colombia, and Ecuador. Mexican independence had earlier been won between 1810 and 1821. Brazil became free from Portugal in 1831. In the Western Hemisphere—with the exception of Puerto Rico—only Cuba still aspired to live under her own flag. Even so, within the island colony, rivalries existed between Cubans who favored annexation by the United States, and those who wanted a free Cuba.

The Rural Guards

When the war ended in August 1898, three armies shared control of Cuba: Spaniards in the western cities,[278] Americans in the eastern cities and Cubans encircling both in the surrounding countryside. Transfer of authority from Spain to the United States on January 1, 1899, immediately menaced Cuban–

American relations. Armed Cubans, organized in regiments and battalions, represented a threat to the American army command and the stability of the occupation. By preserving its organization into the transition period, the Cuban Army would have emerged as a de facto military co-occupier of the island.

Disarming 40,000 Cuban soldiers and releasing them—without jobs—into a devastated economy was a prescription for trouble. Knowing this, the American government looked for a way to keep the lid on a potential threat to the occupation. The solution was to establish the Rural Guards—a Cuban military police force under command of American and Cuban officers. This shrewd action provided jobs for the demobilized Cuban forces, defused the military threat, and assured peaceful American hegemony.[279] One of the captains in the Rural Guards was Manuel Lavastida.

21

A Star of Astonishing Brilliance

I heard God's voice on that streetcar, and gave him my heart.
—Bartolomé G. Lavastida

Christmas Advent

Into this chaotic matrix of revolution, political rivalry, and international up-heaval, Bartholomew Gregory Lavastida, "a star of astonishing brilliance"[280] and co-founder of the West Indies Mission, was born on 24 December 1887. The infant was promptly named for his two grandfathers—Bartolomé and Gregorio. The new father, Manuel Lavastida, entertained high hopes for his firstborn, determined that his son would live in a different Cuba and under the Cuban flag. From the moment Bartholomew could speak, Manuel infused his eldest son with heavy doses of patriotic activism. When friends dropped in for coffee at the Lavastida home, Manuel would order Bartholomew: "Run and tell the folks what we've taught you!" The compliant toddler would respond lustily with the resounding battle cry, "Long Live Free Cuba!" This sometimes made guests uneasy, for the barracks that housed Spanish troops was nearby.

Insurrection

On 29 January 1895 the order came from the exiled Cuban command in New York to launch the popular insurrection against the Spanish crown. Precisely when he responded is not recorded, but within months, Manuel Lavastida was at the forefront, in command of forty men. His sense of destiny now endan-gered his family of four, who begged him to desist. Their pleas were met with one reply: "My children must live under their own flag." Since Bartholomew was the eldest, it fell to the eight-year-old to post lookout in the top of a tall tree on the family farm. Whenever he detected the sound of gunfire or the muffled gabble of approaching Spaniards, he would give the signal to hurry to safety in the nearby caves of Sábalo. Here they were safe, but not alone. The walls and ceiling of their dark refuge were lined with bats.[281]

Brush with Death

This fugitive lifestyle soon depleted the family food supply, and Manuel knew he must move his wife and offspring. Medín, his older brother, lived at the coast, but the family would have to travel one by one to avoid attracting the attention of the Spaniards. Bartholomew Gregorio ("B. G.") Lavastida was the first to make the trip but, to his surprise, the house was already full of other relatives and there was no room for the rest of Manuel's family. Meanwhile, back at Manuel's base, fighting had erupted, making further transfers of family members impossible. B. G.—far from home—was now left alone with his cousin. As provisions dwindled, the boys foraged for crawfish, rats, and birds. Then malaria struck, weakening the youngster to the point where he could no longer search for food. He found an abandoned *bohío* (Indian hut) and took refuge, his clothing now reduced to rags. Malnourished and ravaged by fever, young Lavastida's life was in danger.

Unaware of his son's whereabouts or condition, an alarmed Manuel Lavastida took two of his men. Armed with a revolver and three machetes they made their way to the coast on horseback. They found B. G. on the floor of the *bohío*, emaciated and near death, his disheveled hair infested with lice. Other relatives had already died. Manuel was overcome. "I want my boy at least to die clean!" he choked. The two soldiers, shaken by the grief of their commander, gathered guayabo leaves, boiled them, and gently bathed the child with the solution while Manuel trimmed the matted hair with his knife. Then, cradling B. G. in his arm as if feeding a newborn, he began to introduce a few drops of milk between the parched lips of his son. Bartholomew Gregorio Lavastida began to revive. It would be two days before he would recognize the father who had nursed him and who had come to take him home.

Manuel Lavastida mounted his horse, and cradling the lad in his arm, began the cautious ride homeward, slipping Spanish troops along the way. At home, they were safe for the moment, but the war was escalating around them, and food became unattainable.

Death Knocks Again

To assure their safety, Manuel now moved his family to a secure hideout near the coast. While there, one of the revolutionaries under his command defected to the Spanish garrison. Knowing this would certainly result in an assault upon their sanctuary the following day, Lavastida laid plans for their reception. Selecting a V-shaped defile between two rock formations through which he knew the enemy must pass; he positioned his men, secured a clear line of fire, posted two lookouts, and waited. At dawn the Spaniards appeared, led by an officer on a white horse. Lavastida's men were poorly armed, and every round would have to count. Each picked his Spaniard. All went according to plan. At the sound of the first shots, the lieutenant fell, and—on cue—the women and children emerged from the forest with a whoop, *"To the machete!"*[282] Terrorized, the Spaniards fled.

Colonel Lavastida now moved his family to another hideout. As the fighting intensified it became unsafe to search for food. Hunger and malaria took their toll. Lavastida's family began to die. One by one, Manuel buried his sons—Roque, then Manolo. Returning from digging the grave of his third son, the Patriot found his wife, Carolina, near death, while young B. G., racked with fever, huddled near the small wood fire. "Son," Manuel whispered, " I have marked the place where I am going to bury you and your mother. Then I will place myself in the thick of battle and all the Lavastida family will have been offered for the freedom of Cuba."

Notwithstanding what seemed a certain prognosis, Carolina recovered enough that Manuel felt safe to leave her and B. G. in the Indian hut while he searched for food. In his absence, Spaniards happened upon the shelter and seized Carolina and B. G. The commander's orders were terse: "Execute them!" At this point a soldier whom the Lavastidas had befriended four years earlier, seized the moment, and implored his superior: "Let me kill them!" Permission granted, the three marched off to the woods. At a safe distance, the angel unaware pointed his carbine to the sky and fired two rounds. "Now, run for your lives!" he ordered his lucky charges. B. G. Lavastida had escaped death a second time.[283]

Halls of Learning

The war ended and life became a colorless routine. A youthful B. G. began to run with the pack. This worried Manuel, who now made plans to send him to America to enter school. With a promise not to embarrass the Lavastida name, the sixteen-year-old sailed out of Havana harbor for the United States, where he became a good student and a churchgoer in the family's Catholic tradition. His first stop was Florida, where he studied English at Rollings College. Then he was off to school in Villanova in Pennsylvania, and finally to Rensselaer Polytechnic Institute in Troy, New York. Here he would earn a degree in Civil Engineering (1912) and additional certification in chemistry. He returned each summer to Cuba to work with his father. While at Rensselaer Polytech, he received the news that would forever change his life.[284]

Treachery

Long before the sinking of the Maine, Manuel Lavastida had been a political activist, working tenaciously for the overthrow of Spanish rule. After the victorious American intervention, he became a captain in the Rural Guards, later rising to Lieutenant Colonel. The outspoken patriot was ousted on 1 February 1909 by the Gómez government for his conservative political opinions expressed in the previous year's election campaign. Indignant over his removal, Lavastida conspired against the regime, influencing the men he had formerly commanded, to follow him. He was arrested at Placetas, Santa Clara in the evening of March 15, and was executed the following night, allegedly while attempting to escape. That was the official report.

In fact, Manuel Lavastida was hacked to death by machete-wielding thugs of the corrupt Gómez regime (1909–1913). Petty, self-serving types, the cut-throats had been offered *asenso* (promotion) in exchange for wasting Lavastida. They had come upon him behind his back. He turned and rebuked them; "You shouldn't kill a man from behind, but to his face!" They obliged, finishing their deadly work just outside of Placetas. This murder would be a turning point in the spiritual history of Cuba.

Conversion

The Lavastida affair caused a public furor, since popular wisdom held his death to be a government-ordered assassination. Official assassinations were usually carried out on the pretext of attempted escape.

When the news of his father's death reached B. G.—he read about it on the street in a Troy newspaper—he became enraged, then sank into depression. Thoughts of revenge soon took shape in a determination to return to Cuba and put an end to the existence of José Miguel Gómez. Numb with the magnitude of his loss, young Lavastida went to the home of an evangelical family that had befriended him. As he shared his grief, his friends were moved and gave him a Bible. As he left the home, the daughter said to him, "I have marked in the book words that will comfort you." The text was Matthew 11:28: "*Come unto me all ye that labor and are heavy laden, and I will give you rest.*"

Lavastida left his friend's house, which was close to the end of the trolley line, and boarded a streetcar to return to his dormitory room at Rensselaer. He opened the Bible at the underscored text and began to read. He read for five hours. The simple invitation arrested him. "Come unto me . . . and I will give you rest . . ." In his dormitory room, Lavastida lifted his tormented heart to heaven: "Oh God, give me rest." Later he would recall, "I heard God's voice on that streetcar, and gave him my heart."[285] In place of revenge came a determination to find his father's slayers and tell them of the love of God. B. G. had grown up in the revolutionary ambience generated in the home by his father. With his conversion to Christ, the desire for a free Cuba continued to burn. However, it was no longer political revolution he pursued, but spiritual. Freedom for the Cuban people through the liberating gospel of Christ became his goal.

Lavastida's conversion in New York changed his plans for an immediate return to Cuba. Instead, he continued his engineering studies and began attending a Presbyterian Church on Sundays—but only after attending Mass. Befriended by one of the Sunday school teachers who helped him understand the Scriptures, he joined the church. After graduation from Rensselaer he returned to Cuba and joined the Presbyterian Church in Havana. He later said, "Without much Scriptural knowledge, but with great zeal I gave myself to the winning of souls. The Lord gave me a special love for children."

Lavastida's compulsion to share the gospel and his love for children revolutionized the Havana congregation. Fifty youngsters in Sunday school sextupled to more than three hundred. Within a year, B. G. was appointed elder and Sunday school Superintendent. Many of the children coming to the church were residents in a nearby tenement building. One of them would birth a vision.

Lavastida now sensed God's call to full time service. Asking the Lord to make provision for his mother, brothers and sisters—all of them dependent on him—B. G. determined to return to the United States to attend school. Through the intervention of a friend, misappropriated pension benefits belonging to his mother were recovered, assuring the family's solvency. It was God's seal, and in 1917, he entered McCormick Theological Seminary in Chicago. During his second year, he married Elsie Lines, an American graduate of Nyack, and professor at Wheaton College. She had come to Chicago as a YWCA officer. Together they pastored a Hispanic church in Chicago. She bore Lavastida two children, Ruth, and Aubert, in Michigan.[286]

After graduation from McCormick in 1920, B. G. returned to Cuba with his wife, Elsie. They went as missionaries under the auspices of the Presbyterian Church. Three Presbyterian pastorates followed: Cardenas (1921–22), Caibarién (1922–1925), and Placetas (1928–1934). Lavastida was then appointed evangelist of the Presbytery of Cuba.[287]

Bartholomew G. Lavastida was the consummate pastor. Although an engineering graduate, he turned down a lucrative political post that would have assured his family a comfortable future, choosing to follow the higher call. His family failed to understand. His son, Elmer Lavastida (by B. G.'s second wife, Fefita], himself later becoming a pastor in Cuba, reflected on his father's surrender to the ministry—It was not the pursuit of a profession, but the expression of his life, "as natural as breathing," adding, "He ceased being a pastor [only] when he ceased to live."[288]

Birth of a Vision

During Lavastida's time in Havana, a little girl from a nearby tenement caught his attention. Eight-year-old America always sat on the front bench at church, her eyes riveted on him throughout the service. Whenever she was absent, he knew that diseased tonsils had again confined her to bed. As her absences became more frequent, he would wrap up the morning lesson after church and make his way to the girl's apartment. Pulling a chair up to her bedside, he would present the lesson to the frail youngster and softly sing hymns.

Visits with America disturbed the young teacher. As he reached the door of the shabby tenement he would pause, straighten his shoulders, and breathe deeply before knocking. It helped calm the frustration he felt. The sight of children in the foul grip of poverty angered him. When the door opened, Lavastida would stride slowly into the cramped apartment, throwing a kindly nod to the child's mother. This tiny room was what the family called home. There were just two cots, a small rocker, two chairs, a stool, and a stove. The only item of apparent value was a sewing machine. With that, America's mother sewed for a local tailor shop and kept the family clothing in repair.

Sitting by America's bed, Lavastida's thoughts drifted to his own childhood— the challenge of climbing a tree, the ecstasy of wading barefoot in the nearby brook, the carefree innocence of normal childhood frolic. In that moment of reverie, B. G. Lavastida asked God to use him to establish a school where children like America might enjoy the beauty of nature, receive good schooling, and be won for Jesus Christ and his service. For one Divine moment, the tenement apartment became a sanctuary and his prayer a sacrament. In December of 1922, Lavastida's entreaty at America's bedside began to take shape. It happened quite by accident and turned on a misfortune.

God Gives the Land

Returning from a campaign in Sancti Spiritus, Lavastida decided to lunch at the home of his aunt, Mercedita. She lived close to the railway station, so there was plenty of time for him to catch the next train. Halfway through the meal he was jolted by the mournful blast of the train whistle, signaling departure. Bolting breathlessly for the terminal, he hurriedly bought his ticket, but already the cars were moving and picking up speed. Running alongside the train, he attempted to board, first throwing his suitcase in the direction of the door in order to free both hands for the mount. The case missed, bounced off the top step, and tumbled to the tracks and beneath the wheels. Exhausted from days of ministry, he had lacked the strength to hit his target. Lavastida had barely escaped the fate of his suitcase, now hopelessly destroyed. There was nothing for it but to return to the house of his aunt for the night and await the morning train.[289]

At daybreak, Lavastida took the train to Caibarién, but the unplanned overnight now obliged him to change trains in Cumbre. Here he detrained, bracing his way through the chill winter fog that enveloped the platform. While waiting, he engaged conversation with a stranger who—as it turned out—had been a soldier under the command of his father, Lieutenant Colonel Manuel Lavastida. Moreover, the stranger and the late Colonel had been friends.

In the exchange that followed, Lavastida expressed his interest in securing a piece of land for a school—provided there were no schools already available in the area. Motioning toward the low hills that could be seen from the platform, the former soldier assured B. G. that another friend of his father, Telesforo Alvarez, lived there and could certainly help him. If B. G. would return to Cumbre on Thursday—this being Tuesday—he would have horses ready to take him to Telesforo's spread. When B. G. reached the *finca* (farm) on Thursday, Telesforo was not there. However, his wife and ten children were. None had ever been to school. Lavastida preached the gospel to the family and left, determined to return on Saturday, which he did.

Telesforo now listened as Lavastida laid out his plans for the school project. What happened next became a moment of historic consequence. In Lavastida's own words:

> He took me on horseback to a part of his farm that he had decided to donate. Much of it was covered with brambles, but I accepted that land as a gift from God.[290]

The bramble patch in Jagüeyes would eventually become the home of Los Pinos Bible Institute. But not yet. Lavastida's dream had been a home and a school for Cuba's children. A Bible institute for training Cuban pastors had not yet entered his head.

Plea for Help

B. G. now had the land, but little else. What he did have was the attention of the Cuban Presbytery, which had followed the project with more than casual interest. Lavastida was still pastor of the Presbyterian Church in Caibarién and this connection provided a broad platform on which to float his vision. The *Heraldo Cristiano* (Christian Herald) was the newspaper of the Cuban Presbytery. It enjoyed a wide circulation and Lavastida was not slow to seize the publicity it offered. In the June 1924 issue, there appeared an appeal over Lavastida's signature. It was a letter to the public and it capitalized on the still lingering luster of his patriotic family:

> I am the oldest son of Captain Lavastida, whom you know personally or by references, since his death was lamented by all Cuba, for whose liberty he sacrificed everything, to the point of opening graves and with his own hands burying three of my beloved brothers, who died in the woods of hunger and fever during the war.
>
> I was educated in the United States, and since returning to my beloved country ten years ago, I have carried a burning desire to do something to help the hundreds of needy youngsters throughout the island. Children

are a nation's greatest treasure and to them governments owe their best attention. Money cannot be used with greater benefit than in the preparation of children for life. The project I hold in my heart is to establish in the province of Santa Clara a school, which will be called the "Los Pinos Nuevos" [the New Pines] school, where children from the countryside and poor children from the villages can be educated in a healthful environment and under a qualified staff who will teach by both word and example. Through the cultivation of crops and livestock, costs will be reduced, putting education within reach of the poorest families.

After further elaboration of plans for the school and explaining that his aspirations for the students were nothing less than God's own ideals for Cuban youth, he continued:

To realize these ideals I need your benevolent cooperation. I have the land, donated by a countryman, but we still lack housing, furniture, and equipment to begin this work. You can help me give the bread of education to needy children next September by leaving me a generous contribution with the *Administrador del Ingenio* [sugar mill administrator] when the sugarcane harvest is in.[291]

Every Hammer Blow

Lavastida's letter, written from the manse in Caibarién, was effective. He approached the owners of sugarcane fields specifically, as these were not so affected by the economic crisis tormenting the rest of the country. In addition to contributions that came from individuals and congregations, he worked to involve the entire community in the project.

The Presbytery released Lavastida from the Caibarién pastorate in January 1925 to free him for evangelistic work and the development of the New Pines school. By April, work was proceeding on the house in Jagüeyes, with seven carpenters volunteering from several towns, each town the seat of a Presbyterian Church. Lavastida pumped his troops: "Every hammer blow for Christ!" People came with lumber, cows, goats, and chickens—whatever they had. The hurry to complete the project may have been fueled by one curious fact. Telesforo had attached a condition to his gift. If the school were not functioning within a year, title to the land would revert to the donor. Whether or not the goad was necessary, the result was the same. Classes began in the Spring of 1925 with an enrollment of thirty students.

The New Pines

For six months, Lavastida had ransacked his head for a name for the school. As the wheels of his train drummed out their staccato dance with the tracks, it suddenly came to him. He remembered José Martí, Cuba's exiled patriot, political philosopher, and martyr. Martí had led the charge for Cuban independence and much of his campaigning had been conducted in the United States.

During the 1890s, Florida was a rallying point for expatriated Cuban nationalists. Ybor City in particular was a hotbed of Cuban politics. Martí had called the cigar factories in Key West and Tampa "civilian camps of the national revolution."[292] Each factory had a reader who read revolutionary pamphlets to the cigar handrollers as they worked. On 27 November 1891, in the Liceo Cubano in Ybor City, Martí gave his now-famous "New Pines" oration. He described his train trip between Tampa and Miami across the "bland Florida landscape of scrub oaks and palmettos." He recalled seeing a burned-over patch of pine forest, and continued:

> The sun suddenly broke through a clearing in the forest and there, in the dazzling of unexpected light, I saw above the yellowish grass around the black trunks of the fallen pines, the joyful bunches of new pines. That is what we are—new pines![293]

The metaphor ignited Cuban imagination and became the watchword of the independence movement. Hope for Cuba's future lay with the "New Pines"— the new generation that would rise from the blackened stumps of past humiliation to secure Cuba's independence and dignity. Subsequent generations of Cubans would appropriate the New Pines metaphor "to signify their nonconformity with the past, and with established norms."[294]

If *Los Pinos Nuevos* had enshrined the political dream of the Lavastidas, B. G. now saw that the name perfectly described his hope for Cuba's spiritual rebirth through the children in his new school. They were the *New Pines* who would bring blessing to his country. The choice was apt. Not only did the metaphor express the purpose of the school; it carried instant recognition throughout the island nation. Pine trees, however, were not indigenous to Santa Clara and the motif of the revolution had come to Martí while traveling in Florida. That did not deter Lavastida. He acquired four Australian pines and planted them across his patio.[295] With the school up and running, Lavastida recruited assistants, but when discord erupted among the families, he had to release them. That is when the letter from Hattie Kirk arrived. We shall meet her in the next chapter.

Almost Presbyterian

By 1927, the New Pines School was firmly established in Jagüeyes. In nearby Placetas the Presbyterian Church hosted the fortieth annual session of the Havana Presbytery. Delegates from twenty-eight churches and seven missions represented a membership of 1,800. In November, when the pastor suddenly succumbed to postoperative complications, the church asked Lavastida to assume the pastorate, which he did the following April. The Jagüeyes school became a model, taking second place only to the venerable Progressive School in Cárdenas. Again, The Herald lavished praise on the New Pines institution and its visionary founder, headlining in its April issue an eminent politician who affirmed, "The triumph of this institution is the triumph of Cuba." By this time, the New Pines was viewed as a Presbyterian institution—at least by Presbyterians.

The denomination subsidized the school through special offerings, and felt some understandable pride of ownership. However, it was soon clear that the Presbyterians wished to control the New Pines School, but Lavastida did not share their vision. In 1934 leaders of the Presbyterian church in the USA came to Placetas with the offer to underwrite the costs of the school on condition that the work pass into the hands of the Presbyterian church. The offer was attractive, but Lavastida declined, noting that he already had his own board of directors. When asked who they might be, he responded, "Father, Son and Holy Spirit."[296]

If the Presbyterians exerted proprietary pressure on Lavastida, it was offset by the influence of his wife. Elsie Lines had been groomed at A. B. Simpson's Nyack College in New York. Nyack was theologically conservative, and unlike the Presbyterians, open to a broader spectrum of evangelicalism. In a classic example of thesis→ antithesis→ synthesis, Elsie's Christian and Missionary Alliance theology tempered Lavastida's more parochial Presbyterian ecclesiology. The result was a man in theological equipoise—unmarked by provincialism.

To the alarm of the North American Presbytery, Lavastida began sending some of his more promising students from New Pines to the Toccoa Falls Institute in Georgia. Founded in 1911, the Toccoa school's primary emphasis was on preparing Christian men and women in the industrial arts. Lavastida's action was not motivated by denominational disloyalty; it was the logical, progressive next step for his beloved New Pines youngsters. He wanted to see young Cubans equipped to step into the market place and industry with competence and dignity.

Among its assets the New Pines facility now counted three buildings, dairy cows, sheep, pigs, rabbits, and the ubiquitous chicken. Bountiful harvests of corn, beans, potatoes, and yams supplemented the student diet. Almost unnoticed in the recital of blessings appearing in the Herald was the statement:

> "In Los Pinos Nuevos there are seven workers—one from Canada, another from Costa Rica. Five of them receive no salary."

It was the "one from Canada" who would—indirectly—change the course of Lavastida's dream.[297]

22

The Catalysts

Those people will take the next boat home.

—E. A. Odell

The Wheatfields of Alberta

Hattie Kirk is hardly a household name, but were it not for her, Prairie Bible Institute would not exist, and there would have been no West Indies Mission. In the human equation, she was the catalyst who coalesced the essential elements of both institutions.

Her father, Andrew Kirk, took root in Cornwall, Ontario, where he was born of Scottish stock. There he met and married Maria, whose family had come from Quebec. Kirk was a dairy farmer, and along with milking cows found time to sire and raise ten children—Mabel, Robert, Hattie, Roger, Edward, Hector, Fergus, Elsa, Amy, and Jessie. Andrew had become a respected Presbyterian lay-preacher, and made certain that his growing brood was grounded in the Scriptures. One by one, five of the Kirk clan left their Ontario nest and pioneered westward across the Canadian Prairie to the wheatfields of Alberta. One by one they settled in the town of Three Hills—Fergus, Hector, Roger, Hattie, and Mabel, who married Jack McElheran. All five were to play a role in the founding of Prairie Bible Institute and the beginnings of the West Indies Mission.[298] Nevertheless, Hattie was the *sine qua non*.

Hattie, Fergus, and Prairie Bible Institute

Determined to receive a formal education in Bible, Hattie Kirk applied to the Nyack Missionary Training Institute in New York, founded by Canadian A. B. Simpson. High School education was an entry requirement, but Hattie had no diploma. Simpson recommended two years of equivalent schooling at Nyack to meet the requirement. Unfazed by this setback, she was delighted to learn that Nyack Principal, W. C. Stevens, taught the two weekly Bible classes in the pre-Institute curriculum.[299] Hattie knew that William Coit Stevens had a reputation. He made the Scriptures live.

Plagued most of her life with a stammering problem, Hattie despaired of ever being used by God. When Stevens presented the Biblical case for healing, Hattie was electrified. She knew this message was from God, and she knew it was for her. Eight years earlier when she was nineteen, the Lord had revealed himself to her in a way she never forgot. That is when the assurance had come that sometime, somehow, this frustrating and humiliating bane would be lifted from her. She asked Principal Stevens to pray for her. He did, and she always remembered his prayer: "Lord, as I am bowing in your presence, I have assurance that it is your will that Hattie be healed."[300] Notwithstanding, four years would pass before the promise became fact.

Three years of academic work at Nyack exhausted Hattie Kirk. When she took a short nursing course in Toronto during the summer of 1911, a nervous breakdown prevented her return to school in the fall. When she recovered, her life took on a nomadic twist.

First, she moved to Blackwood, Virginia to help a school friend do meetings for Christian workers in a mining company. Her long-awaited deliverance came unexpectedly when she was called upon to pray at one of the mining camp meetings. Immediately she opened her mouth, the affliction left her, and the next Sunday she conducted services. When early death claimed her sister three months later (May 1913), she returned to Ontario to help on the farm and care for a sickly brother. When he died, she returned to Alberta, rotating among her relatives in Three Hills, staying with whatever family needed her most.[301]

Fergus Kirk shared his sister's hunger for Bible study. Hattie had brought from Nyack some sheets of questions prepared by W. C. Stevens, her former teacher. He had developed a search-question method of Bible study. The approach was inductive, leading the student to personal discoveries of the Bible message without the aid of commentaries. She now shared this with her brother. He promptly devoured it and was eager for more.

By 1922 "Daddy" Stevens had left Nyack and was teaching at Midland Bible Institute in Kansas City. Fergus Kirk was eager to enroll, and would have moved to Kansas City in a moment, but his wife was too ill to leave Three Hills. As he faced this roadblock to his dreams, a flash of inspiration lit his darkening sky. There was a way! Fergus Kirk had experienced one of those inauspicious moments whose brilliance and magnitude only time and reflection can measure.

Why not use the money he would have spent for travel and support at Midland to bring a Bible teacher to Three Hills? The idea danced in his head, rekindling hope. In Hattie he now had a conduit to Midland and Stevens, so about mid-year 1922 Fergus Kirk wrote Stevens in Kansas to see if someone in the student body would be available to come to Three Hills to teach the Word of God. Hoping for encouragement, he showed the letter to an older brother, whose only cheer was to chide him for fanaticism.[302] However, Fergus had already affixed the three-cent postage stamp, and with nothing to lose, he mailed the letter.

Stevens knew just the man to meet the needs in Three Hills. His prize pupil and protégé, Leslie E. Maxwell, was about to graduate. When the invitation was put to Maxwell, Dorothy Ruth Miller, on the staff at Midland and later a beloved instructor in Three Hills, wired back: "Leslie springs to it!"[303] Maxwell finished his studies at Midland on 22 September 1922. On October 9, he was teaching his first classes on the Canadian prairies. With the birth of Prairie Bible Institute, another drumbeat had begun to resonate around the world.[304] Neither Kirk, nor Maxwell, nor Stevens could have guessed how far the sound would go.

Hattie, Harry, and Costa Rica

Harry Strachan was a Scot and a former student of H. Grattan Guinness. Turned away from a Congo assignment with RBMU for medical reasons, he went to Argentina and from there conducted evangelistic campaigns throughout South America. Settling in Costa Rica, he founded the Latin America Mission in 1921, and later, the Costa Rica Bible Institute. An inveterate traveler, Strachan visited the newborn Prairie Bible Institute in 1923,[305] where he gave a report on his own equally new Costa Rica Bible Institute. Hattie Kirk, now resident in Three Hills, was captured by Strachan's report, and offered her services to the pioneer work in Costa Rica.

She knew the odds were against her. At forty-two, frail of health, and with few financial resources, she was hardly the ideal missionary candidate. Notwithstanding, she mustered courage and talked with Strachan. Expressing first her lively interest in the Costa Rica school, Hattie recited her roster of handicaps—age, stuttering, and health—all obvious disqualifiers. Strachan's response was a shrug of the shoulders. A woman in her fifties—he countered—was already on her way to Costa Rica to participate in the ministry. With the Bible School just getting underway the work was open to anyone willing to learn the language.

Hattie made it to Costa Rica in November 1924. Here she met Efraín Monge, a carpenter, and native *Costariqueño*, recently converted from a life of alcoholism. He was taking Bible courses at Strachan's Bible Institute, and a mutual attraction developed. However, along with her baggage, Hattie Kirk had brought a tenuous health history to Costa Rica, and it did not improve. Physical problems obliged her to leave the country in June 1926. She had been in

Costa Rica less than two years. Her desire for mission work remained unassuaged, as did her interest in Efraín Monge.[306] On her way to Canada she made an extended visit with a cousin in Elizabeth, New Jersey. While there, Efraín came to visit, and popped the question. Interracial unions were frowned upon and Hattie had been cautioned against pursuing a relationship with Efraín, but the chemistry was right, and the advice was declined. Just then, another critical link was forged in the making of the West Indies Mission.

Efraín—who spoke little English at the time—wanted the ceremony in Spanish. It so happened that E. A. Odell, Convener of Missions of the Havana Presbytery, was in Elizabeth that month as pulpit supply for a vacationing pastor. Monge contacted Odell, who performed the ceremony. When the newlyweds expressed their interest in Spanish language work, Odell told them of B. G. Lavastida and his school for children, near Placetas, Cuba. Hattie Kirk Monge, who seemed to do whatever she was determined to do, determined to go to Cuba. Lavastida was building a school, and Efraín's skills in carpentry would be useful in the project now underway. Hattie wrote to Lavastida, and the door opened. With no agency to back them, they set out for Cuba.[307]

The Monges Come to Placetas

A steady November drizzle welcomed the newlyweds when they arrived by train in Cumbre in November 1926. Hattie and Efraín had been married eight weeks when they reached the railway station just two miles from the location of Lavastida's school. Unaware of their exact arrival date, the evangelist was engaged in one of his frequent preaching tours through the Cuban countryside, so was not there to meet them. Neither was anyone else.

Struggling under the weight of their luggage, the middle-aged pair labored their way along a path now turned to muddy slush by the constant rain, their ease with Spanish securing intermittent course corrections from passersby.

The first sight of the school sank their hearts:

> We found a very primitive building of boards—whitewashed—with unpainted floors and thatched roof . . .

Some boys were helping an older man with chores. The man was Anastasio Diaz, a Christian farmer who cared for the grounds and led Sunday services during Mr. Lavastida's absence. His wife, Herminia, was the cook, and with the aid of some young girls, cared for the Lavastida housekeeping and looked after their five small children.

The bedraggled couple were welcomed, and once recovered from their two mile trek, had a look around. A quick tour of the property revealed a dozen or more cows and their calves, three horses, a team of oxen, and a brood of hens. A peek into the single classroom disclosed an old organ, a blackboard, and some desks. The all-purpose room served as the school during the week, with

Nica, one of Lavastida's church members from Placetas, doing the teaching. On Sundays, the room metamorphosed into a worship center for the New Pines family and the few neighbors who regularly joined them.

If the building was disappointingly rustic, the lush tropical beauty of the environs was magnificent. Even while bracing the relentless raw drizzle, Hattie was taken with the stately royal palms that adorned the property—they seemed to be everywhere. This was certainly not Three Hills and it was not Costa Rica. However, this was where God had led them, and Hattie planned to stay. Had she known what Pastor Odell was thinking, she might have been less optimistic. E. A. Odell was Superintendent of the Cuban Presbytery.[308] Just before the Monges left New Jersey for Cuba, Odell had passed his evaluation to Lavastida: "Those people will take the next boat home."

Plunging in

Living quarters were cramped. Hattie and Efraín settled into a small room in the same building where the female students lived. If they felt crowded so did Anastasio and Herminia. They housed the boys in their tiny quarters. Everyone ate in the school's all-purpose room.

Hattie's first duties were to oversee household chores, supervise the washing—done with a washboard in galvanized tubs—and monitor the use of the gasoline iron for pressing clothes. When Anastasio's sweet potatoes and corn were harvested, Hattie kept the boys busy with the grinder, while keeping an eye on the girls and their cooking. She would eventually become Mr. Lavastida's secretary and teach a morning Bible class for the women students.

Soon Hattie and Efraín found themselves in charge of the school, since Lavastida was totally immersed in church activity and evangelistic meetings. While Hattie busied herself with indoor chores, Efraín used his carpentry skills to build the few items of furniture they required. Then Pastor Odell came to visit. It proved a blessing. Seeing their cramped quarters, he gave the Monges enough fiber-cement to build their own home. With money sent by family and friends in Three Hills the couple secured lumber and other supplies and set about constructing a house large enough to accommodate themselves and the additional missionaries they prayed would join them. The finished product looked like a warehouse, but it kept out heat and rain.

Hattie Lobbies for a Bible School

Hattie's frustration grew in quantum leaps. The young Cuban students reminded her of Prairie Bible Institute and of Strachan's Bible School in Costa Rica. She remembered, too, those wonderful days at Nyack. The flashback of each mental cameo underscored her conviction that Mr. Lavastida's pupils desperately needed something more than a primary school education, even with the daily Bible lesson that was thrown in. What they needed was a Bible school!

No longer able to suppress her concern, Hattie approached Lavastida with the suggestion that New Pines be turned into a Bible school. If she had expected enthusiastic endorsement of the notion, she was disappointed. Lavastida knew his people—he reminded her—and Cubans were not ready for something as advanced as a Bible school. Moreover, he must respect the wishes of Mr. Telesforo, the donor of the property. The site had been given specifically for the secular educational of disadvantaged local children. A Bible school would be a breach of that agreement.

No quitter, Hattie turned her frustration to prayer, using the daily noon siesta period to take her burden to the Lord. She also shared her concern in letters home, especially when writing to her brother, Roger.

Roger to the Rescue

Roger Kirk was concerned for Hattie. Her impassioned letters brimmed with excitement, but were always laced with pleas for help. She and Efraín had been in Cuba six months. Roger decided to visit them and see for himself. In May 1927, Roger said goodbye to his sickly wife and their children, working his way east from Three Hills to New York City on a cattle car. Eighteen horses were his traveling companions. The lakes, streams, trees, and mountains sped past his coach window in a kaleidoscope of wonder. It put him in a reflective mood. "Even the rocks are interesting," he wrote. "I guess being surrendered to God's will must have to do with daily joy in everything that comes or goes."[309]

When Roger was twenty, he had sensed a call to missions but failed to act. Ever since, life had trounced him with a succession of financial failures.[310] Hattie's obedience and pleas for help now seemed to present an opportunity for redemption. This time, however, the call was different. With an ailing wife at home, his missionary tour would be limited. Even so, the step offered some comfort and he looked forward to the adventure.

Arriving in Placetas on May 28, Roger was overwhelmed by the endemic poverty. Cows were gaunt. A tethered pig displayed its rib cage, clearly visible beneath a veneer of skin. The Alberta farmer winced. Hattie had alerted the workers that her brother was coming, so everyone had turned out to welcome him. Men and boys came in from the field; the young girls stood proudly, hoping he would notice how well they had spruced up the place. Even Mr. Lavastida had managed to be present to show him the property.

The dry season had arrived. Dust clouds puffed around their feet as they walked the grounds. Barnyard stock scattered before them—hens, goats, cows, calves, rabbits, sheep, and pigs—only this was not a barnyard. With a thrust of his jaw, Lavastida motioned toward the well, now yielding only half a pail of water per draw.

The river that sliced through a corner of the farm had reduced to a trickle. Twenty acres of crusted land was being dug for pasture, but heavy brush and matted roots made the project arduous. There was a garden perhaps ten yards square, five acres of corn, a sweet potato patch, and a plot staked out for planting with banana and orange trees and sugar cane.

Grim Lifestyle

Hattie's living quarters distressed Roger, but he consoled himself that everyone seemed happy. He unloaded his bags in the small room they had assigned him, already aware that his sister and her husband had to eat with all the students in the school's dining hall. The meals brought more surprises. Breakfast comprised a few soda biscuits and coffee. Dinner at eleven o'clock was a generous helping of rice and beans. A quick survey of the table revealed that there was no bread. Roger resumed eating what was before him. When the supper bell rang at five o'clock Roger joined Hattie and Efraín in their trek with the students toward the dining room, where more rice and beans awaited them.

That evening Hattie passed up the main course. Roger noticed that she was discreetly consuming other fare. "I can't handle the beans," was her whispered response to his puzzled look. She had substituted a shredded wheat biscuit with a little milk.

"Why is there no bread and butter?" he asked later.

"We have rarely had butter since I came here. Bread is very expensive."

"Why don't you bake it?" he continued.

"We have no oven."

Hattie's living arrangements troubled Roger. He expressed his concern in a letter to his family:

> All they have for a stove [are] four cast-iron things such as a blacksmith builds a fire in. They burn charcoal. Hattie eats shredded wheat for dinner and supper. For breakfast, they have what would be a quarter of a slice of bread. Whatever milk they have, if it is a cup all around, all right, but Hattie says that sometimes it is not more than a quarter cup each, with nothing else until noon. [She] has been buying one quart of milk for herself each day from a neighbor. She also has some platanos, a green banana that she fries.

> I marvel how she keeps up. She seems always busy. Everyone is up at 5:00 am. She seems to be on the go all day and, since I came, until 10:00 p.m.[311]

Roger decided that Hattie had endured more than enough pioneering hardships. It was time to turn things around at Los Pinos.

Roger Campaigns for a Farm

Roger quickly made Hattie's cause his own. His letters home exude a deep sense of burden to see a Bible Institute established in rural Cuba. His gifts and experience in farming uniquely qualified him as God's anointed activist to ratchet interest in the Placetas farm. He knew that a self-supporting campus was essential if the school was to survive in this impoverished rural setting, and such a campus was impossible without an efficiently run farm. The urgent pleadings in Hattie's letters over the past six months now began to make sense. Back in Three Hills, their nieces, Evelyn and Muriel McElheran, had been too absorbed with personal plans to respond. Roger determined to change that. He would see to it that his nieces would be among the first reinforcements for this work. Meanwhile he continued to walk the property, plotting how best to attack the reluctant acreage and reflecting on the two girls and how they would fit in.

Evelyn's presence was essential. She had all the ideal qualities for this kind of life. In addition, her quiet sense of humor would be a welcome relief for Hattie. Moreover, Evelyn seemed to have a real call to Cuba. Once she and Muriel learned the language, they could lead Bible classes and the work for Christ could begin in earnest.

Meanwhile, the immediate task was to till and tame this root-bound soil. He would also have to sell the farm idea to Mr. Lavastida, and that would call for a convincing case. If Roger could pull that off, the next step would be to teach Anastasio the process of plowing, sowing, and harvest. Educating Lavastida would be difficult—he was away so often, and for long periods. Roger liked him. He appeared to be a true man of God despite his associations with other area ministers whom Roger privately classified as unspiritual. Roger also sensed that Mr. Lavastida was somehow at a crossroads in his thinking— theologically sound, but not fully awake to the dangers of "modernism."[312]

The Monges and Roger often accompanied Lavastida on his visitation work. Hattie noted Roger's interest in the thirty Jamaican families who lived in and around Placetas. Always taking the initiative, she suggested holding services for them. They spoke English and appeared interested.

Neither the Cubans nor the Jamaicans seemed to respect the clock, however, and Roger Kirk's patience evaporated. "We seem to make little headway working the land," he complained, "and time means no more to these fellows than to a cow." Kirk knew no Spanish, which increased his frustration. Hattie had to translate for anything he wanted done. It was an awkward arrangement. Kirk, however, was confident that God had sent him to Placetas, and he was not about to be discouraged. God had plans for Cuba, and Roger Kirk could wait it out.

Lavastida Comes Around

Roger often visited Lavastida in Havana and began to sense a change in the evangelist's attitude toward turning Los Pinos into a Bible School. Perhaps the Cuban visionary was awakening to the larger potential of a Bible institute. Until now, Lavastida had seemed engrossed in his own ministry, wanting little more than to bring needy students to the school, educate them, and convert them. Once settled on their farms they would gradually Christianize their communities. That is how Roger Kirk read Lavastida's philosophy of Christian education.[313]

Lavastida could be gruff, but one day he let Roger know that he would be glad to see a Bible School started as soon as possible. The assurance encouraged the Canadian, who had also taken heart from the class of Jamaican families he and Hattie were now teaching. More often than not, the Jamaicans failed to show up for the three o'clock class until 4:00 or 5:00, but it was worth it. Roger was learning to adapt to the culture, and was becoming surer of his mission:

> The people are quiet, simple living, and seem to be open-minded. The priests seem to be asleep and the Christian church as well. There has been good work done in the past. All the centers seem to have a good body of believers. That means [that] someone [had] worked [at] some time, but now they are just going on with their organizations . . . and forget what they were saved for. I believe the Lord will do a work here and that it will spread.[314]

Taming the Good Earth

Roger acquired a pair of plow horses, noting that they were "the awfullest-looking things you ever saw." He improvised a dual harness and then worked the animals, much to the amusement of everyone at the school. Most of the residents were innocent of farming procedures and thought the Canadian had taken leave of his senses. Roger remained unfazed. Long ago he had given up worrying about what others thought of him. Before God, he would do his part to start a solid missionary work in this little parcel of Cuban soil. His gift was farming, and he would use it to the hilt.[315]

Occasionally, Lavastida invited Roger to accompany him on pastoral and evangelistic visits to nearby towns. Roger found that sharing his testimony on such occasions was invigorating. So was his class of Jamaicans. The desire to do more teaching tugged at Roger, but he knew his priority was to prepare the land and instruct the residents how to provide for themselves and the succession of students who would come to this place after he left. Roger knew in his heart that apart from God's gift of strength and courage, he could easily pack

it in and head for home. The heat and humidity were enervating. Plowing before either sunrise or breakfast, he perspired profusely, often dropping to his
knees at the end of each furrow just to catch his breath. He set small goals—
one furrow at a time. Just getting to the end of each furrow was a victory.

It took weeks, but the equestrian team learned to pull the five-foot harrow up
the steep grades. Their success opened the door for Roger to show the now-
inquisitive neighbors how a yoke of horses was supposed to work. In return,
they invited him to watch them plant bananas. With Mr. Lavastida's plans for
an orange orchard, banana plants, and sugar cane, the challenge of providing
food for the school began to take on the shape of possibility.

Overcoming Inertia

Roger Kirk struggled with more than reluctant soil. Cuban indifference was
an even bigger problem. He felt unable to ignite enthusiasm for either the
farm or the garden. Polite assent was given, but without follow through. The
campesino mindset seemed gripped by paralysis. The proposed one-acre
vegetable garden required a fence; otherwise, it would be vulnerable to the
daily marauding of 150 half-starved chickens. This seemed to produce no
concern. Roger bewailed:

> Even Mr. Lavastida begrudges the land. A garden is viewed as a luxury
> . . .Yesterday I found a couple of pieces of potatoes in my beans. I
> asked where they got them. They had *bought* them! The Lord knows
> my vision is along spiritual things. I see a wonderful prospect here . . .
> May the Lord lay it on our hearts to pray about it. I hope we may be able to con-
> centrate a real force here . . . I expect to be home before long now . . .[316]

Burnout

It was becoming a pattern. Hattie Kirk Monge was ready to cut and run. First
at Nyack, then in Costa Rica. Now, after a year in Cuba, she was again sick
and tired—literally. Lonely, too. Efraín was a good husband and her brother
Roger a constant encouragement, but Cuba had drained her. Roger could see
that his sister was exhausted. There were good reasons—the unrelenting heat,
the sight and smell of rice and beans, the miniscule rations of milk, the non-
chalance of the *Cubanos*. Hattie had developed a classic case of culture shock.

The chickens were particularly offensive. They wandered in and out of homes
at will, including Hattie's. She could tell that Roger was not adjusting either.
He had taken to firing table knives or forks at the intruders. On top of that, the
New Pines school was still not a Bible School and it would be a long time
before it ever became one.

Ready to move again, Hattie reasoned: Let's go home, get some rest, and take
courage in the few achievements we've managed. These sulks troubled Roger,
who constantly implored her to stay. Soon he must return to Canada for the

harvest, but it would be a mistake if they all left at once. Muriel and Evelyn—Roger assured his sister—were willing to come. If they would consent to come soon, Hattie might reconsider. Kirk continued to work the land. He reflected and prayed. B. G. Lavastida was obviously God's man for the evangelistic work. The glow on the Cuban's face told all. Meeting after meeting, young people were coming forward to surrender unbelieving lovers and sinful ways. Notwithstanding, Roger concluded, that seemed to be as far as the work went. Something was missing and he knew what it was.

There was no mechanism in place to conserve this spiritual harvest—nothing to lead these young people into a life of service for Jesus. The average Cuban Christian seemed as wedded to the world as any in Alberta. Worse, most of them could not even read! Roger figured that short of a Bible school, at least New Pines should offer a literacy course to all these new believers. That way they could read the Bible. With that foundation, they could preach.

Cuba Needs a Man!

While Roger plowed and prayed, Hattie wrote to her nieces in Three Hills. Both were keen on missions, and had asked their uncle to give them his assessment of Lavastida's work upon his return. Aware of this, Hattie decided to reinforce Evelyn and Muriel's interest on her own. As she fired off letters to Three Hills, however, a different concern began to invade her thoughts. True enough, Cuba needed the services of her nieces. But two young women were hardly a match for the demands of a Bible school. Hattie understood too well from her own adventures that both their gender and lack of experience promised little success in launching a Bible Institute. If women enjoyed few leadership roles in Canada, Cuba would be worse. For the first time Hattie realized that the work of a Bible school called for a male figure. God must raise up a man. Hattie Kirk would find him.

Hattie was now convinced that she and Efraín could not remain in Cuba when Roger returned to Canada for the harvest. The matter was settled when both she and Efraín fell ill. Convinced that the trip home would restore Hattie's emotional health, Roger gave them his blessing and committed the little mission to God. The Monges left for New York. Roger sailed two weeks later.

Once back in Canada, Roger surveyed his options and turned his attention to Elmer V. Thompson. He had been teaching at Prairie Bible Institute and was now in his second year on staff. During the summers, he had boarded with the Roger Kirk family. Roger had come to know Thompson and now quietly assessed his potential for Cuba, reporting his findings to Hattie. Brother and sister agreed: Elmer V. Thompson was the man they were looking for. Their enthusiasm dropped like a barometer when Thompson declined, citing two reasons. First, he sensed no particular call to Cuba, although admitting that God was speaking to him about missions.[317] Second, he was not equipped to lead a pioneer work. Not easily put off, Roger and Hattie refused to dismiss Thompson from their thinking. Still confident they had found their man, they committed him to God.

The Maxwell Factor

Peering through the window of the McElheran home, Evelyn and Muriel watched the two men approaching the house. As the figures came into focus, the sisters recognized the familiar profiles of Principal Leslie E. Maxwell and Professor Elmer V. Thompson. Their gait betrayed the serious nature of their errand. At the door, they announced that they wished to speak to both sisters and to their parents. It was mid-August, 1927.

Principal Maxwell explained that upon returning to Canada, Hattie and Roger Kirk had approached Mr. Thompson about going to Cuba. At the time, Thompson had declined. Now upon further reflection, he believed God was calling him to the island. This being the case, someone would have to take Thompson's place at the Bible School. Would Muriel consider remaining in Three Hills to teach at Prairie and so free Thompson for Cuba?

The McElherans were stunned. Evelyn's head was spinning. She remembered the evening when Mr. Thompson came to dinner. She had talked non-stop about her plans to go to Cuba. On the fifty-mile ride to church the following day she had sat next to him on the front seat of the car. That had been Muriel's idea. By the end of the trip, Evelyn had taken a liking for this fellow who had been on the teaching staff when she was a student. Could it be that they might work together in a foreign country? The idea seemed fatuous. Even if it were possible, one stubborn question persisted: How could she function without Muriel's presence and support?

As the import of Maxwell's proposal sank in, excitement gripped Evelyn. Then fear. In the snatches of conversation that registered on her racing mind, she could hear Muriel agreeing to stay at Prairie while she went to Cuba. Could this really be happening? She and Muriel were inseparable. When the men had gone, Evelyn escaped to her room and sat in numbed reflection. She threw herself on the bed, buried her head in the pillow, and wept uncontrollably. Life without Muriel was unthinkable. In the hours that followed, Evelyn McElheran took the high ground. She later recalled:

> Before I left my room that day I promised the Lord that I would go to Cuba at any cost. Again I realized I must learn to depend on Him and not on others. I took courage and continued to prepare for an unknown future.[318]

23

First Lady

I determined to embrace the cross, and in a more cheerful spirit, unpacked my bags and put things in place. I would adopt this land to which God had called me as my own.

—Evelyn Thompson

Hurdles

Life had given Evelyn McElheran a rough start. From childhood, she suffered from weeping eczema. The condition was particularly triggered by hot weather and affected her face, arms, and hands. There was no cure. Her fingers had to be bandaged daily—each one separately. The early morning hours would find her mother, Mabel Kirk McElheran, in the milkhouse, praying aloud for her nine children and their three adopted sisters. As she asked that each might become a light for God in a dark world, Evelyn's eczema became a constant subject of those prayers.

By the time Evelyn was eighteen, the McElherans had exhausted medical options for their daughter. Nothing remained but to come to terms with the discomfort and embarrassment of her condition. Hope for a cure had all but evaporated. Then, unexpectedly, the question came to Mabel—almost audibly—"You have tried everything else. Why not try me?"

Was this the voice of God? She knew God *could* heal. She had always prayed for the children when they were ill. But this? Despair bid hard for victory as Mabel looked at her daughter's bandaged hands. Still, as she prayed, the conviction grew that God *would* do something. She shared her growing assurance with friends, but no one seemed interested.

Convinced that other Christians should be involved in this exercise, Mabel wrote to Principal Leslie E. Maxwell, sharing her conviction that God had stirred this concern for Evelyn's healing. Maxwell read Mabel's letter twice and agreed. It seemed that God *was* speaking. If Mabel would select a date for the family to pray, Maxwell would write to others to join in prayer at that time.

The date was set. In two weeks at three o'clock in the afternoon they would hold a concert of prayer. In the interim, Mabel tried to prepare herself, reading Scripture, fortifying her heart with the promises of God—every one she could think of. The sense of burden continued, unrelieved. "You go to the meeting tonight. I don't think I'll go," Mabel said to her husband, Jack. Some days remained before the appointed date and she needed time alone with God. However, the assurance and the peace she sought remained elusive. Then, for the second time, a question challenged her reverie:

"If I heal this girl, are you willing that I have her to do anything I want with her?"

"I stopped crying and praying and faced the situation with the Lord," Mabel remembered.

"Yes, Lord, You may have her for any place you want her and not only Evelyn, but you may have every one of my children."

At three o' clock on the appointed date friends arrived. Evelyn was anointed with oil and prayer was lifted. Later that evening Evelyn asked, "Mother, shall I bind my hands?"

"Do as you like. I know the Lord has touched you."

Six months later, a neighbor offered Evelyn a housecleaning job. It was the final test.

"Should I work for this woman?" she wondered. "What if putting my hands in dishwater should bring the trouble back again?"

"I feel the devil is beginning to come in like a flood," Mabel told her daughter, "but the Lord will raise up a standard against him."

Evelyn McElheran bandaged her hands for two days. A week later her hands, arms, and face were clear. Two weeks later, the scars were gone. The condition never returned.

The healing was a spiritual mile-marker for Evelyn McElheran. Still, her self-assessment as missionary material was not reassuring. When in 1924 God began to nudge her about missionary life, she struggled with inadequacies.

I was timid and backward and I could not meet the public. I shrank from strangers, and when left to carry on a conversation, I found myself greatly embarrassed . . . what mission board would accept such a person as I?[319]

But Evelyn could not escape the insistent, recurring echo of the text: *"Necessity is laid upon me,"* and, *"Woe is me if I preach not the gospel."*[320] Finally, she said "Yes" to God and began to pray about *"Where?"* Confident that she could at least work with children, she wrote her aunt Hattie, then at Lavastida's children's home in Cuba. An affirmative reply brought peace. She prepared for Cuba. In the first graduating class of Prairie Bible Institute, Evelyn would also be the first missionary to go out from the school, but she had no mission board. She worked to earn passage money, and with help from friends, bought her ticket. Then she put together her "outfit." One small trunk and a suitcase took care of it. With twenty-five dollars per month pledged by her parents, she was set to go.

On a morning late in the fall of 1927, the McElheran household was the scene of hushed activity. The solemnity was almost palpable as a timid twenty-two-year-old packed her last bag. Few words were exchanged as all shared the bittersweet moment. At the Three Hills railway station, the good-byes were not easy. The whistle blew. Couplings clanked reluctantly as the coaches lurched forward into their eastward journey. Hattie and Efraín were on board,[321] consoling their tender charge, trying to provide some linkage between the past and the future. Evelyn watched as the little family on the platform diminished until they faded completely into the gray bleakness of the countryside. She slumped into a seat alone and sobbed quietly, her face awash with tears.

The Adventure Begins

The 2,400-mile train ride to New York gradually anesthetized the pain of separation and surprisingly, turned out to be fun. Evelyn thought of it as a prolonged picnic as she and the Monges prepared their own meals in one of the train kitchens while they rumbled eastward. Christmas was spent in New Jersey with relatives, then on December 27 the threesome left for New York to meet the SS *Manchuria* for Cuba. They sailed on December 30.

On 2 January 1928 the trio disembarked in Havana. Evelyn strained to take in the strange sights—billboards she could not read and conversations she could not understand. At midnight, they boarded a train for the two hundred-mile trip to Cumbre, where they would detrain for the final two-mile trek to Lavastida's school. Slumping into her seat, she reflected on the crowded events of the day. One thought seemed to dominate her muse: "How different it all is. Everything is so green, so different from the cold, snowbound Canada we just left."

Dawn was breaking on January 3 when the threesome stiffly detrained at the Cumbre junction. It was still semidark, a persistent drizzle compounding the gloom of the moment. A quick survey of the platform sank their spirit. No one had come to meet them. Like a gray mist, a sense of abandonment now settled on Evelyn. Hattie and Efraín understood perfectly. The first time they had arrived at Cumbre, no one had been there to meet them. Worse, it had been raining.

Rutted roads clotted with mud looked impassable. Leaving their baggage beside the railroad tracks, the two veterans and their novice companion sloshed their way through the three miles to the children's school. Evelyn had worked hard to prepare herself for primitive living while planning her trip to Cuba. Now it seemed she should have worked harder. She had never expected to live in a half-built house. It resembled a box car perched on stilts three feet above ground. Nor had she ever expected window openings with no windows, no protective bars, and no curtains or blinds for privacy. Finding some gunnysacks, she hung them over the rough openings. With a sigh, she sat down. It was her first lesson in improvisation.

The day was chilly and damp, and the house was drafty. Evelyn McElheran was cold, and feeling sorry for herself. This time there was no bed on which to collapse. Just a cot. Stretching herself on its length, she pulled the covers over her and gave way to sobs. It was the train ride from Three Hills all over again.

Thank Heaven for Little Girls

The little orphan girls who lived in the school dorm sensed that Evelyn was blue. Just how they discovered that, nobody knew. Peeking in on the new missionary, the girls nattered at her in Spanish. What they said was incomprehensible to Evelyn, but she understood they were beckoning her to follow them.

Touched by their charm, Evelyn hurried after them. Watching their black hair bob up and down as they ran ahead, she was encouraged by their offer of friendship. Once in their dorm, she shared their smiles as they showed off their pet rabbits and rambled on in the unknown tongue she would need to learn quickly. Returning to her sparse quarters after her visit with the students, Evelyn found herself at peace. The affection of the little girls had found its mark. As she reflected in the quiet of her room, she remembered the commitment she had made to God.

> "I determined to embrace the cross," she recalled, "and in a more cheerful spirit, unpacked my bags and put things in place. I would adopt this land to which God had called me as my own."[322]

24

Elmer

I lacked confidence in my soul about the idea. Maybe it was impetus and courage to wait on God about the matter that I then lacked . . . the idea of launching out alone and leading such an enterprise . . . scared me into complete retreat.

—Elmer V. Thompson

The Choice

Elmer V. Thompson's earthly advent took place in Kiowa, Colorado on 4 August 1901. He was the first-born of ranchers James and Freda Thompson, both devout and dedicated to the work of God.

Patriarch Jim Thompson was an active type, his daughter recalled, "a wonderful Christian man!" He started the Bijou Baptist Church in Elbert County. Of the six children—two brothers and four sisters, Lester would become a Baptist preacher and later president of the Conservative Baptist Association. Of the four girls—Flora, Velma, Alice, and Mary—Mary was the youngest, and would one day marry her childhood sweetheart, Louis Markwood.

The Thompson spread lay seventy miles southeast of Denver in Elbert County, commanding a clear view of majestic Pike's Peak, less than forty miles away. Corn and beans made up the usual crop on the family farm and caring for this and for a small dairy herd allowed little free time. Whether bringing strays in from pasture or checking crops, Elmer grew up in the saddle. The ranch was Thompson's world, and throughout his teens, he knew little else. Although converted at age eleven, he did not commit himself to the Lord until he was twenty-one and "God had broken his self-will through two very personal losses."[323]

As the eldest son, Elmer knew that the family ranch would someday be his—if he would promise to farm it—but that attractive prospect seemed to collide with a growing awareness that God wanted him in the ministry. In the cornfields of the family ranch, Elmer had knelt as a boy to promise God he would become a preacher.

He had been saving to buy a car, but his father's counsel brought him to a crisis: "You've been restless this summer . . . You've thought about the ministry . . . Better decide if you want to use your money to buy a car or study." Retreating to the rows of corn where he had earlier met with God, Elmer Thompson wrestled with the first major decision of his life. Would it be the car? Or would it be Bible school?

His parents had virtually marinated their offspring in Scripture, so Elmer knew the words by rote, and had often read them—*"Not my will, but Thine be done."* (Luke 22:42) He now faced the choice between an automobile and Bible school, and the long-familiar words suddenly assumed a costly intimacy. Now they became *his* prayer. With the yielding, came release. An ebullient Thompson burst into the farmhouse and announced, "I am going to school!" He immediately began his preparation at Midland Bible Institute in Kansas City, where he studied for two years. When Midland closed in 1923, he followed his mentor, W. C. Stevens, to the Simpson Bible Institute in Seattle, graduating in May 1925. The same month Leslie E. Maxwell invited him to teach at Prairie Bible Institute. He would be there for just two years.

Cuba's Call

Elmer Thompson was neither adventuresome nor self-reliant by nature, so in the spring of 1927 when Hattie Kirk Monge began to talk to him about Cuba, she rang no bells. He recalled,

> She bore evidence of a heaven-given burden for this project and was most persuasive in her presentation. She assured me the possibilities for the suggested school were real, the need acute, and helpers available. I [was impressed], but lacked confidence in my soul about the idea. Maybe it was impetus and courage to wait on God about the matter that I then lacked . . . the idea of launching out alone and leading such an enterprise . . . scared me into complete retreat.[324]

Thompson rejected outright Hattie's proposal and determined to spend another winter teaching at PBI. Then, two things happened that changed his mind. PBI was still short-staffed, and there was no one to take Thompson's place. He had earlier tried to interest a friend in the teaching post, but was unsuccessful. Just before the 1927–28 fall term began, the friend wrote to say that he had been wrong in declining the offer and was now willing to relieve Thompson if he wished to go abroad. The letter shook Thompson's confidence in his decision to remain at Prairie. However, it was the second incident that clinched the decision to go to Cuba.

A few days before Evelyn McElheran left for the Caribbean, Thompson was invited to the McElheran home for an evening meal. It was one of the "infrequent dinner invitations that came during those years" and Thompson accepted. He relates the mystique of the encounter:

> Something happened that evening. I do not know how or why, but I came away personally impressed by and attracted to the missionary girl going to Cuba.[325]

Apparently, Thompson had not been attracted to Evelyn until that moment, although not for want of opportunity. She had been a student in his class. "I had not the slightest personal interest in her, neither did she have any interest in me," he affirmed. "Furthermore, I had no convictions then of going to Cuba, the island for which she was leaving." Dinner at McElherans changed all that. The pieces were coming together for Thompson and "things moved fast." With Evelyn in the mix, Hattie's Cuba had become very attractive.

Juxtaposed, the two incidents gave Thompson pause. Reconsidering his rejection of Hattie's Cuba proposition, he gave himself to prayer and noted:

> Within a few days, I became convinced the Lord was leading me to prepare . . . for the gigantic task which I had refused. I still was filled, and justly so, with many fears and misgivings, but I now had assurance from God that he was leading and would help me.

As 1927 ended, Elmer V. Thompson piled into his coupe and drove back to Colorado to see the ranch he had traded for the call of God. There were no regrets. Within a few weeks, he was in the former Spanish colony.

Elmer Thompson had not sailed with the Monges and Evelyn. Catching a *Pacific and Orient Lines* vessel out of Miami, he and Roger Kirk arrived in Havana on January 13, just 12 days after Hattie, Efraín, and Evelyn.[326] Roger had returned to Canada to tend family and farm. Now back in Havana, there were things to do before catching the train to Placetas. A reconnaissance trip took them twenty-five miles into the countryside. They checked out truck gardening, Cuban style, where beans, corn, cabbage, oranges, and bananas were growing. The foray produced a black gasoline stove, which they bought for forty-three dollars. Hattie would make good use of the three burners and the oven. Perhaps her life would be easier now. Roger felt relieved.[327]

Seventeen hours later the men wearily stretched out on a bench in the Havana station to await the train to Placetas. It had been a long day. While Kirk thought about farming, Elmer was enjoying the summer weather—in sharp contrast to the Alberta winter he had left behind. At last, the train belched to a halt along the platform. Exhausted, the two men collapsed on the car's slatted benches, and slept their way to Placetas, where they arrived the next morning.

For Thompson, the first sight of the rustic campus took some adjusting. Colorado was never like this. Same for Alberta. Five years in operation, the school housed twenty-five—four staff members, the rest children and teenagers.

There was a dormitory designed for twenty, a dining and kitchen facility, two simple homes, and a granary. They stood in sharp contrast to the American-style cottage Efraín had built for Hattie. Since it was clear that Thompson would require his own accommodations, plans were made to add a "prophet's chamber" to the Monge residence. Meanwhile, he would stay in Mr. Lavastida's room while the pastor was away.

Settling In

Roger Kirk had intended his second trip to Cuba to prepare the land for farming and to conduct some experiments in irrigation. "If it works good," he wrote his wife, "it can be tried on a larger scale next year. I carried one hundred pails of water from the river today. It has been very hot lately, over 90 in the shade."[328] Thompson, meanwhile, tackled the language. "If I don't learn this," he mused, "leaving Prairie Bible Institute will have been futile."

Evelyn kept the family in Three Hills abreast of events.

> There is hardly a thing here with which to work the farm—no harness, no cultivator, no harrow. I don't know what would have happened to this farm if Uncle Roger had not come.

One thing was clear: Roger's passage money had not been wasted. She continued:

> They have written to the States about harness and wagon. You can't get second hand stuff here. If you could see the plow they have and horses to match! It is hard to get the natives to see as we do . . . Uncle Roger sure is patient and this farm problem is so on his mind that he can't get down to language study. They plant potatoes so close together they don't get back much more than seed. They plant corn and beans in between to save the ground.

Evelyn was pleased with her uncle's skill in handling Lavastida:

> He goes very carefully, studies a thing out so he knows what he is talking about, then he goes to him and reasons it out in a quiet way and finally gets his own way. Mr. Lavastida has given him a piece of land for us, so he is busy getting it plowed. You would laugh if you saw them at it with such horses, but they are working better now. He has some seed in, and if they see what we can raise, it will encourage them, so pray that we have a good crop . . . I am glad Uncle Roger came. The Lord has given him wisdom and is using him here.[329]

While Evelyn watched Roger's farming progress from a distance, she observed Elmer Thompson at close quarters. Aunt Hattie was their language tutor. As she and Thompson studied together, Evelyn found Spanish to be a more pleasant exercise than she had expected.

Adjustments

Evelyn McElheran's lifestyle changed abruptly. There was no refrigerator and no electricity. Clothes were washed at the river by beating them to death on smooth stones. Certain there must be a better way, they combed the town to find a galvanized tub. Then they sent to Canada for a tin plunger. They mounted the wash tub on rocks. Underneath, a wood fire quickly brought the water to a boil. The poor fellow pumping the tub of clothing with the plunger looked like a human motor. Clothes were wrung out by hand. Barbed wire served as clothesline.

Adjustments seemed endless. Uncle Roger had said never to go outside without a hat. Evelyn complied. A radical shift in diet called for special grace—horsemeat, ginnie (a rodent similar to a ground hog), rabbit, codfish, and local beans. Uninvited guests complicated life—spiders, crickets, gadflies, grasshoppers, rats, mice, lizards, ants without number, and that bane of the tropics, the cockroach. "All cockroaches not killed yet." she noted. Perhaps these unwelcome novelties had produced the nightmares. Hattie Monge informed Evelyn that she had cried out in her sleep, making "the same kind of noise" as the day she lifted the curtains and a lizard crawled out . . ." Long hours of language study left her mentally exhausted. Unrelenting tropic heat induced a paralyzing lassitude. Evelyn McElheran, the first missionary from Prairie Bible Institute, had entered the fight for which God had prepared her, no small thanks to her mother, Mabel Kirk McElheran.

Meanwhile, Hattie Kirk Monge's role as a catalyst was nearing completion. Her only reason for coming to Cuba had been "to be a link between Prairie [PBI] and the mission field." Elmer and Evelyn were now engaged to be married. They had a grasp of the language and were accepted by the Cubans. Hattie pondered whether it was time to leave: "Had we done our little part?" A Sunday afternoon was set aside to seek the answer. It came, "almost audibly." It was time to go home.[330]

Fading into History

Hattie and Efraín Monge left Cuba in the fall of 1928, not long after their arrival with Evelyn. They had remained long enough to see Evelyn McElheran and Elmer Thompson established on the island, wedding plans in place. With L. E. Maxwell's installation in Three Hills, Hattie's role as catalyst in starting Prairie Bible Institute was complete. Now her mission to put Lavastida's New Pines school on the road to Bible institute status had also been realized. Her mission accomplished, Hattie Kirk Monge returned to the Canadian prairies to fade quietly into history.[331]

The Wedding

Meanwhile, with Aunt Hattie gone, Evelyn McElheran was isolated and lonely. Still struggling with Spanish, she had no English-speaking relatives or friends. Wedding plans must be made, but she was unaware of local customs, and had little money.

Noting the couple's dilemma, Lavastida summoned his parishioners to the rescue. Isabel Junco,[332] the school matron, stepped in as surrogate mother, helping Evelyn through the details. Days later the church was abuzz with preparations. Isabel took care of the wedding dress. Church ladies worked out the menu. Schoolboys dutifully prepared the limousine—brushing down the mules and shining the saddles! Flowers were abundant. The sanctuary was adorned to perfection, and Lavastida himself would perform the ceremony.

September 10, 1928 was the big day. Evelyn recalled:

> I don't know who was more excited, Elmer and I, or the girls in the school. Did you ever hear of a young couple going to their wedding on mule back? Well, that is what we did. There was no road for vehicles from where we were to Placetas. The boys had the mules brushed down and the saddles shining ready to go. The big, white, sluggish mule was for me, and Elmer mounted the more spirited brown mule. Off we set for Placetas accompanied by our friends from the school and farm. Two happier young people it would have been hard to find.

In the pastor's apartment adjoining the Presbyterian Church, arrangements had been made for the required civil ceremony. To Evelyn's relief, the selected maid of honor spoke English. Inside the sanctuary, three hundred guests had come to witness the wedding of the first Americans to be married in Placetas. Pastor Lavastida brought a brief message in Spanish, which neither Elmer nor Evelyn was able to fully catch. The vows followed: "*Si, Señor*," and "*Yo lo prometo*." That much they understood: "Yes, Sir," and "I promise." The couple knelt together before the Lord while Lavastida asked God's guidance and blessing on their life and walk together. As they rose from their knees, a large paper bell, hanging above them, but unnoticed by the pair, suddenly opened to shower them with fragrant rose petals. In joyous gesture, the people of Placetas Presbyterian Church sent the happy couple on their way. That evening they boarded a train to the coastal city of Cardenas for a ten-day honeymoon, all provided by their Cuban friends. Two weeks later, Elmer and Evelyn Thompson would begin the work of their lives.

25

The Cuba Bible Institute

Right then and there in the afternoon stillness I laid it all on the altar as a sacrifice to God on behalf of the Gospel and those to whom God had planned that I take the message of salvation in Christ. God helped me understand that I must lay aside the arms that Satan was trying to get me to take up.

—Florentino Toirac

A Tree Grows in Cuba

The Cuba Bible Institute opened on 25 September 1928, with twelve students, five years after B. G. Lavastida's New Pines school had first welcomed the community youngsters of Jagüeyes. A dozen years had passed since Lavastida's vision at the bedside of an underprivileged tenement child in Havana. The chrysalis had been long in the making, but God was in the metamorphosis, and the new life to emerge would more than fulfill Lavastida's dream of a free Cuba.

From the outset, all had agreed that name, Pinos Nuevos (New Pines), should continue to designate the new Bible Institute as it had the farm school. The carry over was inevitable. The warp and woof of the Lavastida fabric was deeply dyed with José Martí's patriot dream. Separating the man from the New Pines motif was unthinkable. A bust of Martí would stand in the courtyard of the Institute, a perpetual reminder of Lavastida's hope for Cuban Youth.

It may surprise the reader to learn that there was no West Indies Mission in 1928. The Cuba Bible Institute—as Los Pinos Nuevos would be known in North America—*was* the Mission. The West Indies Mission would not come into being for another eight years—in 1936—with the opening of its first off-shore work in Haiti.

Likewise, everyone had agreed that B. G. Lavastida's original school—constructed on Don Telesforo's bramble patch—would be the site of the Bible Institute. The decision was hardly difficult since there was no other place to go. Thompson knew that the location could only be temporary. Access to both the railway and to the main road was difficult, a fact that would limit growth. It did have a farm, however, thanks to Roger Kirk, and the farm was essential to a Bible school serving country people who had little money. Another factor gave Thompson pause. Converting the orphanage into a Bible school had been a major concession on Lavastida's part. This was no time to press the advantage. Moving the school must wait for a more opportune moment. When the Bible school finally opened, it was with an international faculty. Elmer Thompson was from the States, Evelyn Thompson from Canada, Bartholomew Lavastida from Cuba, and Isabel Junco—the school matron—was from Spain.

A Vision Tested

Thompson was jubilant. He would develop the curricula and program. Lavastida would recruit suitable students while continuing his role as Presbyterian pastor in nearby Placetas. The newlyweds moved into the home built by Efraín and Hattie Monge. Lavastida had scoured the countryside in search of students and brought good news. He had enrolled twelve—six men and six women. Each met the primary qualifications—love for God, willingness to accept a simple lifestyle, and dedication to aggressive study. None, however, had anything beyond a grade school education.

Requirements were simple: A Bible, notebooks, clothing, bed and bedding, and one dollar per month tuition. The school would provide housing and food free of charge. Classes would be held mornings only, Monday through Friday. This left male students free to work the school farm afternoons, from 1:00 to 4:00, Anastasio Diaz directing. Women students were kept busy from 1:00 to 3:00 with household chores under the direction of Mrs. Junco. For four months, life at the institute flowed smoothly. Then the tests came like a succession of earthquakes.

"Mama" Junco became ill and was unable to remain in the women's dormitory, where she lived with her husband. This made it necessary for the newlyweds to surrender their house to the Juncos, so that Isabel might have a quiet place to convalesce. Two small rooms in the women's dorm had been reserved for Mr. Lavastida's campus visits. These now became the Thompson's living quarters. With Mrs. Junco ill, Evelyn joined Mrs. Diaz in the oversight of the women students, kitchen responsibilities, and housekeeping. Notwithstanding, an even greater trial was about to sift the Thompsons.

The Cortes Bank

The Cortes Bank of Placetas held all Bible School reserve funds. It also held the Thompsons' savings and wedding gift money. A few months into the first year of the Cuba Bible Institute, Cortes Bank failed. The Thompsons lost everything. Years later Thompson would remember:

> Had we been members of an organized mission agency we could have laid our situation before its leadership, but we had no such affiliation. The only institution with which we had any link was Prairie Bible Institute. However, the leaders of PBI had made it plain that while they trusted me and would help financially as they could, they would not assume financial responsibility for the school. We therefore were not inclined to even mention our need to these friends. Relatives and friends were the only other recourse. These, however, had already given generously. In fact, some of the money we lost had come from them. We could not and would not appeal to them. We were shut in with God.
>
> Thankfully, we did not feel shut out of His concern and care. We . . . could not feel that He intended to let our project fail. It seemed so needed in Cuba and had begun with such bright prospects. We prayed a great deal. I must confess that I also worried. Evelyn's faith was stronger.[333]

As with H. Grattan Guinness before him, the life and ministry of James Hudson Taylor, of China Inland Mission fame, had influenced Thompson. Taylor's biography, written by Geraldine Guinness, had become a treasured guide, particularly the example of Taylor's unswerving trust in God's supply for all needs. Pursuing Taylor's example, the Thompsons enlisted the prayers of their handful of students to invoke God's supply for the Institute in its crisis hour. The answer came in a steady stream of gifts, at first a trickle, but sufficient to put the books in the black by the end of the year.

The stock market crash of 1929 further tested the mettle of the fledgling work. Increased income had marked the last two months of the school year. Thompson expected this additional inflow to continue during the summer and so allow the fall program to open with reserves in place. It did not happen. When classes ended, giving dropped off. What monies did come in during the summer scarcely covered living expenses for the Thompsons and the three or four workers who remained at the school. Now, with the fall term almost upon them, they were without reserves.

A Brief Respite

Lavastida's wife had gone to Pennsylvania to convalesce from tuberculosis. Wishing to visit her, he asked Thompson to assume pastoral duties at the First Presbyterian Church in Placetas during the summer trimester, an offer

Thompson gladly accepted. He and Evelyn could now enjoy the small apartment in the church. Evelyn was well into her first pregnancy, and the more commodious quarters offered welcome relief from dormitory life.

Each week Elmer trekked from Placetas to the school to help Anastasio with the farm work. Burdened over the lack of finances, he continued to cry out to God for a timely intervention. Upon returning to Placetas one Saturday evening, he put the plaintive question to Evelyn:

"Any money come in this week?"

"Not a nickel, Elmer."

"I can't understand this! Have you been to the post office today?"

"No, I haven't."

"I'm going down right now. Can't stand this tension another minute."

A brisk walk through the darkened streets took him to the post office. Hope was in suspense as he opened Box 131. Surely, there would be a letter and a check. Reaching into the box, he extracted a magazine, the dim light revealing a copy of *Moody Monthly*. Disappointed, Thompson groped the inside of the box once more. Nothing. He shoved the magazine under his arm, plunged his hands into his pockets, and dejectedly started home. Later he would recall:

> My heart was broken. In my prayer times during the week, I had come to the place of assurance that God was going to meet our need. Now this. It seemed He had failed me. Then the thought came, "Could it be that God has something for me in this magazine?"

> When I came to a street light I flipped open the cover page an on the inside, printed in dark letters at the top, these words stared at me: *"Your Heavenly Father knoweth that you have need of all these things."*[334]

> The sharp sword of the Spirit penetrated to the depth of my being . . . I was rebuked for my doubt and at the same time assured that He was aware of our needs in the work we were doing for Him and He would supply all of our needs always."

A chastened Elmer Thompson was walking in the footsteps of his hero and mentor, Hudson Taylor. God beckons all to tread the same path— *"Prove me now, and see . . ."* Few follow. In the darkness of a Cuban post office, God was putting shape to the way of faith that would mark the man and the Mission.

Tensions

Elmer Thompson had been absorbed in the routine of classroom preparation and lectures and was not always aware of the currents of trivia flowing within the school staff. Two of the staff members had been employees in the Lavastida home for children before it became a Bible institute. Anastasio had farmed the land, but was now a student, continuing his farm work outside of classes. Nica was a teacher from Lavastida's church in Placetas. She had developed the curriculum for the Bible institute, and taught the scheduled secular subjects.

Unknown to Thompson, Nica was romantically attracted to Mr. Lavastida, and, knowing his wife was critically ill, began to envision herself as the second Mrs. Lavastida. Also unknown to Thompson, she would take the Cuban aside each time he visited campus to relate, and sometimes question, Elmer Thompson's decisions.

Oblivious to these maneuvers, Thompson began to realize that his authority as administrator of the Institute was being undermined. Whenever the Cuban pastor returned to campus from his church duties or from one of his evangelistic tours, he immediately assumed control, undercutting Thompson's authority.

A confrontation finally erupted when Lavastida arrived on campus one day and reprimanded Anastasio. The rebuke was public and it was severe. Thompson's patience evaporated. Striding swiftly toward the two men, he stepped in. Taking Lavastida aside, he said firmly:

> We cannot have dual leadership here. When problems arise, I seek to handle them immediately, but I cannot do so effectively if you countermand them. I want to be named director of the school.

Lavastida was surprised—more by the allegation than by Thompson's confrontation. He asked forgiveness and agreed to the request. Elmer Thompson was named Director of the New Pines Bible Institute.

If conceding leadership of the institute came with relative ease for B. G. Lavastida, Thompson's next request would not be granted so readily. By the end of the second school year, the new director was increasingly uncomfortable with the location of the School.

The Move

There were good reasons to move New Pines from Jagüeyes. The land—never good at best—failed to produce adequately. For several students the location was hard to reach. Moreover, in five years' time, the buildings had run down and the place was shabby. Lavastida, however, loved the farm. His emotional roots were deep in its soil. Much of the ground he had cleared with his own hands. Nor could he ever forget the providence that had brought it to him— that missed train connection six years earlier. Jagüeyes had been God's fulfillment of his dream, and it was sacred.

Elmer Thompson, unfettered by Lavastida's nostalgia, grew adamant: "We must move!" Lavastida was rock solid. He refused to budge, declaring with a nonnegotiable finality, "No."

Thompson resorted to reasoning: "The nearest town is six miles away but it does not even have a public road. There are no telephones, no electric lights or power and no prospect of any of these benefits. If we are going to make any real progress—" Lavastida interrupted the sentence: "No." Only later would Thompson admit to another, more subjective reason that had made him reluctant to go to Jagüeyes in the first place. "The buildings were like those of the Cuban farmers—thatched, with whitewashed walls and dirt floors," he confessed. "I was prone to think my missionaries and I were above living in such simple circumstances."[335]

In 1929, Evelyn's sister, Muriel McElheran, joined the work. She arrived with a new couple—the John Montgomerys.[336] When the trio detrained at Cumbre, they and their baggage were hauled by oxcart to the Institute. The trip was a torture. Thompson was present for the transfer and thought he had found a new argument. He appealed to Lavastida:

> If we make a transition now, it will be easy to transport personnel to another location. We can use the saddle horses. If we wait until the number increases, we will have to go on foot—hardly an appropriate way to travel in an age of cars and trains.

Lavastida was more than a match for Thompson's arguments. He rejoined:

> God provided the money and lumber to construct the needed buildings here. He blessed the institution as a children's home and He has blessed it even more now that it is a Bible institute. Much prayer and sacrifice has gone into this place. I will not move.

Martin Luther once made the point that when two mountain goats traveling in opposite directions meet on the narrow, precipitous trails of the Alps; one lies down to allow the other to pass over its back. Even nature—Luther had explained—teaches submission as the path to conflict resolution.

The standoff continued for six months. Conversations continued. Slowly, Lavastida began to soften. Finally, Thompson proposed a compromise: "Why don't we go to Don Telesforo and offer to give the deed to the land back to him if he will agree to let us take down the buildings and transfer the lumber to a new site?"

For the first time, B. G. Lavastida softened and agreed to the change. When Telesforo posed no objection, Lavastida agreed to take John Montgomery with him to look for a new site. It would have to be a farm, somewhere in the countryside and away from the distractions of city life. Thirty acres near the proposed transnational highway would be about right. The cap, they agreed, should be $3,000. Within two months, the men had found what seemed to be the perfect parcel. The price was $2,300. Thompson flushed with excitement as he surveyed the beautiful valley at a town called Oliver. The parcel was ideal, studded with thirty royal palms and blessed with an orchard. The soil was rich, and nourished by a spring-fed stream.

The fledgling Mission, already stretched with the care of eight staff members and sixteen students, now faced a fresh challenge—how to pay for the new property. Doubt is never far from faith, and Thompson wondered, "Will this new load sink us?" Then he remembered that lonely Saturday night in Placetas a year before. Under a street lamp he had paused to look at his copy of the *Moody Monthly,* when his eyes fell upon the promise: *"Your Heavenly Father knoweth that you have need of all these things."*[337]

Shortly after they signed the contract for the new property, Lavastida shared a secret. His beloved Elsie, who recently had succumbed after a long struggle with tuberculosis, had willed $600 toward a new property. For Elmer Thompson, the gift was sacred—a token of God's approval of their step of faith. Lavastida personally added several hundred dollars to his wife's gift, and each of the missionaries contributed to defray the outstanding balance. A few gifts from friends in Canada made up the $1,200 down payment. Another $500 followed from various sources. Thompson put in the final $600. It was as sacred to Elmer as that of Elsie Lavastida. It had come from his aged father.

The New Pines Bible School moved from Jagüeyes to Oliver in April 1930, where it would remain for the next 70 years. Cuban Dictator Machado had constructed the new Central Highway, which virtually connected the town of Oliver with Havana. The Bible Institute was now conveniently located just eight kilometers from a major two-lane, transnational asphalt highway that linked the capitals of four provinces.[338] While the Los Pinos school still had no electric lights—they would not arrive until the 1940s—the move had put them closer to that possibility. Meanwhile, they continued to use carbide lamps for study. A tobacco shed was converted into a chapel, only now it was called "The Tabernacle"—just like Prairie Bible Institute's worship center. The first graduation took place in the spring of 1932 in conjunction with the fourth annual convention. Among the six graduates was Anastasio Diaz, who had been caretaker of Lavastida's original school.

Chemistry of an Ethos

The ethos of the Cuba Bible institute emerged from a blend of influences. B. G. Lavastida had been groomed at McCormick Theological Seminary, a Presbyterian school not widely regarded as conservative, even in 1920. When he married Elsie Lines, he married a Wheaton college professor whose theology had been shaped at Nyack, under the influence of A. B. Simpson and the Christian and Missionary Alliance.[339]

When Lavastida and Thompson melded their backgrounds to form the new Bible Institute, a further element was added. Thompson had taught for two years at Prairie Bible Institute before coming to Cuba. William Coit Stevens, also from Nyack and a protégé of Albert B. Simpson, had mentored both Thompson and Prairie Bible Institute principal, L.E. Maxwell. Both men— Maxwell and Thompson—shared Steven's distrust of higher education. Pride of intellect was a danger attendant upon the pursuit of advanced degrees, and the credentials of academia were therefore not to be sought.[340] But there was more.

On cultural issues, both Maxwell and Thompson shared a more narrow view of what constitutes Biblical separation. They reflected their times and to a large extent, the conflict then raging between fundamentalism and modernism. Not that the mores they held and taught were either invalid or unbiblical. On the contrary, the convictions they infused into the Bible Institutes they founded, however onerous to some, produced character. Both men viewed Bible school as a place of preparation for life's highest calling. It demanded discipline and concentration. Fraternization between the sexes was a distraction. So was "worldly" dress. Neither could be tolerated. The problem, of course, lay in defining worldliness as measured against the irreducible content of the gospel message—the *Kerugma*.[341] Within the confines of the Canadian Prairies and a particular stratum of North American evangelicalism, specific codes of conduct and of dress could be applied with relative ease. Exporting these standards to another country and culture was another matter.

Codes and Kerugma

In September 1931, at the age of seventeen, Florent Toirac enrolled in the New Pines Bible school and seminary in Placetas. Born amid the banana, coconut, and sugar cane plantations of Oriente Province in Eastern Cuba, Florent and his siblings had been boyhood playmates of Fidel Castro. He would later found and lead the Spanish World Gospel Mission to a worldwide ministry, winning Oswald J. Smith's accolade, "The Moody of the Antilles." First, as a student and later as a missionary with the West Indies Mission, he knew it well. His bumpy ride as a student at New Pines is an education in the clash of cultures:

Every student had to give three hours of work a day to help maintain the farm. This helped us pay our expenses, and it served to teach us to live a practical and humble life.

The schedule was very strict, starting at 5:30 A.M. and ending at 10:00 P.M. Saturdays were set aside for cleanup and preparation for Sunday and the following week . . . Classes were held in the mornings with afternoons reserved for work. Two hours of required study were reserved in the evenings from 7:00–9:00. Any activity other than study during those hours required special permission.[342]

Toirac immediately collided with code enforcement, quite certain that student rules "were more appropriate for prisoners in a penitentiary than for [Bible] institute students!"[343] He ticked off his grievances:

> The hated khaki uniforms
> No radios (radio music was worldly)
> No short hair-dos for the ladies
> No make-up other than powder
> Hem lines below the knees
> No bobbysox—only hose for the ladies (too costly and hot for the tropics)
> No conversation between the sexes
> No greetings between the sexes[344]

Toirac described his impatience with the regulations on gender separation:

> We went out to the city four times a month on Monday afternoons from 1:.00 p.m. to 5:00 p.m. However, men and women were not allowed to leave together on the same day. We had to take turns: the men went one Monday, the women the next. So, in reality we got out only twice a month. Men and women could not converse unless a teacher was present. We could not even greet each other! I really disliked that rule, since I was outgoing and considered myself a man. On our farm, we had been used to saying "good morning" to everyone, even to the dogs! Here I could not even greet the opposite sex.[345]

While Toirac's resentment simmered, the infection was spreading.

> Outside the school gates, no one lived like that. But at the Institute, any lifestyle other than the one depicted was considered worldly.

Toirac wrestled with his rebellion. Should he leave the school? The crisis came on an afternoon when his classmates had gone to town. Alone, he poured out his heart to God for victory and for a solution to the problem. The answer came:

Right then and there in the afternoon stillness I laid it all on the altar as a sacrifice to God on behalf of the Gospel and those to whom God had planned that I take the message of salvation in Christ. God helped me understand that I must lay aside the arms that Satan was trying to get me to take up. The Bible was to be my absolute authority for resisting evil. To be a successful man of God that He could freely use meant to deny one's own desires, [and] take up the cross . . . God gave me the victory to hang on in spite of what I didn't like at the institute.[346]

Toirac had learned the quintessential qualification of the man or woman God uses: Submission is the path to liberation, and "almost always means submission to someone He has put over us." [347] The template was in the Godhead itself—in the Son's submission to the Father. In the God-designed hierarchies of life—family, government, and even angelic realms, submission to authority is the basis of a harmonic universe. Florent Toirac met God clearly, fully, and finally. The evidence? He encouraged his three brothers—Rafael, Moises, Eliseo—and his sister, Juanita, to attend Los Pinos. They did.

Toirac's surrender to the Institute rules was no evidence that his grievances were without warrant. On the contrary. Nevertheless, his attitude had changed. Were the regulations justifiable? To ask is to miss the point. For Toirac, they had served as God's litmus test of character. Once that lesson had been mastered, the propriety of the institute codes could be examined objectively. Did they reflect Biblical values? On the other hand, were they simply cultural imports? One alarming fact had gone unnoticed: The conduct and dress codes introduced at Los Pinos had been interpreted by many Cubans as normative marks of the Christian message, and were transferred by the emerging Cuban leadership to new congregations as the standard of Biblical conduct. In Toirac's words:

> The strict rules governing the life of the Bible Institute were automatically passed on to the new converts. In the same way, these rules became normative in the local churches, making them synonymous with Christianity. Therefore, some new believers left the Institute and its affiliate churches.

> Worst of all, as the missionary association grew and the times changed, new missionaries from less strict backgrounds in Canada and the United States arrived in Cuba. They came with short curly hair, hemlines at the knees or above, wearing makeup and bobbysox, listening to radios, et cetera. The students, other believers, and national pastors were horrified. The Bible Institute had caused them to equate the rules with a godly life, and now the new missionaries were tearing down what had been built up over the years by the first missionaries.[348]

Toirac viewed this importation of cultural baggage not only as an accretion to the Biblical message, but as a practice which had dire consequences:

The original missionaries tried to tell the new ones that these rules were part of Cuban Christian culture. This set up a conflict between the nationals and the older missionaries. It was all a result of man trying to act as God for another man and replacing the power of the Holy Spirit with man-made rules of conformity. It began in the conservative schools the original missionaries attended and was transmitted to them by their converts. As cultures and sub-cultures change and flow with the changes of modern times, it is inevitable that man's rules will fail. Only that which is solidly founded on the Word of God will stand. Anything else causes division.[349]

In consequence, some of the Bible Institute rules were tempered. The immutable principle of submission to authority as the *sine qua non* of Biblical leadership had not changed and would become one of the emerging principles of Worldteam—the concept of servant leadership. None of these inconveniences dismayed Toirac to the point of quitting. After his meeting with God, he would assess the Institute in positive terms. And the lessons learned by the new Mission would become part of the essential orientation of all new missionaries—all teaching and practice introduced by expatriates into a new culture must be examined for its nonnegotiable Biblical content, and that content expressed in culturally relevant terms.

The Annual Conference

To awaken Christians and challenge them to the evangelization of Cuba and the West Indies, Thompson and Lavastida designed a three-day annual conference to coincide with graduation exercises. The gatherings, held just before the spring rains, had three objectives: Win people to Christ, help Cuban Christians grow in knowledge and service, and honor graduating students.

The annual conferences became a Cuban mecca. Hundreds poured into New Pines on foot, on horseback, or in trucks and busses. On Friday, the meetings began. To accommodate guests, hammocks were slung in designated areas. Folding cots lined the tabernacle and men's dormitory. Ladies occupied the women's dormitory and some of the missionary homes. Students gave up their beds to guests, making their own sleeping platforms with blankets on piles of dried banana leaves.

Mr. Lavastida, fluent in both English and Spanish, became the translator for English-speaking guests. Dr. Oswald J. Smith, a major supporter of the school, was one of the early conference speakers. Dr. Allen Fleece, Dr. Marshal Morsey, Dr. L. E. Maxwell, and others, followed him. In a short time, conference attendance soared to an average of one thousand. The impact was dramatic. The Institute began to attract new students, new missionaries, and new exposure in North American churches. Financial support increased, and the Holy Spirit was poured out. Through the ministry of the students, the influence of the school began to spread throughout Cuba.

The Cuba Bible Institute (Los Pinos Nuevos) Faculty and Students, 1936–1937

The Cuba Bible Institute Campus, 1999

26

A Spontaneous Model

The roots of an indigenous church are in the first converts. The training of the first converts is the important matter.

—Roland Allen

The Open Secret

Exactly when the decision was made, no one is certain. From inception, the West Indies Mission adopted a ministry philosophy that would become its distinctive, while winning the admiration and emulation of other agencies. What set WIM apart in Cuba and in its subsequent fields of ministry was the Bible Institute. Bible schools were used to train national workers to reach their own people as opposed to depending on American missionaries to do the preaching and evangelizing. This method was not new, as it had been conducted successfully in Korea and elsewhere. Known as the "Nevius method," after Dr. John Nevius, whose emphasis on preparing nationals to take the initiative in evangelism contributed to explosive growth in the Korean church early in the century. It would become the hallmark of the West Indies Mission.

In the Spring of 1928, Thompson had stood on a hill at the geographical center of Cuba, near to the Jagüeyes property where he nurtured the vision for the Cuban people. He counted five hundred thatch-roofed homes identifiable within the range of his gaze—a radius of three miles. He wrestled with the question: "How, Lord? How can my young wife and I reach so many people in our lifetime?"[350] The answer did not come quickly, but when it did, it was patently Biblical, and it worked.

He found the secret in the Apostle Paul's missionary experience in Ephesus. For three months, the magnum evangelist had preached faithfully in the synagogue, only to meet opposition and abuse. Faced with lack of positive response, the Apostle left, taking twelve disciples with him to the lecture hall of Tyrannus. In this locale, Paul trained his protégés for two years. They then went forth to preach. The result was that "all the Jews and Greeks who lived in the province of Asia heard the word of the Lord."[351] The revelation came like a flood of light. For Thompson, this was beyond question the Biblical model for mission.[352]

They were all novices in this business—both the faculty and the students. It was on-the-job training, with the Holy Spirit as instructor. Thompson explained:

> They were taught in God's school of pressures and challenges. They learned the reality of prayer as the problem solver. They discovered the practicality of faith in God's promises for supplying needs. They came to appreciate the power of the Word of God for transforming human character. They came to understand . . . the West Indian people, their ways, their needs, and the ways to work with them.[353]

Instilled into the missionary staff through the hard knocks of experience, this practical wisdom was in turn infused into the students of the Cuba Bible Institute through both precept and example. While North American seminaries were slow to learn the importance of combining practical experience with classroom academics, Elmer Thompson "had reached the conclusion that spiritual formation of leaders could not happen in isolation or detachment from ministry." It was an open secret—the same method Jesus had employed in training the twelve. New Pines students were plunged into the preaching and teaching process during the academic year. Allen Thompson would later describe this didactic model as:

> A holistic approach to curriculum where ministry formation needed to be formation in and for mission . . . This was not superficial involvement in some type of Christian service in existing churches. Rather, it was frontier evangelism, penetrating the villages and towns of central Cuba with the gospel . . . what John Mackay has called doing theology "on the road" instead of "from the balcony."

> Consequently, immature students began to wrestle with the implications of the gospel. Classroom discussions were transformed from theoretical critiques to applying the gospel to immediate and practical concerns . . . [354]

Thompson also concentrated on life-changing theology with his students. Leaving to others the teaching of standard Bible school curricula, he brought his disciples to grips with the critical issues of godly character—practical holiness, the cost of discipleship, and reliance on the grace of God. For this, his syllabus was the book of Romans:

No one escaped immersion in Romans. And no one was the same after that experience with God. Through that course [he] established the *core values* of what became the Evangelical Association of Cuba and influenced hundreds of leaders in every denomination on the island.[355]

Infused with this instruction, New Pines students conducted regular forays into densely populated areas near the campus and established community Sunday school classes. Nevertheless, the bigger question remained. How to replicate the second part of the Ephesus model so that *all* Cuba might hear the Word of the Lord?

The answer took Mission leadership by surprise. Revival frequently broke out in local churches following the annual Bible conventions. New and higher spiritual standards became the hallmark of those congregations attending the yearly "happening." This brought a new sense of urgency both to New Pines Bible Institute and to participating churches and individuals.

The Forerunners

Following one of the conventions, Macedonio Leyva and Rafael Rodriguez, both seniors in the Institute, approached Lavastida and Thompson, sharing their desire to move out into unevangelized farming districts during the summer months to share the gospel.

The young men sought approval and requested modest financial assistance to implement their vision. Lavastida and Thompson were moved, and readily agreed to the venture. Money was another matter. The school could offer no financial support. They would, however, cover tuition costs for the students' final year.

The young men had already seen God meet the financial needs of the school. Now they must trust him for their own. With few resources and no promise of lodging, the two moved out in opposite directions for the summer. When they returned, they were jubilant at the response of the communities they visited.

In Mamey, ten miles north of the school, a church of twenty-five had been established. In Jagüeyes, five miles to the south, a congregation of fifty was now meeting. From the date of their return to campus, New Pines Bible Institute had entered a new era. It had become much more than a place of cognitive theological input. It was now a center of spiritual vision and outreach. Thompson recalled:

> Rafael and Macedonio stirred up evangelization fervor among the students. The very next spring several other students committed themselves to the Lord for gospel service and sought out for themselves places in the farm districts where they could follow the example of the two forerunners . . .

Petitions from country areas and adjoining small towns began to come
in to the Bible Institute asking for workers for their areas . . . Both
sexes responded to these calls. Some of the young women proved to be
very effective church planters. They were highly respected by the men
as well as by the women.

Following graduation, some students returned to the communities where they
had earlier worked in evangelism, and became pastors. That summer laid the
foundations for a work "that in the next ten years was to see several hundred
thousands of Cubans reached with the gospel message and some 10,000 won
for the Lord."[356] Churches sprang up—self-supporting, self-propagating
churches. Preaching points dotted the island and the momentum carried
throughout the country.

It is no wonder—Allen Thompson later mused—that in this atmosphere
of study and action [followed by] obedience in mission and reflection,
God developed some of the influential leaders for the church in Latin
America and through them the ripple effect to countless thousands. Cu-
ban evangelists went to Haiti, the Dominican Republic, Jamaica, the
Canary Islands, Venezuela, and North Africa . . . [357]

The young Mission had found the secret to planting churches, and God had
answered the prayer lifted by Elmer Thompson in the spring of 1928 on a
high hill in central Cuba.[358]

Lavastida Comes Full Time

B. G. Lavastida's plate was full. In addition to pastoral duties at Placetas and
the teaching schedule at the Institute, he had been named moderator of the
Havana Presbytery. Added to this was the burden of separation from Elsie and
their two children. Her illness with tuberculosis required frequent trips to the
US for treatment, and in 1923, her permanent residence in the States became
necessary. This fact called for periodic visits by Lavastida, pulling him away
from church duties until Elsie's home-call seven years later in August 1930.
While these factors limited Lavastida's involvement in the early years of the
Bible Institute, he remained active in all major decisions affecting the New
Pines work.

After Elsie's death Lavastida visited the Presbyterian Church in *San Jose de
Los Ramos* in Matanzas Province. Here he met María Josefa Alvarez, a
teacher he had led to the Lord nine years earlier. Now twenty-five, "Fefita"
was the new spark Lavastida needed, and the seventeen-year age differential
mattered little. They were married on 20 July 1931. Fefita would teach at New
Pines for forty years.[359] The marriage produced two children, and the integration of B. G.'s offspring, now four in number, was solid. Fefita had already
taken Elsie's two into her heart.

In 1934, six years after the founding of the Bible Institute, B. G. Lavastida determined to resign as pastor of the Presbyterian Church of Placetas. He had served the Cuban Presbytery for fourteen years. Now, with the rapid growth of New Pines he sensed that God was leading him to identify more directly with the school, especially with those students dedicated to evangelism. Through the Institute, he could more effectively multiply his efforts in the evangelization of Cuba. He determined to relocate his family to the Institute campus. One day he advised Thompson:

"I have determined to resign my church."

"What has happened?"

"Nothing."

Lavastida explained his shift in priorities, but Thompson was cautious:

"You have been used to a much higher standard of living than we can offer—will you and your wife be content to live on the same economic level as the Institute staff?"

Lavastida nodded affirmation. They had fully considered the matter and believed God would give them the grace to live as did the students and missionaries.

The presence of B. G. Lavastida brought fresh dynamism to the school. Fefita joined the teaching staff. By 1935, *New Pines* was exploding with new life. Sixty students were enrolled while forty-one graduates served in the loosely knit association of churches that Lavastida would eventually organize into the Evangelical Association of Cuba. By the time Fidel Castro's Communist regime took over the country twenty-five years later, the Association had matured to a muscular consortium of one hundred churches and preaching points.

As the New Pines school faced its financial struggles, B. G., out of his meager stipend from the Presbyterian Church, often helped from his own pocket. He, too, had been greatly influenced by the life of George Mueller of Bristol. Mueller's orphanage had its parallels in New Pines, and on its fiftieth anniversary in 1978, the Institute was lauded as "A Work of Faith."

Oswald J. Smith

In the fall of 1935, an unexpected visit brought a timely infusion of hope and encouragement to the New Pines staff. Oswald J. Smith of Toronto's famed Peoples' Church had been speaking at a conference elsewhere on the island, when on a whim he decided to visit the Bible institute, which had caught his attention. He hopped a bus, traveling all night, and at four in the morning arrived, unannounced, at New Pines. He had to leave at 10:00 the same morning, but in six hours Smith was so taken with this work of God, that he gave fifty dollars to Thompson on the spot, inviting him and Evelyn to the People's Church missionary conference in Toronto the following April.[360]

The Thompsons jumped at the invitation and at the close of the conference, Smith called his new friend to his office to announce that People's Church would assume full support of all 17 members of the New Pines staff.[361] More excitement followed. Peoples' Church underwrote construction of a new tabernacle, dining room, several missionary homes, and provided start-up funds for the new work in Haiti.

The boon was timely and the staff was euphoric. The Los Pinos missionaries had scrimped desperately to finance the new move to Haiti, each member sacrificing out of pocket. They now moved ahead in joyful confidence that God was indeed in the effort.[362] From the outset, evangelization through a trained national leadership had been Elmer Thompson's vision. He saw that Bible trained evangelists and pastors were the primary and urgent need of all the gospel agencies working in Cuba. Unfettered by provincialism, the Cuba Bible Institute freely offered its graduates to other agencies.

Several groups in Cuba reciprocated heartily with the Institute during the early years, encouraging their young people to enroll. Several became pastors upon graduation. Later, however, some agencies expressed concern over two of the Institute's practices—the "mass production" of gospel workers and the relatively low level of secular education of a large proportion of its graduates.

Thompson and Lavastida pondered this criticism. Raising academic entry requirements would deprive many Cuban young people of preparation for Christian ministry. This could not be justified in the face of the Great Commission of Christ to his Church. Although other mission and church agencies in Cuba might no longer use New Pines graduates, Thompson and Lavastida determined to continue their policy of Christian education for all.[363]

The Thompson—Lavastida Synergy

The success of the New Pines enterprise may be traced—at the human level— to two primary factors: a highly gifted, God-anointed Cuban evangelist, working in dynamic synergism with an equally gifted theological educator. Lavastida was a national, highly educated, and fluent in both languages. Perhaps more important, he was a Cuban patriot whose pedigree endeared him to the people. He loved them, and they knew it.

This endearment of respect opened doors and won an audience for the gospel that Elmer Thompson could not have achieved alone. If God was to equip and ignite evangelistic fire in Cuban pastors, someone first had to bring them in. B. G. Lavastida was the man. He built a bridge into the Cuban soul.

If B. G. Lavastida was the obstetrician in the birth of the Cuban churches, Elmer V. Thompson was the pediatrician. He provided both the leadership and the theological groundwork for the Bible Institute. These men were two halves of a whole. It was a marriage of distinctive, but complementary gifting. One who knew both men well remarked:

> It would be hard to imagine two more opposite personalities. Lavastida was impulsive, but he had charisma and spoke with poetic charm. While he lacked management skills, he brought people to the Lord in every circumstance. Thompson, on the other hand, was a careful student and teacher, timid to a fault. Speaking of his Cuban colleague, Thompson confessed, 'More than once I thought we could never go on together.'[364]

Notwithstanding, each man gave in to the other. Both had tasted enough of the grace of God to know that each needed the other.

The duality was reflected in the roles that each fulfilled. Lavastida became president of the Association of Evangelical Churches of Cuba, a position he would hold by acclaim until retirement. E. V. Thompson became the director of the Los Pinos Bible Institute and Seminary and general director of the West Indies Mission. The success of this dynamic duo would later lead to the adoption of World Team's maxim; *"Nationals Do It Better."* The synergy of this equally improbable duo likewise modeled a fundamental principle of successful cross-cultural mission—nationals and expatriates must learn to work together in mutual acceptance of the other's idiosyncrasies. Lavastida and Thompson did just that, and good national leadership arose in their wake.

As the Institute work grew, Lavastida grew restless, still burdened for a wider ministry, not only to his compatriots in Cuba, but to the entire Latin American world:

> The Lord enlarged my missionary vision to get the Gospel message not only to the millions of the West Indies, but to the perishing millions who speak my language—Spanish.

In 1941, his wish was about to be fulfilled.

Wings of the Morning

The small missionary family in Cuba had long discussed the dream of an island-wide radio ministry to the Cuban people. Always the roadblock was money. Unless God stepped in with dramatic provision, cost was prohibitive. With no miraculous intervention in sight, the team prayed, left their concern with God, and kept working.

Thompson spent eighteen months in North America to promote the ministry of the Mission. During the itinerary, Dr. Harold J. Ockenga, pastor of Park Street Church in Boston, invited him to participate in their annual ten-day missionary conference. There he met John A. Huffman, an area pastor, who invited Thompson to speak on his morning radio broadcast. While driving back from the studio Huffman asked, "Has the West Indies Mission ever considered radio as part of its ministry?"

Thompson's antennae went up instantly; however, Huffman was an unknown, and Thompson was cautious. "We have." was all he said. Huffman's radio broadcast was called *Wings of the Morning.* It was a daily program and the pastor was sure he could successfully raise funds if Thompson were serious about launching radio as an evangelistic medium in Cuba.

Huffman then assured Thompson that the project would be at no expense to the West Indies Mission. Huffman would raise the money himself. Ever on guard, Thompson parried:

> Well, brother, when you have the money and can come to Cuba we will take it as God's sign to go with radio.

Thompson was confident that he had heard the last from Huffman. Then came the surprise. Unannounced, John Huffman turned up at the Cuba Bible Institute on a Sunday afternoon. He had just three days to give them. Could they whip up a singing group, go to Havana, and record ten programs? Huffman's New England audience had come through, providing him with all the funding necessary to pay for the recordings and airtime.

Thompson needed no further prompting, and the WIM staff scrambled to comply. Joe Jesperson, Eleanor Hansen, Louis Markwood,[365] and his fiancée, Delphine Rasmus, quickly assembled a package of mixed quartette numbers and duets with Delphine on the piano and Joe doing tenor solos. Louis Markwood would emcee the programs and, naturally, B. G. Lavastida would do the preaching.

The impromptu ensemble hopped a bus and took off for the two hundred-mile, four-hour ride to the Havana studio. When their established contact with the Blue Network fell through, the team retired to the hotel to pray for direction. Through default of a client, a one-half hour window was opened to them on CMQ Net—the largest coverage on the island! [366]

On 27 December 1941, *Alas del Alba,* a translation of the title of Huffman's US broadcast, *Wings of the Morning,* was on the air. Weekly Sunday morning programs began in January, offering one half-hour of music and gospel, all in Spanish.

Thompson described the early effort:

> It was the Christian music—Gospel hymns played and sung from the heart—that brought the most results. Over the course of two or three years, we saw a change in the listeners. Gospel radio was breaking

down spiritual indifference and religious prejudice. Thousands who had considered Protestants as heretics or near atheists were seriously considering the claims of Jesus Christ. Hundreds of listeners enrolled in the Bible correspondence courses offered over the radio. In time, many of these courses were introduced to pastors of gospel churches in Cuba.

Seven Chased Three Hundred

WIM's radio ministry achieved a popularity that penetrated the marketplace. In 1943, thousands of Cubans were working in the island's many tobacco factories. Most had never heard the gospel with understanding, and Christians working among them felt a responsibility to share the good news. Evelyn Thompson described the contest that followed one group's effort:

In one factory employees contribute five cents a week to provide radio facilities. Programs run full blast from 7 a.m. to 5 p.m. daily, and what trash is heard! Seizing the opportunity this radio offered for gospel work, seven Christian employees asked the man in charge to air WIM's program, *The Bible School of The Air.*

"I put on the programs the majority favor," he replied, "and I fear these people will not want an evangelical program."

Next morning, to please the seven, he tuned in our program. At once, uproar began. Some shouted, "Turn off that rot!" Others threatened, "If you don't turn that off, we will break your radio." The place was in confusion. Finally, four big men went to the manager and demanded that he turn it off.

"These seven pay the same as you do," the owner replied. "You ought to let them hear the programs they like at least twice a week."

Thereafter the program was aired two mornings a week, but the opposing employees made noise and in every way tried to hinder those who wanted to hear the message. Two weeks later they stirred up another rebellion. Unless *The Bible School of the Air* was turned off, another man would be asked to bring in his radio.

"We shall vote about this thing," said the superintendent, "and regardless of which side wins, I want the losers to keep quiet."

While they were voting, the seven Christians raised a petition to God. Three of the opponents gathered the votes. The owner of the radio stepped up to announce that the evangelical program had the majority! Even some of the rebellious ones had voted for it and the program was put on daily.

Just after the gospel had gone over the air the next morning, an official stopped by one of our students and said, "Do you know why you folks won?"

"Yes, but do *you* know?"

Pointing heavenward, he said, "The people fear Someone!"

Fueled by the radio outreach, WIM's ministry soared. Hundreds of letters poured in from *Alas Del Alba* listeners and the Bible School of the Air programs. Each received a reply. Some sought advice, others comfort and encouragement with personal problems. A Saturday children's broadcast enrolled 210 students in a children's radio class. Radio messages were sent free upon request. It was a rare week when there was not at least one profession of faith.

Radio Shapes WIM Strategy

The West Indies Mission had begun as a rural ministry. Response to the gospel by Cuban farmers formed the core of the early work. Radio changed that. As farmer families migrated to the towns and cities, WIM followed, opening work in Santa Clara, Colon, Placetas, Cienfuegos, and Tunas. Havana was not touched until the 1950s. While normal migration to the urban centers accounted in part for this shift in strategy, the greater factor was the impact of radio. As one wrote, "Our Sunday broadcast over the most powerful and prestigious radio network CMQ put us on the map." Radio integrated the growing movement and created a sense of community among the churches.[367]

And Others . . .

The war years (1941–45) imposed little hardship upon the work of the West Indies Mission. Instead, wartime demand for sugar and war materiel brought prosperity to the country. Some shortages did exist, and travel was limited, and the armed forces of North America absorbed the work force that otherwise might have found its way to the Caribbean basin. Nonetheless, while Europe was in anguish—and the mission agencies based there—Cuba enjoyed the sunshine of Heaven's favor in a harvest time that could never have occurred in the days of Iberian dominance. A sovereign God was grooming his Church in preparation for its own time of testing—long after the global conflict ceased.

By the end of 1945, the New Pines Bible Institute had an enrollment of 120 men and women. B. G. Lavastida was president of the Evangelical Association of Cuba, with seventy-five national workers serving one hundred churches and an aggregate of 7,000 believers. Six Cuban missionaries had been sent out—Zeida Campos, Florentino Toirac, Efraín Raimundo, Mr. and Mrs. Cecil Samuels, and Mr. and Mrs. Secundino Bermudez.

With the close of World War II, the West Indies Mission had enjoyed seventeen years of vigorous and productive life. WIM's Cuba staff had grown with the addition of the Louis Markwoods (1940), the J. K. Jespersons, Irene H. Nims, the Patrick Arnolds (1943), Elizabeth Parkhurst, Betty Piepho, Jean L. Henningson, the Henry Werners, and the Robert Dalkes. Delma Jackson had arrived as secretary to Elmer Thompson. The Graham Wilkersons were running WIM's press, and publishing *El Misionero Bíblico.* Jean Vanderburgh had joined the Cuba-based headquarters staff, and in 1943, Mr. R. M. Maxwell, of Charleston, West Virginia, became WIM's superintendent for the US.

Looking back, it had been a good run.

West Indies Mission Spring Conference, Cuba, 1948.

27

Live Coals in Voodoo Darkness

You intended to harm me, but God intended it for good, to accomplish what is now being done, the saving of many lives.

—Joseph

The *Machadato*

World War I brought boom times to the Cuban sugar industry and demand for labor outstripped supply. Lured by Cuba's better economy and good wages, Haitians poured into eastern Cuba. It was easy to get there. Haiti's western tip lies just a hundred miles due south of Cuba's eastern extremity, the two islands separated by the Windward Passage. Faced with a labor shortage, Cuba required neither passports nor visas. One hundred fifty thousand Haitians made the trip.[368] Like the Jewish exiles in Babylon, they came, sank their roots, raised families, and worked the cane fields. Cuba became home.

In Cuba, thousands of Haitian immigrants came under the sound of the gospel and hundreds became Christians.[369] Students from the Los Pinos Bible Institute had a hand in this harvest, among them Florent Toirac, whose fruitful ministry among them would eventually lead him as a missionary to Haiti itself. He recalled their welcome and generosity:

> I loved to go to their homes to share the gospel and they in turn shared with me their limited provisions. The little old women covered my cheeks with kisses and hugs to show their love. I was indebted to them for their affection and friendship and their hearts, which were receptive to the gospel.

By 1930, however, the tide had turned. The Great Depression dried up jobs, and sinister winds began to blow for the expatriated Haitians. Cuba was in the grip of an economic and political crisis, popularly known as the *machadato,* a derogatory reference to the incumbent president, Gerardo Machado.[370] Cubans petitioned their government for better wages and benefits. Amid cries of "Cuba for Cubans!" they complained that Haitian immigrants were eroding the job base and demanded the repatriation of wartime foreign workers in their country. Havana listened. Haitians were ordered out. In the four years between 1933 and 1937, fifty-five thousand Haitians were forcibly repatriated.

Florent Toirac assessed the government's action:

> It was manslaughter to push them out of Cuba to suffer hunger, sickness, and death in Haiti. But nothing could be done about it. The rural guards went throughout the eastern fields in Cuba and gathered up the Haitian families, rudely forcing them to leave everything that they had . . . They herded them into open sugar cane cars on trains and took them like cattle to the boats that would take them to Haiti. Once in Haiti, they were abandoned.[371]

This callous measure devastated an already impoverished people. Even while in Cuba, Haitian immigrants had lived in harsh conditions, their homes nothing more than Indian huts with palm-leaf roofs and dirt floors. Repatriation dumped thousands of them on the doorstep of their homeland—indigents without connections, shelter, family, or friends. Forced to live on the streets, many of them suffered hunger. Deprived of medical care, they succumbed to tuberculosis, pneumonia, or died of malnutrition. Many of their children, born in Cuba, had never seen Haiti. For them, Cuba was the only home and *patria* they had known.

There was a bright side. What appeared to be a tragic sociological blunder was a tool in a Sovereign hand. Like live coals from a brazier, Haitian believers had been scattered in Haiti's darkness. Fire-seeds of God's sowing, they ignited the gospel flame throughout their homeland, sharing the message of Christ wherever they went. An unwitting Machado government had been God's instrument in preparing Haiti for the Good News. The Psalmist understood. He sang: *"The wrath of man shall praise thee."*[372]

Ethnic migration has always attended the growth of the Church. Fifteen ethnic groups were present in Jerusalem at Pentecost. Persecution sent them on their missionary way. As the great Sower, God was in the demographics. The pattern had been repeated throughout history. With the repatriation of the Haitian cane cutters, the Lord of the Harvest had set the stage for what he was about to do.

Haiti's Darkness

On 6 December 1492 Columbus made landfall at Mole Saint-Nicolas on Haiti's northwestern coast. He named the island *La Isla Española* (later anglicized as Hispaniola). Spanish settlement was thin, giving way to French pirates, who established plantations and the French West India Company.

French importation of 500,000 African slaves to the sugar plantations gave Haiti its predominantly black population, with only a five-percent minority of mulattos. The slaves revolted, defeating Napoleon's army, and in 1804 established the first black republic in the Western Hemisphere.

With slavery had come voodoo—a potpourri of African animism combining white magic, black magic, spiritism, witchcraft, and other dark arts.[373] Just how dark may be judged by the pervasive fear of demons that held Haitians in the thrall of hopelessness. God was good—they would agree—and the best of the gods, but demonic threats lurked everywhere, demanding appeasement. Haitians feared the dark. They feared the dead. They feared death, which might come by mysterious cause or curse. Each fear required protection. Witches and sorcerers, in plentiful supply, provided it, demanding animal blood, sometimes human. It was the price of survival. Florent Toirac spoke of conducting burial services for children found with their chests opened, veins cut, "their blood and heart taken to pacify the demons."[374] Even President Aristide, on taking office, conducted the so-called *Bois Cayiman* ceremony.[375] All of this pervasive evil was nonetheless acclaimed as "the cultural heritage" of the country. In 1791, Haiti had been dedicated to Satan, while in 1991, President Aristide rededicated the country to voodooism—a fact that may help explain modern Haiti's anguish as the most impoverished nation in the Western Hemisphere.[376]

France had introduced Roman Catholicism to the island, where it became the state religion. All natives and slaves were obliged to be baptized as Christians. Their voodooism, spiritism, and magic posed no obstacle to the accommodating prelates, who without compunction could as readily sprinkle dedicatory water on a witch doctor's drum as on an infant's brow. Haiti slipped, unprotesting, into that bane of Rome's universal legacy in developing lands—folk Christianity.

Into this realm of voodoo darkness, the Lord of the Harvest sowed the Sons of the Kingdom in 1933. President Machado's makeshift flotillas unloaded most of their human cargo at a port town called Les Cayes.

Haiti shares old Hispaniola with the Dominican Republic (popularly known as the "DR"), occupying the western third of the island's landmass. Nearly all of Haiti is mountainous and boasts a curious geography. To the southwest, a peninsula extends 125 miles westward from Port au Prince, the nation's capital, and primary port. A backbone of forested mountains is coextensive with the peninsula. On a map, this spit of land looks much like a long finger, pointing west across the Jamaica Channel. In the southwest of this peninsula lies the port city of Les Cayes.

New Challenge, New Name

Back in Cuba, New Pines Bible Institute was thriving, but as 1936 dawned, the West Indies Mission had not yet been born. New Pines was a Bible institute—with Cuba its sole theater of operation. Beyond its impressive vision for the Island Republic, there were no plans. That was about to change.

Alexander Mersdorf had joined the missionary team in Cuba in 1931. A friend of Elmer Thompson, he had come to Los Pinos from Prairie Bible Institute and from a background in missions in Venezuela. Fluent in Spanish and a capable leader, Mersdorf was both gifted and outspoken. He exuded a benign affability and a confidence that everyone was entitled to his opinion. Comments, suggestions, criticisms—all were freely offered both to nationals and missionaries alike. Mersdorf's manner was neither acerbic nor pretentious, but it did create tensions. Missionaries began to express their grievances to Thompson. Mersdorf's manner had also been encroaching on Thompson's comfort zone, for Thompson had begun to pray about "this troublesome person," and had spoken to Mersdorf several times. True to character, Thompson took the matter to God in prayer, advising the Lord that he felt his missionary coworker was ambitious. As Thompson prayed it became clear that ambition was not the problem. Mersdorf simply needed a bigger job—something equal to his gifts. But the only bigger job was Thompson's, and he was confident that God was not asking him to surrender that.

The Lord's reply, as Thompson relates it, was startling. It came in the form of a question:

"Is Cuba the only needy island in the West Indies?"

Until that moment, the idea had never occurred to Thompson.

> I had never before that hour thought of extending our little Bible Institute enterprise beyond the shores of Cuba. However, that was the challenge that came.[377]

Thompson realized that in his concern to develop the perfect Bible training center, he had left no room for the personal development of his staff. Calling the Institute leaders together, he shared what he believed God was saying. They prayed. Accord was immediate, and the group agreed that it was time to investigate the needs of a second island in the Antilles. With no funds available for what seemed an untimely expansion, the missionaries pooled their meager resources to finance a trip to the DR and chose Alexander Mersdorf as the vanguard.[378]

Mersdorf launched his exploratory expedition to the DR in 1936, the same year that Florent Toirac had graduated from New Pines Bible Institute. Stopping in Haiti on the way—Haiti being the western third of the same island—Mersdorf was stunned by the poverty and appalling need of the people.

While in Port au Prince, he met Ruben Marc, the leading Baptist pastor of Port au Prince. Marc was aware of the repatriated Haitians in the Southern Peninsula, having had some contact with them. He encouraged Mersdorf to investigate the possibility of ministry among them. Ruben Marc's advice confirmed Mersdorf's conviction that Haiti was the place to begin the new work. He decided that further exploration (of the DR) was unnecessary and returned to Cuba with his findings.

About this time, California pastor Dr. Marshal Morsey had been a convention speaker in Cuba for the New Pines work. He related the experience of a US Marine Corps medical doctor who had served with American troops during the first occupation of Haiti. The marine was a Christian, and his exposure to voodoo's infection of Haitian society produced an intense burden to pray for this darkened land. Enlisting others, he maintained this intercessory vigil daily for years, and on his deathbed implored Morsey—who was his pastor—to carry on the prayer torch for the evangelization of Haiti. Morsey did so. This witness to the Holy Spirit's groundwork seemed to confirm both Ruben Marc's recommendation and Mersdorf's conviction that God had prepared Haiti for harvest.

Thompson, Lavastida, and the others concurred, and the little band agreed to expand their work to Haiti. They also agreed that the move demanded a new name for their eight-year-old enterprise. They would call it the *West Indies Mission.*

To Port au Prince

Alexander and Mary Mersdorf went to Haiti in November of the same year, accompanied by Zeida Campos, a Cuban graduate of New Pines, and a proven soul winner. Zeida had already worked with Haitians in Cuba and had been sent out by the Cuban churches. They made their base in the capital, Port au Prince, giving themselves to language study for nine months.[379] The following August they packed their belongings in a truck and made the tortuous 125-mile trip to Les Cayes.

Lizaire Bernard

Ninety-five percent of the 55,000 Haitian repatriates had been landed at Les Cayes—30,000 of them in 1936 alone.[380] Among them was Lizaire Bernard, now a hapless refugee in his homeland. The tall, lean Mulatto knew that no family member would be there to welcome him. Innocent of theological education, he had nothing but the clothes on his back. However, Christ had found and saved Lizaire in Cuba, where he had been a lay worker among the Haitian immigrants. Now back in his homeland, he yearned to lead his compatriots to the light.

"What if all these repatriated Haitian Christians could be scattered throughout the country?" he mused. "If each were to win just a few to the Lord it would be a good start in this battle for Haiti's soul."

Barefoot, and with a bit of dried fish for provisions, Lizaire set out to walk the 125 miles to the capital, Port au Prince. He planned to comb the peninsula in search of other Christians. Once he reached Port au Prince, he would try to find a missionary who might help him in his mission.

Florent Toirac

While in the capital, Lizaire Bernard had learned of the Mersdorfs and sought them out, urging them to come to the needy Southern Peninsula. By August 1937, the trio had relocated in Les Cayes, where boatloads of Spanish-speaking Haitian repatriates were still being offloaded.

For two years, Lizaire prayed for help. When he met Florent Toirac, who arrived in 1938, Lizaire was in extreme poverty, still working selflessly with Haitians. The two men joined hands and prayed for the country. Even before the repatriation, Haiti had not been without gospel witness. Denominational works had been active for years, and congregations existed in many places. The Methodists had established churches in all of Haiti's major cities. However, they failed to extend their work beyond the urban centers. Having reached the upper class populations, they stopped short of evangelizing the masses of peasants scattered throughout the countryside. In this way in 1936, Mersdorf had stumbled upon a vast unreached people group numbering hundreds of thousands. In particular, the malaria-ridden Southern Peninsula was crowded with Spanish-speaking Haitians and peppered with six hundred sorcerers. It was ripe for harvest.

Toirac and Lizaire laid plans to evangelize the peninsula's two million inhabitants.[381] They worked together for several months. When repeated attacks of malaria threatened Toirac's life, the men knew they were in a spiritual contest with demonic power. Moses-like, Lizaire lifted holy hands in prayer for healing. It came instantly. Florent Toirac was immunized from disease for his remaining twelve years in Haiti.[382] He stayed five years in the Southern Peninsula, preaching and teaching with Lizaire Bernard, his faithful co-worker. During that time, the WIM team saw 109 congregations planted, with 25,000 new believers in the Southern Department.[383]

Lizaire Bernard's blitz of the towns and villages of the peninsula had turned up many clusters of Haitians. Several hundred Christians were among the repatriated cane-cutters. Groups of fifty to 150 believers were scattered everywhere—the fruit of spontaneous and joyful witness on the part of the fire-seeds Providence had sown. However, dampening the joy of this discovery was a somber reality: These Haitian believers, mostly poor and illiterate, were sheep without a shepherd. There were no organized churches. And there were no pastors.[384]

Members Only

Zeida Campos was plucky. Fully qualified as a Bible teacher and proven soul winner, she had come to Haiti with a clear call from God to work side by side with the missionaries of the West Indies Mission. By policy, WIM could not provide nationals with essential support. Nor could a national join the North American Mission as a full member. Technically, nationals did join the Mission, but their support had to be provided by the Cuban churches. This left Zeida Campos working side by side with WIM personnel whom she knew and with whom she had trained, but with whom she technically did not share support parity.[385] WIM personnel lived on extremely meager allowances, but the Cuban churches could afford even less. Notwithstanding, Campos fit happily into this arrangement, as WIM personnel freely shared accommodations and amenities with their Cuban colleagues.[386]

Unlike Campos, Florent Toirac was not pleased with this arrangement. He was a graduate of New Pines and had gone to Haiti in 1938. Like Campos, the Cuban churches had sent him. Also like Campos, he was technically a member of the WIM team. He and Campos worked side by side with WIM personnel and with Lizaire Bernard, the de facto leader of the Southern Peninsula effort. Though Toirac likewise shared the meager amenities of the WIM family, he disagreed with what he saw as a two-level status.

Toirac traced his pedigree to Spanish nobility. So could most Cubans—as a wry wit observed. His gifting and dedication to Christ in thirteen years of subsequent ministry in Haiti were of sterling quality. However, as a Cuban, he did not enjoy parity with the West Indies Mission, a fact that he seemed to find irksome. Toirac eventually founded the *Spanish World Gospel Mission,* but indigeneity as practiced by WIM had relegated him to what he perceived as an inferior status. Notwithstanding, Toirac, Campos, and Lizaire valiantly continued their work at a subsistence level, without financial assistance through the West Indies Mission. Such unfortunate disparities were inevitable in a process where all players were learners in an evolving missiology.[387]

While Toirac's nationality precluded his acceptance as a full-fledged member of the Mission, his language skills as a national gave him instant bonding with the people, while newly-arriving North Americans were still struggling with French and Creole. The disparity produced an awkward situation, humiliating to Toirac. In retrospect, he wrote:

> With blood, sweat, and tears, Lizaire and I developed several works only to see the foreign missions take the leadership and claim it as their own. I am ninety-nine percent sure that the credit for the work the Lord

did through me and any other national will not appear with our names on the pages of the missionary version of the history of missions, for the simple reason that we were nationals.[388]

The problem of national worker status was not unique to the West Indies Mission. It was practically universal, and flowed from the concept of indigeneity popularized by Presbyterian missionary John Nevius in Korea at the turn of the century. In essence, it intended to encourage national church support of national workers—which was good—and to discourage foreign support of nationals by western church paymasters—which had led to many problems. Both the West Indies Mission and the RBMU would grapple for decades with this difficult issue—right up to the time of merger in 1995, when new, creative approaches were adopted. From the outset, WIM's policy had been to facilitate development of missionary outreach by Cubans through Cuban structures—not to absorb nationals into the American mission agency. This policy disturbed Florent Toirac.

In Toirac's judgment, these disparities, and consequent lack of cooperation between national workers and missionaries retarded the systematic training of nationals. Nevertheless, a more severe test was still to come. In 1939, American Dorothy Lee came to Haiti with the West Indies Mission. She and Toirac fell in love, posing a still greater problem for WIM's leadership. Marriage to a national was frowned upon.[389] Asked to meet with the WIM leadership in Cuba, Toirac was counseled that the relationship would not work. He was then advised that the West Indies Mission had assumed responsibility for the work in the Southern Peninsula. If he wished to return to that work, it would be on condition of his breaking the relationship with Dorothy.

In the personal struggle that followed, Toirac concluded that God's time had come for him to leave the Southern Peninsula, where he had now been for five years. He did so, turning it over to Lizaire and the West Indies Mission. Florent Toirac and Dorothy Lee were married in December 1942, in Les Cayes. They would spend the next seven years in Port au Prince in a great work for God before going on to found the Spanish World Gospel Mission.[390] Florent Toirac's splendid contribution to the Southern Peninsula work included organizing scores of new congregations to meet the Biblical standards of a local church. At the same time, the Association of Haitian Churches was established, of which Lizaire Bernard became president.

WIM Establishes in Les Cayes

By the end of 1937—the Mersdorf's first year in Haiti—steps had been taken to reach out to the repatriated Haitians in Les Cayes. Haitians coming from Cuba spoke Spanish. This was a great advantage for the new Mission making its Haitian beachhead. Mary Mersdorf recalled:

We were new to the country and we spoke Spanish . . . It seemed [to be] just the right time. We sent out a SOS to our friends in the States for help. God answered our prayers. Money came in enough to rent a large house near where they disembarked. This was a shelter and gave them time to get themselves together.

Lizaire Bernard became caretaker of the WIM hostel, encouraging, and sharing the Word of God with all. "He contacted everyone . . . and how he followed them up!" Mary wrote in praise of Lizaire's astonishing dedication. "They had gone through a terrible time and suffered together and it seemed to draw them closely together."[391]

To those who were penniless, Mersdorf gave a little money to help them re-establish. Many returned to their relatives in the forested hill country. All were given the gospel and a friendly welcome. As they settled throughout the countryside, hundreds were converted and primitive churches sprang up everywhere. Demand for pastors multiplied, driving WIM to set up a Bible school before they were ready.

Revival historian James Edwin Orr was in Haiti in the 1940s, and noted the problem:

> The Cuban-based West Indies Mission followed repatriated Haitians back to Haiti, and were assigned the southwestern peninsula, of which the principal town is Les Cayes. A remarkable awakening began, as many as 10,000 professing conversion, 5,000 baptized as members in 1940. This movement brought problems, chiefly that of supplying pastors to the hundred congregations.[392]

The Haiti Bible Institute

To address the explosive growth of the Haiti Church, Walter Wunsch and Wolfe Hansen transferred from Cuba in 1938.[393] Elsie Scott, a nurse, and Dorothy Lee followed in 1939, with plans to teach in the nascent Bible Institute. A small farm was purchased near Les Cayes. While crashing through French language courses and curriculum preparation, the team worked furiously to construct missionary homes, dormitories, and classrooms for the new Bible Institute. Classes had begun in 1938, with five young men, some scarcely able to read or write, but by February 1940 the first full-fledged Bible Institute in the history of Haiti was in place, with thirty students.[394] They called it the Haiti Bible Institute. In 1958, the name would be changed to *Institut Biblique Lumière* (Bible Institute of Light). This later name was an accident of growth.

As new missionaries arrived in Haiti, housing, offices, clinic, and school buildings sprang up on WIM's *finca*—the farm three miles outside of Les Cayes. The locale was still referred to as "the *finca*," a plebeian cognomen innocent of polish. When casting about for a name for the new radio station, David Hartt suggested the apt title, *Radio Lumière* (Radio Light). He wanted to illuminate the entire country with the gospel message, and radio was the way to do it. Hartt had got the idea from a Sunday School teachers' paper produced by a Haitian Christian, Raymond Joseph. It was called *Rayon Lumiè* (Ray of Light). As the Mission complex blossomed with more buildings, it became commonly known as *Cité Lumière* (City of Light). The *light* motif was apt and was eventually applied to each of WIM's ministries in Haiti, among them, Institut Biblique *Lumière,* and Hospital *Lumière*.[395]

Admission of female students to the Bible school was another "accident of expediency" which proved to be of God's design. Medical doctor Dudley Nelson explains:

> In the early years, each Haitian church had one person who was teacher, preacher, and evangelist, and was usually the founding pastor. They had no other teachers; consequently, they had no Sunday schools. One of the reasons the Mission began admitting women to the Bible school was to train them as Sunday school teachers.
>
> Later . . . a few missionary women taught the Haitian women how to conduct VBS and helped them develop their own curriculum in Creole. Through the years this proved to be one of the most fruitful ministries, reaching many children for Christ, who later became preachers in the Haitian church.[396]

Exponential Church Growth

The Gospel grapevined throughout Haiti's Southern Peninsula along the family web. Bible school students walked or mulebacked from house to house, leading father, or mother to Christ. As the entire household became Christians, they witnessed to neighbors until there were enough families in an area to form a church. Dudley described the way these new groups were accommodated:

> They would build a coconut-leaf shelter, called a *tonnel* where they would meet. Next, they obtained a piece of land, sometimes gifted by one of the members or purchased by the newly formed church. The country church was built of the same materials as their homes—thatch and lime, a little cement for the walls, and a thatch or tin roof. The usual form was a rectangle with double doors in front, a single door toward the front on either side, or one in the rear. Three or four windows—no glass—provided light on both sides, and openings for doors and window would remain without frames until money was available for their installation. Often the building remained without a cement floor, and frequently the last thing to be added was the platform and

pulpit furniture. At first people came with their own chairs, until little by little benches were added.[397]

Rapid multiplication of Haitian churches soon called for an infrastructure to provide for the more efficient deployment of pastors, and for effective pastoral care. To achieve this, the peninsula was divided into eight districts, the founding senior pastor becoming superintendent of the district. Younger pastors under his care were either Bible school trained or mentored by him as lay pastors.[398]

John and Dorothy Depew had come out in 1941, John Depew replacing Mersdorf as field leader.[399] Mersdorf had left the Mission following furlough in 1939 to relocate in Northern Haiti with the Unevangelized Fields Mission. Eventually, health and climate forced the Depew's retirement from Haiti, but their transfer to Jamaica from 1951–1958 would lead to the growth of the Jamaica Bible Institute.

During Depew's leadership, the Haiti Bible Institute achieved an enrollment of one hundred men, with the same number of women in the summer course.[400] For years, James Smith, with his consummate fluency in Creole, became the primary trainer of national church leaders. The Institut Biblique Lumière would become the *pièce de résistance* of WIM's work in Haiti for the next fifty years, feeding the church that God had grown in such astonishing fashion. The missionary's role had been almost entirely one of training, the multiplication of churches having been conducted by students and graduates of the Bible Institute and the lay persons they had trained.[401] By 1998, the Bible school extension department was teaching more than six hundred students in twelve regional centers.

The Clinic

On the back porch of the Depew residence in Les Cayes, aspirin and liniment were available to students working on construction of the first dormitory of the Haiti Bible Institute. The porch became the first aid station and dispensary for the school. When neighbors learned of these basic remedies, they were soon lining up at 4:00 a.m. seeking treatment for a variety of ailments.

Graduate nurse Elsie Scott had come to teach in the Bible Institute, but the growing number of health problems among the students called for attention. She set up a tabletop dispensary to care for the recurrent quota of emergencies, but as the daily queues of patients grew longer, she despaired of coping. WIM missionaries began to pray for nurses and for a doctor. With the arrival in 1944 of Jennie Razumny, a nurse, a small storeroom was converted into a clinic. Nurse Bernice Johnson appeared in January 1946. When medical doctor Dudley Nelson arrived the same year, WIM's medical work grew exponentially.

With hundreds of patients arriving daily, Nelson initiated a community health care program, rotating weekend clinics in remote areas, usually close to a church. Some of these outposts were accessible by Jeep, others only by horse, mule, on foot, or a combination of all. The joy of ministering to so many in this fashion was dimmed only by the distress of having to leave so many unattended. Historically, medical work has been the handmaiden to the gospel, and Haiti was no exception. Medical care had been virtually unavailable. Now WIM's clinic offered hope at two levels, for dispensary schedules always included chapel services where the gospel was presented.

Profile in Grace

Joseph Lemeuble Joseph typified the astonishing work of the Spirit in the Haitian community.[402] He surrendered his heart to God at a street meeting and immediately began to preach in his hometown of Aquin. Conversions resulted, and the little house his father had left him became a church. While his ministry quickly won local acclaim, Joseph knew he lacked the qualifications of a preacher—he was not even baptized. Preaching one day by the riverside, he challenged his hearers, "Those who want to let the world know that we are on the Lord's side, come forward." Delicat—his brother—came, and three others. Delicat baptized Joseph; then Joseph baptized Delicat and the others.

The church grew, but Joseph remained troubled. Separated from his common-law wife he questioned whether he had the right to lead others. Gathering some of the leading members of the church, they prayed: "Lord, show us what to do." Precisely as their prayer ended, a pith-helmeted man rode by on horseback. It was Florent Toirac. Joseph ran to catch him. Breathless, he shot the question, "Who are you and where are you going? Toirac explained that he had come from the Bible School in Les Cayes and was on his way to L'Asile. It was clear to Joseph, if not to Toirac, that God had answered his prayers. He replied to Toirac, "Well, my friend, turn around and come with me. You are the one to bring us God's Word, are you not?" Unable to gainsay the earnestness in Joseph's eyes, Toirac returned with him to the church, where Joseph explained the story.

Toirac immediately sent word to Les Cayes, and two missionaries soon arrived in Aquin. They welcomed the little group into the fellowship of evangelical churches, and on leaving, commissioned Joseph: "Brother Joe, we're putting you in charge." Reluctantly, he carried on. When the missionaries returned in the spring for a district Bible convention, the plea went out for those who wished to enter full-time service. Joseph's hand shot up, and two others followed.

In the fall of 1940, Joseph entered Bible School in Les Cayes. At the end of the school year, 4000 Christians gathered for the convention, many walking thirty miles to attend. It was a glorious time. Back in Aquin, several hundred were now attending services in Joseph's church. He organized a three-day convention, inviting WIM missionaries to attend. When he returned to Les Cayes for his second year of Bible School, a letter reached him from Port au Prince. The wife he had abandoned had written, asking him to take her back. While she was ill and unable to walk, someone had led her to the Lord. The next day she was healed. For the first time, she went to a Bible study in a Protestant church. The message was on "Pardon for Sin." She said to herself, "My man preaches like that. I know he will pardon me." He did, and in 1943, they were married. The same year Joseph finished his schooling and returned to pastor the Aquin church. Hundreds found the Lord. Joseph became district superintendent and treasurer of all the churches then in the Evangelical Association of Haiti.[403]

Joseph Lemeuble became president of MEBSH (the Association of Haitian Churches), which he led with "spiritual excellence." He became the bridge between the Haitian churches and the missionary community. His son, Raymond, took Greek at Moody Bible Institute and became chief translator for the American Bible Society's Creole translation of the Scriptures. Outspoken politically under the Duvalier regime, he was placed on a death list, and for safety went to New York City, where he ran a daily radio broadcast and newspaper.[404] Due to his son's political activity, Joseph Lemeuble was likewise obliged to leave Haiti for personal safety. He and his wife went to French-speaking Guadeloupe, where God gave him a fruitful evangelistic ministry and where he eventually died of natural causes.[405]

Hospital Lumière

By 1974, Allen Thompson's emphasis on the primacy of church planting—as distinct from institutional ministries such as medicine—had dimmed any prospect of further development of WIM's medical work in Haiti. That changed when Dudley Nelson had a visit from another Dr. Nelson in the summer of '74. Medical doctor *Donald* Nelson had spent seven years in Africa with the Conservative Baptists, and gave Dudley some advice:

If you ever want to get American physicians, you must have a hospital.

The good doctor took his advice to the next level and spoke directly with Thompson and the WIM board.[406] His persuasive powers won the day—WIM approved the construction of a hospital. Then Donald Nelson went a step farther. He and his wife, together with his son and daughter-in-law, returned to Haiti in November.[407] Soon Dr. Dudley Nelson had a new hospital—*Hospital Lumière.*[408]

After a Decade

By the close of World War II, the Association of Haitian Churches—organized by Florent Toirac—was in place, with pioneer Lizaire Bernard as acting president. The Association counted 130 established churches, with 80 national workers ministering to 25,000 believers. The Haitian Bible Institute had developed into a resident three-year program for training Sunday school workers. A four-year seminary program offered ministerial training at a level comparable to North American Bible schools, with 140 students in the combined programs. Eighteen WIM missionaries were in the country.[409] Reminiscing in 1948, Elmer Thompson summarized the events of 1936–1948:

> The new staff in Haiti, by choosing to go to the southern province of that land, came into an unanticipated opportunity. Several thousand Haitians had been repatriated from Cuba, and among these returnees were about five hundred Christians. As soon as they learned that missionaries from Cuba were settling in their part of Haiti, they came to our staff and asked to be identified with the West Indies Mission. A Bible School was established for the training of Haitian preachers. Within a dozen years more than a hundred churches had been established and believers numbered between twenty-five and thirty thousand.[410]

This magnificent work of the Holy Spirit in Haiti had been established in a single decade, through two primary channels—The Haitian Bible Institute and The Hospital of Light. The Haiti-wide broadcasting network *Radio Lumière* was still ten years away. By 1989, however, the West Indies Mission would disengage from both.

28

Old Quisqueya

The fact is, North American missionaries experienced little success until several Cuban missionaries were added to their number.

—Elmer V. Thompson

Fatigued by the sweltering heat, five thousand of the DR's faithful inched their tortured ascent toward the summit of Santo Domingo's *Holy Mount*. George Little had never seen anything like it. This was the first anniversary (4 July 1940) of the death of Father Fantino, a priest whose hermit lifestyle had won him reputation as a fanatic. After his demise, Fantino was lionized, and his eccentricities were hailed as marks of saintliness, suffusing his memory with reverential awe. Burial in the temple of the Holy Mount assured Fantino's sainthood—at least in the hearts of the ascending faithful.

"If Ephraim was joined to his idols," thought Little, "Hosea's comment perfectly describes the people of Santo Domingo."

Santo Domingo was founded in 1496 and held distinction as the oldest European settlement in the Hemisphere. Its turbulent history began in 1501, when Spanish settlers introduced the first African slaves into the New World. Ironically, they named the city *Santo Domingo* (Holy Sunday). By the eighteenth century, seven million Africans had crossed the Atlantic in chains, a traffic that would forever change the ethnic composition of much of the Caribbean and the United States. A barbarous blight upon the human race, slavery left its diseased legacy in the current conditions prevailing in some Caribbean countries, in contemporary racial tensions, and in the horrific catharsis of the American Civil War.

Caribs and the Caribbean

The Dominican Republic's indigenous population of Carib and Arawak Indians was soon decimated by Spain's greed for gold, with only the name of the Caribbean Sea left to mark their passing. In 1999, two-thirds of the country's eight million inhabitants were of mixed Afro-European descent (mulatto) and the remainder mainly of African extract. When in 1821 the DR declared independence from Spain, the nation was invaded by Haitians, who were eventually repulsed, but not before losing the western third of the island to the French. The DR became a republic in 1844, only to lose control to Spain from 1861–1865. This turbulent history finally issued in a plea for annexation by the United States in 1869. The request was denied, but when economic chaos later threatened the country's 3.5 million inhabitants, the US Marines occupied the DR for eight years, from 1916 to 1924. The thirty-year rule of Dictator General Rafael Trujillo ended with his assassination in 1962, and was followed again by intervention of American Marines.

WIM's Stormy Debut in the DR

Into this maelstrom of social unrest, the West Indies Mission made its debut in 1939. Cecil Samuels, a bilingual Jamaican graduate of the Cuba Bible Institute, was sent to reconnoiter the country and evaluate ministry options. It became WIM's practice before formal entry of any new field to send someone ahead for a period of one year to engage in survey and evaluation.[411] WIM had been accepting nationals as regular missionaries long before this became common practice among mission agencies.[412] He discovered a population pocket in central DR where at least half a million people were without the gospel.

Before the Littles arrived, Samuels had obtained a modest house in one of Santo Domingo's slum sectors where he began Sunday school classes. Initial curiosity quickly drew crowds, but feeling threatened, the Roman Catholic clergy instigated vigorous opposition, and attendance fell off.

For eleven months Samuels worked largely alone, primarily as an itinerant evangelist, though he had many other jobs to do. His rugged physique took him by foot or horseback to nearby villages, where several small groups of believers were formed.[413]

Samuel's presence was welcomed like the plague. "Away with this *Protestante!* Send him from our country! We follow the Sacred Heart!" Children chanted their prepared script as they followed Samuels through the streets of Santo Domingo. Theologically clueless, the innocents had been marshaled and orchestrated by Roman priests. The pattern was universal throughout Latin America wherever Protestant missionaries went. Spain had done its work well. The reception accorded Samuels was enough to unnerve the dauntless, but there was more to come.

Sunday evening services were disrupted by the cacophony of a thousand drumbeats, as stones pelted the corrugated zinc roof of their meeting place. The attacks were effective, for they instilled fear and dispersed the courageous few who had come to listen. Amazingly, Samuels remained undaunted throughout this Satanic opposition, and he began to visit nearby towns and villages.

La Vega is a town on the trans-Dominican highway that runs from the Republic's capital on the South Coast to Monte Cristi on the island's northern shore. The highway skirts the mountainous regions, which make up the western half of the Dominican Republic. La Vega, which would win reputation as "the toughest spot" in the country, is seventy miles from Santo Domingo. Geographically central, the town was also free of other religious groups. Here Cecil Samuels made his base.

Reinforcements

Meanwhile WIM's Executive Committee considered reinforcements for the DR effort. Thompson reported:

> For some time, the burden of leadership for Santo Domingo has been upon our hearts. We rejoiced last year when God gave us entrance into that needy Republic. Mr. Cecil Samuels has done splendid work in the short time he has been there, but we have felt the necessity of a married couple to establish a home and central base from which to direct the work.

In 1939, Thompson, Lavastida, and Mersdorf comprised the entire Executive Committee of the West Indies Mission, so decisions were readily expedited. In April they agreed to release Mr. and Mrs. George Little from the faculty of the Cuba Bible Institute to join Samuels in the DR. The Littles were briefed:

> Don't do any evangelistic work until we so direct you. You are not to consider yourselves field directors . . . It should be clearly understood that no plans are to be made to begin a Bible school until we give permission, and no propaganda related to the possibility of a school is to be circulated.

Armed with a list of things not to do, the Littles moved to the DR, where they arrived in May 1940. The sight of five thousand votaries climbing Santo Domingo's Holy Hill astounded the couple. In Cuba, they had never seen such a degree of "voluntary and willing slavery." Little elaborated:

> There are idols and graven images of every size and for every occasion, and each idol must be baptized. A very popular saint is the image of a

woman fastened upon a box and enclosed in glass. They pass it from one house to another where it remains for twenty-four hours at each station. She is said to "appear." Each family must give the saint twenty-five cents or more . . . Only yesterday a poor woman came begging money that she might pay her dues to the saints . . . Ignorance is bad enough, but to be content in it is tragic.

WIM's DR staff grew. Frank and Dorothy Butler arrived in 1942. Butler, described as "one of the finest men that ever entered Worldteam," would have just nine years.[414] Then Ida Peterson, Doris Mileson, and May Leslie joined the Samuels and the Littles. They plodded on with personal work, tract distribution, and house-to-house visits.

In the mountain town of Jarabacoa, Ida and Doris opened a small preaching station and a Sunday school. Results here were more encouraging than in La Vega. Then in 1943, the Dominican Bible Institute was opened with six students.[415] Eventually the work spread into some of the major cities, and a few churches were formed. However, something was missing.

Different Playbook

WIM's highly successful experience with Spanish-speaking Latin Americans in Cuba had been followed by similar victories in Haiti, in spite of the additional hurdle of the French language. Work in Haiti had begun with a spontaneous movement of the Spirit among a large population of repatriated Haitians, many of whom had become Christians in Cuba. Flushed with this success, the West Indies Mission logically expected an early harvest in the Dominican Republic.

Enthusiasm soon tarnished, however, when missionaries found that the DR called for a different game plan. The work was slow and arduous. Opposition was unbudging, and the attacks relentless. Over the years, missionaries came and went. Few were equipped to weather the wear and tear of ministry with few visible results. Expatriate attrition was alarming. Thompson lamented that:

Work in the DR has been a desperate struggle from the very start. Never has there been a period of respite from the fight, and never complete victory won.[416]

These obstacles were not due to "human resistance or conniving," Thompson noted, but were attributable to "the mysterious, the metaphysical" and to the "essential spiritual enemy of the gospel—Satan." In fact, WIM had encountered no opposition from the DR government and local officials had extended "every consideration." The people were friendly. Notwithstanding, the Mission's work "had been almost smothered out of existence more than once."

On three occasions serious illness forced WIM leaders to leave the field. The loss to a rare disease of respected field leader, Frank Butler, threatened morale. Butler had opened the Bible Institute. Sensing the Satanic origin of these calamities, Thompson called upon the wider WIM family to "a persistent crusade of faith and prayer" for the overthrow of this miasma from the nether regions.[417]

Slim returns led to further problems. Few converts meant fewer national workers to train for evangelism and pastoral roles. Unlike Cuba with its Lavastida, or Haiti with its task force of repatriated Christians, the DR had no existing cadre of believers waiting to be mobilized. Consequently, appeals for Cuban evangelists to assist the missionaries became standard procedure, as Elmer Thompson explained:

> The missionaries were not accompanied by a nucleus of national Christians, as in Cuba and Haiti. We had to begin at the bottom. It took a long time to begin without the basic confidence of the people. The fact is, North American missionaries experienced little success until several Cuban missionaries were added to their number.[418]

After twenty-three years of "difficult sowing in tears," the Dominican Republic had yielded a scant harvest of fifteen congregations and 900 believers.[419] The country had scarcely been evangelized. The disappointment was not unique to WIM. Other mission organizations might have said the same of their own work. It would remain for Allen Thompson to diagnose the problem and identify a solution. That would not happen until 1963.

World War II

The Second World War failed to exert the impact upon the West Indies Mission that it had upon British RBMU and their fields in Africa and Asia. Snuggled beneath the underbelly of the North American continent, the Caribbean was largely protected from the conflict that engulfed the European and Pacific theaters of operation. Cuba remained neutral and prospered economically as a source of war materiel. Most affected were the economies of America and Canada. They faced shortages, but no hardships. Because the Cuban churches were largely self-supporting and staffed by national pastors, the war failed to retard their growth and development. After the war, however, the West Indies Mission would ride the global wave of diaspora, following its track to new worlds in the old, and to old worlds in the new.

Part 3
When the Lights Came on Again
The Regions Beyond Missionary Union
The Postwar Years
1946–1995

Ebenezer G. Vine
Founder, North American RBMU

29

A Man on Borrowed Time

*November 2, 1950. New Guinea. Said to this mountain, 'Be
thou removed in the mighty name of Jesus.'*

—Ebenezer G. Vine

When the atomic cloud blossomed over Hiroshima on 6 August 1945, the
world entered a new era. In one nuclear flash, four centuries of global domination by colonial powers evaporated. Like a tidal bore racing into a fjord,
Third World countries rushed to proclaim independence and national sovereignty. The global conflict had scattered men and women of the armed forces
throughout the countries of Earth, exposing them to peoples, cultures, and
conditions most had never seen. Many of these GIs were Christians who purposed to return to former combat zones with Words of Life. While the war
seemed to have ended civilization, peace would usher in a new epoch in world
evangelization.

Ebenezer G. Vine: His Work in North America

Ebenezer G. Vine had joined the board of RBMU in 1939, and saw the Mission through its darkest years. For many in our society, age sixty-five means
retirement. For Vine, it was the beginning of his magnum opus, launch pad
for his life's greatest venture. In 1948, he left postwar Britain to introduce the
work of the RBMU in the United States and Canada. He planned a three-
month visit. He stayed fifteen years. He not only launched the ministry of
RBMU, founding councils in Philadelphia and Toronto, but his vision and
tenacious faith prized open new fields—Borneo and Dutch New Guinea.

The Dutch Connection

In 1929 Vine was traveling by train south of London. The only other occupant
of his railway compartment was a young woman. A Hollander, she was

visiting friends in England. She explained that she was a 1926 graduate of Moody Bible Institute and had been trying to find a place for herself in some mission working in New Guinea, but had been refused because of a slight deafness. In fact, three different boards had turned her down! Ever sympathetic, Vine felt that her deafness could hardly be a handicap, since she spoke five languages. Believing her call to be from God, he knelt with her in prayer and together they committed the future to the Lord. Neither Vine nor Greet "Grietje" van't Eind were connected with RBMU at the time, but the prayer meeting in the railway carriage was the first link in a chain of events that would catapult the British Mission to new frontiers.

Early Life

Ebenezer G. Vine was born in London in 1885, the youngest of four. His mother, Mary, was a chronic invalid, but she enjoyed the devoted attention of a loving family. His father was a strict disciplinarian, ensuring that family chores assigned to each sibling were executed properly and on time. Excuses were not tolerated. Church and Sunday school attendance was obligatory and meticulously observed, as were family prayers; but religious duty was serious business and not necessarily something to be enjoyed. While sports were permitted—cricket being a notable example—there was little room for laughter and frivolity in the Vine household. Charles Arthur Vine was earnest about religion, and cared for his family, but not surprisingly, he lacked assurance of his salvation. In this, he reflected his Strict Baptist connections.[420] Later in life, it was Ebenezer's privilege to lead his father to that place of peace and assurance. In celebration, they sang together,

> My sin, oh, the bliss of this glorious thought
> My sin, not in part but in whole
> Is nailed to the cross and I bear it no more
> Praise the Lord, praise the Lord, O My soul.[421]

Watershed

Ebenezer studied hard and did well at school, but for economic reasons was unable to go on to college. Obtaining a good job in a glass factory, he was quickly given more responsibility. When he saw that some of the bottles they were making were used to market beer and hard liquor, he knew he could have no part in it, and turned in his notice. His employer, who was also owner of the plant, did not wish to lose him and offered enticements if he would stay. Vine was adamant. So long as any bottles were used for wrong purposes, he could not remain. Not taking kindly to such nonsense his employer chided, "You young fool, don't you realize that this whole business will be yours one day?" Ebenezer left it all with no prospect of another job. For many years, he would face financial struggles, but never regretting that decision.

Marriage

In 1907 he married Elizabeth (Bessie) Harris, "a beautiful woman four years his senior." The home they established was happy and secure. It was also as free from rules and regulations as his childhood home had been strict and unbending. The union was blessed with a son, Gordon, followed by three girls—Bertel, Eunice, and Muriel. Bertel Grace Vine would play a significant role in RBMU, first as a missionary to India, later—upon the death of her mother—as companion and support to her father in the establishing of the North American councils of the RBMU.

Preparation

Vine's intense missionary vision had its roots in early life. Though denied a formal college education, Ebenezer was a lifelong student. From youth, he determined to prepare himself for Christian ministry. His conversion in London as a teenager soon expressed itself in preaching the gospel in a disreputable district known as "Thieves Kitchen." He continued to study and to read widely, taking evening courses when available. An evening school taught by Dr. Dinsdale Young, one of Britain's foremost Bible scholars (who followed C. H. Spurgeon) gave Vine a coveted opportunity for which he never ceased to be grateful. He attended regularly, often at the cost of walking across London.

Pastorates

Early in his marriage, Ebenezer was called to the pastorate of a small village church. Pastoring poor churches became a trademark, and he supplemented his income by working in the building trade as builders' merchant and quantity surveyor. His pastorates were successful, partly because people valued his preaching, rich in Bible truth, but also because of Bessie. She was a bulwark of support, caring for the entire village, ministering to all, regardless of their church status. This she did through two world wars as well as in times of peace.

Vine Joins the London Board of RBMU

Vine's activism for world missions won respect and in 1939, he was invited to join the London Board of RBMU. A year later he gave up a successful business to devote his full time to missions, a step taken in the face of heavy criticism from his friends. By this time, Great Britain was fully absorbed with the war effort. Building construction halted. Demand for his skills all but ceased. Vine's company closed. He now gave his time increasingly to RBMU. In 1942, after three years on the Board of Directors, he was appointed General Secretary of the Mission.[422]

India Tour

Ebenezer Vine was now working daily in the RBMU office while German air raids carpeted London with high explosives. Nerves were tense, but Harley House was never hit. Vine became a stabilizing presence to the RBMU staff. "His genial presence, and loving personality," wrote Betty Pritchard, "cheered headquarters during the final dreary years of the war. His tremendous faith and vision and his power in prayer revitalized the noon prayer meeting held daily in the office."[423]

With the war winding down, Vine was requested to go to India as a trouble-shooter, where personnel problems called for mediation. Travel was severely restricted, but Vine, now sixty years of age, signed on as chaplain aboard a troop ship.

India was a triumph. He successfully addressed the problems he had gone to resolve, but God surprised him with an unexpected ministry. Doors began to open to him as conference speaker to many mission agencies and churches all over India. This was a tremendous joy to him while it brought refreshment to many weary workers who had plodded without respite through the long years of war. Some had been on the field for ten years or more without a break. Betty Pritchard, RBMU missionary and author, was in India during Vine's three-year tour, and later shared her recollections:

> Wherever he went missionaries and nationals alike were warmed and encouraged by his sincere personal interest in their affairs. The nationals in particular felt the magnetism of his personality as he addressed them. They listened intently no matter how lengthy the sermons [plus interpretation] became. Moreover, his sermons could be very long! It could be said he gave the nationals their first real interest in needy people outside their own country.
>
> I recall a scene during a later visit [when] a group of Christians in our courtyard [sat] cross-legged on the grass around the remains of a communal supper, the moon lighting up the scene as if it were day . . . Every eye [was] on Mr. Vine, as he told them of the wild men of Borneo and the cannibal tribes of West Irian coming to the Lord Jesus Christ.[424]

During his period as Field Superintendent in Bihar, he displayed amazing physical stamina. Over sixty years old, he bore the rigors of the Indian climate without even a passing complaint. He would use a bicycle if no other vehicle were at hand, weaving his swift way through the crowds of jaywalkers, the cycles and tongas, cows, goats, pye-dogs, and bullock carts that throng an Indian bazaar, however hot or wet the day. Sitting up all night in a crowded railway compartment, eating strange and unpalatable food—these things he took in stride. Nothing daunted him.

Vine's ministry in India was preparatory. His magnum opus yet lay before him. It would take him to North America and would open a new and dramatic chapter in the saga of frontier missions.

Call to North America

Shortly after Vine's return to Britain, World War II ended. Much of Europe lay in ruins, including Great Britain. Mission opportunities now began to multiply, rising phoenix-like from the ashes of six years of devastation and hardship. Open doors beckoned everywhere, but there were no funds to enter. Peace had been declared, but the economic cost of the conflict was still in force. Britain was so impoverished that her government restricted charitable agencies—including missions—from sending overseas any funds more than what their average remittance had been over the previous five years. Since remittances to missionaries during the war years had been sharply restricted, postwar monetary regulations simply protracted the hardship. Frozen below subsistence levels, allowable field remittances permitted no advance whatever.

Vine Comes to America

The crisis forced the London Board of RBMU to a course of action that would prove of momentous consequence. They commissioned Vine to cross the Atlantic in hope of raising both funds and personnel to embrace the opportunities now before the beleaguered mission. With a three-month return ticket in his pocket, Vine boarded a transatlantic liner in Southampton and sailed for New York. He would stay fifteen years.

Near the end of his first three months in the States—the intended length of his visit—Vine was pressed by friends to stay on longer. He immediately wrote Bessie to ask her opinion. On receiving the letter she said to her children, "If the Lord wants Dad to stay, I'm not going to hinder him, but I am going, too!" She did just that. At seventy-one, never having been out of England, she left children and grandchildren and crossed the Atlantic on the SS *Queen Elizabeth*—alone. Her support for Ebenezer and his God-given work was rock solid to the end.

On 20 April 1948 Ebenezer G. Vine arrived at the Cunard Line's Hudson River berth in Manhattan, roost for the transatlantic behemoths of the era. Walter Allen had driven from Paterson, New Jersey, to meet him. Neither man knew the other. Allen was an accountant with little notion of the adventure awaiting him. How and why they connected is a story of its own.

The Sirag Saga

Several mission boards had begun work in West Borneo in the nineteenth century, but by 1930, none had entered the Landak River area of the island. Then, in 1933 Greet van't Eind—the young woman Ebenezer Vine had met on the train four years earlier—rose to the challenge. Although cheered by Vine's support, she remained without a mission board to sponsor her. Defying the odds, she went alone. Her singular courage may be judged from the fact that when she embarked on the steamer *Glengarry* at King George dock in London, Ebenezer G. Vine was the only person to see her off.[425] From the coastal city of Singkawang, van't Eind made her way to the inland village of Perigi. This became her home base. She learned the Dayak language in five months, and traveled deep into the interior, spreading the news about Jesus and helping people who were sick. After contracting an unknown illness, she died on 2 May 1935, a month short of her forty-first birthday.

Before the war, William Sirag had been a missionary to the Canary Islands, where he met and fell in love with Sylvia Cushing. She was an Iowa girl who had responded to the missionary challenge through the ministry of Dr. Howard Taylor of the China Inland Mission. Graduating from Northwestern Bible School in Minneapolis, Sylvia had done a stint in Venezuela before going to the Canaries. Bill was a graduate of Moody Bible Institute and a member of Madison Avenue Baptist Church in Patterson, New Jersey. Bill Sirag had previously planned to go to Borneo, but was unable.

The Scripture Gift Mission (SGM) had a warm interest in Borneo's Dayaks, and at their request, Vine wrote up the story of Greet van't Eind. A copy fell into the hands of Bill Sirag and Sylvia Cushing, now missionaries in the Canaries. Vine's account of Greet's work and early death captured the young couple. When forced by the Spanish civil war (1936) to leave the Islands, Bill and Sylvia determined to go to Borneo—as husband and wife.

Wartime travel constraints obliged Sirag and Cushing to leave the Canaries via England, where they arrived armed with nothing but the address of the Scripture Gift Mission. The agency directed them to Ebenezer G. Vine. The Borneo Prayer Fellowship, led by Vine, had been praying for a couple to pick up the work laid down by Greet van't Eind at her death in 1935. Convinced this was the finger of God, Vine married the pair in his home, and after a few months of training in Islington Medical Mission in London, Mr. and Mrs. Bill Sirag sailed for the Dutch East Indies.[426] Bill Sirag would be the second Moody Bible Institute graduate to enter Borneo. Grietje had been the first.

The Sirags had three years among Borneo's Dayaks, where two of their three children were born—Mark and Paul. In March 1940, Sylvia returned on furlough with her boys to Paterson, New Jersey, where a third son, David, was added to the family. Bill had remained in Borneo, and when news of his serious illness (tuberculosis) reached her, she sailed for Java from New York on 30 November 1941, taking with her Mark and Paul, now three and two years of age. Infant David was left in the care of Christ's Home, then in Paradise, Pennsylvania. Sylvia sailed into a nightmare. Eight days later the Japanese bombed Pearl Harbor. Under sealed orders and total blackout, the vessel zig-zagged across the South Pacific, eluding Japanese submarines. From Austra-lia, they finished their journey to Java in a convoy of fourteen ships. The trip had taken three months.

The family was reunited, but their joy was short-lived. Within a year, the Japanese Imperial Army occupied Java. Again, Bill Sirag was separated from his family, this time for three years of internment. He would never see them again. He died in a concentration camp on 8 June 1945. Held in a different camp, Sylvia and the two children survived barbaric conditions that took many lives.[427] When war's end brought liberation, she returned to New Jersey. With her heart still in Borneo, she determined to go back. Throughout their years in Borneo (1937–1945), the Sirags had been sustained by Ebenezer Vine's Borneo prayer group in London, and by the Madison Avenue Baptist Church in Paterson, New Jersey. To facilitate the Sirag venture, the church had formed an agency incorporated as *West Borneo Christian Missions.*[428] Now back in Paterson, Sylvia was among comrades in vision.

Barnstorming for Borneo

Sylvia now turned to these friends for support in her personal campaign to establish a mission agency for Dayak evangelization. She immediately plunged into an aggressive itinerary, criss-crossing the country—Minneapolis, Chicago, Three Hills, Los Angeles—challenging churches and students to rise to the plight of Borneo's Dayaks and recruiting candidates for an agency that did not yet exist. Her old friend, Ebenezer Vine, had not only helped her and Bill to get to Borneo before the war, he had also kept their work before the public in prayer meetings and at the RBMU Slavanka missionary conference. Sylvia now turned to him to see what he could do. Early in the war, Vine had already nudged the London Board to formally adopt the venture. There had been no response.

Notwithstanding, activist Sylvia Sirag was undeterred by bureaucratic paraly-sis and pursued her goal with dogged tenacity. Vine referred admiringly to her "unquenchable ardor."[429] Already encouraged by candidate interest in the States, she determined to place a formal proposal before the RBMU board in London that "Mr. Vine might see his way to cross to America and take steps to establish RBMU interest in the US." She sent her petition to the board by the hand of Ebenezer G. Vine. Nevertheless, a canny Sylvia had already hedged her bets. Independently of the brief she had lodged with Vine, she had earlier contacted one of Vine's close friends in America. Dr. A. E. Harris, one of the founders of Eastern Baptist Theological Seminary, took up her cause and wrote to the Board in London. The weight of his proposal combined with that of Vine's advocacy, led the RBMU in London to conclude, "it would certainly be right to respond to this appeal."

She called at Moody Bible Institute, having been invited to address a missions class. In that class was Gudrun "Goodie" Lima and her brother, Harold, both graduating in August 1948. Gudrun was a Physical Education instructor. High school classmates had bestowed the nickname, "Sam," a chauvinist nod to her athletic talents. Gudrun was taken with Sylvia, irresistibly drawn by her harrowing wartime adventures and her love for Borneo's Dayaks. Sensing God's leading to give her life to the Dayak people, Gudrun determined to accompany Sylvia upon her return to Borneo.[430] The blonde-haired Norwegian—"Goodie" to her colleagues—became the first RBMU recruit in the States and the first of many to go to Indonesia.[431]

While Sylvia continued to beat the drum for Borneo on the Bible school campuses, she and her three children found refuge at Christ's Home in Warminster, Pennsylvania. Her brother, Ralph Cushing, was a student at Philadelphia Bible Institute, where he had a small apartment. In Paterson, accountant Walter Allen put Ebenezer Vine on the train for Philadelphia. Sylvia Sirag was at the station to meet him. It was April 1948. They had not seen each other for twelve years.[432]

Greet van't Eind

30

He Brought the World to Our Home

We did not know when we opened our little home to the RBMU—we called it 'the stable of Bethlehem'—that God would give us a worldwide outreach. I wanted to go into all the world. Instead, he brought all the world to our home.

—Leona Bauman

This Lady Is Special

The voice on the telephone belonged to a secretary at Philadelphia Bible Institute.

Leona, could you possibly take a missionary and her twelve-year-old son into your home for the next week?

Leona Bauman was aghast. Their brick-front row house in Philadelphia's Kensington section was in shambles. Leona and Walter were remodeling. Chunks of plaster covered the floor. Electrical wires hung limp from jagged holes in the ceiling. Plaster dust blanketed everything.

'Impossible!' she mustered.

The voice persisted:

This lady is special! She has just got off a troop ship with her two sons. Three years in a Japanese prison camp in Borneo. Her husband died there.

The Sacrament

Leona Bauman always wanted to be a missionary—to Africa! God, however, had clearly shut that door. One day while cleaning house, she dropped to her knees in the living room and surrendered her home to God. It was a divine moment. She began to move from room to room, repeating that sacrament of dedication until the Holy Spirit seemed to say, "Enough!" Always practical, Leona and Walter Bauman put deed to word. They promptly informed the Philadelphia Bible Institute that their home was available to missionaries passing through Philadelphia! It was no mere gesture. They left the key.

The Bauman Residence: Port of Call

The telephone call should have been no surprise. The former prisoner of war was Sylvia Sirag. She was speaking at Philadelphia Bible Institute, where both Walter and Leona had graduated. The year was 1947. Sylvia stayed in the Bauman home for a few days, where she unburdened her heart for Borneo's Dayaks. The Baumans bonded with their guest, and over the next two years, Sylvia would make frequent recourse to this prophet's chamber. Pressing her advantage, Sylvia shared her vision to establish a mission board in North America. Then she told them about an Englishman—Ebenezer Vine. If he came, would they have room to put him up? Leona Bauman was not pleased—anyone could see there was no room in their tiny Kensington home. Nevertheless, God was in this thing and Lee Bauman knew it. Softening, she agreed—"Well . . . maybe. But just for a few days."

When Ebenezer G. Vine got off the train in Philadelphia, Sylvia first took him to her brother's center city digs. Ralph Cushing's cramped, third floor apartment—complete with children—left Vine with neither space nor solitude. He turned to Sylvia and queried,

> "Did you say that the Walter Baumans had a spare bedroom for guests?" [Sylvia had told him].

> "That's correct. And I have the key," she replied.

The Baumans were away at their summer cottage in Ocean City, New Jersey, and had left instructions that any missionary guest was free to access the house. Armed with the key and totally innocent of Philadelphia neighborhoods, Vine boarded a cab.

> "Nineteen thirty-five Willard Street, Kensington," he said, instructing the driver.

> "East or West?" asked the cabby.

It was critical information since Willard Street was numbered in both directions. The detail had escaped Vine. Taking an educated guess, the driver dropped his fare curbside at 1935 East Willard Street. It was midnight and the choice was right. Nineteen-thirty-five *West* was an unsavory neighborhood.

Vine tried the key in the front door. It worked. Unable to find the light switch, he crawled on hands and knees in the darkness until he felt a sofa. Boarding it, he promptly fell asleep. First light revealed a piano, some hymnbooks, and a couple of Bibles—the evidence erased all doubt. He was in the right house!

The Baumans enjoyed immediate rapport with Ebenezer G. Vine as he explained the nature of his three-month mission in America. He would not only get Sylvia Sirag back to Borneo; he would become God's instrument in establishing a beachhead for an old mission in the New World. Not even Ebenzer knew that his mission would take a lot longer than three months.

A Room, a Bed, and a Table

The spare bedroom in the Bauman home became the first office of RBMU in North America! Somewhere they acquired a second-hand desk, managing to shoehorn the unwieldy item into the already-cramped sleeping quarters. The desk fit—almost. With no room for adjustment, the door refused to shut properly. Walter Bauman resolved the problem by cutting a hole in the door to accommodate the protrusion! The nerve center of the new Mission was complete. The address was 1935 East Willard Street, Philadelphia. It would adorn the RBMU letterhead for months to come—and hundreds of personally handwritten or typed letters in the months ahead.

Leona Bauman, who did not type, became RBMU's first secretary! What she lacked in typing dexterity she made up for in people skills. Leona had contacts. Prominent leaders—Dr. Richard Seume, pastor of Madison Avenue Baptist Church in Paterson, New Jersey and later chaplain to Dallas Theological Seminary; Dr. Whiting, dean of Pennsylvania Bible Institute; Dr. Lehman Strauss, well-known conference speaker; Dr. Ralph Mitchell, of the Pocket Testament League, and Walter Allen—the accountant from Paterson. On 23 July 1948, Vine could thankfully report "the coming into being of councils[433] of the Regions Beyond Missionary Union here in North America," listing for the US Council the following names:

Ralph W. A. Mitchell (Chair)	Richard Seume
Donald F. Ackland	Lehman Strauss
Walter C. Allen (Treasurer)	A. B. Whiting
Leona Bauman (Secretary)	

In the same letter, Vine listed the charter members of the RBMU council for Canada:

Watkin Roberts (Chair)	William Parlane
J. C. Horning (Treasurer)	A. C. Simmonds
M. S. Flint	

Harvested from Vine's campus tours, new recruits descended on the Bauman residence. At first, there were no candidate schools. Just candidates! They slept three in a bed, on the sofas and on the floor. They went to the ends of the earth—to India, Nepal, Congo, Peru, Borneo, and Dutch New Guinea. Through the years, Walter and Leona Bauman became catalysts for missions, their home a way station for those who went out "for the sake of the Name." Leona was a true "Mother in Israel," and always had a fresh, uplifting word from God for all comers. Her Bible study groups nourished hundreds. She later recalled, "We didn't know when we opened our little home to the RBMU—we called it 'the stable of Bethlehem'—that God would give us a worldwide outreach. I wanted to go into all the world. Instead, he brought all the world to our home."

The Bauman Home—Ebenezer G. Vine's First Port in America, 1948.
Left to right: Leona Bauman, Ebenezer Vine, Walter Bauman.

31

A Tiring War of Movement

An astute businessman coming on to the campus and seeing the crying need remarked rather casually, 'You could use a million dollars here.' I replied, 'It would utterly ruin us! We would become so self-sufficient that we would not need to call on God for help.'

—Leslie. E. Maxwell

Beachhead

Arriving in North America in April 1948, Ebenezer wasted no time. Sylvia Sirag's vigorous itinerations had already paved the way, and numerous contacts awaited him, especially for Borneo—the John Tolivers, the Bud Merritts, Gudrun Lima, and the Elmer Warkentins.[434] He followed trails already blazed. Doors opened everywhere, among them, the Bible Institute of Los Angeles, Moody Bible Institute, Columbia Bible College, and Prairie Bible Institute. In twelve months he traveled between thirty and forty thousand miles in what he called "a constant, tiring war of movement."[435] Dr. A. E. Harris, of Eastern Baptist Seminary, who had written urging the London Board to bring Vine to the US, now opened doors for him all over the country. By January 1949— eight months after his arrival—six new workers had been appointed for service in Indonesia, Congo, and India.[436]

Vine had more than one contact in Canada. John B. Leech, a former RBMU missionary to India, was well known to Ebenezer. Leech was British, but had retired to Toronto with his Canadian wife. Watkin Roberts had been a missionary to the headhunters of Assam in northeast India, and had been instrumental in the founding of the Indo-Burma Pioneer Mission. Andrew McBeath, a former RBMU missionary to Congo, was also in Toronto (He joined the Canada Council in 1951). Vine cemented these contacts, forming the Canada Council of the RBMU in Toronto on July 13. Watkin Roberts would serve as chairman for nine years.[437]

The Peru Inland Mission

A. C. Simmonds, a Canadian electronics manufacturer, had for years sponsored the independent work of Annie G. Soper in Peru, known as the Peru Inland Mission (PIM). Soper had stayed in the Simmonds home while attending Toronto Bible Institute before her departure for Peru in 1915. The inauguration of the Canada Council of RBMU in 1948 and its linkage with Simmonds assured the integration of the PIM with RBMU. The amalgamation was formalized on October 1 of the same year.[438]

The 31 May 1949 meeting of the Canada Council is noteworthy, as Elmer Warkentin, together with Bud and Dora Merritt of Vancouver, attended. Warkentin was formally appointed for the work in Borneo. Also present was Ernest Olsen, who had worked with the PIM since 1940 as director of the Bible school at Lamas. At the 28 January 1950 meeting of the Canada Council, Mr. and Mrs. Watkin Roberts opened their home to begin a monthly RBMU prayer meeting on the second Tuesday.[439]

Hands Across the Sea

Since one of Vine's primary missions in North America on behalf of the British board of RBMU was to generate support for financially beleaguered British missionaries, a special joint meeting of the Canadian and American Councils convened in Toronto on 29 June 1950. For the British board, May had been the bleakest month in memory. No allowances could be sent out, and debit balances were being carried forward. This generated disparities, since North American missionaries (Dale Leathead, Ralph Sarver, and Dick Perkins—all in language school at Landour) had ample support, and were willing to share, but support—which went through London channels—could not reach them.[440]

The June 29 meeting addressed the emergency. The China Inland Mission offered their facilities for the purpose. Extended periods of waiting upon God marked the three sessions. In a leap of faith, the joint North American Councils agreed to assume the support of British RBMU in the non-sterling (dollar] areas of operation, namely, Congo, and Peru. The commitment was more than $78,000. The step led to a continent-wide advertising effort through the Christian media, and it gave the fledgling Mission its first large-scale visibility in North America.

Japan's Open Door

By 1950, Ebenezer Vine's cas campusrances had generated collateral interests, especially for entering Japan. He had been approached by a number of students in various schools and universities, eager to enter that country under RBMU. A large group of Japanese students from the University of Tokyo had come to the University of Wisconsin and were attending a church where Vine was preaching. They were keen for action. Likewise Ralph Mitchell of the US Council who was with the Pocket Testament League and heavily engaged in the distribution of ten million New Testaments in postwar Japan, pressed the councils to seize the opportunity, offering all the help that PTL might muster.

Watkin Roberts had received a letter from a missionary in Matsuyama, pleading for additional laborers. She urged the new Mission:

> With the readiness of the people to receive the gospel, it seems a crime not to give them a chance to hear. Because the gospel agencies are so slow, the people are returning to their old faiths. Temples and shrines are on the increase. A well-educated lady with whom I have just been talking had never heard anything about the gospel. There are multitudes like her. May the Lord guide you definitely into all his will for your mission.

It was not to be. When the opportunity was urged upon both the Canada Council and the London Board, the economic straits of postwar Britain were again raised as insurmountable obstacles. American RBMU was still in its infancy. Beholden to its parent board in London, it could not press the matter further.

Prepare for War

For all the activity, life was never without a splash of humor. Vine's hearing loss made him oblivious to the high-pitched whir of the gearbox of his aging Plymouth as he raced the New Jersey Turnpike—in second gear—at speeds that sometimes exceeded his age.

There were frequent trips to New York to the docks to see missionaries off. Air travel was expensive. Freighters and occasionally passenger vessels not only offered cheaper fares, but also allowed on-board time to relax, with stops at exotic ports of call along the way. It was something most British missionaries looked forward to on return from a term of service, as it provided time for R&R before plunging into the frenzied round of deputation assignments waiting for them on arrival home.

Missionary departures were celebrated. Friends readily traveled in automobile caravans the one hundred-plus miles from Philadelphia to the New York docks, although the round trip would consume an entire day. When Marinell Park embarked for Peru in 1949, Christine Eggers accompanied her to New York, together with the customary entourage of RBMU council members, family, and friends. Both Marinell and Chris were graduates of Prairie Bible Institute, where each senior class traditionally adopted a motto, having worked for weeks to design a large plaque on which the class watchword was artistically emblazoned. Nurse and linguist Park was in the class of '49, and their chosen motto was *"Prepare for War!"* referring, of course, to the spiritual conflict of missions.

In the crush of well-wishers straining to wave farewell at the quayside was a stranger with a black valise bearing the United Nations emblem and seal. As the ship loosed her hawsers and began to slip away and the handkerchiefs were waving, Christine Eggers looked up at Marinell waving back from the ship's rail. At the top of her lungs, Chris emitted the battle shriek, "Prepare for War!" The man with the United Nations briefcase looked Chris up and down, surveyed her crowd of well-wishers, and without further ado turned heel and bolted from the crowd.

A Present Help

Bertel G. Vine, the eldest of Ebenezer's three daughters, had gone to India in 1938 with the RBMU. She worked in the villages of North Bihar, mainly with women and children, until the blow fell that would redirect her life. Her mother, Bessie, who had returned to Britain for a brief holiday, died in 1953. Bessie had sailed on November 27 to minister to her daughter, Eunice, who had contracted polio, but she herself was stricken with a heart attack a few days after landing. On receiving the news Ebenezer flew to Britain and was with his wife when she expired on December 13. Vine was now bereft of his helpmeet. Without her, the rented house they had shared on Jeannes Street in the Fox Chase section of North Philadelphia was no longer a home.

Within a few months Bertel received letters from both the US and the British boards asking her to consider returning to the US to be with her father in his work. Both boards expressed the confidence that such a move would benefit the whole Mission. At the same time Ebenezer wrote his daughter to assure her that he was not requesting what he knew would be a sacrifice for her and that he would be very happy for her to remain in India.

After consultation with the Mission leadership in India and well-exercised in prayer, she agreed to come, arriving in Philadelphia early in 1955. From 1955–1964, she became her father's adjutant, travelling with him on many of his tours throughout North America, endearing herself to all as RBMU's hostess and spiritual mother to scores of missionary candidates. Upon her father's death in May 1964, Bertel returned to India the following year for a further term of service with the Duncan Hospital in Bihar Province. She was there until 1971, when she came back to Philadelphia to serve as host and board member until the Mission merged in 1995.

The Man

Vine's efforts in planting RBMU in North America were prodigious. He had no typist-secretary, but the staccato rhythm of his manual typewriter from his bedroom-cum-office assured a steady flow of missives to consulates, expressions of thanks to supporting friends, and encouragement to missionary candidates. Seemingly tireless, Vine had the rare gift of snatching ten-minute naps at will, rising refreshed and recharged.

Ebenezer Vine's frugality stood in sharp contrast to the American lifestyle, even in the immediate postwar years. While others flew to speaking engagements, he took the bus, thinking nothing of a thirty-hour bus ride. Not only was it less expensive, but his ability to catnap on these drafty and rumbling vehicles afforded solitude for meditation in preparation for his assignments. When the treasurer for RBMU Canada expressed inability to understand how Vine was managing on his miniscule "allowance," all members urged that it be increased. In his inimitable English, Vine promised that he would let the council know "if grave consequences were experienced," adding that "so far, with considerable care, this has been avoided."

He knew firsthand what British missionaries had suffered through the war years, many of them living on sharply reduced allowances, or going without furlough. Even a decade after the conflict, within the community of British missionaries, it was rare to receive a birthday or Christmas card that had not been recycled—the original signature scissored out and replaced with that of the current sender. These realities honed Vine's frugality and sharpened a keen sense of husbandry for the resources that had been given, often at personal sacrifice. It would be a long time before Vine exhausted the supply of the little bars of hotel soap carefully squirreled away from his constant itinerations. When in 1957 the Mission finally secured one-half of a vintage three-story duplex to serve as headquarters, all furnishings were second-hand. Costly upgrades were frowned upon, and improvisations were the order of the day.

His hearing loss eventually called for two hearing aids, which he sometimes wore simultaneously, and employed with annoying habit, turning them off when he deemed that a conversation—or someone's prayer—had run its course.

Ebenezer G. Vine was a spellbinding storyteller who made missions live, his trademark circumlocutions notwithstanding. Anything that might be said effectively in one hundred words or less, Ebenezer could deliver in two hundred, but with mesmerizing effect. The forward thrust of his jaw had a determined set which seemed to lead his body, projecting an intensity and a seriousness that commanded respect, while suffusing sufficient expectancy in the audience to hear him out.

His Letters

Vine cultivated personal relationships. His letters were a wellspring of encouragement to many a spiritual foot soldier. In the early days of the North

American work, every gift was honored with a hand-written note. However, his greatest legacy to aspiring missionaries was that of a man who had the ear of heaven. He prayed.

While Ebenezer Vine was a visionary and a motivator, it is fair to say that he was undistinguished as an administrator. Bringing structure to what God was doing through the American Mission would be left to others who would follow. He pointed to the dream of what could be, and people followed him to the ends of the earth.

His Selflessness

Betty Pritchard, who was with him in India, had her own brushstrokes to add to Vine's portrait when she said:

> Ebenezer Vine had attained a degree of selflessness reached by few of us. In his life, God was truly first, others next, himself last. Because he was completely unselfconscious, he could listen to others as if nothing else mattered in the world. He never discouraged confidence by appearing impatient to be getting on with the next job, or by matching others' troubles with an account of his own.

A Daughter Remembers

His daughter, Bertel, who knew him as well as anyone, recalled:

> Nineteen fifty-five through nineteen sixty-four were very happy years, full of joint ministry with my Father. There were many problems, but also many joys. The Lord allowed Dad to be active until just two weeks before He took him home. His diary was full of engagements until that time, and then it was suddenly blank. The Lord himself had surely planned it. I often wondered if Dad puzzled about the sudden lack of engagements, or if he understood. That was the year 1964, shortly before his eightieth birthday. What fruitful years those were! In Borneo and New Guinea particularly, there was tremendous response, so that from Stone Age people came a vibrant, witnessing church.

Ebenezer G. Vine was "on the stretch" to the end, and was pleading the case for world evangelization from a Philadelphia area pulpit the morning he was stricken with his final illness. His legacy sings in many once-dark places of Earth.

32

A Severe Test

I entreat, I implore our dear brethren not to think of the petty shopkeeping plan of lessening the number of stations, so as to bring the support of them within the bounds of their present income. But instead to bend all their attention and exertions to the great object of increasing their finances to meet the pressing demand that Divine Providence makes upon them.

—William Carey

Man on Borrowed Time

Ebenezer Vine had been in the States for a year when he came down with hepatitis—an illness that nearly took his life.[441] Bessie was with him through the seven-week crisis, and though alone in a new land, she had resigned herself to releasing him, should God have willed.[442] E. J. Pudney, director of the Unevangelized Fields Mission, opened their facilities to Vine for his convalescence.[443] For Ebenezer, the episode became a perpetual reminder of his mortality, and ever after, he referred to himself as "a man on borrowed time."

Tension with Toronto

Vine's critical illness sent shock waves throughout the fledgling Mission. Watkin Roberts of the Canada Council expressed his fears to American chairman Ralph Mitchell "that Mr. Vine's recovery might not be very soon" and that: "conditions would justify London sending their best man to this continent," adding that "Such must be a good mixer."[444] At sixty-five and seriously ill, Vine's viability was at stake, and with it the future of the North American RBMU. Roberts was understandably concerned to hedge all bets on Vine's recovery. But there was more.

The Canada chairman held misgivings about Vine's acceptability to North American audiences, complaining that "his ministry in public is unfortunately such that few places seem disposed to invite him a second time."[445]

This concern, expressed repeatedly by Roberts, partly explains the reluctance of the Canada Council to subsidize Vine's living expenses in North America and their opposition to the purchase of a headquarters facility for the new work, the latter a matter which Vine had repeatedly pressed. It also explains the Canadian determination to identify a younger man to represent the RBMU in Canada. A number of efforts to fill this gap would prove abortive until the appointment of Rev. Elmer Austring in 1970.

Meanwhile, Vine had gone to Britain in 1951 for a three-month visit to reestablish connections and to discuss with his daughter Bertel the possibility of her coming to Canada and the States to bring "a first hand report from the field."[446] During Vine's stay in Britain, Roberts continued to question his [Vine's] return to North America. However, both the American Council and the London Board followed their convictions and affirmed to the contrary, the London Board going so far as to encourage the Canadians to provide financial assistance.[447]

Vine was aware of the Canadian criticism, which would have discouraged lesser men. While generously conceding the questions about his suitability, with equal generosity he pressed London to release someone for the North American work. When such was not forthcoming he expressed to the Board "his deep sense of duty" to return to North America.[448] Notwithstanding, the hurt was scarcely concealed in a note to the Canada Council written on board the RMS *Queen Mary* (23 April 1951). Responding to a cabled greeting received on shipboard, Vine referred to his send off in New York:

> I was equally blessed in the States, where . . . there must have been at least 15 who showed their warmth by "accompanying me to the ship." They did not weep over me, as another company did over Paul, declaring rather that "they hope to see my face again," in which desire I also share.[449]

These tensions were more than trivial. In 1952, RBMU's entry of Dutch New Guinea was expected shortly. The acute deprivation suffered by postwar British missionaries demanded large infusions of funding from North America. Vine had played a magnum role in securing such support from both the US and Canada.[450] However, the Canada Council could not see its way to release its limited income (most of it earmarked for other purposes), particularly for opening a new field. On the question of entering New Guinea and Japan (Vine had already recruited one candidate for Japan), the two councils simply agreed to disagree.[451] Compounding the tension had been the London Board's mandate to Vine upon his return, "not to undertake any kind of public work in Canada"—an embarrassed concession by London to the Canadian position.[452] However, the standoff was soon to be resolved by practical considerations. Ebenezer Vine's recruitment efforts—particularly at Prairie Bible Institute with its nearly equal ratio of Canadian and American students—had begun to produce a crop of candidates of both nationalities for RBMU fields, particularly for Dutch New Guinea. This was the proof of the pudding and could not be gainsaid.

Call to Prayer

Vine's gifting as a spiritual motivator may be judged from his efforts in mobilizing prayer for missions. The Borneo Prayer Group, arising from his contact with Greet van't Eind in 1929, continued through the war years. On New Year's Day 1953, he successfully brought Mission representatives and friends of mission together at the Philadelphia Bible Institute for a day of prayer, the writer among them. Upwards of four hundred were present for the event. It was a precedent maintained for several years. Vine had convened a similar gathering three years earlier in Toronto.[453] His voluminous correspondence was shot through with impassioned calls to prayer. When financial straits had brought the British board to an impasse, he wrote from Britain to the Canadian Council:

> For myself, I feel the necessity of waiting upon God in deep, unhurried prayer. I do not believe anything other than that will solve our problems. Here in Britain, I am entreating the Board to set aside a special day for humiliation and prayer before God . . . May I beg that a similar day be called for on your part? Eternal issues are at stake, and lesser things should make their less imperious call.[454]

Pakistan

By 1955, RBMU had several North Americans in India—Dale and Jeanette Leathead, Chris Eggers, Ralph and Lorraine Sarver, Rosella and Roy Smith, and Vera Mikkelson. With increasing restrictions on foreigners and the possibility of their not being able to reenter the country, their future service was in jeopardy. Vine exhorted the London Board to consider entering neighboring Pakistan with its one hundred millions of people. He challenged, "there is a tremendous interest in the States in the sub-continent of India generally. Potential carries with it responsibility. Can we rightly ignore it?"[455] Again, however, the London Board was unable to take up the gauntlet.

Borneo Pioneers, Gudrun and Clara Lima, share the Moody Bible
Institute Alumnus of the Year Award.

On board the SS *Santa Maria.*
Left to right: Leona Bauman, Christine Eggers,
and Peru-bound Marinell Park, 1949

33

Among Men of Blood

No man is worthy to succeed until he is willing to fail. No man is morally worthy of success until he is willing that the honor of succeeding should go to another if God so wills.

—A. W. Tozer

Back to Borneo

Backed by Ebenezer Vine and the Borneo Prayer Fellowship in London, the Bill Sirags (whom we met in an earlier chapter) also enjoyed the support of Bill's home church—Madison Avenue Baptist—in Paterson, New Jersey, where Edward Drew was pastor. These friends had incorporated the West Borneo Christian Mission*s,* an agency to facilitate financial remittances for the Sirag venture. On 24 June 1937, a cluster of well-wishers saw the couple off from London's Victoria Station for Dover and the channel crossing to Calais. Then it was a train to Marseilles, where they boarded the *Jean La Borde* for the Indies via the Suez Canal. One month and three days later, they arrived in Singkawang, West Borneo.[456]

While studying the Malay language in Singkawang, the Sirags reconnoitered the Landak district, but without any leads on where to find the Christian Dayaks left by Greet van't Eind. One day Bill Sirag "set out on foot through the jungle accompanied by his Bible, a hammock, and his God." A few letters left by Greet had mentioned the names of three converts—Oejang, Ranti, and Ilak. Suddenly, the figure of an approaching native appeared, and "After a little conversation [Sirag] found that this man knew Oejang—one of the faithful Christians," and led him to Oejang's village. The Dayaks pled with him to stay and teach. Darit was close to Perigi and had often been visited by Greet, so with this linkage, the Sirags selected Darit as their base. For two and one-half years they witnessed to the Dayaks, and saw conversions, but the response was not large. They baptized nine believers and started a small church near Perigi.

By the end of 1939, the Sirags had spent themselves. Insufficient food and rest had taken their toll. They decided to return to the States and—trusting God for travel money—moved to the coast to await the mail boat. The letter it brought contained the awaited funds—but only enough for one passage. Children traveled free, but with Sylvia seriously ill, Bill would have to remain in Borneo.[457] This painful decision sealed Bill's fate at the hands of the Japanese, as we have seen.

After the war, ill of health and bereft of her husband, Sylvia Sirag had embarked on her campaign to establish a mission in Dayakland. Her indefatigable efforts had secured both Ebenzer Vine's support and the establishing of RBMU councils in Philadelphia and Toronto. With recruits in the pipeline, Sylvia was now free to return to her beloved Dayaks to await the arrival of the new RBMU workers.

Delayed by a dockworkers' strike, she finally sailed from New York for West Borneo on 8 November 1948.[458] Vine had a board meeting, but Richard Seume and Walter Allen saw her off. California appointees, Mr. and Mrs. John Toliver, had also been delayed to await the birth of their daughter Joy, born on December 12. Gudrun Lima would not follow for another six months, sailing on 19 May 1949. The two women would together pursue their vision to reestablish the work that the Sirags had started before the war. They went inland to the Landak River region, settling in the town of Darit, the seat of the government district in which Perigi was located.[459] Perigi was the town where it had all begun in 1932 with Greet van't Eind's solitary foray, and where it faltered temporarily with her death in 1935. What they found was not encouraging. Under the Japanese occupation, imperial troops had searched out professing Christians and confiscated their Bibles, which they then burned. "Fear gripped their hearts," and many turned back to village ways."[460]

Dayak Darkness

"Village ways," as Gudrun Lima would discover, was a daily litany of terror. The Dayak were animists, their life driven by the need to appease malevolent spirits. These abounded everywhere, inhabiting rocks, abnormal tree formations, and certain bamboo groves. In the call of a bird, a spirit speaks. A chirp to the left of the path was an evil omen, requiring a change of plan—sometimes abandonment of a harvest just begun. A chirp to the right was an omen of blessing. Spirit-sources of evil omens had to be bought off—placated with offerings of grain and often with the blood of pigs, dogs, or chickens. *Shamans* (witch doctors) would "capture" souls that cause illness, imposing taboos, which in turn would often deprive "patients" of health-giving foods. With no sense of inconsistency, this lifestyle was often conducted behind a thin veneer of Islamic duty or within a syncretistic blend of Roman Catholic profession.

Not far from the mission house in Darit stood a gruesome *ironwood man* amid a clump of tall trees, a familiar figure to Gudrun Lima:

> From time to time one may note that he has a new set of clothes, or that the woven red and white headband has a newish look to it, as weather and insects have caused its decay . . . The crude shelter with its roof of platted palm leaves . . . undergoes a major repair job periodically, as dampness and mold silently labor in their destructive pursuits. But the wooden man stands much the same, year in, year out, his outstretched arms ever symbolizing protection to those whose trust is in him.

The village of the ironwood man was typical of Dayak villages in Kalimantan in 1949:

> There is the longhouse with its muddy pig population below, its cackling, egg-laying occupants in the rafters above, and the in-between layer being the mingling of human and canine dwellers of various ages and temperaments. Silence is a rarity, found only when all are away in the rice fields. Before every door, one would note bits of dried leaves, shaven bamboo sticks, or other evidences indicating to whom allegiance is given.

> Though [closest] to the church, [the village of the ironwood man] has maintained an almost solid front against the entrance of gospel light, [its residents] content to leave their future in the hands of the little wooden man whose sightless conch-shell eyes stare blankly through the maze of jungle undergrowth.[461]

Key to the Fortress

From the outset, Sylvia Sirag and Gudrun Lima knew that nationals were the key to evangelizing the Dayaks, and that these must be trained:

> "We are much concerned for native workers, for the great burden of the work must be carried out by such," Sylvia wrote, "The Dayaks know their own people . . . Gudrun and I have talked over the need to establish a Bible school . . . For the present we do not see how this is to be worked out, but we are asking the Lord to show us the pattern."[462]

Obstacles seemed to abound, and in the same letter Sylvia reported:

> The new government of Indonesia find themselves in need of funds to run the country. Lacking these, they have just served us notice—with all other residents and nationals—that all the money which we now possess is to be halved. The owner takes one half; the government takes the other. In respect of this the government proposes to issue

bonds bearing the nominal value of the amount taken and which will be redeemable in 40 years [1991]."[463]

This was no currency devaluation. It was, in fact, a government appropriation of private wealth—a 50% tax of all assets.

Breakthrough

How would two single ladies bridge into this Dayak culture, deep in Borneo's jungle, where human skulls adorned the average thatch-roofed family residence, and where animism held its victims in a thralldom of fear, and where their very name identified them as *men of blood?*[464] God held the key. It was revealed in a most unexpected way.

Two Meters of Cloth and a Phonograph

In 1949, the Indonesian government offered two meters of cloth to every Dayak family in Kalimantan. The good will gesture was part of the new government's plan to bond and unify the ethnically diverse nation now called Indonesia. Cloth was a prize to the forest people, and twenty-year-old *Sati* could not resist. He walked a full day from his home in Sapat to the distribution center at Darit to collect the treasure. Here he met Gudrun Lima and Sylvia Sirag, recently arrived. A *Gospel Recordings* platter was spinning on the phonograph. Curious, he listened. Sati was a bright youngster and quickly caught the attention of the missionaries. Needing someone to help with chores such as hauling water and collecting firewood for cooking, they invited him to work for them.

They could hardly have suspected that God had brought them a man who would become not only the first Dayak convert, but also a faithful witness and co-laborer for the next four decades! Sati, however, felt he must first return home to tell his father of the job offer. The women gave him a Bible and a songbook. He promised to return in three days. True to his word, Sati returned three days later to work for the missionaries in Darit. In nearby Ansang they had bought a piece of land where they would build a house. Sati helped clear the land. He washed dishes and performed other household chores, sleeping nights nearby in the home of a Moslem family he knew.

As the weeks passed, he accompanied the women on their trips to preach the Gospel in the outlying villages. Their rigorous effort went unrewarded. The following year they repeated the schedule, but with little result. Only a handful of women and a few children cared enough to listen. Then something happened. It not only proved Sylvia right in her conjecture about Dayak evangelism, it also dropped into their laps the key to the explosive growth of the Dayak church that lay ahead.

Sati was sent home to his village of Sapat for a three-week holiday. During his stay, he assembled the village children each morning at five o'clock to teach them the songs he had learned. Returning triumphantly to Ansang, Sati assured the women that they could now find a willing audience in the Anik area, especially in his own village. Persuaded, the women went with him. He took them first to Anik, where they stayed the night and held a service. Then, they weiᴠ off to many other villages. The trails were muddy and slippery. Neveɪ.heless, their joy was full. Dayak hearts were at last open and receptive to the gospel.

Since Darit was the seat of the government district of Menyuke, village headmen frequently assembled there for meetings. Sati made a point of inviting these leaders to the missionaries' home in nearby Ansang to hear the gospel. One of these men was Bapak Sabit (meaning, the father of Sabit). Better educated than most in the area, he had served with the Dutch army. Excitedly, he related a dream he had experienced about a woman coming to his village with a message from God. Clearly, Gudrun Lima and Sylvia Sirag had fulfilled that dream. Bapak Sabit listened to their message and gave his life to God. His conversion had momentous impact. His education and Dutch army experience commanded respect wherever he went. Many were ready to follow his example. Even better, Bapak Sabit was eager to help spread the gospel, and often accompanied Sati to witness in the villages.

In Dayak culture, major social decisions for the group are normally made or strongly influenced by clan or family leaders. As village headmen gave their lives to Christ, they returned to their villages to tell everyone the good news. Soon scores of Dayaks decided to follow the path their headmen had taken, and the fledgling church began to grow.

Reinforcements

Sylvia Sirag's dreams of a Bible school were about to materialize. Elmer and Ruth Warkentin arrived in 1951. Both were Prairie Bible Institute graduates from the Frazer Valley of British Columbia. Elmer Warkentin's ardor for missions had been honed in boyhood through missionaries entertained in his parents' Saskatchewan home. The war interrupted his Bible school preparation, and for the duration he was "grounded to four years' truck driving." Just before returning to finish Bible school, "Elmer and his sister stopped at Pitt Meadows where they met Ruth Froese, a shy sixteen-year-old girl." He never forgot her. Both Elmer and Ruth had been dedicated to the Lord by Christian parents. In his third year missions class at PBI, Elmer's attention riveted on Sylvia Sirag as she pled the case for Borneo's Dayaks—"We need men, not just women!" Warkentin loved trucks, and when he heard that Sylvia had a 1½ tóh truck waiting to ship it was all the prompting he required. On 10 June 1950, he married Ruth, and on 20 February 1951, the couple boarded the *Ocean Mail* at the Seattle docks. Seven weeks later, they were in Borneo.[465]

Within weeks, fellow Canadians Bud and Dora Merritt joined the Warkentins. By mid-year nurse Clara Lima—Gudrun's sister—had mustered in. American nurse Gloria di Valentino and Australians Jim and Freda Giblett followed her in 1952. The RBMU task force now stood at ten. The same year di Valentino and the Merritts opened the Anik Medical clinic. However, by March, Sylvia Sirag's wartime ordeal had caught up with her health, and she was obliged to return to the States. The little woman from Iowa who had been the catalyst of RBMU's entry to Borneo would never return to Indonesia.[466]

In 1948, E. G. Vine had taken his message to the Bible Institute of Los Angeles (BIOLA), where Joe and Paulene Goodman heard the call of Dayakland. Graduating in 1949, the Goodmans sailed from Los Angeles 28 April 1953 on board the *Elizabeth Bakke*, of Norwegian registry. A breakdown of the vessel in San Francisco Bay gave the couple an unexpected three-week vacation in San Francisco. They arrived in Singapore a month later in June 1953.

By the time of Goodmans' arrival the Gibletts had left Borneo for medical reasons, and did not return. The Borneo roster was now down to seven, but not for long. American Alice Shelley had been scheduled to travel with Gudrun Lima, who was returning from her first furlough. However, Shelly's visa was delayed and she followed later by air, surprising everyone by arriving in Singapore several days before Gudrun! Together they sailed from Singapore to Pontianak.

In 1954, Olav Nyheim left WEC—an agency also working in Borneo—to marry RBMU nurse, Gloria di Valentino. Elmer Warkentin performed the ceremony. The Nyheims opened Ulu Tayan, a distant area where they established many churches and a medical clinic. Nyheim later won distinction as business manager for the Mission and as liaison officer between RBMU and Indonesian government offices. Mr. and Mrs. John Toliver—Sylvia Sirag's first contact at PBI—had also responded to Vine's plea for Borneo, and in 1949, awaited support. They did not make it.[467] However, the Borneo task force continued to grow. Scottish nurse Isabel Cowman joined them in 1959, remaining for one term. Australians Don and June Singer came in 1962. Jack and Ruth Wilson arrived in 1963, as did Ingrid Stippa and the Henry Thiessens.[468] These were the vanguard of RBMU's Borneo venture. Many others would follow.[469]

Gateway to Dayakland

Pontianak is a teeming port city in Southwest Kalimantan, the present name of Borneo. It is the principal gateway to Dayak country and connects with Darit by fifty miles of roadway, now partially paved. In 1949, travel between the two towns was a tortuous trek over rutted earth roadway, negotiable only by four-wheel drive vehicle. This could take a full day, sometimes three. As all supplies and personnel had to enter by this route, the Dodge four-wheel-drive

Power Wagon became the vehicle of choice. At times the front-mounted winch was the only means of extracting truck and cargo from ruts four feet deep and filled with water. By 1969, Mission Aviation Fellowship would anesthetize much of the pain of travel in Borneo's interior, but by then the Dayak Church had already been established, thanks to the Chrysler corporation's workhorse.

GPPIK Organized

On 17–19 March 1954, the Dayak churches associated with RBMU organized as the Fellowship of Gospel Proclaiming Churches, or GPPIK. (GPPIK is the Indonesian acronym for Gereja Persekutuan Pemberitaan Injil Kristus). The statutes of the association were officially adopted 22–24 May 1954. Two years later (June 1956), the GPPIK decided to build more schools in which to educate its people.

Berea Bible Institute

With the GPPIK decision to educate the Christian community, young people drawn from all the churches in the Landak River district of Kalimantan were invited to attend a six-week short-term Bible school. Encouraged by attendance far exceeding expectations, the RBMU staff laid plans for a permanent, full-scale Bible school. On 11 August 1957, twenty-seven enthusiastic young men and women began studies at *Sekolah Alkitab Berea* (Berea Bible School), with Elmer Warkentin as director and anchor.

Entry qualifications called for completion of sixth grade. An annual youth conference held in conjunction with Bible school graduation ceremonies became one of the largest feeders of the school. While Elmer and Ruth Warkentin, Gudrun Lima, and Alice Shelley comprised the early faculty, national teachers Atok, Otto, Njangkuy, and Njerom soon joined them. By 1989, the three-year Berea program had graduated 320 men and women. Berea graduates provided staff for other agencies such as OMF and the Conservative Baptist Hospital. Elementary school teachers, pastors, and evangelists throughout northwest Kalimantan were equipped at Berea.[470]

From inception, the Berea Bible School attracted students with little or no secondary education. After several years of grappling with this issue, the GPPIK Executive Committee in 1989 opened a four-year degree program, changing the name to Berea Theological Institute, with high school or Berea Bible School diploma as entry requirements. By 1989, students from both Kalimantan and Irian Jaya were studying at the Evangelical Seminary of Indonesia in Jogyakarta, completing college level programs, and planting churches. At the ESI, planting a church was a prerequisite to graduation.

Primary Schools

In primitive tribal contexts, RBMU had always been at the forefront in providing elementary education wherever government approval permitted, and always as a means to the end of developing evangelical leadership. The Mission opened more than fifty schools—the first at Anik in 1951 under Bud Merritt, then at Ansang in 1952 with Elmer Warkentin, again at Kampet in 1955 under Joe Goodman. Christian primary schools were not normally opened in a village until a church had been established. Since a 1954 government ruling prohibited foreigners from teaching in the schools, all instruction was carried out by Indonesians, while administration and properties remained under the control of the GPPIK church association. Since religion was a compulsory subject in Indonesian schools, teachers were free to present the gospel and provide Christian nurture.

How the Harvest Came

During their occupation of the Dutch East Indies from 1942–1945, the Japanese declared the islands a republic. As the war progressed and the outcome became clear, the Japanese Imperial Army encouraged Indonesian nationalists to prepare for independence and gave them freedom to organize. With Japan's surrender, the Nationalist Party led by Achmed Sukarno proclaimed Indonesia free on 17 August 1945.

The Dutch attempted to repossess the archipelago, which had been their domain for three hundred years, but the world had changed. Four years of hostilities ensued between the Dutch and Indonesian nationalists. The conflict ended on 27 December 1949, with the Dutch conceding independence to the United States of Indonesia. President Sukarno assumed dictatorial powers and promptly forged ties with Communist China. An attempted coup by Indonesia's pro- Peking Communist party was put down in 1965 by the Indonesian military with great loss of life. These events significantly affected the work of missions in Indonesia, and specifically in Kalimantan.

The Open Door

The overthrow of the Sukarno regime created an opportune climate for Christian evangelism. The new government—determined to unify and develop the unique diversity of a nation made up of 3,000 inhabited islands, three hundred ethnic groups, and more than two hundred languages—adopted a staunchly anti-Communist platform. All Indonesians were urged to adopt some form of religion, whether Hindu, Muslim, Buddhist, Roman Catholic, or Protestant.

Large sectors of nominally Islamic–Animistic Kalimantan now opened the door to Christian missionaries. Many were eager to distance themselves from Chinese communism, so it was common to be approached with the request: "We have registered with the local government as Protestant Christians. Now we want to become real Christians." Opportunities to present the gospel outstripped the availability of workers. Other agencies such as OMF reported thousands turning to Christ in Sumatra, Sulawesi, and elsewhere.[471] It was a time of momentous spiritual release. Later, the screws would tighten as Islamic leadership saw Christian growth as a threat to the dominant Muslim profile of the nation. For the time, however, God had opened a window, and a fair wind was blowing for the Church.

The breeze filled the sails of the growing GPPIK. Typical was a report from Elmer Warkentin in 1964. He had just returned from an eight-day trip into an unreached area:

> On April 8, a company of 64, composed of both students and Berea teachers, divided into eighteen groups and branched off in all directions to spend a week in villages where the gospel message had never been heard. Never before had such a venture been attempted. Satan did his utmost to stall this move into his territory. Rain fell till 10:30 a.m. Some groups left in the rain, others left immediately it had stopped. Our group walked four solid hours in pouring rain.

> The first night in the village of Djelajan 17 families and five single men came to know the Lord. In spite of weariness, we sat up to teach them God's word and some simple hymns. Then, with everyone watching, we crawled into our nets and slept till awakened at 5.00 a.m. by the calling of pigs. The next day the process was repeated, the entire village assuring us that all would receive Christ if we would promise to place a national pastor there. We could not. Thirteen years in Borneo and this was the first time we had been able to visit the region.

> The third day we trekked all morning through leech infested jungle. That night after pulling many of the blood sucking parasites from our bodies, we had another make-your-heart-ache meeting. The headman and most of the village people declared they would only believe if we would promise to guide and instruct them. We could not make that promise.

> For a whole week, our eighteen teams trekked like this, repeating the simple gospel message. There was little opposition. Many Catholics were among the listeners and many of them came to the Lord. There were many physical discomforts—unpalatable food, changing clothes in front of the entire village population, sore backs from the hard bamboo beds, mosquitoes, heavy packs, and wet clothes—all giving contest to a joyful spirit. Still, as with the 70, we "returned again with great joy to report all that God had done" through our 64 students and the missionaries who accompanied each team.[472]

Rampage

In November 1967, a Dayak rampage forced the Chinese to flee the region. The crushing of the 1965 communist coup, which had stigmatized the Chinese and slaughtered many Chinese immigrants, triggered the anti-Chinese vendetta. Another factor had played into the hands of the Dayaks. The Chinese, reputed as "the Jews of the Orient," were successful merchants. Their shops and enterprises, scattered throughout Kalimantan's Dayak communities, had monopolized the market, generating a long-simmering resentment within the Dayak community.

The 1967 uprising vented Dayak wrath and plunged Kalimantan into crisis. Chinese stores were savaged and looted. Once banned by the Dutch, headhunting reappeared. As many as three hundred Chinese were murdered, missionaries were endangered, and most were evacuated. Fifty thousand Chinese refugees crowded the coastal cities of Pontianak and Singkawang.[473]

By December, rioting had subsided and conditions had stabilized to the point where mission personnel could return to their posts. Notwithstanding, the brief reign of terror forever changed the complexion of the Berea Bible Institute. Before 1967, 25% of the student body was Chinese. After the uprising, they never returned. On 15 January 1968, the Berea Bible Institute reopened, with fifty-eight students enrolled. Atok—from the first graduating class—was on the teaching staff.

Expansion

During the 70s the Mission pushed into large unreached sectors of West Borneo—Ketapang, Sempatang, Serimbu, and Lumar Behe, placing Berea-trained Dayak evangelists and pastors. Working from widely separated bases, the Goodmans, Thiessens, Wilsons, Hoekmans, and Nyheims—fielded and coordinated teams of Dayak evangelists.[474] Clara Lima, Ginny Crapser, and Australians Don and June Singer staffed the Anik medical clinic, treating 8,000 patients a year. As Dayak leadership developed so did the desire for higher education. To accommodate the growing number of Christian students relocating in Pontianak, the Mission established a student hostel for Dayaks from inland areas, maintaining the facility for ten years. Under Henry Thiessen's leadership, RBMU opened an evangelical bookstore and constructed the first GPPIK church building in the port city. The Pontianak Mission house, which for forty years had provided rest and haven for missionaries, was released to the GPPIK.

To Pay or Not to Pay

By the 1970s, unprecedented Dayak receptivity to the gospel severely outstripped the ability of the RBMU staff to redeem the opportunities. Even the Berea Bible Institute was unable to supply the exploding demand for village evangelists. Since Dayaks lived at subsistence level, dependent on slash-and-burn farming, national church workers became unable to give themselves to evangelistic work without some form of subsidy.[475]

With growing pressure on western churches to share their financial resources with nationals, the Kalimantan team devised a plan to provide subsidy to qualified workers, permitting them to leave their secular activities for the work of evangelism. Individual missionaries were free to raise money to assist native evangelists. While the RBMU team was strongly committed to indigenous church principles and to the development of self-supporting and self-reproducing mission churches, most missionaries saw that this ideal could not happen overnight. The issue produced some tensions within the Mission team.

Throughout this period RBMU men met monthly for prayer and strategic planning on how to exploit the open door God had set before them. Torn between the 'no subsidy' ideal and the overwhelming opportunity, most were convinced that subsidy was the way to go. However, subvention was provided on a matching funds basis with local church participation. Few national pastors received full support during this exceptional period of harvest. The few who did were deployed in distant areas where no churches yet existed. World Vision International agreed with the subsidy approach and underwrote as many as seven evangelists for a period of three years.[476]

During this period the GPPIK fielded one hundred evangelists and teams, and in consequence experienced phenomenal growth and geographical expansion.[477] By 1989, 16,500 Dayaks had professed Christ, while 3,500 had been baptized. Of the 157 congregations, most of the pastors were virtually self-supporting.

Fifty Years Later

The closing decade of the twentieth century was not the brightest for the Dayak church in northwest Kalimantan. Due to increasingly restrictive government policy, by 1999 World Team no longer had resident missionaries in Borneo. Veteran missionary Joseph C. Goodman described the GPPIK of the 1990s as "a church under siege," citing a number of contributing factors:

First has been government restriction of missionary work and presence, with consequent persecution of Christians and burning of churches. Indonesia is a predominantly Muslim country. In 1995, a plague wiped out the domestic hog population, depriving the Dayaks of an entire year of income. This was followed in 1997 by unprecedented drought, which produced widespread forest fires and loss of crops throughout the island.

In three years (1994, 1997, and 1999) major tribal warfare erupted between the Dayak and Madurese people, leaving the church shaken and confused as to its responsibility and role amid the turbulence.[478] When the Indonesian economy collapsed in 1998 and 1999, church giving fell off sharply. Building projects were aborted. Lack of resources has led to apathy and tensions within the churches.

The political upheaval that engulfed Indonesia in 1999 led to the resignation of President Suharto. Rioting, killing, church burning, and vendettas followed. The secession of East Timor late in the year produced national unrest, UN intervention, and uncertainty respecting the political future of this diverse nation.

While widespread national distress had been reflected within the Dayak church, there was a bright side. Many Christians remained faithful in church attendance, evangelism, and visitation. New churches continued to spring up, and some building programs went forward. In 1999, World Team Asia Director designate, David Enns, stressed the ongoing need for expatriate missionaries in Kalimantan. The Dayak church—for all its illustrious history—is still emerging from third world status and requires the encouragement that western Christians may offer. In 1999, retired workers Joe and Paulene Goodman continued to make biannual pastoral visits to their old haunts in Borneo's forests. Senior men—such as David Enns and Henry Armstrong—continued ministry on a shuttle basis, conducting seminars, conferences, and Bible teaching in stints of three weeks to three months in length.

When in 1948 Ebenezer G. Vine took up Sylvia Sirag's challenge on behalf of the Dayak people, he lifted the latch of heaven's door to Borneo's Men of Blood. Thousands pressed in to sit down with the family of God. For any man that might have been achievement enough. However, in 1953, an even more bizarre chapter in the RBMU story was about to unfold. As always, the sovereign Lord of the harvest took the initiative.

34

Shangri-la

We went to a place called "Evil Spirit" or "the place where I die." It became this for me. Jesus allowed me to be crushed, to agonize, and to die to all that I held precious. The enemy's heavy attacks made deep inroads in our marriage and our health, but I would not exchange a day of it. For God, by his grace and faithfulness, kept me there.

—Helen Dekker

Dutch New Guinea

On 13 May 1945, World War II was in its final convulsions and General Douglas MacArthur's leapfrog New Guinea campaign was in the flush of victory. The Japanese had been ousted from Hollandia the previous April (1944) and allied military aircraft controlled the coastal airspace of the island as preparations were made for the Philippine and Mariana campaigns and the final assault on Japan.

The Archbold Expedition

Seven years earlier (June 1938) explorer Richard Archbold had entered the Grand Valley of the Baliem River, daringly landing the *Guba,* a PBY-2 Flying Boat, on Lake Habbema, 11,342 feet above sea level and 175 miles southwest of Hollandia. The expedition, sponsored by the American Museum of Natural History, had two main objectives. The first was to gather fauna and flora specimens from the north slopes of the Snow Mountains, which form the spine of New Guinea. The second was to make the first aerial circumnavigation of the globe along the line of the equator. An astonished Archbold and his party of scientists described a valley of "some 60,000 people whose existence had not been recorded, and who had never seen a white man." Weeks later, with mission accomplished, Archbold left behind a ton of supplies in order to lighten the load for the Guba's risky high-altitude take off. This bonanza ensured a friendly reception for what would happen next.[479]

Gilt-edged Disaster

With the war's end in sight, fly-overs of Dutch New Guinea's Baliem Valley became a popular tourist attraction for off-duty service personnel based in the Hollandia—Sentani coastal area. Because of its seclusion in the mountain fastness of the Oranje range, few outsiders had ever seen the Baliem.

Overnight, New Guinea's centuries-old secret became a curiosity among military personnel. Here, in the high plateaus of the central Oranje Mountains, communities of tribal people were still living in the Stone Age. From the air, their neatly manicured sweet potato gardens etched symmetrical patterns on the hillsides like so many patchwork quilts. A couple of war correspondents, awed by the bizarre discovery, nicknamed the Valley, "Shangri-la." Visits to the Baliem became so frequent that the number of service personnel flown over the Grand Valley grew large enough to form an organization. Dubbed "The Shangri-la Society," certificates were issued to members, giving the dates of their flights over the valley. For some of these visitors, the war would end on 13 May 1945.

A US Army DC–3 transport threading the Baliem Valley crashed high on the palisade and was consumed by fire. On board were twenty-four service personnel, including seven members of the Women's Army Corps, based at Hollandia. While five of the twenty-four survived the wreck itself, including three members of the WAC, within twenty-four hours two of the WACs succumbed to their injuries. One WAC and two servicemen survived.

Responding to the emergency, medical corpsmen and engineers parachuted to the valley floor with supplies and food. After bringing relief to the survivors, they began construction of an airstrip on which a glider could be safely landed and picked up again by a low-flying transport plane. Walkie-talkie equipment, also dropped from the sky, maintained communication with the base camp. To the surprise of the rescue party, the local people were neither friendly nor unfriendly. They kept a respectful distance from the white men, but brought food to them. Was this gesture the legacy of the Archbold party, seven years earlier?

The rescue took seven weeks. The extended retrieval focused public attention on the stranded party and on a tribal society forgotten by time. Newspapers made capital of the story. The presence of WAC Corporal Margaret Hastings, who survived the crash, infused the rescue operation with high adventure, as her personal narrative was widely reported throughout the United States.

The events of the crash and the fresh discovery of this tribal population and their strange culture gripped the attention of at least one American service member. Paul Gesswein was stationed in the Biak islands, just off the northern coast of Dutch New Guinea. He had been involved in the search operation and in his heart the conviction was growing that God was calling him to take the gospel to this Stone Age society. Upon discharge from the military some time later, Gesswein enrolled at Prairie Bible Institute in Western Canada. That is where he met Ebenezer G. Vine.

The PBI Connection

In the fall of 1948, Vine made his first visit to Prairie Bible Institute.[480] He was an instant celebrity. Elmer Warkentin, soon to make his mark among Borneo's Dayaks, lived in "K" dormitory. On the PBI campus there was a "J" dorm and an "A" dorm, and a "C" dorm. These imaginative designations allowed for future egalitarian expansion of the campus—at least up to twenty-six! The writer, then a first year student, was roommate to Warkentin, a senior classman, while Paul Gesswein occupied the adjoining dorm room. After the war, mission fever was running high. Ebenezer Vine's visit drew students like bees to honeysuckle. It was an opportunity Gesswein would not miss. Benevolently buttonholing the Calebesque Englishman, the ex-navy veteran closed on the dream he had pursued for nearly three years.

> "Mr. Vine, I have two questions to ask you. The first is, Does the Regions Beyond Missionary Union realize there are tens of thousands of tribespeople isolated without the gospel in the interior of Netherlands New Guinea?"

> "How do you know they are there?" Vine countered.

> Gesswein responded: "A military aircraft was missing on a flight over the interior. I took part in the search operations. As we flew over many uncharted areas of the interior, we were amazed to find valley after valley dotted with villages surrounded by extensive garden areas."

> Vine pursued the matter: "What is your second question?"

> Gesswein replied, "Will the Regions Beyond Missionary Union help me take the gospel to those people?"

> Awed by all that a positive answer to his question would entail, Vine first informed him that the Mission was already heavily committed to five fields—India, Nepal, Congo, Peru and Borneo—and then caught up in the excitement of it all, he added, "I'll see what I can do!" [481]

What Vine did would fill the remaining fifteen years of his life.

The Door Opens

Approval from the London Board of RBMU to rise to the unexpected challenge of Dutch New Guinea was the easy part. Getting approval from the Dutch government was another matter. Before the war, the Association of Baptists for World Evangelism (ABWE) had conducted a survey of DNG. When they sought entry after the war, their petition was denied. They never entered. Permission to enter Dutch New Guinea seemed impossible. Vine had made repeated visits to the Dutch Consulate in New York and three visits to The Hague (the Netherlands seat of government) to no avail. Each time the reply was the same:

> New Guinea is dangerous apart from armed protection, and such protection is not available.

Vine's tenacity eventually moved the Dutch Consul in New York, for on 26 May 1951 he received a letter from the Consul advising:

> In answer to your letter, I communicate to you that His Excellency . . . L. A. H. Peters, Minister for Union Affairs and Overseas parts of the Realm, will grant you an interview on Friday, June 1 at 3 p.m. in his office, The Hague.[482]

Wearied but undaunted, almost every day during Vine's stay at the Bauman residence—Leona Bauman recalled—"he and I would get down on our knees beside the couch and pray to God to open Dutch New Guinea. One day we came upon the verse, *"And the heathen shall know that I am the Lord God when I shall be sanctified in you before their eyes."*[483] Ebenezer rose to his feet, and—as if he had never seen the text before—said, "That's it! God must be sanctified in me before that door shall be opened." Evidently, the condition was fulfilled, for the door opened at last, and the first RBMU workers sailed for the East Indies in 1953.

The Vanguard

Two candidate couples for Dutch New Guinea had appeared before the newly formed RBMU council in 1949—the Gessweins (Paul and Joy), and the Widbins (Bill and Mary). Although appointed, they were put on hold for four years, awaiting visas. At last, in September 1953 the Widbins and Joy Gesswein departed for Holland, where they would take some language study and continue to await their visas. Paul already had his permit and went ahead to make preparations. He left the US West Coast in December, arriving in Dutch New Guinea in February 1954. He immediately set out to construct housing for the two couples.

Robert A. Jaffray

RBMU was not the first to challenge Dutch New Guinea's forbidding interior. That dream had been born in the heart of Canadian Robert A. Jaffray, whose missionary fires had been ignited by A. B. Simpson of the C&MA.[484] After distinguished service in China and French Indo-China, Jaffray trained his sights on (what is now) the Indonesian archipelago. World War II interrupted his plans for an island-hopping campaign throughout the archipelago. He died in a Japanese concentration camp in Makassar two weeks before the end of the war. However, others would carry his torch.

Before the war, Darlene Diebler and her husband had pioneered the C&MA work among the Kapaukus of eastern Dutch New Guinea. Like Jaffray, Diebler later died in a concentration camp at Pare-Pare. Mrs. Diebler had been imprisoned with Jaffray in the same facility. She recalled his undimmed vision for the tribes of the Dutch East Indies:

> I remember . . . an afternoon in 1942 when I saw an old man dreaming dreams. Sitting in the corner of a little house in which we were imprisoned, Dr. Jaffray was intent in the study of a map of that great sweep of islands then known as the Netherlands East Indies. How often we've poured over that map and mentally checked off the cities and islands as they were invaded and fell . . . Singapore, Sumatra, Java, and Celebes. "There, lassie," he said as I knelt beside the chair, "are the areas we must enter as soon as the war is over."

Though a prisoner, Jaffray was unfazed by the war. He had neatly assigned the global cataclysm of World War II to its subservient place in God's redemptive sweep through history, as Darlene explained:

> My thoughts were so full of the fears and anxieties, separations, and tales of atrocities that had become such a part of our daily life. Suddenly I realized that to him they were but passing events that never altered the program of reaching the unreached, events that never marred the dream! His fingers traced a path through the Natuna and Anambas groups of islands, encircled central and southern Sumatra, [and] passed over the haunts of the nomadic Punans in the hinterlands of Borneo. [He] caressed Bali with a prophecy that God would again reopen that door to the gospel, then moved on to Misool, the Isle of Demons, the Bird's Head of New Guinea, the Swart and Mamberamo River Valleys . . . at last coming to rest over the Baliem Valley.

> [Said Jaffray] "This is our task and I can hear the sound of going in the tops of the mulberry trees, the noise of the marching feet of the mighty army of young men and women that God is preparing for the occupation of these areas!"[485]

Among the marching feet were those of C&MA pioneer, Lloyd Van Stone, whose missionary vision was awakened when he fought in New Guinea with the First Cavalry Division. His assignment took him to the *Kapaukus* in the Wissel Lakes region of Dutch New Guinea. Likewise, Einar Mickelson had transferred in 1942 from Borneo to New Guinea, working among the Kapaukus for a year before the Japanese invasion. At war's end, C&MA was on the move again, and by 1949 had reoccupied their pre-war stations in New Guinea. Now their goal was *Shangri-la*—New Guinea's Grand Valley, which Jaffray's fingers had caressed prophetically on his map in his prison quarters. In the fall of 1950, Mickelson made the first contact with the Western Dani of the Ilaga Valley. These men broke the first ground for the gospel and paved the way for those who would follow.

Discovery of the Stone-age Dani of the Baliem Valley drew missions like a magnet. Among them were the APCM (Australian UFM), UFM (North America), ABMS (the Australian Baptist Missionary Society), and RBMU—which had been knocking on the door since 1949.[486]

Beachhead

Upon Gesswein's arrival in February 1954, he selected Sentani as the base for RBMU's jump-off to the interior highlands. It was hardly a difficult choice, since C&MA and UFM were already established there, and Dutch New Guinea was no place for loners. Sentani had been General Douglas MacArthur's operational HQ, and a number of concrete slabs and some Quonset huts were already in place. These now served as provisional housing for the missionary advance. High on a hill, the new quarters commanded a panoramic view of Sentani and offered easy access to the airport, just a mile away. Twenty-five miles to the northeast lay the deepwater port of Hollandia (now Jayapura) on the Teluk Bay. The town had been the terminus of MacArthur's logistical supply line during the war. It would now serve like purpose for a different kind of invasion. Meanwhile, Bill and Mary Widbin and Paul's wife, Joy, were still in Holland, awaiting visas. When the permits were finally granted, the trio traveled out together, joining Paul in May.

Carrying a party of C&MA missionaries, Al Lewis, former Canadian Air Force ace, made the first flight into the Grand Valley of the Baliem River on 20 April 1954, piloting a twin engine Sealand amphibian. The Dutch government had made twin-engine craft mandatory for flights from the coast to the interior.[487] Lewis' copilot was Edward W. Ulrich, an ex-US Navy flier. A Christian Kapauku family accompanied them.[488] The following morning brought C&MA linguist Myron Bromley. Other C&MA personnel quickly followed. Robert Jaffray's vision was about to flower.

Mission is always cruciform, and Dutch New Guinea was no exception. TEAM missionaries Walter Erikson and Ed Tritt, encouraged by the prospect of air service with the arrival of the C&MA aircraft, were murdered in 1955 while conducting a survey trip of the Bird's Head region of the island. Their death stirred students of Columbia Bible College to fund the purchase of an MAF *Piper Pacer,* which arrived in Sentani in September of the same year. Appropriately, they named it the *Pathfinder.* It had not come too soon. The previous April—one year after the first C&MA flight into the Baliem—Al Lewis failed to make it through the cloud-shrouded pass into the valley. The wreckage of his Sealander amphibian was spotted a month later. He became the first pilot to give his life for the evangelization of Dutch New Guinea's tribes.[489] He would not be the last.

The Arena

With a shape often likened to that of a prehistoric bird, New Guinea is the world's second largest island. Superimposed on a map of the United States, it stretches from New York to Denver. With its eastern tail dipped in the Coral Sea, its western extremity—known for its contour as the *Bird's Head*—appears to be in pursuit of the Philippines. The island is bisected by the 141st east meridian, the eastern half being Papua New Guinea [PNG], the western half retaining the name 'New Guinea' under the Dutch, and later, 'Irian Jaya' under Indonesian rule. Like the bird's giant spine, the Snow Mountains (*Pegunungan Maoke*) extend 430 miles, forming the western segment of New Guinea's Central Highlands. Much of the range lies above 12,000 feet, one peak—at 16,502 feet—capped with perennial snow.

This mountain fastness cradled 300,000 Dani tribal people as well as many smaller groups. For centuries, the rugged terrain had imposed geographical isolation and insularity on scores of tribal communities, not only from the outside world, but also from each other. In this way, God had preserved them for the coming of the gospel, as the Apostle Paul makes clear.[490] In 1954 the year of their visitation had come.

MAF Arrives

Earlier efforts by the APCM to enter Dani territory overland from the north were thwarted by hostile and impassable terrain. Now, with several agencies grouping at Sentani, it was clear that air service offered the only hope of reaching the interior.[491] Since APCM was already working with Missionary Aviation Fellowship (MAF) in neighboring PNG, the linkage was in place to open MAF service in Dutch New Guinea.[492] In 1955, the wings of heaven came to Sentani.

Room to Work

Within three years of the first landing in the Baliem, five mission agencies were on the scene, the Dani clans in their cross hairs. At the outset, some tensions were present as the several groups jockeyed for comity rights. Stone

Age tribes were a prize, and everyone wanted a share of the action.[493] Eventually, territorial agreements were reached. Missions with available personnel were free to enter unevangelized areas so long as they "did not compromise the geographic or cultural integrity of existing stations." Consequently, ABMS settled in the upper North Baliem, APCM on the northern slopes of the Halbifloerie River system, UFM in the upper reaches of the Rouffaer or Nogolo region, while RBMU entered the Swart Valley.[494] C&MA occupied the central and south Baliem, the Ilaga, and the Sinak Valleys.[495]

Sentani became the base for all the missions and later for MK schools, hostels, commissary, and Regions Press.[496] The RBMU print shop later fed the voracious appetite for literacy primers and Scripture translations generated by five mission agencies and explosive church growth.

Bokondini

On 24 April 1956, MAF flew Bill Widbin to Lake Archbold (where the floatplane could land), Gesswein following a day later. Leaving the Lake on 28 April, the men began the four-day trek to Bokondini, the proposed APCM base.[497] It was no Boy Scout outing. Cutting jungle track, clambering up steep slopes, picking their way for hours through a stony river bed, all the while negotiating with carriers, some reluctant, some cooperative. Friendly eye in the sky was pilot Dave Steiger, who made food drops along the way.

They arrived late afternoon May 1 and before dark were surrounded by two hundred natives—all friendly! Carriers were paid off and food items purchased with cowry shells, the coin of the realm. The men had brought plenty. With five hundred showing up for work the next morning, it was a good thing. Work began immediately on the first interior airstrip. It opened a month later, 7 June 1956.[498] Bokondini now became the springboard for the construction of other airstrips for missions working the interior. Within six years of the first landing on the Baliem River twenty mission stations dotted the Dani settlements, each dependent on the airstrip at its front door and the pilots who dared to land their tiny craft.[499]

Karubaga

Forty miles west of Bokondini in the Swart Valley lay the Dani settlement of Karubaga with a (then) estimated 12,000 inhabitants. Its 4,900-foot elevation offered an invigorating climate as well as an ideal airstrip site. Gesswein and Widbin had checked it out the year before after the opening of the Bokondini base. This would become RBMU's first station in the Central Highlands. In mid-April 1957, Gesswein and Widbin set out from Bokondini with six Senggi carriers.[500] Armed with food, gear, and thousands of cowry shells, they had flown the 170 miles from Sentani to the Bokondini strip. Now came the overland trek to the Swart Valley—three days this time. On the last day, a welcoming committee of two hundred natives came out from Karubaga to meet them. Accompanied by this exuberant crowd, they arrived at Karubaga.

First Airstrip

The men reached Karubaga on 14 April 1957, where 400–500 Danis—all yelling, dancing, and chanting in a cacophony of glee—expressed their joyous welcome. Unwitting, the jubilant Danis were fulfilling Isaiah's prophetic ejaculation, "How beautiful upon the mountains are the feet of him that brings good tidings!"[501] The next day work began on the airstrip. In multiple air-drops, MAF delivered 1,500 pounds of food and supplies. Through smiles and mute gestures—they had only a smattering of Dani—Paul and Bill marshaled a labor force of hundreds, all willing to work for a per diem of one cowry shell. Within three weeks, the strip was completed and Paul Pontier made the first landing on 7 June 1957.

With this precarious toehold at Karubaga, the RBMU mission began in earnest. Over the next three years, construction of housing, storage sheds, dispensary quarters, and schools became urgent priorities. Vegetable gardens were planted and cultivated, and livestock imported. New missionaries were arriving—nurse Victoreen Bigart and Hollanders Cornelius and Louise Vink (1957), Bill and Barbara Mallon and David Martin (Feb. 3, 1959).[502] New arrivals meant an endless succession of supply flights from Sentani, bringing in survival equipment. Native housing—rustic, smoky, thatch-roofed huts—was not an option. Health and viability in the austere and chilly environment demanded adequate shelter. Building supplies, stoves, rudimentary furniture, generators, and a sawmill—all had to be brought in by tiny Cessna aircraft. It was the price of ministry in New Guinea's highlands. The arrival of the Vinks left Bill Widbin free to return to Mary and their two boys at the Sentani base. From there, Widbin would coordinate the supply line.

Vine's Visit

No one yet knew the Dani language, and there was neither grammar nor dictionary to consult. In 1959, Ebenezer G. Vine, then seventy-five years of age, came to Dutch New Guinea to encourage his troops and to see first hand the fruit of his vision. He returned armed with graphic accounts of tribal warfare, unforgettable vignettes of cruelty, and fresh concerns for the safety of the missionary vanguard. The Swart was a habitation of darkness. Little girls, their fingers freshly amputated by stone axe, and boys whose ear tips had been hacked off, were common sights—both practices were expressions of mourning. Before his eyes, wounded warriors were carried to the dispensary, victims of spear and arrow wounds from the constant bloodletting that seemed to swirl around the Mission base as warring clans engaged in an endless cycle of vendettas. Karubaga was stress city, and not for the fainthearted.

As these accounts were shared in the Bible colleges and churches, volunteers stood in line to sign up—John and Glenna McCain, Phil and Phyliss Masters, Winifred Frost, Judy Eckles, and Bruno de Leeuw. John and Helen Dekker arrived in February 1960, then two couples came from Australia—Stan and Pat Dale, and Frank and Betty Clarke. Later (1961) they would be joined by Jacques and Ruth Teeuwen.

By March 1960—eleven years after Gesswein's encounter with Vine at Prairie Bible Institute—a handful of neophyte missionaries was about to witness one of the most spectacular dramas in the annals of mission history. What happened next must be seen in the context of some surprising antecedents.

Hai, Kelangin, and Father Kammerer

Ninety miles southwest of Karubaga in the Ilaga Valley, C&MA missionaries Don Gibbons and Gordon Larson had been working with a mixed population of Damal and Dani people. Knowing little of either language, the two men communicated with the Damals through an interpreter—the son of a local Damal leader who had learned to speak Indonesian in a Roman Catholic school. Damal mythology—they discovered—was dominated by the hope of a future millenarian existence called *Hai,* a concept that immediately resonated with the Christian message.

In 1938, Roman Catholic priest Tillemans had trekked into the Wissel Lakes region, where he spent a month. This was followed by two attempts (1952,54) by another priest, Father Kammerer, to reach the Baliem. On the second trip he took with him Moses Kelangin, a Damal who had graduated from a Roman Catholic teacher training school in 1953. The trip took them through the Ilaga Valley, where Kelangin encountered fellow Damal tribesmen. On his own, he began a preaching ministry, encouraging the Damal to burn their fetishes in preparation for the coming of *Hai.* The movement spread, and in 1955, some fetish burnings took place.[503]

Surprisingly, Kelangin's success met with reprimand for acting without authority, and the Ilaga Valley Damal expectation of *Hai* remained unfulfilled. In this way, the C&MA missionaries to the Ilaga in 1956 "stepped into a highly primed atmosphere and did not have to wait long to experience dramatic results . . . Within nine months of their arrival in the valley the first fetish burnings were taking place."[504] As the word spread, other Damal groups began fetish burnings, and by December 1958 the Ilaga Dani had begun to share the Damal enthusiasm and likewise began to burn fetishes. Missionaries now feared a mass movement void of Biblical moorings. Some questioned the motivational force behind the burnings. Was it an expression of discontent with their culture? Was fetish burning seen as a ticket to the fulfillment of *Hai*—the millennial expectation long buried in the Damal culture? White men seemed to descend from the sky and arise from the sea, disgorging untold wealth from their giant birds and ships. This had given rise to the cargo cult phenomena in many South Pacific islands. Had the missionaries unwittingly fueled the cargo cult expectations?

Finger of God

Another problem that disturbed missionaries accustomed to "the personal decision for Christ" was the mass movement aspect of the burnings. Within the Damal and Dani culture social decisions for the group were made by consensus and under the guidance of the clan leaders. Burning fetishes was the decision of an entire people. How could the Christian message effectively filter through such a process, which seemed to by-pass a *personal* decision for Christ?

In fact, motivation for the Damal fetish burnings (and later, those of the Dani) was an admixture of all of these elements. Moreover, receptivity to the missionary message was further influenced by a Dani creation legend—*Nabelan-Kabelan*—with its similarities to the Damal idea of *Hai*.[505] At the outset, there was little clear theological grasp of the gospel message. However, through this spontaneous movement God had opened the door to an otherwise closed culture and to the effective proclamation of the gospel. Culturally sensitive, C&MA's Don Gibbons and linguist Gordon Larson saw in the burnings the finger of God. It was pointing the Damal and the Dani to the One who would fulfil all their hopes of *Hai* and *Nabelan-Kabelan*.[506]

As news of the Ilaga Valley fetish burning filtered into other Dani settlements beyond the Ilaga, missionaries knew that the message must be rescued from becoming a garbled amalgam of half-truths, fiction, and superstition. Immediate steps must be taken to put the message into a simple credal form—a truly *authorized version*—easily transmitted and free of corruption. However, no one was able to do this as most missionaries working with the Dani were still wrestling with language learning. Addressing this need, the wider mission community invited Larson and a party of Dani Christians from the Ilaga Valley to conduct a teaching and preaching tour of all the mission agency bases among the Dani. However, before that took place, a critical visit was made to the Swart Valley.

In October 1959, Gordon Larson flew to Karubaga, accompanied by Jimbitu and Mejagome, two Christian Danis from the Ilaga. On the same day, Don and Eunice Richter (then with Gospel Recordings) joined them. The Richters had gone to the Ilaga in July—four months earlier—where they had made recordings in both the Damal and Dani languages, using different speakers for each lesson. Several speakers were used to assure the integrity of the message. Richter worked closely with Larson throughout this exercise, and at that point encouraged Larson to accompany his leading Dani believers on a visit to the Swart Valley. The proposal was cleared with RBMU-Karubaga and with the

C&MA, but with some apprehension as the Swart and Ilaga Dani were bitter enemies. So bitter, in fact, that when the MAF flight landed at Karubaga, the two Ilaga men were terrified to leave the aircraft.

Swart Valley Dani Chief Tibagalak orchestrated the encounter and for three days "the Swart Danis heard the gospel clearly explained to them for the first time in their own language and by their own kinsmen."[507] They heard how the Ilaga Dani had forsaken fighting, fetishes, and the taking of additional wives.[508] Gordon Larson now taped more gospel lessons, using his trusted Ilaga Dani duo. The Richters did likewise.[509] Excitement was running high. During the three-day visit, the two Ilaga Danis were in quarantine—for their own safety. A Dani hut had been constructed for them close to the missionary homes, lest the "enemy" should become victims of food poisoning or a surprise attack. They need not have worried. Don Richter was awakened at 3:00 a.m. by what he thought was a radio. Leading Dani men had come to the makeshift hostel to ply the Ilaga Dani with questions about the message. They talked all night. The "fullness of time" had come for the Dani of the Swart Valley.

Three days of recording sessions completed, hundreds of Danis gathered at the airstrip where Larson and the two Ilaga messengers awaited the MAF plane that would take them home. Jimbitu turned to Swart Dani Chief Tibagalak and said:

> "Why don't you take Jesus now?" Open and receptive, Tibagalak responded,

> "Am I ready?"

Jimbitu affirmed that Tibagalak was indeed ready and instructed him what to do next. Rising to his feet, Tibagalak raised his right arm toward heaven, and prayed:

> Greetings, Lord. We have never met before, but I come to you now. We here in our valley have heard your words for the first time. Make me strong in this newfound way, so that I in turn might teach my people. That's it![510]

Over the next weeks, Larson sent tapes from the Ilaga Valley. These were played over a public address system to groups large and small. They provided a vital transition during the early months at Karubaga while RBMU missionaries struggled to learn the language.

Power Encounter

The following month (22 January 1960) the bicultural Ilaga Valley team led by Gordon Larson embarked on a forty-six-day teaching itinerary which took them to all the primary Dani centers, finishing up with an extended stay in

Karubaga. Errors were corrected and a true response to the gospel was encouraged. Then the long-prayed-for breakthrough came. It was a cosmic
power encounter that must have shaken the corridors of hell. David Martin
was there:

> On Tuesday, they had a very large feast to celebrate the ending of their
> old ways and [their] desire to follow the truth. The next day [9 March
> 1960] they gathered . . . their fetishes and put them all on the fire—a
> fire about 150 feet long and six feet wide. All that had to do with war,
> spirit appeasement, and magical rites, was committed to the flames.[511]

While this pyrotechnic drama thrilled the missionaries, it also struck a note of
alarm:

> On both Tuesday and Wednesday, we had long services with the peo-
> ple, questioning their motives and . . . explaining that [burning their
> fetishes] did not signify that they had eternal life. The Ilaga Christians
> [then] diligently explained these things to them.[512]

Fears were allayed when Martin queried the local chief why he wished to burn
his fetishes. He replied, "I am going to burn them because they are bad. I want
to have eternal life. I want Jesus' blood to wash my heart. I want to go to
heaven."[513]

Dani warriors had always invoked the secret names of certain ancestors for
supernatural strength in battle—the *anggin kunik.* Few knew these names,
which were never spoken publicly, since—if learned by an enemy—they
would immediately lose their power. The Swart Valley Dani now began to
openly confess the sacred names, Karubaga's Dani chief Tibagalak leading
the way.

Thousands of preliterate Stone Age Danis had turned their backs upon the
dark side of their culture, but there was little time for triumphalism. A far
greater task now challenged the missionaries—a concern Ebenezer Vine had
expressed when he wrote, "Let us take to heart the basic fact that turning from
tribal war, the burning of fetishes, or any other outward reformation, cannot
become a substitute for inward change of heart."[514]

Change of heart could come in only one way—through assimilation of the
Living Word of God. The mass movement was a blessing in disguise, as it
immediately precluded that bane of mission—where missionaries succumb to
the lure of becoming pastor to new converts. There were simply too many of
them. Missionaries were thus forced from the outset to plunge into the preparation of national leaders as the key, not only to church multiplication, but
also to the very survival of the movement! Moreover, if leadership training
were an urgent imperative, it would have to be predicated upon an even more
basic necessity—teaching the Dani to read and write.

By 1961, airstrips had been opened at Kangime (20 miles from Karubaga in the Swart Valley) and at Mamit (an eight-hour trek north). Both sites had high concentrations of Dani settlements. The John Dekkers were posted to Kangime,[515] while the Frank Clarkes (Australia) and the Jacques Teeuwens settled at Mamit. Costas Macris had arrived in 1961, and promptly put his skills to work helping Dekker construct a motorbike trail between Karubaga and Kangime. This prodigious feat would facilitate oversight of the growing church.

Witness Men

Happily, linguist Gordon Larson had made progress in Dani translation. RBMU's Bill Mallon had also developed some language notes as had Dave Martin at Karubaga. Don Richter's earlier GR recordings completed the meager arsenal of teaching tools. Modeling on a successful pilot program begun by C&MA men in the Ilaga, the "witness school" was launched at both Karubaga and Kangime. Selected by their peers, the more able among the Dani males were designated as "witness men." For four days a week, these were instructed in simple credal statements of the gospel message, which they committed to memory. Returning to their hamlets the men shared what they had learned. As this process was recycled the truth was relayed to the hills and hamlets throughout the region and the audience was multiplied. In this way, the Danis shared the gospel freely throughout the region and the mission employed no paid evangelists.

Meanwhile, as missionaries wrestled with the language, they raced to construct literacy classrooms—ten classrooms for ten levels, with a primer for each. Everyone wanted to learn. At Kangime, 15 men in the witness class became the first literacy students. Using the Laubach method, those completing the third primer were assigned to teach primer one, with graduates of each successive level becoming teachers of what they had learned. In six months, they had completed all ten primers. This program was conducted throughout the Swart Valley. Scores of literacy teachers were trained, and thousands of Danis learned to read and write in this way. Later, Judy Eckles (who had arrived in May of 1962) coordinated the literacy program, with Danis doing the teaching.

New Hand on the Tiller

On 15 August 1962, the Netherlands agreed to transfer control of Dutch New Guinea to Indonesia. The United Nations monitored the transition, and Indonesia assumed full control in May 1963. Hereafter DNG would be known as Irian Barat (West Irian), and later, as Irian Jaya. With 14 RBMU appointees awaiting entry to New Guinea, the news created a stir, as Indonesia's policy toward missionaries was uncertain.[516] Some tribal factions resented the change and would later create trouble for both the Indonesian government and for the missionary community.

Meanwhile, at Kangime Dekker was coping with a growing Dani hunger for the Word of God as "every morning hundreds, sometimes as many as 2,000, mostly men, came to hear what God had written in his book."[517] These teaching sessions led to the first baptisms in the Swart Valley in February 1963 as thousands witnessed.

Church Government

As the church grew and Dekker worked to develop leadership-training materials, it became evident that some form of church organization would be essential. No effort was made to impose an imported ecclesiastical government on the young church. Instead, a few senior Dani pastors to whom other pastors normally looked for advice formed the first Kangime Church Council, selected by consensus of the twenty-four churches meeting in the area. Churches in Karubaga and Mamit developed along the same lines. Instead of leaning on the missionary, people with problems or disputes were referred to the Church council for resolution. In this way the Dani church moved easily into a form of self-government based upon the existing decision-making patterns within the culture, and leadership of local churches was in the hands of Dani Christians as soon as a church was established.[518]

Stewardship was taught from the start, and congregations provided for their pastors by cultivating their vegetable gardens and otherwise providing foodstuffs. From the outset, no foreign funds were used in developing the churches and no paid evangelists were employed.[519]

By 1965, the population of the Swart Valley was firmly estimated at 20,000. Twenty churches were functioning in the Kangime region, with an equal number planted both at Karubaga and Mamit. Danis had been trained to dispense medicines, but with the death of Ebenzer G. Vine (May 1964), the Vine Memorial Hospital was constructed at Karubaga the following year. A team of thirty-five RBMU missionaries was now deployed among five different tribes—the *Dani* at Karubaga, Kangime, and Mamit, the *Yali* at Ninia, the *Kayagar* at Kawem, the *Sawi* at Kamur, and the *Kimjal* at Korupun. A Christian Leadership Training Center at Kangime (1964) had proved so successful that it was moved to Karubaga, where it opened the following year as the Sekolah Alkitab Maranata (The Maranatha Bible Institute). SAM would train hundreds of Danis for Christian service and deploy scores of cross-cultural Dani missionaries to other tribal groups on the island.

When the Indonesian government decreed (August 1978) that expatriate missionaries must nationalize all work by 1981, RBMU moved to accelerate a process already begun—training accountants, administrators, and linguists. Until 1978, all teaching had been conducted in the Dani language, but now that DNG was part of Indonesia, the Dani church had no one qualified to represent their interests before the government. To remedy this, Maranatha Bible

Institute teachers were sent to the coast for further instruction in the Indonesian language, while Dani young people were packed off to Indonesian language high schools. By 1981, *Sekolah Alkitab Maranata* (SAM) was fully nationalized, with a Dani principal installed. So the church grew. In just a few years, light had triumphed over darkness in the Swart Valley. It was only the beginning of what God had planned for Dutch New Guinea.

Paul Gesswein and Bill Widbin
entered Irian Jaya's Swart Valley in April 1957.
See Page 258.

35

Lengthening the Cords

With all the problems of taking a family to live among stone-age people, learning a strange language, and adjusting to a different climate, I find it easy to become fearful and uneasy. Yet being confident of this very thing, that He who has begun a good work in me will perform it until the day of Jesus Christ, I can look with peace and anticipation to the mountainous task head.

—Phil Masters

Ninia

With the Karubaga base firmly established, RBMU looked eastward to even more forbidding valleys, where aerial surveys had spotted unknown tribal settlements clinging precariously to rocky forty-five-degree slopes. Ninia, peopled by the Yali, lay in the Heluk Valley, east of Karubaga. At 6,700 feet it was—and remained— the highest elevation of all RBMU stations. It took eleven months to carve the airstrip out of the mountainside. Mixtures of ground fog and chilling rain swept Ninia and the Yali people were as cold to the gospel as their habitat was inhospitable.

Whereas the Dani had turned out by the hundreds for airstrip work parties, the Yali flatly refused. Stan Dale, former Australian commando, and Canadian Bruno de Leeuw faced a near-impossible task. With a handful of imported Dani helpers they dug a trench one hundred feet wide and three hundred feet long carting "scores of tons of rocks [and] many tons of gravel" to level the strip site and correct the grade. As always, MAF supplied the workforce with airdrops. Early in 1962 John Dekker and Phil Masters trekked in from the C&MA base at Hetigima to lend their efforts, and the Ninia airstrip was inaugurated on March 22.

The Yali were hostile toward any change in their way of life—a life torn by incessant tribal war, taboos, ancient animosities, and witchcraft. One-third of the adult males were involved with clan witchcraft, replete with secret practices, feasts, and ceremonies. For the Stan Dale family the environment was austere and the work slow. It tried the spirit.

Meanwhile, Phil and Phyliss Masters had sailed with their three children for Irian Jaya in 1961. Eager to be at the cutting edge of frontier evangelism, the Masters likewise accepted assignment to the Eastern Highlands at an equally rugged site called Korupun, home to the Kimjal people. An airstrip was finally opened on 21 December 1963.[520] This would become RBMU's fifth Irian Jaya station. Within three years, the mountainous task began to yield to faith's tenacity. Three sons of the local chief became the first Kimjal converts.

Ten days' trek to the west in the Heluk Valley, Stanley Dale was troubled by the slow trickle of response to the gospel among the Yali, near neighbors to the Kimjal. He appealed to his support partners in Australia:

> "Please continue to remember us in prayer. Unfortunately, there is not much interest in places where visible results are small. We trust that something will be done in our areas to bring glory to God, even though we may be unknown." The prayer was answered, but the answer would shock the world.

On 25 September 1968, while trekking between Ninia and Korupun, Phil and Stan were followed by a band of Yali warriors from the village of *Wikbun* in the northern extremity of the Seng Valley. Conscious that they were being watched, the men waved their hands in friendly greeting, palms open. It was a cultural blunder. To the men of Wikbun village, waving the open palm was a signal of intent to kill. In a narrow gorge—a tributary of the Seng—a hail of arrows propelled the two men into the presence of their Lord. Phil Masters was 36, Stan Dale 52. Two carriers survived the tragedy, while Ndengen, a national worker, died from exposure at 12,000 feet while trying to cross the high ranges to the safety of the German mission post at Anggeruk.[521]

The dangers had always been present and the risks were real. Nevertheless, when the telegram reached Philadelphia HQ that September day, all were wounded:

PHIL AND STAN MISSING ON TREK. BELIEVED KILLED. SEARCH IN PROGRESS. 9/30/68 a.m.

In the inscrutable mystery of Providence, Phil and Stan were expendable, but their loss was not in vain. Their martyrdom focused fresh attention upon the unreached tribes of Irian Jaya, sparking a surge of missionary volunteers to that island. Among them were Orin and Rosa Kidd, from Portland, Oregon, and Elinor Young, from Chattaroy, Washington. The *Wikbun* people—legend held—were the historical elders to both the Dani and the Yali people, and their superiors in witchcraft. Moreover, Stan had earlier been warned: *"Don't go into the Seng. That's where Satan's seat is.*" The Seng would prove to be the key to unseating the regnant foe.

Three months after the murders, an MAF aircraft carrying pilot Menno Voth and the Gene Newman family (MAF) crashed in the Seng, killing all on board but 9-year-old Paul Newman. This second tragedy opened the way for the return of missionaries. The Orin Kidds took the Masters' place at Korupun, while British workers, John and Gloria Wilson picked up the gauntlet laid down by Stanley Dale at Ninia. Two martyrs had won the bloodied highland beachhead. Now the Kidds, Elinor Young, and the Wilsons would nurture the church won at such great cost, and give them the Word of God in their own tongue.

Aftermath

Twenty-five years later (January 1993) thousands of Yali tribals gathered on the airstrip at Ninia to celebrate the publication of the Yali New Testament, while at Korupun a vernacular translation of the New Testament neared completion. Hundreds from both tribes had become Christians. By 1999 a multitribal consortium of churches, including the Yali, Hupla, Kimjal, and Momina groups was led by nationals; among them, District Leader, Otto Kobak, who served on several ministry boards and on the translation team for the Yali New Testament. With the advent of men like Kobak, the Church of Jesus Christ in the Eastern Highlands of Irian Jaya had been widely planted and deeply rooted.[522]

Not on My Agenda

After the death of her husband in 1968, Phyliss Masters continued her work in Irian Jaya, returning to the United States years later to represent the work of RBMU in the churches and on the college campuses throughout the country. Reflecting upon the heavy price that had been paid to open the Seng Valley, she shared her experience of God's call upon their lives:

> Being a missionary to Dutch New Guinea had not been on my agenda! Phil and I felt no special attraction to the tribal peoples of Dutch New Guinea, nor did we feel specially gifted for this type of work. Nor was there any compelling sense of burden for the Yali people over what we felt for the lost here at home. What we did want more than anything was to be obedient to God's will. The Lord put within us the willingness to exchange the comfort of life in the States for the rigors of pioneer work in Indonesia.
>
> Would we have gone had we foreseen the future? Would we have left the security of the established work among the Dani tribe to open a totally new effort among the Kimjal people of the Eastern Highlands? Why did the Lord protect Phil on the three earlier trips he had made

through the Seng Valley, but not on that fateful journey in September of 1968? Had we somehow missed God's will this time, stepping outside of that protective envelope of His care? Had Phil and Stan somehow been culturally insensitive in their approaches, inviting an otherwise avoidable disaster? Like the arrows that felled Phil, these questions rained upon my mind, inflicting their own special torment.

I am thankful to our living Lord for the way He prepared us for the blow that would fall. Just before we heard the news on the radio, God had spoken to me so clearly— *"When you pass through the waters I will be with you."* During the long sleepless night that followed the grim news, God seemed to etch Psalm 18:2 upon my heart— *"The Lord is my Rock!"* When my heart seemed to scream, "Lord, I can't face life without Phil" the answer came so clearly, *"My grace is sufficient, and as your days, so shall your strength be."* [523]Stored in the heart, the promises of God are not trite cliches, but timely instruments of the Holy Spirit through which He infuses courage and strength at the point of our need. Two years before the blow fell, I had pledged myself to memorize Scripture. By the time of Phil's death, I had committed nearly six hundred verses to memory. That arsenal was wonderfully there for God to use!

South Coast

Six years before the death of Masters and Dale, new frontiers still challenged the Mission. In 1962, RBMU turned from the rarified elevations of Dutch New Guinea's Central and Eastern Highlands to the gospel-neglected tribes of the island's less-hospitable south coast, where sweltering mangrove swamps buffer the waters of the Arafura Sea. This was home to a number of smaller tribes, two of which became the focus of RBMU ministries. These had to be serviced by floatplane. None of these forbidding regions could have been accessed and serviced apart from the tiny aircraft of MAF and the courageous pilots who flew them.

The Kayagar

The Kayagar (pop. 10,000) had been served briefly (1960–61) by the Elmer Schmidts, TEAM missionaries who left soon after arrival, for health reasons. Living conditions in these malarial areas were harsh in the extreme. The language was difficult and dismal isolation challenged the most robust. Compounding difficulty was the Roman Catholic influence, dominant in 80% of the population. RBMU's John and Glenna McCain, who arrived in 1962, made their base at Kawem on the heels of the Schmidt family. McCain was a seaman from Louisiana and was at home in the estuaries of New Guinea's south coast. The McCains' faithful persistence against incredible odds birthed the Kayagar church. They retired from Kawem in 1973 after ten years in

DNG—but not without having left a legacy. They were followed by the David Tuckers in 1976, and later by the Thomas Goldsches in 1978, both couples later taking reassignment elsewhere in Irian Jaya. McCain had won two Kayagar men to the Lord, Haram, and Haimam, who lived wholeheartedly for God until their death in the early '90s. Haram led many to Christ, and often stood alone for the Truth. The people respected him, appointing him Area Chief, a government-recognized position.

The Dani Mission

When the western missionaries withdrew, Christian Danis from the Central Highlands took interest in the Kayagar, with as many as six Dani families living among them.[524] They introduced agriculture and learned the Kayagar language well enough to become effective in evangelism. They encouraged Kayagar youth to take higher education. Many did, moving to the area capital of Merauke. While there, some accepted free Bible School training on the island of Biak with the Pentecostals, a move that created some tension with the Dani Church Association. By 1999 many Kayagar had graduated from high school and Bible school, some going through university. Widely scattered throughout Irian Jaya, they had a significant influence. Seven churches functioned with about five hundred believers. With few vernacular Scriptures, most Kayagar knew the Indonesian language and did well with their Indonesian Bible, but many still awaited the Word in their mother tongue.[525]

The Sawi

On 16 July 1962, David Martin, then Irian Jaya field director, cabled Ebenezer Vine in Philadelphia:

> Kamur Station opened among the Sawi tribe on Kronkel River. Richardsons situated there. MAF water landing near house.

John McCain, already settled among the Kayagar at neighboring Kawem, had joined Dr. Ken Dresser (TEAM) and Don Richardson in the exploratory trip, which selected Kamur as RBMU's next tribal base. Vine conveyed his admiring assessment to A. C. Simmonds in Canada:

> The Sawi . . . people are very primitive . . . have scarcely seen a white face before . . . the matter needs to be covered with much prayer. I marvel at the composure and *sang-froid* of these dear fellows—and their wives! Surely this courage is God-given—how else account for it?[526]

Don and Carol Richardson spent 14 years with the Sawi, a story graphically told in the book, *Peace Child,* and in the popular film by the same title. While the Richardsons left Kamur in 1976, Don continued to make pastoral visits. Jim and Joan Yost opened work in Comoro, another Sawi area.[527] John and Esther Mills arrived in Kamur in 1971 to work with the Richardsons in translation and in the nurture of the Sawi Church. After 22 years, and a revision of the Sawi New Testament and the development of literacy materials, the Mills withdrew on schedule in 1994. RBMU considered it unnecessary to maintain personnel at Kamur any longer. Of a population of 3,300, 1,500 Sawi became baptized believers in five organized churches. Dani and other Indonesian Christians played a significant role in this growth.[528] As with the Kayagar, many Sawi have taken higher education, and one with a B. A. from TEAM's school in Manokwari was leading the Sawi Bible Institute in 1999.

The Missions Fellowship

Nearly half a century of evangelism in former Dutch New Guinea has been marked by a rare camaraderie among the nine mission agencies privileged to reap the harvest.[529] This bonding was intensified—if not generated—by several factors. The first was the presence of the Mission Aviation Fellowship. New Guinea terrain was hostile and virtually impenetrable by pedestrian means. The missionary community lived in absolute dependence for survival upon MAF pilots and their fragile aircraft. The second factor was the single sideband radio network, integral to MAF and to the missionaries. News and prayer requests were shared daily by radio. When tragedy struck, it was felt by all. This fact alone barred the door to any form of provincial or parochial insularity. Expertise in linguistics was a shared commodity. C&MA provided highest-standard school facilities for all. There was no competition. The Mission Fellowship (TMF) provided a single interface with the government and a commissary for all. For the collective family of 180 missionary couples and singles deployed in 40 stations over seven hundred miles of rugged mountain and coastal swamp, the TMF was in every sense a fellowship of the mutually dependent.

Faced with the need to provide both Bible training in the Indonesian language and trade skills for the Dani church, UFM and RBMU opened the Irian Jaya Bible and Vocational School (SAKIJ) in February 1973, a cooperative effort of the two missions. Scores of literacy centers had led to the formation of many schools, institutions, and numerous Bible institutes. In fact, the Mission had become facilitator to ten different Bible schools throughout the interior of Irian Jaya in six different languages.

By 1999 the GIDI in former Dutch New Guinea had identified 775 churches with an estimated 135,000 members in thirteen different tribal groups.[530] Eight Bible translation projects had either been completed or were in progress. More than half a century before, Robert Jaffray—against all odds—had sounded the drumbeat for the Dutch East Indies. Paul Gesswein and Ebenezer Vine picked up the rhythm. So did those who followed them. Paul, the great missionary apostle, would agree: *"Their voice has gone out into all the earth, their words to the ends of the world."*[531]

36

MAF Was Not Enough

The expert finger cutter moved throughout the area, recruiting children who resolutely placed their fourth and fifth fingers on a board and looked away while the finger cutter lowered the stone adz and chopped off the fingers at the second joints. The children seldom cried out, but often their fingers became badly infected.

—John Dekker

Costas Macris flashed his trademark smile as he loaded fifty-five-gallon drums on the truck in Fox Chase, Pennsylvania. The drums contained his "outfit"—all the household stuff he would need for the next four years in Irian Jaya, Indonesia. Philadelphia was in a deep freeze on this February day in 1963 and heavy ice and snow choked the residential street in front of the Elberon Avenue Headquarters of RBMU. Macris was headed for Irian Jaya on his first assignment, but already he had his own plans—big ones! Cheerily, he shared his dream of buying a custom launch to evangelize the islands of Indonesia, particularly the vast Van Rouffaer island off the south coast of Irian Jaya. Macris was used to thinking in grandiose dimensions—an entrepreneurial gift inherited from his father.

Architect Thanos Macris designed pavilions, and he did one for the 1964 New York World Fair. Ebenezer G. Vine had met him somewhere in Europe and, sensing his spiritual need, pointed him back to God. When the senior Macris lost five companies to bankruptcy, Vine wrote him a letter, urging him to take his distress to Christ. He filed the letter, but failed to act upon Vine's advice. Son Costas likewise wrote his father. It, too, was filed without action. Bankruptcy pushed Thanos over the edge and he determined to take his life. First, however, he would set his house in order. Going through his personal papers, he discovered the letters, which now won his full attention. Convicted by the Holy Spirit, he fell on his knees and gave his heart to God.

Years before his father's conversion, Costas Macris graduated from Millar Memorial Bible Institute[532](1957) and returned to Greece to enter the army. In a magazine, he learned of Dutch New Guinea and of tribes yet without the gospel. "This is for me," thought Costas. Three missions—the magazine said—were working there. Macris wrote to all three. Replies from two were routine. The third was different. Ebenezer Vine wrote a two-page personal letter to Costas Macris.

Vine's response lit Macris' fires and confirmed his call. In Irian Jaya, his talents for landscaping turned otherwise bleak mission stations into places of beauty. He played critical roles in work among the Sawi, Yali, and Kimjal tribes. When he heard about the vast Lakes Plain area of Irian Jaya, he knew he had found the challenge to match his energies.

The Lakes Plain

Without the Mission Aviation Fellowship, it is fair to say there would be no churches in the interior of Irian Jaya. The light Cessna 185s coupled with the skills and courage of MAF pilots, not only facilitated, but really made possible the scores of landing strips precariously hewed out of the rough mountainous terrain. These aircraft and the radio network bonded the island's missionary community into an interdependent family. MAF had serviced the community well—and continued to do so—until Macris tackled the evangelization of the Lakes Plain.

Lying north of the Central Ranges, the Lakes Plain is a vast area drained by the Idenberg (*Taretatu*) and Rouffaer (*Tariku*) rivers. Like a giant pair of ice tongs in the open position, the rivers meander toward each other from opposite directions, converging to form the Mamberamo, which then flows northward through the sago swamps of the flood plain. As if to throttle its final attempt to reach the sea, the Mamberamo gorge constricts and churns the great river into a boil of dangerous rapids before releasing it to the Pacific Ocean.

At an elevation of less than two hundred feet, the Lakes Plain harbored immense swamps. The climate was hot and humid, enervating the most robust. Pilots flying over the region assumed it uninhabited. In the Lakes Plain Macris discovered a number of small nomadic or semi-nomadic tribes, obviously of different origin than the people of the Central Highlands. While their aggregate population was no more than 5,000, they represented seventeen different groups. Vast swamps, great distances, and a diversity of languages separated them. There were no trails and all travel was by canoe.

It was soon clear that to place western missionaries in each group would be logistically impossible and strategically ineffective. This was a job for nationals, and Macris devised a plan to place a "witness man" in each of the language groups. In addition, a teacher would be necessary to provide Indonesian language instruction, medical aid, and radio communication capability. However, this feat called for effective means of transportation, and the airplane was the only answer. Seventeen tribes meant seventeen airstrips. Constructing them was a formidable challenge. Macris went to work, transporting hundreds of Dani workers by air from the highlands to the various sites. Serviced with food and supplies by airdrops, they were furloughed back to their homes for periodic R&R.

When MAF could no longer meet the demands of the Macris operation—its nine aircraft were taxed to the limit—Macris decided that RBMU needed its own air service. Back in Philadelphia, leadership shuddered. The technical demands of operating and servicing aircraft made the Macris proposal an administrator's nightmare. Sensitive relations with good friends at MAF were in jeopardy. Financial implications were colossal. Qualified pilots would be necessary, and lots of money! Moreover, establishing uncompromising technical standards would be imperative. Arguments for starting an air arm of RBMU had to be strong, given the respected presence of MAF. They were the experts who had got us into the Swart Valley in the first place in 1957. Macris lacked a high tolerance for bureaucratic obstacles and immediately went to work.

Regions Wings

Hank Worthington was a veteran MAF pilot who knew the treacherous and unforgiving airstrips sculpted out of Irian Jaya's rocky ravines. Paul Goodman, building contractor and World War II pilot from the Burma Road, was an RBMU council member. Both men rose to the challenge, and came on board, bringing expertise and credibility to the operation. Both lived near the MAF base (then) in Fullerton, California. They comprised the first Regions Wings Board. Two Cessna 185s were acquired. Pilots were recruited—first Jesse Loffer, then Cliff Scott, then Bill Rush, then Roger Stuber, and finally, Kevin Cain. The program hewed strictly to MAF standards of technical excellence and pilot qualification. A major base was established at Taijeve in the southern Lakes Plain, close to the foothills of Irian's Central Highlands.

Soon joined by Frank Clarke, an Australian missionary whose initial vision had prompted exploration of the Lakes Plain, RBMU's "Alexander the Great" had conquered, and *Regions Wings* was born. Within ten years, fourteen airstrips were in operation and seven more under construction. Two–way radios crackled from fourteen locations, while twenty-two national evangelists and thirty-seven teachers had been deployed throughout the region. A children's educational hostel was established at Taijeve. Church planting in this hostile environment was slow, with just two churches organized and twenty preaching points.

Mission is cruciform and victory has a price tag. For Costas Macris, it was the dreaded hepatitis B, contracted from his exhausting work in the malarial swamps of the Lakes Plain. Diagnosis in Australia confirmed the worst. Malaria, filaria, and amoebae had compounded the hepatitis. At the 1979 Field Conference at Karubaga, Macris was too weak to walk unaided and was carried into the meeting room on a chaise lounge. Betty Baum, a UFM doctor was present. She confided: "This man has 75% liver damage. He will not survive and does not have long to live."

Costas Macris did survive. After months of therapy in St. Louis, Missouri, and bathed in intercession, he recovered. Unable to go back to the hostile climate of the Irian Jaya's Lakes Plain, he returned to Greece, his homeland, where he founded the Hellenic Missionary Union. In 1999, he was still evangelizing—and Regions Wings[533] was still flying.

RBMU Field Conference, Irian Jaya.

37

A Bigger Umbrella

Am I not justified in saying that when God wants someone to serve him, he at times chooses even the weakest, often the most physically unfit, to carry out his purposes? All He asks of us is that we trust and obey.

—Annie G. Soper

PIM's Union with RBMU

With the founding of the North American RBMU councils in 1948, the Peru Inland Mission took shelter beneath the umbrella of the Regions Beyond Missionary Union. The merger was a natural outcome of Annie Soper's relationship with her benefactor, A. C. Simmonds, in whose home she had found friends and family while a student at Toronto Bible Institute, and before going to Peru. In 1936, Simmonds set up an office for the PIM in Toronto, and through the years, the two sustained a vigorous correspondence. However, the decision to merge with RBMU was not made without a struggle.

Since the Evangelical Union of South America (EUSA) had been formed in 1911 by amalgamation of earlier RBMU efforts in Peru and Argentina and the Help for Brazil Mission, a PIM merger with EUSA was an equally attractive option seriously considered by Soper. EUSA Secretary Stewart McNairn was a product of Harley College and Soper's linkage with him and with the old RBMU work was strong. At the time, she was convinced that if there was to be a merger it should be with the EUSA, "as from every point of view it seemed the reasonable thing to do."

But she put McNairn off with the hypothesis that EUSA would be unable to bring the allowances of 16 PIM workers up to EUSA standards. The greater reason was left unspoken. She had already received a letter "from Mr. Bamber and Leonard [Soper] to say that they would both resign unless we [PIM] agreed to amalgamation with RBMU, and that I would need to go home and form my own committee." At this time Theodore Bamber was both pastor of Rye Lane Chapel—her home church—and chairman of the RBMU Board in London.[534] Moreover, "the majority of the senior PIM workers favored uniting with RBMU." Feeling the pressure from both quarters, Soper took the prudent course.[535] However, the matter would not die.

Since the war, financial straits had plagued British RBMU and bank loans had become an expedient means of maintaining missionary allowances. While real assets secured the loans and the Mission never actually went into debt, RBMU's fiscal status was at best precarious, and in the eyes of some, compromised. Annie Soper and the PIM had never gone to the bank to sustain her work, and had brought PIM into RBMU "only on condition that all our funds were kept separate, and that only earmarked gifts be sent to us."[536] Even as late as 1954, Soper conjectured that "it may be that God is asking us to join forces with EUSA."[537] But the die was cast. New recruits from the US and Canada had already joined the PIM, and positive changes in London Board policy were afoot.

The postwar years brought rapid changes to the PIM work.[538] Megan Jones, an energetic Welsh nurse, arrived in February 1947. She promptly revolutionized the Lamas hospital, endearing herself to hundreds of patients for whom hospital doors became salvation's gate. Fred and Ruth Webb brought evangelistic and nursing skills from Yorkshire. Ebenezer Vine's peripatetic campus ministry had won North Americans to Annie Soper's cause. Marinell Park arrived in 1951, her heart set upon Quechua translation. Ole and Vera Sorell came from the Canadian prairies in 1954 to run the PIM farm, not guessing that God had a much larger agenda planned for them. Within the next few years, several others swelled the ranks, among them Marguerite Hale, Grace Forgrave, the David James-Morses, and the writer, who arrived in January 1956.

AIENOP

San Martin's churches organized in 1952 as the *Association of Evangelical Churches of Northeastern Peru* (AIENOP), linking together the (then) sixty churches scattered throughout the "eyebrow" of the Selva. Few pastors had secondary education, and the demands of the family subsistence farm—the *chacra*— left inadequate time for pastoral ministry. The Lamas Bible School continued to produce a flow of Christian workers, but supply always lagged behind the need. In 1979 only four of the sixty churches supported their own pastors, the rest being cared for by lay leaders.[539] Ted Ball taught and developed the concept of tithing throughout the AIENOP, but the jungle churches faced an additional difficulty.

Retaining stable, qualified leadership in the sparsely settled farming communities of the montaña was daunting. Population drift to the larger urban centers, especially to Lima, assured a continuing hemorrhage of upwardly mobile types. Air transport and improved roads steadily siphoned off the more venturesome to the lure of improved economic opportunity in the nation's capital. Scores if not hundreds of people who had met Christ in the villages of the Huallaga Valley left the area to relocate in the cities. For these, it often meant exchanging one set of hardships for another. However, God was in the demographics and these changes carried an advantage, as we shall see.

Annie Soper had addressed the shortage of pastors when she introduced the junta system. Taking a page from the existing political district councils in Peru, the regional junta[540] became responsible for the pastoral care of the churches within its district. In this way, district resources could be shared with greater effect, including circuit-riding pastors.

AIENOP churches set up several such juntas throughout the Huallaga Valley, each with representation from the churches within its district. While this functioned well, it failed to resolve the perennial question of foreign subsidy of national workers—a dilemma that has harried mission agencies ad infinitum. Some missionaries—a la Nevius—were opposed to any foreign funding of nationals. Others held a variety of positions ranging from full or partial subsidy of pastor/evangelists to full or partial subvention of hardware projects such as buildings or vehicles. Most agreed that national churches must support pastors without foreign funds. Whatever the ideal, there were always compassionate hearts who found ways to bend the rule.

A. C. Simmonds had proposed setting up a fund to subsidize national workers, but Soper countered:

> The problem is that Ted [Ball] does not like foreign money used for workers. He very strongly believes in indigenous methods, [that] the national church [should be] self-governing, self-propagating, and self-supporting. That is good in principle, and has been our aim from the beginning. We have, however, lost a number of workers because the churches are absolutely unable to support them, and even in instances where possibly they could support them, they have not learnt yet the joy of giving. Thank God, there are splendid exceptions . . . I am afraid I differ from Ted in that I feel we should help at least those who travel from place to place.[541]

Fifty years later the debate continued—with few variations on the theme.

Sand in the Oyster

Meanwhile, Roman opposition to the PIM work remained alive and well. Riding the advantage of a state-supported religion, Catholic priests continued to harass evangelicals. The writer remembers a promising young woman high school teacher who in 1957 had joyfully professed conversion, only to fall away when threatened by authorities with the loss of her teaching position.

Evangelical children faced discrimination in school, and in spite of constitutional religious liberty, clerical pressure intimidated believers. Soper always kept Simmonds up to date, and reported:

> A [petition] was sent from the members at the convention to the [Peruvian] government asking permission to again have meetings in private houses, as the bishop has been making tours and frightening people very much, forbidding absolutely any services where there is not a church."[542]

Herbert Money, then secretary of the Evangelical Council in Lima, reassured the PIM missionaries:

> Indications [now] are that victory is on the way in the fight for religious liberty. Mr. Ball's petitions were just right . . . [The] deputy for Juanjui called on the Minister of Justice and Religion . . . When he was shown the poster put out by the Evangelical Council, he saw . . . that the law could not possibly be interpreted in that way . . . He was impressed with the record of public service rendered by the Moyobamba and Lamas Missions, and [admitted] that a gross injustice was being done by applying the bishop's interpretation of the decree . . . the documents sent by Mr. Ball prove conclusively that the Decree in San Martin is quite unconstitutional.

Notwithstanding, two years later (1954) clerical clout was still in place, and Soper again advised Simmonds:

> Ellen Buckle has just finished a Vacation Bible School. I was nearly put in prison for allowing her to carry on a school without a license. Fortunately, I remembered that we still had a license for our old school, and went and searched it out. The Inspector of Schools—who is friendly— accepted it, and the priest was told we couldn't be put into prison because we had been granted a license and [the inspector] was able to give the number of the resolution. The priests are just trying one thing after another. They have publicly said that we will all be turned out this year.[543]

If grassroots harassment was not enough, Rome's authority reached to the seat of government:

> A Congress is to be held in Lima, its purpose to solve the problems of these troublesome Protestants. The people tell us that the priests do not preach about spiritual things, but use all their eloquence in . . . trying to prove the errors of Protestantism, and forbidding the people to come near us, or read our books. The authorities are very afraid of them. Evidently, they have power to get them the sack, and little by little this constant opposition is having its effect on a proportion of the people,

though we still have plenty of friends. I believe the Lord will give us some years of freedom yet, in spite of all their efforts.[544]

Annie Soper had too long observed the explosive power of the gospel to be intimidated by satanic capers, and never lost her sense of humor. She tweaked A. C. Simmonds on his proposed visit to the Eternal City:

> Certainly, it would be good to call on the Pope and tell him he needs a Savior, and if he doesn't accept him, he will not get into heaven! He certainly would never believe that despised Protestants could do any good work. You won't kiss his toe, will you?[545]

In 1962 Soper wrote:

> A bill has just gone through Congress asking for the abrogation of the law forbidding meetings in private houses and open air. It was a marvelous document gathered together by a member of parliament who is a Christian, giving details of the many abuses committed under cover of this law—five hundred pages and every one proved and stating that there are 200,000 evangelicals and demanding liberty for them. It received great applause in Congress and they passed it, but it has yet to pass the Senate.[546]

Stepping Down?

Soper was seventy-two and still directing the Peru Inland Mission when she informed the 1955 Field Conference that "the time had come to hand over the leadership of the Mission to a younger person." Unanimously, the missionaries elected Ted Ball to the post. However, Annie did not easily surrender a position she had held for twenty-five years. She remained something of a co-regent with Ball for several years thereafter.

She continued in active ministry until retiring at eighty-three to her native England. On her retirement in 1966, she left behind sixty rural churches, 2,000 baptized believers, and a team of RBMU missionaries.[547] In 1964, the Peruvian government awarded her the Congressional Medal of Honor. The following year (1965), Her Majesty Queen Elizabeth II appointed Annie Soper Member of the Order of the British Empire, an honor tempered only by the fact that the Beatles rock group had received the same award that year.

God Keeps a Promise

Meanwhile, God had not forgotten the outpoured prayers of Edyth Vinall and the prayer groups in England. If the apostle Paul saw himself in the priestly role of presenting Gentile ethnic groups as an offering to God,[548] he had ardent imitators in Edyth Vinall, Marinell Park, Grace Forgrave, Keith Anderson, and others who longed to lay the Quechua at the feet of Jesus Christ. But there was yet one to come, perhaps as improbable a candidate as the Apostle himself, for whom God had reserved the role of apostle to the Lowland Quechua.

Victor Cenepo made his premature advent into a world of pain in the village of Chazuta, a Quechua town on the west bank of the Huallaga River a few miles from Lamas. From infancy, arthritic pain racked his limbs, gradually immobilizing his hip and elbow joints, and ultimately forcing him to leave his schooling. His brother José had come to Christ through an illness that brought him to the Lamas hospital and under the care of Welsh nurse, Megan Jones— a doctor without title—who led him to Christ. Brother José went to work on Victor, who soon became a believer.

Then a nurse from Milwaukee arrived in 1951 with a clear call from God to give the Lowland Quechua the Scriptures in their own language. As a means of immersing herself in the Indian culture, Marinell Park went to Chazuta to do Daily Vacation Bible School (DVBS), medical work, and to conduct baptismal classes for a handful of believers. Here she met Victor Cenepo, who became her language informant. When baptisms followed sometime later, Victor and his brother were among the candidates. A year later, during a visit to Chazuta, Jessie Norton encouraged Victor to attend the Lamas Bible Institute.

Academic work was hard—his education had peaked at third grade—and Victor struggled. One day in class he laid down his pen in quiet despair and cradled his head in his arms. A friendly hand on his shoulder supported the whispered question:

"Brother Victor, what's the trouble?"

"I can't do it!" was the pained reply.

The voice continued:

"You must not give up! Stay, and see it through."

He took the advice. Victor Cenepo was bilingual, speaking fluent Quechua and Spanish. He had come to the Spanish language Bible school at Lamas in 1957, hopeful of preparing for Christian service. But with little academic advantage, the path to his dreams was not easy. That year the writer set up bachelor quarters with Victor in the town of Cuñumbuque on the banks of the Mayo River. It was a memorable night when Cenepo gingerly chose his steps through the muddied and refuse-strewn path of a nearby Quechua village on the bank of the Mayo River. Going door-to-door among the thatch-roofed homes and gathering a crowd of perhaps 50, he hung his pressure lantern on a pole and began to tell the gospel story—in Quechua. Every eye was riveted on this little man with the twisted frame. It was the beginning of an apostolic ministry.

Victor completed his LBI studies in 1960 and became one of the primary language informants and translation assistants to Marinell Park in the production of the Lowland Quechua New Testament. He went first to Maceda, where Park and Grace Forgrave were based, later going to the Sisa Valley to follow up on the ministry of Edyth Vinall.

Forgrave was a certified teacher from Michigan and worked with Victor to conduct the first Lowland Quechua literacy program in 1961. When two teenage Quechua girls learned to read in twenty-two days—one of them becoming a Sunday school teacher in the Sisa church—the Quechua thirst for literacy was confirmed and led to the formation in 1967 of a Quechua Literacy Committee, staffed by nationals. Adapting the Laubach *Each One Teach One* method, scores of Quechua were soon reading. Many of these fed into Extension Seminary classes taught by Victor Cenepo. Although selected gospel portions had been translated, Quechua lesson material remained in short supply until the complete New Testament had been dedicated.[549] Cenepo became God's instrument in leading scores of Quechua families to Jesus Christ. When hundreds of Christians crowded the services, the AIENOP leadership turned out to help construct the first Quechua church in the Sisa Valley. With the founding of the Association of Lowland Quechua Churches, Victor represented them as delegate to the Billy Graham Congress on Evangelism in Amsterdam in 1983.

The Chayahuita

Lowland Quechua was not the only aboriginal group east of the Andes. The Peruvian selva was home to at least thirty-five original tribes worked by a number of agencies such as the South America Mission, the Swiss Indian Mission, and Wycliffe Bible Translators. One of the larger tribes was the *Chayahuita* (pop. 4,000 in 1966, 15,000 in 1999), among whom Wycliffe's George and Helen Hart had begun translation work. When RBMU's Everett and Alice Brown arrived in Peru 1966, the Harts had already spent ten years with the Chayahuita. The Harts alone had responded to Brown's written inquiries for information on Indian work and their reply was not in vain. The Oregon couple was drawn to the Chayahuita—and to the Harts. From their base in Yurimaguas the Browns would work side by side with both for the next thirty years.[550]

Plying the rivers in their Johnson outboard, they administered medicine, distributed and monitored gospel cassette recorders, taught literacy and then the Scriptures, repaired pecky-pecky[551] engines, and as ombudsmen to an otherwise exploited people, won the friendship of hundreds of Indians. By the time the Chayahuita New Testament was dedicated in 1979, the Harts and the Browns could rejoice in a vigorous Chayahuita church. Twenty years later Chayahuita believers numbered 2,000 in sixty local churches and continued to multiply.[552]

Peru's steaming selva stretched northward to the Ecuadorian border and the Napo River. This remote and isolated region was home to an assorted Naparuna and mestizo population and was later entered by Canadians, Paul and Liz Ghent. [553] In 1999, they were still there.

Transitions

In 1968, the first of several earthquakes struck Lamas, seriously damaging the hospital and Bible School facilities. It signaled the end of an era. The medical ministry so essential to the early development of the work was no longer needed, as the Peruvian government began to establish hospitals and clinics in the region, staffing them with qualified nationals. Looking down the road, both Mission and National Church saw that the pivotal center of the area was shifting to the town of Tarapoto, and relocated the Bible School under the new name of the San Martin Theological Center (CETESAMA).

CETESAMA opened coincidentally with the completion of a new highway connecting San Martin with the coast. This link ended the isolation of the interior province. Commercial goods began to flow in both directions over its axle-breaking ruts, bringing unprecedented prosperity to the area. When the jet age reached the jungle in 1975, Tarapoto became the air hub for eastern Peru. In 1979 microwave telephone service arrived, making communication with the rest of the world just a dial away. In 1981, television arrived, and the following year saw the advent of a university offering four different degree programs.

Strategic Withdrawal

RBMU had been in San Martin province for nearly fifty years when in 1970 the Mission made the first move toward disengagement from the national church structure. At the time, there were sixty churches in the AIENOP association, served largely by graduates of the Lamas Bible Institute. Academic level was not high, since San Martin was still a frontier state, remote and isolated from the capital. Few students had more than a high school education. Still, the Huallaga Valley churches were strong—though economically poor—and it was time to recognize their maturity.

RBMU considered several options, among them, *integration*—a policy then popular with some denominational missions. Integration called for complete disengagement of the Mission from the national churches. This would have included surrender of mission assets and sovereignty, including the assignment of expatriate missionaries by the national church. [554] In the conviction that this would be neither right nor timely, the Mission opted for a different course—*strategic withdrawal*. [555] The plan called for a five-year phase-out of missionaries and funding from the older, well-established church centers. AIENOP would take full responsibility for its Christian education program. During the transition, only specialized expatriate personnel would remain to teach Bible Institute and Theological Education by Extension programs (TEE) and to develop Christian education materials. Association offices would be housed in the new Christian Education complex, for which plans were being drawn. Peruvian delegates to the Mission's field conference welcomed the proposal with enthusiasm, and began to plan their own program of leadership training and outreach. In 1971, foundations were laid for the new Christian Education and Bible Conference Center at Morales, near Tarapoto. The two-story complex provided facilities for the Bible Institute (Centro Teológico de San Martin), TEE, youth camps, retreats, Bible conferences, and spiritual life conventions. It became the headquarters of the AIENOP churches.

Within two years from implementation, *strategic withdrawal* was working. Churches were entirely in the hands of Peruvian leadership, administered from a central office in Tarapoto, and assisted by a modest $2,000 annual subsidy from the Mission. Expatriate missionaries were freed to address unevangelized areas in church planting and thus provide a model for the association. Nevertheless, the plan had drawbacks. In 1972 there were only four salaried Peruvian pastors in the region, the best paid receiving forty-six dollars per month. Circuit evangelists were paid from funds pooled within the juntas. As (then) Field Director Ole Sorell noted:

> In an agricultural, non-industrialized community, money is scarce, and spiritual initiative is often lacking. It is easier to talk about turning over administrative responsibility to the national church than to implement it. Exposure to the influence of cults is on the increase.[556]

A veteran Peruvian leader, less optimistic than Sorell, assessed the struggling San Martin churches in this way, "We will do what we can, but the rest will have to go; fifty years of seed sowing has been done with weeping, but the harvest will be lost."[557]

Not exactly. In spite of economic struggles, by 1999 AIENOP had grown to 121 churches, with fourteen preaching points. Leadership remained strong, and the short term Bible school working out of the CETESAMA center continued to sharpen the skills of lay pastors, while the Lowland Quechua Church counted twenty-six congregations. *Radio Amistad* (Radio Friendship), a public service FM stereo station linking the AIENOP's widely scattered churches, was launched in 1990. A five-hundred-watt transmitter offered a variety of gospel programming and community services and volunteers from the AIENOP churches staffed the station.

Tension and Expansion

In 1971, a long-simmering tension among missionaries over the glossolalia issue required arbitration. That year field conference defined two regions where personnel who were comfortable with this view might be free to work.

In May 1972, British workers Cherry Noble and Jackie Howe became the first RBMUers to work in Peru's southern Department of Apurimac among the Highland Quechua, while Fred and Ruth Webb took up ministry in Chachapoyas in the Department of Amazonas. This unfortunate decision can be understood only in the light of RBMU's international structure at that time, addressed in Chapter 42.

Lima and ADIBEL

The history of missions demonstrates that "the gospel has always spread along the prevailing currents of the day," as Ernest Oliver once noted. RBMU's shift of focus to Latin America's great metropolitan centers began in the same way. In Peru, it started with a strong evangelical family in the Huallaga Valley town of Juanjui.

Vicente and Rogelia Grandes were converted in the early fifties through reading a gospel tract and through the influence of a daughter who introduced them to the PIM missionaries. They raised eleven children to love God. When Vicente graduated from the Lamas Bible Institute, he became pastor of the Juanjui church. In the mid 1960s, lured by the prospect of greater economic opportunity, the family made a quantum leap from their small farm in the jungle to the congestion and bustle of the capital, five hundred miles distant.

In their baggage was a vibrant, New Testament faith, and Vicente soon had a church going in their home. Their winsome family—which included five preachers, musicians, and career nurses—did not lack for talent, and soon their house-cum-church was overflowing with seekers of truth. In 1971, Cooper and Dorothy Battle had transferred to Lima to set up the Regions Press[558] and provide liaison with the missionaries in the interior. The Battles, who had earlier been posted in Juanjui, knew the Grandes family and looked them up. Battle immediately saw the potential of this church-in-the-home and set about to secure building lots in a new subdivision. In 1980, the first twenty-five by fifty-foot chapel was constructed through gifts from American Christians. The *Tungasuca* church prospered, weathering Peru's economic collapse in 1988, and remained a vital witness in Lima's population of seven million.

In Peru, RBMU had defined its objective to penetrate the middle and upper-middle classes of the Peruvian capital (By 1980 this strategy had been expanded to include the Chilean capital of Santiago). In a society highly stratified by economic disparities, the middle class had long been neglected. Addressing this, a second church was planted in 1978 in Lima's Maranga district by the Robert Hamiltons and a third in San Borja by the Steve Varners, both efforts successful.[559] In 1979, RBMU church plants joined with those founded by sister agency, TEAM, to form the Association Of Bible Churches of Lima. (ADIBEL)

The Drug Era

The communist Shining Path (*Sendero Luminoso*) guerillas systematically destroyed the Peruvian infrastructure and murdered upwards of 30,000 citizens from 1970–1992. The capture of founder and leader Abimael Guzmán Reynoso in a daring police raid in Lima on 12 September 1992, effectively brought to an end the two-decade reign of terror. While the communist guerillas' primary base was in the southern province of Ayacucho, they infiltrated most of the country. Peru's idyllic Huallaga Valley was not spared.

One of scores of swift tributaries that discharge their turgid waters into the Huallaga river of inland Peru, is the Biabo River. Five hundred miles north of Lima, the Biabo laces its way through the tropical selva—a region of the eastern Andean foothills marked by gentle slopes and carpeted with lush jungle, and referred to as the eyebrow of the mountain (*ceja de la montaña*). To this region the intrepid Annie Soper brought the healing of the gospel in 1922, leaving a legacy of some 120 churches which made up (in 1999) the Association of Evangelical Churches of northeastern Peru, known by their acronym, AIENOP. Soper would not have recognized the Biabo of the early 1990s. Peru's narco terrorists concentrated their forces in this valley, winning for the Biabo notoriety as the Red Zone. Most of the coca paste reaching the United States in the 1980s was produced in the Huallaga Basin. As Shining Path and Tupac Amaru guerilla groups worked to destabilize and overthrow the government, they provided protection for the drug lords in exchange for narco-dollars. The once idyllic pastoral setting of the Huallaga basin—home of the AIENOP churches—became a zone of terror.[560]

Pedro Sangama

Pedro Pascual Sangama—his surname revealing his Quechua Indian roots— little realized the trial by fire that awaited him in this normally gentle community of peasant farmers. Converted in 1982 in a Quechua village, Pedro immediately saturated himself in the Scriptures and began sharing his faith. Turning casual conversations into winsome witness for Christ came naturally and artlessly. His single status facilitated an apostolic mobility, allowing him to trek the lonely jungle trails, evangelizing villages up and down the Biabo. His only encumbrances were a Bible, a machete, and a change of clothing. Like a contemporary Francis of Assisi, Pedro prayed that God would lead him to families needing an extra set of hands to replace those of a sick father, or of a widow unable to tend her crops. Wherever a need was present, Pedro was there to help! Love won hearts and opened doors. Churches were established in the villages of the Biabo valley.

Alarmed and outraged by Pedro's growing popularity, guerrilla terrorists served notice: Leave the area or be eliminated. Pedro had been held by the terrorists on an earlier occasion and knew he had run out of options. It was time to go. Preparing to depart the region meant first returning to a nearby village to fetch his few belongings. This time, however, on nearing the village, he was apprehended by a band of guerrillas, who escorted him to the village. The terrorists also seized the mayor of the town, and at gunpoint demanded a meeting of the townspeople. Pedro and the mayor were on trial by a kangaroo court, narco style. Charges were brought against the two—for the hapless mayor, adultery. For Pedro: pernicious influence.

"Do you want any more of this preacher and the Bible?" the Narcos demanded. The menacing barrels of their weapons dictated the peoples' terrified verdict: "No!" Both the mayor and Pedro were sentenced to death. The mayor was summarily dispatched by gunshot. Horrified onlookers now appealed Pedro's sentence as unjust and undeserved. Ordered to mutilate the back of the mayor's body with his machete in exchange for his release, Pedro refused, protesting his inability as a Christian to comply. Then, mysteriously and miraculously constrained by a higher Authority, the guerrillas freed Pedro and ordered him to flee. Having escaped with his life, Pedro Sangama was no longer free to visit his evangelistic circuit on the Biabo River, which remained under the control of the terrorists until 1995. He resettled in another of the river valleys of the Huallaga basin, continuing his ministry for Jesus Christ.

Social unrest occasioned by the drug traffic endangered the national church through its close association with the missionary community. A one point Peruvian helicopter gunships descended on the once pastoral community of Morales, locale of the Bible Institute. For several unsettling days, Peruvian troops bivouacked in the Bible Institute dormitory and classrooms. The region was no longer stable and RBMU personnel were endangered, making necessary their temporary withdrawal from the zone in 1990.[561]

Annie G. Soper's Homecall

The lady who started it all slipped quietly into the presence of her Lord on 3 November 1979. Annie Soper was 96. The founder of the RBMU's work in Peru, formerly known as the Peru Inland Mission, continued active ministry in her adopted land for fifty years until she retired to a ministry of prayer in her native England. Weak and frail, she had defied the odds. Durable, she had breasted hardship, opposition, persecution, and discouragement to take the liberating truth of the gospel to one of the forgotten places of earth. Her life— like Congo's drums—still resonates across the splendid Andean foothills in a hundred peasant villages and in as many congregations of the redeemed. Bearing witness to God's sovereign grace, she left us with this admonition:

> Am I not justified in saying that when God wants someone to serve him, he at times chooses even the weakest, often the most physically unfit, to carry out his purposes? All He asks of us is that we trust and obey.

38

The Empire Strikes Back

If a man lacks humility, tact, compassion, tenderness, and versatility, he will not make much headway with the heathen. We must weed out the men who refuse the cross of Christ.

—H. Grattan Guinness

When Dale Leathead and Ralph Sarver sailed from New York on 23 February 1950, they became the first North Americans to join RBMU's work in India, then half a century old. Leathead had graduated from Bob Jones University, Sarver from Northwestern College in Minneapolis. The two bachelors were soon followed by other American and Canadian workers. Three years earlier Major Ernest Oliver, demobilized from the Indian army, had returned to India to lead the RBMU field into the challenges of the postwar years. Undaunted by North India's disheartening lack of response to the gospel, the team renewed their efforts to address the desperate plight of Bihar's masses.

They rejuvenated school programs, developed literature evangelism, and opened dispensaries in various centers, each crowded with sick and suffering. All received prayer-bathed presentations of the gospel. The Muzaffarpur Leprosy Home, taken over by the Mission in the early 50s, developed into a thriving and efficient hospital under the eye of Dr. Margaret Owen. She cared for several hundred cases on both inpatient and outpatient basis and the hospital became the center of lively Christian witness in the town of Muzaffarpur. The Motihari Christian Girls' Home, established in 1911, continued to shape the lives of scores of young women who otherwise had little future. The Duncan Hospital initiated a dazzling building program, expanding into new wings and facilities, much of the construction supervised by Dale Leathead. A Christian bookstore opened in Motihari and became the launch pad for regular Christian literature forays into the towns and villages of the region.

By any measurement, the Sonepore Mela was a spectacular showcase of India's anonymous masses. This annual festival brought hundreds of thousands of vendors and shoppers to a vast outdoor market in a seething maelstrom of humanity. Mission teams strategically located their makeshift bookstall tents throughout the crowds, selling thousands of Scripture portions, New Testaments, and Bibles. These were bravely offered with a bright smile, though often in the face of curled lips and muttered maledictions. Such efforts met with large response in hundreds of requests for Bible correspondence courses. But missionaries looked in vain for any large-scale turning to Christ.

Indianization Hits

Noted British scholar C. S. Lewis once said, "Hinduism will take on any pattern but will hold none. Hinduism absorbs you. Christ is accepted as another god. The difficulty with preaching in India is that there is no difficulty." While that may have been true in Lewis' day, difficulties were yet to come, and plenty.

By 1967, the Indian government required Commonwealth missionaries to obtain a certificate of registration and residential permit. No other category of Commonwealth citizens was required to obtain such documents. A number of Indian states, among them Orissa, Madya Pradesh, Assam, Mysore, and Bihar, enacted anti-Christian legislation through so-called Freedom of Religion bills, prohibiting conversion from one religion to another "by use of force or allurement." The bills required Christian nationals to report the name, age, sex, caste, occupation, income, benefits, and dependents of each convert. Mission agencies, of which there were more than two hundred in Bihar at the time, recognized the warning signs.

When RBMU dismissed the Indian principal who had taken over part of the school property, and had refused to clear out, the Bihar Christian Council encouraged the Mission to take the case to court. RBMU lost the case with the ominous ruling; " No protection shall be given to institutions founded by foreign missionary bodies." The Patna high court ruled that "Schools, colleges, and seminaries do not have the protection of the constitution."[562]After seventy years of effort there were just 132 baptized Christians in the entire RBMU field of Bihar. Eight local churches had been established, the largest at Muzaffarpur, with seventeen members, most of these employees of the leprosy hospital. While nearly all the staff of the Duncan hospital at Raxaul were believers, most were tribal Christians from the German Lutheran area in South Bihar. They were not local converts.[563]

Why did the RBMU—and many others—continue this dauntless pursuit of an ever-elusive harvest? While a number of answers might be given, one bright gleam suggests God's strange design: In 1954 the RBMU border hospital center at Raxaul became a primary gateway to the forbidden kingdom of Nepal and opened the door to a harvest of thousands of Nepali believers. The early vision of Gordon Guinness, Cecil Duncan, and Ernest Oliver, had been fulfilled. Apart from the long years of hope deferred in North Bihar, the Nepal harvest might never have happened.

In 1969, Indian government policy took aim at ideological and religious propaganda by foreigners financed from overseas. While the policy was directed as much against communism as against Christian missions, mission agencies took the heat. RBMU saw the warning and took steps toward total indigenization of its work.

Emmanuel Hospital Association

First to feel the winds of change was the 120-bed Duncan Hospital at Raxaul—the Mission's largest ministry in India. One of six teaching hospitals serving Bihar's 53 million inhabitants, the Duncan Hospital had five full time doctors logging 4,000 inpatients and 40,000 outpatients annually. Like many other Christian mission hospitals in India, the Duncan faced closure. Underscoring the crisis was the fact that eighty percent of Christian medical missions had been founded in rural India, where the need was greatest, while eighty percent of India's doctors were in the cities. Christian missionaries alone had the motivation to live and work in the marginalized sectors of Indian society. Now the prohibition of foreign funding of Christian medical work became part of India's policy to prevent foreign subsidy of any ideology within the country.

In response to this emergency, the Emmanuel Hospital Association was formed under the aggressive leadership of RBMU's Dr. Keith Sanders. It was India's first association of mission hospitals. Comprising fifteen evangelical hospitals formerly operated by foreign missions, the EHA offered a framework for continuing evangelical work and witness through medicine, free from the stigma of foreign control. In 1972, the Duncan Hospital joined the EHA. For the Christian Indian medical staff, adjusting to the new, national leadership was not easy—although they were compatriots. Indian medical staff found it difficult to transfer their loyalties from the missionaries—with whom they were comfortable—to senior officers of their own nationality. "Still," wrote Sanders, "we find ourselves not on the edge of a salvage heap, but on the threshold of unprecedented new life."

Demise of the Mission Compound

Next to feel the axe of the government's move to Indianization were the Mission *compounds*, an anachronism in India's national consciousness. Like most other agencies, RBMU had its share. The *compounds* were missionary residences, dispensaries, clinics, or schools—buildings usually a cut above the surrounding village housing, often enclosed by a wall. In the past, they had provided some degree of privacy, seclusion, and relief from India's heat, all at safe distance from the eyes of the curious, while at the same time offering protection from intrusions by foraging cows. What once had been a necessary refuge for emotional survival, had gradually become a wall that distanced the foreign missionary from the village people he wished to reach. The mission compound had to go.

In 1960, Herbert Pritchard organized ETANI,[564] a government-recognized holding trust, to facilitate transfer of mission-held property to the control of Christian nationals. At that point, thirty-two missions had not yet arranged for transfer of foreign-owned properties. It was a complex process. RBMU's Motihari compound, for example, was made up of seventy different property units, each requiring to be matched with its own deed. At Gopalganj, there were eighteen such units. Some of the Mission dwellings were sold to needy Christians at a nominal fee. Others were turned over to the Mar Thoma Evangelization Association, the missionary arm of the large Mar Thoma Church in South India. Literature and Bible correspondence work was also transferred to Indian evangelical groups.

Subsidy Phase-out

At the April 1974 RBMU field conference a further step was taken—phase-out of all recurring financial assistance to India by 1974, with the exception of missionary allowances. India's incremental squeeze on foreign mission activity was effective. In 1962, the RBMU contingent of expat workers in North India stood at twenty-nine. Twenty years later it had been reduced to two. Actual attrition was much greater, as over the years workers came and went, often unable to bear the emotional drain of unrewarded toil. However, all was not dark. Under capable Indian leadership, the Duncan Hospital at Raxaul continued as a thriving center of Christian witness with a steady trickle of conversions, baptisms, conferences, and evangelistic efforts. But the longed-for, larger harvest did not come. After one hundred years of faithful gospel ministry, the church in North Bihar remained "a poor, huddling flock"—but with a difference. One hundred years later, eighty-six million Biharis occupied the same space where Banks and Hicks had found twenty-two million in 1899.

Was the work in vain? Let Ernest W. Oliver answer in the text from which he loved to preach: *He that goes forth weeping, bearing precious seed, shall doubtless come again with rejoicing, bringing his sheaves with him.*[565] Happily, Indian groups such as the Friends Missionary Prayer Band, the Indian Missionary Society, and the Swedish Institute continued their efforts in evangelism and Bible translation. When the fullness of time comes for North Bihar, the Lord of the Harvest will say to the reapers, *"Other men labored, and you have entered in to their labors."*[566]

39

Forbidden Kingdom

All of history is moving toward one great goal, the white-hot worship of God and His Son among all the peoples of the earth.

—John Piper

The Duncan Hospital

Mt. Everest thrusts its windswept crag five and one half miles into the sky on Nepal's northern border with Tibet, defying eight attempts to conquer it before Edmund Hilary succeeded in 1953. Equally defiant, the Hindu-dominated Rana Dynasty of this Himalayan fortress had for two hundred years firmly closed its doors to foreign influence.

RBMU personnel had prayed, worked, and waited for decades to enter this forbidden territory, half the size of the British Isles. A giant step toward this goal was taken in 1930, when Scottish doctor, Cecil Duncan, built a hospital at Raxaul, in Bihar Province. Perched on India's northern border with Nepal, Raxaul was a gateway town—a primary crossing point for travelers coming into India from Katmandu, the Nepal capital. Duncan was the hospital's first doctor. He had the text of John 3:16—in the Nepali language—inscribed on the outside wall of the north-facing hospital wing. Nepalis trekking down from the hills could hardly escape the mute announcement as they came into Raxaul. The bold text also expressed Cecil Duncan's heartbeat for the forbidden kingdom. The hospital developed into a highly respected treatment center and training facility in North India, where both Nepali and Indian personnel qualified as nurses and medical technicians.

Duncan Hospital became a primary center of RBMU activity in North Bihar. With the outbreak of the 1951 rebellion, which led to the opening of Nepal to foreigners, casualties from both sides were treated at the Duncan hospital.

The Road to Katmandu

In 1951, getting to Katmandu was high adventure. From Raxaul, a narrow gage railway ran north for twenty-five miles to Bhimpedi in the Himalayan foothills. From that point, vintage buses plied another twenty-five miles of twisting roads, climbing high into the foothills until ascent by vehicle was no longer possible. The determined Katmandu-bound traveler then faced a third twenty-five mile ascent on foot over terrain so rugged that the approach itself seemed to forbid entrance to the Gurkha kingdom.[567]

Ernest W. Oliver

With one eye on Nepal, Oliver had gone to India in 1935, certain that God would one day open the door to the still closed kingdom. When in 1938 he led a Nepali nobleman to the Lord, it was a down payment on his dream. Serving as a major in the Indian army during World War II brought Oliver into touch with the famed Gurkhas, one of them serving as his *batman,* or officer's valet. It was another link in the chain. Sharing Oliver's vision were British doctors Trevor and Patricia Strong. In 1948, they reopened the Duncan Hospital, closed since 1941 because of the war. With the 1951 overthrow of Nepal's ruling dynasty, and with anti-foreign restraints now lifted, the two men decided to have a look.

Traveling the seventy-five miles from Raxaul in the south, Oliver and Strong had their first glimpse of the Katmandu Valley in June 1951. From an overlook on the 7,000-foot pass they paused and thanked God for the privilege of standing upon this once forbidden ground, still without a Christian witness of any kind. Ernest Oliver described it as "the greatest moment of my life—the beginning of the fulfillment of God's call to me." While deeply aware of the history of this exotic kingdom, both men were quick to confess "their insufficient awareness of God's power to overcome the total ignorance of Himself" which marked the Nepali people.[568]

The Gurkhas

The Gurkhas had descended from the Hindus who fled North India during the Muslim invasions, intermarrying with the tribes west of Katmandu. Their intellectual and cultural advantages led first to the conquest of Katmandu and then the entire country. The Gurkha dynasty—under the ruling Rana family of Prime ministers—remained in control for 180 years, until the National Congress Party broke their rule in 1950.

King Mahendra rescinded Nepal's isolationist policy in 1954, bringing his country into the UN and the World Postal Union. He established new and helpful laws. Nevertheless, Nepal remained firmly under the influence of its Brahmanical advisors who denied to all the right to convert from Hinduism. This policy assured a baptism by fire for the church, which then existed only in the mind of God. Overtures were made to the Nepali government to allow the beginning of a medical work in Katmandu. Permission was granted on condition that no Christian proselytizing would be conducted.

The United Mission to Nepal

As other independent and denominational agencies had also been waiting for a crack in the door, the Nepal government laid down a second stipulation: All agencies entering the country must do so under a single administrative umbrella. It was a practical measure, but it meant entering a working accord with a variety of agencies of assorted theological persuasions. Whatever tensions this approach may have posed for some, one fact was inescapable: God was opening the long-awaited door for what he was about to do. In this way, the United Mission to Nepal was created in 1954, with Ernest Oliver as one of its primary architects and its first executive director. Ten denominational boards and agencies (including RBMU) signed as charter members under a ten-year, renewable contract.

The purpose of the UMN was defined:

> To minister to the needs of the people of Nepal in the name and in the spirit of Jesus Christ, and to make Christ known to them by word and life.

> To train the people of Nepal in the care of the sick, prevention of disease, and in education, agriculture, and industry.

> To help strengthen the church in its total ministry.

Following the Currents

Nepal's new open door was quickly entered by a rush of developers from both Communist and Capitalist countries. Hospitals and dispensaries, small industries, schools, and highway networks sprang up everywhere. Referring to this abrupt plunge into the twentieth century, Ernest Oliver wrote, " The history of Christian missions shows us that the Gospel has always spread along the prevailing currents of the day, and the Holy Spirit urges us along them now."[569]

RBMU followed the currents, cooperating with other agencies in the opening of a general hospital in Katmandu, which trained nurses and lab technicians and networked village clinics. The first facility granted to the UMN was the old Cholera Hospital in the city. This was followed by construction of a leprosy hospital, schools, a technical institute, and other clinics in outlying places with exotic names such as *Tansen, Amp Pipal, Pokhra, Okhladunga,* and *Butwol.* British and American RBMU personnel fed the swelling stream of workers. Shanta Bhawan, the palace of a member of the former ruling family, was converted into a hospital.

In 1959, Dale and Jeanette Leathead were reallocated from Raxaul to Nepal, Dale becoming Treasurer of the United Mission in 1963. The names of Chris Eggers and Betty Strothers—the first RBMU nurses to enter Nepal in 1954—Mabel McLean, Mildred Ballard, Betty Young, and Anne Avis, became the currency of UMN newsletters, with RBMU reaching a total contingent of about sixty-five by 1968. In the early 1970s, Drs. Trevor and Patricia Strong took up residence in Katmandu.

Hybrid Work of the Spirit

Many tributaries converged to establish the Nepali church. William Carey had translated the New Testament into Gorkhali in 1828. By 1900, the entire Bible had been published. For years missions had worked along Nepal's border with North India. In 1940, the Nepal Border Fellowship was formed to coordinate the work and prayer of these agencies.

Nepalis were converted to Christ at the Raxaul hospital. Nepali language literature was developed, while Bible School work in the Darjeeling district on Nepal's eastern border trained Nepali students. Far Eastern Broadcasting Company blanketed the country with Nepali language programming. Hundreds of Nepalis began taking Bible correspondence courses from bases in India. Gurkha soldiers, converted in Britain, returned to Nepal with their new-found faith.

Each of these threads was woven into the tapestry of the Nepali church. The thrust of the United Mission to Nepal was unique. Traditional approaches to evangelism and church planting were impossible under the laws of a Hindu society intolerant of conversions from Hinduism. Thus, there were no baptisms or church plants by foreign missionaries. To do so would have meant expulsion. The Nepali church grew up alongside the United Mission to Nepal, with no organizational connection, but nourished by the love and support of a worldwide network of praying people. At the same time a cosmopolitan amalgam of missionaries conducted the holistic ministries that not only brought the country into the twentieth century, but also provided the gospel culture in which God would grow his church. These facts assured that the emerging Nepali Church became totally independent and wholly self-reliant from the beginning. In the late 1970s, however, denominationalism made its appearance and subsequently became firmly entrenched.

The Harvest

In 1954, God's moment of providence had come for dark Nepal. A sovereign hand drew the curtain, and the light shined. RBMU was part of that history. In 1952, Ernest Oliver had baptized Col. Nararaj Shumshere Jung Bahadur, the Nepali nobleman he had led to the Lord in 1938. In 1955, the first Protestant church in Katmandu met in the Colonel's house.

Just before leaving Nepal in 1961, Ernest Oliver helped form the Nepal Christian Fellowship. He encourage the (fewer than one hundred) Christians in the Katmandu Valley and in West Central Nepal to unite. By 1966, there were five hundred active Christians in the entire country. In 1998, there were more than 200,000.

The NCF grew into The National Churches Fellowship of Nepal with a membership (in 1998) of hundreds of local churches. Other major groupings of churches were also formed. In 1968, the Churches of Nepal were represented at the Asian Congress of Evangelism.[570]

Why the Nepali Church Grew

Betty Young, who served with RBMU in the Administrative Office of the UMN since its formation in 1959, and later as the archival historian of the UMN, cited a number factors contributing to the explosive growth of the Nepali Church. Two of the more significant were:

> *Nepali Leadership.* Evangelization of Nepali émigrés who settled in India's Darjeeling district in the nineteenth century had produced a cadre of ready-for-use leadership. When Nepal opened to the gospel, these repatriated nationals filled leadership roles that otherwise would have been denied to expatriates.

> *Persecution.* While legal persecution, arrests, and imprisonment have been widely publicized, the social ostracism of converts by family and friends has been more prevalent and harder to bear. These include rejection by family, loss of inheritance, loss of rights to the village water supply, and the like. Such was the price of standing for Christ in Nepal. Rice Christians[571] were few, and hundreds of Nepalis testify to their faith being strengthened through suffering.

Prem Pradhan

One of the classic examples of persecution's fruitful work was that of Prem Pradhan.

Prem Pradhan was the son of a well-to-do Nepali. Educated by the Sadhus,[572] he was indoctrinated in the Hindu religion and later became an officer in the Indian army. In 1951 he heard some Indian Christians tell how Christ had died as a sacrificial Lamb. Prem remembered that the Vedas (Hindu sacred texts) had prophesied that one day a lamb would be nailed by its hoofs and die. Then it would come to life and save the world. As he listened, he said to himself, "That is Jesus."

Prem resigned his army commission and returned to Nepal to tell his family about Christ. They disowned him. For three years, he witnessed without visible results. One day he entered the home of a woman who had been paralyzed for six years. She listened with a receptive heart and turned to Christ in faith. In response to prayer, God healed her completely. The miracle marked a change in Prem's ministry. He began to see conversions. Persecution set in with a vengeance. In November 1959, Prem—together with five men and four women he had baptized—was pushed into a windowless, heatless room in Tansen Prison for the crime of changing religion. The converts' sentences were for one year, but their leader's was for six. One day he was manacled hand and foot and forced into a low-ceiling, narrow cell that had served to store dead bodies of prisoners for claim by relatives.

While Prem was in prison, a guard heard him talking to someone. When the guard could bear the suspense no longer, he asked, "With whom are you talking?"

"Jesus," replied the prisoner.

"How did Jesus come in?"

"He's with me all the time."

The guard brought his flashlight and knelt to peer in as he threw its beams into every corner. He was bewildered. "I can tell you how to find him," volunteered Prem. As the guard stood outside his door the prisoner explained how Christ came to earth and died, how he rose again, and how he now lives in the hearts of Christians. The guard listened and became a believer. In five years, Prem Pradhan was in seven different jails. An estimated seventy-five guards and prisoners became his converts, including a powerful political prsioner.[573]

Official persecution ended with a change of government in 1990, when Nepal became a democratic state, but only after five hundred martyrs had given their lives.[574] Amnesty was extended to all religious prisoners and outstanding court cases were dismissed. Hundreds of pastors and believers had suffered imprisonment. Among the first was Prem Pradhan, whose six-year prison sentence drew worldwide attention. It set in motion the amnesty that was to come twenty-five years later.

In 1960, the Nepali Church was about to enter its finest hour. Seven thousand miles away, another national church was about to face the test of its life.

40

Trial by Lions

After independence when the Simbas came, I thought God could have stopped this. I saw people killed and stuffed in sacks. But God saw we were too proud and inflated since independence, and God taught us we must look to him.

—Congolese Christian

Congo's Independence

With the close of World War II, former African colonies rushed pell-mell to seize the prize of national sovereignty. Within fifteen years, twenty-six African states had declared independence from their former colonial rulers.[575] The Belgian Congo was one. In 1960, the country erupted with jubilation as Belgium's fifty-two-year colonial rule (1908–1960) passed to Congolese leadership. Fifty years earlier in the scramble for Africa, colonial powers had imposed their will at gunpoint. Through brutal atrocities, Africa's forests had surrendered their treasures to European greed. Now, in the euphoria of independence, the tables were turned. Payback time had come. Missions should not have been surprised.

The Belgian Failure

Belgium had done much to develop the infrastructure of the Congo, but failed to plan for the inevitability of independence and a smooth transition of government to native rule. Under the 1908 Colonial Charter, the Congolese were excluded from democratic participation in their own government. Eighty percent of the children enrolled in schools were restricted to a primary school education. A white European elite denied the Congolese admission to all but the lowest civil posts. When independence came, fewer than thirty university graduates could be counted among a population of 13.5 million.[576]

This paternalistic repression produced simmering resentment, and was first expressed publicly in 1956 in a Catholic schools' periodical, *The African*

Conscience. The article decried Belgian domination, demanding political expression, and involvement in the future of the country. Shortly thereafter, the Alliance of Bakongo issued a manifesto demanding a full bill of rights. Belgium remained shortsighted, projecting a thirty-year timetable for emancipation. However, France would spoil Belgian indifference.

France Takes the Lead

In 1958, France offered full independence to her African colonies. The impact of this action in Leopoldville (Kinshasa) was dramatic. Patrice Lumumba—who would become Congo's first prime minister—petitioned the Belgian colonial minister to "prepare the masses and the elite to take control of public affairs and free the Congo from Colonialism."

Independence, 30 June 1960

Six days after Lumumba's speech, on 4 January 1959 riots broke out in Leopoldville and chaos ensued. The army mutinied. Atrocities followed. A wave of anti-white feeling swept the country. The time had come to collect the legacy of Leopold's predatory reign of terror. Releasing its grip on the "African Cake" and with less than two weeks notice, Belgium declared Congo independent on 30 June 1960.[577] Independence had rocked the nation. Now it would also rock the Church.

While shouts of "Go home!" were still ringing in the ears of foreigners, Congo embarked on the rocky road of selfhood. For months, a groundswell of nationalist feelings had been building. Expressing itself at first in insubordination by school children, it then erupted in widespread riots, wrecking of property, and molesting of Europeans. United Nations troops were called in to keep the peace.[578] For missionaries, the outlook was bleak. The RBMU-sponsored Association of Evangelical Churches of Lulonga (CADELU) had imbibed deeply of the nationalist spirit. For many, independence meant much more than merely throwing off the yoke of colonial rule. With the prize in hand, many Congolese saw independence as a complete reversal of roles. Now Congolese would be in charge. Foreigners would take orders.

While not all shared this attitude, many church leaders hotly demanded complete relinquishment of all missionary controls—funds, properties, and institutional administration. Church-mission tensions developed. Fellowship was strained. Missionaries went home. Most Europeans—traders, administrators, and missionaries—fled a volatile and precarious situation. On 22 July 1960, all female RBMU personnel were evacuated.[579] After the exodus, RBMU missionaries, Mr. and Mrs. Lawrence Walling, and two Portuguese traders were the only foreigners in the entire area, where previously there had been over a hundred."[580]

Even after the crisis had subsided, Congo's independence continued to sharply reduce the expatriate presence.[581] As a few missionaries began to trickle back, they found chaos. Hundreds of primary schools were in the hands of headmasters who had nothing more than elementary schooling. The sudden flush of power had unmasked an unsuspected spiritual adolescence within the national church leadership. Baptisms were conducted without adequate Biblical instruction. Principles instilled carefully over years were cavalierly discarded or waived in the expediency of the moment. Standards were lowered as patriotic fervor infused a revived respect for former tribal superstitions and the animism of yesteryear.

Ebenezer G. Vine's visit to North America in 1948 had championed the cause of RBMU's postwar British missionaries in Congo. Many had been without adequate support—even at the abstemious British levels then prevailing. In the US and Canada, Vine effectively generated "Friends of Congo," who for years faithfully supported workers they had never met. He also pled the need for fresh troops. Canadian Muriel Langley left for Congo the same year of Vine's arrival in North America, followed by Canada's Jane Hirsch in 1953. The Allen Petersons were soon on their heels—the first RBMU missionaries for Congo from the States. Allen was a graduate of Bethel College and PBI, while Marcie took her degree from Northwestern Schools. After language study in Belgium, they were posted to RBMU's first mission station on the upper river—Lulonga. Three years later, health forced their return to North America, where they would serve the rest of their working years on the faculty of PBI schools, catalysts for world missions.

The Changing Role of the Congo Protestant Council

Protestant missions in Congo, long cited as a showcase of mission comity among evangelicals, marked out their territories with a minimum of friction. The 1946 missions map of Congo displayed this remarkable cooperation.[582] Since 1902 the Congo Protestant Council (a cooperative affiliation of Protestant missions) represented the Protestant cause before the state and provided a vehicle for comity agreements. This greatly helped avoid duplication of efforts while promoting inter-mission cooperation.[583]

For years all Protestant work in Congo had been known collectively as "The Church of Christ in Congo," but in 1956 the Congo Protestant Council (CPC) changed from a council of Mission agencies to a council of *churches*, with Congolese voting. When national independence came in 1960 the CPC determined that its leadership would no longer include foreigners, but would be comprised of Congolese nationals only. Foreigners would remain only as technical aides. Pastor Pierre Shaumba was elected CPC Secretary-general in 1960.[584]

This change in the ethos of the CPC from that of a consultative body to one with executive powers forced the organic fusion of all Protestant churches in Congo, including dialogue with the Roman Catholic Church. Amalgamation of all former Protestant mission-birthed churches was predicated upon a popular notion that equated church union with patriotism—"One Church, One Congo." This political spin intimidated evangelical leaders from speaking out against theological ecumenical union, and missions were castigated as the cause of church division. Total integration of mission agencies with the national church in terms of personnel, property, and funds was pressed. To counter this trend, the *Evangelical Alliance of Congo* was formed, presenting a "Declaration of Convictions" to the Congo Protestant Council at Kisangani in 1969.

The Congo Churches—CADELU

By 1960, RBMU had planted more than 1,000 churches in Northwest Congo with 40,000 baptized communicants. Forty-five missionaries serviced a region roughly the size of England and home to three major tribal groups. Integration of so many churches posed a problem. No public transportation existed and mission aviation was unknown. To provide cohesion for hundreds of isolated churches, the Community of the Association of Evangelical Churches of the Lulonga (CADELU) was formed, the name deriving from a primary tributary of the Congo River and from the oldest and westernmost center of RBMU work, home to the Lingombe-speaking Ngombe people.[585] Five hundred miles to the east lay Yoseki, center of the Longando-speaking Bongando tribe, with two hundred churches and 18,000 believers. Midway between the two lay Baringa, opened in 1899, and site of the Baringa Bible School. The third major tribal group is the Mongo, distributed east to west between Basankusu and Mompono, and north to south between Bongandanga and Yuli.

At the time of independence, CADELU churches were "mostly self-supporting and self-governing, and to a certain extent, self-propagating. Pastors were functioning and evangelists were living in bush villages, touring the scattered churches to teach and advise."[586] Within a space of three years—to cite a typical case—supervising pastor Samuel Iseeli had visited each of the two hundred churches in the Yoseki region.

The Congo Christian Institute

The Congo Balolo Mission had established hundreds of primary schools (through grade 6) with 9,000 students. In a late effort (1958) to plug the gap in education, the government requested mission agencies to open additional secondary schools to absorb those children leaving grade six with no where to go. The result was the ICC—the only large Protestant secondary school in Equator Province. Located at Bolenge, just outside of Mbandaka (Coquilhatville), this government-recognized cooperative effort was launched by four missions—Swedish Baptists, Evangelical Free Church, Disciples of Christ, and RBMU. Among the teachers were RBMU's Lily Shield (first to serve), Joan Sledmere, Elsa Morgan, and Joyce Ferguson. Teachers were required to take the Colonial Course in Brussels for certification. Opened in 1962, this school proved a strategic effort since ICC graduates later filled many government leadership posts.

The Maringa Christian Institute (ICM), an educational complex three miles outside of Baringa, was (in 1999) the site of the only High School in the CADELU region. It was launched in 1961 following transfer at independence of all Mission-operated primary schools to Congolese control. ICM took housing in the fine building complex of the former Baringa leprosy colony, combining the Bible Institute and CADELU's secondary school under the banner of the Maringa Christian Institute. In 1962, the Featherstones began a two-year catechist training school. Maimie McIntyre and others later developed this into a three-year pastoral training program. The Bible Institute passed to national leadership in 1970 and continued to upgrade course offerings, becoming in 1980 the Baringa Institute of Theology. A central accounting office in Basankusu managed the payroll for two hundred schoolteachers throughout the region.[587]

RBMU mission hospitals functioned at Baringa, Yoseki, and Yuli. Under the skill of British surgeons, Arthur H. Wright[588] and Edgar R. Wide, hospitals and leprosaria flourished,[589] while many nationals were trained as nurses, medical technicians, and therapists. The Belgians did develop an excellent health infrastructure throughout the villages, towns, and cities of Congo. By 1960, they had virtually eradicated malaria and sleeping sickness.[590] Anticipating independence, the Mission had wisely encouraged CADELU to secure its *personnalite civile*, a legal status essential for the holding of funds or property. Notwithstanding, while so much had been achieved, missionary Joan Sledmere noted that RBMU

> Had left the church ill-equipped to meet the new dangers of the day; we had left them almost totally unequipped to obey Christ's commands to heal the sick [there were no Congolese doctors] . . . and unable to cope with the rising demand among the young for better education.[591]

The latter charge would be the Achilles heel of RBMU's great work in Congo. Independence had fueled an unprecedented migration of Congo's youth from their forest homes to the cities—all in eager pursuit of higher education and economic opportunity. With this migration, the old Congo of the Guinness era passed into history and with it the effectiveness of the old approaches to mission. Anticipating this movement, the Roman Catholic Church shrewdly constructed Lovanium University in the Kinshasa capital in what

Ernest Oliver termed, "The Roman Catholic stake in Congo's future." The strategic coup would assure Roman Catholic dominance in the new nation.

Neighboring denominational works such as the Disciples of Christ likewise provided scholarship funding for the growing cadre of students aspiring to secondary education, enabling many to pursue graduate degrees in the United States and elsewhere. British RBMU did not enjoy the financial resources of the denominational missions to match such efforts, and the disparity of opportunity generated some tensions within the CADELU leadership. If in 1999 this deficiency is met with raised eyebrow, we must remember that at the time of Congo's independence, British missionaries were receiving an "allowance" of $50 monthly.

Neither was the Mission able to launch seminary level education within the CADELU region. Founded in 1938, the Bible School had produced more than one hundred pastoral graduates in its twenty-five-year history. Most of them did not attend high school, but many of them were distinguished men of God who grew and nourished the churches. However, the Simba uprising in 1964 forced closure of MBS.[592] While RBMU did provide scholarship grants for some, sending a number of CADELU leaders to France and Switzerland for theological training, the larger need for an indigenous seminary remained unmet.[593]

The Simba Rebellion

In 1960, the CADELU churches faced trial by independence, but 1964 plunged them into a more painful crucible. The secession of mineral-rich Katanga (Shaba) province in 1960 led to the *Simba*[594] rebellion of 1964–65, leaving scars that would not be erased. A few weeks before the UN force withdrew from Congo (June 1964), an army of Congolese rebels who called themselves "Simbas"—the Swahili word for lions—ravaged the country, occupying an area the size of France. The Simbas were rabidly anti-American, due to US support of the Lumumba government. Thirty-four Protestant missionaries, including several children, met violent death. Three hundred whites and "tens of thousands of Congolese" were massacred.[595] The debacle led to one reporter's cynical observation that the Congo was "virtually ungovernable."[596] While no RBMU missionaries were killed, property losses to affected missions tallied in the millions of dollars. Of several thousand foreigners in Kisangani (Stanleyville) at independence, by 1967 their number had plummeted to ten.

The rebellion sharply tested the church. The severity varied from tribe to tribe. Some were killed for their faith or for their opposition to the cruelty of the rebels, or for their schooling, or for their western dress. Many Christians died.[597] Notwithstanding, the church grew. The Simbas overran half of the CADELU area, including Bongandanga, Mompono, and Yoseki. The latter,

RBMU's most eastern zone of operations, and closest to Kisangani (Stanleyville), was hardest hit. Mission property was destroyed and Christians were killed. As fugitives in the forests, many entered a new dimension of experience with Christ. Pastors emerged to preach and witness with new power. During the writer's visit in 1969, the question was put to a number of CADELU leaders, "What did you learn during the rebellion?" Among the replies was this from Jele Marc, a Mompono nurse, and pastoral assistant:

> I was completely alone for three weeks. God taught me to pray. Before the trouble we used to think of things as everything—as he pointed to a radio and a lamp—but we had to abandon all and God taught us the important thing is eternal life.

Another leader, Simon Lokuli, added:

> After independence when the Simbas came, I thought God could have stopped this. I saw people killed and stuffed in sacks. But God saw we were too proud and inflated since independence, and God taught us we must look to him.

The Simba uprising chastened the Church, and in its wake, missionaries were again welcomed with open arms. Christians danced in the streets, waved flags, sang hymns, and hugged and kissed the missionaries. Even local government officials went out of their way to greet them."[598] Any lingering resentment from independence had evaporated. Nevertheless, even more severe tests awaited the chastened CADELU Church.

Back to African Authenticity

On 24 November 1965, avowed anti-Communist Colonel Mobutu Sese Seko seized power in a military coup, launching a rapacious thirty-two-year dictatorship that soon collapsed the country's economy.[599] Calling for a return to "African authenticity," Mobutu banned official religious services on national days. Christian congregations were ordered not to pray for him or for the government of the country. This anti-Christian attitude was defended on the ground that Zaire must maintain its true African authenticity. Christianity was the white man's religion and therefore incompatible with African indigeneity. Following the same reasoning, the use of Christian first names was suppressed.

Throughout this cacophonous uproar of "Africa for Africans!" Some CADELU pastors stood rock-like for truth and sanity at great personal cost. Benjamin Lofinda, pastor of the Ikau church, wonderfully influenced Christians to distance themselves from a hysterical nationalism, a stand for which he was bitterly accused of favoring missionaries. Simon Mokala, the Ngombe supervising pastor of the Lulonga Church, was appointed to the leadership of

CADELU, since "he had borne bitter persecution in the past with all the grace and meekness that only Christ can give."

Some church members were not so strong, as Maimie McIntyre explains:

> As the nation of Zaire pursues its understandable policy of seeking a Bantu identity of its own, the effort to shake off western shackles assumes different forms. For some the answer is a "Bantu-isation" of theology, principles, and practice . . . It is difficult for the average Zairois Christian to maintain a Biblical and balanced perspective against a background of radio propaganda, chanting of political slogans in schools, party rallies, and other means employed to evoke a sense of national patriotism . . . We shall never fully appreciate the temptations facing our African brethren to compromise, to switch priorities, [and] to excuse sins as being some ancestral custom.[600]

CADELU Becomes Autonomous

In 1970, RBMU still had twenty-nine missionaries working in Zaire,[601] but a year later the Mission reached an agreement with the CADELU churches transferring full autonomy to the church association and integrating all RBMU personnel into the CADELU structure.

By edict of Mobutu, the 51,000 member CADELU churches had become part of the United Church of Christ in Zaire—effectively a state Church and the sole permitted Protestant body in the country. While the move was imperative, the fusion effectively surrendered the autonomy of the Mission as a church planting agency in Zaire. From that point forward the expatriate missionary presence in the CADELU region steadily diminished.[602]

By 1980, CADELU reported a membership of about 50,000. While many of these were committed believers "praying for revival in the Church," at least as many were "nominal Christians with little outward evidence of faith in everyday life." CADELU continued to play an important role in community life, notably through a network of primary schools run by the Church with teachers paid by the state. Hospitals at Yoseki, Baringa, and Bosodjafo, plus seven dispensaries, continued to serve the region. CADELU maintained links with several agencies, including RBMU, missionaries working as members of the church association and under its administration. CADELU remained dependent on Western economic aid, opening "the door to theological pressures" from contributing agencies.[603]

Action Partners

After the disbanding of the British RBMU, the Mission's historic service to the CADELU churches of Congo was transferred on 1 January 1991 to Action Partners, the agency that had been founded by Karl and Lucy (Guinness) Kumm as the Sudan United Mission.[604] Action Partners continued the work of the Baringa Institute of Theology, which had thirty-six students enrolled in 1999. Rebel movements and civil disturbance continued to beset the school. The old problem of moneyed denominational influence has been repeated with the entry of at least one German mission group offering CADELU leaders funded scholarships to theologically liberal institutions. This remains an irresistible attraction for many and does not encourage optimism for the future of the Church. Moreover, Congo's history of unrest continues. In 1999, rebel activity and civil disturbance flared up again not far from Baringa, besetting the work at the Baringa Institute of Theology. Serious intertribal fighting resulted in many deaths in the Bunia area northeast of Basankusu.

Notwithstanding, in 1999 the CADELU churches remained a viable Christian presence in a troubled land. They witness to the triumph of the gospel and to the dedication both of the early pioneers and the noble company who followed them.

41

Where Magellan Sailed

Dogmatically I assert that no man can hold seriously to the biblical concept of God, of Christ, of the gospel of God and the lostness of man and not experience crises in his mind and life. These tensions will create a state of emergency that will drive the honest and spiritually minded man to drastic action.

—George Peters

Returning from Southeast Asia in 1979, British RBMU's Ernest Oliver remarked to the writer that the Republic of the Philippines appeared ripe with opportunity. In spite of seventy-one Bible Schools, seminaries, and thirteen national agencies sending Filipino missionaries into cross cultural ministries at home and overseas, church planting opportunities abounded. North Americans were not only needed—they were still welcome in the island Republic.[605]

RBMU had been looking for an open door in Southeast Asia. Indonesia—the Mission's largest theater—had begun to restrict the flow of visa approvals. Worse, government policy was aggressively limiting the time which experienced resident workers might remain in the country—a measure designed to harass and discourage the evangelical presence in the predominantly Muslim nation. With one hundred missionaries in Indonesia, RBMU's viability was jeopardized. Redeployment options were now a critical concern.

Spain's Legacy

The Philippines was a logical step. Like Indonesia, it was an archipelago—a stunning galaxy of 7,000 islands with a cultural nebula of one hundred tribal groups. For a century, RBMU had specialized in frontier evangelism, ethnic church planting, and Scripture translation. In the Philippines there was no shortage of "regions beyond." Unlike Indonesia, the Republic had friendly linkage with the United States, a fact that presented real advantages.

Backed by Charles I of Spain, Portuguese navigator Ferdinand Magellan discovered the Philippines in 1521, one of his ships becoming the first to circumnavigate the globe. Magellan's discovery staked the archipelago for the Spanish crown, bequeathing Iberian architecture, language (nearly a third of the Bicolano dialect employs Spanish words), and Spain's universal export—syncretistic, nominal Roman Catholicism.

When Admiral Dewey destroyed the Spanish fleet in Manila Bay in 1898, America emerged as a world power and wrested the Philippines from nearly four centuries of Spanish control. The ouster of Spain assured the introduction of the American educational system and made the Philippines an American sphere of influence with English a major lingua franca. It also assured an open door to the gospel. This advantage was affirmed with American deliverance of the islands from the Japanese in World War II. That epic victory not only hallowed the name of American general Douglas MacArthur in Filipino history, it set the stage for the Philippines to become one of the most gospel receptive lands in Southeast Asia.

We Have Been Waiting for You!

On 14 September 1979, Southeast Asia veterans David Martin and Don Richter met in Manila. Commissioned by the North American Councils, they plunged into a five-week feasibility survey of the Philippines, looking for linkage with existing evangelical agencies. From the outset, the Mission determined to avoid duplication of effort and to work wherever possible with established ministries. The welcome was euphoric.

"We've been waiting for you!" one agency greeted the survey team. Scripture translation had produced many conversions among the tribespeople of Northern Luzon. Churches had sprung up everywhere through the light of the written Word. "We've been looking for a group like RBMU to train tribal leadership for the churches that have grown out of our work in the mountains of northern Luzon."[606] This sister mission—in keeping with its general practice—had established a target date to complete their translation projects and withdraw. For RBMU, the marriage was made in heaven, and God was in the timing.

The survey disclosed numerous ministry options. Luzon was the home of nine different tribal groups. Others were scattered throughout Mindanao, the Sulu archipelago, and Palawan. Aboriginal groups made up 12% of the Republic's (then) 44 million inhabitants. Agencies pressed RBMU to provide leadership training and to place church planting teams in several such groups. With shadows lengthening in Indonesia, God had opened wide a new window of opportunity. For a number of reasons, the Philippines would quickly become a giant enterprise for RBMU.

Racine, Wisconsin

In October 1980, the annual meeting of the IFMA[607] convened in Racine, Wisconsin. RBMU seized the occasion to piggyback a proprietary conference of officers and staff. Meeting at a local hotel they decided for RBMU's entry of the Philippines, with specific focus on Luzon's Bicol Peninsula and the tribal populations of Ifugao and Mountain Provinces. David W. Martin, seasoned by years of leadership roles in Irian Jaya, was designated Field Director. By August of 1981, seven new workers had joined the Martins.

The Manila Base

"Would God give this to us?" Finding $106,000 for the spacious, two-story, six bedroom facility in Manila's St. Ignatius Village seemed impossible, but a central headquarters facility was critical to RBMU's advance. "Manila Headquarters" became the subject of earnest prayer. Gifts poured in from the US, Canada, and Australia. Capped by a timely legacy bearing the unmistakable print of God's provision, settlement was made on 31 January 1982, giving the Mission title to its first base of operations in the Philippines.

Since no specific target areas within the agreed parameters could yet be defined, a three-member team was commissioned to conduct the first survey of the Bicol. The peninsula is a two hundred-mile long rocky appendage that twists and turns in a southeasterly direction from its slender connection with the major island of Luzon. The Bicol was one of the most gospel-neglected areas of the republic. David Martin, Marvin Krueger, and Trevor Douglas comprised the survey trio and set out 22–25 January 1982.[608]

We Enter the Philippines

With the arrival in Manila of the Martin family on 30 June 1981, RBMU set to work. The objectives were clear: evangelism, church planting, and the training of church leaders. From the outset, efforts were conducted in maximum consultation and cooperation with existing evangelical agencies and with existing national church structures. These guidelines were followed in a model of cordiality and led to a high degree of cooperation with the Association of Bible Churches of the Philippines (ABCOP)[609], the Association of Ifugao Bible Churches (AIBC), and the Highland Evangelical Church Association (HECA). OMF and SEND were also among the consulting agencies.

Recommendations urged by a sister mission[610] in 1979 led to an in-depth survey of Ifugao and Mountain provinces in Luzon, 10–21 May 1982. Extensive interaction with a dozen workers and national leaders defined conclusively what RBMU's Luzon agenda would be:

> That in cooperation with the existing churches that are seeking our assistance, we establish vernacular Bible Training Centers for [the] Ifugao and Balangao people.[611]

As with many appointees awaiting visas for Indonesia, Trevor Douglas[612] accepted reassignment to the Philippines. Here he had spent his childhood with his missionary parents, never dreaming he would return. They would later join the staff of Prairie Bible College, where Alban Douglas became a beloved professor. In one of God's surprise diversions, Trevor Douglas was assigned to Ifugao Province. He would develop the Ayangan Bible Training Center, grooming leaders from among the ninety churches and 6,000 believers of the Association of Ifugao Bible Churches (AIBC), the fruit of Scripture translation. In March 1993, the center completed its first academic year with twenty-one students.

When Douglas arrived in 1982, an active agency requested that he refrain from church planting, noting that "you may stifle what the Ifugaos are already doing." Douglas complied with the unusual request, for his calling was clearly to teach and train. "Consequently," he reported in 1999, "churches are mushrooming so much that [there remains] only a handful of Ayangan villages which have not yet been reached." The Ayangan mandate had changed from evangelism to one of promoting cross-cultural missions.[613]

Deployments elsewhere continued briskly as new missionaries arrived. The David Teaters settled among the Balangao tribe (1983), famous for the translation and church planting work of Jo Shetler. They prepared Balangao believers for church leadership.[614] Naga City in Camarines Sur province, the educational and economic hub of the Bicol Peninsula, became RBMU's initial target in the Bicol with the Marvin Kruegers, the Lee Rempels, the Buster Roalsens, Brenda Woods, and Heather Miller making up the initial team.[615]

Naga City

With 15,000 university students, Naga was a logical target for the Mission's first Project Timothy Team in the summer of 1983.[616] Setting up a coffee house ministry in the main plaza, the seven young people (five from Faith Community Church in Roslyn, Pennsylvania) engaged students in evangelism and discipleship, using English as the medium. The outreach built bridges, produced many contacts, and brought an abiding reciprocal stimulus to the sending church and to RBMU.[617] ABCOP missionaries Mel and Pity Reynales joined the group in 1984, forming the first Filipino-expatriate RBMU team. In 1989, Mark and Sherida Gray joined the team in Naga City, followed shortly by Gordon and Brenda Wiens and Pete and Cindy Zull. Among the fruit of their combined efforts was the Bicolandia Bible Christian Center, fully independent with its own Filipino pastor, Basil Santos. Heather Miller, gifted in pioneer evangelism, spearheaded a new church north of Naga City, the Canaman Bible Christian Fellowship (CCBF), pastored by Romy Azul, a former convict who came to Christ under Miller's prison ministry. He became an important leader in Canaman, helping to establish two satellite churches in nearby Poro and Casuray. In 1999, Marvin and Marjorie Krueger returned to Naga City after ten years in the US. Bob and Koleen French joined the Camarines Sur Team *to* begin a church planting training institute.

Catanduanes

Pear-shaped Catanduanes island (pop. 172,000) became RBMU's first Hidden People target (1984) and the first unreached people group to be adopted by a local church in North America—Faith Community Church of Roslyn, Pennsylvania. A distinctly Filipino Catholicism was stronger here than in other areas of the republic—"An indefinable mixture of animistic spirit-appeasement, seventeenth century Spanish Catholicism, and twentieth century western materialism."[618] First to be assigned were Doug and Phyliss Trick, Jerry and Marilyn Hogshead, Koleen Matsuda (French), and Colleen Orr. As some team members rotated out, others were added.[619] Several were trained to pastor the fledgling church and start new ones, among them, were Totoy Sebastian, and Teng Candelaria. By 1995 the *Virac Bible Christian Fellowship* (VBCF) was nationalized, and pastored by Dennis Abados, one of the few full-time pastors ever to serve on Catanduanes. In 1999, Totoy Sebastian, one of Jerry Hogshead's early converts, became pastor of VBCF.

In 1993, Gail Smith pioneered a new church plant in Viga, a remote town in northern Catanduanes frequently cut off from the south by typhoons and mudslides. Joining her the following year were Teng and Edna Candelaria, Filipinos converted and trained in the VBCF. Together with the Pfannenstiels they formed another Filipino-expatriate RBMU team.[620] Virac, a major town in southern Catanduanes, had been RBMU's first point of contact on the island. Totoy Sebastian, an early convert of Jerry Hogshead, was pastoring the Virac church in 1999.[621] Other churches were planted in Metro Manila.

In 1990, the Mission deployed its first team to Muslim groups in the southern Sulu archipelago, a difficult and dangerous zone for the courageous few who ventured there. They faced extreme isolation, religious/political activism, and most difficult of all, the anonymity essential to the survival of their work.[622]

Returning to North America in 1983 to join the US RBMU administrative staff, David Martin took up the role of Asia Coordinator for RBMU work in Southeast Asia. David Meade replaced him as field director, a post he and Trevor Douglas would alternately fill effectively for ten years.[623] Kermit Carlberg, in turn, replaced Meade in 1992. In 1999, the Mission had twenty-eight missionaries in the islands. In the eighteen years since the arrival of RBMU, seven churches had been established with Filipino pastors, a Bible school had been started in Ifugao, and numerous national pastors had been trained in the Ifugao and Catanduanes.

42

Every Twitch and Grunt

Do you know your besetting sin? Do you weep in secret about it? It is a manly act, an act of a good soldier of Jesus Christ.

—Alexander Whyte

Pierre Trudeaux, former prime minister of Canada, once remarked to an American politician, "Living next to you is in some ways like sleeping with an elephant. No matter how friendly and even-tempered is the beast, one is affected by every twitch and grunt." Similar "friendly and even-tempered" differences existed between the US and Canada councils and between them and the parent board in Britain. Most missionaries will agree that the mix of international backgrounds within RBMU was an enriching experience. International relationships were marked—with rare exceptions—by mutual respect, cultural enlargement, and abiding friendships. Within any international fellowship, there are always a few flag-waving types, but these were rare. Support level disparities between postwar British and American missionaries did exist (RBMU was always at the low end of the scale). While these created some tensions, a healthy body life was operative and people shared freely with one another.

Corporate relationships were not so easily resolved. This was traceable to several factors. First was the lack of centralized leadership. From the outset, RBMU had no international board with defined parameters of authority. Even during the Guinness days, the Congo Balolo Mission had its separate home council, as did also the combined India and South America Mission. The London Board came later. Ebenezer Vine's commission in North America had been to extend British interests. In the late 1940s, this presumed the parental role of the London Board and compliance by the new overseas councils with

British policy. Little thought had been given to handling the administrative issues certain to arise in the different cultural milieu of North America.

At the same time, national distinctives between Canada and the US were also present, though in lesser degree. The American branch, because of its larger size and initiative, at times placed Canada in a defensive posture, validating Premier Trudeaux's humorous, but serious observation. Policy initiatives taken by the American Council could not always assume approval by Canada. Occasional disparities existed between support policies on either side of the border. More important, Canada's historic commonwealth loyalty to Britain looked askance at any American motions toward independence or divergence from London's practice. In consequence, both were reluctant to surrender even a limited autonomy to the other. The philosophical tensions between the London Board and Ebenzer Vine have already been described in chapter 37.

At this time—at least in North American RBMU—there were no policies in place governing medical insurance, costs of furlough travel and living arrangements, ministry expenses and least of all, retirement plans. These were hammered out on an ad hoc basis as emergencies arose.

Increasingly, however, both American and Canadian governments had begun to scrutinize and control the use of tax-exempt funding by international organizations. Legalities imposed on mission agencies by both countries escalated. This led to the formation in 1972 of the Joint North American Councils of RBMU, a board of balanced representation from each council. Meetings alternated between Toronto and Philadelphia, sometimes midway between the two, in Syracuse, New York. Wherever possible, actions were taken jointly. However, by 1975 international meetings had replaced joint meetings of the North American councils.

The Australia Council—so far away and clearly a junior partner both in terms of the number of personnel and income ratios—often felt removed from the decision-making process. Both distance and differing cultural nuances minimized possibilities for full-bodied, practical cooperation.

Adolescence

Ebenezer G. Vine had not come to America in 1948 to launch a new mission agency, but to seek help for British RBMU. For that reason the new councils in Philadelphia and Toronto remained under the direction and policies of the British board. At the time, documentation of London's operational policies was virtually non-existent.[624] Britain was emerging from war's devastation and little thought had been given to refining prewar mission policy and procedure. Missiology as the highly articulated and widely diffused science it has become today was unknown. While Vine's efforts brought a welcome infusion of new life, British RBMU was soon to find itself dealing with a trouble-some adolescent.

Rapid development of the Mission in North America was due to two factors: First, was the effectiveness of Vine as spokesperson for the Mission. Second, was the intensified interest in global missions after the war. Vine's gifting was seamlessly woven with the romance of attractive new frontiers in Indonesia. In Kalimantan (Borneo) and in Irian Jaya (Dutch New Guinea) the mystique of headhunting Dayaks and primitive Stone Age tribes proved an irresistible lure to would-be candidates. God was at work, and Ebenezer Vine had come to the kingdom for such a time as this.

Notwithstanding, from the outset of Vine's debut in North America in 1948, tensions existed between his visionary and expansionist efforts and the cautious conservatism of postwar Britain. The war had jaded Great Britain and had all but bankrupted the Mission. The visionary faith required to launch new fields—while British missionaries remained literally destitute—was in short supply. Vine, on the contrary, exuded Caleb-like confidence—*"Let us go up at once and possess it!"*[625] He had little patience with what he saw as lack of vision, nor had he forgotten London's failure to share his enthusiasm for either Greet van't Eind or Bill Sirag in their burden for Borneo's Dayaks. Similar lack of enthusiasm had greeted his expansionist vision for Dutch New Guinea, Japan, and Pakistan. We must not lose sight of this backdrop as we consider RBMU's later moves in North America.

In 1961, Ernest Oliver, returning from outstanding service in India and Nepal, was named Executive Secretary of British RBMU. He immediately planned a visit to the US and Canada, accompanied by Chairman Charles Strong. In a logical and laudable effort to consolidate the new fields in Indonesia (and the North American councils) under a centralized British administration in London, Oliver floated the proposal in a letter to the three RBMU councils in the US, Canada, and Australia.[626]

From the British perspective, it was a reasonable suggestion. Ebenezer Vine was 77, with no successor in view. However, his reply to Oliver on December 23 could not be faulted for ambiguity:

> That which I now write . . . is the [united] expression of the . . . [American] Council . . . Everything that has transpired with respect to these newer fields [Kalimantan and Irian Jaya] serves to demonstrate that . . . the London Board of Directors have lacked all sense of the Lord calling them to this responsibility. To imagine for one moment that it has been just merely an absence of finance that has kept them back would be to make a fatal mistake. There has been almost a complete absence of interest and initiative, with one or two notable exceptions.

This cause, with all its demands, its sorrows, and its joys, has been carried through, alas, without the evidence of any deep concern on the part of the board as such. It is with sorrow that this has to be declared, but it is true! . . . The profound concern . . . essential to the safe development and guidance of the work on these fields has not existed and does not exist . . . Before God Himself, we dare not violate such vital and fundamental realities . . . This statement is made in all Christian grace, kindness, and courtesy, but it is essential that it be understood from the outset.

Vine's retort was unequivocal and precluded further discussion. There would be no global unification of RBMU fields under the umbrella of the British board. This historical background set the stage for the North American Mission's eventual move to autonomy in 1977. Nevertheless, other factors were at work:

By 1975, Indonesia had become RBMU's largest field, with one hundred missionaries in place. Popular buzz in mission circles referred to Indonesia as a "go-go" field—the adjective a take-off on a popular dance of the early sixties. Everybody wanted to go there and there was no shortage of candidates. The fading of Congo's relevance and the increasing antiforeign posture of India had diminished RBMU's profile and viability in these historic fields. With the groundswell of new recruits, the ratio of missionaries was shifting from the UK to North America. Still, there was another factor.

Cultural Tensions

The three councils—USA, Canada, and Australia, the latter having started as the Australia Mission to Nepal—had been subsidiaries of the Board in London. Since RBMU structure provided for neither an international director nor board, tensions inevitably developed.[627] This difficulty was compounded by cultural and theological factors so that in North America, both the Canada and American councils remained technically and legally independent of each other. In Canada, Commonwealth loyalties remained strong. These tensions would lead to a partial solution, as we shall see in a moment.

The Three Issues

In the late 1960s the issue of theological and ecclesiastical separatism intruded ominously within conservative evangelical circles in North America. British RBMU remained largely unaffected by these concerns. There were three primary issues: neo-evangelicalism, glossolalia, and moratorium.

The term "neo-evangelical," popularized by Billy Graham and *Christianity Today* magazine, became a lightning rod for the concern held by many conservative churches and Christians.

Dr. Harold Ockenga, then pastor of Park Street Congregational Church in Boston and president of Fuller Theological Seminary, appears to have coined the term. In a news release on 8 December 1957, he said:

> The new-evangelicalism is the latest dress of orthodoxy as neo-orthodoxy is the latest expression of theological liberalism. Neo-evangelicalism differs with fundamentalism in its willingness to handle the social problems which fundamentalism evaded . . . The Christian faith is a supernatural personal experience of salvation and a social philosophy.

This "latest dress of orthodoxy" sought to exhibit a more friendly attitude toward science, a more tolerant attitude to varying views of eschatology, a shift away from extreme dispensationalism, and an increased emphasis on scholarship, social responsibility, and a willingness to dialogue with liberal theologians.

Many conservatives of fundamentalist persuasion were not pleased, and "neo-evangelical" soon became a pejorative. As with most labels, the nuances of meaning were lost in the emotion of polemics. Many churches and individuals comprising the RBMU support base, particularly in America, condemned neo-evangelicalism. They wanted reassurance that the missionaries they supported (whom they knew) and their mission agencies (whom they did not know as well) also condemned these trends. Frequently, this entire range of concern distilled down to one defining question: Where do you stand on Billy Graham? For many, Billy Graham stood condemned for the inclusivist platform that marked his evangelistic campaigns. The question became a touchstone of Biblical separation.

Questionnaires calling for definition of RBMU's position on separation became frequent fare at mission headquarters, and many letters were written defending the Mission's position. RBMU's British-authored doctrinal statement was orthodox; but failed to satisfy American preoccupation with a calendarized eschatology and dogmatic millennial forecasting.[628]

Nor did it speak specifically to the then-raging concern over glossolalia. It also failed to satisfy those who took issue with RBMU's cooperative posture toward theologically liberal agencies within the United Mission to Nepal. These facts placed a young and relatively unknown American RBMU in an awkward and defensive posture and the Mission became unwelcome on a few Christian college campuses.

On one occasion, more than a dozen mission executives, including the writer, were requested to appear before a group of some thirty pastors in New England. The ministers, seated behind a phalanx of tape recorders and note pads, called for each agency representative to define his board's position on a prepared roster of issues, including those above-mentioned. The sincerity of these men in defense of the truth was beyond question. The future of mission-aries, whose support depended upon the right answers, was not.

In 1971, a cluster of students on the campus of Prairie Bible Institute—where RBMU enjoyed great respect and popularity—besieged the writer, challeng-ing the Mission's involvement with the United Mission to Nepal. Notwith-standing the fact that only a handful of North American RBMU people were involved—the rest being British—student perceptions brought RBMU to the docket. In support of the charge, a list of the (then) twenty-seven cooperating denominations and agencies was produced, an asterisk against the name of each agency that was a member of the World Council of Churches. The pro-test was sufficiently strong on campus to have the writer called before the PBI Board to defend the RBMU position. Such matters were non-issues with most British evangelicals and American concern was met with a bemused smile and misgivings about the sanity of American evangelicals. History proves the folly of deciding within which frameworks the Holy Spirit is free to work and the danger of capitulating to those who so insist, but at that time both the credibility and viability of North American RBMU was on the line.

Glossolalia

The second touchstone of orthodoxy during this period was the highly visible charismatic movement and the issue of glossolalia. Dr. Samuel Rowden, then Principle of London Bible College, reportedly affirmed that 60% of the stu-dents in the London Bible College held an open view on the glossolalia ques-tion.[629] From this school, British RBMU was drawing many of its candidates. What was a non-issue in Britain became a point of contention in North America, particularly in the United States. Conservative American mission agencies scrambled to define their position on the charismatic question, seek-ing conciliatory approaches to friends and supporters on both sides of the is-sue. A formal appeal from the American council to the British Board had been mimeographed on yellow paper. It was good-naturedly referred to as "The Yellow Peril." While most persons of either persuasion were mature enough to live in peace, some could not, and therein lay the issue. Throughout these exercises, American RBMU was not free to define proprietary doctrinal and policy statements for North America. To complicate matters, most RBMU fields were integrated internationally.

Moratorium

A third tension point was moratorium. This related primarily to RBMU's Congo field, and was not so much an issue of principle as it was of timing. Missiologically, the call for moratorium on western missions and their per-ceived imperialism was being raised in the developing countries in the 1970s and was vigorously championed in some denominational circles. Sovereignty of the national churches was defended. The time had come, it was said, for expatriate missions to withdraw and no longer interfere with the national church. Evangelical missions struggled with the tough questions of disengagement. When was it time to leave an established work? American agencies hammered out a wide assortment of accommodations to the mood of the day, including withdrawal, merger of mission and national church, partnership, and sundry variations on the theme.

Particularly affected was RBMU's Congo field. Following independence and the Simba uprising of 1964, CADELU churches became independent in 1971. President Mobutu's policy of *African Authenticity* imposed its own moratorium and subsequent history demonstrated that the CADELU churches (the fruit of RBMU work in Congo) were not adequately prepared for independence. The practical effect was a gradual diminution of expatriate involvement in the Lulonga Association of Churches and a corresponding loss of interest in the sending countries.

For the North American RBMU councils—still subsidiary to the British Board—it became clear that for RBMU in North America, policy on sensitive issues vis-à-vis the Christian public must be decided independently of contemporary British views.

Rift in Peru

The first separation came to the Peru field of the Mission, where British and Americans divided sharply on the glossolalia issue. In 1971 a remedial approach defined separate ministry spheres, leaving the work in southern Peru (Abancay) and in the west (Amazonas) to British workers, while historic ministries in the provinces of San Martin, Loreto, and Lima remained under North American administration. This rupture was painful and longstanding personal relationships were strained. For some, the scars would remain.

North American Autonomy

In 1977, an ad hoc international meeting of RBMU convened in the town of Battle, England (November 8–11). Delegates from the three RBMU councils were present, hosted by the London Board, with representatives present from all RBMU fields. The outcome was an action plan conceding the independence of North American RBMU from its parent Board in Britain. The agreement conceded North American leadership in the Indonesian fields of the Mission. British missionaries working in Indonesia—there were seven at the time—would be governed by North American policy. The plan was finalized the following spring at a smaller conference in Keswick, New Jersey. The separation was amicable. Fellowship and cooperation remained intact, but American RBMU was now free to tailor policies in keeping with the expectations of its North American constituency.

43

Hidden People

Missionary societies are not beggars holding out their caps for the friendly coin of charity. These societies are a channel of privilege, a clearinghouse enabling us to wipe out an awful debt. Have we ever sensed that we are heavily in debt? Has the emancipation proclamation freed us? Dare we deny this freedom to others?[630]

—L. E. Maxwell

A New Yardstick

Cameron Townsend, father of Wycliffe Bible Translators, saw the need to translate the Scriptures into every language on earth. In 1934 the linguistic diversity of earth was only dimly perceived, as captured in the film title, *O For A Thousand Tongues*. With Townsend's vision the *people group* approach to world evangelization was born. The world was a vast mosaic of languages—each one like a piece in a global jigsaw puzzle waiting for the liberating Word of Truth. As the years passed, incremental discovery of new languages and dialects reached the astonishing count of more than 6,000. Far from producing dismay, this discovery—for the first time in the story of redemption—had *quantified* the remaining task of world evangelization. The job was now finite and measurable, and missiologists began to speak of closure theology in terms of Matthew 24:14. Each language was viewed as a distinct *ethnos,* or people group, to be reached with the salvific Scriptures in their own vernacular. Eventually the concept of people groups as legitimate targets for evangelism would receive sharper definition and visibility in the great congresses on World Evangelization. The Berlin Congress in 1966 highlighted the ethnic diversity of the church:

The great challenge confronting the Church today is to identify and to locate every person in the world by the end of this century. There is no individual, no people, who cannot be reached with the gospel if we set ourselves to this supreme task of the Church. We can truly go to every creature.

It would fall to Dr. Ralph Winter[631] at the 1973 Lausanne Congress to elevate people group thinking to an unprecedented level. Winter's mathematical and analytical genius graphically thrust *people group* thinking into the evangelical consciousness and led to the Adopt-A-People movement. The AAP called upon local churches and mission agencies worldwide to target specific people groups for prayer, penetration, translation, and church planting. The count-down was on.

In March 1982, RBMU established a Hidden Peoples research department. The term pointed to the fact that thousands of groups had been overlooked by missionary effort. The designation was later changed to Unreached Peoples to avoid the misleading notion that such groups were somehow yet undiscovered in the forests of the planet. Following the RBMU-Worldteam merger in 1995, this strategic concept was retained, but with yet another name change to Least-evangelized Peoples (LEP). RBMU embarked on a project to identify and prioritize ten unreached groups for evangelism and church planting. The list was later increased to twenty groups. *Regions Beyond* editorialized:

This is no flag-waving idealism of inexperience. The long history of RBMU—and of all true work of God—is punctuated with costly and often painful offerings of time and strength and life itself. As a mission, we know not only the joy of bountiful harvest, but also the long years of self-expenditure in areas and among peoples that have yielded little fruit. Any call to advance into unevangelized areas must inevitably meet with resistance, with difficulty, and with the assault of doubt. Only those who are fully persuaded that what God wills is possible, will tenaciously see it through."[632]

The first three groups targeted were in the Philippines—the island of Catanduanes, Isabela Province on the East Coast of Luzon, and Sibutu, a Muslim area in the Sulu archipelago. The Mission went on to identify, prioritize, and enter the Esimbi, Assumbo, Baka, and Fulani in Cameroon; the middle to upper middle class sector of the city of Santiago, Chile; the Naparuna of Peru, the Muyu of Irian Jaya, and the Sulu archipelago of the Philippines. While a few of these projects could not be developed for external reasons, most had been entered with successful translation and church planting projects in progress by 1999.

Faith Community Church

In 1982, Faith Community Church of Roslyn, Pennsylvania, was the first to enter formal partnership with RBMU in the adoption of an unreached people group. Catanduanes, an island off the East Coast of Luzon in the Philippines, became the first Hidden People group on a roster now increased to twenty targets. Catanduanes (pop. 176,000) had no evangelical activity apart from a small Bible study group. Faith Community Church rose to the challenge. Pastor Richard Krueger went to the Philippines to minister to the RBMU Field Conference. This visit—plus other similar visits to RBMU fields—had a tremendous influence on the church. In 1983, five FCC young people went to Naga City in the Bicol Peninsula, setting up a coffeehouse for student witness in this university town. They toured Catanduanes, and on their return from the Philippines, became catalysts of prayer and interest, with the island remembered each Sunday morning from the FCC pulpit. The church supported RBMU missionaries to Catanduanes. Two churches were established, while this intelligized prayer interest remained strong fifteen years later. As for the "coffeehouse kids" from Faith Community Church, two couples went into full time missionary service.

Cambodia

Notorious for its killing fields of the Vietnam war era, Cambodia came into RBMU's focus in 1993 as a least-evangelized people target. With fewer than 15,000 Christians among this Buddhist nation's 15 million people, Cambodia had several groups without a viable church. Three were selected for church planting—the Tempuan, the Kreung, and the Cham. Tom and Debbie Seckler, veterans of four years' teaching ministry among the Dayak people of Kalimantan (1991–95) were appointed to pioneer this work and began their ministry among the Khmer people of Phnom Penh in 1996.

44

Hinge of Africa

Lord, I give up my purposes and plans, all my own desires, hopes, and ambitions, and accept thy will for my life. I give myself, my life, my all, utterly to Thee, to be Thine forever. I hand over to Thy keeping all my friendships; all the people whom I love are to take second place in my heart. Fill me and seal me with Thy Holy Spirit, work out Thy whole will in my life, at any cost, now and forever. To me to live is Christ.

—Lois Newman

Bismarck's Invaders

When the gunboat *Möwe* landed a party of German bluejackets in Cameroon on 14 July 1884, everyone was surprised. Especially the British. By the late nineteenth century, English merchants had established trading posts along the West Coast of Africa and some native kings on the Cameroon River had petitioned Queen Victoria to make the region a British protectorate. The paperwork was complete when Bismarck's invaders hoisted the German flag in the name of the Imperial Chancellor. With the European *Scramble for Africa* at full tilt, the area we know as Cameroon passed into German hands.[633] It would not be for long.

British and French troops drove out the Germans in World War I and in 1919 the protectorate was divided between Britain and France. When independence from France came in 1960, French and British Cameroon united as a one-party republic, making Cameroon the only officially bilingual country in Africa. It was also the most linguistically complex region in the continent.

RBMU launched its Unreached Peoples effort in 1982 to identify and enter ten new unreached people groups.[634] Research began immediately. Congo (at that time called Zaire) was no longer an option, but the Mission's historic presence in that country made Africa a logical candidate for study. Employing the databases of Operation World, Wycliffe Bible Translators, and the unreached people profiles then taking wing under the Missions Advance Research and Communication Center (MARC), Cameroon and Togo became priority options. Togo was later dropped because of visa restrictions.

A speaking assignment at the Sioux Falls North American Baptist Conference seminary in 1983 ignited the new venture when Don Richardson found the evangelical Baptist group sympathetic and willing to cooperate with RBMU plans. The Baptists had been established in Cameroon for a hundred years. Permission to enter could be had only beneath the umbrella of a recognized agency already in the country.[635] Agreement was reached and RBMU's Elmer Austring and Jonathan Lewis were commissioned to conduct the first survey in May 1984.[636] Their report issued in the resolution the following month that "RBMU International move to open a new field of service in Cameroon." The initial thrust would be church planting among the Esimbi people, with additional targets to include the Baka Pygmy, the Kotoko, the Bobili, and the Fulani. When the Mission councils met concurrently with the RBMU Candidate Orientation Program (COP) in June of 1985, the appointment of a vanguard of three couples was simultaneous—Dan and Karen Jealouse, Dean and Laurie Pankow, and Douglas and Lorna Warkentin. This was the first instance of pre arrival team selection based on compatibility, gifting, and mutual consent.

Cameroon took its name from the River of Prawns (*Rio dos Camarões*)—the cognomen given to the Wouri River estuary by early Portuguese explorers. The country (pop. 11 million) is a mosaic of more than 260 language groups, making it the most complex geopolitical unit on the continent and deserving of its nickname, *the linguistic crossroads of Africa*. Its singular location in the crotch of the continent won another epithet—the *Hinge of Africa*. For a century Presbyterians, Baptists, and Lutherans had developed strong ministries among the larger ethnic groups. Notable among them was the work of the Cameroon Baptist Convention. These efforts had produced churches, schools, seminaries, and medical facilities; however, the older denominations became institutionalized, lacking either vision or resources to evangelize the many smaller tribal groups still without the gospel. At the time of RBMU's entry, twenty-four tribes remained unserviced.

Working with the Baptists

In April 1985, the writer and Elmer Austring visited Cameroon to negotiate an agreement with the national church. This accord was ratified later that month (April 22–26) by the RBMU International Conference in Wongabrai, Australia. At this point, seasoned Irian Jaya workers Graham and Elizabeth Cousens had been on extended pastoral sabbatical in Britain. They joined the team, with Graham leading the Cameroon mission from Britain on a shuttle basis and conducting further survey work in 1985. Cousens continued oversight until the field was well established and Dan Jealouse assumed the role of field director in 1993.

From the outset, RBMU's purpose was to cooperate with existing evangelical works. In primitive areas such as Borneo and Dutch New Guinea, where no evangelical bodies had existed before the Mission entered, churches formed their own nonaffiliated associations. In Cameroon, with the Baptist Conference already in place, RBMU agreed that any churches resulting from its ministry would ipso facto become members of the Cameroon Baptist Conference.

The Tribes

The Esimbi tribe (pop. 20,000) became the first unreached people group to be entered by the Mission with the arrival of Dan and Karen Jealouse in 1987. Doug and Lorna Warkentin and Arnie Coleman joined the Jealouses the following year. [637]

In 1988, RBMU entered the Assumbo, a grouping of small tribes whose sparsely settled villages straddle western Cameroon's border with Nigeria. Seventeen thousand Assumbo speak ten different dialects, each one belonging to the Tiv family of languages, the largest language group in Nigeria. Three Assumbo dialects—Oliti, Icheve, and Ipulo, are mutually intelligible. Magic, sorcery, and fear of death dominated the worldview of the Assumbo. Dean and Laurie Pankow and linguist/medical specialists Ray and Paula Yoder established the first base among the Assumbo in 1989. Later joined by Bert and Annette Mull, work began on Scripture translation, and Yoder became coordinator for the Assumbo dialects. Pankow withdrew from the Assumbo work to coordinate the Theological Education by Extension program for the national church.

A People Bruised in Spirit

Of all the groups overlooked by both time and missions, none was more wrenching than the Baka Pygmy. Their ebony faces peered suspiciously from the arched doorways of their crude mongulu leaf huts, offering no welcome to the visitor. Their home was the Cameroon rain forest, deep in West Africa. Isolated by geography, backwatered by society, and disadvantaged by their small stature, the Baka were viewed as the dregs among earth's people groups. Neighboring tribes regarded them as subhuman—fair game for abuse and exploitation. To a people bruised in spirit, the arms of the rain forest offered welcome refuge from society's contempt.

Most of Cameroon's 25,000 Baka Pygmies were semi-nomadic hunter-gatherers, living part time in temporary forest camps, part time in permanent villages that bordered the larger Bantu towns. The forest camps were makeshift settlements of mongulu leaf huts, periodically abandoned, as the supply of game and forest foods would dictate.

The Baka were animists, living in a world of spirits. They believed in a creator god called Komba, but the perversity of people drove the creator god away. *Jengi*—the spirit of the forest—became their real god, dangerous if disturbed, but also the source of well being. Since ritual disharmony with Jengi was the cause of sickness and misfortune, Baka life was tightly controlled by a complex of religious rituals designed to preserve a good relationship with Jengi.

Between 1992 and 1997 the first RBMU church planting team entered the disadvantaged Baka Pygmy group (pop. 25,000). The team comprised Phil and Reda Anderton, Claude and Jenny Daoust, Sheila Joshi, and Desma Bosch. By 1993, four North American churches had "adopted" the Baka in keeping with the effort to link sending churches with unreached people groups.[638]

In 1993, Hugh and Susan Griffiths opened work among the Muslim Fulani. The Griffiths' background in animal husbandry uniquely qualified them to identify with the cattle-raising Fulani culture. They later recruited Randy and Shawn Olson, who continued the work the Griffiths had begun.

In 1998, the Mission turned to the Yemba tribe with the reassignment of veterans Dan and Karen Jealouse. The largely animistic Yemba scored as one of the larger of Cameroon's unreached groups, with 800,000 speakers concentrated primarily in the country's mountainous Western Province. As with many African people groups, life for the Yemba was tightly laced with the pacification of evil spirits. January of the same year saw entry of the Oroko tribe with the Mike Scotts and the Dan Friesens. They worked with Mbonge, one of nine Oroko dialects.

The Mission's presence in Cameroon quickly grew, and by 1999 counted a task force of thirty-eight missionaries working among six tribal groups. Poor roads, unreliable telephone service, and political instability hampered work in this isolated, multicultural setting.

45

Standing By the Stuff

I give on the basis of 2 Corinthians 9.6. I sow, expecting to reap. The test of a gift is that God is praised, not the giver.

—Bill Volkman

Scripture is clear that the Church functions like the human body—a miraculous organism composed of innumerable interdependent parts. The metaphor is beautiful, for it assigns equality of worth to every believer yielded to the will of Christ our Head. It is worth remembering that human society could never function if all were identically gifted. Some are designed to govern nations, others to perform menial chores. Between the two lies the infinite variety of skills and callings upon which productive society depends. The distribution of gifts and callings affirms the wisdom of our sovereign God.

The work of missions is no different. Truisms may become trite—and boring—but not invalid. It is said, "Some are called to go, others to give, others to pray." The truth is that all are called to do all three, but with obviously different emphases. If God is sovereign, he is also just. David reflected that truth and laid down the golden law of parity when he said, "The share of the man who stayed with the supplies is to be the same as that of him who went down to the battle. All will share alike."[639]The roster of those who stood by the stuff within the RBMU family is without number, and to mention any is to disparage many. Assuming that risk, here are a few—

Accountant Walter Allen of Patterson, New Jersey, put Ebenezer G. Vine on the train to Philadelphia in 1948, little imagining that he (Allen) would serve as treasurer and coordinator of publications for the new mission for the first three years of its existence. Allen passed the baton to structural engineer, Edwin H. Castor, on 23 March 1951. Castor agreed to help with the Mission bookkeeping for "one evening a week," little dreaming that the office of Treasurer would occupy his nearly full-time voluntary service for the next twenty-one years. Like Topsy, his work grew until almost any morning would find him in the office at break of dawn. Canada Council charter member and foreign exchange trader Jack Horning did the same for the Canadian Council until his death in 1979—a span of 36 years.

Mertise Philipson became Ebenezer Vine's first salaried secretary, replacing Leona Bauman, until an early Home-call took her in 1961. Evelyn Brady, a consummately efficient typist, logged 18 years as secretary to the writer. Staff wives—Eileen Conley, Margy Martin, and Barbara Humphries—kept the Fox Chase office humming. In 1969, Dale Leathead returned from twenty years' service in Nepal, anticipating a normal Stateside life in the business world. When implored in 1970 to join the Philadelphia headquarters staff, he did so, staying on as associate director and business manager until his retirement in 1995. Christine Eggers returned from twenty-five years in the "forbidden kingdom" to fill an office role at headquarters. For years, Carl Weber, retired from banking life, coaxed an ailing NCR machine to perform beyond its normal lifespan in tracking the Mission's financial records.

Anna Mae Marshall arrived in 1957 to keep the mailing department running for years. Her perennial cheerful smile and domestic touch brightened Mission headquarters. Fresh flowers and curtains were her specialty. Bertel G. Vine returned to India after her father's death in 1964, but came back five years later as resident hostess at Mission headquarters, a post she held until her retirement in 1995. Invited to join the Home Staff, Dave and Kathy Tucker returned from Irian Jaya in the mid-1980s. Dave became a highly successful campus recruiter. David Martin, after distinguished service in Irian Jaya for many years, and having opened the Philippine field of the Mission, came on board as an associate director in 1982. Following the RBMU merger with Worldteam in 1995, he served as Asia Director for the new Mission. By this time, the 8102 Elberon Avenue property was bursting at the seams, all four floors of the ninety-year-old structure having been converted into offices.

US Headquarters

In 1992, Helps International Ministries (HIM) and a host of skilled volunteers contracted the design and construction of the two-story, 10,000-sq. ft. headquarters facility in Warrington, Pennsylvania. Working under chief architect Ray Miller, Doug Leathead—son of Dale and Jeanette—brought his own architectural skills to the project. Paul Kline's able participation in the project from start to finish combined with that of the others to save the Mission thousands of dollars. After two years in temporary quarters, the RBMU staff took occupancy in August 1994. The building was dedicated on 23 April 1995.

Canada Headquarters

Before merger talks began between RBMU and Worldteam, the Canada offices had been looking for a way to share headquarters facilities with six other missions. In July 1994 eight missions[640]joined to form the ACTS corporation (Association of Christians Together in Service), and purchased a large office complex close to Toronto's airport.

Hands in Service

Ron and Dot Hilsabeck began this Canadian counterpart to World Team Associates in 1984 with a work project to the Philippines. Since then, Hands in Service mobilized 165 laypersons on nine overseas trips to the Philippines, Peru, Bolivia, Spain, and Greece. Team members were drawn from nearly all the Canadian provinces and nine different churches. In addition to their personal investment in mission projects, Hands in Service missionaries saw lives changed, prayer for missions mobilized in the sending churches, and six members become fulltime missionaries. In 1999, *HIS* was operating out of the Hilsabecks' home church in Clive, Alberta.

Semper Fi

Californian Don Richter served with the First Marine Division in the Solomon Islands, fought on Okinawa, and did occupational duty in north China until 1946. Upon demobilization, he returned to the US, unscathed, and armed with a litany of war stories, cultural insights, and a vision for the lost. As with many servicemen, Richter had been awakened to the lostness of thousands of the South Pacific's Melanesian population. Graduating from Prairie Bible Institute—where he and the writer met as dishwashing crew supervisors—Don returned to the Pacific theatre in 1953 under the auspices of Gospel Recordings.

While overseas he met and married Eunice Holley, a gifted Australian linguist with Wycliffe Bible Translators. In the course of seventeen years, the Richters recorded salvation's story in eight hundred tribal languages. Their launch—the *Overcomer*—was a familiar sight along the estuaries of the New Guinea coastline. Armed with recording equipment, Don and Eunice were among the first handful of missionaries to enter the Baliem Valley of Dutch New Guinea in 1959, where their work was a critical factor in conserving the astonishing movement of the Holy Spirit among the Dani people.

In 1970, the Richters left their island-hopping itinerant lifestyle for a more family-friendly missionary involvement. Don came on Board with RBMU as campus recruiter and American West Coast Director. His disarming blockbuster smile and his mesmerizing gift in narrating missionary adventure quickly won the hearts of students and endeared him to his peers on the RBMU team. Their San Gabriel home became an orientation center and a sleep-on-the floor bivouac for RBMU candidates, as the Richters continued to touch scores of lives for world missions. Many World Team missionaries (former RBMUers) look to Don as the "Pied Piper" who won their hearts and moved them to join the mission family. Don and Eunice served RBMU for twenty-five years and in 1999 resided in San Gabriel, California.

It would be impossible to record the men and women whose unfailing and often unseen support has been integral to the achievements recounted in this story. Thousands of hours in board and committee meetings, prayer gatherings, airport shuttles, hosting of missionaries and other forms of service must remain unnumbered and their donors unmentioned. It is a task that must be left for another book—the one composed by the great Head of the Church, who said, "I know your hard work . . . and your perseverance."[641] He alone can fulfill the promise not to forget the work and the love they have shown him as they have helped his people in the great march toward the consummation of redemption's story.[642]

World Team Headquarters, Warrington, Pennsylvania.

46

Where the Sun Had Never Set

Our duty—our vocation—is not to enslave but to set free; and I may say without any vainglorious boast . . . that we stand at the head of moral, social, and political civilization. Our task is to lead the way and direct the march of other nations.

—Lord Henry J. T. Palmerston,[643]

British RBMU Disbands

The greatest dominion the world had ever known relished her well-earned aphorism, "The sun never sets on the British Empire." The cartographers' choice of the color red to designate Britain's far-flung commonwealth of countries gave the nineteenth century planet a decided roseate hue. Lord Palmerston's boast was not all pomp. For all her well-deserved indictments, the United Kingdom left a benevolent mark upon humanity as none other has. Britain gave the world the industrial revolution and a universal language. Through her Tyndales, Wesleys, Whitfields, Wilberforces, Guinnesses, Bible societies, and missionaries, she bequeathed the liberating Word of Truth to an otherwise dark and lost humanity. Among her spiritual offspring was the Regions Beyond Missionary Union. When, after a century of glory, the founding agency in Britain disbanded in 1991, it was a melancholy day for many. Betty Young, veteran of years of missionary service in Nepal, put it tersely—*We were shattered!*

She defended the painful action:

Nevertheless, we were very fortunate in having a field visit ten days later from Geoff Larcombe (Executive Secretary for British RBMU at that time),[644] so quickly heard something of the inside story, and the reasons for this move. As with any group of people, there were mixed reactions and a few fought the decision. But most of us quickly realized that for Geoff it meant a real Gethsemane, and he would never have led

RBMU into that situation without being totally convinced that it was God's clear leading and he had no choice. There were many others involved, too, of course, but as Executive Secretary Geoff took the brunt of the heart searching and criticism. He was a superb leader, and we completely trusted him. On that basis, I accepted the decision as God's direction. I think most of my colleagues felt the same, and we have assurance that it was right, though hard.[645]

The Reasons

By 1988, British RBMU had initiated discussions on the future of the Mission in Great Britain. Changing times and shifting patterns of mission methods dictated the need for clear direction. Geoffrey Larcombe, who had served with RBMU in India, was now director of the Mission in Britain. His colleague and pillar, Richard Burton, was strength to Larcombe and together they carried a vision for the growth of RBMU–UK. That vision was dimmed when Burton contracted leukemia, and died some months later. While lack of financial resources did not play in the decision to disband, what did concern the London Board was that up to 30% of Mission income was then being absorbed by administrative costs—a disproportionate ratio for the maintenance of relatively few missionaries.

Larcombe explained the reasons for the decision:

> We felt we were trying to do mission with a largely nineteenth century structure and that we were failing to adequately serve our personnel with the know-how and resources they deserved. We [believed] it was better for them to link with others who had specialist input into that part of the world where they were serving.[646]

It was agreed that British personnel with RBMU in Peru would join the new Latin Link.[647] Others affected by the decision would be obliged to explore other alternatives. Missionaries in Congo would integrate with Action Partners, the agency founded as the SUM by Karl and Lucy Guinness Kuhm. Missionaries in Nepal, already linked with the United Mission to Nepal, were free to remain in that country, but without an RBMU identity. Those in both India and Nepal would be free to join Interserve or other agencies. Arrangements were made for the seven British workers in Irian Jaya to link with UFM International, which in turn seconded them to North American RBMU. In this way, the seven remained in Irian Jaya, preserving continuity of ministry in fellowship with colleagues of longstanding.

Reaction

In defense of RBMU–UK's global, multifield spread, some reasonably argued that a diversity of fields is essential in a day when countries may close at a moment's notice, and that redeployment options must be maintained. No one seemed to have considered retaining the British office as an extension of North American RBMU and thus saving alive a historic pedigree. Perhaps the differing ethos of the two had been underscored in 1961 and again in 1977 to the point where the cultural gap was viewed as insurmountable. Perhaps a reversal of roles between North America and Britain was likewise unthinkable. Perhaps no suitable personnel remained to be keepers of the flame. Prompted by a combination of factors, British RBMU chose to draw the curtain upon a century of Kingdom work.[648]

The UK decision wounded many—particularly RBMU's longstanding supporters in Scotland. Among the missionaries, John Wilson, working in Irian Jaya, was a third generation RBMU missionary whose parents and grandparents had served in Congo—a span of one hundred years. For many, British RBMU was family, and breakup was painful. In 1991, the Regions Beyond Missionary Union in the UK closed its offices. All existing personnel continued their work through other agencies. The corporate élan of RBMU was gone. Perhaps a century of glory had been enough.

47

Pass the Baton

Thou mayest add thereto . . .

—King David

Great Britain

Life is a continuum of transitions, where change is the only constant. Men build briefly upon foundations laid by others, only to move on. RBMU had its share.

H. Grattan Guinness founded and directed the East London Institute for Home and Foreign Missions from 1873 until he relinquished leadership to his son in 1884. He and his equally gifted wife, Fanny, led the Livingstone Inland Mission (as a subset of the ELI) from 1881–1884, when that work was ceded to the American Baptists. Son Harry took the baton from his parents, directing both the ELI from 1884 and the Congo Balolo Mission from its formation in 1888 until his death in 1915. A Board of regents[649] conducted the affairs of the CBM and the North India work until 1920, when the beloved Fredrick B. Meyer—co-director since 1898—assumed the leadership. In 1927 Canon Gordon Meyer Guinness, a third-generation Guinness, and one of Dr. Harry's three clergymen sons, joined the Board of Directors. He raised expectations for resurgence of RBMU's life.

Then at Easter, 1929, F.B. Meyer died. Compounding the blow was the death of two other directors about the same time—Dr. Inwood and Reverend Gordon Watt. When illness forced Gordon Guinness to retire, Mr. H. G. Gamman was named director. He had spent years in Congo and since 1923 had worked for years in the London office as assistant to Dr. F. B. Meyer.[650] In 1939, Ebenezer G. Vine donned the mantle as general secretary, leading British RBMU until 1948, when he came to North America. Theodore

Bamber, pastor of Rye Lane Chapel in Peckham, home church of a number of PIM missionaries, followed him as chair of the British Board from 1947 until his resignation in 1954. Ernest Oliver carried the leadership from 1961 until his retirement in 1976. Geoffrey Larcombe, former missionary to India, followed Oliver until British RBMU disbanded in 1991.

Australia

The Australia Nepalese Mission merged with RBMU in 1942, becoming the Australia Council of RBMU. In 1950, Pierson Harrison was its first secretary. Frank Manning, who retired in 1972, followed him. George Lazenby, vice principal of Melbourne Bible Institute, followed him as chairman, a post he filled for twenty years (1972–1992). Ron Willis held the chair from 1979–1985. Don Richter went to Australia, where he served as director for three years (1986–89). He was followed in turn by David Morley (1989–1995), Dennis McCurdy (1986–87), and by Brian Billing in 1997.[651]

Canada

When the Canada Council was formed in 1948, charter member Watkin Roberts became its chairman. After ten years' service, he resigned in 1957 and was followed by A. C. Simmonds. Stanley Plunkett served as secretary (1953–1955), but returned to Britain after a brief term. Claude Simmonds assumed the chairmanship upon the death of his father, A. C. Simmonds, in 1966. Halsey Warman, former missionary to India, represented the Mission from 1 July 1957–31 January 1970. Elmer Austring followed him in June of the same year. While awaiting visas for Irian Jaya, the Austrings had worked for three years (1966–69) with the Hawaiian Islands Mission before Elmer's appointment as director of the RBMU Canada Council, a position he would hold for twenty-five years until the merger. Warnar Spyker became associate director for Canada in 1984. Following Spyker, Ken Bennett, a veteran of service in Peru (1979–1988) and field director, returned to Canada for family medical reasons. He served as mission representative (1988–91), as associate director (1992–95), and was named Director of Canada RBMU in 1995.

Transitions

In August 1962 the writer and his family returned from Peru for emergency medical reasons, which prevented their return. By November, he was at the side of Ebenezer G. Vine to assist with the growing administrative demands of the Mission. Eighteen months later (10 May 1964), the seventy-nine year-old patriarch was called Home, stricken with a cardiac infarct while in the pulpit. He was in hospital for two weeks—apparently recovering—when the call came.

While Vine's death should have been no surprise, the American Council seems to have given little thought to leadership continuity in a work that had begun 15 years earlier through the gift and vigor of a 65-year-old, who sooner rather than later would require a successor. Immediately upon Vine's death, the writer was appointed to the leadership of the American Council of RBMU.

Ebenezer G. Vine had been an inspiring motivator, visionary, and spiritual giant. In every way, he was equipped with the outlook of Caleb, his Biblical predecessor. Caleb's courageous plea—*Give me this mountain!*—epitomized the final fifteen years of Vine's life.[652] Whatever gifts Vine may have had as an administrator were preempted by the urgency of opening new fields, recruiting workers, and inspiring congregations. Development of the administrative policies and structures essential to the viability of his work fell to his successors.

By the spring of 1987, the writer had led American RBMU for twenty-three years. During this time, the headquarters staff was enlarged to include Dale Leathead (1970), Don Richter (1970), David Tucker (1975), and David Martin (1981), veteran missionaries with many years overseas. They brought to the American base in Philadelphia a variety of gifts. New ministries were opened in the Philippines (1979), Chile (1982), and Cameroon (1985). In 1982 an *Unreached Peoples Department* (first called Hidden Peoples) identified, researched, and began entry of 20 unreached people groups with church planting teams.

8102 Elberon Avenue

In 1953, the writer had pastored a small church in the Germantown section of Philadelphia. In 1957, the old stone structure—formerly a Protestant Episcopal church—was sold and the proceeds divided between two mission agencies. RBMU was one. The money was used to purchase one-half of an old (circa 1905) duplex in Fox Chase, Pennsylvania. The three-story-plus-basement structure served as RBMU headquarters for more than thirty years, remodeled and outfitted with offices on each of its four levels, although unsuccessful attempts had been made to move to other facilities.

By the fall of 1987, it was clear to the writer that it was time to pass the baton to other hands. With a view to this transition, David W. Martin had been invited to the US staff six years earlier. The writer submitted his resignation from the leadership, effective 31 December 1987. Retiring to South Florida, he continued active involvement in Hispanic ministries as director of RBMU's Latin America fields. He later resumed the editorship of *Regions Beyond Advance,* continuing through its transition to the new World Team newsletter, also called *Advance.* In 1998, having served briefly on the Joint Ministry Council of World Team, he was commissioned to write the joint histories of the Regions Beyond Missionary Union and the West Indies Mission, a task resulting in the present volume.

In Boca Raton, Florida from 1988–95, the writer led a successful church planting ministry within the Hispanic community in collaboration with Carlos Vera and others. Vera was a gifted Argentinean evangelist. With start-up assistance from Boca Raton Community Church, within five years the Iglesia Hispana de Boca Raton (IHBR) had become autonomous. This Hispanic church conducted vigorous evangelistic outreach to the South Florida community through radio, audio, and videotapes, and ministry to migrant workers. Its membership drawn from a dozen Latin American republics, IHBR carried out a number of evangelistic campaigns in South and Central America, particularly in concert with RBMU church plants in Lima, Peru. In 1999, Peruvian Jesus Villalobos, one of its first converts, effectively pastored this work.

The Boca Raton effort brought the IHBR into fruitful linkage with master musicians, Charles and Betty Pugh. Under the wing of RBMU (and later, World Team), the Pughs' prodigious effort and creative skills in ethnomusicology developed more than seventy-six church choirs throughout Latin America and South Florida, providing culturally relevant music and techniques for teaching it to the people.

Part 4
A Mission Grows
The West Indies Mission
The Postwar Years
1946–1995

48

A Mission Grows

The training of native workers is the crowning missionary method. The missionary's true aim should not be to make himself indispensable, but rather the very reverse, by raising up native agents to take his place. The missionary who successfully does this may be said to work by multiplication instead of mere addition.

—Robert Hall Glover

At War's End

World War II had little impact upon the work of the West Indies Mission. Neutral Cuba had prospered economically and the Caribbean basin emerged unscathed from the global conflict that had devastated Europe and Asia. In fact, the war had a positive effect upon the West Indies Mission (WIM), for it unleashed demographic forces that would lift the Mission's horizons far beyond the lands of the Caribs.

In the wake of the conflict, former colonial possessions shook off imperial chains in the global rush to independence and national sovereignty. Dutch Guiana became independent from the Netherlands in 1979, becoming Suriname. St. Lucia and St. Vincent became parliamentary democracies the same year, gaining independence from Britain. French Guiana retained its status as an overseas department of France, the former penal colony showing little interest in independence.

Guadeloupe, the former French colony, became an overseas department of France in 1946. Trinidad and Tobago became independent from Britain in 1962 as a parliamentary democracy. Cashing in on their new freedom, colonial subjects emigrated by the thousands to Great Britain, France and other countries in Europe. The new ethnic diaspora had come with a rush, presenting the West Indies Mission with new cultural targets in the Old World.

Homer City

In 1945 the West Indies Mission was seventeen years old, but still had no North American Headquarters. From WIM's beginning in 1928 as the Cuba Bible Institute, both L. E. Maxwell (PBI) and Elmer Thompson had agreed that the Canadian school would assume neither administrative responsibility nor financial support for the Cuba Mission. Although Thompson had many friends at Prairie and interest in Cuba was warm, it meant that support gifts for WIM were receipted directly from Placetas, Cuba. New recruits were met, interviewed, housed, and inducted into the Mission in private homes in North America. As the Mission grew, it was easy to see that this system would enjoy a short life.

God is always previous—runs the maxim—and He had not overlooked WIM's need for a North American headquarters facility. In 1945, Mrs. Carrie McCrory, wife of the late J. G. McCrory of five and ten-cent store fame, lent a large mansion to the Mission. Nestled in Pennsylvania's Appalachian Mountains just east of Pittsburgh, Homer City was a long way from Cuba and hardly rang with metropolitan importance. But it was a timely and welcome provision. It gave the West Indies Mission its first headquarters facility in North America, an induction center for new candidates, a home base for furloughing personnel, and a farm!

In 1950 Elmer and Evelyn Thompson left Cuba and moved to the farm with their family, where they continued to administer WIM's affairs. Frances Alexander became the first office secretary. Mr. and Mrs. Weir Gillespie, close associates of Home Counselor R. M. Maxwell, managed both the farm and the home. B. G. Lavastida remained in Cuba. From that base, he conducted frequent itinerations in North America on behalf of the Mission.

Mrs. McCrory died in 1950, and two years later her three daughters deeded the entire 925-acre estate to the West Indies Mission. WIM now possessed five houses on the property—an office building, a chapel, a conference building, and four barns. The barns led to WIM's curious involvement with milk production![653]

Seventeen years earlier, Elmer Thompson had brought to Cuba the cultural model of Prairie Bible Institute—a self-supporting school in a rural setting, where a farming operation run by the students subsidized the cost of a Bible school education. The model had worked well on the Canadian prairies of the 1920s and fared well for a time in Cuba. In 1945, Thompson transferred this model to Homer City, Pennsylvania. The West Indies Mission office staff lived on the farm—living on-site was not optional—took communal meals, helped work the garden plots, and milked the cows. In postwar Pennsylvania, it seemed an unlikely way to run a mission.

Notwithstanding, WIM remained in Homer City for the next twenty-five years. Within the first year, the operation had grown to include three milk cows, nine calves, and two horses.[654] Five hogs awaited the ultimate sacrifice, providing food for the residents. Fifty turkeys and one hundred broilers were raised for personal use or for sale. There was one milk goat, three hundred baby chicks, and thirty-five laying hens, while the farm produced eight hundred bushels of corn, fifteen tons of hay and a vegetable garden.

The home and its directors were supported in the same fashion as the work in Cuba—by faith and through designated contributions. Crops and livestock subsidized the cost of living for staff. Homer City became the nerve center of the West Indies Mission. In the first year eleven candidates were housed and fed while going through orientation. Missionaries came and went, serving the Pennsylvania community through a weekly Bible class and prayer service.

Coral Gables

In 1965 Allen Thompson was soon to assume the leadership of the West Indies Mission. The world had changed, and in the modern milieu, the Homer City property was no longer logistically practical. Mission offices had to be close to major airports, with ready access to ministry fields, while allowing metropolitan interaction with the larger mission community. The new director opted to relocate the entire West Indies Mission office complex to Coral Gables, Florida. The Miami suburb offered ready access to the entire Caribbean basin as well as to the newer fields in Europe. The move was made in stages, Thompson relocating in 1965, other staff following later. During the transition, they worked out of a local church. The Homer City property lingered a while, but was eventually sold in 1970 to Triple DEL Farms of New Florence, Pennsylvania. During WIM's sojourn in Homer City, the Mission had grown from 98 missionaries to 220 and from four islands to nine, plus two countries in South America.[655] WIM's new International Office Building in Coral Gables was dedicated on 8 March 1970, with Elmer Thompson remaining as chairman of the Board.[656]

Whitened Harvest

Canadians Max and Ena Inglis made their first home on WIM's Homer City farm in 1954, where Max designed some of the Mission's early literature and ran the press. For thirteen years, Inglis brought his writing skills to the publication of *Whitened Harvest,* the mission magazine, then with a circulation of 3,000. When Worldteam moved to Coral Gables, Max and Ena were among the first of the home staff to make the move (1966). Here *Whitened Harvest* became *Harvest Today,* and grew to a much larger circulation.

Mission to Orphans

Early in WIM's history, John Montgomery had been moved by the plight of Cuba's homeless children. In Cuba, orphans were everywhere, "destitute and without hope," to quote their advocate. Montgomery initiated an effort to salvage them. With their plate already full, the WIM Board was uncomfortable about taking on another ministry and declined Montgomery's proposal. Undeterred, he obtained a farm and some homes in Santa Clara, Cuba's central province. In 1945, the Mission To Orphans (MTO) was born as an entity independent of the West Indies Mission. However, MTO missionaries continued to work alongside their WIM colleagues.

In 1954 the MTO launched a second project in Haiti, located "within a stone's throw of the WIM center at Aux Cayes," in the Southern Peninsula. Ron and Velma Vasselin joined this ministry, and later the Bob Stewarts. Eight years and scores of orphans later, MTO leadership concluded that consolidation with the West Indies Mission would relieve the increasing burden of administration, reduce costs, and free MTO personnel for more effective use of their time with the children. Thanks to the Castro revolution, the Cuba orphanage in Santa Clara had by this time been phased out and the children housed with relatives or friends. In June 1962 leaders of the two groups met in Homer City to seal the merger agreement. This became legally effective on 31 March 1963. George McKerihan, general director of MTO at the time, remained in Haiti to continue as superintendent of that work. Years later, WIM's orphanage ministries were turned over to Compassion International.[657]

WIM's Literature Venture

In 1932 the Nuevos Pinos Press was launched with "a special gift of one hundred dollars," enabling production of the first issues of *Whitened Harvest,* official newsletter of the new Mission. Its counterpart, *El Misionero Biblico* (The Bible Missionary) became the official organ of the *Association of Los Pinos Nuevos Churches.* It was the oldest self-subsisting evangelical paper in Cuba, entirely supported by national funds.

Literature work had not been a major focus of the West Indies Mission, but that changed with the arrival of Leslie and Mary Thompson in 1954, both graduates of Prairie Bible Institute. In Cuba, Allen Thompson had been director of the Bible Institute and Seminary, where he trained Cuban Obed Gorrin, who in turn trained eighty youth groups. Les Thompson supplied them with youth-oriented literature using a *Power* magazine format titled *Juventud* (Youth). From its first base in Cuba, *Juventud* developed into *Latin Youth Publications* (LYP), later moving to Bellingham, Washington, and finally, to Miami. The transnational, market-based nature of this literature ministry assured that it could not remain within the structure of WIM. In 1968, following the Mission's move to Coral Gables, LYP separated from WIM and became an independent corporation. Under Les Thompson's direction, LYP eventually metamorphosed into LOGOI (words), an auto-didactic Bible study ministry in wide use throughout Latin America.

Resolving Cultural Issues

Florent Toirac's stormy encounter with regulations and dress codes at the New Pines Bible Institute helped sharpen WIM's approach to cultural issues. In a cross-cultural, multi-national agency, such issues occur with dismaying frequency, at times producing tensions, but more often generating perplexities on what is right and what is wrong. Add to this mix the variety of denominational and cultural backgrounds that missionaries bring to an interdenominational agency and the agenda has been set for interesting discussion.

In the modern missions milieu missionaries are well-primed in cross-cultural skills and contextualization of the message. Pre-field exercises in form-versus-function at least remove the element of surprise when the worker is confronted with translation conundrums and cultural taboos. The writer has wry recollections of earlier missionaries in Peru who taught with sincere conviction that permed hair—not to mention make-up—signaled a worldly heart. It worked well until a young woman missionary arrived with naturally curly hair. Nationals whose theology had been shaped by missionary example could not be persuaded that the new worker fresh from England did not engage in clandestine permanent wave sessions.

The WIM executive had its share of guidelines governing church polity, but the process of thesis/antithesis/synthesis was inevitable. Was tithing a duty or an obligation? Elmer Thompson saw a distinction between the two. Windward Islands' Field Director Henry Werner taught tithing as a duty, but stopped short of excommunicating believers for failure in this grace. He took a less severe approach, restricting nontithers from participation in the church business sessions. Thompson affirmed that "Any teaching that touches on obligation is taken by the listeners legalistically, and we must lean the other way." Werner noted that Christian women in St. Lucia believed that hats must be worn in church. Thompson countered that hats are not important, "so long as there is no law imposed. No one should set about correcting another on this type of thing." Walter agreed, noting that "such things do come up in Haiti, and we must lead national believers away from all types of legalism." He added, "I used to feel it necessary to be severe in the beginning. Now I see the mistake. We must *lead* young people —both new missionaries and students— into the work rather than into a spirit of opposition or antagonism."

WIM leadership was learning—with bumps and bruises along the way—what all transcultural missionaries must learn if they are to be successful: Leave all taboos, shibboleths, and cultural baggage at customs. Teach biblical principles and trust the Holy Spirit to interpret his Word in the life of the maturing church.

49

The Jamaica Venture

It costs to be missionary-hearted. It costs parents their sons and daughters. It costs churches their best young people. It costs prayer. It costs material sacrifice. But that is how preachers are sent out.[658]

—Elmer V. Thompson

Puerto Rico

In 1945, Puerto Rico seemed the next logical move for the West Indies Mission. In WIM's eastward sweep through the Greater Antilles—Cuba, Haiti, the Dominican Republic—Puerto Rico was next in line. George Little was certain. The Littles had been based in the largely unresponsive Dominican Republic. Ready for a change, they had spent months touring this island of the *Borinquens*[659] and decided that Puerto Rico was an ideal location for a Bible school.[660] Little shared his enthusiasm with the Executive Committee:

> In our travels by car, bus, train, and horseback, we have freely distributed gospel literature. Wherever we have gone, we have found a readiness on the part of the people . . .Many opportunities have been given us to preach the gospel and the Lord has been pleased to bless in the salvation of 116 souls to date. Puerto Rico has great need for a Bible Institute.[661]

Some people in Puerto Rico shared Little's view and offered their cooperation if WIM would come; however, the Mission remained unconvinced. Puerto Rico already had well-established churches. Sensing pressure, WIM leadership—now comprising Thompson, Lavastida, Depew, and Butler—were uncomfortable. Retreating for corporate prayer on the matter, the men later broke up for a time of personal prayer in search for wisdom. When they reconvened to discuss the matter in-depth, a consensus was reached—better to release the Littles to pursue their personal sense of direction, but apart from WIM. Reaching an amicable accord with the Mission, the Littles were freed to work with another agency in Puerto Rico, and the West Indies Mission permanently bypassed the island.

Oswald J. Smith

During this protracted deliberation over Puerto Rico, Jamaica had come to WIM's attention. Dr. Oswald Smith of People's Church in Toronto had visited the island, and urged the West Indies Mission to enter. Jamaica was a significant territory in the Greater Antilles, just west of Haiti. As in Puerto Rico, there were established churches. Anglicans, Moravians, Baptists, Methodists, Congregationalists, and Presbyterians—all had worked the island since colonial days. As early as 1783, a freed American black had gone to Jamaica as a missionary. By 1842, George Lisle's church had sent forty-five Jamaican missionaries to Africa. In terms of need, it hardly fit WIM's profile of unevangelized. Thompson was disinclined to follow Smith's suggestion. Then something happened to change the picture.

Ernest Clark

In the summer of 1944, Ernest Clark, a prosperous Jamaica plantation owner and influential evangelical leader, invited Thompson to speak at a Bible conference—the Jamaica Keswick. Here was the chance to see firsthand what had so enthused Oswald Smith. Thompson accepted Clark's invitation and planned to conduct his own survey of the island. He took Evelyn with him and stayed a month.

Before leaving for Jamaica, Thompson had put Wolfe and Muriel Hansen on alert. If Jamaica in fact should prove to be the next step for the Mission, the Hansens would be the ideal vanguard. They remained on standby, prepared to leave in September for one year once a decision was reached. During his stay in Jamaica, Thompson invited Clark to visit New Pines Bible Institute in Cuba. Clark did so, arriving just before the annual spring conference. He was astonished at the sight of the many New Pines graduates who were evangelizing Cuba. "This could happen in Jamaica!" he thought. "A school like this . . . reaching our own people in the same way."

Upon his return, Clark immediately shared his vision with two Christian executives. Together they agreed to purchase land and invite WIM to begin a work on the island. There would be one proviso—the West Indies Mission would not establish churches. They would teach Jamaicans.

The Jamaica Bible Institute

As agreed, the Hansens—who were on standby—came to the island and were brought to the farm that Ernest Clark and his friends had purchased. The site was happily located high in the cool hills of Jamaica, just a mile from the town of Mandevelle. Two large buildings and three smaller bungalows were already in place. Unlike Cuba, Haiti, and the Dominican Republic, facilities were ready and waiting when the missionaries arrived—including a warm welcome! The Jamaica Bible Institute (JBI) opened on 1 November 1945 with nine students.

Not everyone shared Clark's excitement about the new Bible school. Curiously, the opposition came not only from unbelievers, but also from Christians. Grievances were twofold.

First, economically disadvantaged parents had expected the school to provide a ticket to prosperity for their children. JBI's Bible curriculum disappointed these expectations. Its purpose was to train Christians for service, not to prepare students for respected salaried positions in the marketplace. More than one parent bewailed, "What will become of my son after this?"

Second, well-to-do parents were equally offended. JBI opened its doors to all levels of society without respect to social standing. This policy was offensive to those who felt it beneath their dignity to mix with lesser mortals. As one parent remarked, "I didn't train my child to dig yam hills and scrub floors!"

Despite some initial hostility, students continued to come and the school continued to grow. Jamaica Bible School and College soon was matriculating an average of fifty students, providing Christian leadership training not only for Jamaican churches, but for English-speaking youth from other British Islands of the Lesser Antilles. JBI also cooperated with as many as forty churches in a variety of evangelistic activities, helping them to reach their communities for Christ.

John and Dorothy Depew

After health problems forced them to leave Haiti, seasoned missionaries John and Dorothy Depew came to Jamaica in 1951. The move was possible only because superior medical facilities not available in Haiti were available in Jamaica. Under Depew's leadership, the Bible Institute grew, and graduates eventually moved offshore to serve in Hong Kong, Africa, South America, and several Caribbean islands.[662]

By 1964, nearly one-third of the student body was from abroad. "We have new students from Surinam, British Guiana, Trinidad, Tobago, Aruba, Panama, Barbados, Haiti, and the Turks islands," wrote Dorothy Depew. " Better-prepared young people are coming to us and are expecting a higher level of training. If we cannot provide it, we will have failed in meeting the need of the hour. After much waiting upon the Lord, plans are now underway for our school to become a Bible college."[663] That same year construction was completed on a one-and-one-half-story library. Music rooms, study halls, and classrooms flanked the new facility. Twenty-six Bible correspondence courses were offered, with more than 13,000 lessons riding the postal mail, and 276 students professing faith in Christ. JBI's success was exhilarating, but for the West Indies Mission, even success had its limits.

Time to Leave

More students were graduating from JBI than there were churches in which to place them. Saturation had been reached, and WIM began to question its continuing role on the island. Escalating operational costs and increasing difficulty in securing visas was leading to the obvious: WIM's job was done. It was time to leave Jamaica. The Jamaica decision pressed Mission leadership to re-examine the larger question of the its mandate. Until now WIM had been a Bible institute mission employing training institutions as a means to foster evangelism and church planting. It had worked well. Now, with well established churches throughout much of the Caribbean, the West Indies Mission saw the danger which lay ahead—that of becoming an agency burdened with expensive institutions, not only in Jamaica and Haiti, but on other fields as well.

Patrick Arnold, former president of WIM/Worldteam expressed the consensus: "The Lord had not called us to be an institutional mission. We came to the deliberate decision to close the Jamaica Bible Institute, and turn the property over to a Jamaican Board." For WIM, it was the right thing at the right time. The JBI became a Jamaican community college with a Christ-centered emphasis. In two decades of existence, the Jamaica Bible Institute had served its purpose well.

50

A Hartt for Guadeloupe

An occasional missionary Sunday, an isolated missionary of-
fering, or a few missionary speakers throughout the year, will
never make the people of any church realize that the task of
world evangelization is of vital importance.

—Paul Smith

Like a string of pearls, the Caribbean islands of the Lesser Antilles trace a
gentle, eight hundred-mile arc from Puerto Rico in the north to Trinidad and
Tobago in the south. The island of Guadeloupe lies close to the midpoint of
the chain, buffering the Caribbean Sea on the west from the Atlantic Ocean on
the east.[664] Guadeloupe, a French possession, counted 300,000 inhabitants in
1947, mostly descended from slaves, without Christ and with no way of
coming to know him. Lying a thousand miles east of Santiago de Cuba, where
the West Indies Mission had begun twenty years earlier, Guadeloupe was
about to become WIM's farthest frontier.

The Haitian Vision

John Depew—at that time director of WIM's Haiti work—visited the French
and British islands of the Lesser Antilles to evaluate gospel opportunities
(July–August 1946). Haitian Christians initiated the visit. Their concern for
other Creole-speaking islands had moved them not only to pray about such a
survey, but also to gather several hundred Haitian dollars to underwrite the
venture. With additional help from missionaries—much of it from the Hartts'
wedding gifts and from friends in the US—Depew mounted a survey of Guadeloupe, Dominica, Martinique, and other islands farther south.

His first stop was Pointe-à-Pitre, Guadeloupe's chief port, and commercial
center. Reconnoitering the island over several days, he inquired everywhere
for a Christian or a copy of the Bible, but without success. Depew's report

immediately led to Elmer Thompson's mandate to the David Hartts—in Haiti since 1942—to take assignment to Guadeloupe. However, unlike WIM's experience of phenomenal church growth in Haiti, winning a beachhead for the gospel in Guadeloupe would be bitterly contested.[665]

David Hartt

Bremerton-born David Hartt trained at Prairie Bible Institute, where his father had taken his skills as an electrician and served on staff. Elmer Thompson's PBI connections made the school a favorite fishing hole for West Indies Mission recruitment. While at Prairie, Dave met Erma Anhorn, and in 1941, still single, the pair signed on with WIM, and went to Cuba for orientation. After their engagement, they were appointed to Haiti, where they arrived in May 1942. Wedding bells followed their first year of teaching at the Haiti Bible Institute. Engaged couples were required to defer marriage for one year after arrival on the field. This policy was instructive, as it taught some prospective candidates to marry first and apply later! The Hartts continued to work in Haiti until the call came that would shape their future. The Mission asked David to survey ministry possibilities in Guadeloupe.[666]

Armed with a new mandate and a one-month visa, Hartt attempted to visit the island, but a shipping strike obliged him to fly to neighboring Antigua, since Guadeloupe had no airfield. Here he chanced to meet a Syrian cloth merchant about to fly to Guadeloupe in a war surplus aircraft. He planned to land in a cow pasture. Fifty dollars bought his passage, and Hartt arrived on the island on 6 March 1947. Waiting to meet him was a solitary gendarme, who turned out to be the immigration officer. Hartt did not know it, but he would have to deal with this man for the next two years.

Acting in mercy, Hartt had left his wife and infant son in Haiti to await completion of the survey. Frugality now dictated his choice of accommodations. He took an attic room in the *Imperial Hotel,* a run-down hovel with an unsavory reputation where flour sacks served as bedsheets. In the aftermath of World War II, both cloth and food were scarce. Guadeloupe was a French possession and had not shared Cuba's wartime industrial prosperity. Everything was rationed. People waited in queues, scrapping for the few available staples. French forces had done little to provide for the population during the war. Years of inadequate diet had left a legacy of tuberculosis and poverty.

Hartt spent the next ten days visiting towns and population centers. He was well-received, everyone curious about the contents of the black briefcase that he always carried. The case contained his survival kit—seven hundred dollars and a passport. In three weeks, he had surveyed the island and had developed a list of hundreds of names—mostly people who wanted to buy Bibles.

Encouraged by this reception, Hartt proceeded to befriend the local police, since their station was directly across the street from his hotel. Enlisting their aid, he typed out a request to the governor of the island for permission to remain in Guadeloupe, and to represent the West Indies Mission. When an apprehensive Hartt went to the palace to request an audience with the governor, the answer was a polite, "Not today." However, the governor did agree to a later appointment, and on the date indicated—20 March 1947—he returned to the palace, letter in hand.

Hartt was not nervous, but felt keenly the importance of his appeal. WIM's future in Guadeloupe now depended on his success with the governor. In passable French he presented the work of the West Indies Mission and his purpose in coming to Guadeloupe. The visit lasted no more than a few minutes and the outcome was disappointing. Appropriate papers would have to be sent to France, and nothing could be done until French authorities replied. Inexperienced with face-saving French diplomacy, Hartt was not aware that he had been turned down.

Having lodged this formal request and with many friends praying, Hartt now approached the immigration department for permission to remain on the island until the awaited reply might come. The extension was approved and he used this waiting period to begin a more extensive survey of the island.

With money in short supply, Hartt began taking his daily meal at a local *pension*.[667] It was cheaper, and one meal a day was all he could afford. This abstemious lifestyle would continue for nearly fifteen months. Curiously, the West Indies Mission had placed a $15.00 per month cap on missionary support.[668] This across-the-board support rate for all workers was based upon living costs in Cuba, where things were plentiful, and where food from the Mission farm subsidized missionary living costs. Guadeloupe was different. Two American churches had pressed the Hartts to accept $50.00 a month. However, Director Thompson—who had not been to Guadeloupe—was unyielding. Egalitarian standards must be maintained and the offer was declined. Later, when the Hartt family had been reunited on the island for six months, symptoms of serious nutritional deficiency began to show, particularly in little Paul, who was losing his hair. When Elmer Thompson was able to visit Guadeloupe and assess the situation first-hand, the support ceiling was eased.

Hartt's first convert was a shoemaker. Wilfrid Espere was attracted to the stranger from America, but he was suspicious, since rumor had it that Hartt was a spy. So he prayed (apparently having enough light to do so): "Lord, if this man is an imposter, condemn him, but what he has to say is so wonderful it has to be the truth." Then, as Wilfrid later testified, he saw a vision of Jesus standing at the foot of his bed assuring him that Pastor David was a man of God and could be trusted.

Stonewalled

Hartt soon had three men who showed interest in the gospel, and he began to hold services in his hotel room.[669] The three became Hartt's advocates and petitioned the government to allow him to remain in the country. Their efforts were denied. Hartt later learned that his friends were not socially qualified to ask favors of French government officials. An appeal to the American Consul proved even worse. The consul wrote Washington, requesting Hartt's recall as one who was straining French-American relations.[670]

At the end of July—nearly four months after Hartt's arrival in Guadeloupe—the governor replied. Far from the hoped-for smile of approval, the official response grimly challenged the young American:

> Where do you hold your meetings? Who are your converts? Who works with you? What are their names, addresses, professions, and nationalities?

Hartt knew he was being stonewalled. To say he had no meeting place, no members, and no services would provide the governor with the pretext he seemed to be fishing for. Since proselytizing was illegal, there would be no reason to permit him to remain on the island.

On 23 June 1947, he wrote home: "These people are very open to the gospel and I find more open doors for visits than I can possibly fill." On August 1 a jubilant Hartt began public preaching services, "to let the world know that the gospel had come to Guadeloupe." He began to meet regularly with a few business people during lunch hour. Much of his time, however, was taken up in the slums where people professed to accept Christ, but quickly seemed to forget their interest in spiritual things.

By November 10, the picture was not so bright: "This work is not going so fast as I thought it might. The blitzkrieg has already slowed down to hand-to-hand slugging it out with the enemy for a few souls. I have had evening meetings almost every night for two months. Several have professed conversion."

A Church Is Born

In four months, Hartt had made the acquaintance of a handful of nominal Protestants. Though unconverted, they were friendly and sympathetic to the gospel message. Since they were his only resources, he called them together and explained the crisis. The group immediately began to pray for an open door. Within a few days, they found a place on one of the busiest streets in Pointe-à-Pitre. The room was tiny—just ten-by-twelve—but it *was* a front room and opened onto the street. They promptly rented it for 5,000 francs a month—nearly $150—thanking God for his mercy. Benches were essential, but Hartt played by the book, refusing to invest WIM money in the project.

From the outset, this would be the responsibility of nationals. So it was. The handful of Christians agreed to the policy and began to give sacrificially.

His three friends embraced the gospel. On 10 April 1948—just a month before his reunion with Erma—Hartt baptized them in the sea, with many curious townspeople watching the ceremony. The otherwise peaceful procedure was punctuated by at least one angry shout from the crowd— "Drown the lot!" David Hartt had been in Guadeloupe fourteen months.

Hartt now had both a meeting place and members. He drafted a charter document for his "little evangelical association" and wrote another letter to the governor. Now wiser in bureaucratic ways, Hartt had the petition signed by everyone he knew—saved and unsaved alike—even the saloon keepers to whom he had preached the gospel. The tide was turning and Hartt was confident.

The Advocates

Meanwhile, something happened that changed Hartt's standing before the government. In a chance meeting with a French soldier who proved to be a Bible-believing Christian from a reformed church in France, Hartt had explained his difficulties with the immigration department. "Come and meet my commanding officer!" was the soldier's reply.

Paul Verdier was commander of a "CRS" group—French shock troops comprised of former felons who had paid their debt to society. Verdier was a no-nonsense military who had served in Madagascar. When things got out of hand, he knew what to do. In Madagascar, he told the Roman Catholic bishop who had been hassling missionaries: "Lay off, or I will blow up your headquarters!" The CRS commander rose to Hartt's defense, and took care of things with the prefect. Thereafter, neither Hartt, nor any WIM missionary had problems with Guadeloupe immigration.

Another incident at this time evidenced God's imprimatur upon WIM's Guadeloupe venture. An agronomist and reputed geneticist, Dr. Henry Stehle, was a Protestant by birth but had not met Christ personally. He befriended Hartt, who later led him to the Lord. Stehle informed Hartt that a French judge, Liotard, had just been assigned to a post on Marie Galante, largest of Guadeloupe's five satellite islands.[671] This information would become a highly significant development in the planting of the evangelical church in Guadeloupe.

WIM Gives the Nod

Months passed. Converts increased and the church grew. Hartt launched a two-week Bible school for the nurture of the little flock. It was now clear that God was nudging the West Indies Mission to a new effort, and WIM's executive committee of May 1948 decided "that the West Indies Mission consider Guadeloupe as a prospective department of the Mission."[672]

During the long process of establishing the Mission's base David Hartt had technically been an illegal—operating for more than a year on a one-month visitor's visa.[673] Hartt had been separated from his wife and young son, who were still in Haiti. Repeated visa applications for Erma and Paul had been denied. Even a promised tourist visa fell victim to a shipping strike and a breakdown in mail service. The intervention of Paul Verdier changed all that. The governor wired Erma's visa to the French Consul in Haiti. Within days, Erma and Paul flew from Haiti to Guadeloupe. On 13 May 1948 the Hartt family joyfully embraced. They had been separated fifteen months.

Early Efforts

Hartt had not been the first to bring gospel light to Guadeloupe. Earlier efforts had failed to produce converts, but seed had been sown. A Frenchman converted in Canada had gone to Guadeloupe in 1912 to distribute Scriptures. Of Plymouth Brethren persuasion, Louis Germain planted no churches, but had either offered, given, or sold Bible portions and tracts in every home in Guadeloupe; a fact later confirmed when David met the aged Louis in Ottawa about 1950. Forgotten by most, the Frenchman passed into history. In 1926 Henry Dutton, a middle-aged, bearded Englishman established a shop where he sold English china as a means of staying in the country to promote the gospel. Roman persecution eventually drove him to the island of Marie Galante. He recorded no conversion. Germain and Dutton had sown the seed. David Hartt was entering the harvest part of the cycle. It would give fresh meaning to the words, *"Other men labored, and you have entered into their labors."*[674]

Etienne Liotard

Before his reunion with Erma and Paul, David had suppressed his excitement at the news of Judge Etienne Liotard's arrival on Marie Galante—the largest of Guadeloupe's five satellite islands. What raised his eyebrows was the fact that the judge was a Protestant, reportedly converted from Catholicism. This was a significant contact and they determined to investigate. Turning the trip into a family outing, Dave, Erma, and little Paul made the journey by sailboat, booking into a hotel on Marie Galante while pursuing the acquaintance of the Liotards. The judge's conversion from Roman Catholicism proved to be a matter of convenience—he had divorced his first wife and had remarried, becoming Protestant in order to have a religious ceremony.

Notwithstanding, the Liotards were cordial and welcomed the Bible studies Hartt held in their home each morning, afternoon and evening. Hartt recalled:

> I told them that I would ask the mayor's permission to preach in the park and play my trumpet. Both found it amusing and outlandish, but I assured them it would be solemn and in good taste. They joined us for this strange and unusual type of Protestant service. I played my trumpet. Erma and I sang a duet.

A crowd gathered and listened attentively as I preached on repentance and faith in the finished atoning work of Christ on the cross.

But when Hartt pressed the gathering to confess Christ publicly, there was no response. A mute hush fell upon the listeners. Mayor Tirolien finally broke the silence with a question:

"Is not such a decision a private matter?"

Hartt responded,

"Jesus Christ died publicly and in shame."

The missionary continued:

"Are there not some who will stand publicly to renounce their lives of sin?"

Again, silence reigned. Hartt prayed and bid them all good night. As he parted from the Liotards, he assured them that the service had not been in vain. Fruit would certainly follow. The next morning as he conducted a final Bible study with the Liotards, he asked them to pray. His prediction of the previous evening was on the mark:

They bubbled over with joy that they were now saved and had scarcely been able to sleep during the night. I then asked when this had occurred. Their faces radiated the joy of the Lord as Etienne replied, "Since we could not sleep thinking about what we heard last night, we knelt at our bedside and invited the Lord Jesus Christ into our lives by faith." Thus began their walk with God.[675]

Meanwhile, God was preparing other assets for what he was about to do in Guadeloupe. Roy and Margaret Bergquist—both graduates of PBI—had gone to Haiti in 1945, where they developed a warm camaraderie with fellow Washingtonians, David and Erma Hartt. When Guadeloupe called the Hartts two years later,[676] Erma turned to the Bergquists (David had gone ahead alone for the survey) and said wistfully, "Wouldn't it be wonderful if the Lord would send you two to work with us in Guadeloupe?" The Lord did just that, but not in a way expected. First would come a test of faith.

The Bergquists' tour of duty in Haiti came to a grudging halt when pain in Margaret's perforated eardrum became unbearable. Remedial measures had failed, including a trip to Cuba for better professional attention. Reluctantly they said good-bye to their Haitian students on 5 December 1947. Six days later they were in Seattle, the future unclear. They had been in Haiti less than three years.

Back in Washington, Roy took a pastorate and Margaret gradually recovered. Bergquists' vision for the islands never died, and over the months they maintained vigorous correspondence with the Mission. Then the letter came from Director Thompson—would they be willing to work with the Hartts in Guadeloupe? Roy and Margaret needed no prompting. Knowing that visas for Guadeloupe were impossible, they advance booked a December passage on a ship out of New York (sailings were infrequent in the wake of the war).

In August they put their crates on the Seattle docks for transshipment to New York and connection with the Guadeloupe-bound December sailing. Still no visas. Railway tickets in hand and booked to leave the following day, the essential visas still failed to appear. A persistent voice said, "Wait one week." They did. By midweek the visas had arrived at the French consular office in Seattle. God was in the details. Assured of their call, the Bergquists arrived in Guadeloupe on 20 December 1949.

The Bergquists' return to the Caribbean was more important than anyone could have imagined. The Hartts were weary, and Erma was nearly crippled and in pain with a severe back condition. Bergquists' spirit sank when the Hartts flew north for Erma's surgery. Elmer Thompson's prognosis did little to lift Roy's spirit when he wrote in May, "Unless the Lord does a miracle for Erma she will not be able to return to Guadeloupe."[677] The Bergquists, virtually alone (they had been joined at the end of December by Nettie Tiessen), now faced daunting responsibility without their veteran colleagues.

Erma Hartt faced a long recuperation from back surgery. It would prevent their return for a year. The news came by telegram, and Bergquist shared it with the congregation on a Sunday morning. The people were stunned. The David Hartts were greatly loved, and Bergquist felt ill-equipped to fill his shoes. "Sometimes I think they almost worship David," Roy said ruefully. However, God had prepared the Bergquists for this moment. The previous week the word had come through a devotional booklet: "Has God called you to take on extra responsibility? Shirk it not! Trust him and see what he can do through you."

Bergquist was certain that the people thought the church could not survive without Pastor David. Further reflection suggested that the loss might be for the best. Perhaps God had removed the Hartts for a short time so that Guadeloupe's young Christians might learn to lean upon God rather than upon any person.

That Sunday, Roy Bergquist took the offensive with the young congregation:

> "If anything can be accomplished this year, it will be up to you!" he challenged the subdued gathering.

> "You know I can hardly speak the French language. You are going to have to do the speaking and preaching out in the surrounding communities and here in the city. All who are willing to forget petty differ-

ences, willing to forgive one another for things said, and willing to share God's message of love with your relatives, neighbors, and with those you do not know, will you stand?"

Everyone rose. The Pointe-à-Pitre congregation made a commitment to trust God for the 300,000 people of Guadeloupe. The service ended and the people left—united in their love for God, for each other, and for the evangelization of Guadeloupe.[678] In the struggle for maturity, the work had turned a corner.

The Liotard Factor

The Liotards' enthusiasm for sharing their faith was infectious and during their years in Guadeloupe God used them effectively to share their new life in Christ. Nevertheless, Judge Liotard was to play a more critical role in the life of the evangelical church of Guadeloupe than anyone could have guessed. Roy Bergquist explained:

> Once, as he [Liotard] accompanied David Hartt on a visit to the mayor of Capesterre, he saw a book on a shelf in his office, and promptly begged to borrow it. The book outlined the legal procedures for organizing a church body under French law. We missionaries had no understanding of French law regarding church organization and wondered how we would ever go about it. This [book] was like a table let down from heaven, for it enabled us to organize our churches, declare our existence, and obtain legal recognition. Judge Liotard drew up these important papers.[679]

On 5 July 1951—four years after David Hartt's arrival—the church constitution was presented to thirty-two baptized believers who organized as The Evangelical Association of Guadeloupe (*L'Association Evangelique de la Guadeloupe*). The assembly elected four elders. The missionaries laid hands on them and commended them to God for service. Joy overflowed and God's providence in the conversion of Judge Liotard was on full display.

That November (1951) Hartt and Bergquist began a mini Bible school in the Pointe-à-Pitre church, continuing the course in February and April of the following year. New believers joyfully sacrificed time and resources as they launched into the construction of the first church building of the Evangelical Association of Guadeloupe. Though hampered by the usual Romanist efforts to prevent their securing of a building permit, Guadeloupe's first evangelical church was dedicated on Sunday, 18 May 1952.

WIM's Guadeloupe family now grew quickly, and the 1952 New Year's Eve watch-night service counted the David Hartts, the Bergquists, Albert Waechter, Nettie Tiessen, the Ben Heppners, Lila Inglis, and the Tom Addisons. Within two years the Harold Alexanders, the Wayne Potters, the Benjamin Walls, and the Lloyd Ogbornes had joined them.

With the deployment of these reinforcements, WIM moved into new centers—Basse-Terre (the capital), Capesterre, Sainte-Anne, and Moule. A five-acre plot of land was purchased near Bananier, beautifully located several hundred feet up the mountainside. Bergquists' house was moved from Basse-Terre to the new site, where it served as dormitory, dining hall, kitchen, and classroom for the Bible school started that fall. The 1955 Easter conference at Pointe-à-Pitre drew 245 attendees. Their missionary offering fueled the outreach by Bible school students and missionaries to the five satellite islands of Guadeloupe. The Hillside View Grade School opened at the Bananier center to accommodate the growing missionary family.

Five years earlier, David Hartt had rebuilt the radio frequency section of Radio Guadeloupe's one hundred-watt AM transmitter. The amateur band transmitter was the only station on the island and had been seized by the government at the outbreak of the war. In appreciation for Hartt's services, free time had been offered to WIM. When Judge Liotard was transferred in 1952 from Marie Galante to Basse-Terre, he took responsibility for one of the weekly Sunday morning broadcast, a ministry he would maintain for twenty years. Liotard's impeccable French coupled with his eminent political and social stature in the French judicial system gave the evangelical message prestige and respectability throughout the island.

Not all was sunlight. Both Church and Mission weathered satanic opposition, natural disasters, and tragic losses.[680] A fruitful ministry begun by a national in Pointe-à-Pitre faded after a few months for lack of leadership, a problem that seemed to dog the churches. In the early stages, missionaries tended to paternalism, performing functions that should have been conducted by nationals. The church was slow to support its own workers. Hindsight is perfect and such problems would yet be addressed. In spite of all, in just twelve years the Church in Guadeloupe had been firmly rooted. May Day 1959 was a historic triumph, when the first four graduated from Guadeloupe Bible School's four-year program, where Harold Alexander was principal.

David and Erma Hartt left Guadeloupe in 1954 to apply David's radio engineering skills to the development of Radio Lumière in Haiti. Margaret Bergquist's perforated eardrum—resulting from childhood scarlet fever—had again become intolerant of the tropical humidity. They left Guadeloupe in 1961. However, WIM was not without a leader. Walter and Adeline Wunsch, senior veterans of years in Haiti (1938), arrived on 9 December 1960. Walter took the helm. The Mission was in good hands.[681]

In 1987, no hall in Guadeloupe was large enough to accommodate the annual conference, attended by three to four thousand.[682] By 1995, WIM had planted twenty-nine congregations throughout the entire island's population centers. Walter Wunsch reported:

Most of our churches are full to the doors every Sunday morning. Hundreds have professed receiving Jesus as Lord. Our churches are remarkable for being filled with young people—and young men. This year we have 250 students enrolled in our extension seminary program. Of our ten teachers, all but one are Guadeloupians, and they teach in 13 different places so the classes are available to all the Christians. The new [hurricane-proofed] conference center, which seats 4000, is constructed with galvanized steel of French manufacture. The land was bought and dedicated 15 years previously and Guadeloupian Christians are paying for it.[683]

Fifty years after David Hartt's arrival the Evangelical Churches of Guadeloupe celebrated their golden jubilee (1998). World Team President Albert Ehmann, present for the event, reported: "Today thousands of Christians in 49 churches celebrate their freedom in Christ. The bond between Dave Hartt and a French judge was a moving thing to witness."

The judge was the same Etienne Liotard whom Hartt had led to Christ on the island of Marie Galante so long ago. Long since retired in France, Liotard had made a special trip to Guadeloupe to celebrate with his friend the wonderful works of God.[684]

David, Paul, and Erma Hartt, 1947.

51

Threading the Necklace

Let the whole church put world evangelization where it be-
longs. It is not a by-product, but the product.

—Paul Smith

With work firmly established in Cuba, Haiti, the Dominican Republic, and Guadeloupe, WIM turned an evangelistic eye to the remaining islands of the Lesser Antilles. Sending missionaries to the Bahamas had earlier been considered, but that island group was already well-evangelized, and failed to offer the pioneer conditions to which the West Indies Mission felt called. In any case, Cuban nationals would later enter the Bahamas. The chain of islands known as the Lesser Antilles looked like a necklace—like so many beads on a string—with Guadeloupe at the midpoint. Threading the rest of the necklace was the logical next step for the expanding mission.

St. Lucia

After Guadeloupe, St. Lucia was the next Windward Island pearl in WIM's expansion. Dominica and Martinique, while larger, had also been passed over since well-established evangelical ministries were already present. However, postage-stamp size (619 sq. km) St. Lucia had long been neglected by gospel messengers, though not by imperial powers. Ever since British Admiral Rodney captured Grenada, St. Vincent, and St. Lucia in 1762, the tiny island had been the pawn of bitter fighting between French and British troops. It changed hands seven times before winding up a British possession.[685] While that made English the official language, most of its 81,000 people spoke French or Patois (Creole) and ninety percent were Afro-Caribbean blacks. The towering Qualibou volcano (3,145') with its boiling sulfur springs had given birth to the island, making it a draw for tourists.

St. Lucia's idyllic tropical paradise masked a sinister underside. Nightfall distilled a peculiar terror upon the people of St. Lucia. That was when malignant

spirits—the *gahza*—sallied forth. Children raised on tales of dreadful en-
counters on dark and lonely roads at night did not easily shake off such fears
on becoming adults. The *gahza* haunted the darkness. Any enemy skilled in
witchcraft could call up the *gahza*—any enemy with a grudge. Taking the
form of a predatory beast, the *gahza* might enter one's yard to bleed the livestock. People told of waking at night to see a large fire in their yard, only to
find in the morning no sign of anything having been burned. Superstition
paralyzed St. Lucians.[686]

In October of 1949, Henry Werner arrived in St. Lucia, which he soon judged
to be the most neglected of the islands. Looking for a place to settle with his
wife and family, he selected a site in Souffriere. It was not to be. When the
owner learned of Werner's purpose, he reneged on the contract. Vieux Fort
was the island's southernmost town, and here Werner rented a large structure
from the American Air Base, known as Beane Field. The Werner family arrived in December, together with Max Inglis. Edna Anhorn had been in Guadeloupe visiting her sister, Erma Hart. She joined the new arrivals in St. Lucia
in January, and the foursome spent most of the year blitzing the island's
towns, preaching at street meetings and wherever the doors might open to
them. The team was cheered by the arrival of Sam Harms in the fall of 1950
and immediately Max and Sam—both bachelors—moved to the town of Dennery on the east coast. Here several young people opened their hearts to the
Lord, four of them forming two-thirds of the first class of the Windward Bible
School, which opened in 1953. Three more workers joined the ranks that fall
(1950)—Walter and Ann Grymaloski, who based in Soufriere, and Gertrude
Herbert, who joined Edna Anhorn in Micoud.

Everywhere meetings were packed. Whenever possible, halls were rented for
gospel services. In Dennery, you could get the dance hall free of charge. In
Micoud, you could rent one for fifty cents.

Plainview Christian School

In Vieux Fort, on St. Lucia's south coast, the Werners conducted cottage Bi-
ble studies three times weekly.[687] When a Baptist group entered St. Lucia,
WIM agreed to their offer to work the northern part of the island. In this way,
WIM's ministry was concentrated largely in the south, and the Vieux Fort
Evangelical Church became the first established body of the *Evangelical
Church of the West Indies* (ECWI) and the "mother" church of several others.[688] Later they moved to the island of St. Vincent. In Vieux Fort—and
elsewhere on the island—children of evangelicals were openly persecuted in
the parochial schools. This moved Art Harms and the Walter Grymaloskis to
open a Christian day school. In time, the facility grew in popularity through
the influence of many missionaries and St. Lucian Christians. In 1999, *Plainview Christian School* had an enrollment of 746.

In one year, 130 Bibles, 285 Testaments and 881 Gospels were sold on the island and 15,950 tracts were distributed. However, old ways were hard to change and missionaries confronted sinister exhibitions of satanic darkness. In addition, Roman Catholic opposition took shape in slanderous rumor and boycott of meetings. Other meetings were disrupted, and Bibles and New Testaments were confiscated.[689] Gospel work in St. Lucia was not easy and every step was contested.

By 1952, the team had established a church and convened the first Bible convention. These advances were encouraging, but the missionaries were still appalled by the vice that chained so many of those they tried to reach. One of them had seen it all:

The *Old Folks' Home* in Dennery was nothing more than a tiny hut, eight feet square. We passed it one day and saw an old woman lying on the floor. Determined to visit her, we took penny-bread in hand and went to see her. The scene was devastating. She was seventy-five years old and dying.

The hut was void of furniture. She lay on dirty rags, surrounded by filth. I gagged. Her body was emaciated, her fingernails claw-like. I prayed fervently that this wretched soul would not see my struggle.

No one seemed to care for this human being. Sucking her cigarette, she lay there day after day. I went often to visit her and told her of the Savior, hoping to lead her to pray the sinner's prayer. She did repeat it, but her mind seemed too dull to understand the words.

She realized that she was near death, and her fears intensified. Religion and witchcraft offered no consolation. The roof of her hovel leaked severely, deepening the gloom and accelerating her inevitable demise.

One day someone called. Marguie had died. I walked to the hut, where two candles burned to light her spirit's passage to heaven. The stench overwhelmed me, so I went outside, sat down on some rocks, and spoke to the people who had gathered. I told them of the Savior who lights the valley of death for all who trust in Him!

That night there was the customary wake. Friends and relatives gathered to sing hymns all night. The hymns were nothing more than a talisman to keep evil spirits at bay, for the people did not believe the words. Liquor flowed freely. All had a great time, without cost to the celebrants. To such we had come with the light of the gospel.

A Demographic Mandate

WIM had been in St. Lucia twenty years before tackling the capital city of Castries, at the northern end of the island. Deferring to a longstanding agreement with the Baptists, WIM had largely confined its efforts to the Vieux Fort region—in the south. By 1970, changing demographics demanded a shift in strategy. Church members from the rural south in pursuit of economic opportunity had begun to migrate to the capital—a syndrome common in developing countries.

While the loss of these elements weakened the southern churches, it also presented a fresh opportunity. Christian émigrés from the rural south, dislodged from the familiar, were often out of their cultural comfort zone in the big city. They were a nucleus in need of a shepherd, and offered an immediate bridge into the Castries metro area.

Grasping the opportunity, Dean Franklin and Albert Ehmann arrived in Castries early in 1970. They saw that a strong city church in the capital would meet the needs of their migrant charges, while providing an anchor church for the wider organization of ECWI. The West Indies Mission formed a partnership with ECWI to plant a church in Castries.

Fresh from his apprenticeship with Elmer Thompson in Jamaica, Albert Ehmann addressed this task. His two-month acculturation tour in St. Lucia included such improbables as helping organize and operate a small supermarket, loading trucks, sweeping floors, and doing security. His bachelor meals—hosted by a national—consisted of West Indies cuisine, not particularly enjoyable to the Canadian, especially the twice-weekly course of pumpkin soup.

Notwithstanding, Ehmann—"Vibrant, optimistic, dedicated"—threw himself into a schedule of Bible study groups and open-air meetings, ably assisted by national Christians. In 1971, Daniel Ehmann—Albert's brother—joined the team. Soon the Jeremie Street meeting-place overflowed, and conversions followed. So, in 1973, Albert Ehmann headed north to Canada to raise monies for a church building.[690] His success translated not only into a new church facility in Castries, but into a second, daughter church in Guesneau-Tiroche in 1975.[691] In June of that year, Ehmann was posted to WIM's new work in Sicily.

Fifty years after Henry Werner landed in St. Lucia, World Team could count fourteen established churches, ranging in size from 40 to three hundred members, with a total membership of 1,200. Even greater than the numbers was their strength. They had walked through the fires of persecution and had come out strong.

St. Vincent

Looking south on a clear day from St. Lucia you can see the island of St. Vincent—just twenty-one miles away. Often called the "Gem of the Lesser Antilles," the island was once home to ferocious Carib Indians. As early as 1675, Native Africans, shipwrecked near the island, swam to shore and were kindly received. A struggle for possession between France and England left the British in control in 1763.

When WIM missionaries from St. Lucia arrived here in 1951, St. Vincent's population was not large—less than 100,000—but prospects here were brighter than in St. Lucia. Unlike her near neighbor, St. Vincent had earlier entertained Protestants and was more open to the gospel. Even more significant was the fact that Roman Catholicism had never played a dominant role. The people were generally regarded as more dependable than in St. Lucia—and more receptive.

Sam Harms might not have thought so. Preaching on the subject of sin in Troumaca, he was mobbed one Sunday afternoon. "Things were tense for awhile," he said, but he was left unscathed.

The Windward Islands Bible Institute

Just outside of Kingstown, a forty-acre site for the proposed *Windward Bible School* came to WIM's attention in 1953. Only a few young people were ready for Bible school that fall—perhaps five or six—but it was a start. Gospel witness quickly spread from town to town, largely through dedicated Christian laymen and the influence of the young Bible institute.

The St. Vincent WIM staff grew quickly, and within three years of entry, twenty-three workers were on the island. Led by Field Superintendent, Henry Werner, were the Walter Grymaloskis, the Sam Harmses, Gertrude Huebert, the Leonard Messengers, the Harvey Mohrs, the Otto Derksens, the Edwin Sharpes, Muriel Hayne, Doris Bauman, the Arthur Harmses, and the Donald Shonkwilers. Ill health obliged the withdrawal of the Leon Tiedes in 1952. Max Inglis, who had come from St. Lucia, replaced them. He was in St. Vincent long enough to meet WIM missionary Ena Thayer, whom he married in 1954 in Homer City. For Inglis, Homer City was a bend in the road, and marked the beginning of a long career as publications editor for Worldteam.

By 1964 Dean Franklin could report, "The enrollment at Windward Islands Bible Institute is up this year with a total of 20 students—ten new ones and ten returning." However, Franklin tempered this encouragement with the fact that "False cults and religions are gaining ground in St. Vincent."[692] Early in 1969, four miles from Kingstown, the struggling Belair church recorded "an overwhelming breakthrough" with the conversion of twenty-five adults. This spiritual renewal was repeated throughout St. Vincent. The phenomenon was clearly traceable to a special seminar for church leaders conducted in the Southeastern Caribbean two years earlier.

Desperate over the spiritual stagnation that had immobilized many Christians, church leaders conducted an intensive, yearlong study. Mass meetings for evangelism had become commonplace. Islanders joked about American evangelists who "felt called" to the Caribbean in January and February. The study sought to determine the cause of the malaise. Later, in cooperation with *Men in Action*,[693] representatives from seven evangelical denominations structured a one-year program of intensive evangelism.

In February, the Men In Action team met with thirty-one pastors from six denominations to outline principles and a program for the crusade. A small core of laymen was trained—two or three from each congregation. The following month, 180 prayer cells sprang up as people prayed for neighbors, relatives, and businessmen. Mass evangelistic crusades followed, but this time the campaigns were coupled with consistent personal witness and follow-up. By 1970, twenty renewed and growing congregations dotted the island, all members of ECWI. By 1996, World Team-related churches were led by ten national pastors with an aggregate membership of 650. In 1998, Cliff and Reathel Gross—the only remaining World Team personnel—were conducting a radio ministry to the people of St. Vincent.

Nine miles off St. Vincent's lee shore is Bequia, a small speck of land bypassed by all mission agencies—including WIM—until the 1950s, when Otto Derksen began a ministry among its population of 5,000. From 1951 to 1965, the Derksens divided their church planting/training ministry among the three islands—St. Lucia, St. Vincent, and Bequia. When they left, local churches were flourishing under national leadership.

Grenada

Another island passed over by WIM in earlier surveys was Grenada, a tiny (120 square miles) emerald splash of mountainous beauty set in the turquoise of the Caribbean. As the southernmost pearl in the Windward chain, the "Isle of Spice" lies between St. Vincent and Trinidad. In 1957, with work well-established in the major islands, the Mission took another look and appointed Art and Margaret Harms.

When the Canadian couple arrived in the fall of that year, little evangelical work existed outside the capital city of St. George's. Grenville was the island's second largest town, and as it had no church, they selected it as WIM's beachhead. The pair created a stir as they trundled into town each evening, their motor scooter groaning under the weight of an accordion, gas lantern, public address system, and songbooks. Open-air meetings drew consistent crowds in spite of efforts by the priests to foment public boycott.

Not even the pain of extra penance or excommunication failed to dampen public enthusiasm. People were converted and, by 1961, WIM had constructed two chapels in the towns of Grenville and Byelands. Basil and Ada Bickel, Regina Bears and Susan Giesbrecht joined the Harmses.[694] By 1998, Grenada counted seven mission-birthed churches—all under national leadership.

The Evangelical Churches of the West Indies [ECWI]—with the help of World Team—was grooming one hundred students through the lay training program known as the *Evangelical Institute of Christian Education* programs in Grenada, St. Lucia, St. Vincent, Trinidad, and Tobago. By 1987, all Worldteam missionaries had left Grenada. The association also launched a cross-cultural mission to the island of Carriacao, where they planted a church. In cooperation with ECWI, World Team united the English-speaking Caribbean island churches under the name of the Southeast Caribbean (SEC).

French Guiana

In 1986, ECWI (Evangelical Churches of the West Indies) began a missionary effort in this former French penal colony, sending Nazaire and Mary Ann George to plant churches in this needy country. Jay and Beth Weaver joined them in 1988.

Trinidad

Christopher Columbus was on his third voyage when he first sighted Trinidad on 15 August 1498, although the island was not settled until the 1570s. It then became a Spanish outpost and a frequent target for British, French and Dutch buccaneers. It was finally ceded to Britain in 1797, becoming (in 1888) part of the two-island crown colony of Trinidad and Tobago. This assured two things: fine schools and a flood of immigration from another part of the world's greatest empire—India.

Lloyd Cross arrived in Trinidad in 1951.[695] Housing was hard to find and accommodations were austere. Cross was in Trinidad to survey the island for WIM. Concluding that Trinidad would be "a very wise move," he reported:

> Everyone has a religion to which he adheres. Some have two. You may be a member of a church body or denomination, while in secret—or even openly—practicing Hinduism, or following some other cult. I feel that I now know how to meet, interest, and deal with such people and I realize it is not going to be easy.

> Trinidad's population of 600,000 falls into three equal [in size] religious groups: Roman Catholic, Hindu, and another made up of 30 different sects. Anyone who is not Hindu or Moslem is considered "Christian." Anyone born again is referred to as "a saved soul."

Of all the islands in the Windward chain, Trinidad is the largest. East Indians make up forty percent of the 1.5 million population, and everywhere the island reflects Hindu culture and religion. Fifty percent of Trinidad's people are of Afro-Caribbean origin. Ancestors of the East Indian residents came to the island as contract laborers from India and the East Indies. Trinidadians had forty religions and cults from which to choose and theological confusion was no surprise.

Remarkably, Trinidad was no primitive outpost. The tiny country abounded with schools and medical facilities. The people lived well and lacked little. This upscale lifestyle bred an attitude of self-sufficiency. Trinidadians had no need for missionaries bringing schools and clinics. Nor had they any need for the gospel. The West Indies Mission did not agree.

Dooknie—Brand from the Burning

WIM's early years in Trinidad were unsettled because of frequent changes in field leadership during 1955 and 1956. Lloyd Cross had begun the work in 1953 but by 1956, three additional field leaders had served the area. Despite turnover, the work grew. Starting along the rural northern coast WIM found little response. East of Port of Spain, however, congregations were established in the more progressive towns of San Juan, Arouca, Arima, Valencia, and Sangre Grande. WIM missionaries moved into Tobago, then branched out to the south where a church was established in the small town of Siparia. Next was the capital—Port-of-Spain.

Ramdehal "Sonny" Dooknie had been born of Hindu parents in Trinidad. At nineteen and near death from tuberculosis he was converted in 1953 through the witness of five TB patients in the hospital, where he spent more than two years. After six years as a missionary in India, where he met his wife, Nancy, he returned to Trinidad.

Dooknie knew that God performed miracles and he wanted to see one in the town of Sangre Grande. He asked God for a plot of land, a new church build-ing, and "other sheep" who would gather to praise God. After several weeks of praying for the land, Sonny called the believers together and announced, "We shall fast and pray until the land is provided." He later added, "the Holy Spirit seemed to be saying to me, 'Why don't you start praising God for souls, for the land, for the building, and for everything you need?'"

A few days after Dooknie's praise meeting, a couple from the group ap-proached their visionary leader and exclaimed jubilantly, "Brother Dooknie, we think we have found the land. The owner is asking only $7,000!" They hurried to see the proprietor. They had no money, but boldly assured him, "Sir, your land is sold." Sonny Dooknie got his miracle. In a few months, the cost was fully subscribed and Sangre Grande chapel became a monument to vibrant faith.

On a trip to India, the Dooknies enlisted two missionary couples from the sub-continent and God began using them among the Hindu people in Trinidad. Former Hindus were now effectively reaching Hindus. It was already axio-matic in the West Indies Mission that nationals did a better job of reaching their own than expatriate missionaries ever could. This had been the secret of phenomenal church growth in Cuba and later in Haiti. Now in Trinidad's ethnic casserole, Indian Christians were proving the principle among the Hindu population—*nationals do mission best!*

For Men Only

That is what Edith Johnson thought in 1962 when asked to take over a start-up work in Arima, Trinidad. "This is a man's job," she argued with WIM leadership. "I can't stay here, you've got to move me out." Johnson's comfort zone was working with women and children—not planting churches. Gradually, her protests yielded to the mounting evidence of her gifting as a mobilizer—youth camps, women's Bible studies, *and churches*. Her talent for "getting things going" was later complemented with the arrival of Donna Williamson, whose music and skills in youth work paired with Johnson's gifts in Bible teaching. Three and a half years later, the duo left a growing, maturing church in San Juan, a large town on the outskirts of Trinidad's capital, Port of Spain. Other church plants would follow.

Doors opened to them as they displayed a willingness to do what genteel white ladies in Trinidad did not do—clean house. One dwelling they rented had been a machine shop, and the floor was black with oil and grease. They set about to make it habitable. It took them a month. The community noticed. Soon their new meeting place was overflowing.

Asked to start a religious education class in a private school of three hundred students—religious education was a government requirement—the school facility was soon offered to them for church services, and another church was born. Thirty-five years after Johnson's reluctant takeover of the work in Arima, she had been a primary instrument in starting and nurturing five Trinidad churches and in mobilizing ECWI churches to pray for missions.

ECWI Reaches Out

Approaching the new millennium, the Evangelical Church of the West Indies (ECWI) experienced an awakening to global missions. On 26 July 1998, they established their own missionary sending agency, *Advance International,* with Nazaire George as director. Leaders agreed to a five-year strategic and tactical plan, which included the training and commission of two national church planting teams, with five couples in each. Guess who the men of the new mission agency asked to join their ranks? Edith Johnson.

52

Into Mato Grosso

That land is henceforth my country that most needs the gospel.

—Count Nicholas Zinzendorf

Lowell Bailey

When Pope Alexander VI tried to arbitrate territorial rivalry between Spain and Portugal, he selected a meridian just west of the Azores. All discoveries to the west of the line would belong to Spain, while everything to the east would go to Portugal. A further agreement in 1494 moved the line 1,100 miles farther west—just in time for Pedro Álvares Cabral's discovery of Brazil, part of which now fell within the Portuguese zone. Later, raiding groups from São Paulo would push the border far to the west. In this way, a country half the size of the entire South American continent inherited the Portuguese language.

Angola-born Lowell Bailey was fluent in Portuguese, a skill he studied to maintain throughout his high school years in South Carolina. That is where he met Katharine (Kathy) Powlison, another "MK" from Bolivia. Both graduated from Columbia Bible College (CBC). In 1953 Lowell had conducted a survey of Brazil as part of a CBC course requirement.

That year he joined the CBC staff and married Kathy, confident that God was leading them to Brazil. Bailey's extensive research on Brazilian Bible schools—they were few at that time—combined with his intensive effort to upgrade his Angola Portuguese to its Brazilian form. This led to his teaching the language during the 1954–55 academic year at Columbia. Kathy was one of his students. His missionary father had spoken highly of the West Indies Mission, and subsequent contacts with Elmer Thompson and Louis Markwood convinced the aspiring couple to apply to WIM. Letdown was keen when the Mission replied flatly, "WIM has no work in Brazil." When a survey of other mission Boards proved unproductive, the Baileys reapplied to WIM. This time they were encouraged to prepare a case for WIM's entry to Brazil.

The WIM Board considered Bailey's brief at a meeting in Trinidad. Shortly thereafter, Lloyd Cross appeared at CBC with the news that the Mission had approved Bailey's proposal to launch pioneer work in Brazil. However, in a country larger than the United States, just where to start posed a problem.

Through a CBC contact with Neil Hawkins, director of the Unevangelized Fields Mission Indian ministries, Bailey was invited to the Indian convention at Dourados, Mato Grosso. The *Caiuá Evangelical Mission*—the only all-Brazilian mission to Indians—was working alongside the largest Indian reservation in Brazil and had invited guests from three tribes. With a financial boost from two South Carolina churches, Bailey flew to Belém—at the mouth of the Amazon— and from there accompanied Hawkins to Dourados, a frontier town close to Brazil's border with Paraguay.

Bailey saw an encouraging response to his ministry at the convention and the Dourados contact resulted in an invitation from the Caiuá Mission to offer Bible training to Indian Church leaders. The Mission also invited WIM to develop a curriculum for a small group of preachers who wished to take the gospel to the Guarani, Terena, and Caiuá tribes. With these arrangements in place, the Baileys were sent to Jamaica for the 1955–56 school year, where Lowell taught in the Jamaica Bible School. They arrived in Brazil in March 1957. Within two weeks they were writing materials and teaching classes in Dourados.

Rio Grande do Sul

Within a year Sam and Edna Harms (Edna was Elmer Thompson's daughter) transferred from the Windward Islands to join the Baileys in Mato Grosso. At that time, Dourados was still a small city, so WIM commissioned the Baileys to survey other Brazilian states for a permanent location. They selected Rio Grande do Sul, Brazil's southernmost state, and in 1960, the Harms and Bailey families made the 1,000-mile move. Rio Grande enjoyed the distinction of having large concentrations of German and Italian population. It also proved to be one of the most gospel-resistant areas in all Brazil, on a par with secular Uruguay. The Baileys settled in Porto Alegre, the state capital, while the Harmses located in Novo Hamburgo, an industrial city an hour's drive north.

Sam Harms quickly displayed gifting as a church planter, and he and Bailey soon had a congregation going in Novo Hamburgo—Bailey making weekend bus shuttles to team with Harms. However, the church in Novo Hamburgo never reached critical mass, its members later transferring to another work. Jerry and Marge Hildebrand, Canadian Mennonites, were next to join the group, locating in São Leopoldo, not far from Novo Hamburgo. Soon a small church was up and running. Howard and Virginia Barrigar were next in the pipeline, taking up their post on the other side of São Leopoldo. They would later leave WIM to work independently, taking with them the two churches they had started. Harms' next target was Sapiranga, a city northeast of Novo Hamburgo. Meanwhile, Lowell Bailey was kept busy in the area of his primary gifting.

Bailey's command of Portuguese made him a natural for radio work. In 1962, a group of Christian businessmen pooled resources to establish a Christian radio station. Soon, forty programs were being recorded weekly in WIM's studio. Bailey maintained the radio ministry—five broadcasts a week, aimed at three different target audiences. The programs offered Source of Light Bible courses, and the resulting correspondence school achieved an enrollment of several thousand. When Everett and Norma Jean Lamberson transferred from Haiti, Everett became director of WIM's radio outreach in Brazil. His skills as a radio technician brought professional excellence to the broadcasts.[696] Then Alden and Virginia Barrows arrived, going to work in the city of Montenegro. However, amid the flurry of newly arriving missionaries, something insidious was happening.

A Lesson Learned

The radio ministry tended to attract middle to upper class listeners, whereas the work of church planting was happening among the urban working classes. WIM studios were inundated with responses to the correspondence courses—many coming from hundreds of miles away. Driven by the urgency to reach all Brazil, the Mission placed new recruits in different cities often separated by great distances. Lack of telephone contact—a telephone line cost $2,500 at that time—combined with distance to hamper communication among the missionaries. It was a shotgun approach to reaching an entire state of 100,000 square miles, and it backfired. This failure to concentrate resources in a few critical areas produced tensions. Widely scattered, missionaries felt isolated and lost the sense of cohesion and teamwork. Church planting goals suffered and some church plants failed to prosper. Unintentionally, WIM personnel in Brazil had begun to operate in a "Lone Ranger" mode.

By contrast, when Jerry and Marge Hildebrand teamed up with Sam and Edna Harms they enjoyed one of the most successful church planting efforts in the early days of the work. Working as a team, in 1957, the Baileys and Lambersons planted the Bible Alliance Church in Porto Alegre. The success enjoyed through close proximity to each other demonstrated the importance of limiting the number of targets. A lesson had been learned—concentrate on those target areas where teamwork is possible. Perhaps unaware, they had put into practice one of the ten axiomatic principles of military warfare—the calculated massing of overwhelming force. WIM would carry this approach to its work in Europe.

WIM's early work in Brazil began at a time when the Mission leadership believed that the Cuba model was transferable to any field. In the Dominican Republic and now in Brazil, they discovered otherwise. In both Cuba and Haiti, Christian applicants to the Bible institutes—primed by national evangelists—arrived in a steady stream, then went out as pastors to their communities. Churches multiplied. In the Dominican Republic, and now in Brazil's secular Rio Grande do Sul, the Mission did not have Christians with whom to work. Nor were there national pastors to bring young people in for training. Expatriate missionaries had to begin from the ground up, winning families to Christ, and starting churches. Had WIM's meager resources been concentrated on a couple of teams, they might have seen a telling impact on major urban centers. Instead, limited funds were thinly allocated among isolated workers. This restricted procurement of preaching locations to affordable but less strategic locales.

Bailey later reflected:

> If we had been able to begin our ministry in the way the Caxias do Sul work was begun, our ministry might have borne much more fruit. Had we worked as teams in that period when we had so many missionaries in Brazil, and had we avoided isolation from one another, we might have made a greater impact. [697]

By 1972, WIM's church planting efforts had seen few results. Sam and Edna Harms had poured ten disheartening years into Novo Hamburgo, Campo Bom, and Sapiranga, and had come to believe that "we did not know how to plant a church." Relocating to Caxias, they decided to try again for two more years. If God did not work there, they would quit. [698]

Caxias do Sul

Caxias do Sul was an intensely Roman Catholic city of Italian immigrants located in the mountains a couple of hours' drive north of Porto Alegre. Harms was attracted to the city, since a teacher there was using WIM's Bible correspondence material with his students. WIM's ideal model for successful church planting was soon to be realized.

The Harmses began with a nonreligious approach, offering courses on how to have a happy home and later setting up a coffeehouse that attracted many young people. Edna recalled:

> We hardly knew what to pray for or where to begin, when *The Taste of New Wine* by Keith Miller fell into our hands. It marked us deeply. Caixas was a city very resistant to the gospel and Miller's idea of friendship evangelism seemed the only way to go. We dropped our ti-

tles of "missionary" and "pastor" and then tackled some of the approaches we felt were closing rather than opening doors . . . We decided to drop common church terminology that would not be understood by non-Christians or that had negative connotations among these people—terms such as *believer*. We also decided we were not going to go house-to-house with a Bible under our arms. Our children visited in our neighborhood and invited young people for a fun night at our home. We sang folk songs, ate, and showed slides. A couple of weeks later we set up a game room in the basement and soon had six young people from several parts of the city.

Interest grew. They offered courses on Bill Gothard material—*Six Areas of Youth Conflict*. Edna taught a course on *Fascinating Womanhood*. Conversions followed and hope revived. As new believers were discipled, Christian homes were established. A large, solid church developed, which in turn planted daughter churches in other cities, both in the original Italian-immigrant area and as far away as Rio de Janeiro. In 1978—WIM's fiftieth anniversary—a large grant made possible acquisition of a lot and construction of a four-story building which became an all-purpose church center.[699] By the mid-80s, the newly completed church in Caxias do Sul had become an active training center for outreach. Brazilian Florentino Romais oversaw construction of a church in the city of Sapiranga, while the congregation in Taquari, led by Paulo Rech, successor of Ken Richard, began reaching out to the twin towns of Lajeado and Estrela. Nationals were now working side by side with the missionaries, reaching their own country.

In 1970, Bailey had established the Theological Education by Extension (TEE) program in Greater Porto Alegre, which he led until 1978, assisted by several Brazilian pastors. *Bible Alliance* and other evangelical groups were involved. This led to the formation of AETTE, an association of all Theological Education by Extension programs in Brazil. Bailey served as president, turning AETTE over to national leadership in 1978. The name has since been changed to AETAL, the Bible institute and seminary accrediting association for all of Latin America.

In 1978, the Baileys left Brazil to serve for fourteen years in the Coral Gables offices of Worldteam. They returned to Brazil in 1992, joining Jeff and Jannette Smith, Bryan and Terry Harms, Mickey and Cherie Counter, Jim and Beth Himsworth, and Mark and Stephanie Watkins. In 1999, World Team in Brazil continued its focus on leadership training and the planting of self-reproducing cell churches, while Brazilian workers in twelve cities (ten in Rio Grande do Sul, one each in São Paulo and Rio de Janeiro) spread the gospel through cell multiplication.

53

Suriname

Lord help us to rise above our sense of failure and realize that your purposes are not limited by our apparent failures or success.

—Gene Friesen

Perched on the north-central coast of South America, Suriname had been a Dutch colony since the seventeenth century. It left behind its old name of Dutch Guiana when it became an autonomous territory of the Netherlands in 1954. When the original inhabitants—six Amerindian tribes—failed to satisfy the demand for plantation workers, Dutch colonists imported their own, a potpourri of ethnic diversity—Bihari Indians, Javanese, Chinese, Laotians, and Negroes. Intermarriage produced yet another cultural subset—the Creoles, now the largest and most influential group. Suriname's multiracial influx brought a casserole of religions to a population of less than half a million— Animism, Hinduism, Confucianism, Mohammedanism, and Roman Catholicism—plus the legacy of nominal Christianity left by the early Dutch settlers.

WIM Enters Suriname

A strange quirk brought the West Indies Mission to this swatch of South American jungle. The Ludwig Van Kantens, a Suriname-born Negro couple, embraced the gospel (the wife, Ilse, in Aruba; the husband, Ludwig, in Holland). They married in Holland and later returned to Suriname, praying that God would send someone to their homeland with the Good News.[700] That prayer was answered when a Surinamese girl found the Lord. Philo Brandon was of mixed racial extract and of Roman Catholic background. While in Aruba in search of employment, she met some TEAM[701] missionaries who encouraged her to enroll at Prairie Bible Institute in Canada. When in 1954 Elmer Thompson came to PBI on one of his many visits, Philo approached him, shared her vision for her homeland, and urged him to consider launching a WIM ministry in Suriname.[702] Impressed with Philo and the need she had described, Elmer Thompson gave the idea some thought. Moreover, he knew just the man to send.

David and Letitia Neff had joined the West Indies Mission in the fall of 1951. After working in Haiti for nearly two years, they were commissioned to conduct a survey for WIM in Brazil, but Neff's exploratory correspondence was never answered. Meanwhile, Thompson returned from PBI in the spring of 1954. With Brazil now uncertain, he turned to Neff to explore possible open doors in Suriname. David arrived on 7 April 1954—"the end of a long journey for me, but the beginning of a new chapter of the West Indies Mission." Just how exciting the chapter would be, he could not have guessed. He had left Letitia in Trinidad with WIM missionaries until lodgings could be secured. Although Philo Brandon was a Surinamese national and had urged WIM to enter the country, she was unable to supply contact information, and Neff arrived in Paramaribo without introduction.

Diagnosis

Neff's report to the WIM Board was realistic. Paramaribo would be no easy mark. The city abounded in churches—Moravian, Dutch Reformed, Evangelical Lutherans, African Methodist, Baptist, Pilgrim Holiness, Jehovah's Witnesses, Swedenborgians, Adventists and Roman Catholic—all addressing a population of 100,000. The Moravians had been active in Suriname since 1735, becoming the largest and most influential religious group in the country. They had eight churches in the capital, one with 6,000 members. Nevertheless, the ardor of first love had cooled, the fire had all but gone out, and in 1954 there were few groups in Paramaribo with an aggressive, vibrant gospel message.

Neff assessed the spiritual climate, noting that in spite of the presence of large Protestant congregations, "their faith—if it can be called such—does not seem to have effected any vital change in their lives." Preachers appeared more concerned with pleasing people than with leading them to repentance. Worship services were perfunctory and wooden, with most churches empty on Sundays. (He had attended the 6,000-member Moravian church to find a scant one hundred present at morning and evening Sunday services) Sectarian loyalty was fierce, even among those who rarely attended. "Christianized, but not converted," Neff concluded. The clergy seemed more like mercenaries than men called of God. With some pastors receiving large stipends from the government, the spiritual apathy of the people was understandable.

A Strategy

If Neff's analysis of spiritual life in Paramaribo was bleak, it was not pessimistic. Viewing the multi-lingual cosmopolitan mix of the city, he was confident that the West Indies Mission could meet the need. Nevertheless, the answer would be found in placing effective national evangelists in each of the target subcultures. "The situation is a challenge, and only our God can intervene and change it." He urged the WIM Board:

> Send young people from their own races that are on fire for Christ! The Lord must give us key men from each racial group who can work together as a team to get the message of salvation to their own people in an effective way.

Spelling out possible approaches, Neff continued:

> Street meetings, house to house visitation, child evangelism work, a tract ministry, correspondence courses, mass evangelism and radio." These would be effective. In addition, of course, the proven sine qua non of WIM's ministry in the Caribbean to that point: a Bible school!

Paramaribo boasted other advantages: Compulsory education for all children ages seven to thirteen, coupled with a fine school system, would accelerate the evangelistic process. Missionaries would be free from teaching literacy, as had been necessary in Haiti. Neff urged one final point: *"Center the work in Paramaribo."*

Impressed with Neff's assessment, the WIM Board endorsed the move to Suriname, assured that this was the finger of God. The Neffs would spearhead the new work. However, the hurdles had just begun. Neff would make forty appearances in Suriname's government offices before permission would be granted for the West Indies Mission to enter the country.

Entry

David Neff arrived in Paramaribo in April 1954, Letitia following twenty weeks later. They faced a nominally Protestant population largely indifferent to the gospel message. A neighbor expressed the prevailing apathy: "You can't expect to change all of Paramaribo. That may be all right for America, but we do it differently here. People will come once or twice to hear you; then you will not see them anymore."

With this warm welcome, the couple set out to disprove the discouraging forecast. As the primary population center of the country, Paramaribo was strategic. The capital's multiethnic mix was a concentration of the best-educated elements from each racial group, many of them young people with the country's future in their hands. Youth work became a major thrust in this early ministry. In spite of the forecasts, harvest came. Youth clubs were established throughout the city, and an evening Bible school became an avenue for evangelism with evangelistic junkets into rural areas.

By 1959 Suriname's WIM staff totaled seven—two American couples, a German couple (Hansjurgen and Gertrud Sturz), and Philomena Brandon. The Walter Jacksons arrived in Paramaribo on 18 March 1957.

Now an even greater test awaited the WIM vanguard. In December 1962, illness forced Letitia home. It would claim her life less than three months later. They had just a little more than eight years together in Suriname.[703]

Why had Philomena Brandon urged Elmer Thompson to come to Suriname? Why had the West Indies Mission entered? Why had the David Neffs negotiated permission for WIM's entry at such great cost, only to face a largely unresponsive metropolis? God was about to do something in Suriname for which the preparatory work in the nation's capital would be a launch pad. It was bigger than even David Neff could have imagined.

Wayana chief, with Scriptures,
Suriname.

54

Operation Grasshopper

The gospel message had been built into Wayana and Trio cul-
ture. Jesus Christ is the One who lifts us up! An infant was not
regarded as a member of the tribe until lifted up. Then it would
be loved and cared for. It was a message the Indians clearly
understood and it became the first key to the effective sharing
of salvation's story.

—Missionary to Suriname

In 1950, while working with the Unevangelized Fields Mission among the Wai-Wai Indians of British Guiana, Claude and Barbara Leavitt began to pray for the neighboring Trios. However, the border of Suriname lay between them and that unreached tribe, and no evangelical group had yet been given permission to reach the Amerindians of Suriname.[704]

Nine years after Leavitt's prayer for the Trios, Walter Jackson sat on the end of a pier, lazily watching the eddies of the *Marrowijne*—the river that marks the frontier between Suriname and French Guiana. So far, his fishing equipment was worth more than anything he had caught, but this was how Walt relaxed from a busy missionary schedule in Paramaribo. Suddenly, the muffled drone of an outboard motor invaded his reverie. Coming from upriver, the sound grew louder until he could see the long dugout canoe, filled with Indians—Wayanas, as he would soon learn.

Jackson was in the frontier town of Albina. Apart from some coastal Arawaks in the area, he knew little of the tribal dwellers in Suriname's remote interior. He approached the group, and attempting to show himself friendly, inquired as to their identity. They had come into town for supplies, having traveled two hundred miles from their forest home upriver. In that instant, God spoke to Walt Jackson. It was one of those oracle moments, indefensible as courtroom evidence, but with a clarity beyond question: Take the gospel to this people!

Walt shared his mandate with Marj who, as always, encouraged him. Still, both were perplexed as to how this thing could be. The West Indies Mission in 1959 was still a Bible Institute Mission. Pioneering efforts among frontier jungle tribes had never been on WIM's agenda and was not likely to be. The Mission had no experience with noncognate language groups, nor with the complex logistics of accessing primitive people. Three years earlier, Nate Saint's innovative use of small aircraft to reach the remote Auca people of Ecuador was a pioneering leap and mission aviation was still in its infancy.

In 1956, the Jacksons had been studying Spanish in the Dominican Republic when, unexpectedly, a visa for Suriname became available. They were abruptly transferred to Suriname to strengthen the hands of the David Neffs. Walt began digging into the Dutch language. Finding it easier than Spanish, he was soon ministering in a church in the capital city. The Wayana encounter was about to interrupt that ministry and nudge the West Indies Mission out of a comfort zone.

Price and Friesen

God had simultaneously, placed the burden of the Wayanas and Trios on the hearts of Bob Price and Eugene Friessen, co-founders of the *Door To Life Ministries* (DTL)[705] of Philadelphia. In June 1959, the two winged their way in a single-engine Piper Super Cub from Philadelphia to Suriname. Winning favor with the Suriname officials, they penetrated the uncharted interior in a government-approved survey. The door had been opened.

Price returned to the US to recruit workers for the Trios and Wayanas. He found Ted Lepper, pilot and aircraft mechanic, and his medical doctor wife, Nancy. In the process of applying to the Mission Aviation Fellowship, they eagerly rose to the challenge, helping to pioneer the Indian work in Suriname with DTL before proceeding to their permanent MAF assignment.

Jackson's hunch was prophetic. Thompson and the WIM leadership wanted no part of pioneering the Wayana Indians. "We have no experience in this kind of ministry," Thompson protested. Nevertheless, Jackson could not stifle the insistent voice within, even if it meant finding a vehicle other than WIM. He eventually persuaded Thompson to come to Suriname to have a look.

In 1959, there was no Mission Aviation Fellowship in Suriname,[706] but the Suriname government was eager to open its undeveloped interior. When the government saw what foolhardy American missionaries could do with a tiny Piper Cub, they went to Florida and bought four of them. When DTL crashed their Piper on the beach near a Wayana village, the government asked DTL pilot, Eugene Friessen, to fly for them. Many jungle airstrips would be necessary to develop the country, so the project was dubbed, *Operation Grasshopper*.[707] Since these airstrips would be essential to the advance of the gospel, a little prompting from a couple of missionary enthusiasts had made the government of Suriname a partner in the Great Commission.

Meanwhile, on a trip from British Guiana in a small commercial aircraft, Elmer Thompson did a flyover of Suriname's Wayana villages. Looking down upon the distant specs of human habitation, he was gripped by their utter isolation from the outside world. The Wayana were without visible hope of hearing salvation's message, and Elmer Thompson again heard the voice of God. Without further hesitation, WIM seconded Walt and Marj Jackson to Door To Life Ministries.

The Jacksons spent the summer of 1960 at the University of Oklahoma at Norman, poking their way through phonemes, morphemes, and the techniques of linguistic analysis in preparation for their work with the Wayanas. Here they met Morgan and Mary Jane Jones, who became the next recruits for DTL's tribal outreach.

Meanwhile, God was preparing another couple for the Suriname venture. Ivan and Doris Schoen were attending the BIOLA School of Missionary Medicine. When they received a DTL brochure on Suriname's Indians, they knew that they had found the pioneer field for which they had been asking God. In 1960, they joined DTL, and arrived in Suriname in 1961. They would stay for nearly forty years.

Walter and Marjorie Jackson returned to Suriname in April 1961, and were soon deep into the work of reducing the Wayana language. With five couples now posted in the vast expanse of Suriname's interior—all with Door To Life—radio contact became imperative.[708] In August, Don Draper, an RCA radio technician, joined the task force. He and his wife, Doris, established a base in Paramaribo, where they provided hostelry, radio contact, and purchasing services for the pioneer team.[709]

Making the Paper Talk

It took the Jacksons and the Schoens two years to establish an alphabet in the Wayana language. Simultaneously, the Leavitts (on loan to DTL from UFM) and the Joneses addressed the same task among the Trio Indians. Primers were later compiled and mimeographed to teach the Indians to read and write in their own language. There were no Christians, and the Indians were highly suspicious of the missionaries' motives. Later they would learn that on more than one occasion the Wayana had considered killing their visitors. Nevertheless, the essential foundation of Scripture translation was well on its way.

"Make the paper talk," both Wayana and Trio implored as they began to grasp the relationship between the phonetic symbols on paper and their own spoken words. Like flicking a light switch, the connection was electric. Soon it was impossible to satisfy their appetite for Bible stories, songs, and doctrine. The

Bible text became *God's Paper.* For the first time, the Amerindians of southern Suriname were hearing the voice of God in their own language. As it always does, "God's Paper" would change their lifestyle.

The One Who Lifts Us Up

Both the Ivan Schoens and the Walt Jacksons were constantly on the alert for cultural insights that would aid them in making the gospel understandable to the Wayana. This meant constant note taking, and they filled many notebooks with vocabulary and frame sentences. All of this was built into the daily routine of clearing jungle, building homes, schools, airstrips, and finding food for the table.

Trained at BIOLA's School of Missionary Medicine, the Schoens attended to the Indians' medical and dental needs, together with Mary Jane Jones, a nurse, and Nancy Lepper, a medical doctor. For *Operation Grasshopper,* the medical team was a rare and winning combination—reassuring to the missionary families who likewise depended on them for care. Medicine became an ever widening circle of influence for the gospel, as government workers, Bush Negroes, and tourists came for help, not a few of them finding Christ in the process. Short-wave radio allowed couples to coach each other when emergencies arose—and to share linguistic insights.[710]

One day, as the Schoens were delivering a baby, the father suddenly shouted, "If it is a girl, I will kill it!" The Wayana regularly practiced infanticide. Up until this time they were killing as many as eighty percent of their babies.

"What will you do?" The question was directed to the father.

"I will not lift it up."

The missionaries were nonplussed at this reply. Had he said, "I'll kill it with a stick of firewood!" they would have understood. What could he mean by "I will not lift it up."?

When they pressed for an explanation, the answer came like a blaze of light. Wayana mothers bore their children on the dirt floor of their huts. There the newborn must remain untouched by anyone until the father lifted it. If he lifted the child, it would live. By refusing to lift it, he had pronounced the death sentence. The infant would be taken to the jungle and left to die or be buried alive in the hut along with the placenta.

The missionaries wasted no time in applying the analogy. The gospel message had been built into Wayana and Trio culture. Jesus Christ is *the One who lifts us up!* An infant was not regarded as a member of the tribe until lifted up. Then it would be loved and cared for. It was a message the Indians clearly understood and it became the first key to the effective sharing of salvation's story.[711]

Door To Life Merges with WIM

In December 1962, a throng of Wayanas crowded the airstrip at Lawa, on Suriname's border with French Guiana. One of four Door To Life's interior stations, Lawa was the station to which the Jacksons had been assigned the previous year. The welcome mat was out for Elmer Thompson, WIM's director, and Walter Wunsch of WIM's Guadeloupe field. The visit by these dignitaries would formalize the already functional relationship of DTL missionaries with the West Indies Mission. Common goals and a harmonious working relationship with the Jacksons assured the DTL team that the WIM umbrella offered a more effective advocacy in North America for their work with Suriname's tribes. The merger was signed without fanfare and approved by the West Indies Mission Administrative Committee on 7 January 1963. The action brought the entire DTL[712] staff into the West Indies Mission, with the exception of the Leavitts, who continued with UFM (but on loan to WIM), and the Ted Leppers, who left Suriname for their MAF assignment.[713]

Trio Breakthrough

By 1963, many Trios had become Christians. The breakthrough came when Tamenta, a revered Trio witch doctor, took a daring step. Facing his fellow tribesmen, he took his heathen fetishes and, one by one, explained their devilish purposes. He then handed them to the missionary by his side. Seconds later the eyes of the entire group followed the trajectory of these venerated charms as they skimmed through the air to disappear forever in the depths of the jungle river.

Tamenta was not the first Trio to receive the Lord Jesus as Savior. However, he was an important man in the tribe and, because of his clear break with heathenism, a strong Trio church was established at Paloemeu. Another Trio church was birthed at the Alalaparoe Station in the southwest corner of the country. The Wayana of central Suriname were also responding to the gospel. All but a few of the seventy-plus Wayana at the village of Big Arrow had professed faith in Christ.

Since the Wayana Indians of southeastern Suriname had more contact with the outside world than the Trios, they were at first not as ready to receive the gospel. Then a Wayana witch doctor received Christ and renounced his witchcraft. Like a drumbeat, the impact of this action resounded throughout the tribe, bringing many to Christ.

Suriname's Sanballats

At WIM's Paloemue River station, the government had lengthened the airstrip to accommodate larger aircraft. The Trio now became a tourist target. Groups of twelve to sixty sightseers flew in on weekends from Paramaribo in hopes of watching the Trios dance and chant the songs of the spirits. On one occasion when asked to perform a tribal dance, the Indians, after meeting privately, replied, "Dancing belongs to the old life; we will not do it now. If the visitors wish, we will sing songs, show how we can shoot arrows, and read stories from God's Word."[714] Disappointment in finding a community of Christian Indians who had put away their former lifestyle vented itself in vicious rumors which found their way into one of Suriname's newspapers: "Let's get this influence out . . . The Indians are slaves . . . [and] live in fear of the missionaries." Another paper, however, consistently defended the work of the Mission.

In 1998, there were five indigenous churches among the Wayana and Trio Indians. One Wayana church was on the Lawa River, one on the Tapanahoni River and one at the mouth of the Paloemeu River. Trio churches functioned on the Paloemeu and Sipalawini Rivers—each church with multiple leaders, referred to as elders and deacons, plus their own Indian missionaries. Sharing the responsibilities of the ministry, none were paid.

The tribes are hunter-gatherer-farmers who live in a mostly subsistence economy. Nevertheless, they support their missionaries to the best of their ability, sometimes with food and supplies, sometimes with money. They receive the money from the government through the sale of handcrafts, wild meat and fish, et cetera. Their missionary activity is within Suriname, but also extends to French Guiana, Guyana, and Brazil. Most of those they reach are from other Indian tribes, some of whom are distant relatives. A few of these Indian believers have had the opportunity to witness to a king, a queen, a princess, and to prime ministers and lesser government officials—just as Paul the Apostle had done before them.[715]

Trio and Wayana churches meet throughout the week except for Wednesdays and Saturdays, which are hunting and bread-making days. They conduct prayer meetings and meetings for children, women, and men. Most of the civil leaders are fine Christians as well as church leaders. Led by the Holy Spirit, the churches function on their own, with timely encouragement and teaching by missionaries who make periodic visits.

Roy and Margaret Lytle, Fred and Trudy Vermeulen (no longer with World Team, but still very much in the work), Fred and Jan Blind, and Ivan and Doris Schoen, continued their ministry to the churches. The Schoens, actively retired, continue (1999) to translate Scripture in the Wayana language, having completed the New Testament in 1979. As of 1999, they had completed twenty-four books of the Old Testament. Claude Leavitt completed translation of the Trio New Testament in 1979. Both Testaments were dedicated the same year. Leavitt translated much of the Old Testament, a project continued by Fred Vermeulen.

From these beginnings, WIM expanded its work throughout this multicultural republic, which is perched on the northern shore of the South American continent. In 1962, work was begun among the Bush Negroes, descendants of African slaves who had escaped to the interior. They inhabit central Suriname. Here World Team personnel trained Christian leaders. In Paramaribo, World Team ministered to a cosmopolitan spectrum of Hindustani, Creole, Guyanese, and Javanese peoples, employing radio, literature, short-term Bible schools, church-starting teams, and the training of health workers.

Letting the Fire Die

In 1968, Art and Evelyn Yohner joined a party of missionaries and Christian Indians—Trio and Wayana—in search of the nomadic *Wayarekules,* one of a number of presumed "lost tribes" in Suriname's jungle fastness.[716] In the course of several expeditions they learned that the Wayarekules were few in number and widely scattered in several tiny cluster groups. Wayarekule, which means "savage," was not their real name. It was the cognomen with which outsiders had labeled them. Their real name was *Akurijo* (ah-kúd-ee-oh). More amazing was the extremely primitive lifestyle of this Stone Age people. Making fire—a skill learned only by the men—was so complex a process that they always carried fire with them in their nomadic search for food. "Letting the fire die" became a synonym for death.

When the gospel was explained to them by Trio Christians in song and message, the Akurijo were receptive. When invited to come out of their jungle isolation and live among the Trio, they agreed. Like seventy other Amazon tribes before them, the Akurijo were dying out, and leaving their isolation was their only hope of survival.

The ultimate test came when they laid down their fire sticks, which could not be taken aboard the evacuation canoes since they were fitted with gasoline outboards. In this act of faith—letting the fire die—the Akurijos exchanged their old life for the new. Their families were taken in and adopted by Trio Christians. Most of the Akurijos became Christians. The Wayana, the Trio, the Akurijo, the Bush Negroes—each one is a story in itself. Like the book of Acts, the drama continues and much remains to be written.

Philomena

The astonishing Suriname venture began with Philomena Brandon, the catalyst who prompted Elmer Thompson and the West Indies Mission to enter the country. After graduating from Prairie Bible Institute, Philo joined the Mission and served for several years in Paramaribo, where she met and married Erwin G. Levens, a young layman who had made profession of faith in Christ. In keeping with Mission policy,[717] Philo resigned from WIM upon her marriage and, with her husband and two children, said good-bye to Paramaribo and to the WIM family in 1973. The marriage did not fare well, and Erwin subsequently revealed a dark side of his personality. Traveling to the Netherlands for a time, the family eventually settled in the town of Bassano in Alberta, Canada. On 7 August 1980, Erwin Levens removed his rifle from its rack on the wall of their bungalow in Bassano. In a twisted moment and for reasons known only to God, he took aim at his two children and Philomena, and shot them dead. Then he took his own life. They had been married seventeen years.[718]

55

On the Air in Old Hispaniola

*We want men and women who are easy to get along with, who
have died to self and self-will, who can keep sweet and can
submit themselves to their superintendents until they have
learned the language and become qualified to be leaders. Who
can keep rank as David's soldiers; who are adjustable, good-
natured, ready to meet persecution and insult without getting
angry, and who can live the gospel of Christ among the heathen even as the Master did.*

—A. B. Simpson

The New Medium

In 1956, the West Indies Mission had 60,000 new Haitian Christians to shepherd and few pastors to go around. The country's communications infrastructure was hopeless. Postal and telephone service was unreliable, roads were in
deplorable condition, and schools were few. The three hundred churches of
the MEBSH association had no means of interface, since travel was mostly
limited to muleback. The Church faced false doctrine from without, and division from within. Radio receivers were few and in the hands of the elite.

While WIM searched for answers, David Hartt was planning. The Bell Research Lab team had invented the transistor in 1947. Within a short time, the
revolutionary electronic device had found its way into a variety of miniatur-
ized applications, including the transistorized radio. Hartt envisioned placing
a pretuned receiver in every congregation in Haiti's Southern Peninsula. In
this way, the three hundred groups could be networked by radio and those
without pastors could be serviced.

Fluent in French and Creole, David Hartt was the logical choice to head this
effort. He was an ardent ham operator with a background in electronics, and
had opened Guadeloupe for the Mission in 1947. He had already upgraded a
government-owned amateur radio station in the French possession. An

enthusiastic Hartt was prepared to cover Haiti with gospel radio. Elmer Thompson was not so sure.

WIM's director was not an easy mark for innovative approaches to evangelism. For Thompson, the Bible institute was both biblical and a proven success. Radio was not part of the WIM arsenal, in spite of the fact that John Huffman's *Alas del Alba* program had enjoyed success in Cuba. Thompson saw ownership of a radio station in the same terms as the classic definition of a pleasure boat—a hole into which you pour money. The West Indies Mission had little to spare. Thompson vetoed the notion. David Hartt, however, proved a scrappy defender of his convictions and persisted. Thompson remained unbudging. Then Hartt released a final salvo. If WIM failed to authorize a radio station in Haiti, David Hartt would resign and launch an independent radio effort. Thompson backed off.

Hartt's response was not petulance. Professionals at HCJB (the missionary radio station in Quito, Ecuador)[719] had strongly advised him against launching a radio station under the auspices of the Mission. Prevailing anti-foreign sentiment in Haiti would preclude social and political acceptance of a foreign-owned station—a fact with which Elmer Thompson agreed. For radio to succeed in Haiti, support of the Association of Bible Churches would be essential, and only WIM could sell the idea to MEBSH. Without Thompson's backing, Hartt would have to go to the MEBSH churches on his own. Hartt was so convinced that radio was the answer to the evangelization of Haiti that he was prepared to work outside of WIM if necessary.

With some misgivings, WIM's executive committee gave Hartt the green light, but with three conditions: First, cost to the Mission would not exceed $750. Second, Hartt would not be permitted to publicize the project, and third, he would have to raise any additional funds on his own—exactly how was not clear.

David Hartt signed the agreement. Of course, the issue created tensions, for missionaries had lined up on both sides of the question. Hartt was an alumnus of Prairie Bible Institute, where his parents were on staff. The school was his alma mater and he had many friends on the campus. One of them was Fergus Kirk, who was also chairman of the PBI Board. Kirk was elated with the logic of the radio project and immediately wrote Hartt a check for $1,000, promising to advocate the need within their mutual circles of interest at Three Hills. Hartt had another advantage—Kirk was also the Canadian representative of the West Indies Mission. With Fergus Kirk on his side, Hartt had no further trouble fundraising for the radio project.

In 1957, he went to work. Four twenty-foot lengths of three-inch irrigation pipe lashed together with two-by-fours comprised the makeshift antenna, and Radio Lumière (Radio Light) went on the air Christmas Day 1958. Pioneer

Hartt had taken the first step in what would become a major Christian broadcasting network serving the churches and the people of Haiti. At his side was his wife, Erma, who served as program secretary. In 1960, Haitian pastors received the first of 450 fixed-frequency transistor radios placed throughout the island. Radio infused new life into the Haitian churches. It also stirred Jesuit ire, with priests forbidding parishioners to listen to the broadcast—even entering homes to turn off sets. By 1962, *Radio Lumière* was also beaming Spanish language broadcasts to Cuba, which by then had shut down Christian broadcasting within Castro's dictatorship—just as David Hartt had predicted.

When hurricane Flora struck Haiti (3 Oct. 1963), Radio Lumière broadcast emergency bulletins to the people, winning the appreciation of civil and military authorities. No other broadcast station had ever before warned the public of impending storms. Eleven months later, on 22 August 1964, hurricane Cleo slammed the island, creating even greater havoc. The Bible school campus, the transmitter, and the studio at Les Cayes in the southern peninsula—all were devastated. While Radio Lumière had enjoyed success at Les Cayes, Hartt knew that relocation of the station to Haiti's teeming capital was critical to reaching the nation. This now became his objective. Government permission for the move could be readily attained, but not without conditions which would have compromised the Mission—a price Hartt was unwilling to pay.

Authorization to build a radio transmitter in Port au Prince had to come from the highest level of Haiti's government. Hartt enjoyed cordial contact with the army chief of staff, but such favors were beyond even the general's ability to broker. So Hartt was taken by surprise when a summary order from the top was delivered to him through the health officer in charge of post-hurricane rehabilitation Les Cayes: Get Radio Lumière back on the air immediately! With rebel activity in the Haitian hills, national security was now at stake and the Les Cayes transmitter was critical to government interests. Pressing the advantage Flora and Cleo had bestowed, Hartt agreed to restore the Les Cayes facility, but argued for location of the main studio and transmitter in the capital, Port au Prince. The Les Cayes location could serve as a relay station. With back to the wall, the government gave Hartt carte blanche. In three weeks, he had the Les Cayes transmitter back on the air.

Meanwhile, with help from the Back to the Bible broadcast, Hartt bought a lot in Port au Prince. It came complete with a reinforced concrete building—hurricane-proof—all for less than $10,000. Almost miraculously, additional properties quickly followed, and radio became a catalyst of growth and unification for the Haitian church. Moreover, it won the respect and cooperation of Haitian authorities.

Ed and Mary Lee Walker had been based in Les Cayes, where Ed had been Principal of the Bible Institute since 1963. Following Cleo's 1964 devastation of the campus—including the loss of their home—the Walkers relocated to Port-au-Prince to establish the new radio station. Walker was named director of Radio Lumière in 1967, a position he held for twelve years.[720] Arising from a personal audience with President Francois Duvalier on 19 November 1968, WIM leadership received permission to expand coverage on the island.[721]

Dave Hartt continued in engineering until 1972, and after studies at the University of Haiti and Wheaton College, he returned to Haiti in 1974 as director of research. In 1976, Radio Lumière began broadcasting FM stereo. When WIM adopted its policy of disengagement in 1987, Radio Lumière was already well established in the hands of nationals, and remained largely unaffected by the change. Meanwhile, across the border in neighboring Dominican Republic, God was doing a new thing.[722]

Radio Lumière Staff, Haiti.
Front center: David and Erma Hartt.
Front right: Edwin and Mary Lee Walker.

56

Quisqueya para Cristo!

*It is no use dreaming of other places, other gifts, and other
personality traits that we see in someone whom we admire.
First, that is destructive. Secondly, it is offensive to our Lord,
who gifted you, created you, and placed you where you are
right now.*

—Luis Palau

After twenty-four years in the Dominican Republic, WIM's ministry had
stagnated. Allen Thompson became field director in 1963 and promptly put
his finger on the problem. Bible institute ministry in both Cuba and Haiti had
crowned WIM's early efforts with success beyond their dreams. Graduates
evangelized. Churches multiplied. WIM applied the same successful formula
in the Dominican Republic, but without success.

In Cuba and Haiti, national workers had done the work of church planting,
while the Mission concentrated on equipping the planters through the Bible
Institute. By contrast, in the Dominican Republic, when missionaries began
the task of starting new churches, there was no Cuban B. G. Lavastida to
evangelize the people and bring students into the Bible Institute. Nor had
there been any providential sowing of repatriated Christians, as in the case of
Haiti. For missionaries in the Dominican Republic, church planting was a cold
start—unprimed. While successful Cuban pastors had been brought to the
Dominican Republic to help the North Americans, the churches they planted
tended to become autonomous cells—ingrown and without a vision for the
nation.

The Cuba Bible Institute, on the other hand, had championed the vision of
winning all Cuba to Christ. Lavastida's evangelistic gift and national recognition had made the Bible institute a distinguished base of missionary operation
for the entire country—a launch pad with Cubans reaching Cubans. This advantage was largely absent in the Dominican Republic.

Transitions in Training

By pushing the Bible institute model in the Dominican Republic—a practice successful in Cuba and Haiti—WIM had overlooked its most critical assets: the nonprofessionals. Local church members had never been discipled in the art of soul-winning and church multiplication. A few had been brought to the Bible school for short periods, but while these were away studying, the local church was deprived of their ministry. What Thompson now proposed was to shift the locus of training. Rather than send church members off to a distant Bible institute, every local church would be turned into a training center. This would bring Bible training within reach of greater numbers, but without the disruption of leaving jobs, home, and family.

Thompson called on Hilario Diaz, a well-known and gifted Cuban pastor then ministering in the capital city of Santo Domingo.[723] He used the Diaz church as a pilot institute for training laymen. Two missionaries would give themselves to a six-week teaching stint in the capital, then another six weeks in La Vega. Later they would rotate among other important population centers. In this way the Bible institute could remain open to supplement the task of training in the local churches.

To promote this new thrust within the Mission, Thompson knew that a revision of WIM's ministry philosophy would be necessary:

> Without stifling missionary thinking, operating principles must be adopted and carried through. We must encourage missionaries to read, to study missionary methods in various fields, and discover where improvements can be made. Then we must promote a uniform means of implementation.

In April 1965, *Evangelism-In-Depth* (EID) brought two hundred national pastors and workers to the Mission conference center in La Vega—a remarkable achievement in the wake of the national economic chaos following Trujillo's assassination. Thompson reported:

> Many felt that the DR had never seen a demonstration of God's power in the salvation of souls during its history of Christian missions . . . [Hopes had been] dashed to the ground at the sight of bloody revolution.

In the wake of the assassination, hope now began to rise from the ashes of despair, and the Evangelism-In-Depth campaign lifted the Church. For thousands of Christians, *Quisqueya para Cristo!*[724] (The Dominican Republic for Christ) became the rally cry. Allen Thompson led the cooperative effort involving four hundred churches.

As the EID effort ran its course, 164 prayer cells were organized throughout the country. The groups met weekly in homes, churches, and shops to pray for the salvation of men and women and to be instructed through a visitation program. Spiritual expectancy charged the atmosphere. Believers displayed an eagerness to open new fields and to enter unreached areas. One layman from the Azua church began such an effort and reported forty conversions. Another in Las Yayitas saw seventy persons come to Christ. Neither missionary nor national pastor had visited either area. Laymen had taken the initiative and God had anointed their efforts.

The record was impressive. A year of Evangelism-In-Depth had added two churches, eight preaching points, and seven hundred new believers. Nine hundred Christians had been mobilized and 164 prayer cells organized. Four hundred thirty graduated from the WIM's training course in evangelism. Three hundred and five of these participated in house to house visitation.[725]

For the first time in the history of WIM's efforts in the Dominican Republic, nonprofessionals were rising to leadership roles in the churches. Evangelism advanced on three fronts—youth groups, men's groups, and women's organizations. Hopes ran high as an awakened Church began to penetrate society with the Gospel. At last, the West Indies Mission had tapped into the evangelistic potential of the Dominican churches. Notwithstanding, another test was waiting in the wings.

A Premature Move

By 1970, WIM's ministry had begun to shift to Santo Domingo, the country's strategic center. Other cities such as Santiago, Azua, Cotui, and the original starting point of ministry, La Vega, were growing nerve centers. However, the major action was in the capital. Not only were the churches growing, they were also organizing.

Eighteen congregations formed a church association called *Templos Evangélicos* (Evangelical Temples). In Santo Domingo alone, four *Templos* congregations enjoyed successful outreach among the city's one-half million people. Other churches and groups followed WIM's cue and began to set goals to reach other cities in the Dominican Republic with the gospel message. Dominican believers had learned to witness effectively and now, Bibles in hand, they confidently challenged the faithful on their annual pilgrimage to George Little's "Holy Hill."

Transition

With the formation of the Templos Evangélicos association, WIM confidently passed the leadership baton to the national church in a triumphant "next step." Now-familiar aphorisms had already become working principles within the West Indies Mission long before becoming popular missiological buzzwords: *"Nationals evangelize their own better." "No success without a successor." "Foundations are forever."*

Since 1939, WIM had practiced basic three-step, missions-by-the-book in the Dominican Republic: Evangelize→ Teach→ Nationalize. It was not hard to see that national Christians, unfettered by language or cultural barriers, could reach their compatriots more effectively than linguistically challenged foreigners. The true measure of a missionary's success had always been the viability of the work he leaves. If he has trained successors who will replicate and multiply his ministry, he has been successful. Failing this, his work remains incomplete. Nationalization of the Dominican Republic church had been a worthy goal, but the process had been flawed. One veteran missionary explained:

> The men given leadership were not biblically qualified for eldership. This later became a source of contention. Once on the playing field and given the ball, they wanted to run with it. That is when the troubles began.

Templos Evangélicos had groomed its own bureaucracy. Chain-of-command disputes bred controversial decisions. Annual conferences produced lively quarrels, often over trivia. Groups polarized, refusing to work with one another. Lacking spiritual maturity, leaders often failed to reach consensus on important issues.

Rupture

Eager to model the servant spirit, WIM missionaries had placed themselves under the direction of the national church, but the move was premature. National leadership had not been grounded in Biblical principles of church administration. Attempts to redirect the focus of Templos Evangélicos leadership were interpreted as manipulation. Unable to support their pastors, the churches looked to WIM to provide a purse—but without interference. While these tensions were not unique to the West Indies Mission, in the Dominican Republic they would lead to rupture. By the mid-70s, simmering animosity between national pastors and missionaries reached boiling point. The Mission was forced to withdraw five families.

To repair the breech, WIM sent a delegation to the Dominican Republic. Pat Arnold and Harold Alexander accompanied Allen Thompson—then executive director of WIM. Thompson hoped to arbitrate agreement between the two bodies. He also planned to develop a philosophy of church-mission relationships that might be applied throughout WIM's various fields.

However, by 1980 the leftist element within the church association had gained control. In 1981, all but two of the Templos Evangélicos severed their relationship with Worldteam. Because Templos Evangélicos had been legally incorporated, opportunistic church leaders took control of the church structure (1986), seized the properties, and put pastors and people on the street. These developments stunned WIM leadership. In the rush to nationalize, the West Indies Mission had made a critical misstep. They had failed to verify leadership qualifications before turning over the keys. It was a lesson they would not forget. In November 1988, in a retreat of thirty-five leaders, the principles for a new Center for Ministerial Training (CEM) were established under the guidance of field leader Al Ortiz.[726]

While the 1965 Evangelism-in-Depth campaign had logged 12,000 professions of faith nationwide, subsequent experience evidenced little continuing church growth either numerically or spiritually. Out of many early conversions, few had been integrated into local churches as effective, functioning members—a fact confirmed in an island-wide study conducted by Dr. Peter Wagner. The study led to an examination of the reasons for this failure. What they discovered led Thompson to the conviction that a church-multiplying peoples' movement could be sustained using cyclical reinforcement approaches—systematic, repetitive instruction and motivation employing witness tools, manuals, and prayer cells. These materials were subsequently developed and used effectively in Haiti.

The tensions in the Dominican Republic also strained relationships within the mission family. At times, missionaries had carefully groomed nationals for leadership roles, only to be overruled by their own Mission. Projects or programs begun by missionaries were changed without prior consultation. Nationals affected by such top-down decisions became embittered. Conflicts erupted between missionaries and supervisors when months of work were discarded at the seeming caprice of a new director with a different agenda.

By the late 1980s, however, the shadows had begun to lift over WIM's work in the Dominican Republic. During the 1988 Easter weekend, four hundred believers gathered with Allen Thompson, Al Ortiz and the Dominican Republic team in the second annual church-wide spiritual life conference, built around the theme, *Doing Greater Works with God.*[727] When the exposition came to the high priestly prayer of the Lord Jesus in John 17, congregational prayer followed the exegesis of each paragraph. In small groups, participants scattered throughout the auditorium to pray for themselves the way Jesus had prayed. The work of the Holy Spirit was profound. Unity of purpose and an appetite for the things of God pervaded the gathering. The work in the Dominican Republic had turned a corner.[728]

57

A Storm Breaks in Cuba

Sainthood springs out of suffering. It takes eleven tons of pressure on a piano to tune it. God will tune you to harmonize with Heaven's keynote if you can stand the strain.

—A.B. Simpson

Upheaval, 1959

Civil war had smoldered underground for years in Cuba's eastern province of Oriente with only sporadic outbursts to demonstrate its presence. The excesses of the Batista regime had fueled a growing public anger. It erupted with fury in the island's central province of Las Villas in November 1958, and ended abruptly with President Fulgencio Batista's abdication on 1 January 1959.

The West Indies Mission lay directly in the path of the advancing rebel forces. On the same evening that thirty-two-year-old Fidel Castro took the town of Placetas, seven miles east of the West Indies Mission campus. Santa Clara—the Provincial capital—fell to Castro without resistance. Had government forces been able to mount a defense, the Los Pinos Bible Institute might have been destroyed. Instead, the West Indies Mission locale was now in rebel hands, but the missionary staff, Cuban pastors, and all property, had been providentially spared.

If Castro had carefully orchestrated his revolution, he had also planned for its aftermath. Within forty-eight hours of the cease-fire, handpicked men had assumed new roles as mayors, governors, and military officers. Several sound, evangelical men were among those assigned to posts in the new government. Cubans were wild with joy at Batista's overthrow and the cessation of hostilities, and Fidel Castro was hailed as hero and liberator. The euphoria would soon subside.[729]

New Pines Closes

Cuba declared itself a socialist state, and anti-American feeling was running high. Early in 1960, the government ordered all persons holding foreign residence visas to leave the country. Those failing to do so would no longer be free to leave at will. WIM leadership knew it was time to go. In 1961 the Los Pinos Seminary closed. The *Alas del Alba* radio program fell silent. Evangelical bookstores closed, as imports became unavailable. Notwithstanding, the Evangelical Association of New Pines had reached a maturity and strength that would stand firm for the next four decades against the dark winter of the Castro Regime.

One hundred thirty churches were alive and well; the seminary was strong, and with a large student body, provided nurture to the growing church. With the ominous forecast now clear, one by one the contingent of West Indies Mission personnel left the country. A handful of Canadian workers remained, but the high drama of political tension between the United States and Cuba effectively closed the door to the return of Americans. By August 29, all American WIM families had left the island, with the exception of a few singles, who soon followed.[730] Delma Jackson, of White Rock, British Colombia, was the last to leave. She had been Elmer Thompson's secretary.[731]

By 1967, seven years of economic sanctions had reduced the beautiful New Pines campus to a drab shadow of its former self. The faculty had shared the common pool of funds with the missionaries. With the missionaries gone, there were no funds to maintain the faculty. The gender-mixed student body had diminished, as had the curriculum. It was now a two-year education course training thirty female students as Sunday school teachers and children's workers. The Cuban Military and forced labor camps had swallowed up many of the men. Street meetings were banned and the annual Bible conference subjected to a rigid protocol of approval. Leaders of one group that failed to secure the required permissions were imprisoned for six months. Offshore guest speakers were banned, and *Alas del Alba* shared the same fate.

Fidel Castro continued to show his true colors. In his 1969 New Year's speech to the nation he promised:

> In 1969 we will do away with the celebration of Christmas. Instead, I am calling upon the people of Cuba to join me in bringing in a ten-million-ton sugar harvest, and from now on, July 26 (the anniversary of the revolution) will be the day of celebration.

To bolster the battered economy, the *Year of the Great Leap Forward* was announced as a time for Cubans to put their hands to the industrial and agricultural plow. Ten years of economic decline had produced strict rationing and a black market. One by one, freedoms eroded. After 1967, small farms were confiscated, including that of the West Indies Mission. Activities were monitored and reported by incognito government agents. Public transportation dried up as vehicles wore out. Busses issued two classes of tickets—"reserved" and "standby."

The Noose Tightens

Restrictions began to throttle the Church. Six hundred Catholic priests were expelled, denominational schools and colleges were closed, and gospel broadcasts were banned. While overt persecution was not practiced, the government employed harassment tactics to discourage the practice of religion. Religious leaders were singled out. One pastor, accused of harboring a Cuban youth who was fleeing the country, had been away in Havana—absent from his home—the night the youth slept in his church. He received a four-year prison sentence.

Church attendance dwindled. Pastors who touched on the biblical themes of Egypt and Israel's bondage were accused of double-talk. All churches were required to register with the government. When they complied, they could function. Those refusing were shut down. Church board minutes had to be submitted to the government. No one could preach unless ordained, licensed, or granted special rights by the government in consultation with the church organization.[732]

The Thaw

As the Cuban economy continued to deteriorate, some welcome changes came in 1990 when President Castro declared: "We have built many towns without churches. There is going to be one church per town." A more relaxed attitude toward the Church followed, with greater freedom to minister. Anti-government speeches were forbidden, as were open-air meetings, and house-to-house distribution of evangelistic material. Beyond such limits, Cubans were legally free to engage in all other normal evangelical activity.

During the 1990s, a spiritual hunger pervaded Cuba, with thousands turning to Christ. Of a population of eleven million, the number of active Christians approached ten percent. By 1999, an estimated 3,000 Protestant house churches functioned throughout the island.

Finger of God

Retrospect disclosed the wonderful providence of the Lord of the Harvest in his plans for Cuba. God had removed the religious/political yoke of Roman Catholic Spain in 1898, opening wide the door to Protestant missions. When the West Indies Mission came to the island in 1928, God opened a thirty-year window through which the gospel exploded into Cuban life. Within that frame, the church grew rapidly with the founding of a Bible institute and the planting of more than one hundred churches, a work that became the key that unlocked the door of life for thousands throughout the West Indies. When the storm of Castro's revolution broke in 1959, the seminal work had been completed, the Cuban church was prepared, and the window closed. The events of history simply underscored the authority of our Lord Jesus Christ when he said, *I will build my church.*

One of the men whom God had brought to the kingdom for such a time as this was Otoniel Bermudez.

Otoniel Bermudez

Otoniel Bermudez grew up in the Dominican Republic, where his Cuba-born parents had been the first missionaries sent to the DR by the Cuba national church. They returned to Cuba just before Fidel Castro's 1959 revolution and the restrictive measures of a new regime. Here, their son would play a critical role on behalf of the Cuban Church in its struggle for viability.

Otoniel saw that the Castro regime lacked understanding of the nature and purpose of the Church. Failure in this would lead to misunderstanding and conflict. In this conviction, Bermudez began building bridges of understanding between the government and the evangelical churches of Cuba. His courage and faith won him favor with government officials. At times misunderstood, his most severe critics were often other pastors who opposed what they saw as compromise. In the face of painful misunderstanding, Otoniel refused discouragement. His winsome diplomacy brought the Church in Cuba greater freedom and growth in the later years of the Castro regime.

In 1999, Bermudez was serving as executive secretary of the Cuban Council of Churches, and as pastor of the *Los Pinos Nuevos Church* in Old Havana. Often called upon to mediate conflict between Christian leaders and government officials, he became World Team's principal contact in Cuba. Throughout a difficult time in Cuba's history, Bermudez remained faithful to his preemptive call—to serve the Church of the Lord Jesus Christ.

Old Soldiers Never Die

B. G. Lavastida had welcomed Castro's revolution. The old patriot still hoped that a new day had arrived for his nation. He earnestly prayed for the success of Castro's forces in the movement against Batista. When it became obvious that Castro was a communist, Lavastida's disenchantment was overwhelming.

"How could I have been so gullible?" he chided himself. Disillusionment turned to bitterness when both his youngest son and his son-in-law were placed in Castro's forced labor camps.

Nevertheless, B. G. Lavastida knew his God, and a confident faith, matured by years, brought him through yet another personal crisis. Lavastida continued to preach Christ at every opportunity, disdaining the edicts of mere men, and without fear of personal cost.

Nineteen years after the revolution, Lavastida stood before a gathering of students, professionals, and church leaders who crowded Havana's *Evangelical Church.*

"I am asking God for 1,000 conversions this year!"

The trembling, yet firm, voice of the ninety-one-year-old patriarch brought a hush to his audience. He continued:

"For over a half century, God has given me the joy of winning men and women to Him all over Cuba. Is it too much to ask Him for this display of His grace in 1978?" Then, bowing his head he said, "Father, I want to present you 1,000 souls as a gift at the end of this year. Nothing is too hard for you. Encourage my brothers and sisters here to embrace this challenge with me."

The embattled patriot, weathered by a century of life, received his upward call on 30 September 1992. The previous day he had lifted a favorite hymn, *Jesus Paid It all.*[733] At 105, he was, like Job, *"old and full of days."*[734] God had abundantly vindicated the vision of Hattie and Roger Kirk,[735] of Elmer and Evelyn Thompson, and not least, of Bartholomew G. Lavastida.

Fefita and B. G. Lavastida, 1988

58

Florida Gold

If your objects are large, the public will contribute to their support: If you contract them, their liberality will immediately contract itself proportionately.

—William Carey

Anthony Rossi

His ingenuity revolutionized the American citrus industry. His orange juice fueled the widening outreach of the West Indies Mission. *Tropicana Products* was the brainchild of Anthony Rossi, Sicilian innovator, and entrepreneur from Bradenton, Florida. At twenty-one,[736] Rossi had arrived in New York City, a penniless immigrant with an image of the Madonna in his pocket. Before the day ended, he had found a job. Within six months he had bought a used Buick and got into the taxi business. Upscaling to a newish Packard, he hired out as private chauffeur at $450 a month. Always ahead of the curve, Rossi was soon operating a small, self-service grocery in Jackson Heights, called Aurora Farms. When his interest in the grocery business cooled, he sold out for $30,000. When New York winters became too cold for his Sicilian blood, he began to think Florida—and farming. Looking for books on agriculture in the 42nd Street library, a volume caught his eye. It was *The Life of Christ*. The story absorbed him and he read for hours. It drove him to the Bible, which he began to read avidly. The simplicity of the gospel posed questions that now cast doubt upon his religious upbringing:

Why do I need to fear purgatory? Why do I need to do penance for sins, [or] pray for the dead whom I have loved? Christ has already died to pay for all my sins.[737]

Rossi took these questions with him to Florida in 1941. Back in Jackson Heights, he had married one of his grocery store clients, Florence Stark, the daughter of a Methodist minister. The couple came to Bradenton, where they joined the Methodist Church.

In Florida, Rossi's entrepreneurial instincts continued to probe new options—tomato farming, a cafeteria, and a restaurant. Citrus ended his search. In Miami, he took to shipping gift boxes of fruit. Here he made two pivotal discoveries. First, citrus could be bought cheaper direct from the groves, so he moved back to Bradenton, leaving someone in charge of the Miami enterprise. Bradenton would bless him for the decision.[738] Second, as the packers sorted citrus, they selected the choice oranges, discarding the smaller ones. "Such a waste," he thought, "these little things ought to be useful for something." Rossi's fertile mind attacked the problem. What he discovered changed orange juice forever.

Until Rossi, long-distance shipping of fresh orange juice was impractical, since fresh juice readily spoiled and existing refrigeration methods were inadequate. Rossi found a way around the problem. His solution defied conventional wisdom and turned the citrus industry on its ear. Fresh citrus juice and fruit segments could be chilled and preserved without reconstituting. With a combination of carefully engineered insulation and large frozen slabs of juice (later ground to slush), Rossi refitted a sea-going tanker and filled it with 1.45 million gallons of refrigerated orange juice, delivering it—on time—to a Long Island pier at Whitestone, New York. The marketing miracle made Tropicana Products the world's largest producer and distributor of chilled Florida gold. It would also make Anthony Rossi a billionaire. But something was missing.

Conversion

Growing up in Sicily, Rossi had been taught that getting to heaven might be earned by complying with a formula: recite the *Lord's Prayer*, the *Ave Maria*, and the *Credos* twice a day—morning and evening—for seven years. It was a tall order, but Rossi wanted to get to heaven, and hewed fervently to the prescription. In seven years, he never missed a beat. However, for all his effort, the assurance he sought remained elusive.

In Sarasota he learned of a group of men who met to study the Bible, and joined them. Driving to the weekly meeting with a new friend, he heard the question for which he had no answer—

"Anthony, if you were to die tonight, would you go to heaven?"

"I want to, but I cannot say. It's up to God," he answered.

During the evening's study, Rossi learned something they had never taught him in Sicily—that salvation flows freely and solely from the death of Christ in our place and from his supernatural resurrection, not from anything we might attempt to do for him. For the first time, Anthony caught the distinction and welcomed Jesus Christ as his Savior. There would be no more Ave

Marías, Hail Marys, or mechanical repetitions. It was Jesus Christ *alone*. Assurance of forgiveness and life eternal flooded the Sicilian's heart. Rossi immediately became concerned for the people of his homeland and purposed to share with them his discovery of God's grace. He would return to Sicily and tell them himself.

Family First

By 1952, Rossi's father had weathered 81 winters and his final one could not be far off. Rossi knew that to share Christ he must begin with his own family, especially Papa. That year he went to Sicily.

Sleep eluded him for most of the night flight to Rome. He spent hours reading the book of Romans, pondering what he would say to his father. Towering at six feet, the senior Rossi cut an imposing figure with his white hair, goatee, and handlebar mustache. Every bit the patriarch, and staunchly Roman Catholic, he enjoyed the respect of the community. The prospect of speaking to him about salvation made Anthony cringe inwardly. Although he was fifty-one years of age, Anthony still felt the timidity of filial reverence in the presence of his father. It would take courage to confront him with the gospel.

His brother Constantino and his wife met him at the Rome airport. Boarding a southbound train to Reggio, at the toe of Italy's boot, they caught the train ferry to Messina, just across the Messina Straits. The Rossi clan was waiting.

Praying fervently for the right words and the right moment, Anthony had worked up an arsenal of Scripture texts and the points he wished to make with his father. He felt comfortable with his weapons. Now, like a hunter watching for the flush of a quail, he remained alert, waiting for the right moment to share his newfound peace in Christ.

Attempts to talk one-on-one with his brothers and sisters were unproductive. Each one seemed to cut him off mid-sentence. Papa was different. One day when all the family was together, Rossi asked his father permission to pray. The old man was receptive, and affirmed that he, too, would henceforth pray in Jesus' name. The patriarch's moist eyes confirmed the quiet transaction that had taken place in his heart. Anthony Rossi was convinced that his father knew Christ in a personal way. Rossi resolved to reach other Sicilians. Thereafter, he returned to Sicily each September for vacation and Bible studies with the family. In the summer of 1966, he took the annual junket a step further and planned an open-air meeting.

CBC and Sicily

Tom Petty was on the staff of Columbia Bible College (CBC) when he learned of Sicily's need for a visitation from heaven. He began to enlist students, pastors, and lay people to join him in asking God to raise up an evangelical church in the tiny country.[739] At the time, Dr. Allen Fleece was president of CBC.

Rossi had been generous to the college,[740] and Fleece, who had been on the West Indies Mission Board since 1961, introduced Rossi to the Mission.[741] When the Tropicana magnate planned his five-day evangelistic mission to Messina, then a thriving city of 300,000, he tapped his nephew, Ralph Nicosia, to arrange the details. Nicosia was a CBC student. On arriving in Messina, he was flatly advised that the proposed effort was futile. No one would come to his meetings. Frantic, he telephoned the States and explained the rebuff to his uncle. Anthony Rossi would hear none of it. "The Lord has put it in our hearts to come and we are coming to preach the Gospel," Rossi advised his anxious nephew, "Continue to make arrangements."

Against this background, Rossi's expectations were not high when he arrived in Messina, so he was surprised to find more than 250 of his compatriots at the first meeting, all waiting to hear what he had to say. "I was scared," he confessed, "but the Lord gave me strength." For five nights the once-penniless immigrant preached to his people. Twenty-four accepted Christ. The reception awakened even larger dreams in Anthony Rossi.

The Tropicana Connection

In 1970, he invited Dr. Mario DiGangi to conduct a weeklong evangelistic mission in Messina. DiGangi was a well-known Bible expositor, former pastor of Tenth Presbyterian Church in Philadelphia, and fluent in Italian. He preached nightly at the fairgrounds to a consistent crowd of three hundred. In the wake of Vatican Council II,[742] a new openness to the evangelical message was in the air, and both DiGangi and Rossi were encouraged by the response. The Messina meetings brought a new challenge to the West Indies Mission. Sicily was the underbelly of Europe and it seemed that God was opening the door to an even wider ministry on the continent. Cuban missionary Emiliano Acosta had already gone to the Canary Islands, and Worldteam had eyed the potential of Caribbean immigrants in France,[743] but it took the Sicily campaign to nudge them into Europe.

When Rossi sponsored another Sicily crusade two years later, seventeen responded to the gospel. The Tropicana magnate was no longer standing alone against the darkness. He had found an ally in the West Indies Mission. Matt and Charlotte Garippa were the first WIM missionaries to enter Sicily's open door. Working with Bob and Janet Jones, they co-pastored *Chiesa Biblica Cristina*, a church strategically situated on the *Viale Europa* in Messina. David and Anne Calhoun, who transferred to Sicily after their first term at Jamaica Bible College, later joined the new team. John and Maureen Gilmore followed, then Albert and Janet Ehmann. God had another assignment in mind for Albert Ehmann, but that would come later.

The Urban Challenge

If Rossi's vision had opened Europe to the West Indies Mission, the timing could not have been better. It coincided perfectly with a shift in WIM's strategy, already in the works. In the spring of 1967, J. Allen Thompson was preparing to succeed his father as director of the West Indies Mission.[744] During a tour of Latin America, the magnitude of world-class cities arrested Thompson, as did the urgency of reaching them for Christ. He distilled his impressions in an editorial:

> After visiting the jungled plateaus of Suriname and flying over the endless Amazonian rain forest, I thought the huge cities of our neighboring countries made [the] waste hinterlands [of these countries] appear strongly out of character. I was . . . drawn to these population centers by an interesting paradox—the stupendous vitality of gigantic industries . . . [coexisting] with physical misery, economic inflation, political stagnation, and general continental unrest.

This challenge of the city was not new, as Thompson noted, citing God's concern for Ninevah with its 600,000 inhabitants. Jesus had wept over Jerusalem, and the Apostle Paul had chosen the major cities of Europe as strategic centers for evangelism. Thompson concluded, "Can we—dare we—chart a . . . strategy of evangelism without giving priority to the cities?" The question was rhetorical, but the answer was already echoing from the Messina experience. Anthony Rossi and Tropicana Products had infused the West Indies Mission with a fresh vision. If B. G. Lavastida was the national who had bridged a path into the Cuban soul, perhaps Sicilian Anthony Rossi would become Lavastida's counterpart in Italy. To the cities they would go.

WIM Writes a New Chapter

Fresh leadership, creative vision, and a new challenge to reach the cities were about to launch a new phase of WIM's venerable life. Expectation and excitement surged within the mission family. Forty years of WIM's history read like the book of Acts. Now they were about to write a new chapter. The secret of the Mission's growth had been a tried and true modus operandi. It was simple, but effective—reach nationals for Christ and teach them to evangelize. The Bible Institute was the tool.

However, by 1968, the predictable model that had assured WIM's success for forty years was passé. It was valid, but no longer adequate. Mission had changed. The world was shrinking. New demographic forces were at work. To survive effectively, missions had to discover ways of meeting the challenge of global mobility. Specifically, missions had fallen short of the Acts model, where the Holy Spirit had harnessed the bold and joyful witness of the entire community of believers to permeate society with the gospel message.

How could this be done within the West Indies Mission spheres of operation? How could local churches catch the vision of global evangelism in such a way as to become self-reproducing multipliers of missionary-sending churches? It was clear that a new kind of training was called for, and that meant a new kind of missionary, specially equipped for a new era. Achieving that goal would require reexamination of existing mission approaches and institutional efforts.

The Thompson Men

All three of Elmer and Evelyn Thompson's sons had grown up on the mission fields of the Caribbean. All three became missionaries—Leslie in Cuba, Allen also in Cuba and (after the revolution) in the Dominican Republic, and Paul in Spain. Theirs was the priceless heritage not only of being raised biculturally—speaking Spanish before they learned English—they had watched the birth and phenomenal growth of the national church in a variety of contexts. In their parents, they had the best of mentors. They understood the Latin mindset, relationships between nationals and expatriate missionaries, and the problems encountered in growing cross-cultural churches. Not always do the sons of leaders inherit the legacy of their parents' calling, gifting, and vision. The Thompson sons did, and would leave their own special legacy to World Team. All three displayed a passion for education, particularly in the training of nationals.

Leslie Thompson—together with other media professionals—would develop the communications arm of the West Indies Mission in publishing, before spinning off the literature work in 1968 as a separate corporate entity.

J. Allen Thompson was a developing missiologist who would take the fundamental principles of missionary work instilled by his father and lift them to a higher level of articulation and application in a changing world.

Paul Thompson's reflective nature and his strength as a motivator and theologian of biblical missionary practice traced a different path for him, one that lay outside of the traditional structure of mission administration. He and Allen would define and develop a theology of church planting and team dynamics that would become the operational model for the new World Team. Paul would develop into a respected church planting consultant both to Worldteam and other agencies.

Elmer Thompson had left a legacy of devotion and theology, but little on the theology of the church. It fell to the Thompson sons to develop and apply a biblical ecclesiology to the missionary scene, answering the questions, "What are the marks of a church?" And, "How are biblical churches planted?"

WIM's New Director

When Allen Thompson took the helm of the West Indies Mission in 1967, he stepped into the long shadow of his father. The decision was at first opposed by the senior Thompson, who was at pains to avoid any appearance of nepotism or establishment of a family dynasty. G. Allen Fleece, president of Columbia Bible College, saw the younger Thompson's gifting and persuaded the father to yield to the obvious consensus within the board. Yielding to that consensus posed an even greater struggle for Allen, who wrestled with his own sense of inadequacy—"How can I fill my father's shoes?" Once both men had come to terms with the decision as God's leading, Elmer and Evelyn Thompson accompanied Allen on a tour of WIM fields as they passed the mantle to the new leader.

Elmer Thompson's influence continued to permeate the life of the Mission. Within the board, among the missionaries, and throughout the wider circles of the Mission constituency, the aura of the patriarch's legacy was ever present. For Allen's leadership, that legacy was at once a credential and a cross. Winning respect as the new leader of a mission still peopled with venerable veterans, many of them his senior in years, was essential if the West Indies Mission was to exchange the past for an expectant future. To facilitate the transition, Elmer and Evelyn Thompson wisely removed themselves from the scene for five years, taking up residence in Jamaica, where Elmer taught in the Bible Institute. Upon their return, Allen called on his father to assume leadership of the Worldteam prayer ministry. Both men continued to enjoy a deep camaraderie, not so much as father and son—though that was present in full measure—but as coworkers in the West Indies Mission, the grand opus which God alone had orchestrated.

Change

J. Allen Thompson brought WIM to a new level of relevance in a world where all the rules had changed. He began by introducing several radical measures. The first was *strategic management*. Until 1967, the WIM Board had been comprised largely of field missionaries from within the mission family. Field directors enjoyed full autonomy within their regions, but the Mission lacked corporate direction and unified planning. Thompson wisely built trust by appointing seasoned and respected men as assistant directors. Both Walter Wunsch and Louis Markwood had distinguished service records on WIM fields. G. Allen Fleece was the widely known and trusted president of Columbia Bible College. As co-leaders the three brought stability to the transition.

Thompson surrounded himself with energetic and creative thinkers who were attracted to his groundbreaking leadership style. Together they conducted critical assessments of methods and programs that had been institutionalized by years of unquestioned practice. One of the first things to change was the care of WIM's most treasured resource—the missionaries themselves. They also were people with needs, hurts, and hang-ups. For the first time, the West Indies Mission began to nurture its personnel.

Anthony Rossi had earlier become an active and dedicated member of the Worldteam Board and began to contribute substantial sums to the Mission, designating these gifts for the operation of the US ministries department and for the funding of missionary projects, especially in Haiti. Rossi was utterly committed to world evangelization,[745] and his gifts resulted in new efforts, which would otherwise have been impossible. Everyone rejoiced in God's supply of the means to achieve their collective dreams.[746] Among the first changes to be implemented through Rossi's generosity was the mission magazine.[747]

Whitened Harvest, the newsletter published by WIM since 1940, became *Harvest Today.* The new format began to share the real-life problems faced by missionaries—adaptation to new cultures, marital struggles, burnout, MK conflicts, and dead prayer times. Traditional reports of field accomplishments were blended with updates on trends in missions and leadership styles. Think tank sessions addressed strategy. They also consumed time and energy and not everyone saw the changes as improvements. Some felt that the Mission had become too cerebral.

The second change Thompson introduced was in the *philosophy of missionary support.* Elmer Thompson had modeled WIM after Hudson Taylor's approach to finances. All Mission income had been pooled—an egalitarian ideal that generated both hardship and tensions for many. Under J. Allen Thompson, WIM moved to a personalized support structure. With one of Anthony Rossi's annual grants, $250,000 was used to set up a pension fund for missionaries.[748]

A third change was in *mission promotion.* Thompson had never been comfortable with the direct mail approach to fund raising. With the arrival of the annual Tropicana grants, the need for such fund-raising appeals was removed, and Worldteam turned to a different kind of interface with the Mission's partners. *Harvest* magazine was redeveloped to feed the constituency with information designed to provoke thinking and missiological awareness. "Value" ads in magazines like *Christianity Today* dealt with issues in contemporary missions, such as teamwork. These approaches were made possible through Anthony Rossi's largess. Thompson also began to develop the idea of a *strategy for church planting,* another area calling for change. Out of this would come the WIN Institute in 1986, with its focus on the selection and training of church planters and the redirection of Worldteam's thrust as an agency specialized in promoting church planting *movements.*

In structure, WIM was moving from the simple to the complex. It began to track people groups and to explore new methods of reaching the unconverted.

The traditional modus operandi—the Bible institute—would no longer predominate, even in those fields where such institutions already existed. To reach more pastors and lay people, theological extension programs (TEE) would be introduced at the local church level—where the people were. Local churches were composed of lay persons who could be and must be marshaled into an evangelistic force. But the first step was to put Bible education on the lower shelf, making it accessible to all. Closely tied to these developments were impending changes in *church/mission relationships* which would recognize the maturity and sovereignty of the national churches, nudging them out of paternalistic dependence upon the Mission to assume their biblical role as self-supporting centers of global missionary witness. It would be a salutary transition—but not without pain for both.

God had clearly brought J. Allen Thompson to the kingdom for such a time as this. Likewise, Anthony Rossi's stewardship of wealth had provided the fuel essential to strategic change. Notwithstanding, the new munificence was not without its dangers and would prove to be a mixed blessing for Worldteam.

59

Secret Weapon

Missionaries are not to consider themselves individually or corporately as central or enduring, when compared with the local Christians and churches that have resulted from their ministry. In the final analysis, national Christians, and local congregations, by their permanence of existence and possibilities of continuous outreach, are God's tools for preaching the gospel to every creature.

—Arthur Glasser

Measuring Success

On the threshold of WIM's fifth decade, Director Allen Thompson reminded the family that successful mission is not measured solely in quantitative terms. Not that these were lacking. In 1968 WIM had good reason to indulge in a God-honoring triumphalism of sorts, as Thompson reported in an editorial:

> In 40 years of missionary work . . . progress can be reported in precise arithmetic—three hundred churches scattered through the Caribbean and South America, five hundred graduates from six Bible schools, 220 missionaries serving in 8 fields . . .

Nevertheless, Thompson challenged, "We are anxious to measure our success in terms of Servanthood." Quoting a European Christian, he elaborated:

> Most New Testament letters to younger churches contain neither exhortation to organize evangelism campaigns nor methods of increasing members. These letters are prefaces to martyrdom, and mission is not concerned with statistics, but with sacrifice.

The term *servanthood* appeared with increasing frequency in mission articles. So did *synergy*, which the dictionary defines as "the interaction of two or more forces so that their combined effect is greater than the sum of their individual effects." Closely related to both was *teamwork.* All three were becoming missiological buzzwords in WIM's vocabulary. And all three were threads of the same cloth. Paul Thompson developed the theological basis of teamwork in an article entitled, *"Synergism—a New Word and a New Way for Missions."*[749]

Biblical Roots of Teamwork

The brief defined the biblical roots of teamwork, beginning with the Genesis pronouncement, *"It is not good that man should be alone."* Jesus had amplified the concept when he said, *"Where two or three are gathered together in my name, there am I in the midst."*[750] The Trinity further reinforces this principle of efficient unity in plurality, as does the marriage of a man and a woman. Thompson then demonstrated that teamwork was clearly present in our Lord's training of the twelve. Jesus coached them, not so much one-on-one, but as a group. Interdependent and complementary in their temperaments and gifting, their corporate expression was greater than the sum of its parts. The apostolic example likewise underscored the importance of teamwork, for the Apostle Paul never chose to work alone, and "every single missionary initiative conducted by the church was a team effort."

The application for Worldteam was clear—teams made up of competent, compatible, servant-minded missionaries are the only logical response to the biblical norm. The article defined the difficulties often faced by western missionaries in a second culture:

> Take a missionary and put him in a foreign city with a strange culture and an even stranger language. Give him a job description that includes planting a church that [must] extend itself over the whole city in a mighty wave of vigorous evangelism. The missionary works tirelessly, fighting a thousand cultural devils each time he sets out to accomplish anything, facing his ugly foreign accent every time he opens his mouth.
>
> Soon he finds that the first converts for whom he so earnestly prayed took the "step of faith" in order to get an easy visa to New York. The young man he was discipling to become pastor turns out to be a polygamist, while the girl his wife was so excited about is pregnant by an unidentified father. The city traffic, the smog and noise pollution is beyond anything he can describe in the monthly newsletter.
>
> Soon at the end of his tether, the missionary either returns home in disillusionment or retreats from the crucial task of evangelism and church planting or settles down in some form of missionary institutionalism.

Thompson went on to make his point, defining the new paradigm shift that Worldteam was about to make:

Take the same missionary and place him with a *team* of competent fellow workers [preferably including nationals and foreigners to form an international, bicultural team]. Then inspire that team with solid church planting goals, back it with prayer and financial support, and you have the makings of a dynamic, positive witness in any culture.

Integrating competent nationals and westerners into a focused church planting task force so that their combined effect is greater than the sum of their individual effects. This was WIM's new paradigm—body life at its biblical best.

Body Life: One Man's Journey

Teamwork and synergy became practical realities to Paul Thompson in Spain. Before that could happen, the third of Elmer Thompson's three sons had to come to grips with his own deficiencies. While engaged in a house-to-house visitation campaign in western Canada, Paul found himself preferring to stand on a windy corner for hours rather than confront total strangers with a gospel tract. While in seminary, a small Spanish-American church nearly expelled him for his inability to evangelize. In his second pastorate, the deacons grilled him one night about his apparent inadequacy as an evangelist. He sat silent, unable to give them an answer.

This is Not for Me

While surveying Spain in 1971—the following year Spain would become WIM's second field in Europe—Paul Thompson imagined doors being slammed in his face as he tried to share Christ. He found himself muttering Peter's ultimate contradiction, *"Not so, Lord."*[751] This is not for me. The question haunted him—If a missionary does not have the gift of evangelist, what use is he?

Paul Thompson's venture into the Iberian Peninsula had been no capricious impulse. It was the outcome of a promise he had made twenty years earlier. Max Inglis explains:

When Frank Butler died in 1952—the leader of WIM's Dominican Republic field—a young man who had always held Butler as his hero was at the funeral. That day, Paul Thompson vowed to the Lord that he would someday take Butler's place. What he did not realize was that Butler's deep desire had been to someday open a work in Spain.

After successful pastorates in Mexico City and Phoenix, Thompson was reading the Mission magazine one day and discovered for the first time Butler's keen interest in Spain. His course was set.

In 1972, Paul Thompson and his young bride set out for the land of the Moors and flamenco. Notwithstanding, his success in the pastorate and God's clear call to Spain had not prepared him for the discomfort he felt when faced with door-to-door evangelism. Breaking new ground as an evangelist was not his gift. However, God was in the crisis, and Thompson's dilemma was about to end in a fresh and liberating discovery.

The Dynamic of Body Life

God is the Author of diversity. The body of Christ was never intended to function as a multiplicity of identical clones. The gifting is diverse so that by the mutual interdependence of one upon the other, the many may glorify God and so fulfill the purpose of the Head, who is Christ. Thompson explained the revelation that had gripped him so dramatically:

> God's plan is that we work *together* to achieve what we cannot do alone . . . God has chosen to work principally through a body, a group of persons bound together by love to Christ and committed to one another. As that body properly functions, the Holy Spirit expresses the divine life of Christ through a dynamic instrument. The body becomes greater than the individuals who comprise it. Missionaries working as a body perform with a strength that they could never achieve in isolation.

> Like so many things God does, the Spain team *happened* to us. It was neither preplanned nor were its members handpicked. It *emerged*. God *planned* the team. God *selected* its members. We were left only to observe and reflect upon what He was doing.

> Within two years the Lord brought together a core of fellow-strugglers from six nationalities and began the process of welding us into a body solidly united. Our desire was first to *be* the church. We felt that the church must be incarnated in our experience if we were to plant it successfully.

> We determined so to live as a group that our lives would demonstrate the values of the kingdom of God. To this end we drew up a covenant centered around commitment to one another, accountability especially in areas of our lives where we were weak and needed support, all resting upon openness, honesty and trust.

> From this vantagepoint of togetherness and support, we began working toward the accomplishment of our evangelistic goals.

If Paul Thompson felt handicapped as an evangelist, he was now discovering that God had bestowed upon him a different gift—the ability to motivate others. He wrote:

> My role is to ignite the team and keep it fired into action. The team gave me confidence and the assurance I needed to work where I belong.

WIM Takes a New Name

While WIM leadership had demonstrated team dynamics over four decades, it took a second generation of leaders to define the formula for developing effective team relationships. With the process articulated and in place, it remained to find a new name for the Mission—one that would reflect both the new working dynamic and the wider horizons implicit in the Mission's entry into Europe. In January 1978, after two years of reflection, they chose the name, *Worldteam.* However, it would take more than a new name to make a team.

Tensions in Sicily

While the Spain team tested its new synergism, the work in Sicily was experiencing unique struggles. The Messina church—*Chiesa Biblica Cristiana*—had grown numerically through the annual crusades, but discipleship training failed to keep abreast. Under Matt Garippa, pastoral leadership emphasized outreach, but lacked focus on leadership development. In an effort to accelerate training and local ownership of the vision, two men were selected and inducted as deacons. The move proved premature. Conferring leadership responsibilities upon immature Christians produced tensions, particularly since one of the deacons was a distant relative of Rossi. Attempting to arbitrate the disputes, Rossi called in his brother, who was not a part of the church. Because of these defective patterns, effective team dynamics failed to materialize in Sicily.

Working amid these difficulties, Albert Ehmann discovered the power of radio. Messina had a poorly run station on which he purchased airtime. Contacts through the radio broadcasts soon proved more productive than those made through the Messina church.

In just two years, Catania—a large city south of Messina— saw conversions through the broadcasts sufficient to start a church. However, considerable turnover of missionary personnel and the instability of the Sicily team crippled growth potential.

Lessons Learned

The early debacle in Sicily forced Worldteam to address issues yet unresolved. The concept of teamwork had not been fully grasped by all. Some team members lacked church planting experience. The intensity of the spiritual conflict disabled the immature, and field leadership was not equipped to cope. The need for prior screening of church planting candidates became clear. Spiritual maturity, emotional stability, and practical skills were now recognized to be essential markers in the recruitment process—qualities that must be identified in would-be church planters *before* they arrived on the field. Since effective teamwork could not be expected to happen spontaneously, the

Mission began to expound the principles of team relationships as part of the pre-field orientation process.

Sound Advice

Philip Armstrong, executive secretary of Far Eastern Gospel Crusade, had become a close advisor of Director Allen Thompson. A respected thinker, Armstrong in 1969 indicated three dangers within growing mission structures:

1. The loss of men to the organization who are effective in ministry.
2. The loss of mobility, when the mission becomes a thing instead of an act.
3. Missionaries assuming roles that make them extra rather than intra-church agents.

Armstrong called on Worldteam to "test every ministry" in terms of its service to the church. The product of effective evangelism must be healthy churches. Workers within the churches must be trained to assist the church to define its structure. Danger is present—Armstrong noted—when a mission removes itself from mainstream evangelism and devotes its energies to technical ministries such as radio, literature, and medicine. Similar pitfalls snare national churches when excessive emphasis is placed on organization, staff, and buildings.

Worldteam took Armstrong seriously and began to reexamine its focus. With radio ministries on nearly every field, hospital work in Haiti, and missionaries in a pastoral role in several countries, concern was justified. Thompson already sensed God's redirection from rural areas to urban centers. Worldteam's future must lie with the masses in the world's megacities. Converts in the cities could then focus on the less populated zones within their countries. While this thinking was valid and timely, it called for qualifiers.[752]

Cloud on the Horizon

Forty years of WIM's ministry had birthed the Church in eleven fields. Centers of intercessory prayer and financial partnership had multiplied, nourished through systematic contact from the Mission. By 1973, Worldteam's *Harvest* magazine enjoyed a circulation of 28,500. Newsletters approached 20,000. Partnership gifts were running 2,000 every month, while *Interaction*—another publication—served a select list of five hundred.

Anthony Rossi was now on the Worldteam Board, and through his giving, the Mission was able to expand its ministry in North America. Leadership developed a series of promotional audio-visuals and redesigned the magazine, *Harvest Today.* Directed by Bobby Clinton, the *Learning Resource Center* produced self-study materials to enhance church planting initiatives. These enjoyed increasing circulation among mission enthusiasts. Ads in *Christianity*

Today and *Moody Monthly* enunciated Worldteam values. Accommodating this ministry growth was a commensurate enlargement of the Mission's American staff.[753] Think tanks and strategic planning sessions probed new ministry options. All seemed well. However, trouble was brewing. Anthony Rossi, who had done such great good for Worldteam, became increasingly manipulative.[754] This would lead to Allen Thompson's unexpected resignation and the cessation of large grants to the Mission.

60

When the Brook Dried Up

Money matters may be, must be, a means of grace to those whose only banker is their heavenly Father.

—Fanny Guinness

Tensions

The crisis came early in January 1982 when Allen Thompson received a telephone call from Lloyd Fesmire. Fesmire was a member of Worldteam's board and Anthony Rossi's pastor.[755]

"Allen, you need to come to Bradenton. We've got a crisis on our hands."

"What's up, Lloyd?" Thompson replied.

"I can't tell you now. Come up and we'll talk."

Thompson was in Coral Gables at the Worldteam office. Packing hurriedly, he jumped in his car and was off to Bradenton, on Florida's gulf coast. Niagara-like, his thoughts cascaded as he sped north on highway 41—the early days of God's blessing in Messina—the many trips to Bradenton to explain Mission policy and strategy to Anthony Rossi—the unbending nature of the Sicilian benefactor once he had fixed upon an idea. What could it be this time? How would God intervene?

In Bradenton, Fesmire went straight to the point:

"Mr. Rossi wants to see you with an urgent demand."

"What's it about, Lloyd?" Thompson pressed.

"He wants you to make an adjustment in the executive personnel of the Mission."

Thompson and Fesmire drove across town to Rossi's home, where they were warmly welcomed. After the usual pleasantries, Rossi clarified his position:

"Mr. Thompson, you have a leader in your midst that is not trustworthy—the overseas director. I cannot continue participating in the Mission unless you fire him."[756]

"Mr. Rossi, what has he done to merit this treatment?" Thompson queried. "Why have you lost confidence in him? I can deal with evidence, but not with personal wishes."

Thompson's insistence on a rationale for the judgment led to extended discussion, but Rossi remained unyielding: the leader must go. Thompson could not agree to what he viewed as an unwarranted demand. The two men reached an impasse.

Allen Thompson returned to Miami with a heavy heart. For more than a decade he had dealt firmly and repeatedly with Anthony Rossi on many mission matters. The stress of these constant exchanges had worn him to a point where his health was now at stake. Compounding the pressure was the fact that the Worldteam Board was unaware of these tensions. Until this latest exchange, Thompson had been successful in bringing Rossi to reconciliation with mission policy and standards. Now with Worldteam facing severe financial need, and a long-standing relationship under strain, would Thompson surrender to Rossi's wishes for the sake of future revenue?

Resignation

Desperately needing time to pray and think things through, Allen and Marilyn Thompson retreated to the country home of a friend in New Hampshire. As they prayed, pondered Scripture, and sought the Lord for guidance, it became clear that there was no justifiable reason to accede to Anthony Rossi's demand. For Allen Thompson, this conviction left him with but a single course of action—to resign as general director. The decision was wrenching, compounding the stress he had already experienced in previous altercations with Rossi. With twenty-six years of service to Worldteam, Thompson wrestled with his sense of duty. He knew that his proposed action would be a letdown to nationals and missionaries alike, not least to the father who was counting on his continued leadership. The supporting public, innocent of the background, would find it hard to understand. In the absence of clear transition plans, Worldteam would certainly lose momentum. Nevertheless, having carefully weighed the consequences, the Thompsons knew they had but one option—resignation.

Shortly after returning to Miami, in a meeting of the executive committee, Allen Thompson submitted his resignation as general director of World-team.[757] Once the news broke, the entire Mission felt the pain, though most knew nothing of the underlying circumstances. The May 1982 issue of *Worldteam Today* editorialized:

> Shock is the word that best described the reaction of Worldteam's family when J. Allen Thompson recently announced his resignation as president. Mr. Thompson, who gave 15 years of effective and creative leadership in this post, explained his deep desire to get back into a direct ministry of the Word and the developing of leadership for the church.

Patrick Arnold Appointed

Expressions of affirmation, love, and appreciation for Thompson's years of leadership flowed freely from many within and outside the mission family. Responding to the resignation, the board of directors appointed Patrick Arnold as interim president. Though other leaders around Thompson aspired to the leadership position, Arnold had been with the Mission since 1943 and knew it as well as any. Maintaining trust throughout the crisis was now the primary concern. Elmer Thompson agreed to continue serving as chairman of the board.

Uncertainty followed Allen Thompson's resignation. Within a year, Anthony Rossi was no longer on the board, having left at the end of his normal term. He did not return. Patrick Arnold and Dean Franklin shouldered leadership responsibilities. Harold Alexander resigned, as did Bobby Clinton, who departed for doctoral studies at Fuller Theological Seminary. Don Bjork—director of North American Ministries—had terminated prior to Allen Thompson's departure. This abrupt leadership vacuum sent tremors through the headquarters staff and the entire mission family. Some felt deserted and faced the more subjective question: How will this affect my ministry? There were few answers.

Damage Control

Allen Thompson had foreseen the financial crisis and its effect upon the headquarters and North American staff. Mission partners continued to faithfully support missionaries and their related overseas ministries, and overseas operations had not become unduly dependent upon Anthony Rossi's annual contribution (which amounted to twelve to fifteen percent of the total World-team budget). However, Aurora money had become the lifeline of the North American headquarters' staff. Since Headquarters staff was not required to raise their support through pledges, fully twenty-five percent of the North American budget depended on Anthony Rossi's contributions. The remaining budget came from the ten percent administration fee levied upon all mission income, plus all undesignated contributions.

In 1980, Thompson had requested Donald Bjork, North America ministries director, to present a plan of operation that would reflect less dependence upon the Aurora Foundation. In his report to the Worldteam Board, Bjork made an honest appraisal:

> We are now facing an era that will require not only the highest dedication, but the soundest management as well. Worldteam is not facing an immediate financial crisis, but could well find itself in such a situation a year or so down the road.

Bjork knew that the North American department would suffer severely if Rossi's monthly contributions stopped. He also knew that Tropicana stock was earmarked by the board primarily for overseas projects and not for North America operations. He continued:

> This means that a quarter to a third of the Mission's [North American] funding base [must] be replenished from new grants and/or from other sources [or] we'll have to cut back severely.

But no other grants or sources were in sight. This was due primarily to the Mission's strict policy against direct solicitation of gifts. From its early history, the West Indies Mission had walked by the faith principle. Allen Thompson continued to apply his father's conviction that needs could be made known, but without request for donations. But in 1988, Worldteam softened its fund-raising policy to read:

> It shall be the policy of Worldteam to prayerfully depend on God for all the needs of Worldteam efforts. In our fundraising, (1) We will accurately share the vision, the victories, the challenge, and the magnitude of the task; (2) We will make known the needs so that God's people can intelligently pray with us for God's provision, and, (3) We will invite God's people to prayerfully consider sharing financially as the Lord leads and enables them. Solicitation shall stop short of asking for or suggesting that donors consider giving a specific amount.

Even with a strict nonsolicitation policy, however, very little work was done during the ten years of Anthony Rossi's largess to establish a solid funding base for North American operations. Don Bjork presented a roster of remedial measures, which focused primarily on strengthening the department charged with resource development:

1. Develop a corps of dedicated representatives.

2. Use computers to track income against expenses.

3. Cultivate friends of the Mission that may lead to new support.

4. Develop and implement an ongoing deferred giving program.

But time was running out. Austerity measures spawned fresh tensions throughout the Mission. Few felt the strain as keenly as the headquarters leadership group. The sense of harmonic purpose began to erode. The supporting public likewise sensed that all was not well. The last issue of Worldteam's historic magazine, *Harvest Today,* was dated Winter, 1981.

Old-timers at Worldteam's Sixtieth Anniversary, 1988.
Left to right: Louis Markwood, Delma Jackson, Fefita and Bartholomew Lavastida, Evelyn and Elmer Thompson, Muriel Hansen.

61

Into Europe

Remember that your parish is not your field. The field is the world. Your parish contains a force committed to you by God to train for him that he may reach the field, which is the world.

—A. T. Pierson

Anthony Rossi's evangelistic campaigns in Sicily opened the door to Europe. Paul Thompson's assignment to Spain followed. However, Worldteam would learn that secular, materialistic Europe would not yield the ready successes the Mission had known in the Caribbean. Notwithstanding, while tensions and turmoil followed the loss of the Tropicana legacy, the newly imposed hardships failed to hinder Worldteam from launching new efforts in Europe—first, Italy, then Spain, France, and England.

Italy, Spain, and France

Italy had become a post-Christian nation plagued by a history of unstable governments. Once the hub of the Roman Empire and seat of the long-powerful Roman Catholic Church, by late in the twentieth century, Roman Catholicism ceased to be the state religion, and the R. C. Church had lost nine million members, together with much of its influence. In a land of fifty-seven million inhabitants, fewer than 2,000 towns had an established evangelical church and 30,000 were without gospel witness. Occultism became widespread, with more consulting magicians in Italy than Catholic priests. While church planting proved difficult, churches were established, particularly in the cities of Catania and Siracusa, Sicily, largely due to the Messina-based radio ministry.

Once fixed in the cross hairs of the Apostle Paul's missionary vision, Spain had been guardian of the Mediterranean gateway to the Roman Empire. For seven centuries, the Iberian Peninsula was dominated by Islamic influence.

Spain not only launched the Age of Discovery and the Inquisition, but also left her indelible mark upon the Western Hemisphere in language, culture, and religion in the form of Roman Catholicism.

In the final century of the second millennium, civil war, dictatorships, religious intolerance, and economic instability marked Spanish history. While constitutional guarantees of religious equality were later established, the Spanish people in 1999 remained secularized and disillusioned with the church.

Worldteam entered Spain in 1972. Fifteen million of her forty million people lived in towns or districts without an evangelical church. Muslim influence remained strong, and Madrid could boast Europe's largest mosque. Sixteen years later, Paul Thompson could report a growing momentum with three strong cluster churches established, and three church planting teams "working together in harmony."[758] But even with this progress, Spain remained a Roman Catholic land, and the Christ of the crucifix was powerless to change the Iberian heart. Luis Palau would later refer to Spain as "possibly the most difficult field in the free world." The long-awaited gospel harvest lingered.

The Mission next turned to France, renowned for its culture and sophistication. France had never recovered from the Inquisition and the expulsion of the Huguenots. At the height of the Reformation, forty-eight percent of the population was Protestant; by 1999 it had shrunk to a mere two percent. Forty-three million of her fifty-seven million inhabitants had no vital link with a Christian church. Noted historian Stephen Neil in 1964 pointed to Europe's drift from spiritual values:

> We seem to be watching a steady diminution of the spiritual capital of Europe, the disappearance of the old European synthesis of religion and culture, and a desiccation of the human spirit, as a result of which men not merely are not religious, but can see no reason why they should concern themselves with anything beyond the world of senses.[759]

The Diaspora

This was the soul-numbing reality of missionary work in modern Europe, as any missionary who has worked there knows. However, in the wake of World War II, relaxed immigration laws prompted an unprecedented wave of ethnic migration to the homelands of former colonial powers, including France. Growing migrant communities of Turks, Iranians, Afghans, and other minorities flooded Europe. France soon had more Arabic-speaking immigrants than any other country, playing host to a steady stream of Muslims from her former colonies in Morocco, Tunisia, and Algeria. Thousands of French-speaking immigrants from the West Indies settled in greater metropolitan Paris. Many of these migrants, without church affiliation, came to Christ in

Guadeloupe, a Worldteam field. This diaspora opened a new window of opportunity to missions in Europe.

Worldteam's interest in France began to stir as the evangelical Church in Guadeloupe awakened to the hemorrhage of émigrés now thinning its ranks. Antillian youth were pouring into France in search of jobs. Many mission agencies were discovering that the phenomenon of global ethnic migration was no sociological accident, but a diaspora divinely engineered to accelerate worldwide evangelism. Transplanted ethnic enclaves, especially in urban centers, were emotionally receptive to the new culture and largely free from the paralyzed mindsets and cultural restraints of their homeland.

In the case of evangelical youth from Guadeloupe, the call was not so much a matter of evangelistic opportunity as it was one of concern. France was a materialistic, secular culture, and its people devoid of life-sustaining commitment to biblical truth. How would young Christian immigrants from Guadeloupe fare in the spiritual chill of this environment? Did they possess the inner strength to resist the overpowering influences of secularism? Were there any churches in France to provide the nurture they needed? The evangelical Church in Guadeloupe was concerned for the spiritual welfare of their expatriated, upwardly mobile youth. And with good reason. Reports coming back to the islands suggested that some had cooled in their walk with the Lord. Others had fallen away.

There was another facet to this concern. Most Antillians were black, reflecting their ancestral African origins. How would blacks from Guadeloupe be received by white French Parisians? Had some sought spiritual shelter in local congregations, only to feel the sting of racial ostracism once inside? Could such prejudice have driven sensitive immigrant Christians to jettison their faith?

A Call for Help

These questions exercised Worldteam and prompted investigation. Spurred by a French missionary couple on the island, church leaders in Guadeloupe requested a survey. They selected Harold Alexander, the last expatriate missionary president of the Association of Churches in Guadeloupe before its nationalization. Alexander visited France and conferred with church leaders. The result was a formal request to both Worldteam and the Guadeloupe Church Association to send missionaries to France to minister to the expatriate Antillian population. Antoine Poulain, the new association president, received the same inquiry.

Steve and Ann Miller were the logical choice to spearhead the effort. As missionaries in Guadeloupe, they knew the language, the culture, and the issues faced by the émigrés. In 1978, together with schoolteacher Eliezer Helmet, they prepared to relocate to France by the end of the following year 1979.

Within three years, Worldteam established two churches on the outskirts of Paris. In Noisy-le-Grand, a congregation of forty-five West Indian immigrants was developing. Another team in Cergy Pontoise began a work in association with a French church, training men for leadership. Twenty-one thousand Muslims in the *St. Denis* region were also targeted. By 1998, World Team had sixteen workers in France.

Bridging the Moat

Despite early successes, France—like Spain—loomed as an impenetrable fortress, shut off from the life of God by centuries of secularistic, superficial Christianity. England would present the same challenge in 1986, when Worldteam made a similar effort to reach a large Asian subculture in London. Traditional evangelistic approaches were not working. The challenge was to find new ways of bridging this encircling ring of indifference.

In Spain, basketball clinics and soccer were introduced as door openers for friendship evangelism. In France, missionaries coached American football and Little League teams to make contacts with parents and children.

London

Paul and Lorraine Abeyta came to Worldteam in 1984 with a keen interest in Brazil, but a summer spent among Afghan immigrants in New York City awakened them to the need of Muslims. Islamic studies confirmed the call. When asked to spearhead Worldteam's first pioneer church planting effort among the Muslims and Hindus of Southhall, England, they knew this was God's path for them. The Southhall project became a team effort in 1988 when Haiti veterans, Ralph and Shirley Walbridge, reinforced the Abeytas. The Walbridges opened their home to neighborhood children, many of them Sikhs. London had two million Asian immigrants, most of them Muslims. Abeyta described the open door:

> We're seeing a crack in the Koranic curtain. There is great upheaval in the Asian families here. For the first time young adults are resisting their parents and making their own decisions. This upheaval is making people receptive to the gospel.

The Abeytas applied "creative evangelism," which they defined as "entering a situation, assessing the needs, and devising a strategy to meet those needs."[760] They hosted an open house during the Christmas season. They became active in community centers, distributing clothing, and food in France. They helped Asians with language study. Whatever might be done to break down barriers, establish friendships, remove prejudices, or otherwise garb the gospel with winsome appeal—all means were courageously tried, and covered with prayer. Notwithstanding, progress remained at a crawl. Here and there, small beachheads were made, but much land remained to be possessed. It was a hard lesson for a mission that had witnessed breathtaking movements of the Holy Spirit in the islands of the Caribbean. The sharp—and disappointing—contrast raised serious questions.

Perennial Question

How long should missionaries work a field without visible results? When is it right or wise to pack it up and move on? The question was not new to British workers in India with RBMU, who for decades faced similar sterility among the Hindus of North Bihar. The people-group movement thesis of respected missiologist, Dr. Donald McGavran, enjoyed both novelty and popularity in the 1960s and 1970s. People come to Christ by groups (communities)—McGavran maintained—when the gospel is presented in a manner that poses fewest cultural hurdles for the receptor group.

But there was a corollary to which the best missiology must yield—the fact that *the wind blows where it pleases.* The questing Spirit remains the sovereign Architect of harvest. He alone defines the times and seasons when groups respond to the message, so the axiom is clear: Look for groups and cultures where God appears to be already moving.

For all the theoretical approaches, Worldteam missionaries in Europe still wrestled with fundamental questions: Are we doing it right? Are we moving too fast? Too slow? Do the people like me? Can we really pull this off? What will our support partners think if we have not been successful in planting a church within this first term?" In a letter home, one of them bared his soul:

> These and many other questions have haunted us and kept us awake at night. A sense of desperation has sometimes made us think of breaking [out of] the pack to attempt some daring things . . . However, we have resisted our doubts and fears and have held steady to our course . . .We are beginning to see cracks in the indifference of many.

Not all were equipped to stand the strain of unrequited toil. Some went home.

62

Redefining Mission

*The mule church works hard, is faithful, pulls a great load,
and seems to be doing fine, but it is sterile. Over 90% of all
churches founded today are mules. The donkey church is the
same as the mule with one difference. It reproduces.*

—Paul Thompson

A Weakened Mission

The departure of Allen Thompson was devastating. Few understood the reasons for his decision, nor could he share them publicly without compromising others.[761] The grant fund established with the proceeds of Tropicana stock was steadily decreasing. Long-range planning gave way to the more urgent concern of surviving on a drastically reduced budget. The volume of material flowing from Worldteam presses slowed to a trickle. Busy with new ministry frontiers and with no concern for means, Worldteam had failed to develop the fresh corps of praying and giving partners essential to the success of new initiatives. While churches and individual supporters developed over four decades remained faithful, many were now aging and unable to continue their original involvement. Replacement of an aging generation of givers was not pursued. The departure of leaders important to the Mission caused some supporters to question the viability of Worldteam, and they turned elsewhere for participation.

Throughout the pain, Patrick Arnold took the helm, his hand providing the stability so desperately needed throughout the crisis. With two years before retirement, Arnold knew the principles that had brought the Mission to its well-deserved place in the sun. He would preside over a catharsis that thrust the agency into the sharply defined ministry philosophy that marks it today. There was a lot to do.

Arnold rehearsed the development of God's pattern in the West Indies Mission which had brought national leaders to the forefront on every field—men such as Norberto Quesade, president of the churches in Cuba. Brezil St. Germaine, overseer of 270 churches in Haiti, and Guadeloupe's Eliezer Helmet, who had gone to France as a missionary to his own people. WIM had enjoyed an impressive achievement in global missions, and beleaguered Worldteamers could take heart. "As we have seen God work in [the past], so we anticipate his continued working," Arnold reassured the faithful. " We have made mistakes. There have been problems. Satan has sought to bring in division and defeat. However, in God's mercy and grace a large body of national fellow servants has emerged."

Recovering the Apostolic Function

While Arnold wrestled with mission finances, projects, and the care of personnel, Paul Thompson struggled with missiological concepts. "Mission" and "church planting" were familiar terms, but what did they really mean? Could they be defined in terms of New Testament practice? What were the biblical 2 models and how might they be applied in Worldteam's contemporary ministry?

In 1984 Thompson had conducted a ministry values workshop which he called, *Lord, Plant Your Church!—The Apostolic Function Today.* Drawing heavily from sources such as Robert Brow, Arthur Glasser, Ray Stedman, Alan Tippett, and South American church leader Juan Carlos Ortiz, Thompson zeroed in on their use of the word "apostolic."

"The apostolic function is the most neglected and yet most necessary gift for the worldwide Church," wrote Brow.

"The apostolic function must be recovered today. We have too many Timothy's tied to local churches, just blessing the saints." said Glasser.

"It is part of the apostolic gift to start new churches," affirmed Stedman.

"The word apostle is not confined to the twelve," added Tippett.

"We need the apostolic ministry in the Church today . . .leaders who can draw up God's blueprints and equip believers to put the building together," asserted Ortiz.

As Thompson examined the apostolic function and compared it with that of the evangelist and that of pastor, a thesis began to emerge. There was a difference between *form*—the *way* something is done, and *function*—the essence of the thing itself.

If the twelve Apostles were unique in terms of *form* [They had seen the Christ], and that *form* ceased upon their death, then apostolic *function* [the ministry they exercised] was still available to the church today. Martin Luther had obviously confused form and function when he affirmed that the Great Commission had been given to the apostles only. Thompson noted that:

This apostolic function must be recaptured if we are to plant and multiply churches in the yet unreached areas of the world.

Since a large number of evangelical teachers hold that the apostolic role [i.e., the function] has ceased for today, it is clear that the concept has not been properly understood or defined, and therefore, most contemporary church planters fail to differentiate between the apostolic and the pastoral roles. For this reason, most church planters do not function apostolically, but pastorally.

Thompson elaborated the distinction:

We believe the New Testament distinguishes between structured local congregations (churches) and the structured apostolic band called by God to evangelize the heathen and plant new churches. Whereas the apostles were of the Church, their corporate ministry of missionary outreach necessitated among themselves patterns of leadership and organization, recruitment and finance, training and discipline, distinct from comparable patterns within local congregations. This significant distinction gives biblical sanction to today's structured missionary fellowship.

Confusing these distinctive roles has seriously handicapped effective church planting efforts and is the root of many tensions between the mission agency and the national church. Blurring this critical distinction often deprives us of a truly biblical basis for decision-making in church planting strategy, in personnel recruitment, and in training.

Worldteam's Three Phases

Thompson saw Worldteam's fifty-year history falling neatly into three phases: *Institutional, Pastoral,* and *Apostolic.* The West Indies Mission had begun with a primary emphasis on evangelism and the training of nationals through resident Bible schools. For years, the WIM banner had been, "For the training of a national gospel ministry," and the engine of that training had been the Bible institute. This phase—which Thompson viewed as the most fruitful era of WIM's history—was *institutional* in form, but *apostolic* in function.

The second phase was *pastoral.* On Worldteam's newer fields, the focus was on church planting. On older fields, Bible institutes [*institutional*] were closing, being replaced by Theological Education by Extension programs.

The third phase grew out of the question; "Just what is it we are planting?" In search for the answer, mission leadership became absorbed with the *nature* of the church. Allen Thompson developed a course, *"Lord, Make Us Your Church."* These exercises gave rise to the aphorism, "We must be the Church before we can plant it." Gradually, the emphasis of Worldteam's ministry began to shift to the *development* of existing churches.

Thompson's musings were not mere semantic exercises. A philosophy of mission and ministry was taking shape, which would permanently affect the way Worldteam did mission. This philosophy would become the groundwork for a new approach to the orientation of missionary candidates.

The Challenge

Pointing to Brazil, Sicily, Spain, and France as Worldteam church planting fields, Thompson posed a series of questions.

1. What has been our record of accomplishment on these fields?
2. Are we planting churches?
3. How many?
4. More importantly, are we training leaders in our churches?
5. How many churches can we point to on these new fields that are functioning under local national leadership that we ourselves have trained?
6. It would be interesting to put a dollar value on the churches we have planted. How much has it cost us to plant a church? How much time has it taken us?

Convinced that God had used WIM's *pastoral* phase as a precursor to the apostolic, Paul Thompson challenged Worldteam to redefine its mission:

> Barnabas and Saul were pastors (Acts 13). They were involved in the ministry of a local church before God pushed them into apostolic ministry. In my own case, I spent six years as a pastor before God began the upheaval that was to thrust me into church planting. As an organization, Worldteam has also passed through its *pastoral* phase. Now we know what it is that we are to plant. So, let us plant it. However, there is a right and a wrong way to go about that. We will bog down as church planters unless we recognize the apostolic calling and clearly define it.

What Is a Team?

Paul Thompson's drive to shift Worldteam into the apostolic mode posed a further question: What constitutes a team?

For him, the issue had been resolved in Spain, where missionaries had learned the meaning of *synergism*—people with differing gifts working together in organic harmony, just like the human body. As Thompson addressed the need for the Mission to adopt this pattern of apostolic church planting, he again defined the biblical concept of a team:

> The Apostle Paul's conversion, training, and call took place *after* Pentecost, clearly identifying him wholly with the Church age. He and his fellow workers were the vanguard—the prototype—of the apostolic function at its best. Paul's team was international and multicultural. The Jews in that early band were all born in Gentile lands, except John Mark. All spoke Greek. Paul himself was a Roman citizen. They were sent out from Antioch, the congregation in which God's purposes for this age first came to full fruition.

Looking at the well-known list of gifts in Ephesians 4, Thompson rejected the notion that it is merely a list of Spirit-gifts. On the contrary, the Apostle identifies individuals to whom God has given specific, *complementary*, and essential spheres of ministry. Thompson defined them in this way:

The Apostolic Approach

> The practical aspects of apostolic church planters must center on the following functions:

The Apostle—	Initiates
The Prophet—	Awakens
The Evangelist—	Proclaims
The Pastor/teacher—	Cares and instructs

While functions may overlap, Thompson explained, each requires a cluster of gifts to facilitate the particular calling. The Apostle's modus operandi was to plant a *string* of churches, and then visit them cyclically to help them develop. He did this at times through letters, and at times by sending a team member to minister to them for a period. Always he ordained elders or encouraged those already in place (Acts 20). To assure doctrinal purity, he visited or wrote to the churches whenever they strayed from the path of truth, the letter to the Galatians being a prime example. Paul also *left* the churches he planted, confident that the leadership he had appointed would be empowered by the Holy Spirit. In this way, he avoided their becoming dependent upon him.

This *watchcare* ministry explained the Apostle Paul's remarkable success in starting new churches. His continuing relationship with these churches by letters, visits, and emissaries assured their viability. Working cyclically with a *string* of churches, he avoided their becoming dependent upon him, thus assuring their development.

Properly understood—affirmed Thompson—the apostolic technique is the key to successful church planting. He distilled its essence in terms of contrasting activities:

Camping vs. Moving. A pastor's outlook is settled; he is a camper . . . the apostolic function is temporary in a given locality; he is a mover . . .

Growing vs. Planting. A pastor grows a church; an apostle plants a church, which a pastor then grows . . . The apostle plants the seed, waters it, and believes God for its sprouting. The pastor's call is to patiently cultivate the plant.

Broad vs. Focused. The pastor's ministry is broad, all-inclusive . . . his job is pictured beautifully in John 10 in the person of the Good Shepherd . . . The apostle is equally concerned, but his motivation is different. He focuses attention on people who will be able to lead and carry on the pastoral ministry . . .

Local vs. Foreign. The pastor is "one of the flock," or if not brought up through the local situation, he is certainly a native of the country where he is pastor . . . The apostle, by the very nature of his task, is an outsider.

Contextual vs. Transcultural. A pastor applies the gospel within a given culture. While a church planter must be sensitive to the culture, his primary emphasis is upon those transcultural aspects of the gospel, which may not and must not yield ground to any cultural accommodation.

Process Education

The success of the apostolic approach likewise depended upon the training of local church leaders, not merely through cognitive input, but through *process education*. This was the method Jesus had used—not training the disciples *for* ministry, but training them *in* and *through* ministry, that is, *on-the-job*. It was the same discovery that Elmer V. Thompson had made in the early days of the Cuba Bible Institute. It made the church grow. Process education meant that missionaries must resist the temptation to become pastors. Instead, as a mother bird momentarily abandons the fledgling on its first attempt at flight, so the apostolic missionary must periodically leave his leaders-in-process to their own devices, free to test their knowledge and develop their skills. He then returns as coach, counselor, and encourager.

The New Breed

Worldteam had defined the biblical paradigm. Now the larger task remained—communicate this apostolic concept to the missionaries of Worldteam. Then make it the modus operandi of the new Mission. While they had plenty of experience in planting churches, the fresh summons was to plant *clusters* of *self-multiplying* churches using the apostolic technique, and so generate church planting *movements* among the least-evangelized peoples of Earth. The fact that the remaining blocs of unreached were no longer to be found primarily in rural areas, but in the world's large, urban centers, called for an equally radical shift in strategic planning. It would also be more expensive.

But these considerations paled before an even more drastic necessity. The proposed shift in strategy demanded a new breed of missionary—people with demonstrated gifting for church planting and the ability to function in a team relationship. Escalating costs demanded increased accountability. Cost-effectiveness called for careful assessment of missionary candidates. In the past, if candidates could raise support, the mission organization was ready to send them. Now higher standards were necessary. This implied both the screening of missionary applicants (easy to do) and discreet selection of those suitable (difficult to do).

If the new agenda was drastic, it must also be resolute. Not everyone would welcome the implications, especially those who might be rendered redundant, or whose lives might otherwise be affected. The new axiom was simple: *The formidable expense of sending missionaries is justifiable only as they demonstrate the ability to multiply themselves by equipping national leaders who in turn will train others.* Otherwise, the Mission motto—*No Success Without a Successor*—becomes an empty cliché. The aphorism had to become a working axiom and it had to be rigorously applied.

WIN: Getting It Done

The process began with the development of a four-day assessment program to determine how well candidates might adapt to cross-cultural, pioneer church planting. This grew in usefulness and popularity and led to the 1986 launching in Sacramento of the *Worldteam Institute* (WIN), an annual four-week "family experience" for novices and veterans alike.[762] Living together, participants learned to understand themselves, their colleagues, and the issues that affect church planting worldwide. Assignments, case studies, workshops, readings, projects, and conflict resolution made up the curriculum. Participation of all Worldteam personnel—old and new—would be essential to achieve uniformity of philosophy and objective on all fields. Worldteam summarized its new philosophy and purpose:

Our Mission: To proclaim the good news of Jesus Christ to the lost in such a way that the Church of Jesus Christ is established and the nations of the world are impacted.

Our Vision: To influence the nations (*ethnos*) we serve through a church-multiplying movement.

Our Principles:

Think Together: A movement can only progress to the degree that church planters and the churches they establish possess a unified philosophy of evangelism and the church.

Think Total: A movement can only result through careful planning with a complete strategy.

Think Teamwork: Responsible teamwork is essential if we are to escalate evangelism into an expanding movement—one that goes beyond the establishment of isolated, individual churches.

Think Training: Church multiplication takes place only to the degree that all believers are indoctrinated in the movement's distinctives and where potential lay leaders are both trained and deployed.

A venerable Mission had mustered the courage to take a critical look at itself. Willing to break with the past, it had made some radical changes—changes that would bring pain and struggle. However, Worldteam was confident not only that a new path was necessary, but also that God was leading them. In a world of change, other Christian organizations, fearful of change, had become moribund. Someone had written:

We will not be afraid to change. We will stand on tiptoe, like the whole creation that groans and waits for His redemption. Ours will be a posture of expectancy. We will revere our past and build on the foundations laid. But we will move on as God leads into uncharted territory.

The tests were yet to come.

63

Church and Mission Collide

There is a war going on and we do not expect Satan to surrender easily.

—Elmer V. Thompson

While Worldteam leadership grappled with the dual issues of radical financial cutbacks and redefinition of its ministry philosophy, serious problems were brewing in Haiti. In fact, the impending Haitian difficulties had their roots in the very issues the leadership was now struggling to address—money and the philosophy of mission.

Fifty years of ministry on the island had witnessed prolific harvest. Two hundred seventy local congregations counted 50,000 believers. Keeping pace with this growth, Worldteam had gradually moved to a supporting role in Haiti. Missionaries served primarily as teachers, administrators, and as technicians in radio and medical work. Only on exceptional occasions did a missionary serve as pastor.

For a few decades after entering Haiti, the West Indies Mission enjoyed government recognition as an official organization. That changed in 1970, when at WIM's initiative, a formal agreement with MEBSH (*Mision Evangelique Baptiste d'Sud Haiti*—the WIM-related Association of Churches in Haiti), established MEBSH as the official, government-recognized organization with WIM as its foreign affiliate.[763]

Two critical elements marked the contract: MEBSH would assume title to all properties, while mission personnel would act as administrative advisors. Louis Markwood, Worldteam field director for Haiti at the time, would serve as chief advisor, with all correspondence over the signatures of MEBSH officers. With this agreement in place, the Haitian Church was now sovereign, but not solvent. Economic disparities between the relatively affluent Mission and its impoverished offspring were easy to see and hard to ignore.

Haitian church workers struggled financially. Mandated to serve their churches, they were hard pressed to make a living on the side. Local churches were unable to provide the subsidies essential to free a pastor for the full time care of his flock. Although Haiti remained the poorest country in the Western Hemisphere, the West Indies Mission stuck to its indigenous church support policy.

"No foreign support to national workers" was axiomatic to WIM's mission philosophy. The only wiggle room was the subsidy of institutional ministries. In this, WIM excelled. However, even this generosity had a fatal flaw. A marked disparity developed between the wages of pastors, teachers, and evangelists, and the wages paid to employees in institutions subsidized by the Mission. If that seemed wrong, the solution they adopted would hasten a crisis.

Sharing the Bounty

Worldteam had long enjoyed generous grants from the Aurora Foundation, cheerfully sharing its bounty with Haitian churches and with ministries on other fields. MEBSH programs also received subsidies. Pastors welcomed liberal help with transportation costs. Medical, radio and other works shared like blessing. However, the most significant beneficiary of financial refreshment was the Workers Fund. This fund permitted monies to be channeled through the Mission for deposit with MEBSH for scheduled distribution to pastors and teachers. There were no guarantees, but the new slush account helped workers make ends meet, as funds became available.

If national workers enjoyed the new revenues, the Church Association was euphoric. Greatly encouraged, MEBSH leadership was now able to refresh limping programs and launch new expansion. "You can't count on this indefinitely," the Mission would intone gently almost every time a fresh disbursement was made to MEBSH. However, in the elation of their newfound fiscal freedom the national leadership had moved out of earshot. They were no longer hearing Worldteam's oft-repeated caveat.

The Gathering Storm

With the dawn of 1983, a grim awareness began to settle upon Worldteam leadership. Benefactor Anthony Rossi's final term on the board had expired and he was not reelected. Prior to Thompson's resignation, Anthony Rossi had ceased giving large grants, requesting that distributions be made from the Tropicana stock he had already gifted, so that early in 1980, Worldteam understood that Rossi's munificence to the Mission was drawing to a close.

Many of the Mission's large overseas projects were funded by this large stock grant, including Haiti's Hospital Lumière, a church in Santo Domingo, apartments in Madrid and Catania, and a church building in Brazil. The larger grants for churches and apartments were for city evangelism, where costs were exorbitant and otherwise out of reach for Worldteam. Tropicana stock likewise helped set up revolving fund loans to churches in several countries and brought refreshment to the Haitian Church.[764] It had been God's provision. Like Elijah at Cherith's brook, MEBSH was not prepared for what would follow. With grant monies running out, subsidies to MEBSH fell off. The Haitian Church Association was not pleased.

Compounding the disappointment and dilemma facing MEBSH were rumors that Louis Markwood, field director in Haiti since 1959, was to be replaced. Markwood was nearing retirement, but his leadership was pivotal in the eyes of MEBSH. Haitians had linked him with the growth and prosperity of their best era, and with good reason. Markwood had transferred to Haiti from Cuba in 1959 to lead WIM's Haiti work, where he became "one of the best known and most influential men in Haiti,"[765] a reputation earned through his daily broadcasts over Radio Lumière, delivered in flawless French and Creole. Protestants and Catholics alike listened to his *Morning Encounter with the Workers.*

MEBSH disappointment notwithstanding, Lamar Myers was installed as Haiti Field Leader. The move disturbed the national leadership. Despite a plan that provided for Markwood's phase out over a two-year period, MEBSH saw the decision to replace him as an imposition by the Mission. Stress fractures in the relationship between Worldteam and the Haitian Church began to show.[766] MEBSH viewed Myers as an intrusion. He had requested a five-year plan in 1983. It never materialized. Discord intensified when a core of twenty disgruntled workers called for reforms in the administration.

Early in 1984, Patrick Arnold went to Haiti to join Markwood and Myers in a meeting with the MEBSH Executive Committee. Their message was not welcomed: All Worldteam subsidies would cease by the end of the year.

"How can we face our workers with this news?" the Haitians responded. "We need MORE financial help—not less!" Then came an onerous request: Would Patrick Arnold go to Haiti and personally deliver the unwelcome news? He agreed. It would take three months for the Haitian leadership to formulate their response to Worldteam.

Polarization

Arnold was unaware of the test awaiting him in Haiti. Having thought through the issues, he returned in March. Expecting fraternal dialogue and some

Q &A, he was optimistic that the difficulties could be resolved. It would not be that easy.

When Arnold, Markwood, and Myers arrived for their meeting with MEBSH, they were advised that the general church council would meet first in private sessions. At the conclusion of business, they would call for the Worldteam representatives. The trio waited patiently, paced the floor, rehearsed possible scenarios, talked, and prayed. Three hours passed.

The MEBSH Proposal

Finally, at noon the three were invited to meet with the Haitian executive committee. They were handed a typed statement. Reading it, they stared in disbelief. The paper requested a monthly commitment of $16,500. There was a second demand—A one-time grant of $30,000 for the purchase of two vehicles.

Restraining shock and disappointment, Arnold responded: "I do not think this will be possible. I cannot respond to this on my own. I will have to take it to the board of directors. But while we are together, let's discuss the implications should the response from Worldteam be 'No'."

"We have already thought about that," the committee replied, explaining that the action had full approval of the general council. Should the mission fail to commit to significant financial assistance, certain Worldteam missionaries (whom MEBSH considered expendable) should be repatriated immediately. Remaining Worldteam personnel would be free to stay on for three years or longer, length of time to be determined upon MEBSH evaluation. Worldteam would cease to exist in Haiti.

It was a solar plexus punch and it devastated many Worldteam missionaries. Reaction ranged from pain to anger. "Have we wasted our lives here?" one asked. Others had no time for questions: "We're going to pack up and leave now!"

MEBSH to the US

As word circulated that some missionary families were making plans to leave Haiti, many national workers became alarmed. They assumed the full content and nature of the proposition and resolution submitted to Worldteam had not been disclosed to the general membership. At least, it had not been understood.

With missionary morale sinking, and confusion reigning within the Haitian Church Association, Patrick Arnold stepped into the breech. He invited MEBSH to send a delegation of its leadership to Worldteam's upcoming International Council (IC) in the States. There they would be free to present their case in person. The invitation was accepted.

Before the council meeting, Myers had written the MEBSH Executive Committee on behalf of the missionaries, reiterating Worldteam's commitment to the Haitian brethren. He had also underscored the Mission's earnest desire to continue a working relationship with the nationals.

A Conciliatory Gesture

As International Council deliberations ended, someone suggested an offering from the IC members to MEBSH. Nearly $2,500 was raised. It was a high watermark. The MEBSH committee returned to Haiti encouraged. They had not received the requested promise of more financial assistance, but the generous gift reassured them of the Mission's care. By September, the Haitian church had agreed to continue working with the Mission and had asked Worldteam to remain in Haiti. However, hurts were slow to heal. Some Worldteamers felt that neither the Mission nor MEBSH leadership had really heard their case. High-level dialogue between Worldteam and the Haitians had failed to include the missionaries, whose life and work were on the line. Predictably, relationships were strained. While Worldteam and MEBSH worked through the details of their new relationship, the tempest subsided. Nevertheless, it was only the eye of the storm. The full blast was yet to come.

Redefining Mission

The ultimatum laid at the Mission's doorstep by the Haitian Churches was painful. It signaled the need for radical measures. Paul Thompson had challenged mission leadership to take a hard look at Worldteam's profile. The Mission had become institutionalized—comfortable in traditional patterns of ministry, perhaps smug. Success had become the norm. It was easy to assume that Heaven's smile was an unconditional part of the Worldteam franchise. The blow-up in Haiti shattered that illusion and called for healthy introspection. Paul Thompson had been watching the weather and had already made a critical analysis of the Mission's goals. He had forged his thesis on the anvil of personal ministry struggles, and articulated his confident grasp of the "apostolic" approach to church planting. The material was in place and ready for road test. Patrick Arnold—who had seen the Mission through a stormy transition—was closing out his two-year duty tour as president. The timing seemed right.

Thompson Takes the Helm—Again

For five years, Worldteam had struggled with a welter of concerns—alarming turnover in leadership, painful financial stringency, program cutbacks, and perhaps worst of all, the hemorrhage of its historic support base.

Not least of these concerns was Worldteam's philosophy of mission vis-a-vis a now mature national church. Historic commitment to institutional ministries such as hospitals, radio, print shops, and even Bible schools—once essential entrées to evangelism— was now increasingly in tension with the Mission's primary reason for existence—multiplying new churches. In the absence of the Rossi capital, financial shortages preoccupied everyone's thinking. Procurement of medical and other essential supplies continued to drain reserves with no relief in sight. Corporate peace was eroding. With Arnold's term expiring, the Worldteam Board was unable to find a new president. They turned again to Allen Thompson. Would he come back?

The Great Divide

At this time Morrie Cottle, one of Wycliffe's seasoned field leaders from the Philippines, had taken a pastorate in the US and was now chairman of the Worldteam Board.[767] Cottle saw advantages in Wycliffe's administrative separation of North American and overseas ministries, and encouraged Worldteam to adopt a similar model. The board agreed, restructuring the Mission in late 1984.[768]

Two operations centers were established: one for North American Ministries, the other for Overseas Ministries. Each had its own director, board, and budget. The action was intended to decentralize the Mission—shifting administrative work in the United States to the Miami-based board (with its Canadian counterpart in Toronto), while freeing the Atlanta-based international board to concentrate on strategy and the selection, training and deployment of church planting missionaries. Role and function of the US and Canadian boards would be to communicate with their constituencies, recruit and select missionaries, and develop resources of prayer and finance. The new structure would also allow other sending countries to establish national boards under the umbrella of a single Worldteam International Council without increasing the administrative burden of the IC. In considering Allen Thompson's return, the division of labor reflected in the new structure was viewed as a means of releasing Thompson from excessive burden of administration, should he agree to return to the international leadership.

Early in 1985, Lloyd Fesmire, board member and chairman of the search committee, telephoned Thompson—then in Denver—with the proposal. Thompson pondered the invitation. He was encouraged by the Mission's commitment to a radical break with old patterns. Administering institutions and social programs had served their day, at least in Worldteam's experience. If closing that chapter had taken courage, even greater boldness would be called for in taking the next step—an exclusive commitment to church multiplication. Turning the ship around would be a painful process. Stormy weather lay ahead. Notwithstanding, Allen Thompson agreed to take the helm again.

Move to Atlanta

He began by moving to Atlanta in September, where he established a small Worldteam international office. Atlanta was strategic as an international hub. It also afforded some insulation from administration of Worldteam's North American concerns. Ed Walker, newly installed as president of Worldteam USA, began his work in the Miami office (Coral Gables) the same month, while Albert Ehmann established the Worldteam Canada office close to the Toronto airport.

As international director, Thompson was now free to move from an administrative role to what he did best—that of motivator, facilitator, and creative strategist. Setting himself "to figure out how to ignite church planting vision," Thompson brought his brother Paul to Atlanta to help develop church planting vision tools. Another team in Miami led by Deputy General Director Dean Franklin addressed the mobilization of Worldteam as a force for church planting.

At the time, the restructure seemed to spell relief for Allen Thompson, freeing him for the higher priority of a training ministry. Unfortunately, what had worked well for Wycliffe did not do as well for Worldteam. The practical effect was to create two distinct mission entities with two directors. This duality had decided merits, but would ultimately prove detrimental to the unity of the Mission. Tensions arose between the two boards, particularly over funding.[769]

Notwithstanding, Thompson's return brought a fresh sense of lift. He introduced Worldteam's decavision—*Horizon 2000*—a strategic plan and vision statement projecting a faith path to the new millennium, still thirteen years away. Launched in June 1987, *Horizon 2000* posed the question, "What may God wish to do through us in the immediate future?" Plan and Pray workshops were taken to Europe, the Dominican Republic, Brazil, Suriname, and Trinidad, with each field called upon to articulate a purpose statement. Horizon 2000 captured the imagination of the Worldteam family—new fields would be entered, thirty-six new teams of church-starters would deploy, least-evangelized people groups would be identified, researched and targeted, and Worldteam would take the cities for Christ.

To facilitate the effort, *Prayer Pacesetters* were enlisted—persons available to be matched with church planters overseas, to pray for the target group and the evangelistic effort of the team. By 1989, forty-two *Pacesetters* from nine countries had been linked with thirty-two church planters.[770]

Into this milieu of organizational change, financial shortfall, and uncertain plans, J. Allen Thompson had returned to the leadership of Worldteam. He had conditioned his return upon a personal commitment to bring the Mission into a merger relationship with another agency, but the timing proved unpropitious and the notion of merger failed to win popularity. Notwithstanding the bright promise of a new agenda, misgivings had begun to rise. Great plans called for great means, not only financial, but also human. Launching new fields demanded seasoned leaders, and these were in short supply. Thompson's unwillingness to compromise these ideals of leadership qualifications would cause him to falter in the implementation of ventures to which the leadership team was already committed by consensus. If Worldteam had changed, so had J. Allen Thompson. Administration of an increasingly complex mission society had begun to lose its attraction. His passion had begun to shift to a larger challenge—the training of missionaries in church planting skills.

Worldteam USA: First Steps

When the Mission restructured in 1985, Ed Walker became the first president of Worldteam USA (in September) and vigorously addressed his mandate to reshape the North American Ministries division as a leaned-out and supple agency. Together with his team of leaders,[771] Walker developed long-range plans, fine-tuned the accounting department, and reestablished relationships with a long-neglected constituency. He introduced an approach to resource development not previously practiced by Worldteam. For ten years, the Aurora Foundation endowments had made fund-raising unnecessary. By 1985 the Mission had grown accustomed to this abundance, and "was not entirely wise in the stewardship of these massive gifts."[772] Unhealthy spending and operational habits developed, and lacking a resource development department, no plans had been made to compensate for the inevitable cessation of Aurora income. That changed with the intensified development of donor relations and the streamlining of operations. A Deferred Giving Program (DGP) was launched in 1986. Within five years, the DGP had begun to generate significant returns. These efforts soon returned Worldteam USA to a sound fiscal position. Morale lifted and expectations soared.

The Institute for Church planting

With Allen Thompson as facilitator, Walker and his team of leaders also developed selection criteria for identifying workers with potential church planting gifts, while Paul Thompson defined and developed the biblical and practical philosophy of church planting. These elements, critical to Worldteam's restructure as a focused church planting agency, were now in place.

Keystone of the strategy shift was the *Institute for Church Planting* (WIN).[773] With Allen Thompson's return to the leadership, the first WIN Institute was conducted in 1986 in Sacramento and annually thereafter in different locations. Its purpose—"to train effective missionary church planters who can be counted on to plant multiplying churches." Worldteam faced a problem common to many agencies: organizational drift and loss of focus. New candidates often arrived poorly equipped in skills essential to church planting—training that most divinity schools failed to provide. The WIN curriculum effectively addressed these issues. By 1989, WIN was successfully integrating apostolic church planting principles into the life of the Mission with a goal to expose all Worldteam personnel to this new standard—veteran missionaries as well as new recruits. Within four years, nearly eighty percent of mission personnel had passed through the program. Revitalization was underway, a refreshed corporate focus was in place, and virtually all Worldteam personnel had made the new philosophy their own.[774]

Worldteam Canada

Meanwhile, in 1985 Worldteam Canada had organized as an autonomous agency with legal identity including its own board, naming Albert Ehmann as director. An apprenticeship program was in place for the training of church planters. Forty Canadians were now members of the international organization.

Fresh ministry thrusts had been launched in London (1984) and French Guiana (1986), and new church planting teams were being deployed among the Bush Negroes of Suriname, the Guyanese, and the cities of Bejar in Spain, and Porto Alegre and São Leopoldo in Brazil. Two additional teams entered Santiago in the Dominican Republic. Church multiplication ministries continued in Cuba, Guadeloupe, and the Southern Caribbean. Many of the new efforts had been made possible through redeployment of experienced personnel, ready, and willing to establish new beachheads for the Mission. Worldteam was committed to a missiological quantum leap—total revamping as an exclusively focused church planting mission. The most painful test of that commitment lay just ahead.

64

Disengagement

When considering foreign missionary service, don't look for an easy field in order to avoid difficulties and hardships. Choose the difficult place where you will be tested and challenged. It is in the hard place that you will be made strong.

—B. G. Lavastida

Disengagement had probably not been the right word to describe the Worldteam action. It sounded too much like abandonment—precisely what the Mission was not doing. Even *bar mitzvah* would have been better. The Haitian church had grown up, and no one could argue against cutting parental strings. Everyone agreed: "It was the right thing to do. It was the wrong way to do it!" Years after the event, that impromptu verdict would still resonate around the water coolers at Worldteam Headquarters. Predictably, casualties had resulted from the way in which disengagement in Haiti took place. Could it have been done differently? Who could say? One thing was certain: Hindsight is perfect and history is not subject to edit.

The June 1987 minute of the Worldteam board had sent tremors throughout the missionary community in Haiti:

> Worldteam recognizes its responsibility to the Haiti field, to the established national Church organization, and to the institutions it has established. Worldteam recognizes that a plan of action must be devised to disengage direct Worldteam involvement in these institutions, while maintaining the Church's vital ministry and witness through these institutions, to the society that they serve.

Reaction among missionaries was swift, and questions rained like hail on a tin roof.

"Sounds like we'll be leaving Haiti."

"When will this 'disengagement' take place?"

"How will it take place?"

"Will there be a place for missionaries in Haiti ten years from now?"

"Was institutional involvement a mistake from the start?"

"Is it not too disruptive to leave at this point?"

"Can't we do both institutional ministry as well as apostolic church planting?"

"Where does that leave me?"

Some felt discarded. Others felt demeaned—as if suddenly relegated to second class status. "I'm a nurse-doctor-technician, not a 'church planter.' Does this mean that I am no longer a missionary?"

No one seemed to have an answer.

The National Church Reacts

While missionaries struggled to regain their balance, the Haitian Church was sure of one thing: Worldteam's announcement had been in response to the MEBSH proposition and resolution dropped on the Mission the previous year.

Lamar Myers tried to calm the fears.

"No. Not at all!" he responded. "This action consummates years of study and struggle by Worldteam to redefine its role in world missions. We have no timetable to impose. The important thing is that we begin the process. Together we can determine how long the process will take. Responsibility for the work must be turned over to the Haitian church—for her own good."

Haiti Speaks

Once the initial shock subsided, the picture began to clear for both the missionaries and the Church: After fifty years, it really *was* time for the Haitian church to stand on its own feet. Chavannes Jeune, coordinator of the MEBSH departments, was among the first to grasp the necessity and importance of what was to happen. In a public statement, he captured the providence of the moment:

As I analyze the situation, the MEBSH is being offered an excellent opportunity to do what some other church associations in the country would like to bring about, but do not know how.

In the summer of 1986, MEBSH leadership adopted the document, "Policies Relative to Worldteam Haiti Disengagement." They had agreed to assume total responsibility for the work. In December, Allen Thompson and Dean Franklin went to Haiti to finalize terms of the contract. MEBSH would assume full responsibility for the Haitian churches on New Year's Day, 1987. Radio Lumière and Hospital Lumière would be incorporated as separate entities.

The 1959 revolution in Cuba had taught WIM what national churches could do best. The revolution had forced the separation of the Cuban Church from the West Indies Mission. Through this experience, WIM leadership learned that institutions—hospitals and radio stations—could become a burden to the church and thereby greatly hinder church vitality and growth. Moreover, in Cuba the communist government did not confiscate the New Pines Seminary property (although it did take part of the farm) because all property was registered in the name of the Evangelical Association of Cuba—a local entity, not foreign. Mission-owned properties also cast a shadow of paternalism upon the national churches. Fearing future political tensions in Haiti, all properties were transferred to MEBSH, while Worldteam in Haiti established three separate organizations, each with board representation—*Radio Lumière, Hospital Lumière*, and MEBSH.

Thompson reported to the March meeting of the Worldteam International Executive committee:

> Attitudes among the Haitian leaders have moved from hesitancy, hurt and unbelief to trust, warmth, and eagerness. I think the reason is a clearer understanding of our motives and recognition of the opportunities it gives them to lead. The talks were straightforward with no hidden agendas. I was invited to speak at the annual conference in April.

So far, so good.

Postmortem

For medical missionaries, disengagement was simply impossible—philosophically, emotionally, and ethically. They had poured their lives into the *Hospital Lumière*. God had called them specifically to medical ministry. The same Lord of the Harvest had confirmed that call. Witnessing one-on-one to thousands of patients over the years, they had seen many come to the Savior. Many among Haiti's desperate masses still depended on the touch Lumière's doctors and nurses could provide.

Recognizing the need for continued leadership in the medical ministry, Louis Markwood postponed retirement and became the head of Lumière Medical Ministries, one of the agencies that Worldteam spawned by disengagement. Markwood and others would continue to work with the medical community on the island and later move to Gastonia, North Carolina to set up offices to coordinate the new ministry in North America. Lamar Myers would stay on for one year as advisor to the Secretariat's office of MEBSH. Radio Lumière more easily weathered the shift in policy. The radio network already had a national director and a responsible board, so the island's radio ministry continued without significant disruption.

MEBSH celebrated its fifty-first anniversary in April 1987. The occasion signaled the healing and mutual understanding that had taken place between church and mission. Allen Thompson was one of the plenary speakers. He participated in the ceremony of transfer, presenting a large wooden key to Pastor Lozama on behalf of Worldteam, symbolizing the changeover. Following appropriate remarks and prayer, the two embraced before the 10,000 guests. The Haitian Churches had risen with dignity to responsible corporate selfhood. Under Thompson's leadership, Worldteam had taken a courageous and costly step. Other mission agencies in Haiti were watching. Later, some of them would follow Worldteam's example.[775]

The Price of Courage

Everyone agreed that Worldteam's disengagement from institutional ministries in Haiti was good missiology, but the action brought immediate and painful consequences. Most Worldteam personnel in Haiti were involved in institutional work—hospital, radio, print shop, dental clinic, and Pioneer Girls. Now redundant, most would have to leave, transfer to other work, or remain in Haiti independent of the Mission. While some Worldteamers did remain on the island and others were reassigned,[776] not a few went home. Broken and bruised, they never returned.[777]

Disengagement also inflicted financial pain. Worldteam's institutional ministries had been largely supported by overseas contributions. When these ministries were discontinued, their support income went with them. The same was true of missionary personnel made redundant by the action. The Mission administrative budget depended upon the ten percent administrative assessment applied to all project and missionary support. Withdrawal of this revenue resulted in a $160,000 annual erosion of operating capital. Since no other plan was in place to replenish this loss, the resulting emergency demanded an unwelcome increase in the administrative fee for all Worldteam missionaries. But that was not all.

The disengagement process exacted a heavy toll on the energy of the Mission. Time and attention that would normally have been invested in Worldteam's other fields and in the forward thrust had been absorbed in the myopia of the Haiti crisis. Ripples of discontent began to reverberate throughout the mission family. The strong bond linking missionary and Mission administration was weakened through a rising sense of isolation and neglect. In happier days, furloughing personnel cheerfully plunged into deputation assignments during furloughs. Mission administrators regularly visited the fields. Communication was warm and frequent. The sense of family was alive and well. Now the halcyon days were gone. Communication deteriorated, though Worldteam was now worldwide. From modest beginnings in Cuba sixty years earlier, Worldteam had grown to a workforce of 250 missionaries serving in Europe and South America as well as in the West Indies. Administrators still visited the fields, but things were not the same. Missionaries lamented privately, "We never know what is going on. First we hear the Mission is heading in one direction, then we hear nothing more and it seems it has taken a turn somewhere else." Worldteam, once muscular, cohesive, and focused, had lost something.

Setting the Sails

In his *International Director's Communiqué* of 3 February 1989—*Setting the Sails*—Thompson addressed the crisis. He reviewed the state of Worldteam since his return four years earlier, outlined the financial emergency, and defined a three-year recovery plan. Diagnosing symptom and cause, he expressed it in a prayer:

> Father, we confess we have not been obedient leaders. We have too often fallen into the world's mold of going our own way and not submitting to You.

> Specifically, in this situation, we deferred hard decisions when things were going well. We planned poorly, using money unwisely and making funds available for projects without long-term planning. We did not seek your guidance sufficiently. We did not build a broad base of prayer and financial partnership with your people. Instead, we developed unhealthy dependence on single sources of support. Forgive us, Lord, for our inordinate attention to image and tasks at expense of relationships. Forgive us for our careless attention to missionary's needs. Forgive us for pride of ideas thinking we had a handle on biblical strategy. We are grieved that we have failed to show a true submission both to You our Master and to our brethren.

> We solemnly commit ourselves to cooperate more actively with the Holy Spirit in having a learning attitude, to be guided by your Word in our decisions, and to aggressively engage in prayer. Be merciful unto us, O Lord. Amen."[778]

Grasping the Nettle

Grasping the nettle called for more than confession, as Allen Thompson knew. Worldteam was not in debt, and held reserves sufficient to cover all missionary support and designated obligations, but funding sources were insufficient to meet the current level of operations beyond September of 1989.

He fired off an appeal for prayer to all Worldteam fields. Replenishment of financial resources was urgent, but more than that, God's wisdom and direction were critical. Calling for days of prayer throughout the Mission, he urged field leaders to study, discuss and debate the issues with all personnel—and return their recommendations to the International Center. Then he announced a leadership conference to precede the upcoming board meetings in May. Answers must be found. Meanwhile, a vexed administration mandated emergency measures:

1. Overseas-related goals and ministries were cancelled for six months to devote full energies to raising support.
2. Salaries were frozen to 1988 levels; and support pooled among teams.
3. Missionaries were alerted to the possibility of salary cuts.
4. International Office secretarial staffing was cut. Four were laid off.
5. *Worldteam Today* was reduced to a less costly format.
6. Worldteam Associates became an affiliate in church planting.
7. Worldteam Canada released its five percent earnings share of the International Reserve Fund and paid staff expenses for WIN training modules in Canada.

Reduced to bare-bones austerity, Worldteam hovered on the brink of collapse. Leadership had thinned, and continuity suffered. Resignations had left three fields without directors. A significant gap now existed between older, experienced leaders and the upcoming crop. Offices in Miami, Atlanta, and Toronto might have eased the pressure by pooling resources, but distance and cost factors were prohibitive. Still, the problems had been addressed and unpleasant medicine had been swallowed. Then, in a timely providence, God brought a paraclete to Worldteam's side.

World Team Associates

Life changed radically for Clayton ("Clayt") E. Irmeger in 1967 when he took part in a Worldteam missions tour to the Dominican Republic. The experience convinced him not only that he should be involved in missions, but also that lay people can energize the local church and make a positive contribution to world evangelization. As early as 1985 Irmeger had informally begun to mobilize laymen, sending volunteer construction teams to Worldteam fields. The concept of *Worldteam Associates* (WTA) was born. Ron Vasselin had been Irmeger's contact with Worldteam. The idea was floated with the Worldteam board and Vasselin and Irmeger made contact with Dr. Howard "Hod" Getz about becoming the first president of WTA. Dr. Getz had been the associate Dean of the University of Illinois Medical Center and a high-school classmate of Irmeger. Retired at fifty-five, he had taken a number of mission trips and shared Irmeger's enthusiasm. At a Worldteam board meeting in July 1988, this body of volunteers, committed to Worldteam's mandate and vision, was released to form a separate corporate structure. On 1 January 1989 WTA took flight, with Getz as first president.[779]

Irmeger had studied the experience of similar organizations such as *Wycliffe Associates* and saw that the new arm of Worldteam could better function as an independent affiliate of the Mission. Within the year, WTA had organized and secured its non-profit and ECFA[780]status. The formation of Worldteam Associates was timely, for within sixteen months a great door of opportunity would swing open for the Mission. Already working as a subset of Worldteam, WTA laymen were being used to strengthen donor relations. As an incorporated entity, WTA would make it possible for the Mission to seize this new opportunity. Like a relief column coming to the aid of a beleaguered garrison, WTA would arrive just in time.[781] But before that happened, another blow would fall upon the Mission. It would not easily recover.

Allen Thompson Leaves Worldteam

Although he had spearheaded the disengagement from the MEBSH and had accomplished changes critical to Worldteam's future,[782] Allen Thompson would soon leave the Mission to which he had brought so much lift. The smooth passage which marked his first leadership tour had not attended his second cycle as international director. Following Thompson's *Setting the Sails* communiqué in February 1989,[783]questions over ultimate authority began to surface, causing confusion and mistrust. Criticism was directed at the international director, calling for more decisive leadership. Transfer of some field leaders to fill posts in the US and Canada had left older fields with a leadership vacuum and a resulting sense of neglect. Erosion of working capital had begun to paralyze vision for new fields and fresh ventures of faith.

Requested by the board to become minister-at-large, and to relinquish the post of international director, Allen Thompson left the Mission for the second and last time in September 1989. Earlier that summer (June) the Worldteam board had commissioned Steve Miller as CEO to assist the international director in the implementation of the Mission's plans. Steve and Anne had followed Guadeloupe's migrant believers to the suburbs of Paris in a new ethnic ministry, where Miller had become field director for Worldteam in France. With Allen Thompson's resignation, the mantle of international director now fell upon Miller. He assumed the leadership of Worldteam International as the fourth executive director in its sixty-one year history.[784]

65

Turning the Page

Far better is it to dare mighty things . . . even though check-
ered by failure, than to take rank with those poor spirits who
neither enjoy much nor suffer much, because they live in the
gray twilight that knows not victory nor defeat.

—Theodore Roosevelt

Steve Miller

In his new role as general director,[785] Steve Miller was suddenly thrust into unfamiliar waters with respect to the International Board, its functions, and attendant responsibilities. Miller had returned to a new Mission, different in structure and dynamic. Ed Walker continued as president of Worldteam USA, a position he would hold until 1992.

The *Setting the Sails* communiqué and Thompson's subsequent departure drained the *Horizon 2000* plan of its momentum. The loss of Allen Thompson's creative leadership seemed irreparable, dealing a blow to Worldteam from which it would not fully recover. Steve Miller and Ed Walker closed ranks to face the lingering challenges. The drastic cuts mandated in Thompson's May 1989 board report remained in place, with all projects on hold. Nonessential staff had been laid off. Worldteam was out of debt with reserve funds on hand to cover all missionary support and scheduled obligations. Ed Walker continued his effective development of the donor base and deferred giving program. Even so, income remained inadequate to permit the aggressive level of operation the Mission wished to pursue. The loss of important leaders further dampened Worldteam's ability to conduct the aggressive expansion envisioned in Horizon 2000.

As Miller and Walker—in their respective roles as international director and president of Worldteam USA—analyzed the Worldteam corpus, the conviction was growing that for all of Mission's innovation and progress, the critical mass essential to a vigorous future was not present. They began to sense that merger might be the answer. While not all agreed, exploratory merger talks did begin with another agency. Considerable energy was expended over a period of nine months, but fell short of consensus. Then some things happened that would call for cheers.

Beyond the Iron Curtain

The first was a political event that stunned the world. The collapse of the Soviet Union in 1990–91 was triggered by American President Ronald Reagan's 1987 imperative to the Soviet Leader— *"Mr. Gorbachev, tear down this wall!"*[786]

Reagan's verbal blast at the infamous Berlin Wall signaled the end of communism's seventy years of failed experiment in social engineering and the fall of what Winston Churchill had called *The Iron Curtain.* Rushing to fill the economic and spiritual vacuum left by atheistic oppression was a fresh breeze of freedom and independence. "Bodies politic in eastern and central Europe began to reject the alien regimes that had been grafted on to them."[787] Ethnic enclaves and satellite states whose existence was unsuspected by many Westerners, suddenly began to define their borders and lift the cry for freedom.

Emerging phoenix-like from the rubble was the Commonwealth of Independent States (CIS), with its new openness to the West and to the gospel of Christ. Mission and Church agencies rushed to fill the void. Since no one knew how long the window might remain open, immediate and concerted response was urgent. Eighty mission organizations joined hands to form the *CoMission.*[788] Worldteam seized the opportunity and fielded professional and nonprofessional workers to teach English and conduct Bible lessons, with Steve Miller heavily involved in the planning. Between 1992 and 1998 Worldteam sent thirty-two team members to Petrozavodsk and several other cities.[789] CoMission had offered a fresh approach to biblical networking and an efficient means of focusing evangelical energies. Worldteam Associates— formed in January 1989—was born for this moment. Hod Getz marshaled recruits and coordinated the Worldteam effort, placing workers in Keralia through the CoMission. It was a fresh page in the Worldteam story, and all took courage.

Alliance for Saturation Church Planting

The second event was also a direct result of the disbanding of the Soviet Union. Riding the wave of the new freedom in former iron curtain countries, *The Alliance for Saturation Church Planting* was formed with the express purpose of equipping existing national leaders in Eastern Bloc countries for church planting and multiplication. The idea had come to Dwight Smith, then president of the United World Mission, to equip Eastern Bloc pastors as church planters. Joining forces, Smith, Worldteam's Steve Miller, and Jim Montgomery, president of DAWN ministries, signed a mutual assistance agreement. Releasing seasoned personnel from other fields, Worldteam began training church planters behind the former Iron Curtain. The missiological breakthrough of Allen and Paul Thompson in the creation of WIN now began to pay off in this unexpected and long neglected region of Eastern Europe. Worldteam's Jay and Beth Weaver and Glenn and Mary Jo Livingstone joined the effort, making their base in Budapest. By 1999, the Alliance had seen 2,400 new churches planted in former Eastern Bloc countries.

Church Partnerships

Encouraged by the CoMission experience, Worldteam became aware of the need to close ranks and join hands with the larger body of Christ for the greater glory of God. The advent of e-mail and satellite communications had begun to move evangelical missions toward a refreshing biblical synergy with other evangelical groups whose common denominator was to get the gospel message to every man, woman and child on earth. From its beginnings, Worldteam had worked in cooperation with nationals. Now a persistent question begged reply: Why must Christian agencies cling to organizational identity while the magnitude of the task is crying out for us to lay aside pride of pedigree in the interests of a more efficient use of resources through cooperation?

Xenos Christian Fellowship

If CoMission and the Alliance had seemed to answer that question, a group in Columbus, Ohio would erase all doubt. In the late 1980s, *Xenos Christian Fellowship,* a forward-thinking local church, had identified within their ranks a team committed to fulfill XCF's mission vision and purpose.[790]Members of the Xenos team already shared the same sense of calling, demonstrating compatibility with one another in personality and gifting.

XCF became the first local church to enter partnership with Worldteam, sending a team to Indonesia. From this starting point, Worldteam developed the *Church Partnership Program,* engaging in strategic planning in cooperation with individual congregations already burdened for a particular world area or people group. Under the program, participants remained accountable to their local church during their tour on the field, while the Mission provided liaison between the team and their church. Ken Campbell and Don Ropp would later coordinate the Church Partnership Program.

God was awakening Worldteam to a yet larger world. Horizon-lifting partnerships could infuse new life and maintain freshness and viability in a world of constant change. The Lord of the Harvest was preparing the Mission for a greater and more radical partnership than anyone had thought.

66

Requiem

God is not interested in what you do for him until he is satisfied with who you are.

—G. Allen Fleece

Character Matters

Elmer V. Thompson stood tall among the giants with whom he had so much in common: Enoch, who walked with God; Abraham, whom God called, *"my friend;"* Jacob, who in dying, worshipped; David, who in old age got the answer to his prayer—*"let me show thy strength to this generation."*[791] The rancher from Colorado who founded the West Indies Mission fulfilled all the prototypes.

In the phosphorescent wake of his life, he left hundreds of churches and countless thousands of Christians. He also left a virile and vibrant agency that would perpetuate his God-given vision into a new millennium. By the time his upward summons came on 20 October 1998, Elmer Thompson's drumbeat had echoed throughout the earth—from Caribbean isles to the cities of Europe and to the forests of South America. Only then did he learn how far the sound had gone.

Elmer Thompson was a focused man. Described by one who knew him best as "detached, intense, formal, stern, disciplined," with a prayer life "almost unearthly," he was unaffected by the common interests which distract most men. His appetite for lesser things was dulled—as a son remembers—by his hunger for God.[792] How else can one explain a man who had little interest in keeping up with the latest book, or film, or fashion, who appeared to stand before a narrow window on the universe, his gaze absorbed with the Eternal? And Thompson was always at the window, as his son Paul remembered—this man who with bowed head prayed at parties, who, though he watched very little television, prayed during commercials, who seemed at times to those closest to him, aloof and distant.

The intensity and constancy of his prayer life appeared at times to eclipse even the common intimacies of family life. Son Allen remembered:

> Praying became a habit of the heart, a spontaneous and frequent conversation with God. As a young boy, I often joined him on his evening walks up Windy Hill, a bald elevation near Los Pinos campus. As we walked hand in hand, I would hear him mumble a phrase.

> "What were you saying, Dad?"

> "Nothing, son, I was just talking to my heavenly Father."[793]

This intimacy nurtured a rich pulpit life. He had few peers. The authority and conviction with which he spoke were formidable. At ninety years of age, he gave an address to the students of Columbia Bible College. It was received with a standing ovation. The fact that hundreds of young people gladly followed him into the ranks of the West Indies Mission bears witness to the Elijah-mantle that he wore.

In the home Elmer Thompson was a strict disciplinarian who sought to balance the "goodness and severity" of God in the work of parenting. Where an offense was clearly moral in nature, the consequence was nonnegotiable. Thompson offspring would be led to their father's office and dealt with firmly from the Scriptures. Prayer—and the strap—followed. If the matter was known openly, a public confession was expected. The pain of confessing before the entire student body of the Cuba Bible Institute was sufficient deterrent to further transgressions. Scottish pulpiteer Alexander Whyte once noted that "God humbles us through humiliation." The Thompson children understood.

As a leader of men, Thompson was not without flaw. He could be authoritarian, so sure of Divine leading that at times decisions would be made without prior consultation with those affected. Changes were not easily conceded. Everyone knew that a confrontation with "*el viejo*" (the old man) was serious business. Spirited confrontations with Thompson caused some to leave the Mission. Evelyn, on the other hand, brought a balance that was recognized by all, including the Cubans. When second son Allen succeeded him as director of WIM, the comment was directed to Allen, "*Tienes el empuje del viejo y la ternura de tu madre.*" ("You have the push of your father and the tenderness of your mother.") That *empuje* notwithstanding, E. V. Thompson's true stature was displayed in his willingness, when wrong, to make things right, even to the point of public confession. In this self-humbling and submissive transparency lay his greatness as a man used by God.

Allen knew that his father's achievements stemmed from the fact that he had led the West Indies Mission, not from his abilities, but from the strength of his character. Elmer Thompson did not possess all the abilities essential to leading a great mission, but:

> He knew he could surround himself with a team of people that complemented his deficient areas. He also knew instinctively that [even these complements] were not sufficient. He knew the evil lurking in his own heart enough to recognize that gift-deficient areas would undermine him unless he compensated with godliness. So, in addition to staffing to his weaknesses, Dad covered his weaknesses with godly character. He developed a leadership style that was not only effective but gave him power and ministry.[794]

Eldest son Leslie, founder of LOGOI, described his father as a "matchless giant" who exemplified a disciplined intimacy with God throughout his long life. If children are the most reliable assayers of a parent's character, then let a son place his father on the scales:

> Imagine, if you can, growing up in a family where every day, at four in the morning sharp, the father got up to pray. Imagine every evening after supper that same father gathering his children about him to lead them in singing, Bible study, and prayer. Imagine a father, who by spiritual example taught his children to deal with sin and keep the heart from evil. Imagine a father who—in a superlative way— gave his best for the Lord Jesus.

If the Thompson offspring followed their parents into the work of world evangelization, it was not through parental admonition or a sense of dynastic obligation, but by the compulsion of example. The four eldest grew up within the community of the Cuba Bible Institute, its students and faculty.[795] This environment modeled the high calling, shaped their character, and inspired their values. The consistent dedication and commitment of Elmer and Evelyn Thompson to the will of God was itself the altar call to world evangelization.

The senior Thompsons retired from the leadership of the West Indies Mission in 1966, serving in Jamaica for five years as members of the Jamaica Bible College staff. After Jamaica, they became directors of Worldteam's prayer ministry. In 1995, accompanied by his lifemate, Thompson attended the merger ceremonies of the two missions in Mississauga, where at ninety-four he delivered a stirring exhortation to the assembled delegates. The following year (1997) Evelyn Thompson rose to the skies. She was ninety-two. Elmer would follow in just eighteen months.

With ever-increasing debility limiting his activity, he lived with his daughter and son-in law[796] until the demands of constant care obliged his retirement to the *Life Care Center* of Columbia, South Carolina. Here he was resident for a year and here he won the hearts of his caregivers through his witness and daily prayers for the staff—at their request. Sometimes he read Scripture to them in the language of heaven—Spanish—oblivious to the fact that they did not understand, but seemed to enjoy. The summons came on 20 October 1998. The "matchless giant" was ninety-seven. He and Evelyn had given seven decades to the service of Christ and Cuba.[797] His career had spanned twenty years as a missionary in Cuba, eighteen as general director of the Mission, and twenty in active retirement.

Thirty-nine years earlier, Elmer V. Thompson had composed a letter. It remained sealed, to be opened and read only after his death. On 1 October 1959, he had written for posterity:

> I believe this work has been divinely kept on its course through the years and divinely supplied as to its material needs. Rather than to conceive the Mission's first human leader as a benefactor of the enterprise, let him be remembered as chief among the benefited. I rejoice that my God has granted me in mercy the privilege of working so many years among you. I dare not say I have done my best, but I believe I have given my heart and strength to the work. [798]

As usual, he was right. As all know who surrender all to God, Thompson was "chief among the benefited." It is a fitting epitaph for the founder of a great work of God—and an example for his successors.

Elmer and Evelyn Thompson

Part 5
Treading a New Path
The Merger of
The Regions Beyond Missionary Union
and
The West Indies Mission
1995–2000

67

The Rationale for Union

Two are better than one, because they have a good return for their work.

—Solomon

Until the 1980s, most North American mission efforts could be described as "a cluster of isolated lifeboats, each one struggling alone against a monstrous wave of unbelief around the world."[799] New mission agencies proliferated, each with a fresh sense of "call." By 1990, nearly a thousand North American societies were at work. Many operated in studied isolation of what others were doing. Duplication of effort was inevitable. Not a few had existed beyond their justifiable lifespan. For recruiters and resource developers, survival became an endless cycle of competition for a diminishing supply of human and financial resources, all drawn from the same pool. Merger offered a solution of sorts, but called for courage not always present, for the survival instinct is strong, and loss of identity, pedigree, position, or control, resists change.

By nature, entropic regression is at work in every human enterprise, moving inexorably from vision to machine to monument. Mission agencies, like denominations, outlive the vitality that birthed them, and must be replaced by fresh bursts of Spirit-life. That this process results in a continuous proliferation of new agencies is not necessarily to be lamented. The Holy Spirit is eternally creative, at times breathing new life into old structures, but more often creating new vehicles and innovative methodologies under a leadership willing to discard what no longer works in exchange for what—to the surprise of many—proves effective.

Past Experience

Mission mergers were not new to RBMU and Worldteam. Economic and administrative weakness led RBMU in 1911 to surrender its South American fields to a localized merger, which became the Evangelical Union of South America. While the Mission soldiered bravely on during the decades of the 20s and 30s, it had lost much of the elán it had enjoyed under the stellar Guinnesses, a vivacity that would not be recovered until after World War II and the advent of Ebenezer G. Vine.

RBMU in turn absorbed the *Australia Nepalese Mission* in 1942 and the *Peru Inland Mission* in 1948. The West Indies Mission assimilated the *Mission to Orphans* in Cuba in 1963 and the *Door to Life* mission in Suriname the same year. None of these were true mergers of equals, but absorption of weaker agencies by the stronger, with the smaller surrendering their identity to the larger in the interests of efficiency. True mergers of equals in a shared identity remain rare, though in the economic convulsions of the final decade of the millennium, corporate giants have led the way.

Together We Can!

By the 1990s, the days of "Lone Ranger" agencies had begun to yield to a refreshing biblical ecumenism. No longer obsessed with divisive issues, the church seized upon a theology of closure—a church for every people. The goal was finite, measurable, and attainable. However, it could not be done alone. *Networking* slipped into the evangelical vocabulary. The information explosion, the advent of global telecommunications, and the worldwide internet accelerated the trend. The three major evangelical short-wave radio stations adopted a common goal to blanket the earth with the gospel.[800] Staid Southern Baptists opened their vast unreached people database to all comers. The CoMission amalgamated the efforts of eighty mission agencies to give the gospel to a Russia emerging from seventy years of lethal social experiment. *"Together we can!"* became the mood of a new generation.

Setting the Mood

In 1990, RBMU formed an international council (the UK excepted). While this step failed to reduce overhead and created logistical problems, it served the practical purpose of separating the growing weight of overseas concerns from those of home administration, a pattern a number of societies were following at this time. David Martin became director of American RBMU in 1988, following the writer, and with the formation of the International Council in 1990, assumed the role of international director. David Meade, commended by a solid, ten-year record of accomplishment in the Philippines, succeeded Martin as director of American RBMU in early 1992. At this time a number of serious concerns stressed the leadership. The Mission was emerging from an internal shortfall of $186,000 (covered by real assets). A valued and effective staff recruiter resigned,[801] the health of another officer was in question, a resource development department was in the birth process, a major move to the new Warrington headquarters was underway, and tentative merger feelers (not with Worldteam) were in progress. Combined, these factors enhanced a growing mood in favor of merger.

Worldteam had traced a similar path. By the mid-1980s, foundation grants which had carried the Mission through a decade of aggressive expansion had been exhausted,[802] leaving Worldteam in a weakened position. Redefinition of the Mission's philosophy had changed its role vis à vis the national churches from that of patron to partner. Radical redirection of mission energies occasioned the loss of gifted leadership and a hemorrhage of missionary personnel.[803] In 1992 Worldteam had not fully recovered from these reverses and had begun tentative explorations of merger, although not with RBMU.

Rationale

While both agencies remained economically viable in 1993, additional factors—common to both—nudged them to consider merger. Loss of missionary vision and a decrease in giving within North American churches did not augur well for the future. The diminishing number of candidates signaled danger. Increased operating costs and a growing complexity in the recruitment and care of workers weighed heavily. Leaders of both agencies were overextended. It was also clear that small-to-medium sized North American agencies would face increasing difficulties as these trends continued. Aggressive solutions were needed. Both groups had addressed merger prospects with other agencies, but without consummation.

Then, in 1993, at the annual IFMA fall consultation in Houston,[804] delegates David Martin, Graham Cousens, Steve Miller, and Bob Vetter informally floated the subject. Martin and Miller were international directors, respectively, of RBMU and Worldteam. Vetter was then director of World Team USA, while Graham Cousens was director of RBMU's Asia operations. Comparing the ethos of the two missions, the foursome agreed that compatibility on fundamental issues was present and further talks were warranted. This led to a summit meeting on 3–4 December 1993 in the Toronto office of RBMU, with several other representatives present.[805]

As talks progressed, arguments multiplied in favor of merger. Both missions were highly compatible in purpose, vision, core values, and philosophy of ministry. A stronger staff would allow sharper focus on priorities, providing financial stability, and more efficient use of resources. These reasons were reinforced by a prevailing sense of unity, peace, enthusiasm, and transparency in the discussions. Neither mission had accepted earlier merger proposals.

With Eyes Open

Both were aware of the downside. Some unrest was inevitable. Relocation of staff would be disruptive and costly. Loss of historic identity would inflict its own kind of pain and some board members and staff would face redundancy. Such factors posed a threat to unity and would require time for healing.

The Toronto meeting confirmed consonance and the absence of any non-negotiable elements in the respective profiles. Accordingly, the meeting recommended formation of a steering committee[806] to perform an in-depth study and to provide formal recommendation to the boards. Officers from both missions agreed to relinquish their positions as a condition of merger. There was one non-negotiable agreement. In 1990, RBMU had completed construction of a 10,000 square-foot headquarters facility in Warrington, Pennsylvania. Both groups agreed that the new mission would locate its American headquarters in Warrington. The trade-off came in selection of a name for the new agency. RBMU had for some time been looking for a new name, and *Worldteam* aptly reflected the vision and methodology of the two agencies. Both agreed the choice was logical—with one change: The new mission would become *World Team* (two words). The agreement was sealed with the steering committee's request for a budget of $20,000 for the research that lay ahead.

RBMU director for Canada, Ken Bennett, noted in his January 1994 report to the steering committee that "oneness of spirit," openness, and an absence of maneuvering or manipulation had marked the discussions. Bennett's report reiterated the harmony of both groups with respect to core values, philosophy of ministry, and doctrine. It also expressed unanimous agreement to draft a firm proposal for merger to the respective missions by June 1994.

The steering committee outlined procedural steps toward merger, including the formation of a transition board (comprised of weighted representation from each of the six legal boards) and a full-time action team to execute the mandates of the transition board. By August, a questionnaire had been sent to all personnel in both missions soliciting viewpoint and comment on a variety of issues pertinent to the proposed union.

The Nuptials

In June 1995, in Mississauga, Ontario the two agencies blended their significant histories in merger nuptials in the presence of three hundred missionary delegates and friends of world evangelization.[807] Six months later, in December, the two missions ceased to exist as legally distinct entities when signatories from both groups formalized incorporation documents creating the new mission, World Team. The merger resulted in a combined force of four hundred workers, plus active retirees, deployed in twenty-six world areas and in all five continents.

The New Structure

The new World Team would coordinate its ministries locally through legal boards in each sending country, and globally through its Joint Ministry Council, made up of delegates from each national board. The terms of this cooperative relationship were defined in a statement called the *Joint Ministry Agreement*. This pact incorporated *World Team Essentials,* a defining document, which includes World Team's statement of faith, operating principles, and procedures. *Essentials* defined one of the new mission's primary strategies: decentralization. This concept minimized the de facto domination of the sending boards in the traditional sending countries by identifying potential missionary "sending communities" in other countries, establishing national boards within those countries, and extending to them the right to sit as full-fledged international World Team boards with voice and vote.

Under the umbrella of World Team Essentials—universal policy standards applicable in any country—each national board was free to function autonomously with respect to the recruitment, orientation, and fielding of its national missionary personnel, including selection of its fields of ministry. Under this broad umbrella, each sending country was also free to develop proprietary policies governing local legal and cultural requirements. A Joint Ministry Council was established to monitor compliance. National boards would be free to define their own policies in terms of their nation's proprietary legal requirements.

Adjustments

Among the first to pay the price of the new move was the Worldteam staff then living in Miami and Atlanta. Eleven Worldteam families based in greater Miami found the 1,200-mile move to Pennsylvania a disruption greater than they felt able to make. They resigned from the Mission. Three families did make the move—the Steve Millers from Atlanta, the Joel Dingledeins, and the Ralph Walbridges. A fourth family—the Albert Ehmanns—relocated from the Toronto area.

Synthesizing the administrative policies of two missions was a major task that took weeks, and became an ongoing process. Initiating the process was a task force made up of three senior men, two from Worldteam and one from RBMU—Morrie Cottle, Ed Walker, and Joe Conley. This demanding job was begun in the fall of 1995 and was completed in stages, with referenda repeatedly circulated to all personnel for comments and approval. The final document, designated World Team Essentials, was completed in 1998. Later editions would follow.

For all the forethought given to the merger process, glitches were inevitable. Failure to allow adequate transition time for coordination of two computerized accounting systems produced months of chaos in the merged accounting department. Delays and mix-ups in transmission of funds to missionary accounts dismayed both missionaries and donors. Severe snowstorms in greater Philadelphia in the winter of 1995–96 complicated these transitions. As expected, months of administrative staff time were consumed in development of the five-year action plan that would take World Team into the new millennium.

Not everyone was happy about merger. For those unprepared to relocate, merger spelled the end of years of service with Worldteam. For some who stayed the course, a bumpy ride lay ahead. Much like a marriage, it took time for the newlyweds to get to know each other and to make the adjustments essential to harmonic bliss. Merger had promised a greater economy of both human and material resources. Whether this was achieved will be mooted from the expertise of hindsight. Bigger was not necessarily better, as the new international director Albert Ehmann noted:

> Missions today must change to remain both cost and ministry effective in serving the sending churches. Bigger is better only if it permits a higher degree of effectiveness with little or no increase in the use of administrative resources. Doubling our missionary staff does not in itself make us more effective. However, as in a marriage, each partner brings complementary strengths to the union.[808]

And there *were* complementary benefits. RBMU's historic emphasis on Scripture translation and frontier church planting among unreached people groups brought a fresh ministry emphasis to the old Worldteam. This focus was intensified and sharpened as the Least-Evangelized Peoples (LEP) strategy of the new Mission got underway.

Strategic Partnerships

Worldteam skills and experience in training techniques for identifying and equipping church planters, emphasis on church multiplication, and development of effective missionary teams brought critical expertise to RBMU. The development of this singular church planting focus had been a courageous missiological breakthrough, developed through undaunted tenacity and painful process. It brought a new modus operandi to RBMU. Both missions had struggled with finding mechanisms to engage and deploy emerging national leadership in global church planting in a way that would place nationals on a level playing field with western missions in the decision-making process. World Team's decentralization of mission authority under a Joint Ministry Council provided the framework for a fresh approach to mission. As the new director Ehmann noted:

> The great challenge to Western missions is no longer simply to take the gospel to unreached peoples—we continue to do that vigorously—but to help equip emerging national churches to become *churches that start new churches*, and to unite with these two thirds world churches in

strategic partnerships to facilitate their own world missionary vision . . . We believe that God has uniquely qualified us to do this.[809]

The New Leader

When the transition team began its search for God's man to lead the new mission, they solicited nominations from the fields. A handful of names emerged—all proven and promising leaders. Professional consultants were called upon to examine each candidate for suitability against an established roster of leadership criteria. Canadian veteran Albert Ehmann emerged as the clear choice. In full confidence that God was in the decision, his name was presented to the corporate body and approved.

Albert Ehmann had been raised on missions. His father was a Colorado cowboy who followed God's call to Prairie Bible Institute in Alberta, Canada. On the PBI campus Albert's parents caught the vision of world missions and prayed that God would use their six children to carry the gospel to the world. All six became missionaries. From childhood, Ehmann was immersed in gospel work, first helping his parents in their ministry to the Blackfoot Indian reservation, later as a Canadian Sunday School Mission worker in camps, vacation Bible schools and church planting ministries. It was a natural next step upon graduation from Prairie Bible College to join Worldteam (then the West Indies Mission). His first assignment was Jamaica, where he apprenticed for one year under Elmer Thompson, co-founder of Worldteam, and one-time professor at Prairie. During the Jamaica ministry, Albert met Jane Kesler, whom he subsequently married. She had been serving in the Peace Corps. In Jamaica, Ehmann formed a church planting team together with his brother, Daniel.

The Ehmanns were next posted to St. Lucia in the West Indies, where they completed a five-year church planting assignment. Next was a ten-year tour in Sicily (1976–1985), where Ehmann launched a Christian radio station in Messina, serving as field director for the second half of their tour. In 1985, Worldteam named Ehmann Executive Director of Worldteam Canada. Here he initiated a church planting apprenticeship program to train church planters, while coordinating Worldteam's ministries to Cuba. With the 1995 merger of RBMU and Worldteam, Albert Ehmann was named International President of the new Mission.

68

The Way Ahead

We have no choice but to think about the future, for the future is all that is left of life.

—Ed Dayton[810]

Like a timely blood transfusion, merger infused World Team with new life and expectancy. Months earlier, a transition board, and six task groups had poured herculean effort into restructuring the mission.[811] The resulting action plan was launched immediately and would carry the agency into the new millennium. Since biblical planning is always a faith-vision for the future— never a presumptuous attempt to forecast the future—plans are always in flux and continuously subject to course corrections. Corporate prayer, careful re-search, and vigilance in monitoring global developments sharpen sensitivity to the Holy Spirit's nudging. New *kairos* moments may appear unexpectedly, calling for immediate response or change of tactic. For this reason, today's projections may be modified tomorrow—even discarded. For the new mis-sion, many adjustments were called for as mechanisms were tested, amended, and refined.

Caliraya

Then, on the eve of the third millennium, the first International Strategic Planning Conference of World Team convened in Caliraya in the Philippines, 26 January–12 February 1999. Eighty delegates from twenty-three countries crafted statements defining World Team's purpose, vision, strategic objec-tives, and goals for the twenty-first century. Topping the list was the over-arching purpose of the new agency:

To glorify God by working together to establish reproducing churches among unreached peoples of the world.

It was an old slogan with a new twist. *"Reproducing"* was the critical adjective, for it represented a new threshold of purpose and a new standard for measuring successful mission. With a century of God-given success in *establishing* churches, World Team now raised the bar, calling for the planting of churches which by nature, training, and express purpose, would become exponentially reproductive—*reproducing* other churches in the biblical pattern. In a word, successful mission is achieved only when local churches become truly *missionary* in purpose and action.

As world population continued to burgeon exponentially,[812] mission strategists saw that the goal of global gospel saturation could be realized only through the multiplication of church planting *movements.* With proven mechanisms already in place, World Team stretched confidently into the new millennium with this goal—*to ignite an explosion of church planting movements among the unreached people groups of earth.* The vision was radical, and the goal would take World Team to frontiers where human resolve alone would be inadequate. With eyes on the finish line, Caliraya's first five-year action plan for the new millennium defined several objectives:

1. Enter Unevangelized People Groups.

The missionary focus of Scripture in both Old and New Testaments is upon the *people groups* of the earth—the *ethnos,* often translated *gentiles,* or *nations.*[813] In support of this emphasis, the great Apostle in Romans 15 cites no fewer than four Old Testament passages,[814] and portrays himself in priestly metaphor as pouring out as an offering to God, the people groups of earth. Since the fragmentation of earth's population into a vast mosaic of ethnolinguistic families was by divine fiat and not a sociological accident,[815] and since Scripture clearly indicates that God did this with a redemptive purpose in view,[816] the mission of the Church shall not be complete until a viable expression of the life of Christ is present in each of these groups.

Grounded in these Scriptural affirmations, we may be assured that our mandate is achievable, measurable, and within the reach of obedient faith. As we step into a new century, an estimated 1, Unreached People Groups remain without a Christian church, many of them located in the 10-40 window.[817] Over the next five years, World Team is committed *to enter 17 of these UPGs with church planting teams.*[818]Beyond 2004, through continuous research and based upon prioritized criteria, the Mission will continue its work of church planting among these ethnolinguistic families until the task is complete.

2. Form National Partnerships.

When Charles Haddon Spurgeon said, "The social element is the genius of Christianity,"[819] he echoed the Apostle Paul, who called it by another name—*koinonia,* a sharing in common.[820] Western churches have shared the riches of

Christ and his gospel, taking salvation's message to the dark side of the world. The result has been a global church "more widely planted and deeply rooted"[821] than ever before in history. As these national churches have matured, thousands of new believers and scores of national church associations have begun to catch the spirit of global missions. No longer a mission *field*, they have become a potential mission *force*. Many, however, have lacked the infrastructures to launch effective programs.

With a little help, they represent a dynamic factor in world evangelization. At Caliraya, World Team pledged to lift *koinonia* to a richer—and costlier— level of expression by *forming church planting partnerships with these national churches and with national missionaries.* In many places, international church planting teams already function. Now, World Team will accelerate these efforts to bring national churches onto the larger playing field of world missions. Ways and means will be sought to provide support for national missionaries by encouraging business ventures and by sharing global resources within a framework of accountability.

3. Focus on Multiplication.

This goal of reproducing churches by multiplication will be achieved only as each newly planted church becomes committed to world evangelization. This means that the missionary cannot be content solely with church nurture, but must also instill an activist missionary vision in the church before his task is complete.

At the time of merger, this near-forgotten principle of the book of Acts was already unleashing a new dynamic for exponential church growth on a global scale. Since its formation in 1992, the Alliance for Saturation Church Planting—of which World Team is a part—saw six hundred new churches formed in former Eastern Bloc countries *annually* over a four-year period.[822] This was accomplished through the training of national leaders in the biblical basis and skills of church multiplication. Training existing national leadership in multiplication principles through workshops, seminars, and coaching teams, World Team has tapped into a potential force for world evangelization. Caliraya purposed *to market the multiplication principle in church planting* throughout World Team's national ministries in twenty-three countries.

Because the multiplication of churches is directly tied to the multiplication of leaders, Caliraya also committed the new mission *to facilitate national churches in the identification, training, and multiplication of national leaders.* Pilot programs have already proved effective, as churches have been challenged with this biblical mandate through workshops, seminars, and the college of coaches.

4. Develop Inter-Agency Partnerships.

The fusion of two venerable agencies in 1995 to form a more muscular servant of the sending churches bears witness to World Team's commitment to
inter-mission cooperation. With an established record of cooperation in the
former Soviet Union, the Philippines, the Caribbean, and elsewhere, World
Team will move aggressively *to forge synergistic partnerships with sister
mission agencies* as a means of reducing overhead and avoiding duplication of
effort. A promising step toward this goal was taken when World Team joined
Next Step, a coalition of North American agencies dedicated to pooling resources among sending churches, mission mobilizers, and sister missions.[823]

5. Vitalize Linkage with Sending Churches.

Long before the dawn of the new century, North Americans had become im-
patient with mission agencies, no longer content to serve as mere paymasters
with little voice and less control. With accelerating global awareness and mobility, many looked for a more direct involvement in the work of cross-
cultural missions. This trend resulted in some churches launching proprietary
mission efforts, independent of traditional agencies. While this has worked in
selective contexts, the practice is fraught with pitfalls both for the sending
church and the workers it commissions.

Because the work of cross-cultural church planting has become a highly
skilled process, demanding exacting cultural and political sensitivity, local
churches can avoid much grief by taking advantage of the cutting-edge expertise which experienced and successful missions can provide. At the same
time, not a few sending churches have been successful in developing a biblical missions program in the selection and equipping of their members for
cross-cultural service. Combining the creative energies of church and mission
in a dynamic relationship of mutual respect is the way forward for the new
century. As noted elsewhere in this history, World Team has already established effective, cooperative relationships with several such churches. Caliraya committed the new World Team to the continuing *development of creative partnerships of mutual trust with sending churches.*

Here, then, is the shape of mission for the World Team of the twenty-first
century. Here is the way ahead—a team of focused missionaries who have
caught the vision of church multiplication, who have seen the larger picture,
who understand that biblical multiplication of reproducing churches results
through a determined equipping of local believers for the work of church
planting. It is a vision that calls for a new breed of missionary. One who finds
fulfillment, not so much in gathering the harvest, but who by investing his or
her life and energy in the training of others, assures the multiplication of that
harvest beyond anything they might have done alone.

69

You *Can* Change the World!

Faith shares the Omnipotence she dares to trust. —Anon

"The power of God has always hovered over our frontiers," observed A. W. Tozer. "It is only released into the church when she is doing something that demands it." In this confidence, World Team rises to the challenge of the twenty-first century. *God will be there for us.*

The drumbeats of an earlier generation inspire us, invoking admiration. Wistfully, we marvel at their achievements, too often convinced that what they have accomplished is beyond our reach. We fail to take into account the *frontier* factor, for it is there—and only there—that we discover the enabling power of God. Once-dark zones of our planet ring today with songs of worship and praise, because men and women of faith stepped out—sometimes fearfully—into the unknown, with nothing to lean upon but the promise of God. Few of them could have guessed the astonishing outcome of their quiet sacrament, for the power of God was not always visible. It awaited them at their frontiers. They discovered, as we all must, that the call to follow is never so clearly given as to make unnecessary that first, trembling step into the unknown. "Can you send me where the communists won't come?" was one would-be missionary's conditional offer. But God extends no pre-audit of his plan, and we walk by faith.

What sets our heroes apart is that they took Jesus at his word. He promised, *"Greater works than these you shall do, because I go unto the Father."* [824]The exploits of the World Team story are the *greater works* of which Jesus spoke. We share continuity with what Jesus began. Do not relegate that promise to the Apostles alone. It belongs to every obedient Christian. His work continues through us. There is a *finished* work of Christ, and there is an *unfinished* work of Christ. The finished work of Christ has secured the Kingdom for us. The *unfinished* work of Christ is the calling out of his own from the nations of earth. When that work is finished, he will come. Jesus died and rose in triumph, not to gather the harvest, but to make the harvest possible. *Harvesting* is what he has given us to do. Once that is understood, missions becomes the most glorious of vocations, for what missionaries and their partners-in-mission do, is nothing less than part of that eternal work of God. It cannot fail.

When the Allied forces secured the beaches of Normandy on 6 June 1944, the outcome of World War II was already decided. The German high command knew it. The allied generals knew it. Still, eleven months of bloody fighting lay between the Allies and the unconditional surrender of Germany on 8 May 1945. Every hedgerow and every village would be contested and taken before victory was complete. In the war for world evangelization, we are poised between Normandy and V-E Day.

As we enter the twenty-first century, our world is convulsed by paroxysms of Satanic fury, unleashed in multiplying violence, terrorism, genocide, and virulent persecution of the holy seed—the Church. Missions are promised no safe-zone. These facts must neither take us by surprise, nor paralyze us with fear. Nor must they be permitted to deter us from obedience to our Lord's commission. They are but "the cheap shots of a frustrated player in the waning moments of a lost contest."[825] In our turbulent century, even more costly service may lie ahead for those who carry the banner into the dark places of earth. But when the white flag is run up and unconditional surrender is signed, we shall have no regrets for anything we have done for God.

History moves swiftly toward its consummation in the supreme exaltation of Jesus Christ, when he shall have gathered his own from among every people, tribe, and nation. Then the day of missions will be past, and with it, the opportunity of harvest. Mission is not forever. It is a temporary mechanism, in place momentarily until Jesus' *unfinished* work is complete. In this brief hour of life, he invites us, *"Go, work today in my vineyard."*[826] Don't miss the moment.

The outcome is assured: *"The earth shall be filled with the knowledge of the glory of the Lord."* "The God of peace shall bruise Satan under your feet." Then we shall sing, *"You are worthy to take the scroll and open its seals, because you were slain, and with your blood you purchased men for God from every tribe and language and people and nation."*[827]

Dr. Harry Guinness, one of the early founders of this work, left us this advice one hundred years ago:

> Gentlemen, find out the will of God for your
> generation; and then, as quickly as possible,
> get into line.

About This Story . . .

[1] British RBMU disbanded in 1991 and lodged much of its historical documentary material in the Centre For The Study of Christianity In The Non-Western World, New College, Mound Place, Edinburgh, EH1 2LX.
[2] Counted from inception to time of merger: RBMU: 1873–1995, WIM: 1928–1995.
[3] Proverbs 4.18
[4] Romans 10.18 (NIV).

Chapter 1   The Man Who Beats the Drum
[5] J. Edwin Orr, *The Light of the Nations* (Exeter Devon: Paternoster, 1965), 100.
[6] ibid.
[7] Robert Sobel, *Panic On Wall Street* (Dutton, NY: Truman Talley Books, 1968), 108.
[8] Samuel I. Prime, *The Power of Prayer* (Edinburgh 1859. Reprint: Carlisle, PA: Banner of Truth Trust, 1991), 24.
[9] J. Edwin Orr, 109.
[10] ibid., 254.
[11] G. F. Barbour, *The Life of Alexander Whyte* (London: Hodder and Stoughton, 1923), 92.
[12] William Temple, *Readings in St. John's Gospel* (New York: Macmillan, 1955), 130. Cited by John Stott in *Evangelical Truth* (Downers Grove: IVP, 1999).

Chapter 2   A Shining Light
[13] Michele Guinness, *The Guinness Legend* (London: Hodder and Stoughton, 1990), Jacket.
[14] Betty Pritchard, *For Such A Time* (Eastbourne: Victory Press, 1973), 49. While other mission conferences had convened before Edinburgh, the 1910 conference was the first truly global missions conference, with 1,200 delegates present. John Raleigh Mott was chairman. He had earlier coined the slogan, *"The evangelization of the world in this generation."*
[15] British Protestants who did not accept the authority of the Anglican Church.
[16] Michele Guinness, 26.
[17] ibid., 29.
[18] ibid.
[19] Kenneth Holmes, *The Cloud Moves* (London: RBMU, 1963), 9.
[20] ibid., 10.
[21] Michelle Guinness, 65, 66.
[22] ibid., 67.
[23] ibid., 68, 69.
[24] ibid., 57.
[25] Malachi 3:10 (NIV).
[26] Michele Guinness, 105.
[27] Kenneth Holmes, 16.
[28] Betty Pritchard, 20.
[29] Kenneth Holmes, 16.
[30] ibid., 10.
[31] Luke 24:47, Rom. 15, Gen. 12:3.

[32] "A group of eight or nine students gathered there four evenings a week after work to study Paley's *Evidences of Christianity*, a book designed to enable its readers to hold their own against Darwin and his supporters." (Michele Guinness, 84)

[33] Mrs. Howard Taylor (née Geraldine Guinness) was Grattan Guinness' eldest daughter. She became Hudson Taylor's biographer.

[34] Geraldine Taylor (Mrs. Howard), *The Growth of a Work* (Lutterworth: China Inland Mission, 1918), 56, 57.

[35] Kenneth Holmes, 13.

Chapter 3   Ashes That Lit A Fire

[36] C. W. Macintosh, *The Life Story of Dr. Harry Guinness* (London: RBMU, 1916), 13.

[37] Karry Kelley (W.T. Spain) confirmed that two "Quemaderos" existed in Madrid, one near the Plaza San Bernardo, where the records offices of the Inquisition were housed. The other site was Puerta de Alcalá, near Retiro Park. E-mail letter to the writer, November 1998.

[38] Michele Guinness, 91.

[39] Lorraine Boettner, *Roman Catholicism* (Philadelphia: Presbyterian and Reformed Publishing, 1962), 428. See also Philip Schaff, *History of the Christian Church*, Vol. IV, Ch. 60, 553–554. Also Jason Slade, internet, 6 August 1996.

[40] Michele Guinness, 91.

[41] H. Grattan Guinness, *Romanism and the Reformation* (London: Harley House (RBMU), 1887. Reprint: Hartland Publications, Rapidan, VA. 1995), 94.

[42] The Roman Catholic Church has never rescinded the maledictions pronounced by the Council of Trent (1545–63) upon those who teach salvation through faith alone in God's judicial acquittal of the believer through the cross-work and resurrection of Jesus. The 1994 Catechism of the Roman Catholic Church cites the CT ninety-nine times. Historically, evangelical missions in Roman Catholic lands have faced this fury to the present day, a position modified only where prevailing political climate necessitates. The inveterate gravitation of the human heart to seek divine approbation through meritorious works first reared its head in the Mother Church at Jerusalem through the Judaizers (Acts 15). It was courageously and vehemently denounced by the Apostle Paul in his polemic to the Galatians, but gradually infiltrated the writings of the church fathers, and later became known as Pelagianism (after the British monk who denied original sin). The watershed nature of the Galatian epistle forever established the irreducible and uncompromising content of the gospel (Kerugma). Those who teach otherwise—Paul affirms—are themselves subject to a far more serious anathema, that of God himself. I am indebted to Dr. Robert Reymond, of Knox Theological Seminary, for his insights on the development of Roman Catholic salvation-by-merit dogma before the Reformation.

[43] H. Grattan Guinness, from his lectures recorded in *Romanism and The Reformation* (1887. 1995 Rapidan, VA. Hartland Publications), 144, 145.

[44] ibid., 22 ff.

[45] ibid., 147.

[46] See bibliography of H. Grattan Guinness' writings on page 491.

[47] De Cheseaux, *Historical, Chronological, and Astronomical Remarks on Certain Parts of the Book of Daniel*. British Museum.

[48] Michele Guinness, 129.

[49] ibid., 204, 205.

[50] H. Grattan and Fanny Guinness, *Light For The Last Days* (London: 1893, Marshall, Morgan & Scott, London, 1917. . . 1934 [eighth impression]).

[51] Michele Guinness, 297.

Chapter 4   The East London Institute

[52] Kenneth Holmes, 14.

[53] Lucy Guinness depicted London's East End in her book, *Only a Factory Girl.* She had voluntarily lived and worked among girls marginalized by the industrial revolution.

[54] H. Grattan Guinness, *Lucy Guinness Kumm: Her Life Story* (London: Morgan & Scott, 1907), 9.

[55] Geraldine Taylor, (Mrs. Howard), *The Growth of a Work* (Lutterworth: China Inland Mission, 1918), 56, 57.

[56] Fanny Guinness, *New World*, 531. (*New World* text states date as March, 1872)

[57] Geoffrey Hanks, *60 Great Founders* (Ross-shire, Scotland. Christian Focus Publications, 1995), 19.

[58] November, 1874 (Macintosh, 12).

[59] Kenneth Holmes, 14, 15.

[60] Betty Pritchard, 19.

[61] Harry Guinness, *Not Unto Us* (London: RBMU, 1908), 41.

Chapter 5   How Far the Sound Would Go

[62] Robert L. Niklaus, with John S. Sawin, and Samuel J. Stoesz, *All For Jesus—God At Work In the Christian and Missionary Alliance Over 100 Years* (Camp Hill, PA: Christian Publications), 23.

[63] Richard Gilbertson, *The Baptism of the Holy Spirit: The views of A. B. Simpson and his contemporaries*, 41. Simpson had left the Presbyterian Church "in order to spend more time in mass evangelism and also to be free to practice believer's baptism." (Ruth Slade. *King Leopold's Congo*. London. Oxford. 1962), 144.

[64] Charles W. Nienkirchen, *A. B. Simpson and the Pentecostal Movement* (Peabody MA: Hendrickson Publishers), 21. Fanny Guinness explains the philosophy, objectives, and structure of Guinness' Institute in *The Wide World and Our Work in It* (London: Hodder and Stoughton, 1886).

[65] Robert Niklaus. All For Jesus: God at Work in the Christian & Missionary Alliance (Camp Hill, PA), 128, 273.

[66] ibid.

[67] Simpson Bible Institute later moved to San Francisco, then to Redlands, CA, its location in 1998.

[68] The 1925–26 and 1926–27 terms. *Whitened Harvest*, Jan.–Feb. 1958.

[69] Geoffrey Hanks, *60 Great Founders* (Geanies House, Ross-shire, Scotland: Christian Focus Publications, 1995), 132 ff.

[70] ibid., 18.

[71] Religious Tract Society, 1894.

[72] Dayton Roberts, *One Step Ahead* (Miami: Latin America Mission, 1969). 13 ff.

[73] *Regions Beyond* (UK) July 1886, 19.

[74] J. Edwin Orr, *The Light of the Nations* (UK: Paternoster, 1965), 183.
[75] J. Edwin Orr, *Evangelical Awakenings in Latin America* (Minneapolis: Bethany, 1978), 37.
[76] J. B. A. Kessler Jr., *Protestant Missions in Peru and Chile* (Oosterbaan & le Cointre N.V. Goes, 1967), 33, 36.
[77] ibid., 38.
[78] Harry Guinness, *Not Unto Us*, 18.
[79] Henry Clay Mabie, *From Romance to Reality* (American Baptist, 1917), 112, 113.
[80] J. Edwin Orr, *Evangelical Awakenings in Latin America* (Minneapolis: Bethany, 1978), 61, 94.
[81] CIM later became the Overseas Missionary Fellowship (OMF).

Chapter 6   Heal This Open Sore
[82] Peter Forbath, *The River Congo* (NY: Putnam, 1973), 204. The Arabs were not solely responsible for slavery in Central Africa. Domestic slavery was already widespread among the Bantu tribes. (Ruth Slade. *King Leopold's Congo* (NY: Oxford U., 1962), 85.
[83] Stanley's Journal, 14 March 1872.
[84] Forbath, 216.

Chapter 7   Frail Craft on a Troubled Sea
[85] Fanny Guinness, New World of Central Africa, 176
[86] Ruth Slade, *King Leopold's Congo* (NY: Oxford U., 1962). P.142 ff. See also, Fanny Guinness, *New World of Central Africa*. (Arthington offered £1000 to the BMS if they would undertake work in the Congo).
[87] Fanny Guiness, *The New World of Central Africa*, 180, 235. Unless otherwise noted, all citations re. the era of the Livingstone Inland Mission (1877–1884) are extracted from the voluminous work of Fanny Guinness, *The New World of Central Africa*, (London: Hodder and Stoughton, 1890), hereafter referred to as *New World.*
[88] They were W. T. Berger, Esq., of Cannes, Lord Polwarth, of Mertoun, N. B., J. Houghton, Esq., of Liverpool, and Thomas Coates, Esq., of Paisley.
[89] Neal Ascherson, *The King Incorporated* (NY: Doubleday, 1964), 85.
[90] A railway line completed in May 1898 links the city to the ocean port of Matadi. Henry Morton Stanley founded Kinshasa as a supply depot in 1881 at a Humbo village site. In 1923 it replaced Boma as the capital of Belgian Congo.
[91] *New World*, 47, 48
[92] John Crawford, *Protestant Missions in Congo*, 2. *Matadi* is the Kikongo word for "stone." Matadi is ninety-three miles upstream from the Atlantic port of Banana and is the last deepwater port before the cataracts.
[93] New World, 315.
[94] ibid., 315–317.
[95] ibid., 405
[96] ibid., 256.
[97] ibid., 246-248. A second SS *Livingstone* was launched on 20 April 1901 for use on the upper Congo as a memorial to Mrs. Fanny Guinness. (Macintosh, 67).
[98] ibid.

[99] *New World*, 206. The writer has adapted this account from Fanny Guinness' material in *The New World of Central Africa*, 202–297.
[100] Ruth Slade,. 72. Reluctance of porters on the lower River obliged missionaries to contract with men of the Kru tribe (east of Liberia) for the journey.
[101] New World, 291.
[102] ibid., 296
[103] Michele Guinness, 222.
[104] New World, 202.
[105] New World, 297
[106] Luke 7:19
[107] New World, 297.
[108] ibid., 298
[109] John 12:24.
[110] New World, 234.
[111] ibid.
[112] Fanny Guinness, The New World of Central Africa, 405.
[113] ibid., 251.
[114] Michele Guinness, 159.
[115] *New World* 238–240, 386.

Chapter 8   Pentecost on the Congo
[116] *New World*, 429. Unless otherwise noted, citations in this chapter are extracted from *the New World of Central Africa*, by Fanny Guinness, referred to as *New World.*
[117] ibid., 429.
[118] ibid.
[119] *New World*, 420, 421.
[120] ibid., 430.
[121] ibid.
[122] ibid. 413–420.
[123] J. Edwin Orr, *Evangelical Awakenings in Africa* (Minneapolis: Bethany Fellowship, 1975) 87, 88.
[124] ibid.
[125] Begun in 1887 (Macintosh, 31).
[126] New World, 393.
[127] ibid., 394.
[128] ibid., 396.
[129] Petterson and Westling, sent out by the Swedish Missionary Society, had joined LIM to learn the language before commencing an independent effort. The Mukimbungu station was transferred to the Swedish Baptist Mission at this time. (*New World*, 402).
[130] They were *Palabala*, LIM's first station, south of the Yellala Falls, and on a hill 1,600 feet high. *Mukimvika*, built on a cliff overlooking the Atlantic, opposite Banana, but separated from it by seven miles of water. *Banza Manteka*, founded in 1879, and site of the first church building. *Mukimbungo*, near Itumzuna Falls. *Lukunga*, "a pleasant place in a populous district." *Leopoldville*, on Stanley Pool, where the steamers were reconstructed. *Equatorville*, near Wangata on the upper river, founded by Pettersen and Eddie among the N'kundu people. Stations at Banana and Matadi were

abandoned, while the station at Banana was moved to Mukimvika. (*New World*, 401,402).

[131] They were Mr. and Mrs. Craven, Mr. and Mrs. Clarke, Mr. and Mrs. Ingham, Mr. and Mrs. Stephen White, Dr. Sims and Messrs. Harvey, Richards, Billington, Pettersen, Westlind, Fredrickson, Banks, Pictorn, Glenesk, Eddie, and Hoste, with the Misses Spearing, Cole, Harris, and Skakle. (*New World*, 401).

[132] Michele Guinness, 216

Chapter 9   The Congo Balolo Mission

[133] C. W. Mackintosh, *The Life Story of Dr. Harry Guinness* (London: RBMU, 1916), 13–29.

[134] ibid., 19.

[135] ibid., 16.

[136] ibid., 31–33.

[137] ibid.

[138] Fanny Guinness, The New World of Central Africa, 465–471.

[139] Baptist policy was to evangelize in one language only, develop a strong central base, and expand radially as strength permitted. The Swedish Mission, formed when the LIM withdrew, followed the same policy. See Slade, 144 ff. McKittrick returned to England early in 1888.

[140] Fanny Guinness, *New World*, 476.

[141] *Regions Beyond*, first quarter, 1968.

[142] Harry Guinness. *Not Unto Us* (London: RBMU, 1908), 85, 87.

[143] New World, 528.

[144] The first CBM party comprised the John McKittricks, the Messrs. Whytock, Haupt, Howell, Todd, and Blake, together with Miss de Hailes. They were reinforced in 1890 by Messrs., Adamson, Luff, and Cole.

[145] The Lower Congo Railway did not open until May 1898.

[146] Dora McKenzie, *How We Entered the Land*, article in *Not Unto Us* (Harry Guinness, London: 1908), 71-78. All citations in this segment will be found on pages 71-78 of *Not Unto Us*.

[147] Guinness sailed with his wife and children for Tenerife on March 19, she going on to visit her home in Tasmania, Harry going to Congo by way of Madeira. (Macintosh, 39).

[148] Harry Guinness' own account of these incidents is found in Macintosh, 41-47.

[149] The writer will not soon forget visiting the Bonginda gravesite in 1969. In the center of a clutch of missionary markers was a four-tiered marble base, atop which was a simple marble cross bearing the inscription in Lingala: John McKittrick/Englishman/A Teacher of God's Word/Greater Love Hath No Man Than this/That a Man Lay Down His Life for His Friends/October 30 1857–November 22 1891.

Chapter 10   The Enemy

[150] Frederick F. Cartwright, *Disease and History* (New York: Dorset, 1972), 138.

[151] ibid., 141. "Malaria might carry off entire expeditions of three or four hundred men with such effectiveness and speed that at first the Portuguese believed they had been poisoned by Africans or coastal Arabs." Jeal, 27.

[152] Fanny Guinness, *New World*, 492, 493, 500.

[153] ibid., 492

[154] ibid., 492, 493, 502.

[155] Side effects of large doses included vomiting, headache, rashes, disturbances of vision, and severe tinnitus (Cartwright, 144).

[156] Cartwright, 138

[157] Lily Ruskin, *Ruskin of Congo* (London: RBMU, 1948), 33.

[158] Commissioners investigated the excesses of Anglo-Belgian Rubber in this region from October 1904 to February 1905. "Some of the sharpest criticisms of the Congo regime had come from the missionaries of the Congo Balolo Mission." Slade, 188.

Chapter 11   This Magnificent African Cake

[159] Peter Forbath, *The River Congo* (NY: Putnam, 1973), 323.

[160] Fanny Guinness, *New World,* 83.

[161] John R. Crawford, *Protestant Missions in Congo*, 1878–1969 (Kinshasa), 9. "Roman Catholic missionaries, Belgian almost to a man, remained strangely quiet until 1906. Protestant missionaries found themselves rebuffed and hindered by State officials and trading companies . . . Missions ready to advance into new areas were repeatedly denied concessions, though land was readily available."

[162] Thomas Parkenham, *The Scramble For Africa* (New York: Avon, 1991), 21.

[163] ibid., 22.

[164] Tim Jeal, *Livingstone* (NY: Putnam, 1973), 377,378.

[165] Ruth Slade, *King Leopold's Congo* (London: Oxford U.), 39-43.

[166] In 1891 the Congo State produced 82 tons of rubber; by 1901 she was producing 6,000 tons a year.

[167] Macintosh, 73.

[168] Colin Legum, *Congo Disaster* (Penguin Books, 1961), 35.

[169] Thomas Parkenham, 590.

[170] The Anthropological Society in Britain, formed in 1863 by followers of Robert Knox.

[171] Philips Verner Bradford and Harvey Blume, *Ota Benga, The Pygmy in the Zoo* (New York: St. Martin's Press, 1992), Cited in New York Times, Sunday, 9 Sept. 1906. Benga had been brought with other pygmies for exhibition at the St. Louis World's Fair in 1904.

[172] Macintosh, 69.

[173] ibid., 76, 77.

[174] Lily Ruskin, *Ruskin of Congo*, 30.

[175] ibid.

[176] ibid., 20.

[177] Ruth Slade, *King Leopold's Congo* (London: Oxford U.), 179.

[178] Macintosh, 69.

[179] *New World*, 78, 79.

[180] C.W. Mackintosh, *The Life Story of Dr. Harry Guinness* (London: RBMU. 1916), 70, 71.

[181] ibid., 71.

[182] Michele Guinness, 274.

[183] Mackintosh, 71–75.

[184] Macintosh, 77. The protest was raised on 19 November 1909. Belgium had annexed the Congo Free State on 15 November 1908. Britain recognized the annexation in June 1913.

[185] Harry Guinness, *Not Unto Us*, 102.

[186] ibid., 85.

Chapter 12   If I Will That He Tarry

[187] John's Gospel, 20:18 ff.

[188] Lily Ruskin, 26.

[189] ibid. 27.

[190] ibid., 18, 20

[191] ibid., 38.

[192] Ruskin, 21.

[193] Harry Guinness, *Not Unto Us*, 112.

[194] C.W. Mackintosh, The Life of Harry Guinness, 47.

Chapter 13   The Congo Church

[195] *Regions Beyond*, September 1995, 4.

[196] ibid.

[197] RBMU Congo brochure, undated c. 1954

[198] Dr. Arthur Wright, with appropriate cultural sensitivity, objected to the common use of the term "leper" in reference to those afflicted with the disease. "Leprosy is a disease, and such a term is no more fitting than to refer to a person suffering from malaria as a 'malaria'." Elizabeth Wright, letter to the writer, 14 August 1999. In 1948 the World Health Organization discouraged the use of the word 'leper' and in 1966 the Mission to Lepers changed its name to The Leprosy Mission, so painful had become the stigma of "leper."

Chapter 14   Lucy Guinness Kuhm

[199] H. Grattan Guinness, *Lucy Guinness Kuhm, Her Life Story* (London: Morgan and Scott, 1907), 5 ff.

[200] ibid., 8, 9.

[201] ibid., 10. The Student Volunteer Movement (SVM) convened in Liverpool in 1896 with 23 countries represented. Their battle cry: *Make Jesus King!* (Macintosh, 50).

[202] ibid., 83.

[203] ibid., 18.

[204] H. Grattan Guinness, Lucy Guinness Kumm, Her Life Story, 19.

[205] ibid., 20.

[206] ibid.

[207] Founded in 1902 at the Sheffield YMCA as the Sudan Pioneer Mission, the mission was reorganized as the Sudan United Mission, a name suggested by Dr. Alexander Whyte of St. George's church, Edinburgh.

Chapter 15   Graveyard of Missions

[208] H. Grattan Guinness, Lucy Guinness Kumm, Her Life Story, 13.

[209] ibid., 13.

[210] Hodge served for years as secretary of the Bihar Christian Council and later (1929) as secretary of the National Christian Council of India, in which he played a formative role. He also wrote *Salute to India*; and *Bishop Azariah of Dornakal.*

[211] Betty Pritchard, *For Such a Time*, 43

[212] John 4.38.

[213] Peter Forbath, *The River Congo* (NY: Putnam, 1973), 200.

[214] 2 Cor. 10:16.

[215] In January 1899, all branches of the work at Harley House were united under the new name. (Macintosh, 48)

[216] Pritchard, 57.

[217] Ernest W. Oliver, autobiographical notes submitted to the writer.

[218] Pritchard, 58

[219] ibid.

[220] ibid., 59, 60.

Chapter 16   A Very Able Major

[221] Personal interviews with E. W. Oliver and autobiographical material shared with the writer.

Chapter 17   Neglected Continent

[222] H. Grattan Guinness, *Lucy Guinness Kuhm, Her Life Story* (London: Morgan and Scott, 1907), 11.

[223] C. W. Mackintosh, *The Life Story of Dr. Harry Guinness* (London: RBMU), 55 ff.

[224] On 11 November 1915, Peru's constitution was modified "to admit forms of worship other than Roman Catholic." John Savage, *Peru Today* (London: EUSA c. 1947).

[225] Efforts of the RBMU pioneers and the advocacy of the Guinnesses led to the securing of religious liberty in Peru "on 20 October 1914, the voting in the Chamber of Deputies being sixty-one against twelve." C. W. Mackintosh, 66.

[226] J. B. A. Kessler Jr., op. cit., expands upon the Cuzco venture, 160 ff.

[227] John L. Jarrett. This account is adapted by the writer from the booklet, *Fifteen Years in Peru* by John L. Jarrett, sent to the writer in 1976 by Jarrett's son, Harry V. Jarrett. (photocopy)

[228] Macintosh, 55. The three trips: 1897, 1904, and 1907. In 1907, his daughter Geraldine accompanied him. Her articles on Peru and Argentina appear in *Not Unto Us*. At this time, RBMU had twenty-two workers in the province of Buenos Aires, Argentina. (Harry Guinness, *Not Unto Us*, 116–127)

[229] By 1908, RBMU Councils had "for some years" been established in Canada and the US. Rev. George Smith, who had spent fourteen years in Argentina, led the Toronto Council.

[230] Betty Pritchard, *For Such A Time*, 39.

[231] For extended treatment of John Ritchie's work with the IEP, see J. B. A. Kessler, Jr., op cit., Chapter 13.

[232] ibid.

Chapter 18   Beyond The Ranges

[233] Betty Pritchard, *For Such A Time*, 39, 40.

[234] *Lamas Evangel*, report of A. G. Soper's Silver Jubilee Celebration, 1947.

[235] TBI later became Ontario Bible College.

[236] *Lamas Evangel*, Nov.–Dec. 1935. Testimony of Rhoda Gould.

[237] ibid.

[238] Peru is divided into twenty-four departamentos, or states, and each of these is divided into provinces. Moyobamba is the capital of both the Province of Moyobamba and the Department of San Martin, in north central Peru.

[239] *Lamas Evangel*, July–October 1940.

[240] J. B. A. Kessler Jr., 146 ff.

[241] *Lamas Evangel*, July–October 1940. "So sure was she of her call that she asked us to paint 'Moyobamba' underneath the labels for Lima."

[242] "Duly repaid before she set out for the interior." *Lamas Evangel*, July–October 1940.

[243] One account, authored years later by Annie G. Soper, states the length of the trip as "one month, three weeks."

[244] An earlier account of the Soper-Gould expedition is given by Phyllis Thompson in *Dawn Beyond the Andes*, (London: RBMU, 1955), 150. Mrs. Vera Sorell, who with her husband subsequently spent a lifetime in the San Martin work, later provided a comprehensive survey of RBMU's eighty years of ministry among the people of the Huallaga Valley in her book, *Los Chasquis del Rey* (*The King's Runners*, Sp.). The English version is titled, *Go, Chasquis, Go!* (Belleville, ON: Guardian Books, 2000).

[245] *Lamas Evangel*, July 1940.

[246] ibid.

[247] Kessler, 150. Mackay arrived on 5 December 1926.

[248] A. G. Soper (Hereafter referred to as AGS) to Herbert Pritchard, 8 June 1930.

[249] Escuela Britanica (the British School) opened in 1933.

[250] *Lamas Evangel*, May 1934.

[251] ibid.

[252] ibid.

[253] Vicente Coral left for Costa Rica on 14 February 1935.

[254] Coral died in May 1990 at the age of 94.

[255] *Lamas Evangel*, May–June 1938, 37.

[256] *Lamas Evangel*, July–October 1940, 103.

[257] *Lamas Evangel*, July 1934.

[258] ibid.

[259] ibid.

[260] AGS ltr. written from Sisa, 27 March 1939.

[261] *Lamas Evangel*, May–June 1938, 36.

[262] AGS to Herbert Simmonds, 19 July 1933.

[263] *Lamas Evangel*, July–August 1941, 138,139.

Chapter 19   Ebb Tide

[264] Kenneth Holmes, *The Cloud Moves*, 27.

[265] C. W. Macintosh, The Life Story of Dr. Harry Guinness, 78.

[266] 30 October 1913 to 11 April 1914.

[267] Betty Pritchard, 46.

[268] Lyle W. Dorsett, *A Passion For Souls: The Life of D. L. Moody* (Chicago: Moody Press, 1997), 180, 181.

[269] Betty Pritchard, *For Such a Time*, 46.

[270] Kenneth Holmes, 28.

[271] ibid., 29.

[272] Pioneer John Z. Hodge had opened the Raxaul station in 1926. Noting its strategic location as the gateway to Nepal, he wrote, "We are not here by accident—we are here for the purposes of God." Pritchard, 53.

[273] *When the Lights Come On Again* was a popular song during World War II.

Chapter 20   Where It All Began

[274] Captain Dwight Charles Sigbee testified before a court of inquiry that there was no smokeless powder on board, just "ordinary brown powder." Brown powder was stable and could be safely heated close to 600° F. This was significant in the attempt to establish the explosion as external in origin. See Michael Blow, *A Ship to Remember.* (New York: William Morrow & Co. 1992), 136 ff.

[275] Responsibility for the loss of the *Maine* remains unresolved. The US disclaimed any intention to annex Cuba, and on 19 April 1898, recognized Cuban independence.

[276] J. Edwin Orr, *Light of t he Nations*, 218.

[277] Charles E. Chapman, *A History of the Cuban Republic* (New York: Octagon Books, 1969), 300 ff. See also *The People's Chronology*, licensed from Henry Holt and Company, Inc. Copyright 1992 by James Trager.

[278] By 1897, there were 200,000 Spanish troops in Cuba.

[279] Cuba's anguish lay in the fact that after a decade of war and loss of 300,000 lives, she remained under American influence even after the ouster of Spain. The objective of a free, sovereign, democratic republic remained unrealized. While independence came in 1902, Cuba remained subject to US intervention.

Chapter 21   A Star of Astonishing Brilliance

[280] Epithet assigned by his son, Elmer Lavastida in *Trayectoria Pastoral del Rev. Bartolomé Diaz*, (Universidad Bíblica Latinoamericana, Junio 1998).

[281] ibid., 3 ff.

[282] A large, heavy knife used (especially in Latin America) for cutting sugar cane and underbrush.

[283] These anecdotes appear in a variety of sources and are frequently retold *in Whitened Harvest*, the West Indies Mission magazine; See also *Cuban Patriot and Soul Winner*, West Indies Broadcast Committee, Cambridge, MA 1940, and *Trayectoria Pastoral*, a thesis by B. G. Lavastida's son on the life of his father.

[284] Trayectoria Pastoral, 8.

[285] The writer's interview with Elmer Lavastida, son of B. G. Lavastida, Kendall, FL, 17 September 1998.

[286] By 1930, Elsie Lavastida would succumb to her long struggle with tuberculosis. She died that year in Asheville, North Carolina.

[287] Elmer Lavastida, *Trayectoria Pastoral*, 1.

[288] ibid.

[289] Trayectoria Pastoral, 41.

[290] ibid., 42.

[291] *Heraldo Cristiano*, Junio 1924, 8. Cited by Elmer Lavastida in *Trayectoria Pastoral*, 44, 45.

[292] José Martí, *Our America*, (New York: Monthly Review Press, 1977) 18, 19.

[293] This extract appears on the wall of the *José Martí* exhibit in Ybor City, FL.
[294] Louis A. Perez Jr., *José Martí In The United States—The Florida Experience.*
(Tempe, Arizona: Arizona State University Center for Latin America Studies)
[295] *Whitened Harvest*, second quarter 1943, 9.
[296] Trayectoria Pastoral, 36.
[297] ibid., 48.

Chapter 22   The Catalysts

[298] Their children were: Mabel Clare Kirk, (m. Jack McElheran; d.1964 In Three
Hills); Robert Telford K., (d.1915 in Ontario); Edward Marshall K., (d. 1970 in Calgary); Harriet Aitken (Hattie) K., (m. Efraín Monge, d.1970 in Calgary); Roger Pringle K., (d. 1967 in Three Hills); Hector Alexander K., (d. 1952 in Three Hills); John
Fergus K., (d. 1981 in Linden, AB); Elsa Maria K., (d. 1913 in Nyack, NY at twenty-
three); Amy Sophia, (d. 1913 in Gallingertown, Ontario); Jessie Georgina, (d.1990 in
Three Hills). All ten of the Kirk children were born in Ontario. The McElherans
moved to Calgary in 1912 and to Three Hills in 1915. Andrew Kirk died in Three
Hills in 1940, his wife, Maria in 1936. (Source: Ray Kirk, e-mail to the writer, 1 June
1998).
[299] Normally, Stevens did not teach the preparatory course. He did so at this time because no other teacher was available. Dorothy Ruth Miller was Hattie's senior preparatory teacher in the other subjects (Hattie Kirk, *Autobiography*, 6). D. R. M. later
became a professor at Midland Bible Institute and then at Prairie Bible Institute. She
authored *A Handbook of Ancient History in Bible Light* (NY: Revell, 1937), for years
a standard textbook at PBI.
[300] Hattie Kirk, *Autobiography*. Chapter 1, p.7.
[301] ibid., 10. Siblings Robert, Hector, and Hattie Kirk had remained on their Ontario
farm. Robert's death in the fall of 1915 freed Hattie to go to Three Hills. Hector went
to Moody Bible Institute and subsequently spent his life in Africa.
[302] W. Philip Keller, *Expendable* (Three Hills: Prairie Press, 1966), 69 ff.
[303] From a Western Union telegram once held by the writer, but submitted to L. E.
Maxwell c. 1950. Dorothy Ruth Miller had been on the teaching faculty at Midland
Bible Institute where both L. E. Maxwell and E. V. Thompson were students. She
later taught at Prairie Bible Institute. She was friend and counselor to WIM from its
inception. She died 1 March 1944 in Charleston, WV.
[304] W. Philip Keller, 44.
[305] Hattie Kirk, 10.
[306] Afflicted with tropical sprue, Hattie left Costa Rica in June 1926. On her way to
Canada, she visited a cousin, Mrs. Jessie Benn, in Elizabeth, NJ. During her stay in
Elizabeth, she continued correspondence with Efraín, who came to visit.
[307] Hattie Kirk, 10, 17.
[308] Elmer Lavastida notes that the great growth of Presbyterian, Methodist, and Baptist Churches in Cuba during the last fourteen years of the nineteenth century was due
to at least two factors: 1. The relaxing of Spanish regulations governing freedom of
the press and political expression. 2. The conversion of many Cuban exiles in the
United States who returned to Cuba to evangelize and plant churches. The political
hegemony exercised by the United States following the Spanish-American war was
extended in the religious dimension, so that Cuban leadership gave way to American

denominational patronage. In 1921 the Presbyterians opened a seminary in Cárdenas. E. A. Odell was one of the professors.

[309] Roger Kirk (Hereafter, RK) ltr. from the CPR 11 May 1927.
[310] RK ltr. 30 May 1927.
[311] RK ltr. written from Placetas, 28 May 1927.
[312] RK ltr. 5 June 1927.
[313] RK ltr. 5 June 1927.
[314] RK to the family, 27 June 1927.
[315] RK to the family, 24 June 1927.
[316] RK to the family, 17 July 1927.
[317] In late 1926, God spoke to Thompson through the ministry of Kenneth Grubb, a missionary from Latin America, "to make me know I was to henceforth serve him as a missionary." *Whitened Harvest*, Jan.–Feb. 1958.
[318] Evelyn Thompson relates these events in *Whitened Harvest*, summer 1968.

Chapter 23   First Lady
[319] *Whitened Harvest*, Jan.–Feb. 1958.
[320] 1 Cor: 9.16
[321] The Monges had come home to Three Hills on furlough in 1926.
[322] The account of Evelyn McElheran's arrival in Cuba is drawn from the Jan.–Feb. 1958 edition (and others) of *Whitened Harvest* together with material from June Vetter's manuscript.

Chapter 24   Elmer
[323] E. V. Thompson, personal testimony in the *Worldteam 50th Anniversary Album*.
[324] *Whitened Harvest*, Jan.–Feb. 1958, 2.
[325] ibid.
[326] ibid.
[327] RK ltr. 12 January 1928. E. V. Thompson noted the date as January 13.
[328] RK 16 February 1928.
[329] Unreferenced citations in this chapter are taken from June Vetter's ms.
[330] Hattie Kirk, 20, 21.
[331] The Monges returned to Alberta, where they set up a tinsmith business in the town of Fairview. Their home above the shop "became a gathering place where the gospel of Christ was taught" and led to the formation of the Fairview Gospel Chapel. The Monges later moved to Three Hills, where they lived for several years. Hattie Kirk Monge was promoted to glory in 1970. (Muriel Hansen).
[332] Mrs. Juan Junco was one of the first five members of the Mission family. Affectionately known as "Mama Junco," she served for many years as matron of the Cuba Bible Institute. She died in 1968.

Chapter 25   The Cuba Bible Institute
[333] Cited by June Vetter.
[334] Matthew 6:33.
[335] *Whitened Harvest*, September–October 1966.
[336] *Whitened Harvest*, 1st Quarter 1943.
[337] Matthew 6:32
[338] Elmer Lavastida, 32.

[339] ibid., 25.

[340] Elmer Thompson later recognized that in a changing world these views could not be defended, and Los Pinos Nuevos graduates were encouraged to take further training to meet the demands of the modern pastorate.

[341] The irreducible content of the gospel message, the Kerugma, dominates the apostolic proclamations in the book of Acts and embraces the sacrificial death of Christ, his resurrection, the divine acquittal of the believer, and Christ's universal Lordship (Acts 13:38–39; 1 Cor: 15.3–11). The duty of missionaries and missiologists is to determine how to proclaim the whole gospel within the target culture, free from the addition of their own cultural trappings and ecclesiastical shibboleths.

[342] Florent D. Toirac, *A Pioneer Missionary in the Twentieth Century* (Winona Lake IN: Spanish Publishers, Undated), 122.

[343] ibid., 123.

[344] ibid., 125

[345] ibid., 123.

[346] ibid., 124.

[347] Elizabeth Elliott, *A Path Through Suffering* (Ann Arbor: Servant Publications. 1990), 30.

[348] Toirac, 128.

[349] ibid.

Chapter 26   A Spontaneous Model

[350] *Whitened Harvest*, September–October 1966.

[351] Acts 19:1–10. NIV.

[352] Elmer Thompson, *"Evangelism By Means of National Workers in Training."* (Whitened Harvest, 1st Quarter 1945, Vol. 10 No. 1).

[353] Elmer Thompson, *"Hitherto Hath The Lord Helped Us."* (Whitened Harvest, September–October 1967).

[354] J. Allen Thompson, *Character Matters*. Allen Thompson's memorial message at his father's funeral.

[355] ibid.

[356] ibid.

[357] Among them: Dr. Ruben Lores, who became a vice president of Latin America Mission, and Regino Loyola, one of the leading evangelists in the 1960 Evangelism-in-Depth movement. —*Character Matters*.

[358] *Whitened Harvest*, September–October 1966.

[359] Fefita Lavastida died on 24 January 1991, exactly one month after her husband's 103rd birthday. She was 85.

[360] Whitened Harvest, 1943 The WIM In Retrospect, E. V. Thompson.

[361] J. Allen Thompson noted that Smith wanted the entire Cuba Bible Institute and its workers to become a People's Church mission, a temptation which Elmer Thompson resisted.

[362] ibid.

[363] *Whitened Harvest*, 4rth Quarter 1945.

[364] Notes from the writer's interview with former WIM director, Patrick Arnold.

[365] Louis and Delphine Markwood went to Cuba in 1940, where Louis served as secretary, treasurer, and Bible school professor. They were posted to Haiti in 1959, where Louis served as field director.

[366] Louis Markwood provided these details of the origins of *Alas Del Alba.*

[367] *Historical Perspectives*, 1976. A WIM teaching syllabus.

Chapter 27   Live Coals in Voodoo Darkness

[368] Florent D. Toirac, 226.

[369] E. V. Thompson stated that the churches in Cuba had led 500 Haitians to Christ. Transcript of EVT message, 18 August 1987.

[370] Elmer Lavastida, *Trayectoria Pastoral*, 34.

[371] Florent Toirac, 197.

[372] Psalm 76:10

[373] *Vodun*, commonly known as voodoo, is based on a Dahomean word meaning *god* or *spirits*, and is the generic term for all deities in a vast pantheon of spirits. See Harmon A. Johnson, *The Growing Church in Haiti*, (Coral Gables: West Indies Mission, 1970), 17.

[374] Florent Toirac, 217.

[375] Letter from Paul Steinhauer to the writer, 24 May 1998. Steinhauer's parents were WIM missionaries in Haiti, where Paul was raised.

[376] Patrick Johnstone, *Operation World*, (Grand Rapids: Zondervan, 1993), 261.

[377] *Whitened Harvest*, September–October 1967,. 3. See also transcript of EVT message, 18 August 1987, delivered at Worldteam's US center.

[378] Mersdorf's transfer to Haiti handicapped the staff of the Cuba Bible Institute, a loss compounded by the departure of Muriel McElheran (Evelyn Thompson's sister), who had suffered an attack of facial paralysis. This left Elmer and Evelyn Thompson the only senior missionary teachers for a student body of 100. (Transcript of EVT message 18 August 1987).

[379] *Whitened Harvest*, third quarter, 1939, 2.

[380] ibid.

[381] Florent Toirac, 226 ff.

[382] ibid. 236 ff.

[383] ibid., 300.

[384] *Whitened Harvest*, December 1937, 2.

[385] Florent Toirac, 346, ff.

[386] This disparity was later resolved when more Cuban missionaries were sent and funds were pooled. The Cuban churches were never able to supply full support for their missionaries.

[387] ibid., 347 ff.

[388] ibid., 350. Lizaire Bernard had, in fact, invited the West Indies Mission to Haiti's Southern Peninsula in 1937 on behalf of the many Haitian churches without pastors. Toirac arrived in Haiti a year later, in 1938. This unfortunate allegation is unfounded and is disavowed by WIM missionaries contemporary with Toirac.

[389] This policy was not unique to the West Indies Mission and was general practice in most missions. The RBMU notes a number of instances where such unions called for the resignation of the missionary.

[390] ibid., 376 ff.

[391] June Vetter.

[392] J. Edwin Orr, *Evangelical Awakenings in Latin America*, (Minneapolis: Bethany Fellowship, 1978), 103.

[393] Wolfe Hansen was raised in Denmark, emigrated to Canada, enrolled at PBI in 1934, and went to Haiti as a missionary with WIM, where he married Muriel McElheran (Evelyn Thompson's sister). He distinguished himself as a teacher of the Word in the Cuba Bible Institute and founded Jamaica Bible College. He died in 1984. Muriel survived him into the new millennium.

[394] *Whitened Harvest*, second quarter 1943, 6, 7.

[395] Ed Walker. Also Dudley Nelson, *As the Cock Crows*. (Franklin, TN: Providence House, 1997), 41.

[396] Dudley Nelson, 40.

[397] I have adapted Dr. Nelson's description. See *As the Cock Crows*, 106. As churches grew, more substantial structures were developed. Canadian Bob Stewart constructed many such churches, bringing work crews from the US and Canada.

[398] Dudley Nelson, 109 ff.

[399] John and Dorothy Depew served WIM for thirty-two years, retiring in 1968. Dorothy was Oswald J. Smith's sister.

[400] *Whitened Harvest*, summer 1968, 12.

[401] Among those who served as principal of the Haiti Bible Institute were Ed Walker, Herb Shoemaker, Don Ropp, and Dominique Gelin. Gelin was the first Haitian to serve as director of the Institute. Other faculty included Walter Wunsch, Zeida Campos, Ken Harold, Pringle McElheran, Elizabeth Peeke, Bob Wagler, James Smith, Willette Smith, and Richard Douliere. By 1999, all the Bible Institute professors were Haitian. James Smith, long-term principal of the Institute, was so fluent in Creole that radio listeners were surprised when they met him in person to learn that he was not a Haitian (Ed Walker).

[402] Joseph's Christian name and his surname are identical.

[403] *Whitened Harvest*, July–August 1967.

[404] Dictator Jean Claude Duvalier was put out of office on 7 February 1986.

[405] Edwin Walker, who served as associate pastor under Joseph Lemeuble, supplied this information.

[406] Patrick Arnold was present at this meeting.

[407] Nelson's son and daughter-in-law worked elsewhere in Haiti, but not on the hospital construction.

[408] Dudley Nelson, 128 ff.

[409] *Whitened Harvest*, fourth quarter, 1945.

[410] *Whitened Harvest*, second quarter, 1943.

Chapter 28   Old Quisqueya

[411] Elmer Thompson, *The Expansion of the Los Pinos Bible Institute*. Message given 18 August 1987.

[412] Elmer Thompson in *Whitened Harvest*, September–October 1967, 5. This assertion was true, but with qualifications. Nationals served as coworkers with WIM missionaries, but only as sponsored by national churches. They did not enjoy full member benefits and privileges accorded expatriate WIM missionaries.

[413] *Whitened Harvest*, winter 1969, 8.

[414] Elmer Thompson in The Expansion of Los Pinos Nuevos Bible Institute. Message, 18 August 1987.

[415] Cecil Samuels' report in *Whitened Harvest*, first quarter, 1944.

[416] ibid. third quarter, 1944.

[417] ibid.

[418] *Whitened Harvest*, September–October 1967, 5. Hilario Diaz, one of this group, remained twenty years and started ten churches.

[419] *Whitened Harvest*, July–August 1966, 8.

Chapter 29   A Man on Borrowed Time

[420] The Strict Baptist Denomination in Britain.

[421] B. G. Vine to the writer, 1998.

[422] "Secretary" was a term commonly synonymous in Britain with the American, "director."

[423] Betty Pritchard, 74.

[424] ibid.

[425] *Regions Beyond*, August 1963, 7.

[426] Sylvia Sirag, *Victory Through Christ in the Midst of Suffering*, Booklet. This is Sylvia Sirag's account of her concentration camp experience under the Japanese.

[427] ibid.

[428] This group was headquartered in Englewood, NJ, with Thomas Clark as president, and Edward Drew on the Board of Trustees. Jeanette M. Loeks in East Grand Rapids, MI was listed as reference.

[429] *Regions Beyond* (UK), North American insert, April 1949.

[430] Letter to the writer from Harold Lima, 6 January 1999.

[431] Sirag had earlier enlisted the John Tolivers at Prairie Bible Institute, but the door failed to open for them under RBMU. They later went to Borneo with the Go Ye Fellowship.

[432] *Regions Beyond* (UK), North American insert. April 1949.

Chapter 30   He Brought the World to Our Home

[433] Since Vine was not establishing a new mission agency, but expanding British RBMU, the designation, "Council" was adopted rather than "Board," as there could be but one "Board," viz., the parent authority in London.

Chapter 31   A Tiring War of Movement

[434] Sylvia Sirag newsletter, 16 March 1948. Vine arrived in New York April 20 and "after a few days in Philadelphia came out to Minneapolis . . . May 4–9 Mr. Vine and I shall be in Los Angeles . . . May 10–27 he shall be working eastward, stopping at Madison, Chicago, Grand Rapids, Fort Erie, and London, Canada. May 27 we hope to meet again in Toronto, then to Buffalo, Philadelphia, and Paterson." —S. Sirag newsletter, 29 April 1948.

[435] *Regions Beyond* (UK), April 1949, North American Insert. E. G. Vine report.

[436] E. G. Vine letter, 17 January 1949 to Toronto (no addressee indicated).

[437] Watkin Roberts left the chair of RBMU Canada in 1957. He died on 20 April 1969.

[438] With Roberts' departure, A. C. Simmonds became chairman.

[439] Data is extracted from copies of the minutes of the Canada Council, RBMU.

[440] E. G. Vine letter to Watkin Roberts and Richard H. Seume, 22 May 1950. Perkins returned home shortly after arriving in India.

Chapter 32   A Severe Test
[441] April 1949.
[442] Vine had been preaching at Calvary Church, Lancaster, PA when he fell ill, and where he was diagnosed with "a rather bad attack of jaundice." Bessie described him as looking "rather like a Chinaman . . . he is so yellow!" (letter, Bessie Vine to Watkin Roberts, 16 March 1949)
[443] Then at 1150 North 63rd Street, Philadelphia.
[444] Watkin Roberts. letter, 19 April 1949.
[445] Watkin Roberts' letters to Richard Seume 16 November 1950 and 4 December 1951; WR to Theodore M. Bamber, chairman, British RBMU, 31 December 1951.
[446] R.H. Seume to Watkin Roberts, 16 November 1950.
[447] T.M. Bamber to Watkin Roberts (Hereafter, WR), 9 July 1951, 23 January 1952; WR to Bamber, 5 March 1952. While in Britain on this trip (1951),Vine had been invited to remain in England as director of the British work. American Council chairman Richard Seume wrote Roberts on 16 October 1951: "While we . . . appreciate . . . the honest opinion of our Canadian brethren (relative to Vine's return to NA) we . . . desire that he be in our midst to take up the responsibilities so diligently handled by him."
[448] ibid.
[449] E. G. Vine letter to "the Canadian Council," circulated 8 May 1951.
[450] This was true notwithstanding Vine's self-deprecating defense that he was not one to press financial appeals before the Christian public. Letter, WR to Theodore Bamber, March 1952.
[451] WR to Theodore Bamber, 5 March 1952 and to Edwin H. Castor of the same date.
[452] T. M. Bamber (chairman of the London Board, RBMU) to WR, 23 January 1952.
[453] E. G. Vine to WR, 5 January 1953.
[454] E. G. Vine to Canada Council, 21 September 1951.
[455] E. G. Vine to London Board, 21 April 1955.

Chapter 33   Among Men of Blood
[456] Sirag newsletters, 2 July and 26 August 1937.
[457] *Moody Monthly*, Feb. 1944, article by Nell Bachman Caley.
[458] Ebenezer Vine circular ltr. 23 Nov. 1948.
[459] Henry Armstrong, *A Biographical History of the GPPIK* (Thesis submitted to the faculty of Providence Theological Seminary, 1997), 9, 10.
[460] Undated letter from Gudrun Lima to Mrs. Roem van't Eind. Pontianak, Kalimantan Barat.
[461] Gudrun Lima, article in *Regions Beyond*, January 1956. 11.
[462] As early as 1938 Bill and Sylvia had written, "God is laying on our hearts the need of a school for the training of evangelists . . . pray for two teachers for this work." Sirag newsletter, 31 August 1938.
[463] *Regions Beyond* insert, 1951.
[464] The Indonesian name of the people was Orang Dayak. (Orang = men + Dayak = blood). Blood sacrifice was common among the Dayak animists. Headhunting had been long outlawed by the Dutch, but has reoccurred at times of political unrest.

[465] *Words About the Warkentins*, Ellen Warkentin, pamphlet. RBMU Scarborough, 1980.
[466] Sylvia Sirag retired to a ministry in Nassau, in the Bahamas, where she was still living in 1999.
[467] The door to Borneo failed to open for John and Frances Toliver under RBMU. Vine deemed their family (then three children) too large to proceed with appointment. They later went out with the Go Ye Fellowship, where they spent ten years south of the Kapuas River before returning to join the Staff at Prairie Bible Institute. Their daughter, Joy, born in 1948, later became an RBMU appointee to Borneo. Just before her planned departure in April 1975, she was tragically killed in an auto accident in Alberta. The writer, en route to Prairie Bible Institute for meetings, was called upon to bring her funeral message.
[468] *Regions Beyond*, Feb. 1963, 4; Feb. 1964, 12.
[469] They were Bill and Diana Gray, Bob and Jeri Jackson (1970), Bruce and Hazel Darby (1971, Karl and Karen Hoekman (1977), Jim and Robin Nottingham (1980), Henry and Janet Armstrong, Loren and Becky Warkentin, Wayne and Carolyn Allen (1977), Darell and Sylvia Davis (1976), Eric and Vangie Thiessen. In 1965—after fourteen years' service— Bud and Dora Merritt left Borneo. They had played a major role in establishing the Dayak church, opening several churches, schools, two clinics, and the vast Lumar area. Both Lima sisters died of cancer, Clara on 7 Dec. 1998, Gudrun on 10 May 1992. Elmer Warkentin died 16 October 1993. Olav P. Nyheim died 28 January 1996.
[470] *Regions Beyond*, second quarter 1971, 7.
[471] *East Asia Millions*, June 1965, 85.
[472] Elmer Warkentin, *Regions Beyond*, August 1964, 11, 12.
[473] *Regions Beyond*, first quarter 1969, 10.
[474] Ketapang is a large area south of Pontianak inhabited by Dayak tribes, Malays, and Chinese. Karl and Karen Hoekman spent six years here developing and expanding the church inland. Later, two Dayak couples were assigned. Sempatang, north of the RBMU area, is close to the Sarawak border. Serimbu, north of the Landak River, was visited by medical teams and posted a national worker. Lumar Behe is north of Anik.
[475] Virtually all GPPIK pastors were bivocational—working as schoolteachers, farmers, rubber tappers, or lumber cutters while caring for their churches.
[476] World Vision believed that recipient churches should be self-supporting within three years.
[477] Some RBMU personnel in Kalimantan did not agree with the subsidy plan, notably Don Singer and Wayne Allen, both at Anik. Consequently, this area accepted no external funding. Uniformity of policy in the realm of church planting methodology was not enforced within RBMU's Kalimantan work.
[478] Thousands of ethnic Madurese (from the island of Madura) emigrated to Kalimantan, where they became a source of tension for the Dayaks.

Chapter 34   Shangri-la
[479] National Geographic Magazine. Articles— *Unknown New Guinea*, and *New Guinea's Mountain and Swampland Dwellers*, March 1941, December 1945.
[480] *Regions Beyond*, October–December 1953. 2,3. Sylvia Sirag newsletter, November 1948.

[481] Don Richardson relates this exchange in *Peace Child*, (Ventura, CA: Regal Books, 1974), 81.

[482] E. G. Vine "SOS" air letter appeal for prayer from England 26 May 1951 to Watkin Roberts.

[483] Ezek. 36:23

[484] Russell Hitt, *Cannibal Valley* (Camp Hill, PA Christian Publications, 1962), 34.

[485] ibid., 47, 48. Both the Swart and the Mamberamo (Lakes Plain) became zones of RBMU ministry.

[486] The Unevangelized Fields Mission was formed in 1931 through the reorganization of missionaries serving in Africa and South America. Of UFM's three sending countries—Australia, UK, and the US—the Australian division had focused on Papua New Guinea and later upon the tribals of Dutch NG, where they began work in 1949. In 1971, Australian UFM changed its name to Asia Pacific Christian Mission.

[487] The Dutch later relaxed this requirement.

[488] Russell Hitt, 16,17.

[489] Bill Widbin, *A View of the World, West Irian Emphasis*. Booklet. 1965. See also Hitt, 105 ff.

[490] Acts 17:24–27.

[491] C&MA had been planning a proprietary air service.

[492] The name, *Missionary Aviation Fellowship* was later changed to *Mission Aviation Fellowship*.

[493] Douglas Hayward, *The Dani of Irian Jaya Before and After Conversion* (Sentani, Regions Press, 1980), 123.

[494] RBMU later expanded to the Central and Eastern Highlands and to the South Coast.

[495] Douglas Hayward, 123.

[496] In 1964, Bill and Mary Widbin, later joined by Bill and Marianne Rosenberger, set up Regions Press in a World War II Quonset hut at Sentani. Back to the Bible Broadcast of Lincoln, Nebraska, largely subsidized funding for equipment. Translation projects throughout the island community of The Missions Fellowship generated an insatiable demand for printed Scriptures, literacy primers, and Bible Institute materials and by 1978 had printed 550,000 books. Dani Christians from the Swart Valley became expert in production and assembly. Regions Press was fully nationalized and remained productive for years until changing market conditions and commercial shops at the coast brought its timely and useful life to an end.

[497] In 1971 Australia UFM became independent and took on the name, APCM.

[498] The log of the Gesswein-Widbin trek appears in the June–July 1956 issue of *Regions Beyond*.

[499] Douglas Hayward, 123.

[500] Senggi was a village on the north coast, some fifty miles inland from Sentani, where UFM had earlier started a work.

[501] Isaiah 52:7

[502] Dave returned briefly to Canada to marry Margaret Colton, who had remained at home to complete nurse's training.

[503] Douglas Hayward, 127, 129.

[504] ibid.

505 The Dani legend, *my-skin-your skin* (nabelan-kabelan), held that the snake (which both sheds and renews its skin) possessed the secret of eternal life. See Dekker. *Torches of Joy*, Crossway, 1985, 59 ff.
506 Don Gibbons had been influenced by Donald McGavran's *Bridges of God*, in which McGavran postulated the importance of people group movements as vehicles for the acceptance of the gospel. See Hayward, 130.
507 Helen Manning, *To Perish For Their Saving* (London, Victory Press, 1969), 15.
508 Christian Dani men remained polygamists—as the gospel had found them. However, such men were ineligible for church leadership. Those who had plural wives at conversion maintained the integrity and responsibility of these relationships. Once converted, they ceased to take additional wives.
509 Don Richter described the recording process: "I worked the battery-operated tape recorder. Eunice gave one sentence of the script (in English) to Gordon Larson, who translated into Moni, in which he was fluent. (The Ilaga Dani were bilingual in Moni and Dani). Jimbitu translated the Moni to the Ilaga Dani dialect, which the Swart Dani speaker could readily understand. The Swart speaker then recast the sentence in the Swart Dani dialect. I recorded that sentence. We continued in this manner until each script was completed. At each point Jimbitu amplified and clarified the content. Larson knew enough Dani to assure the integrity of the translation."
510 Don Richter (Gordon Larson providing the Dani translation), relates this exchange.
511 *Regions Beyond*, August 1960, 11. Martin report. Fetishes represented the spiritual power reserve of a community. They included a variety of objects associated with sorcery and black magic. Hayward cites UFM's Ralph Maynard, who described the inventory of material put to the flames:

> Innumerable bows, arrows, spears, stone and bone knives, shells, beautiful fur headdresses, pig tails, nose bones, bits of string, all sorts and sizes of feathers, large and small bridal stones, pieces of cane, armbands, "feather dusters" (large feather affairs used for waving about to chase away evil spirits), necklaces, rare ornamental shells plus a host of wrapped items which we didn't see (Hayward, 137).

512 *Regions Beyond*, August 1960, 11.
513 ibid.
514 *Regions Beyond*, November 1961. E. G. Vine editorial, 11.
515 Kangime is a Dani word meaning, "The place of death."
516 They were the John Wilsons, the Richard Hales, the Costas Macrises, the Malone Battles, the Jack Lengs, Margaret Crawley, Rose Marshall, David Sirag, and a Miss Horter.
517 John Dekker, *Torches of Joy*, 92.
518 ibid., 111 ff.
519 ibid., 193.

Chapter 35 Lengthening the Cords
520 E. G. Vine to D. W. Martin, 20 December 1963.
521 Phyliss Masters, on a visit to the Seng Valley in May 1999, spoke with some of the Wikbun men who had taken part in the murders. The warriors had seen the missionaries drinking tea, which they assumed was blood. When the missionaries ate meat

from a tin, the warriors assumed the worst. The open hand, waved in greeting, re-moved all doubt as to the evil intent of the missionaries. By 1999, the son of one of the killers had become a Bible College graduate. –Information shared with the writer by Mrs. Masters, 18 November 1999. See also *Return To Silivam*, in *Regions Beyond*, fourth quarter 1970.

[522] The dramatic story of God's sovereign design in the deaths of Masters and Dale is grippingly narrated in the widely acclaimed book, *Lords of the Earth*, by Don Richardson. Regal Books, 1983. (The deaths of Dale, Masters, Voth, the Gene New-man family, and the Dani carrier, Ndengen became the key to the resumption of min-istry in the Seng Valley.)

[523] 2 Cor. 12:9.

[524] Dani missionary Mbitmbet went to the Kayagar with his young family in the late '60s. Thirty years later (1999) they were still serving faithfully.

[525] From material furnished by John Mills to the writer, 22 April 1999. E-mail.

[526] E. G. Vine to A. C. Simmonds, letter, 16 July 1962.

[527] The Yosts acculturated well with the Sawi and won many to the Lord. However, in a painful decision, they left the field in 1995, and later resigned from the Mission.

[528] The first missionaries sent out by the Dani tribe—Yana and Aki Wandik—went to work alongside the Richardsons in 1966. They served there faithfully and with dis-tinction for twenty-five years.

[529] They were MAF, RBMU, C&MA, TEAM, UFM, ABMS, APCM, the NRC (Netherlands Reformed Congregation) and the Zending Gereformeerd Kerken (ZGK—Holland), the latter two holding associate membership.

[530] Figures encompass the ministries of APCM, UFM, and RBMU/WT.

[531] Rom. 10:18 (NIV).

Chapter 36   MAF Was Not Enough

[532] In Saskatchewan, Canada.

[533] The Indonesian name for Regions Wings is *Tariku Aviation*, named for one of the rivers in the Lakes Plain.

Chapter 37   A Bigger Umbrella

[534] Theodore M. Bamber was "a man utterly disciplined, fearlessly outspoken, yet beloved because of his warm, genial, loving spirit." At the same time, "controversial waters swirled about him." See Pritchard, *For Such a Time*, 62, 63.

[535] A. G. Soper to Mr. and Mrs. A. C. Simmonds. 22 January 1956.

[536] AGS to Simmonds, 13 March 1954.

[537] ibid.

[538] While now an RBMU field, the Peru Mission retained the PIM name within the country.

[539] Lucas Grandes, *Regions Beyond*. April–June 1979.

[540] An administrative or legislative council.

[541] AGS to A. C. Simmonds, 19 October, 1961,

[542] AGS to A. C. Simmonds, 6 October 1952.

[543] AGS to A. C. Simmonds, 5 February 1954.

[544] ibid.

[545] AGS to A.C. Simmonds, 8 March 1959.

[546] AGS to A.C. Simmonds, 5 January 1962.

[547] By 1999, the number of AIENOP churches of inland Peru had increased to 120.

[548] Rom. 15:15,16.

[549] Marinell Park's dedication to Scripture translation led to her resignation from RBMU and to her affiliation with Wycliffe Bible Translators for the linguistic technical support this agency could offer. She remained with her Quechua people, and—joined by other Wycliffe friends—triumphantly completed the Lowland Quechua New Testament forty-two years after her arrival in Peru. It was dedicated in 1993. The book of Titus was the first portion, published in 1971. (*Regions Beyond*, Jan.– Mar. 1972, 12,13).

[550] Mark and Ruth Sirag also worked briefly with the Chayahuita, as did Gill College (British RBMU).

[551] Small Briggs and Stratton inboard engines which powered Chayahuita dugout canoes, so named for the sound emitted by the engine.

[552] Elio Solís, a Peruvian brother from Cuzco, married a Chayahuita girl, settled in Yurimaguas, and became a highly effective evangelist to the Chayahuita. In 1999 the Indians were composing and recording their own gospel music on cassette tapes. Portions of the OT had been translated and a Chayahuita dictionary published.

[553] 1992

[554] *Regions Beyond*, third quarter 1971.

[555] Options governing mission/church relationships overseas were expounded the following year at the IFMA/EFMA Green Lake Conference in 1971. See *Forms of Mission-Church Relationships*, Louis King (*Missions in Creative Tension* 1971 Pasadena, William Carey Library), 157.

[556] *Regions Beyond*, 1ST Quarter 1973. 12.

[557] ibid.

[558] Incorporated as the *Asociacion Editora Evangelica*, Regions Press produced hymnbooks, extension seminary textbooks, and VBS material in three languages. (*Regions Beyond*, second quarter 1980).

[559] Varner started another work in the Monterrico section of Lima, called *Roca Eterna* (Eternal Rock). Others who joined the work in Lima: The Andrew Baxters, the Buster Roalsens, the Allistair Parlanes, the Roy Buchanans, the Rex Carlaws, the Gary Clarks, the Len Smiths, and the Jim Riddells. The Riddells became teacher/facilitators to the Maranga church, Jim later serving as field director. The Hamiltons and the Parlanes left Lima in 1982 to open work in Santiago, Chile. The Bill Allans transferred from work in the selva to plant cell groups in Lima.

[560] The Communist Shining Path guerillas systematically destroyed the Peruvian infrastructure and murdered upwards of 30,000 citizens from 1970–1992. The capture of founder and leader Abimael Guzmán Reynoso in a daring police raid in Lima on 12 September 1992, effectively brought to an end the reign of terror. The Communist guerillas' primary base was in the southern province of Ayacucho.

[561] *San Martin Update*, a periodical newssheet, by the writer, July 1992.

Chapter 38   The Empire Strikes Back

[562] From the writer's June 1969 interviews with Indian Christian leaders in Muzaffarpur, India.

[563] By contrast, the Ranchi district in south Bihar had seen an ingathering of 48,000 communicants.

[564] The Evangelical Trust Association of North India.

[565] Ps. 126:6.

[566] John 4:38

Chapter 39   Forbidden Kingdom

[567] Dale Leathead first traveled this route in 1952. In the late 1950s, US Aid constructed a motor road from Raxaul to Katmandu. Before that, vehicles had to be transported on the shoulders of twenty-four to thirty-six porters.

[568] Ernest W. Oliver, *Still In Nepal* (Booklet, Regions Press, London).

[569] ibid.

[570] Ernest W. Oliver, Christmas letter, 1998.

[571] Those who embrace Christianity for social or economic advantage.

[572] In Hinduism, an ascetic holy man, esp. a monk.

[573] This account of Prem Pradhan's prison experience is adapted from a report in *Power For Living*, second quarter 1972.

[574] Ramesh Khatry, Church & Mission Relationship in Nepal—Forty Years Ahead! Monograph 21 May 1996.

Chapter 40   Trial by Lions

[575] Transfer of power was successful in nearly all of the twenty-six with the notable exception of Belgian Congo. See Stephen Neil: *A History of Christian Missions* (Penguin Books 1964), 493, 494.

[576] This shortsighted policy changed in the late 1950s with the approach of independence. See David Reed. *111 Days in Stanleyville*, (New York, Harper & Rowe. 1965), 56 ff.

[577] Peter Forbath, *The River Congo* (NY, Putnam, 1973), 394.

[578] David Reed. *111 Days in Stanleyville*,. (New York, Harper & Rowe 1965), 51. Over the four-year occupation, 93,000 UN troops from 33 countries rotated peacekeeping duty in Congo with a one-time peak of 20,000.

[579] Mrs. Lawrence Walling was the only exception. She remained with her husband.

[580] *Regions Beyond*, November 1960, article by Edgar R. Wide and Arthur Wright, 5.

[581] In 1959 there were 1800 missionaries in Congo. In 1969 only 1200 remained.

[582] J. Edwin Orr, *Evangelical Awakenings in Africa*, 157. "The Roman Catholic missions in Congo were not only outside these comity arrangements but were in a recognized competition for the loyalty of the African Christians." ibid.

[583] John R. Crawford, Protestant Missions in Congo, 10.

[584] ibid., 1.

[585] Lulonga's strategic location on the river route to the capital drew other settlers, so that this church served more than the Ngombe tribe. The trade language (Lingala) is commonly used in Lulonga.

[586] Betty Pritchard, 102.

[587] Unlike the primary schools, the MCI was permitted to have expatriate staff until qualified African teachers would be forthcoming.

[588] Wright commuted regularly over Belgian-built dirt roads between the Baringa and Yoseki hospitals, a distance of 250 miles.

[589] The Belgian government decorated Dr. Wide for his work with leprosy sufferers. He constructed brick duplex housing with cement floors for over 1,000 patients at Baringa. A huge assembly hall permitted movies to be shown (from the British embassy), to the delight of the patients. All bricks were made on site by the patients, using earth from abandoned anthills. At this camp the ICM was started, by which time only 300 burnt-out cases of leprosy remained. The area was beautifully landscaped under the direction of Mrs. Wide.

[590] Following independence in 1960 this victory succumbed to the law of entropy, and malaria again became rampant. (Joyce Ferguson, letter to the writer, 2 September 1999)

[591] RBMU missionary Joan Sledmere quoted by Betty Pritchard in *For Such A Time*, 102. Not all would lay this charge at RBMU's doorstep, including Maimie McIntyre. RBMU continued to upgrade the training of national workers from the opening of the first Bible School in 1938 to the establishment of the current Baringa Institute of Theology. During the writer's visit in 1969, CADELU leaders (Philip Kole) pressed their plea for "theological" training as opposed to (elementary) Bible School level preparation.

[592] A catechists' school opened at Baringa in 1962, gradually upgrading to become (in 1980) the Baringa Institute of Theology. It continued to function in 1999 under the auspices of Action Partners.

[593] It can be argued that the CADELU village churches did not need large numbers of highly-trained theologians; however, the opportunity for such training was lacking.

[594] *Simba* is a Swahili word meaning "lion," and was used to designate the rag-tag revolutionaries who overran much of Congo in 1964, savaging property and populace.

[595] David Reed, *111 Days in Stanleyville* (Harper, 1965), 273.

[596] ibid., 275.

[597] Crawford, 19.

[598] Herbert Kane, *Concise History of Christian Missions* (Baker, 1978), 185.

[599] By mid 1993 Zaire (Congo) had fallen victim to a crumbling infrastructure, thanks to the dictatorship of President Mobutu. Eighty-five percent of the roads left by the Belgians had returned to forest. Basic commodities such as salt and soap were no longer available in rural areas. Soaring inflation eroded buying power to the point where "wealthy" teachers could buy only half a bar of soap with a month's salary.

[600] Maimie McIntyre, *Regions Beyond*, April–June 1974.

[601] Canadian Muriel Langley was the first RBMU recruit from North America to arrive in Congo. Sent out by the Avenue Road church in Toronto, she arrived in the summer of 1948.

[602] Arthur and Elizabeth Wright left Zaire in 1973 in spite of urgings by the Church to "stay a little longer." Wright felt that church leaders were leaning too heavily upon his advice rather than seeking God's guidance. This decision was later confirmed when they wrote, "You were right, Doctor. We felt alone when you left, 'till we remembered what you had said . . . when we prayed to God, truly he has guided us." Elizabeth Wright, ltr. to the writer, 14 Aug. 1999.

[603] From a "1980s" CADELU report.

[604] This date is from a letter to the writer, cited by Elsa Morgan.

Chapter 41   Where Magellan Sailed
[605] *Regions Beyond*, Oct.–Dec. 1983, 3.
[606] *Regions Beyond*, Oct.–Dec. 1979, 3, 4.
[607] The Interdenominational Foreign Missions Association, an accrediting body of which RBMU became a member in 1952.
[608] *Bicol Survey Report*, January 1982, RBMU archives.
[609] ABCOP was later changed to ABCCOP, Alliance of Bible Christian Communities of the Philippines. ABCCOP had 160 churches in 1998.
[610] Intentionally unnamed.
[611] Report on RBMU International Survey in Ifugao and Mountain Provinces, 10–21 May 1982. RBMU archives.
[612] Trevor Douglas later married Norma Leathead, daughter of RBMU missionaries, Dale and Jeanette Leathead.
[613] Trevor Douglas newsletter, September 1999.
[614] ibid., 7–10.
[615] The Rempels arrived in the Philippines in 1982 and were part of the initial Naga team.
[616] Project Timothy was RBMU's summer program for college students, begun in 1972.
[617] *Regions Beyond*, October–December 1983, 4.
[618] ibid., 11. Also, Catanduanes Survey Report, 6–12 September 1982.
[619] Linguist Doug Trick had gone to assess the need for a Catanduanes New Testament. Having determined that Tagalog could be used with sufficient comprehension, he left the island several months later. Others joining the Catanduanes effort were Norma Leathead Douglas (1986), Gail Smith, and Arlene Junta (1989), and the Kerm Carlbergs and the Bill Wiebes (1990). Bob and Koleen Matsuda French followed in 1991. In 1994 the Wiebes pioneered a new work in Cabugao, the largest municipality in eastern Catanduanes. The Chris Wassells and the Randy Pfannenstiels took over the Cabugao effort in 1999, releasing the Wassells to join the OMF team in Manila.
[620] A Philippine missionary sending agency under the auspices of ABCCOP was being formed in 1998.
[621] Totoy Sebastian had earlier joined Chris and Kathy Wassell in Manila and the OMF team to plant the Lord of Life Church (1990–96). Bob and Koleen French together with SEND missionary, Amy Miller, two ABCCOP pastors and a businessman started a cell church in Makati (1996–97), a major business center in Metro Manila— Redeeming Grace Ministries (1996,97). Most national pastors here, as in other developing countries, were bivocational.
[622] Names intentionally omitted.
[623] *Regions Beyond*, April–June 1984, 14.

Chapter 42 Every Twitch and Grunt
[624] In 1952 the writer was given to read—but not to keep—a single copy of the old RBMU *"Blue Book"* of the Mission's principles and practice. Heavily emended, sections no longer applicable had been scissored out, or otherwise marked.
[625] Numbers 13:30.

[626] 7 December 1961. The writer has not seen this letter, although it is referenced in E. G. Vine's 23 December 1961 reply to Ernest Oliver. A copy of Vine's strongly worded reply is in the writer's possession.

[627] To address these concerns, the writer and US Council chairman George Hampshire met with the London Board in 1966 at Herne Bay, England.

[628] Reportedly, Charles Haddon Spurgeon, when asked why throughout his prolific ministry he had preached only once on Revelation chapter 20, replied simply, "I did not wish to divide the house."

[629] Reported by E. W. Oliver.

Chapter 43   Hidden People
[630] *Whitened Harvest*, fourth quarter 1943.

[631] Respected missiologist Winter founded and directed the US Center for World Mission (USCWM) in California.

[632] *Regions Beyond*, April–June 1982, 5.

Chapter 44   Hinge of Africa
[633] Thomas Parkenham, *The Scramble for Africa* (New York, Avon 1991), 200.

[634] Then referred to as "Hidden People."

[635] The Cameroon Baptist Convention (Not to be confused with the American Baptist Convention) is the national daughter church of the North American Baptist Conference, an evangelical body based in Villa Park, IL.

[636] *Regions Beyond*, July–September 1984.

[637] Targeted groups were first referred to as *Hidden People*, a term popularized by the USCWM. This was later changed to Unreached People. Following the RBMU/WT merger, the designation was again changed (within World Team) to Least-evangelized People, and still later, to Unreached People Groups (UPGs).

[638] They were Agape Christian Fellowship, Brattleboro, VT; First Baptist Church, Doylestown, PA; Bethel Gospel Assembly, New York, NY; and Westerly Road Church, Princeton, NJ.

Chapter 45   Standing by The Stuff
[639] 1 Sam. 30:24.

[640] They were Eurovangelism, Jewels for Jesus, Open Doors, RBMU International, Shantymen International, Slavic Gospel Association, World Radio Missionary Fellowship, and Worldteam.

[641] Rev. 2:.2. (NIV)

[642] Heb. 6:10.

Chapter 46   Where the Sun Had Never Set
[643] Lord Henry John Templeton Palmerston, Third Viscount, was British prime minister (1855–65) and symbol of British nationalism.

[644] Geoff Larcombe went to India and Nepal in December 1988 and to Peru and Zaire in the spring of 1989, to discuss the proposed move with British missionaries. (GL ltr. to the writer, 16 December 1999)

[645] Betty Young, ltr. to the writer, 2 July 1998.

[646] Geoff Larcombe, ltr. to the writer, 25 June 1998.

[647] *Latin Link,* formed in 1991, is a coordinating body comprising British RBMU and personnel in Latin America, working in cooperation with the Latin America Mission in North America.
[648] In 1999, RBMU continued to exist in the UK as a legal entity to deal with gifts and legacies. Britain's Charity Commissioners agreed to divide such gifts among those mission agencies which had absorbed the RBMU work.

Chapter 47   Pass the Baton
[649] Directors in 1908 were F. B. Meyer, George Hanson, Wright Hay, George Morgan, Stuart Holden, and Andrew Wingate. The Congo Balolo Mission had its own Home Council as did the South American And Bihar Mission.
[650] Betty Pritchard, 52, 53.
[651] Records of Australia RBMU are incomplete and some data is uncertain.
[652] Josh. 14:12.

Chapter 48   A Mission Grows
[653] *The Way the Lord Led,* WIM booklet, 1962, 15.
[654] By 1963, the WIM farm had a 140-head dairy operation.
[655] *Harvest Today,* September 1970, 7.
[656] *Harvest Today,* May 1970, 2.
[657] *Whitened* Harvest, September–October 1962.

Chapter 49   The Jamaica Venture
[658] *Whitened Harvest,* first quarter 1944.
[659] *Boriquen* is the Amerindian name for Puerto Rico.
[660] The Littles began their survey of Puerto Rico on 23 May 1944. See *Whitened Harvest,* third quarter 1944.
[661] *Whitened Harvest,* first quarter 1945.
[662] *Whitened Harvest,* summer 1968, provides a brief biosketch of the Depews and their work with WIM in Cuba, Haiti, and Jamaica.
[663] *Whitened Harvest,* November–December 1964, 2.

Chapter 50   A Hartt for Guadeloupe
[664] Guadeloupe consists of two major islands and five smaller satellites. Of the two major islands—Basse-Terre and Grande-Terre—Basse-Terre is the larger.
[665] *The Way the Lord Led,* (WIM, 1962, booklet), 39, 40.
[666] Unless otherwise noted, all data relating to Hartt's arrival in Guadeloupe and the establishing of the church, are taken from the writer's telephone interviews and e-mail exchanges with David Hartt in November, 1999.
[667] Usually a home where meals were prepared for live-in or walk-in guests. Erma Hartt later led this woman to the Lord.
[668] The 1941 rate. By 1947, the rate may have been slightly more.
[669] They were Winfrid Espere, Maximilien Bradamentis, and Lionel Arnel. Arnel's working life was with the postal department. He would eventually regard himself a joint founder of the Evangelical Church in Guadeloupe. Hartt agreed this to be the case.
[670] Hartt had a heated exchange with the American Consul, who advised him that he (the Consul) "was not in Guadeloupe to expedite the entry of American missionaries."

It was an indefensible prejudice that Hartt rebutted vigorously on the grounds of his American citizenship.

[671] The island was named for the caravel, *Marie Galante*, chosen by Columbus to lead the fleet on his second voyage to the New World.

[672] The Way The Lord Led, 11.

[673] The gendarme-cum-immigration-officer agreed to wink at this irregularity on pain of disavowing knowledge of Hartt should Hartt have been discovered.

[674] John's Gospel, 4:38.

[675] Roy Bergquist,. *Fifty Years of Adventure with God* (Pamphlet 1995), 20. All data related to the Bergquists' ministry are drawn from this account and from e-mail exchanges with the writer.

[676] 18 February 1947.

[677] Bergquist, 15.

[678] *Whitened Harvest*, second quarter 1948, 10.

[679] Bergquist, 21.

[680] Mrs. Leslie Thompson (Mary Doty) died in childbirth in 1959; six-year-old Philip Alexander lost an arm in a roadway accident; 11-year old Tim Janis was killed in a boating accident in 1967. Twenty-one year old Tim Heppner lost his life in an auto accident in 1971. WIM personnel weathered Hurricane Betsy (11 August 1956), the eruption of 5,000-foot Mt. La Souffriere (1956), and a tidal wave. Spiritual division and revolt briefly affected the church at St. Anne (1956).

[681] Other workers joined the ranks of the WIM team. These included: Don and Carol Janis, Rusty and Norma Young, Mary Heppner, and the Mittons. All shared in establishing the church in Guadeloupe.

[682] Elmer Thompson, The Expansion of the Los Pinos Nuevos Bible Institute, Message, 18 August 1987.

[683] Walter Wunsch report cited by Roy Bergquist in *Fifty Years of Adventure with God*, Chapter 7, p. 13.

[684] Etienne Liotard died of a stroke 28 May 1999, in France. He had taken early retirement from his post in Guadeloupe in order to do full time gospel work in France and in the Middle East. In 1999, Mrs. Monique Liotard was still living.

Chapter 51 Threading the Necklace

[685] St. Lucia became a member of the Federation of the West Indies in 1958 and independent in 1979.

[686] *Whitened Harvest*, July–September 1954, 9.

[687] *Whitened Harvest*, second quarter 1951, 7.

[688] *A History of the Vieux Fort Bible Church*, Wilson Collymore. paper. World Team archives.

[689] ibid.

[690] A revolving fund, established from the sale of the St. Vincent Bible School property, provided ECWI with the down payment on a building lot for the new church. Backed by WIM, Ehmann raised prayer interest and funding for the first phase of the building, which was dedicated in the fall of 1974.

[691] *Castries Evangelical Church*, a paper by Peter Recaii and Mary Tobierre. (World Team archives). Among those who helped establish the Castries church were Peter Recaii, Ignatius Evans, Josephine McDimmed, Lucia Chitole, and Steven Emmanuel.

[692] *Whitened Harvest*, Nov–Dec. 1964, 2.
[693] *Men In Action* was a ministry started by Terry Geiger to develop strategies with national leaders in the Caribbean, of which Haiti's Christ for All campaign was most significant. Geiger later became head of the PCA mission to North America.
[694] *Whitened Harvest*, July–Aug 1962.
[695] Dave Whitermore, Edith Johnson, and Bernhard Penner later joined Cross.

Chapter 52   Into Mato Grosso
[696] *Whitened Harvest*, spring–summer 1969.
[697] Lowell Bailey's notes to the writer.
[698] Edna Harms. The Story of Our Work in Caxias do Sul.
[699] This grant was another instance of Anthony Rossi's generosity.

Chapter 53   Suriname
[700] The Van Kantens were an encouragement to the Neffs. Ludwig helped them with language study and message preparation when they began their first Dutch language Bible studies in their home, mid-1955.
[701] The Evangelical Alliance Mission.
[702] *Whitened Harvest*, July–Sept. 1954, 20. Philomena Brandon became a WIM missionary in 1956. Fluent in Dutch, she tutored Walt and Marge Jackson, who arrived in Paramaribo on 18 March 1957.
[703] *Whitened Harvest*, May–June 1963, 8. David Neff subsequently married Judy Eckles, veteran RBMU missionary to Irian Jaya. The couple served in Paramaribo until their retirement.

Chapter 54   Operation Grasshopper
[704] *Whitened Harvest*, March–April 1963, 6.
[705] Originally, *Door to Life Gospel Ministries*, this Mission had been established in 1956 as a radio ministry in the US. The name was later abbreviated to *Door To Life Ministries*.
[706] At this time MAF was operating in neighboring British Guiana (now Guyana).
[707] During the first twelve months of Operation Grasshopper, thirteen aircraft crashed and two pilots lost their lives. See *I Will Build My Church*, Alice Nichols, 1979, booklet, Paramaribo.
[708] The five couples: Lepper, Jones, Leavitt, Jackson, and Schoen. DTL founders, Friessen and Price, remained in the US but were used of God to make a few of the first landings. In 1979 they revisited Suriname to attend the dedication of the Trio and Wayana New Testaments.
[709] *Whitened Harvest*, March–April 1963.
[710] When the Leppers left Suriname in 1962 to resume their assignment with UFM/MAF, the medical work continued with the remaining personnel. Later, a medical foundation was established, headed by a Surinamese doctor. Nurses were then recruited from the US and the Netherlands. In 1999, the Indians were conducting medical work, counseled via radio by a doctor in Paramaribo. The Walter Jacksons left Suriname in 1965 for reassignment to lead the Dominican Republic field.
[711] WIM missionaries had been on the lookout for this custom, so were not taken by surprise. Claude Leavitt, from his experience with the Wai-Wai, first made WIM per-

sonnel aware of this cultural practice. The Wai-Wai, Trio, and Wayana groups were all of the Carib family and shared many cultural practices.

[712] DTL ceased to exist after 1962.

[713] *Whitened Harvest*, March–April 1963.

[714] *Whitened Harvest*, July–August 1963, 4. Also: Ivan Schoen e-mail to the writer, 25 August 1999.

[715] Acts 9:15.

[716] *Whitened Harvest*, fall, 1968. *The Tribe That Almost Got Away.* The Art Yohners spent fourteen years in Suriname (January 1967–July 1981), Art later becoming Minister of Missions for Worldteam. Roy and Margaret Lytle joined the Amerindian work in 1970 and were involved with the Akurijo contact.

[717] New candidates by marriage were required to qualify independently of the spouse; moreover, nationals from the target country were not permitted to join the Mission.

[718] *The Bassano Tragedy*, Kathleen L. Smith, (England: Pearl Books, 1982, BN11 1QX).

Chapter 55   On the Air in Old Hispaniola

[719] The evangelical radio station in Quito, Ecuador founded by Clarence Jones.

[720] Walker later became president and CEO of Worldteam USA from September 1985–September 1992, and assistant to the president of Worldteam International from September 1992–1994.

[721] *Whitened Harvest*, spring–summer 1969.

[722] David Hartt related events of the establishment of Radio Lumière in Port au Prince to the writer through telephone interviews and e-mail exchanges, November 1999.

Chapter 56   Quisqueya Para Cristo

[723] Hilario Diaz was among the "four or five" Cuban couples sent by E. V. Thompson to the DR and was "the most successful man of that group."

[724] *Quisqueya* is the name supposedly given to the island of Hispaniola (Haiti and the Dominican Republic) in pre-colonial times by the Arawak Indians.

[725] *Whitened Harvest*, July–August 1966.

[726] Praise and Pray with Us, January 1988.

[727] Based on the *Upper Room Discourse*, Thompson gave this series of studies taken from John 14:12.

[728] Worldteam Day of Prayer agenda, 24 May 1988.

Chapter 57   A Storm Breaks in Cuba

[729] *Whitened Harvest*, March–April 1959.

[730] Canadians Don and Elsie Elliot remained in Cuba for another thirty years, under considerable hardship. In 2000 they were serving in Petrozavodsk, Russia.

[731] *Whitened Harvest*, November–December 1960.

[732] *Whitened Harvest*, winter 1969.

[733] Elmer Lavastida, *Trayectoria*, Ch. IV., 8.

[734] Job 42:17.

[735] Roger Kirk became the Mission's first representative in North America. He died in 1968.

Chapter 58   Florida Gold

[736] Anthony T. Rossi was born in 1900, a convenient marker for his age.

[737] *Anthony T. Rossi*, Sanna Barlow Rossi (Downers Grove: IVP 1986), 82 ff.

[738] Tropicana Products eventually employed 28,000 workers in Bradenton.

[739] Now Columbia International University. Petty was director of Christian Service at CBC.

[740] Anthony Rossi established the Aurora Foundation, which generously funded Christian educational institutions and Christian missions. He is reported to have said, "I will be ashamed at the judgment seat of Christ if I have one nickel that belongs to Anthony Rossi." The Rossi Building at CIU bears the following inscription:

> Anthony Rossi lived to honor God. An immigrant from Sicily virtually without formal education, Rossi found Jesus Christ in his beloved America, and America provided him the opportunity for business success through his God-given creative genius.

> He caught the vision of Christian education and missionary training and generously supported CBC.

[741] Dr. G. Allen Fleece served as assistant director of WIM from 1961–1969. He traveled extensively for the Mission in Bible teaching and conference work.

[742] 11 Oct. 1962–8 Dec. 1965.

[743] A French missionary couple in Guadeloupe had drawn attention to the Guadeloupe immigrant population in France.

[744] Thompson was accompanied on this tour by his parents, Elmer and Evelyn Thompson, who introduced him as the general director designate. J. Allen Thompson had been assistant to the GD for two years ('65–67) and became General Director in 1967. He had served as field director in the Dominican Republic from 1963–1967.

[745] His motto was "Love-Obedience-Discipline."

[746] Anthony Rossi had joined the Worldteam board prior to 1970. Over a period of fifteen years His Aurora Foundation invested an estimated ten million dollars in stock and cash in Worldteam.

[747] While Rossi financed the early Sicily crusades, he was careful not to give money to WIM. Beginning in 1970, he made occasional gifts. Only after coming on the Worldteam board (where he saw the large budget needs) did his giving become significantly large and systematic. Thompson never appealed to Rossi for help.

[748] Two grants of $250,000 each were given annually for a period of ten years.

Chapter 59   Secret Weapon

[749] *Harvest Today*, September 1976.

[750] Genesis 2:18; Matthew 18:20.

[751] Acts 10:14.

[752] The history of mission shows that the gospel does not always trickle down from evangelized urban population centers to the marginalized minorities within a given country. The Apostle Paul's strategy to reach those urban centers at the nexus of commercial trade routes marked the history of eighteenth and nineteenth century missions. The failure of this strategy to reach marginalized groups gave rise to the inland missions of the late nineteenth century. It remained for later pioneers of unreached

people groups to correct the dangers of imbalance and to assure that mission would deal with both. In the 1980s, both Worldteam and the Regions Beyond Missionary Union directed a renewed focus upon the great urban centers while maintaining their historic concern for the unreached people groups of earth.

[753] Including Samuel Rowen and Bobby Clinton, members of Allen Thompson's "think tank."

[754] This characteristic had not marked Anthony Rossi's earlier generous relationships with Worldteam. His positive and creative contributions to the Worldteam board had always been motivated by his desire to be faithful to God. Only as he aged (he was now in his mid-eighties) did this symptom appear.

Chapter 60   When the Brook Dried Up

[755] Calvary Baptist Church, Bradenton.

[756] The overseas director, by definition, was in charge of the Sicily operation.

[757] Thompson resigned at the end of February 1982 and went into pastoral ministry from 1982–1985, serving as co-pastor of the Trinity Baptist Church in Denver in what proved to be for him "a marvelous renewal."

[758] Praise and Pray with Us, May 1988.

[759] Stephen Neil, *A History of Christian Missions* (Hazell Watson and Viney, Bucks, UK 1964), 565.

[760] Praise and Pray With Us, December 1987.

Chapter 62   Redefining Mission

[761] Thompson resigned at the end of February 1982.

[762] WIN was a collaborative effort of Allen Thompson, Paul Thompson, and Myles Lorenzen.

Chapter 63   Church and Mission Collide

[763] This insistence on establishing a legal presence for the national church was due in part to the lessons learned in Cuba. The Cuban Association of Churches was not expropriated by the Castro regime, since its assets belonged to a Cuban body and not to a foreign entity.

[764] Information supplied to the writer by Allen Thompson.

[765] Ed Walker to the writer, 28 December 1999.

[766] In an unfortunate coincidence, termination of the grants from the Aurora Foundation coincided with the departure of Louis Markwood, giving the appearance that somehow the phase out of grants to MEBSH was associated with the transfer of leadership to Lamar Myers.

[767] Morrie Cottle was pastor of the Virginia Beach Community Chapel.

[768] The new structure became operational in 1985, and completed its legal incorporation in 1986.

[769] This difficulty was addressed and resolved at the time of the Worldteam/RBMU merger in 1995.

[770] Praise and Pray with Us, April 1989.

[771] They were Terry Harder, vice president of development; Nicholas Dannemiller, vice president of finance; and David Melick, vice president of human resources.

[772] Ed Walker. President's report to the board of directors, 29 May 1992.

[773] See previous chapter.

[774] J. Allen Thompson, Training Church Planters: A Proposal for Lifelong Learning. 1990.

Chapter 64   Disengagement
[775] The Worldteam / MEBSH disengagement process took place at a time when Dictator Jean-Claude Duvalier was being ousted from Haiti (1986). The popular mood was strongly anti-establishment, and it was in vogue for national churches to bash their missionary benefactors. Worldteam was ahead of the curve, relinquishing mission control (of mission institutions) at a time when most agencies retained the reins.
[776] Redeployment from Haiti placed experienced personnel in London, Paris, Miami, Atlanta, Toronto, Cayenne, and Paramaribo.
[777] As a direct or indirect result of this action and the decline of work in Sicily, 100 workers left the Mission. Worldteam's roster of supporting churches and donors was reduced from 6,000 in 1986 to 4,000 in 1990. (Ed Walker report of 8 November 1991). The total annual budget of all Haiti and Sicily ministries was $1,602,000. The ten percent annual administrative loss to Worldteam was more than $160,000.
[778] Setting the Sails, 1989 page 2.
[779] Successive presidents after Getz: Dean Chouinard, Robert Wiedman.
[780] Evangelical Council for Financial Accountability
[781] By 1999, WTA had fielded more than 100 lay teams throughout the Caribbean, South America, and Europe and became directly involved in recruiting workers for the former Soviet Union under the CoMission. From the outset, WTA's purpose was to "encourage, inform, and involve laypeople in missions." In addition to the popular workteam, perhaps the most successful teams from a ministry standpoint were those going to the English-speaking islands of the Caribbean to teach DVBS. Many children and adults came to know the Lord through this ministry. In 1999, WTA's prayer teams continued to grow in number and blessing in support of global gospel advance.
[782] J. Allen Thompson's legacy was considerable. His leadership helped define Worldteam's purpose and vision, brought the Mission to ownership of that purpose, led in the creation of the Worldteam Institute (WIM), helped develop the doctrine of the church, successfully taught and modeled teamwork, led in the development of profile and assessment of church planters, and moved the Worldteam family to become increasingly a worshipping people.
[783] *Setting the Sails* (2/3/89) reviewed achievements, defined the impending financial crisis stemming from the cessation of Aurora Foundation grants, and proposed a three-year recovery plan calling for stringency measures.
[784] The others: E. V. Thompson 1928–66; J. A. Thompson 1967–81, 1985–89; T. P. Arnold 1982–84. The chief executive position in Worldteam had been—at different times—variously designated as general director, executive director, and international director. The term "president" was also used, but primarily to designate the chief officer of the legal corporation.

Chapter 65   Turning the Page
[785] Miller was installed as international director and president of Worldteam on 21 October 1990 in Morton, Illinois.

[786] A reference to the infamous Berlin wall. Soviet-allied East Germany opened checkpoints on the Berlin wall on 9 November 1989.

[787] Former president George Bush at the Brandenburg Gate on the tenth anniversary of the fall of the wall.

[788] Coordination meetings were held in 1992 in California (January), and in Chicago (March). CoMission goals were to 1) Provide CIS teachers with a ten-lesson curriculum on Christian morality and ethics. 2) Start 30,000 Bible studies that would become churches. 3) Equip 600 Russians to teach the Bible in 120,000 schools (Steve Miller's 28 May 1992 report to the Worldteam board).

[789] Worldteam made several commitments. 1) Recruit thirty people for ministry during the convocations, 2) Recruit five teams of ten people including a leader by the end of 1992 for follow-up. 3) Recruit eight teams from 1993 to 1997. 4) Provide supervision for all teams sent out by Worldteam. 5) Raise $60,000 for one four-day convocation." —ibid.

[790] Myles Lorenzen had conducted an ACMC workshop in Illinois, where some XCF members were present, and where their interest was stirred.

Chapter 66   Requiem

[791] Psalm 71:18.

[792] Extracted from Paul Thompson's remarks at his father's funeral service.

[793] *Character Matters*, J. Allen Thompson's message at his father's memorial service.

[794] ibid.

[795] Of the six Thompson children, Edna Harms, Les, Allen, and Paul grew up in the Los Pinos atmosphere and became missionaries with WIM. Paul left Cuba with his parents in 1950 when they moved to Homer City. Grace and Lester Lehman did a two-year stint with the Quisqueya children's school in Port-au-Prince, Haiti. Carolyn, the youngest, was afflicted with MS since Columbia Bible College days and has been an invalid most of her life.

[796] Lester and Grace Lehman.

[797] Evelyn Thompson died in April 1997. Her memorial service was held at Calvary Baptist Church, Columbia, SC on 24 April 1997.

[798] *Word Windows*, December 1998—A World Team monthly newsletter.

Chapter 67   The Rationale for Union

[799] James Reapsome, *Evangelical Missions Quarterly*, July 1988, 211.

[800] HCJB, Trans World Radio, and FEBC, in September 1985.

[801] David Tucker.

[802] Anthony Rossi's significant capital grants and shares of stock were designed to carry the Mission work through interest on investment. By 1985, operating deficits had begun to erode the endowment principal.

[803] Leaving the work of Worldteam had been Allen Thompson, Harold Alexander, Donald Bjork, Bobby Clinton, and Bob Vetter (Vetter in 1995).

[804] The meetings were held in the Embassy Suites Hotel.

[805] This chronology of events derives from notes of D. W. Martin, shared with the writer.

[806] Members of the steering committee were selected by their respective boards and comprised: Morris Cottle, David Martin, Steve Miller, David Newberry, Ken Bennett, Albert Ehmann, Bob Vetter, Graham Cousens, and Spencer Bower. Bower, with the

Christian Service Fellowship, had been invited to the meetings as a consultant. The first meeting was held in facilities provided by the Davisville Baptist Church. Morrie Cottle was appointed chairman. Five task force groups were appointed to address vision, purpose statement, core values, philosophy of ministry, and doctrinal statement (TF1), organizational structures, legal entities, and name (TF2), facilities, finances, and accounting (TF3), personnel resources (TF 4), and resource development (TF5).
[807] Ceremonies took place at the Sangam Restaurant and Banquet Hall, 6991 Millcreek Drive, Mississauga, Ontario.
[808] *Advance*, fall, 1996, 2.
[809] ibid., 3.

Chapter 68   The Way Ahead
[810] Cited by George Otis, Jr. in *The Last of the Giants*. (Grand Rapids: Chosen Books, Baker 1991).
[811] The transition board began operations in January 1994.
[812] On 12 October 1999, world population surpassed six billion.
[813] *Ethnos* translates ninety-three times in the NT as *Gentiles*, sixty-two times as *nations*, and five times as *heathen*.
[814] Rom. 15: 7–21.
[815] Genesis 10 and 11.
[816] Acts 17:26,27.
[817] George Otis, Jr., *The Last of the Giants*, 97.
[818] In 1999, World Team was involved in church planting among sixty-two people groups.
[819] *The Quotable Spurgeon* (Harold Shaw), 271.
[820] *Koinonia* is variously translated, fellowship, communion, contribution. 1 Cor. 10:16, Romans 15:26, 2 Cor. 8:4.
[821] Kenneth Scott Latourette.
[822] In 1995, 500 churches were planted. In 1996, 583. In 1997, 634. In 1998, c. 700.
[823] *Next Step*: North American Partnership in Mission Training has a web site at www.thenextstep.org.
[824] John 14:12
[825] Gorge Otis, Jr., *The Last of the Giants*, 143
[826] Matthew 21:.28
[827] Hab. 2:14; Rom. 16:20; Rev. 5:9 (NIV).

End of Notes

A Chronology of World Team

Regions Beyond Missionary Union

1835   Birth of H. Grattan Guinness.

1873   East London Institute for Home and Foreign Missions opens.

1877   H. M. Stanley descends Congo River to the Atlantic, opening Central Africa to the world.

1878   Livingstone Inland Mission is first society to enter Congo.

1884   ELI cedes LIM and Lower Congo to American Baptists.

1885   Congo Free State established. Rubber atrocities increase.

1887   Regions Beyond Magazine launched with Fanny Guinness as editor.

1888   CBM begins work on the Upper Congo; F. B. Meyer joins the board.

1896   Lucy Guinness goes to India, recruits for India missions. Six CBMers die.

1898   Death of Fanny Guinness.

1899   Banks and Hicks enter India's North Bihar Province.

1900   CBM takes the name, Regions Beyond Missionary Union.

1901   Queen Victoria dies. Boer war bleeds Britain. Cliff College closes.

1908   Dr. Harry Guinness visits Congo. CBMer John McKittrick dies of malaria.

1910   H. Grattan Guinness dies. First global World Missionary Conference convenes in Edinburgh.

1911   RBMU in Peru and Argentina merge, forming the EUSA.

1915   Harry Guinness dies. WW I bleeds Britain. Harley College closes.

1916   Annie G. Soper sails for Peru.

1922   Soper and Gould cross the Andes, begin work in Moyobamba.

1932   Peru Inland Mission is founded in Lamas.

1929   F. B. Meyer dies; Gordon Guinness is named Director of RBMU–UK.

1932   E. G. Vine backs Greet van't Eind's outgoing to Borneo.

1935   Bill and Silvia Sirag enter Borneo.

1939   E. G. Vine named Director of RBMU in Britain. World War II begins.

1942   Australia Nepalese Mission merges with RBMU. Sirags interned in Java by Japanese, where Bill Sirag dies before war's end.

1945	World War II ends. Global diaspora begins. Missions mobilize.
1948	E. G. Vine sails for North America, forms RBMU councils. PIM merges with RBMU. Borneo (NW Kalimantan) entered.
1952	Inland Peru churches organize as AIENOP.
1953	RBMU enters Dutch New Guinea (Irian Jaya).
1954	Nepal opens; United Mission to Nepal formed.
1957	RBMU (US) moves into Elberon Avenue property in Fox Chase, PA. Karubaga airstrip opened (IJ). Berea Bible Institute begins (KB).
1960	Swart Danis burn fetishes. Congo becomes independent; missionaries withdraw.
1961	Ernest W. Oliver named Executive Secretary of RBMU–UK.
1964	Ebenezer G. Vine dies. J. F. Conley named Director of RBMU (US). Simba rebellion ravages Congo.
1966	Annie Soper receives member of British Empire award for her work in Peru.
1967	Abortive Chinese communist coup savages Dayak churches (Kalimantan, Indonesia).
1968	Phil Masters and Stanley Dale are martyred in Irian Jaya.
1970	Elmer Austring is named Director of RBMU Canada.
1971	Urban Church Planting begins in Lima, Peru. Regions Press established (Peru).
1973	*Peace Child* filmed in Irian Jaya.
1977	International conference in England concedes North American RBMU autonomy.
1979	Philippines survey commissioned. Lima churches organize as ADIBEL. Annie Soper dies.
1980	Southern Cone republic capitals (South America) surveyed, Philippines entered.
1981	Urban work begins in Santiago, Chile.
1982	Unreached (Hidden) Peoples Department is established.
1984	Catanduanes entered—RBMU's first 'Hidden People' target.
1985	Cameroon entered. RBMU (UK) disbands.
1987	J. F. Conley resigns as US director (12/31). D. W. Martin named Executive Director.
1994	RBMU enters new 10,000-sq. ft. HQ facility in Warrington, PA.

1995   RBMU and Worldteam merge to form World Team.

1996   Cambodia entered.

The West Indies Mission (Worldteam)

1887   Birth of B. G. Lavastida

1891   Cuban patriot José, Martí gives New Pines speech in Ybor City, Florida.

1898   USS Maine sinks. Cuba wins independence from Spain.

1901   Birth of Elmer V. Thompson.

1909   Manuel Lavastida assassinated. B. G. Lavastida converted in Troy, NY.

1923   Lavastida founds Los Pinos school for Cuba's disadvantaged children.

1926   Hattie Kirk arrives in Cuba, advocates Bible Institute.

1928   Thompsons arrive in Cuba, Cuba Bible Institute founded.

1932   Los Pinos Nuevos Press prints first edition of Whitened Harvest and El Misionero Biblico.

1933   Cuban repatriation of Haitian Cane Cutters begins.

1936   Cuba Bible Institute Mission enters Haiti; becomes West Indies Mission.

1938   Haiti Bible Institute opens with five students.

1939   WIM enters Dominican Republic. Depews and Hansens reinforce Haiti staff.

1940   Alas del Alba broadcast begins. First publication of Whitened Harvest.

1945   WIM acquires Homer City property, relocates headquarters. St. Lucia and Jamaica entered.

1947   David Hart surveys Guadeloupe, WIM enters.

1949   St. Lucia entered.

1950   The Elmer Thompsons relocate to Homer City.

1951   The Evangelical Association of Guadeloupe forms with thirty-two baptized members. St. Vincent entered.

1953   Trinidad entered.

1954   Suriname entered. Hurricane Floyd smashes Haiti; Radio Lumière goes on the air in Haiti.

1955   Grenada entered.

1957	Brazil entered.
1959	Latin Youth Publications begins in Placetas, Cuba.
1960	Castro revolution forces WIM evacuation from Cuba.
1962	Mission to Orphans merges with WIM.
1963	DTL merges with WIM. Hurricane Flora ravages Haiti.
1965	WIM HQ begins move in stages to Coral Gables, FL.
1968	Latin Youth Publications incorporates.
1970	WIM moves into new HQ facility in Coral Gables. Homer City property sold. Italy entered.
1971	Paul Thompson conducts Spain survey.
1972	Spain entered
1978	West Indies Mission changes name to Worldteam.
1979	France entered
1982	Allen Thompson resigns (February) as director of Worldteam; Patrick Arnold becomes Interim general director.
1985	Patrick Arnold retires after three years as general director. Worldteam restructures. Worldteam USA board established, with Ed Walker as president. Canada becomes sending country with Albert Ehmann as director. Canada church planter apprenticeship program starts. Ethnic ministries begin in London. Allen Thompson returns as general director.
1986	Worldteam Institute (WIN) founded.
1987	Disengagement policy implemented in Haiti. Remaining Worldteam missionaries are seconded to MEBSH.
1988	World Team Associates forms. French Guyana entered.
1989	Allen Thompson leaves Worldteam in September; Steve Miller named International Director.
1992	B. G. Lavastida dies. Alliance for Saturation Church Planting forms.
1993	Java (Indonesia) entered. First teams enter CIS (former Soviet Union) entered under CoMission.
1995	Worldteam merges with Regions Beyond Missionary Union, becoming World Team. Albert Ehmann is named International Director. Joint Ministry Council forms. Five-year strategic plan is adopted.
1998	Evelyn Thompson dies.
1999	Elmer V. Thompson dies.

RBMU Books

Listed by category/country. Authors are listed alphabetically by last name.

GENERAL

Guinness, H. Grattan

Light for the Last Days (London: Hodder and Stoughton, 1886). 333 pp.

Romanism and the Reformation (1887. Rapidan, VA: Hartland, 1995). 217 pp.

The Divine Programme of the World's History, 1888.

The City of the Seven Hills, 1891.

Creation Centered in Christ, 1896.

Key to the Apocalypse (London: Hodder and Stoughton, 1899).

History Unveiling Prophesy (London and Edinburgh: Revell, 1905).

Lucy Guinness Kumm: Her Life Story, 1907. 93 pp.

The Story of Job: A Poem, 1907.

The Approaching End of the Age (Contains his astronomical schemes for measuring prophetic time).

Surely I Come Quickly CAFMW, 15 December 1895. Article.

The Coming of Christ: A Stimulus to Missionary Zeal (1896) CAFMW 17, 2 October 1896. Article.

The Second Coming: Will it be before the Millennium? The British Weekly, 24 June 1887, 34. Article.

Guinness, H. Grattan ("Harry")

Not Unto Us (London: RBMU Press, 1908). Hardcover, Pictorial, 191 pp. A record of RBMU's first twenty-one years.

Guinness, Lucy

South America: The Neglected Continent, 1894.

Across India at the Dawn of the Twentieth Century, 1904.

Holmes, Kenneth

The Cloud Moves (London: RBMU, EmPrint, 1971). A synopsis of RBMU history. 52 pp.

Macintosh, C. W.

The Life Story of Dr. Harry Guinness (London: RBMU, 1916). 127 pp.

Pritchard, Betty

For Such A Time (London: Victory Press, 1973). 125 pp. Traces God's faithfulness through the RBMU for a hundred years, 1873–1973. Elizabeth Pritchard was the author of several books.

Sword at the Heart. A historical novel on the life of Jeremiah.

Sword of Elisha. A historical novel on the life of Elisha.

Golden Windows. A novel tracing the steps of a North India boy's revolt against the restraints of his Christian home.

PERU
Sorell, Vera
  Los Chasquis del Rey (Lima, Ediciones Puma, 1998. Spanish). English language
  edition: *Go, Chasquis, Go!* (Belleville, ON: Guardian Books, 2000). 304 pp. A
  comprehensive survey of the work of the Peru Inland Mission.
Thompson, Phyllis
  Dawn Beyond the Andes (London: RBMU, 1955). 126 pp. The life and work of
  Annie G. Soper.

IRIAN JAYA
Dekker, John
  Torches of Joy (Westchester, IL: Crossway Books, 1985). 200 pp. John and Helen
  Dekker's trials and victories among the Dani people of Irian Jaya.
Manning, Helen
  To Perish For Their Saving (London: Victory Press, 1969). 128 pp. The
  martyrdom of Phil Masters and Stan Dale.
Richardson, Don
  Peace Child (Ventura, CA: Regal, 1974). 288 pp.
  Lords of the Earth (Ventura, CA: Regal, 1977).
  Eternity in Their Hearts (Ventura, CA: Regal, 1981). 176 pp.

CONGO
Guinness, Fanny
  The New World of Central Africa (London: Hodder & Stoughton, 1890). 540 pp.
Ruskin, Lily
  Ruskin of Congo (London: RBMU, 1948). 162 pp.

Worldteam Books

Bergquist, Roy
  Fifty Years of Adventure with God 1995. Biography.
Dudley, Nelson, G., M.D.
  As The Cock Crows: Reflections of a Medical Missionary to Haiti (Franklin, TN:
  Providence House, 1997).
Johnson, Bernice
  She Hath Done What She Could. Undated. Missionary journal of Bernice Johnson,
  who spent thirty-seven years in Haiti with Worldteam.
Livingstone, Glen
  Prayer That Strengthens and Expands the Church (South Holland, IL: Alliance
  for Saturation Church Planting, 1999).
Markwood, Louis
  The Sovereignty Of God Working To Form A Mission. Undated. Booklet. The
  story of the West Indies Mission/Worldteam.

Nichols, Alice
I Will Build My Church (Paramaribo, 1979, Booklet). Story of the Trio and Wayana Indian work in Suriname.
Thompson, J. Allen and Bjork, Don, eds.
What Does It Mean To Be A World Christian? (Coral Gables, FL: Worldteam, 1978).
Walker, Edwin S.
Church/Mission Partnership: A Proposal for Joint Team Preparation and Church Planting Among the Unreached (Worldteam, 1992).

Other Bibliographical Resources

—

Cartwright, F.
Disease and History (New York: Dorset, 1972).
Guinness, Michele
The Guinness Legend (London: Hodder and Stoughton, 1990). 330 pp. Definitive work on the illustrious Guinness family with primary emphasis on the Grattan H. Guinness branch of the family. This volume is a rich source of fascinating historical data respecting the personal lives of many members of the Grattan H. Guinness family and their astonishing affect upon world evangelization.
Hayward, Douglas
The Dani Of Irian Jaya Before and After Conversion (Sentani: UFM, Regions Press, 1980), 223 pp. Excellent, well-documented chronology of events related to the culture and conversion of the Dani people.
Hitt, Russell T.
Cannibal Valley (Camp Hill, PA: Christian Publications, 1962).
Kessler, J. B. A. Jr.
The History of Protestant Missions in Peru and Chile (Oosterbaan, & le Cointre N.V., Goes, 1967), 369 pp.
Orr, James Edwin
The Light of the Nations (UK: Paternoster, 1965). 302 pp.
Pakenham, Thomas
The Scramble For Africa (New York: Avon, 1992). 738 pp.
Toirac, Florent D.
A Pioneer Missionary in the Twentieth Century (IN: Winona Lake. Undated. Published by the Author). Autobiography of Florent D. Toirac, "The Moody of the Antilles," who trained under B. G. Lavastida and Elmer V. Thompson at the Los Pinos Nuevos Bible Institute in Cuba.

All other bibliographical resources are referenced in the endnotes.

A